Digital Picture Processing

Second Edition

Volume 1

AZRIEL ROSENFELD

Computer Science Center
University of Maryland
College Park, Maryland

AVINASH C. KAK

School of Electrical Engineering
Purdue University
West Lafayette, Indiana

1982

ACADEMIC PRESS, INC.

(Harcourt Brace Jovanovich, Publishers)

Orlando   San Diego   San Francisco   New York   London
Toronto   Montreal   Sydney   Tokyo   Sao Paulo

ACADEMIC PRESS, INC.
Orlando, Florida 32887

United Kingdom Edition published by
ACADEMIC PRESS, INC. (LONDON) LTD.
24/28 Oval Road, London NW1 7DX

Library of Congress Cataloging in Publication Data

Rosenfeld, Azriel.
  Digital picture processing.

  (Computer science and applied mathematics)
  Includes bibliographical references and index.
  1. Optical data processing. I. Kak, Avinash C.
II. Title. III. Series.
TA1630.R67 1981   621.3819'598   81-17611
ISBN 0-12-597301-2   AACR2

PRINTED IN THE UNITED STATES OF AMERICA

83 84 85   9 8 7 6 5 4 3 2

Contents

Preface

The rapid rate at which the field of digital picture processing has grown in the past five years has necessitated extensive revisions and the introduction of topics not found in the original edition.

Two new chapters have been added: Chapter 8 (by A. C. K.) on reconstruction from projections and Chapter 9 (by A. R.) on matching. The latter includes material from Chapters 6 and 8 of the first edition on geometric transformations and matching, but it consists primarily of new material on imaging geometry, rectification, and stereomapping, as well as an appendix on the analysis of time-varying imagery.

Chapter 2 incorporates a new section on vector space representation of images. Chapter 5 on compression has undergone a major expansion. It includes a new section on interpolative representation of images and fast implementation of the Karhunen–Loève transform based thereon. Also included in this chapter is image compression using discrete cosine transforms—a technique that has attracted considerable attention in recent years. New sections on block quantization, the recently discovered technique of block truncation compression, and error-free compression have also been added to Chapter 5. New material has been added to Chapter 6 on gray level and histogram transformation and on smoothing. Chapter 7 has also been considerably expanded and includes many new restoration techniques. This chapter incorporates a new frequency domain derivation of the constrained least squares filter. The treatment of Markov representation has been expanded with a section on vector–matrix formulation of such representations. Chapters 10, 11, and 12 are major expansions of the first edition's Chapters 8–10, dealing with segmentation of pictures into parts, representations of the parts (formerly "geometry"), and description of pictures in terms of parts. Chapter 10 incorporates much new material on pixel classification, edge detection, Hough transforms, and picture partitioning, reflecting recent developments in these areas; it also contains an entirely new section (10.5) on iterative "relaxation" methods for fuzzy or probabilistic segmentation. Chapter 11 is now organized according to types of representations (runs, maximal blocks, quadtrees, border codes), and discusses how to convert between these representations and how to use them to compute geometrical properties of picture subsets. Chapter 12 treats picture properties as well as descriptions of pictures at various levels (numerical arrays, region representations, relational structures). It also discusses models for classes of pictures, as defined, in particular, by constraints that must be satisfied at a given level of description ("declarative models") or by grammars that generate or accept the classes. It considers how to construct a model consistent with a given set of descriptions and how to extract a description that matches a given model; it also contains an appendix on the extraction of three-dimensional information about a scene from pictures.

The size of this second edition has made it necessary to publish this book in two volumes. However, a single chapter numbering has been maintained. Volume 1 contains Chapters 1–8, covering digitization, compression, enhancement, restoration, and reconstruction; and Volume 2 contains Chapters 9–12, covering matching, segmentation, representation, and description. The material in Volume 2 is not strongly dependent on that in Volume 1; and to make it even more self-contained, the Preface and Introduction (called Chapter 1 in Volume 1) are reproduced at the beginning of Volume 2.

The authors of the chapters are as follows: Chapters 2, 4, 5, 7, and 8 are by A. C. K, whereas Chapters 1, 3, 6, and 9 through 12 are by A. R.

Acknowledgments

A. C. K. would like to express appreciation to his colleague O. Robert Mitchell and his graduate students David Nahamoo, Carl Crawford, and Kai-Wah Chan for many stimulating discussions. A number of our colleagues helped us by providing figures (see the individual figure credits). In addition, many of the figures were produced by Andrew Pilipchuk and others at the University of Maryland; and by Carl Crawford, Doug Morton, and Kai-Wah Chan at Purdue University. Kathryn Riley, Dawn Shifflett, and Mellanie Boes, among others, did an excellent job of preparing the text. To these, and to others too numerous to mention, our sincerest thanks.

The authors wish to express their indebtedness to the following individuals and organizations for their permission to reproduce the figures listed below.

Chapter 3: Figures 1, 4–7, and 11, from T. N. Cornsweet, *Visual Perception,* Academic Press, New York, 1970. Figure 3, from J. Beck, *Surface Color Perception,* copyright © 1972 by Cornell University; used by permission of Cornell University Press, Ithaca, New York. Figure 8, from S. Coren, "Subjective contours and apparent depth," *Psychological Review* **79,** 1972, 359–367. Figures 9–10, from M. Luckiesh, *Visual Illusions,* Dover, New York, 1965. Figure 12, from J. Beck, "Similarity grouping and peripheral discriminability under uncertainty," *American*

Journal of Psychology **85,** 1972, 1–19. Figures 13–16, from M. Wertheimer, "Principles of perceptual organization," in D. C. Beardslee and M. Wertheimer, eds., *Readings in Perception,* pp. 115–135, © 1958 by Litton Educational Publishing, Inc.; reprinted by permission of Van Nostrand Reinhold Company, Princeton, New Jersey. Figures 17–19, from J. Hochberg, *Perception,* © 1964, by permission of Prentice-Hall, Inc., Englewood Cliffs, New Jersey.

Chapter 4: Figure 8, from R. Legault, "The aliasing problems in two-dimensional sampled imagery," in L. M. Biberman, ed., *Perception of Displayed Information,* 279–312, Plenum Press, New York, 1973. Figure 10, from L. M. Biberman, "A summary," *ibid.,* 313–322. Figure 12, from A. Habibi and P. A. Wintz, "Image coding by linear transformation and block quantization," *IEEE Transactions on Communication Technology* **COM-19,** 1971, 50–62. Figure 15, from T. S. Huang, O. J. Tretiak, B. Prasada, and Y. Yamaguchi, "Design considerations in PCM transmission of low-resolution monochrome still pictures," *Proceedings of the IEEE* **55,** 1967, 331–335. Figures 17–19, from T. S. Huang, "PCM picture transmission," *IEEE Spectrum* **2,** 1965, 57–63. Table 1, from J. Max, "Quantizing for minimum distortion," *IRE Transactions on Information Theory* **IT-6,** 1960, 7–12.

Chapter 5: Figures 1 and 3–9, from P. A. Wintz, "Transform picture coding," *Proceedings of the IEEE* **60,** 1972, 809–820. Figures 16–18 and Tables 2–3, from A. Habibi, "Comparison of nth-order DPCM encoder with linear transformations and block quantization techniques," *IEEE Transactions on Communication Technology* **COM-19,** 1971, 948–956. Figures 21 and 22 from E. J. Delp and O. R. Mitchell, "Image compression using block truncation coding," *IEEE Transactions on Communication Technology* **COM-27,** 1979, 1335–1342.

Chapter 6: Figure 14, from D. A. O'Handley and W. B. Green, "Recent developments in digital image processing at the Image Processing Laboratory of the Jet Propulsion Laboratory," *Proceedings of the IEEE* **60,** 1972, 821–828. Figure 15, from T. G. Stockham, Jr., "Image processing in the context of a visual model," *ibid.,* 828–842.

Chapter 7: Figure 3, from J. L. Harris, Sr., "Image evaluation and restoration," *Journal of the Optical Society of America* **56,** 1966, 569–574. Figure 4, from B. L. McGlamery, "Restoration of turbulence-degraded images," *ibid.* **57,** 1967, 293–297. Figure 5, from J. L. Harris, Sr., "Potential and limitations of techniques for processing linear motion-degraded imagery," in *Evaluation of Motion-Degraded Images,* pp. 131–138, NASA SP-193, December 1968. Figure 6, from B. R. Hunt, "The application of constrained least-squares estimation to image restoration by digital computer," *IEEE Transactions on Computers* **C-22,** 1973, 805–812.

Contents of Volume 2

Chapter 1

Introduction

1.1 PICTURE PROCESSING

Picture processing or *image processing* is concerned with the manipulation and analysis of pictures by computer. Its major subareas include

(a) *Digitization and compression*: Converting pictures to discrete (digital) form; efficient coding or approximation of pictures so as to save storage space or channel capacity.

(b) *Enhancement, restoration, and reconstruction*: Improving degraded (low-contrast, blurred, noisy) pictures; reconstructing pictures from sets of projections.

(c) *Matching, description, and recognition*: Comparing and registering pictures to one another; segmenting pictures into parts, measuring properties of and relationships among the parts, and comparing the resulting descriptions to models that define classes of pictures.

In this chapter we introduce some basic concepts about pictures and digital pictures, and also give a bibliography of general references on picture processing and recognition. (References on specific topics are given at the end of each chapter.) Chapter 2 reviews some of the mathematical tools used in later chapters, including linear systems, transforms, and random fields, while Chapter 3 briefly discusses the psychology of visual perception.

1

The remaining chapters deal with the theory of digitization (4); coding and compression (5); enhancement (6); restoration and estimation (7); reconstruction from projections (8); registration and matching (9); segmentation into parts (10); representation of parts and geometric property measurement (11); and nongeometric properties, picture descriptions, and models for classes of pictures (12).

The level of treatment emphasizes concepts, algorithms, and (when necessary) the underlying theory. We do not cover hardware devices for picture input (scanners), processing, or output (displays); nondigital (e.g., optical) processing; or picture processing software.

1.2 SCENES, IMAGES, AND DIGITAL PICTURES

1.2.1 Scenes and Images

When a scene is viewed from a given point, the light received by the observer varies in brightness and color as a function of direction. Thus the information received from the scene can be expressed as a function of two variables, i.e., of two angular coordinates that determine a direction. (The scene brightness and color themselves are resultants of the illumination, reflectivity, and geometry of the scene; see Section 6.2.2.)

In an optical image of the scene, say produced by a lens, light rays from each scene point in the field of view are collected by the lens and brought together at the corresponding point of the image. Scene points at different distances from the lens give rise to image points at different distances; the basic equation is

$$\frac{1}{u} + \frac{1}{v} = \frac{1}{f}$$

where u, v are the distances of the object and image points from the lens (on opposite sides), and f is a constant called the focal length of the lens. If u is large, i.e., the scene points are all relatively far from the lens, $1/u$ is negligible, and we have $v \approx f$, so that the image points all lie at approximately the same distance from the lens, near its "focal plane." Thus the imaging process converts the scene information into an illumination pattern in the image plane; this is still a function of two variables, but they are now coordinates in the plane. (Image formation by optical systems will not be further discussed here. On the geometry of the mapping from three-dimensional scene coordinates to two-dimensional image coordinates, see Section 9.1.2.)

We can now record or measure the pattern of light from the scene by placing some type of sensor in the image plane. (Some commonly used sensors will be mentioned in the next paragraph.) Any given sensor has a characteristic spectral sensitivity, i.e., its response varies with the color of the light; thus its total response to the light at a given point can be expressed by an integral of the form $\int S(\lambda)I(\lambda)\,d\lambda$, where $I(\lambda)$ is light intensity and $S(\lambda)$ is sensitivity as functions of wavelength. This means that if we use only a single sensor, we can only measure (weighted) light intensity. If we want to measure color, we must use several sensors having different spectral responses; or we must split the light into a set of spectral bands, using color filters, and measure the light intensity in each band. (Knowing the intensities in three suitably chosen bands, e.g., in the red, green, and blue regions of the spectrum, is enough to characterize any color; see Section 3.3.) In other words, when we use only one sensor, we are representing the scene information by a scalar-valued function of position in the image, representing scene brightness. To represent color, we use a k-tuple (usually a triple) of such functions, or equivalently, a vector-valued function, representing the brightness in a set of spectral bands. We will usually assume in this book that we are dealing with a single scalar-valued brightness function. Photometric concepts and terminology will not be further discussed here; we use terms such as "brightness" and "intensity" in an informal sense.

Image sensors will not be discussed in detail in this book, but we briefly mention here some of the most common types.

(a)   We can put an *array* of photosensitive devices in the image plane; each of them measures the scene brightness at a particular point (or rather, the total scene brightness in a small patch).

(b)   We need only a single photosensor in the image plane if we can illuminate the scene one point (or small patch) at a time; this is the principle of the *flying-spot scanner*. Similarly, we need only one photosensor if we can view the scene through a moving aperture so that, at any given time, the light from only one point of the scene can reach the sensor.[§]

(c)   In a *TV camera*, the pattern of brightness in the scene is converted into an electrical charge pattern on a grid; this pattern can then be scanned by an electron beam, yielding a *video signal* whose value at any given time corresponds to the brightness at a given image point.

In all of these schemes, the image brightness is converted into a pattern of electrical signals, or into a time-varying signal corresponding to a sequential

---

[§] As a compromise between (a) and (b), we can use a one-dimensional array of sensors in the image plane, say in the horizontal direction, and scan in the vertical direction, so that light from only one "row" of the scene reaches the sensors at any given time.

scan of the image or scene. Thus the sensor provides an electrical or electronic analog of the scene brightness function, which is proportional to it, if the sensors are linear. More precisely, an array sensor provides a discrete array of samples of this function; while scanning sensors provide a set of cross sections of the function along the lines of the scanning pattern.

If, instead of using a sensor, we put a piece of photographic film (or some other light-sensitive recording medium) in the image plane, the brightness pattern gives rise to a pattern of variations in the optical properties of the film. (Color film is composed of layers having different spectral sensitivities; we will discuss here only the black-and-white case.) In a film transparency, the optical transmittance t (i.e., the fraction of the light transmitted by the film) varies from point to point; in an opaque print, the reflectance r ($=$ the fraction of light reflected) varies. Evidently we have $0 \leqslant t \leqslant 1$ and $0 \leqslant r \leqslant 1$. The quantity $-\log t$ or $-\log r$ is called optical *density*; thus a density close to zero corresponds to almost perfect transmission or reflection, while a very high density, say 3 or 4, corresponds to almost perfect opaqueness or dullness (i.e., only 10^{-3} or 10^{-4} of the incident light is transmitted or reflected). For ordinary photographic processes, the density is roughly a linear function of the log of the amount of incident light (the log of the "exposure") over a range of exposures; the slope of this line is called photographic *gamma*. Photographic processes will not be discussed further in this book. A photograph of a scene can be converted into signal form by optically imaging it onto a sensor.

1.2.2   Pictures and Digital Pictures

We saw in the preceding paragraphs that the light received from a scene by an optical system produces a two-dimensional image. This image can be directly converted into electrical signal form by a sensor, or it can be recorded photographically as a picture and subsequently converted. Mathematically, a *picture* is defined by a function $f(x, y)$ of two variables (coordinates in the image plane, corresponding to spatial directions). The function values are brightnesses, or k-tuples of brightness values in several spectral bands. In the black-and-white case, the values will be called *gray levels*. These values are real, nonnegative (brightness cannot be negative), and bounded (brightness cannot be arbitrarily great). They are zero outside a finite region, since an optical system has a bounded field of view, so that the image is of finite size; without loss of generality, we can assume that this region is rectangular. Whenever necessary, we will assume that picture functions are analytically well-behaved, e.g., that they are integrable, have invertible Fourier transforms, etc.

When a picture is digitized (see Chapter 4), a *sampling* process is used to extract from the picture a discrete set of real numbers. These *samples* are usually the gray levels at a regularly spaced array of points, or, more realistically, average gray levels taken over small neighborhoods of such points. (On other methods of sampling see Section 4.1.) The array is almost always taken to be Cartesian or rectangular, i.e., it is a set of points of the form (md, nd), where m and n are integers and d is some unit distance. (Other types of regular arrays, e.g., hexagonal or triangular, could also be used; see Section 11.1.7, Exercise 4, on a method of defining a hexagonal array by regarding alternate rows of a rectangular array as shifted $d/2$ to the right.) Thus the samples can be regarded as having integer coordinates, e.g., $0 \leqslant m < M, 0 \leqslant n < N$.

The picture samples are usually *quantized* to a set of discrete gray level values, which are often taken to be equally spaced (but see Section 4.3). In other words, the *gray scale* is divided into equal intervals, say $I_0, \ldots, I_K$, and the gray level $f(x, y)$ of each sample is changed into the level of the midpoint of the interval I_i in which $f(x, y)$ falls. The resulting quantized gray levels can be represented by their interval numbers $0, \ldots, K$, i.e., they can be regarded as integers.

The result of sampling and quantizing is a *digital picture*. As just seen, we can assume that a digital picture is a rectangular array of integer values. An element of a digital picture is called a *picture element* (often abbreviated *pixel* or *pel*); we shall usually just call it a *point*. The value of a pixel will still be called its gray level. If there are just two values, e.g., "black" and "white," we will usually represent them by 0 and 1; such pictures are called two-valued or binary-valued.

Digital pictures are often very large. For example, suppose we want to sample and quantize an ordinary (500-line) television picture finely enough so that it can be redisplayed without noticeable degradation. Then we must use an array of about 500 by 500 samples, and we should quantize each sample to about 50 discrete gray levels, i.e., to about a 6-bit number. This gives us an array of 250,000 6-bit numbers, for a total of $1\frac{1}{2}$ million bits. In many cases, even finer sampling is necessary; and it has become standard to use 8-bit quantization, i.e., 256 gray levels.

Except on the borders of the array, any point (x, y) of a digital picture has four horizontal and vertical neighbors and four diagonal neighbors, i.e.,

$$
\begin{array}{ccc}
(x - 1, y + 1) & (x, y + 1) & (x + 1, y + 1) \\
(x - 1, y) & (x, y) & (x + 1, y) \\
(x - 1, y - 1) & (x, y - 1) & (x + 1, y - 1)
\end{array}
$$

In this illustration of the 3×3 *neighborhood* of a point we have used Cartesian coordinates (x, y), with x increasing to the right and y increasing upward. There are other possibilities; for example, one could use matrix co-ordinates (m, n), in which m increases downward and n to the right. Note that the diagonal neighbors are $\sqrt{2}$ units away from (x, y), while the horizontal and vertical neighbors are only one unit away. If we think of a pixel as a unit square, the horizontal and vertical neighbors of (x, y) share a side with (x, y), while its diagonal neighbors only touch it at a corner. Some of the complications introduced by the existence of these two types of neighbors will be discussed in Chapter 11. Neighborhoods larger than 3×3 are sometimes used; in this case, a point may have many types of neighbors.

If (x, y) is on the picture border, i.e., $x = 0$ or $M - 1$, $y = 0$ or $N - 1$, some of its neighbors do not exist, or rather are not in the picture. When we perform operations on the picture, the new value of (x, y) often depends on the old values of (x, y) and its neighbors. To handle cases where (x, y) is on the border, we have several possible approaches:

(a)   We might give the operation a complex definition that covers these special cases. However, this may not be easy, and in any case it is computationally costly.

(b)   We can regard the picture as cyclically closed, i.e., assume that column $M - 1$ is adjacent to column 0 and row $N - 1$ to row 0; in other words, we take the coordinates (x, y) modulo (M, N). This is equivalent to regarding the picture as an infinite periodic array with an $M \times N$ period. We will sometimes use this approach, but it is usually not natural, since the opposite rows and columns represent parts of the scene that are not close together.

(c)   We can assume that all values outside the picture are zero. This is a realistic way of representing the image (see the first paragraph of this section), but not the scene.

(d)   The simplest approach is to apply the operation only to a *sub-picture*, chosen so that for all (x, y) in the subpicture, the required neighbors exist in the picture. This yields results all of which are meaningful; but note that the output picture produced by the operation is smaller than the input picture.

1.2.3   Operations on Pictures

In this book we shall study many different types of operations that can be performed on digital pictures to produce new pictures. The following are some of the important types of picture operations:

(a)   *Point operations*: The output gray level at a point depends only on the input gray level at the same point. Such operations are extensively used for gray scale manipulation (Section 6.2) and for segmentation by pixel classification (Section 10.1). There may be more than one input picture; for example, we may want to take the difference or product of two pictures, point by point. In this case, the output level at a point depends only on the set of input levels at the same point.

(b) *Local operations*: The output level at a point depends only on the input levels in a neighborhood of that point. Such operations are used for deblurring (Section 6.3), noise cleaning (Section 6.4), and edge and local feature detection (Sections 10.2 and 10.3), among other applications.

(c) *Geometric operations*: The output level at a point depends only on the input levels at some other point, defined by a geometrical transformation (e.g., translation, rotation, scale change, etc.) or in a neighborhood of that point. On such operations see Section 9.3.

An operation $\mathcal{O}$ is called *linear* if we get the same output whether we apply $\mathcal{O}$ to a linear combination of pictures (i.e., we take $\mathcal{O}(af + bg)$) or we apply $\mathcal{O}$ to each of the pictures and then form the same linear combination of the results (i.e., $a\mathcal{O}(f) + b\mathcal{O}(g)$). Linear operations on pictures will be discussed further in Section 2.1.1. Point and local operations may or may not be linear. For example, simple stretching of the gray scale ($\mathcal{O}(f) = cf$) is linear, but thresholding ($\mathcal{O}(f) = 1$ if $f \geqslant t$, $= 0$ otherwise) is not; local averaging is linear, but local absolute differencing is not. Geometric operations are linear, if we ignore the need to redigitize the picture after they are performed (Section 9.3).

$\mathcal{O}$ is called *shift invariant* if we get the same output whether we apply $\mathcal{O}$ to a picture and then shift the result, or first shift the picture and then apply $\mathcal{O}$. Such operations will be discussed further in Section 2.1.2. The examples of point and local operations given in the preceding paragraph are all shift invariant, but we can also define shift variant operations of these types, e.g., modifying the gray level of a point differently, or taking a different weighted average, as a function of position in the picture. The only shift-invariant geometric operations are the shifts, i.e., the translations. It is shown in Section 2.1.2 that an operation is linear and shift invariant iff it is a *convolution*; this is an operation in which the output gray level at a point is a linear combination of the input gray levels, with coefficients that depend only on their positions relative to the given point, but not on their absolute positions.

In Chapters 11 and 12 we will discuss *picture properties*, i.e., operations that can be performed on pictures to produce numerical values. In particular, we will deal with *point* and *local properties* (whose values depend only on one point, or on a small part, of the picture); *geometric properties* of picture subsets (whose values depend only on the set of points belonging to the given subset, but not on their gray levels); and *linear properties* (which give the same value whether we apply them to a linear combination of pictures, or apply them to each picture and then form the same linear combination of the results). It will be shown in Section 12.1.1a that a property is linear and bounded (in a certain sense) iff it is a linear combination of the picture's gray levels.

We will also be interested in certain types of *transforms* of pictures, particularly in their *Fourier transforms*. These are of interest because they make it easier to measure certain types of picture properties, or to perform certain types of operations on pictures, as we will see throughout this book. Basic concepts about (continuous) Fourier transforms are reviewed in Sections 2.1.3 and 2.1.4, and various types of discrete transforms are discussed in Section 2.2.

1.3 A GUIDE TO THE LITERATURE

Papers on picture processing and its various applications are being published at a rate of more than a thousand a year. Regular meetings are held on many aspects of the subject, and there are many survey articles, paper collections, meeting proceedings, and journal special issues. Picture processing is also extensively represented in the literature on (two-dimensional) signal processing and pattern recognition (and, to a lesser extent, artificial intelligence).

No attempt has been made here to give a comprehensive bibliography. Selected references are given at the end of each chapter on the subject matter of that chapter, but their purpose is only to cite material that provides further details about the ideas treated in the chapter—it is not practical to cite references on every idea mentioned in the text. Annual bibliographies [9–19] covering some of the non-application-oriented U.S. literature contain several thousand additional references, arranged by subject; they may be consulted for further information.

The principal textbooks on the subject through 1980, including the predecessors to this book, are [1–8, 20]. The following are some of the journals that frequently publish papers on the subject:

IEEE Transactions on Acoustics, Speech and Signal Processing
IEEE Transactions on Communications
IEEE Transactions on Computers
IEEE Transactions on Information Theory
IEEE Transactions on Pattern Analysis and Machine Intelligence
IEEE Transactions on Systems, Man, and Cybernetics

Computer Graphics and Image Processing
Pattern Recognition

We shall not attempt to list the numerous meeting proceedings or paper collections here; see [9–19] for further information.

REFERENCES

1. H. C. Andrews, "Computer Techniques in Image Processing." Academic Press, New York, 1970.
2. K. R. Castleman, "Digital Image Processing." Prentice-Hall, Englewood Cliffs, New Jersey, 1979.
3. R. O. Duda and P. E. Hart, "Pattern Classification and Scene Analysis." Wiley, New York, 1973.
4. R. C. Gonzalez and P. Wintz, "Digital Image Processing." Addison-Wesley, Reading, Massachusetts, 1977.
5. E. L. Hall, "Computer Image Processing and Recognition." Academic Press, New York, 1979.
6. T. Pavlidis, "Structural Pattern Recognition." Springer Publ., New York, 1977.
7. W. K. Pratt, "Digital Image Processing." Wiley, New York, 1978.
8. A. Rosenfeld, "Picture Processing by Computer." Academic Press, New York, 1969.
9. A. Rosenfeld, Picture processing by computer, *Comput. Surveys* **1**, 1969, 147–176.
10. A. Rosenfeld, Process in picture processing: 1969–71, *Comput. Surveys* **5**, 1973, 81–108.
11. A. Rosenfeld, Picture processing: 1972, *Comput. Graphics Image Processing* **1**, 1972, 1972, 394–416.
12. A. Rosenfeld, Picture processing: 1973, *Comput. Graphics Image Processing* **3**, 1974, 178–194.
13. A. Rosenfeld, Picture processing: 1974, *Comput. Graphics Image Processing* **4**, 1975, 133–155.
14. A Rosenfeld, Picture processing: 1975, *Comput. Graphics Image Processing* **5**, 1976, 215–237.
15. A. Rosenfeld, Picture processing: 1976, *Comput. Graphics Image Processing* **6**, 1977, 157–183.
16. A. Rosenfeld, Picture processing: 1977, *Comput. Graphics Image Processing* **7**, 1978, 211–242.
17. A. Rosenfeld, Picture processing: 1978, *Comput. Graphics Image Processing* **9**, 1979, 354–393.
18. A. Rosenfeld, Picture processing: 1979, *Comput. Graphics Image Processing* **13**, 1980, 46–79.
19. A. Rosenfeld, Picture processing: 1980, *Comput. Graphics Image Processing* **16**, 1981, 52–89.
20. A. Rosenfeld and A. C. Kak, "Digital Picture Processing." Academic Press, New York, 1976.

Chapter 2

Mathematical Preliminaries

2.1 LINEAR OPERATIONS ON PICTURES

2.1.1 Point Sources and Delta Functions

Let $\mathcal{O}$ be an operation that takes pictures into pictures; given the input picture f, the result of applying $\mathcal{O}$ to f is denoted by $\mathcal{O}[f]$. We call $\mathcal{O}$ *linear* if

$$\mathcal{O}[af+bg] = a\mathcal{O}[f] + b\mathcal{O}[g] \tag{1}$$

for all pictures f, g and all constants a, b.

In the analysis of linear operations on pictures, the concept of a *point source* is very convenient. If any arbitrary picture f could be considered to be a sum of point sources, then a knowledge of the operation's output for a point source input could be used to determine the output for f. The output of $\mathcal{O}$ for a point source input is called the *point spread function* of $\mathcal{O}$.

A point source can be regarded as the limit of a sequence of pictures whose nonzero values become more and more concentrated spatially. Note that in order for the total brightness to be the same for each of these pictures, their nonzero values must get larger and larger. As an example of such a sequence of pictures, let

$$\text{rect}(x, y) = \begin{cases} 1 & \text{for} \quad |x| \leqslant \tfrac{1}{2}, \quad |y| \leqslant \tfrac{1}{2} \\ 0 & \text{elsewhere} \end{cases} \tag{2}$$

10

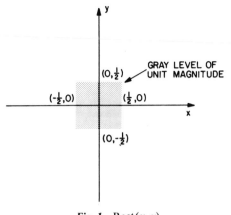

Fig. 1 Rect(x, y).

(see Fig. 1) and let

$$\delta_n(x, y) = n^2 \operatorname{rect}(nx, ny), \qquad n = 1, 2, \ldots \tag{3}$$

Thus δ_n is zero outside the $1/n \times 1/n$ square described by $|x| \leqslant 1/2n$, $|y| \leqslant 1/2n$ and has constant value n^2 inside that square. It follows that

$$\int\int\limits_{-\infty}^{\infty} \delta_n(x, y) \, dx \, dy = 1 \tag{4}$$

for any n.

As $n \to \infty$, the sequence δ_n does not have a limit in the usual sense, but it is convenient to treat it as though its limit existed. This limit, denoted by δ, is called a *Dirac delta function*. Evidently, we have $\delta(x, y) = 0$ for all (x, y) other than $(0, 0)$ where it is infinite. It follows that $\delta(-x, -y) = \delta(x, y)$.

We can derive a number of important properties of δ as limiting cases of properties of the functions δ_n. Thus, in view of (4), we can write

$$\int\int\limits_{-\infty}^{\infty} \delta(x, y) \, dx \, dy = 1 \tag{5}$$

More generally, consider the integral $\int_{-\infty}^{\infty} \int_{-\infty}^{\infty} g(x, y)\delta_n(x, y) \, dx \, dy$. This is just the average of $g(x, y)$ over a $1/n \times 1/n$ square centered at the origin. Thus in the limit we retain just the value at the origin itself, so that we can write

$$\int\int\limits_{-\infty}^{\infty} g(x, y)\,\delta(x, y) \, dx \, dy = g(0, 0)$$

If we shift δ by the amount (α, β), i.e., we use $\delta(x-\alpha, y-\beta)$ instead of $\delta(x, y)$, we similarly obtain the value of g at the point (α, β), i.e.,

$$\int\int_{-\infty}^{\infty} g(x, y)\delta(x-\alpha, y-\beta) \, dx \, dy = g(\alpha, \beta) \tag{6}$$

The same is true for any region of integration containing (α, β). Equation (6) is called the "sifting" property of the δ function.

As a final useful property of δ, we have

$$\int\int_{-\infty}^{\infty} \exp[-j2\pi(ux+vy)] \, du \, dv = \delta(x, y) \tag{7}$$

where $j = \sqrt{-1}$. For a discussion of this property, see Papoulis [8].

2.1.2 Linear Shift-Invariant Operations

Again let us consider a linear operation (or system) that takes pictures into pictures. The point spread function, which is the output picture for an input point source at the origin of the xy-plane, is denoted by $h(x, y)$.

The linear operation is said to be *shift invariant* (or space invariant, or position invariant) if the response to $\delta(x-\alpha, y-\beta)$, which is a point source located at (α, β) in the xy-plane, is given by $h(x-\alpha, y-\beta)$. In other words, the output is merely shifted by α and β in the x- and y-directions, respectively.

Now let us consider an arbitrary input picture $f(x, y)$. By Eq. (6) this picture can be considered to be a linear sum of point sources. We can write $f(x, y)$ as

$$f(x, y) = \int_{-\infty}^{\infty}\int_{-\infty}^{\infty} f(\alpha, \beta)\delta(\alpha-x, \beta-y) \, d\alpha \, d\beta \tag{8}$$

In other words, $f(x, y)$ is a linear sum of point sources located at (α, β) in the xy-plane with α and β ranging from $-\infty$ to $+\infty$. In this sum the point source at a particular value of (α, β) has "strength" $f(\alpha, \beta)$. Let the response of the operation to the input $f(x, y)$ be denoted by $\mathcal{O}[f]$. If we assume the operation to be shift invariant, then by the interpretation just given to the right-hand side of (8), we obtain

$$\mathcal{O}[f(x, y)] = \mathcal{O}\left[\int_{-\infty}^{\infty}\int_{-\infty}^{\infty} f(\alpha, \beta)\delta(\alpha-x, \beta-y) \, d\alpha \, d\beta\right]$$

$$= \int\int f(\alpha, \beta)\mathcal{O}[\delta(\alpha-x, \beta-y)] \, d\alpha \, d\beta \tag{9}$$

by the linearity of the operation, which means that the response to a sum of excitations is equal to the sum of responses to each excitation. As stated earlier, the response to $\delta(\alpha-x,\beta-y)=\delta(x-\alpha,y-\beta)$, which is a point source located at (α,β), is given by $h(x-\alpha,y-\beta)$, and if $\mathcal{O}[f]$ is denoted by g, we obtain

$$g(x,y) = \int_{-\infty}^{\infty}\int_{-\infty}^{\infty} f(\alpha,\beta)h(x-\alpha,y-\beta)\,d\alpha\,d\beta \qquad (10)$$

The right-hand side is called the *convolution* of f and h, and is often denoted by $f*h$. The integrand is a product of two functions $f(\alpha,\beta)$ and $h(\alpha,\beta)$ with the latter rotated by 180° and shifted by x and y along the x- and y-directions, respectively. This is pictorially shown in Fig. 2. A simple change of variables shows that (10) can also be written as

$$g(x,y) = \int_{-\infty}^{\infty}\int_{-\infty}^{\infty} f(x-\alpha,y-\beta)h(\alpha,\beta)\,d\alpha\,d\beta \qquad (11)$$

so that $f*h=h*f$.

2.1.3 Fourier Analysis

Let $f(x,y)$ be a function of two independent variables x and y; then its *Fourier transform* $F(u,v)$ is defined by

$$F(u,v) = \int_{-\infty}^{\infty}\int_{-\infty}^{\infty} f(x,y)\exp[-j2\pi(ux+vy)]\,dx\,dy \qquad (12)$$

In general, F is a complex-valued function of u and v. As an example, let $f(x,y)=\text{rect}(x,y)$. Then it is easily verified that

$$F(u,v) = \frac{\sin\pi u}{\pi u}\frac{\sin\pi v}{\pi v}$$

This last function is usually denoted by $\text{sinc}(u,v)$; it is illustrated in Fig. 3.

Exercise 1.   Verify that the Fourier transform of $\text{rect}(x,y)$ is $\text{sinc}(x,y)$ and, more generally, that the Fourier transform of $\text{rect}(nx,ny)$ is

$$(1/n^2)\,\text{sinc}(u/n,v/n) \quad\blacksquare$$

The Fourier transform of f may not exist unless f satisfies certain conditions. The following is a typical set of sufficient conditions for its existence [5]:

(1) $\int_{-\infty}^{\infty}\int_{-\infty}^{\infty}|f(x,y)|\,dx\,dy < \infty$.
(2) $f(x,y)$ must have only a finite number of discontinuities and a finite number of maxima and minima in any finite rectangle.
(3) $f(x,y)$ must have no infinite discontinuities.

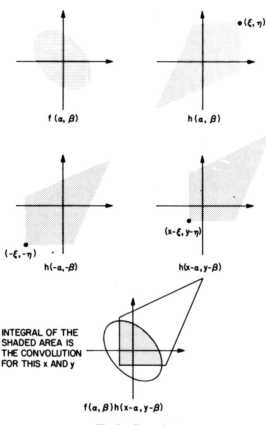

Fig. 2   Convolution.

Some useful mathematical functions, like the Dirac δ function, do not necessarily obey the preceding conditions. Sometimes it is possible to represent these functions as limits of a sequence of well-behaved functions that do obey these conditions. The Fourier transforms of the members of this sequence will also form a sequence. Now if this sequence of Fourier transforms possesses a limit, then this limit is called the "generalized Fourier transform" of the original function. Generalized transforms can be manipulated in the same manner as the conventional transforms, and the distinction between the two is generally ignored; it being understood that when a function fails to satisfy the existence conditions and yet is said to have a transform, then the generalized transform is actually meant [5, 7].

In Section 2.1.1, we introduced the Dirac δ function as a limit of a sequence of the functions $n^2 \operatorname{rect}(nx, ny)$; then by the preceding argument and Exercise 1,

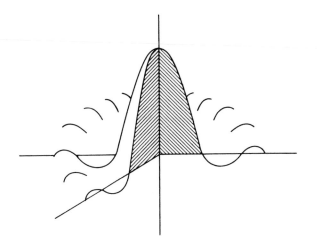

Fig. 3 Sinc(x, y).

the Fourier transform of the Dirac δ function is the limit of the sequence of Fourier transforms sinc$(u/n, v/n)$. In other words, when

$$f(x, y) = \delta(x, y)$$

then

$$F(u, v) = \lim_{n \to \infty} \text{sinc}(u/n, v/n) = 1 \tag{13}$$

By multiplying both sides of Eq. (12) by $\exp[j2\pi(u\alpha + v\beta)]$, integrating both sides with respect to u and v, and making use of Eq. (7), it is easily shown that

$$\int_{-\infty}^{\infty} \int_{-\infty}^{\infty} F(u, v) \exp[j2\pi(u\alpha + v\beta)]\, du\, dv = f(\alpha, \beta) \tag{14}$$

or equivalently

$$f(x, y) = \int_{-\infty}^{\infty} \int_{-\infty}^{\infty} F(u, v) \exp[j2\pi(ux + vy)]\, du\, dv \tag{15}$$

which is called the *inverse Fourier transform* of $F(u, v)$. By Eqs. (12) and (15), $f(x, y)$ and $F(u, v)$ form a *Fourier transform pair*.

Equation (15) can be used to give a physical interpretation to $F(u, v)$ and to the coordinates u and v, if x and y represent spatial coordinates. Let us first examine the function

$$\exp[j2\pi(ux + vy)] \tag{16}$$

The real and the imaginary parts of this function are $\cos 2\pi(ux + vy)$ and $\sin 2\pi(ux + vy)$, respectively. In Fig. 4, we have shown the lines corresponding

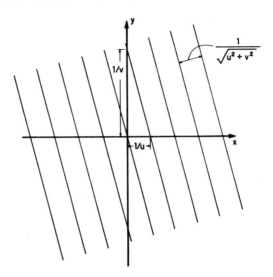

Fig. 4   Lines corresponding to the maxima of cos $2\pi(ux + vy)$.

to the maxima of cos $2\pi(ux + vy)$. The minima of this function would be along lines parallel to these but located in between them. It is clear if one took a section of this two-dimensional pattern parallel to the x-axis, it goes through u cycles per unit distance, while a section parallel to the y-axis goes through v cycles per unit distance. This is the reason why u and v are called the *spatial frequencies* along the x- and y-axes, respectively. Also, from the figure it can be seen that the spatial period of the pattern is $(u^2 + v^2)^{-1/2}$. The plot for sin $2\pi(ux + vy)$ looks similar to the one in Fig. 4 except that it is displaced by a quarter period in the direction of maximum rate of change.

From the preceding discussion it is clear that $\exp[j2\pi(ux + vy)]$ is a two-dimensional pattern, the sections of which, parallel to the x- and y-axes, are spatially periodic with frequencies u and v, respectively. The pattern itself has a spatial period of $(u^2 + v^2)^{-1/2}$ along a direction that subtends an angle $\tan^{-1}(v/u)$ with the x-axis. By changing u and v, one can generate patterns with spatial periods ranging from 0 to ∞ in any direction in the xy-plane.

Equation (15) can, therefore, be interpreted to mean that $f(x, y)$ can be considered to be a linear combination of elementary periodic patterns of the form $\exp[j2\pi(ux + vy)]$. Evidently, $F(u, v)$ is simply a weighting factor that is a measure of the relative contribution of the elementary pattern, the x- and y-components of the spatial frequency of which are u and v, respectively, to the total sum. For this reason $F(u, v)$ is called the *frequency spectrum* of $f(x, y)$.

Exercise 2. Show that if $f(x, y)$ is a circularly symmetric function, i.e., $f(x, y) = f(\sqrt{x^2 + y^2})$, then its frequency spectrum is also circularly symmetric and is given by

$$F(u, v) = F(\rho) = 2\pi \int_0^\infty r f(r) J_0(2\pi r\rho) \, dr \qquad (17)$$

while the inverse relationship is given by

$$f(r) = 2\pi \int_0^\infty \rho F(\rho) J_0(2\pi r\rho) \, d\rho$$

where

$$r = \sqrt{x^2 + y^2}, \qquad \theta = \tan^{-1}(y/x), \qquad \rho = \sqrt{u^2 + v^2}, \qquad \varphi = \tan^{-1}(v/u)$$

and

$$J_0(x) = (1/2\pi) \int_0^{2\pi} \exp[-jx \cos(\theta - \varphi)] \, d\theta$$

where $J_0(x)$ is the zero-order Bessel function of the first kind. The transformation in (17) is also called the *Hankel transform of zero order*. ∎

Exercise 3. Use (7) to show that the Fourier transform of $\cos 2\pi(\alpha x + \beta y)$ is $\frac{1}{2}[\delta(u - \alpha, v - \beta) + \delta(u + \alpha, v + \beta)]$. ∎

Exercise 4. Let us define a comb function as

$$\text{comb}(x, y) = \sum_{m=-\infty}^{\infty} \sum_{n=-\infty}^{\infty} \delta(x - m, y - n) \qquad (18)$$

(see Fig. 5). Show that $\text{comb}(x, y)$ and $\text{comb}(u, v)$ are a Fourier transform pair. ∎

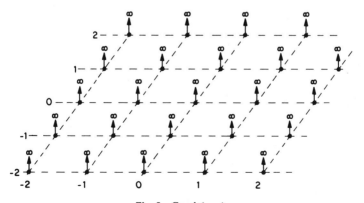

Fig. 5 Comb(x, y).

2.1.4 Properties of Fourier Transforms

Let $\mathcal{F}\{f\}$ denote the Fourier transform of a function $f(x, y)$. Then $\mathcal{F}\{f(x, y)\} = F(u, v)$. We will now present without proof some of the more common properties of Fourier transforms. The proofs are, for the most part, left as exercises for the reader (see the books by Goodman [5] and Papoulis [8]).

(1) *Linearity:*

$$\mathcal{F}\{af_1(x, y) + bf_2(x, y)\} = a\mathcal{F}\{f_1(x, y)\} + b\mathcal{F}\{f_2(x, y)\}$$

$$= aF_1(u, v) + bF_2(u, v) \tag{19}$$

This follows from the linearity of the integration operation.

(2) *Scaling:*

$$\mathcal{F}\{f(\alpha x, \beta y)\} = \frac{1}{|\alpha\beta|} F\left(\frac{u}{\alpha}, \frac{v}{\beta}\right) \tag{20}$$

To see this, introduce the change of variables $x' = \alpha x$, $y' = \beta y$.

(3) *Shift property:*

$$\mathcal{F}\{f(x-\alpha, y-\beta)\} = F(u, v) \exp[-j2\pi(u\alpha + v\beta)] \tag{21a}$$

This, too, follows immediately if we make the change of variables $x' = x - \alpha$, $y' = y - \beta$. The corresponding property for a shift in the frequency domain is

$$\mathcal{F}\{\exp[j2\pi(u_0 x + v_0 y)] f(x, y)\} = F(u - u_0, v - v_0) \tag{21b}$$

(4) *180° rotation:*

$$\mathcal{F}\{\mathcal{F}\{f(x, y)\}\} = f(-x, -y) \tag{22}$$

(5) *Convolution:*

$$\mathcal{F}\left\{\int_{-\infty}^{\infty}\int_{-\infty}^{\infty} f_1(\alpha, \beta) f_2(x-\alpha, y-\beta)\, d\alpha\, d\beta\right\} = \mathcal{F}\{f_1(x, y)\}\, \mathcal{F}\{f_2(x, y)\}$$

$$= F_1(u, v) F_2(u, v) \tag{23a}$$

Note that the convolution of two functions in the space domain is equivalent to the very simple operation of multiplication in the spatial frequency domain. The corresponding property for convolution in the spatial frequency domain is given by

$$\mathcal{F}\{f_1(x, y) f_2(x, y)\} = \int_{-\infty}^{\infty}\int F_1(u-s, v-t) F_2(s, t)\, ds\, dt \tag{23b}$$

(6)   *Parseval's theorem:*

$$\int_{-\infty}^{\infty} \int_{-\infty}^{\infty} f_1(x, y) f_2^*(x, y)\, dx\, dy = \int_{-\infty}^{\infty} \int_{-\infty}^{\infty} F_1(u, v) F_2^*(u, v)\, du\, dv$$

(24)

where * denotes the complex conjugate. When $f_1(x, y) = f_2(x, y) = f(x, y)$, we have

$$\int_{-\infty}^{\infty} \int_{-\infty}^{\infty} |f(x, y)|^2\, dx\, dy = \int_{-\infty}^{\infty} \int_{-\infty}^{\infty} |F(u, v)|^2\, du\, dv$$

(25)

In this form, this property is interpretable as a statement of conservation of energy.

We conclude this section by introducing the autocorrelation and cross correlation of functions. The definitions given here are valid only for deterministic functions. These averages are also used to characterize probabilistic functions, and their definitions for that case are given in Section 2.4.2. Under certain conditions to be discussed later, the two definitions are equivalent (see Section 2.4.5).

The *cross correlation* C_{fg} of two functions f and g is defined as

$$C_{fg}(x', y') = \int_{-\infty}^{\infty} \int_{-\infty}^{\infty} f^*(x - x', y - y')\, g(x, y)\, dx\, dy$$

$$= C_{gf}^*(-x', -y')$$

(26)

Note that for real functions the cross correlation differs from the convolution in that before taking the product of the two functions shifted with respect to one another, no rotation is performed.

Exercise 5.   Using (23) show that

$$\mathscr{F}\{C_{fg}\} = \mathscr{F}^*\{f\} \mathscr{F}\{g\} = F^*(u, v)\, G(u, v) \quad \blacksquare$$

(27)

The *autocorrelation* of a function $f(x, y)$ is defined as

$$R_f(x', y') = \int_{-\infty}^{\infty} \int f(x, y)\, f^*(x - x', y - y')\, dx\, dy$$

$$= \int_{-\infty}^{\infty} \int f(x + x', y + y')\, f^*(x, y)\, dx\, dy$$

(28)

From (27) it is clear that

$$\mathscr{F}\{R_f\} = |F(u, v)|^2$$

(29)

For deterministic functions $f(x, y)$, $|F(u, v)|^2$ is called the *power spectrum*. We see that the power spectrum is the Fourier transform of the autocorrelation function.

2.2 DISCRETE PICTURE TRANSFORMS

Let a matrix $[f]$ represent an $M \times N$ array of numbers:

$$[f] = \begin{bmatrix} f(0,0) & f(0,1) & f(0, N-1) \\ \vdots & \cdots & \vdots & \cdots & \vdots \\ f(M-1,0) & f(M-1,1) & f(M-1, N-1) \end{bmatrix} \tag{30}$$

Note that such an array of numbers could be obtained by sampling a picture $f(x, y)$ on a grid of $M \times N$ points, each number in the array representing the gray level in the picture at the corresponding sampling point.

A general discrete transform of the $M \times N$ matrix $[f]$ is an $M \times N$ matrix $[F]$ defined as the product of the three matrices

$$[F] = [P][f][Q] \tag{31}$$

where $[P]$ and $[Q]$ are nonsingular§ $M \times M$ and $N \times N$ matrices, respectively. The specific transform is determined by the way the matrices $[P]$ and $[Q]$ are defined. The transform $[F]$, which is an $M \times N$ matrix, can also be written as

$$F(u, v) = \sum_{m=0}^{M-1} \sum_{n=0}^{N-1} P(u, m) f(m, n) Q(n, v) \tag{32}$$

for $u = 0, 1, ..., M-1$, $v = 0, 1, ..., N-1$.

Since the transformation matrices $[P]$ and $[Q]$ are nonsingular, their inverses are uniquely defined. Let $[P]^{-1}$ denote the inverse of $[P]$ and $[Q]^{-1}$ that of $[Q]$. Multiplying both sides of (31) first from the left by $[P]^{-1}$ and then from the right by $[Q]^{-1}$, we obtain

$$[f] = [P]^{-1}[F][Q]^{-1} \tag{33}$$

---

§ We will briefly define some of the properties of matrices that we have used in this section.

(1) A square matrix possesses an inverse if its determinant is nonzero; such matrices are called *nonsingular*.

(2) A real square matrix $[T]$ is called *symmetric* if $[T] = [T]^t$ where $[T]^t$ is the transpose of $[T]$. $[T]$ is called *orthogonal* if $[T]^t[T] = [I]$ where $[I]$ is the identity matrix. Therefore, for a real square matrix that is both symmetric and orthogonal, $[T]^{-1} = [T]$.

(3) A complex square matrix $[C]$ is called *Hermitian* if $[C]^{*t} = [C]$, where $[C]^*$ is obtained from $[C]$ by taking the complex conjugate of every element. $[C]$ is called *unitary* if $[C]^{*t}[C] = [I]$. Therefore, for a complex square matrix that is both Hermitian and unitary, $[C]^{-1} = [C]$.

This defines the inverse transform relationship, and we say that $[f]$ is the *inverse transform* of $[F]$.

Before we present special cases of discrete transforms, we would like to mention that if a nonsingular real square matrix is orthogonal and symmetric, then its inverse is equal to itself. Therefore, if the square matrices $[P]$ and $[Q]$ are real, symmetric, and orthogonal, then the transform relationships (31) and (33) become

$$[F] = [P][f][Q], \qquad [f] = [P][F][Q] \tag{34}$$

For the case of complex matrices this is true provided the matrices are Hermitian and unitary.

2.2.1 The Discrete Fourier Transform

Let us define a $J \times J$ transformation matrix $[\Phi_{J,J}]$ whose (m,n)th element is given by

$$(1/J)e^{-j(2\pi/J)mn}, \qquad m,n = 0,1,2,...,J-1 \tag{35}$$

With

$$[P] = [\Phi_{M,M}] \quad \text{and} \quad [Q] = [\Phi_{N,N}] \tag{36}$$

the *discrete Fourier transform* F of an array f is given by

$$[F] = [P][f][Q]$$

or making use of the expansion in (32), (35), and (36),

$$F(u,v) = \frac{1}{MN} \sum_{m=0}^{M-1} \sum_{n=0}^{N-1} f(m,n) \exp\left[-j2\pi\left(\frac{mu}{M} + \frac{nv}{N}\right)\right] \tag{37}$$

for $u = 0,1,2,...,M-1$, $v = 0,1,2,...,N-1$. Even though this expression is similar to the discrete sum approximation of the Fourier integral in Eq. (12), note that (37) by itself is not an approximation; $[F]$ as defined in (37) is the exact discrete Fourier transform of the array of numbers $[f]$.

The inverse matrix $[\Phi_{J,J}]^{-1}$ is again $J \times J$, and its (m,n)th element is given by

$$e^{j(2\pi/J)mn} \tag{38}$$

That this is true can be seen by multiplying the two matrices $[\Phi_{J,J}]$ and $[\Phi_{J,J}]^{-1}$ and noting that

$$\sum_{m=0}^{J-1} \exp\left[\frac{-j2\pi}{J}km\right] \exp\left[\frac{j2\pi}{J}mn\right] = \begin{cases} J, & k = n \\ 0, & k \neq n \end{cases} \tag{39}$$

Since $[P] = [\Phi_{M,M}]$ and $[Q] = [\Phi_{N,N}]$, therefore $[P]^{-1} = [\Phi_{M,M}]^{-1}$ and $[Q]^{-1} = [\Phi_{N,N}]^{-1}$. The inverse transform relationship as given by Eq. (33)

is completely defined and in its expanded form is given by using (38):

$$f(m,n) = \sum_{u=0}^{M-1} \sum_{v=0}^{N-1} F(u,v) \exp\left[j2\pi\left(\frac{mu}{M} + \frac{nv}{N}\right)\right] \tag{40}$$

for $m = 0, 1, \ldots, M - 1$, $n = 0, 1, \ldots, N - 1$. In Fig. 6a we have shown a picture represented by a 16×16 matrix $[f]$. The real and imaginary parts of its Fourier transform $[F]$ are shown in Figs. 6b and 6c, respectively.

In (37) the discrete Fourier transform $F(u, v)$ is defined for u between 0 and $M-1$ and for v between 0 and $N-1$. If, however, we use the same equation to evaluate $F(\pm u, \pm v)$, we discover that the periodicity properties of the exponential factor imply that

$$F(u, -v) = F(u, N-v)$$
$$F(-u, v) = F(M-u, v) \tag{41a}$$
$$F(-u, -v) = F(M-u, N-v)$$

Similarly, using (40) we can show that

$$f(-m, n) = f(M-m, n)$$
$$f(m, -n) = f(m, N-n) \tag{41b}$$
$$f(-m, -n) = f(M-m, N-n)$$

```
0  0  0  0  0  0  0  0  0  0  0  0  0  0  0  0
0  0  0  0  0  0  0  0  0  0  0  0  0  0  0  0
0  0  0  0  0  0  0  0  0  0  0  0  0  0  0  0
0  0  0  0  0  0  0  0  0  0  0  0  0  0  0  0
0  0  0  0  0  0  0  0  0  0  0  0  0  0  0  0
0  0  0  0  0  0  0  0  0  0  0  0  0  0  0  0
0  0  0  0  0  0  1  1  1  0  0  0  0  0  0  0
0  0  0  0  0  0  1  0  1  0  0  0  0  0  0  0
0  0  0  0  0  0  1  1  1  0  0  0  0  0  0  0
0  0  0  0  0  0  0  0  0  0  0  0  0  0  0  0
0  0  0  0  0  0  0  0  0  0  0  0  0  0  0  0
0  0  0  0  0  0  0  0  0  0  0  0  0  0  0  0
0  0  0  0  0  0  0  0  0  0  0  0  0  0  0  0
0  0  0  0  0  0  0  0  0  0  0  0  0  0  0  0
0  0  0  0  0  0  0  0  0  0  0  0  0  0  0  0
0  0  0  0  0  0  0  0  0  0  0  0  0  0  0  0
```

Fig. 6a   A picture represented by an array of numbers. The top left-hand corner corresponds to $m = 0$ and $n = 0$.

v \ u	-8	-7	-6	-5	-4	-3	-2	-1	0	1	2	3	4	5	6	7
-8	0	.14	-.41	.47	0	-1.06	2.41	-3.55	4.00	-3.55	2.41	-1.06	0	.47	-.41	.14
-7	.14	-.20	.25	-.00	-.71	1.77	-2.81	3.41	-3.27	2.41	-1.17	-.00	.71	-.85	.60	-.28
-6	-.41	.25	0	-.42	1.00	-1.60	2.00	-2.01	1.59	-.83	0	.66	-1.00	1.01	-.83	.60
-5	.47	-.00	-.42	.67	-.71	.59	+.40	.23	-.11	-.00	.17	-.41	.71	-.94	1.01	-.85
-4	0	-.71	1.00	-.71	0	.71	-1.00	.71	0	-.71	1.00	-.71	0	.71	-1.00	.71
-3	-1.06	1.77	-1.60	.59	.71	-1.50	1.25	-.00	-1.64	2.85	-3.01	2.12	-.71	-.41	.66	-.00
-2	2.41	-2.81	2.00	-.40	-1.00	1.25	0	-2.25	4.41	-5.43	4.83	-3.01	1.00	.17	0	-1.17
-1	-3.55	3.41	-2.01	.23	.71	-.00	-2.25	5.03	-6.97	7.11	-5.43	2.85	-.71	-.00	-.83	2.41
0	4.00	-3.27	1.59	-.11	0	-1.64	4.41	-6.97	8.00	-6.97	4.41	-1.64	0	-.11	1.59	-3.27
1	-3.55	2.41	-.83	-.00	-.71	2.85	-5.43	7.11	-6.97	5.03	-2.25	-.00	.71	.23	-2.01	3.41
2	2.41	-1.17	0	.17	1.00	-3.01	4.83	-5.43	4.41	-2.25	0	1.25	-1.00	-.40	2.00	-2.81
3	-1.06	-.00	.66	-.41	-.71	2.12	-3.01	2.85	-1.64	-.00	1.25	-1.50	.71	.59	-1.60	1.77
4	0	.71	-1.00	.71	0	-.71	1.00	-.71	0	.71	-1.00	.71	0	-.71	1.00	-.71
5	.47	-.85	1.01	-.94	.71	-.41	.17	-.00	-.11	.23	-.40	.59	-.71	.67	-.42	-.00
6	-.41	.60	-.83	1.01	-1.00	.66	0	-.83	1.59	-2.01	2.00	-1.60	1.00	-.42	0	.25
7	.14	-.28	.60	-.85	.71	-.00	-1.17	2.41	-3.27	3.41	-2.81	1.77	-.71	-.00	.25	-.20

Fig. 6b   Real part of the Fourier transform matrix $256 \times F(u, v)$ of the picture in Fig. 6a.

v \ u	-8	-7	-6	-5	-4	-3	-2	-1	0	1	2	3	4	5	6	7
-8	0	.06	-.41	1.14	-2.00	2.55	-2.41	1.47	0	-1.47	2.41	-2.55	2.00	-1.14	.41	-.06
-7	.06	-.20	.60	-1.20	1.71	-1.77	1.17	.00	-1.36	2.41	-2.81	2.50	-1.71	.85	-.25	0
-6	-.41	.60	-.83	1.01	-1.00	.66	0	-.83	1.59	-2.01	2.00	-1.60	1.00	-.42	0	.25
-5	1.14	-1.20	1.01	-.67	.29	.00	-.17	.23	-.27	.33	-.40	.41	-.29	-.00	.42	-.85
-4	-2.00	1.71	-1.00	.29	0	.29	-1.00	1.71	-2.00	1.71	-1.00	.29	0	.29	-1.00	1.71
-3	2.55	-1.77	.66	.00	.29	-1.50	3.01	-4.03	3.97	-2.85	1.25	.00	-.29	-.41	1.60	-2.50
-2	-2.41	1.17	0	-.17	-1.00	3.01	-4.83	5.43	-4.41	2.25	0	-1.25	1.00	.40	-2.00	2.81
-1	1.47	.00	-.83	.23	1.71	-4.03	5.43	-5.03	2.89	0	-2.25	2.85	-1.71	-.33	2.01	-2.41
0	0	-1.36	1.59	-.27	-2.00	3.97	-4.41	2.89	0	-2.89	4.41	-3.97	2.00	.27	-1.59	1.36
1	-1.47	2.41	-2.01	.33	1.71	-2.85	2.25	0	-2.89	5.03	-5.43	4.03	-1.71	-.23	.83	-.00
2	2.41	-2.81	2.00	-.40	-1.00	1.25	0	-2.25	4.41	-5.43	4.83	-3.01	1.00	.17	0	-1.17
3	-2.55	2.50	-1.60	.41	.29	-.00	-1.25	2.85	-3.97	4.03	-3.01	1.50	-.29	-.00	-.66	1.77
4	2.00	-1.71	1.00	-.29	0	-.29	1.00	-1.71	2.00	-1.71	1.00	-.29	0	-.29	1.00	-1.71
5	-1.14	.85	-.42	.00	.29	-.41	.40	-.33	.27	-.23	.17	-.00	-.29	.67	-1.01	1.20
6	.41	-.25	0	.42	-1.00	1.60	-2.00	2.01	-1.59	.83	0	-.66	1.00	-1.01	.83	-.60
7	-.06	0	.25	-.85	1.71	-2.50	2.81	-2.41	1.36	-.00	-1.17	1.77	-1.71	1.20	-.60	.20

Fig. 6c   Imaginary part of the Fourier transform matrix $256 \times F(u, v)$ of the picture in Fig. 6a.

Another related consequence of the periodicity properties of the exponential factors in Eqs. (37) and (40) is that

$$F(aM+u, bN+v) = F(u,v) \qquad \text{and} \qquad f(aM+m, bN+n) = f(m,n) \quad (42)$$

for $a = 0, \pm 1, \pm 2, ..., b = 0, \pm 1, \pm 2, ...$ Therefore, we have the following conclusion: If a finite array of numbers $[f]$ and its Fourier transform $[F]$ are related by Eqs. (37) and (40), then if it is desired to extend the definition of $f(m,n)$ and $F(u,v)$ beyond the original domain as given by $[0 \leqslant (m \text{ and } u) \leqslant M-1]$ and $[0 \leqslant (n \text{ and } v) \leqslant N-1]$, this extension must be governed by (41) and (42). In other words, the extensions are periodic repetitions of the arrays.

It will now be shown that this periodicity has important consequences when we compute the convolution of two $M \times N$ arrays $[f]$ and $[d]$ by multiplying their discrete Fourier transforms $[F]$ and $[D]$. The convolution of two arrays $[f]$ and $[d]$ is given by

$$g(\alpha, \beta) = \frac{1}{MN} \sum_{m=0}^{M-1} \sum_{n=0}^{N-1} f(m,n) d(\alpha-m, \beta-n)$$

$$= \frac{1}{MN} \sum_{m=0}^{M-1} \sum_{n=0}^{N-1} f(\alpha-m, \beta-n) d(m,n) \quad (43)$$

for $\alpha = 0, 1, ..., M-1, \beta = 0, 1, ..., N-1$, where we insist that when the values of $f(m,n)$ and $d(m,n)$ are required for indices outside the ranges $0 \leqslant m \leqslant M-1$ and $0 \leqslant n \leqslant N-1$, for which $f(m,n)$ and $d(m,n)$ are defined, then they be obtained by the rules given in Eqs. (41) and (42). With this condition, the convolution previously defined is called a *circular or cyclic convolution*.

We will now show that the discrete Fourier transform of (43) is the product of the discrete Fourier transforms of $[f]$ and $[d]$. By making use of (40), we obtain

$$g(\alpha, \beta) = \frac{1}{MN} \sum_{m=0}^{M-1} \sum_{n=0}^{N-1} f(m,n) d(\alpha-m, \beta-n)$$

$$= \frac{1}{MN} \sum_{m=0}^{M-1} \sum_{n=0}^{N-1} \left\{ \sum_{u=0}^{M-1} \sum_{v=0}^{N-1} F(u,v) \exp\left[j2\pi\left(\frac{mu}{M} + \frac{nv}{N}\right)\right]\right\}$$

$$\times \left\{ \sum_{w=0}^{M-1} \sum_{z=0}^{N-1} D(w,z) \exp\left[j2\pi\left(\frac{(\alpha-m)w}{M} + \frac{(\beta-n)z}{N}\right)\right]\right\}$$

$$= \frac{1}{MN} \sum_{u=0}^{M-1} \sum_{v=0}^{N-1} \sum_{w=0}^{M-1} \sum_{z=0}^{N-1} \left\{ F(u,v) D(w,z) \exp\left[j2\pi\left(\frac{\alpha w}{M} + \frac{\beta z}{N}\right)\right] \right.$$

$$\times \left. \sum_{m=0}^{M-1} \sum_{n=0}^{N-1} \exp\left[j2\pi \frac{m(u-w)}{M}\right] \exp\left[j2\pi \frac{n(v-z)}{N}\right]\right\}$$

$$= \sum_{u=0}^{M-1} \sum_{v=0}^{N-1} F(u,v) D(u,v) \exp\left[j2\pi\left(\frac{\alpha u}{M} + \frac{\beta v}{N}\right)\right] \quad (44)$$

where the last equality is obtained by making use of the orthogonality relationship (39). This proves that the discrete Fourier transform of $[g]$ in (43) is $[F] \times [D]$.[§] One can similarly show that the discrete Fourier transform of the "circular" convolution of two $M \times N$ arrays in the frequency domain is equal to the product of the inverse transforms of the two arrays. That is, if we construct the following circular convolution in the frequency domain:

$$G(u,v) = \sum_{w=0}^{M-1} \sum_{z=0}^{N-1} F(w,z) D(u-w, v-z) = \sum_{w=0}^{M-1} \sum_{z=0}^{N-1} F(u-w, v-z) D(w,z)$$

for $u = 0, 1, 2, ..., M-1$, $v = 0, 1, 2, ..., N-1$, then its inverse discrete Fourier transform is given by

$$g(m,n) = f(m,n) d(m,n)$$

for $m = 0, 1, 2, ..., M-1$, $n = 0, 1, 2, ..., N-1$ or

$$[g] = [f] \times [d] \tag{45}$$

A property of the discrete Fourier transform that is often used is the discrete version of Parseval's theorem, which is given by (24) for the continuous case. The statement of the theorem for the discrete case is

$$\sum_{m=0}^{M-1} \sum_{n=0}^{N-1} f(m,n) g^*(m,n) = MN \sum_{u=0}^{M-1} \sum_{u=0}^{N-1} F(u,v) G^*(u,v) \tag{46}$$

This can be proven by substituting in (46) the inverse transform relationship (40) and the corresponding relationship for $g(m,n)$. The result is

$$\sum_{m=0}^{M-1} \sum_{n=0}^{N-1} f(m,n) g^*(m,n) = \sum_{m=0}^{M-1} \sum_{n=0}^{N-1} \left\{ \sum_{u=0}^{M-1} \sum_{v=0}^{N-1} \sum_{u'=0}^{M-1} \sum_{v'=0}^{N-1} F(u,v) G^*(u',v') \right.$$

$$\left. \times \exp\left[j2\pi \frac{m}{M} (u - u') \right] \exp\left[j2\pi \frac{n}{N} (v - v') \right] \right\} \tag{47}$$

Interchanging the summations on the right-hand side, performing them first with respect to m and n, and using the orthogonality relationship in (39), we get (46).

The following relationship directly follows from (46):

$$\sum_{m=0}^{M-1} \sum_{n=0}^{N-1} |f(m,n)|^2 = MN \sum_{u=0}^{M-1} \sum_{n=0}^{N-1} |F(u,v)|^2 \tag{48}$$

[§] Note that this product is *not* the matrix product of $[F]$ and $[D]$ but ordinary multiplication of two functions, which happen to be discrete. If we denote this product by $[F] \times [D]$, then the (m,n)th element of $[F] \times [D]$ is $F(m,n)D(m,n)$.

Exercise 6.   In constrained deconvolution in Chapter 7 the left-hand side below will be used as a measure of "smoothness" of the restored image $f(m, n)$. Prove that the left-hand side is equal to the right-hand side:

$$\sum_{m=0}^{M-1} \sum_{n=0}^{N-1} \left| \sum_{p=0}^{M-1} \sum_{q=0}^{N-1} f(m-p, n-q) \, d(p, q) \right|^2$$

$$= M^3 N^3 \sum_{u=0}^{M-1} \sum_{v=0}^{N-1} |F(u, v)D(u, v)|^2 \tag{49}$$

where the convolution on the left-hand side is circular, as was the case in (43). ∎

Before we end this subsection, we would like to say a few words about the numerical implementation of the discrete Fourier transform. Equation (37) may be written as

$$F(u, v) = \frac{1}{M} \sum_{m=0}^{M-1} \left[\frac{1}{N} \sum_{n=0}^{N-1} f(m, n) \exp\left(-j\frac{2\pi}{N} nv \right) \right] \exp\left(-j\frac{2\pi}{M} mu \right),$$

$$u = 0, \ldots, M - 1, \quad v = 0, \ldots, N - 1 \tag{50}$$

The expression within the square brackets is the one-dimensional DFT of the mth row of the image, which may be implemented by using a standard FFT (fast Fourier transform) computer program (in most instances N is a power of 2). Therefore, to compute $F(u, v)$, we *replace* each row in the image by its one-dimensional DFT, and *then* perform the one-dimensional DFT of each column.

The reader may have noticed that in the discrete Fourier transform shown in Fig. 6, the origin ($u = 0$, $v = 0$) appears approximately at the center of the array. Ordinarily, this will not be the case. If the above described computer implementation is directly carried out, the frequency domain origin will appear at the upper left-hand corner and the rest of the array will contain both positive and negative frequencies. [Note, for example, that $u = 15$ and $v = 0$ corresponds to a negative frequency of one cycle per image width. This can be seen by substituting $u = 1$ and $v = 0$ in the second equation in (41a).] To display the frequency domain origin at approximately the center of the array (a precise center does not exist when either M or N is an even number), the image data $f(m, n)$ is first multiplied by $(-1)^{m+n}$ and then the discrete Fourier transformation is performed. To prove this, let us define a new array $f'(m, n)$ as follows:

$$f'(m, n) = f(m, n)(-1)^{m+n} \tag{51}$$

and let $F'(u, v)$ be its discrete Fourier transform:

$$F'(u, v) = \frac{1}{MN} \sum_{m=0}^{M-1} \sum_{n=0}^{N-1} f(m, n)(-1)^{m+n} \exp\left[-j2\pi\left(\frac{mu}{M} + \frac{nv}{N} \right) \right] \tag{52}$$

Rewriting this expression as

$$F'(u, v) = \frac{1}{MN} \sum_{m=0}^{M-1} \sum_{n=0}^{N-1} f(m, n) \exp\left\{ j2\pi \left[\frac{(M/2)m}{M} + \frac{(N/2)n}{N} \right] \right\}$$

$$\times \exp\left[-j2\pi \left(\frac{mu}{M} + \frac{nv}{N} \right) \right] \tag{53}$$

it is easy to show that

$$F'(u, v) = F\left(u - \frac{M}{2}, v - \frac{N}{2} \right), \quad u = 0, 1, \ldots, M - 1, \quad v = 0, 1, \ldots, N - 1 \tag{54}$$

Therefore, when the array $F'(u, v)$ is displayed, the location at $u = M/2$ and $v = N/2$ will contain $F(0, 0)$. The rest of the indexing will also correspond to that shown in Figs. 6b and 6c.

We have by no means discussed all the important properties of discrete Fourier transforms. Literature abounds on the subject [13].

2.2.2 The Hadamard Transform

If the transformation matrices $[P]$ and $[Q]$ in (31) are Hadamard matrices, then $[F]$ is called the *Hadamard transform* of $[f]$. A Hadamard matrix $[H_{J,J}]$ is a symmetric $J \times J$ matrix whose elements are the real numbers $+1$ and -1. The rows (and columns) of a Hadamard matrix are mutually orthogonal. An example of a Hadamard matrix of order 2 is

$$[H_{2,2}] = \begin{bmatrix} 1 & 1 \\ 1 & -1 \end{bmatrix} \tag{55}$$

The following theorem is useful in constructing Hadamard matrices of orders that are powers of 2 from $[H_{2,2}]$.

Theorem. If $[H_{J,J}]$ is a Hadamard matrix, then

$$[H_{2J,2J}] = \begin{bmatrix} [H_{J,J}] & [H_{J,J}] \\ [H_{J,J}] & -[H_{J,J}] \end{bmatrix} \tag{56}$$

is also a Hadamard matrix.

Proof: The matrix $[H_{2J,2J}]$ is clearly a symmetric matrix with elements $+1$ and -1. We must now show that the rows of this matrix are orthogonal vectors. Let r_j be the jth row of the matrix $[H_{J,J}]$. The rows of $[H_{2J,2J}]$ can then be denoted by (r_j, r_j) or $(r_j, -r_j)$ depending on whether the string of

numbers in r_j is followed by a similar string or by a string of opposite sign.
The dot product of the jth and $(J+j)$th rows of $[H_{2J,2J}]$ is

$$(r_j, r_j) \cdot (r_j, -r_j) = (r_j \cdot r_j) + (r_j \cdot (-r_j)) = J - J = 0 \qquad (57)$$

For any other combination of rows

$$(r_i, \pm r_i) \cdot (r_j, \pm r_j) = (r_i \cdot r_j) \pm (r_i \cdot r_j) = 0 \pm 0 = 0$$

and thus $[H_{2J,2J}]$ is an orthogonal matrix. ∎

By the left direct product $[A] \otimes [B]$ of two matrices $[A_{M,M}]$ and $[B_{N,N}]$
we mean the $MN \times MN$ matrix

$$[A] \otimes [B] = \begin{bmatrix} b_{0,0}[A] & b_{0,1}[A] & \cdots & b_{0,N-1}[A] \\ b_{1,0}[A] & b_{1,1}[A] & \cdots & b_{1,N-1}[A] \\ \vdots & \vdots & & \vdots \\ b_{N-1,0}[A] & \cdots & \cdots & b_{N-1,N-1}[A] \end{bmatrix}$$

$[H_{2J,2J}]$ in (56) can be expressed as a left direct product of $[H_{J,J}]$ and
$[H_{2,2}]$:

$$[H_{2J,2J}] = [H_{J,J}] \otimes [H_{2,2}] \qquad (58)$$

By the preceding theorem $[H_{2J,2J}]$ can be further expressed as

$$[H_{2J,2J}] = [H_{J/2,J/2}] \otimes [H_{2,2}] \otimes [H_{2,2}]$$
$$= [H_{2,2}] \otimes [H_{2,2}] \otimes [H_{2,2}] \otimes \cdots \otimes [H_{2,2}] \qquad (59)$$

provided J is a power of 2.

The order of a Hadamard matrix need not be a power of 2. It has been
conjectured that for J greater than 2, $[H_{J,J}]$ exists for all J equal to a multiple
of 4, but this has neither been proved nor disproved. In the applications of
Hadamard matrices considered in this book, we have restricted ourselves to
those Hadamard matrices with orders equal to powers of 2.

It is easily shown that the inverse of $[H_{J,J}]$ is given by

$$[H_{J,J}]^{-1} = (1/J)[H_{J,J}] \qquad (60)$$

Therefore, the discrete Hadamard transform relations take the form

$$[F] = [H_{M,M}][f][H_{N,N}] \qquad \text{and} \qquad [f] = (1/MN)[H_{M,M}][F][H_{N,N}] \qquad (61)$$

In Fig. 7 we show the Hadamard transform of the pattern in Fig. 6a.

By definition, the determination of discrete transforms involves matrix
multiplications. Let the matrix $[f]$ in (31) be an $N \times N$ matrix. Then $[P]$ and
$[Q]$ are both $N \times N$ matrices. The product $[f][Q]$ is again an $N \times N$ matrix.
Given $[f]$ and $[Q]$ it would require N operations to calculate each element

8	4	−2	2	−2	2	8	4	2	−2	−8	−4	−8	−4	2	−2
4	0	−2	2	−2	2	4	0	2	−2	−4	0	−4	0	2	−2
−2	−2	0	0	0	0	−2	−2	0	0	2	2	2	2	0	0
2	2	0	0	0	0	2	2	0	0	−2	−2	−2	−2	0	0
−2	−2	0	0	0	0	−2	−2	0	0	2	2	2	2	0	0
2	2	0	0	0	0	2	2	0	0	−2	−2	−2	−2	0	0
8	4	−2	2	−2	2	8	4	2	−2	−8	−4	−8	−4	2	−2
4	0	−2	2	−2	2	4	0	2	−2	−4	0	−4	0	2	−2
2	2	0	0	0	0	2	2	0	0	−2	−2	−2	−2	0	0
−2	−2	0	0	0	0	−2	−2	0	0	2	2	2	2	0	0
−8	−4	2	−2	2	−2	−8	−4	−2	2	8	4	8	4	−2	2
−4	0	2	−2	2	−2	−4	0	−2	2	4	0	4	0	−2	2
−8	−4	2	−2	2	−2	−8	−4	−2	2	8	4	8	4	−2	2
−4	0	2	−2	2	−2	−4	0	−2	2	4	0	4	0	−2	2
2	2	0	0	0	0	2	2	0	0	−2	−2	−2	−2	0	0
−2	−2	0	0	0	0	−2	−2	0	0	2	2	2	2	0	0

Fig. 7 Hadamard transform of the picture in Fig. 6a.

of the product, where each operation consists of one multiplication and one addition. Therefore, the total number of operations to compute $[f][Q]$ is, in general, equal to N^3. It follows that the determination of the transform $[F]$ ($=[P][f][Q]$) would take $2N^3$ operations.

Good [4] demonstrated that if a matrix can be expressed as a product of p sparse matrices where p is proportional to $\log N$, then a product of the matrix with a vector can be determined using a number of operations proportional to $N \log N$ rather than N^2. It follows that if $[P]$ and $[Q]$ are such matrices, then the product $[f][Q]$ would require a number of operations proportional to $N^2 \log N$. The total number of operations to compute $[P][f][Q]$ and hence $[F]$ from $[f]$ (or vice versa) would then be proportional to $2N^2 \log N$ rather than $2N^3$. In fact, this forms the basis of "fast" Fourier and Hadamard transforms [2, 13]. Another matrix that lends itself to very efficient factorization is the Haar matrix [6, 11] which comprises ones, minus ones, and zeros [1].

2.3 RANDOM VARIABLES

2.3.1 Outcomes, Events, and Probabilities

Let us consider a statistical experiment. The experiment could be rolling a die or selecting a picture from a collection. The experimental outcomes for the case of rolling a die consist of particular faces of the die turning up. In the second case, the outcomes are the selections of particular pictures. If the set of outcomes in an experiment is $\Omega = \{\omega_1, \omega_2, \omega_3, \ldots\}$, then we can assign a probability p_i to each outcome ω_i in Ω. These probabilities satisfy

$$p_i \geqslant 0 \qquad \text{and} \qquad \sum p_i = 1$$

which correspond to the facts that no outcome can have probability less than zero, and on every performance of the experiment one of the outcomes must occur. Every subset A of Ω in this case also has a well-defined probability which is equal to the sum of probabilities of the outcomes contained in A.

In practice, it turns out that it is necessary to consider probabilities on the subsets of Ω. The subsets of Ω are called *events*. For example, for the case of rolling a die, $\Omega = \{\omega_1, \omega_2, \omega_3, \omega_4, \omega_5, \omega_6\}$ where the outcome ω_i corresponds to the face numbered i showing up. Some possible events for this experiment are

$$A_1 = \{\omega_1, \omega_2\}, \qquad A_2 = \{\omega_3, \omega_4\}, \qquad A_3 = \{\omega_1, \omega_2, \omega_5, \omega_6\}$$

$$A_{\text{even}} = \{\text{event that an even number will show up}\} = \{\omega_2, \omega_4, \omega_6\}$$

$$A_{\text{odd}} = \{\text{event that an odd number will show up}\} = \{\omega_1, \omega_3, \omega_5\}$$

Note that an event occurs whenever any of the outcomes that constitute that event occur. For example, if face 1 shows up, then events A_1, A_3, and A_{odd} have occurred. It is clear that the collection of all the outcomes Ω is also an event. It is called the *certain event*.

If in an experiment A_i is an event, then the complement of A_i, denoted by $\bar{A}_i$, is also an event. The event $\bar{A}_i$ is the nonoccurrence of A_i. Also, if A_i and A_j are events, then the results of set operations on these events would also be events. That is, if A_i and A_j are any two events, then $A_i \cup A_j$, $A_i \cap A_j$ and $A_i - A_j$ are also events. In the probabilistic description of any experiment, we need one other event—the *null event*. The null event is an empty set, that is, it contains no outcomes and is denoted by $\varnothing$. Two events, A_i and A_j, are called *mutually exclusive* if their intersection equals the null event, or, symbolically, if

$$A_i \cap A_j = \varnothing$$

One can now introduce the axiomatic definition of probability. The probability of an event A is a number $\mathscr{P}(A)$ assigned to this event in such a fashion as to obey the following conditions:

    I. $\mathscr{P}(A) \geqslant 0$;

    II. $\mathscr{P}(\Omega) = 1$;

    III. Whenever $A_1, A_2, \ldots, A_n, \ldots$ is a sequence of mutually exclusive events, $\mathscr{P}(A_1 \cup A_2 \cup \cdots \cup A_n \cup \cdots) = \sum_{i=1}^{\infty} \mathscr{P}(A_i)$.

Suppose that in an experiment we assign a number to every outcome. That is, if ω_i is an outcome of the experiment, then to this outcome we assign a number $\mathbf{f}(\omega_i)$, which is then a function over the set $\Omega = \{\omega_1, \omega_2, \ldots\}$ and is called a *random variable*.

Note that the relationship between the outcomes ω_i and the numbers $\mathbf{f}(\omega_i)$ assigned to each of them is deterministic. In other words, once an outcome has occurred, then the value that the random variable takes is a completely determined quantity. What is random is the occurrence of the outcome itself. As an example, consider the experiment of rolling a die. The set of outcomes is $\Omega = \{\omega_1, \omega_2, \omega_3, \omega_4, \omega_5, \omega_6\}$. To each outcome we assign a number as follows:

$$\mathbf{f}(\omega_1) = 5, \quad \mathbf{f}(\omega_2) = 10, \quad \ldots, \quad \mathbf{f}(\omega_6) = 30$$

thereby defining the random variable $\mathbf{f}(\omega_i)$. Suppose we roll the die and the face ω_2 shows; then the random variable takes the value 10. The random variable $\mathbf{f}(\omega_i) = 5\omega_i$ constructed here could be our gain if ω_i shows in a dice game.

We will use boldface lowercase letters to denote random variables. The symbol $\mathbf{f}(\omega_i)$ will indicate the number assigned to the specific event ω_i. Also, we will use the notation $\{\mathbf{f} \leqslant z\}$ to represent a set consisting of all the outcomes ω_i such that $\mathbf{f}(\omega_i) \leqslant z$. Note that z is an arbitrary but fixed number and for any z the set $\{\mathbf{f} \leqslant z\}$ is an event. Similarly, given two arbitrary but fixed numbers z_1 and z_2

$$\{z_1 \leqslant \mathbf{f} \leqslant z_2\}$$

is also an event. The set $\{\mathbf{f} = z\}$ is an event and is a collection of all the outcomes ω_i for which $\mathbf{f}(\omega_i) = z$. In particular, the sets $\{\mathbf{f} = +\infty\}$ and $\{\mathbf{f} = -\infty\}$ are also events, i.e., in general, we may allow the random variable $\mathbf{f}$ to equal $+\infty$ or $-\infty$ for some outcomes ω_i. We shall insist, however, that the set of such outcomes have zero probability.

2.3.2 Distributions and Densities

The probability of $\{\mathbf{f} \leqslant z\}$ is a number depending on z, that is, it is a function of z. This function will be denoted by $P_f(z)$ and will be called the *distribution function* of the random variable $\mathbf{f}$. Thus

$$P_f(z) = \mathscr{P}\{\mathbf{f} \leqslant z\} \tag{62}$$

where $\mathscr{P}(A)$ denotes the probability of event A. We will assume here that $P_f(z)$ is differentiable.

A distribution function has the following properties:

(a) $\quad P_f(-\infty) = \mathscr{P}\{\mathbf{f} \leqslant -\infty\} = 0$ and $P_f(\infty) = \mathscr{P}\{\mathbf{f} \leqslant +\infty\} = 1$

The first property follows directly from the specifications for a random variable in the preceding section. As for the second, the event $\{\mathbf{f} \leqslant \infty\}$ must be the set of all the outcomes and, hence, is the certain event whose probability is 1.

(b) It is a nondecreasing function of z:

$$P_f(z_1) \leqslant P_f(z_2) \qquad \text{for} \quad z_1 \leqslant z_2$$

This can be proved by showing that for $z_1 \leqslant z_2$, $\{\mathbf{f} \leqslant z_1\}$ is always a subset of $\{\mathbf{f} \leqslant z_2\}$ and further by showing that if event A is included in event B in the set-theoretic sense, then $\mathscr{P}(A) \leqslant \mathscr{P}(B)$.

(c) $$\mathscr{P}\{z_1 < \mathbf{f} \leqslant z_2\} = P_f(z_2) - P_f(z_1) \tag{63}$$

Property (c) is equivalent to saying the probability of the random variable taking a value between z_1 and z_2 is equal to the difference between the values of the distribution function at these two points.

The derivative

$$p_f(z) = dP_f(z)/dz \tag{64}$$

of the distribution function $P_f(z)$ is called the *density function* of the random variable $\mathbf{f}$. By property (c) and Eq. (64), we have

$$\mathscr{P}\{z_1 \leqslant \mathbf{f} \leqslant z_2\} = \int_{z_1}^{z_2} p_f(z)\, dz \tag{65}$$

so that $P_f(z) = \int_{-\infty}^{z} p_f(z)\, dz$. Also for Δz sufficiently small

$$\mathscr{P}\{z \leqslant \mathbf{f} \leqslant z + \Delta z\} \simeq p_f(z)\, \Delta z$$

The density function can thus be defined as a limit

$$p_f(z) = \lim_{\Delta z \to 0} \mathscr{P}\{z \leqslant \mathbf{f} \leqslant z + \Delta z\}/\Delta z \tag{66}$$

This equation points to a direct method for determining the density function of a continuous random variable. The steps involved are: Repeat the experiment a large number of times, say N. Count the number of times the random variable takes values between z and $z + \Delta z$ with Δz being small compared to the range of values taken by the random variable. Let this number be $N_{\Delta z}$. Clearly, the probability that the random variable takes a value between z and $z + \Delta z$ is approximately $N_{\Delta z}/N$. Therefore, the value of $p_f(z)$ at z is approximately

$$N_{\Delta z}/N\, \Delta z \tag{67}$$

Note that by Eq. (65) the area under the density function between z_1 and z_2 equals the probability of $\mathbf{f}$ taking a value between these two limits.

The *expected value* or the *mean value* $E\{\mathbf{f}\}$ of a random variable $\mathbf{f}$ is defined as

$$E\{\mathbf{f}\} = \int_{-\infty}^{\infty} z p_f(z) \, dz \tag{68}$$

That this definition agrees with the meaning we commonly associate with averages can be shown as follows:

$$E\{\mathbf{f}\} \simeq \sum_{i=-\infty}^{\infty} z_i \, p_f(z_i) \, \Delta z$$

where the integration has been approximated by a discrete sum. By using Eq. (66), we obtain

$$E\{\mathbf{f}\} \simeq \sum_{i=-\infty}^{\infty} z_i \mathscr{P}\{z_i \leqslant \mathbf{f} \leqslant z_{i+1}\}$$

By the arguments leading to (67), this equation can be written as

$$E\{\mathbf{f}\} \simeq \sum_{i=-\infty}^{\infty} z_i \frac{\text{number of times } \mathbf{f} \text{ falls in the interval } (z_i, z_{i+1})}{\text{total number of times the experiment is performed}}$$

which is the usual definition of an average.

Let $\mathbf{g} = \mathscr{L}(\mathbf{f})$ be a random variable that is a function of the random variable $\mathbf{f}$; then it can be shown that

$$E\{\mathbf{g}\} = E\{\mathscr{L}(\mathbf{f})\} = \int_{-\infty}^{\infty} \mathscr{L}(z) \, p_f(z) \, dz \tag{69}$$

Let μ_f be the mean of the random variable $\mathbf{f}$. Then the *variance* σ_f^2 of $\mathbf{f}$ is defined as

$$\sigma_f^2 = E\{(\mathbf{f} - \mu_f)^2\} = \int_{-\infty}^{\infty} (z - \mu_f)^2 p_f(z) \, dz \tag{70}$$

where the last equality follows from (69). The square root of the variance is called the *standard deviation*.

As an example of a density function commonly encountered, we say a random variable $\mathbf{f}$ is *normally distributed* if its density function is a Gaussian curve given by

$$p_f(z) = \frac{1}{\sigma_f \sqrt{2\pi}} \exp \frac{-(z - \mu_f)^2}{2\sigma_f^2}$$

where it can be shown that μ_f and σ_f^2 are, respectively, the mean and the variance of $\mathbf{f}$.

2.3.3 Conditional Densities

Consider two events A and B. As stated earlier, their intersection $A \cap B$ is also an event. The *conditional probability* of A, given that B has occurred, is defined by

$$\mathscr{P}(A \mid B) = \mathscr{P}(A \cap B)/\mathscr{P}(B) \tag{71}$$

The *conditional distribution* $P_f(z \mid B)$ of a random variable $\mathbf{f}$, assuming B has occurred, is defined as the conditional probability of the event $\{\mathbf{f} \leqslant z\}$; that is,

$$P_f(z \mid B) = \mathscr{P}\{\mathbf{f} \leqslant z \mid B\} = \mathscr{P}(\{\mathbf{f} \leqslant z\} \cap B)/\mathscr{P}(B) \tag{72}$$

where the numerator is the event consisting of all outcomes ω_i such that

$$\mathbf{f}(\omega_i) \leqslant z \qquad \text{and} \qquad \omega_i \in B \tag{73}$$

At the points of continuity of $P_f(z \mid B)$, the *conditional density* is defined as

$$p_f(z \mid B) = dP_f(z \mid B)/dz \tag{74}$$

$$= \lim_{\Delta z \to 0} \mathscr{P}\{z \leqslant \mathbf{f} \leqslant z + \Delta z \mid B\}/\Delta z \tag{75}$$

The last equality follows by arguments similar to those leading to (66).

The *conditional expected value* of the random variable $\mathbf{f}$ is given by integral (68), where $p_f(z)$ is replaced by $p_f(z \mid B)$:

$$E\{\mathbf{f} \mid B\} = \int_{-\infty}^{\infty} z p_f(z \mid B)\, dz \tag{76}$$

2.3.4 Joint, Marginal, and Conditional Densities

A random variable $\mathbf{f}$ was defined to be a function $\mathbf{f}(\omega_i)$ over the set of all outcomes $\Omega = (\omega_1, \omega_2, \ldots)$ of an experiment. Let us define n functions

$$\mathbf{f}_1(\omega_i), \quad \mathbf{f}_2(\omega_i), \quad \ldots, \quad \mathbf{f}_n(\omega_i)$$

over this set of outcomes. From our earlier discussion, the sets

$$\{\mathbf{f}_1 \leq z_1\}, \quad \{\mathbf{f}_2 \leq z_2\}, \quad \ldots, \quad \{\mathbf{f}_n \leq z_n\}$$

are events with respective probabilities

$$\mathscr{P}\{\mathbf{f}_1 \leqslant z_1\} = P_{f_1}(z_1)$$

$$\mathscr{P}\{\mathbf{f}_2 \leqslant z_2\} = P_{f_2}(z_2)$$

$$\vdots$$

$$\mathscr{P}\{\mathbf{f}_n \leqslant z_n\} = P_{f_n}(z_n)$$

where $P_{f_1}(z_1), P_{f_2}(z_2), ..., P_{f_n}(z_n)$ are the distribution functions of the random variables $\mathbf{f}_1, \mathbf{f}_2, ..., \mathbf{f}_n$.

The intersection

$$\{\mathbf{f}_1 \leqslant z_1\} \cap \{\mathbf{f}_2 \leqslant z_2\} \cap \cdots \cap \{\mathbf{f}_n \leqslant z_n\} = \{\mathbf{f}_1 \leqslant z_1, \mathbf{f}_2 \leqslant z_2, ..., \mathbf{f}_n \leqslant z_n\}$$

of these n sets is also an event consisting of all the outcomes ω_i such that $\mathbf{f}_1(\omega_i) \leqslant z_1, \mathbf{f}_2(\omega_i) \leqslant z_2, ..., \mathbf{f}_n(\omega_i) \leqslant z_n$. The *joint distribution function*

$$P_{f_1, ..., f_n}(z_1, ..., z_n)$$

is the probability of this event. That is

$$P_{f_1, ..., f_n}(z_1, z_2, ..., z_n) = \mathscr{P}\{\mathbf{f}_1 \leqslant z_1, \mathbf{f}_2 \leqslant z_2, ..., \mathbf{f}_n \leqslant z_n\} \qquad (77)$$

The nth-order partial derivative

$$p_{f_1, ..., f_n}(z_1, z_2, ..., z_n) = \frac{\partial^n P_{f_1, ..., f_n}(z_1, z_2, ..., z_n)}{\partial z_1 \, \partial z_2 \, \cdots \, \partial z_n} \qquad (78)$$

(wherever it exists) is known as the *joint density function* of the random variables $\mathbf{f}_1, \mathbf{f}_2, ..., \mathbf{f}_n$.

Since $\mathbf{f}_1, \mathbf{f}_2, ..., \mathbf{f}_n$ are defined over the same set Ω, and since the set $\{\mathbf{f}_k \leqslant \infty\}$ for any k must be the collection of all possible outcomes, then by the property of intersections, we have for $i \leqslant n$

$$\{\mathbf{f}_1 \leqslant z_1\} \cap \{\mathbf{f}_2 \leqslant z_2\} \cap \cdots \cap \{\mathbf{f}_i \leqslant z_i\}$$

$$= \{\mathbf{f}_1 \leqslant z_1\} \cap \{\mathbf{f}_2 \leqslant z_2\} \cap \cdots \cap \{\mathbf{f}_i \leqslant z_i\} \cap \{\mathbf{f}_{i+1} \leqslant \infty\} \cap \cdots \cap \{\mathbf{f}_n \leqslant \infty\}$$

Therefore, it follows for $i \leqslant n$ that

$$P_{f_1, ..., f_i}(z_1, z_2, ..., z_i) = P_{f_1, ..., f_n}(z_1, z_2, ..., z_i, \infty, ..., \infty) \qquad (79)$$

where there are $(n-i)$ ∞'s.

It can be shown from (78) that

$$P_{f_1, ..., f_n}(z_1, z_2, ..., z_n)$$

$$= \int_{-\infty}^{z_1} \int_{-\infty}^{z_2} \cdots \int_{-\infty}^{z_n} p_{f_1, ..., f_n}(\xi_1, \xi_2, ..., \xi_n) \, d\xi_1 \, d\xi_2 \, \cdots \, d\xi_n \qquad (80)$$

By making use of (74) and (80), we obtain for $i \leqslant n$

$$p_{f_1, ..., f_i}(z_1, z_2, ..., z_i)$$

$$= \frac{\partial^i P_{f_1, ..., f_i}(z_1, z_2, ..., z_i)}{\partial z_1 \, \partial z_2 \, \cdots \, \partial z_i}$$

$$= \int_{-\infty}^{\infty} \int_{-\infty}^{\infty} \cdots \int_{-\infty}^{\infty} p_{f_1, ..., f_n}(z_1, z_2, ..., z_n) \, dz_{i+1} \, dz_{i+2} \, \cdots \, dz_n \qquad (81)$$

So we see that if we integrate $p_{f_1,\ldots,f_n}(z_1, z_2, \ldots, z_n)$ with respect to some of the variables, we obtain the joint density function over the rest of the variables. Joint density functions thus obtained are called *marginal density functions*.

By making use of Eqs. (72)–(76), one can show that

$$p_{f_1,\ldots,f_k}(z_1, z_2, \ldots, z_k \mid \mathbf{f}_{k+1} = z_{k+1}, \mathbf{f}_{k+2} = z_{k+2}, \ldots, \mathbf{f}_n = z_n)$$

$$= \frac{p_{f_1,\ldots,f_n}(z_1, z_2, \ldots, z_k, z_{k+1}, \ldots, z_n)}{p_{f_1,\ldots,f_n}(z_{k+1}, z_{k+2}, \ldots, z_n)}$$

where the left-hand side denotes the conditional density of $\mathbf{f}_1, \mathbf{f}_2, \ldots, \mathbf{f}_k$ given that the random variables $\mathbf{f}_{k+1}, \mathbf{f}_{k+2}, \ldots, \mathbf{f}_n$ have taken the specific values $z_{k+1}, z_{k+2}, \ldots, z_n$, respectively. The denominator on the right-hand side is the marginal density over $\mathbf{f}_{k+1}, \mathbf{f}_{k+2}, \ldots, \mathbf{f}_n$.

Before we end this subsection, we would like to give the expression for the expectation of a function of several random variables. Let a random variable $\mathbf{g}$ be a function of the random variables $\mathbf{f}_1, \mathbf{f}_2, \ldots, \mathbf{f}_n$ as follows:

$$\mathbf{g} = \mathscr{L}(\mathbf{f}_1, \mathbf{f}_2, \ldots, \mathbf{f}_n)$$

By making use of definition (59), it can be shown that

$$E\{\mathbf{g}\} = \int \int \cdots \int \mathscr{L}(z_1, z_2, \ldots, z_n)\, p(z_1, z_2, \ldots, z_n)\, dz_1\, dz_2 \cdots dz_n \qquad (82)$$

2.3.5 Independent, Uncorrelated, and Orthogonal Random Variables

The random variables $\mathbf{f}_1, \mathbf{f}_2, \ldots, \mathbf{f}_n$ are called *independent* if

$$p_{f_1,\ldots,f_n}(z_1, z_2, \ldots, z_n) = p_{f_1}(z_1)\, p_{f_2}(z_2) \cdots p_{f_n}(z_n) \qquad (83a)$$

where $p_{f_i}(z_i)$ is the density function of the random variable $\mathbf{f}_i$. Similarly, $\mathbf{f}_1, \mathbf{f}_2, \ldots, \mathbf{f}_r$ are called "independent" of $\mathbf{f}_{r+1}, \mathbf{f}_{r+2}, \ldots, \mathbf{f}_n$ if

$$p_{f_1,\ldots,f_n}(z_1, \ldots, z_n) = p_{f_1,\ldots,f_r}(z_1, \ldots, z_r) p_{f_{r+1},\ldots,f_n}(z_{r+1}, \ldots, z_n) \qquad (83b)$$

The random variables $\mathbf{f}_1, \mathbf{f}_2, \ldots, \mathbf{f}_n$ are called *uncorrelated* if

$$E\{\mathbf{f}_i \mathbf{f}_j\} = E\{\mathbf{f}_i\}\, E\{\mathbf{f}_j\} \qquad \text{for all } i, j \text{ with } i \neq j \qquad (84)$$

If μ_{f_i} denotes the expected value of the random variable $\mathbf{f}_i$, then the *covariance* of two random variables $\mathbf{f}_i$ and $\mathbf{f}_j$ is defined by

$$C_{ij} = E\{(\mathbf{f}_i - \mu_{f_i})(\mathbf{f}_j - \mu_{f_j})\} \qquad (85)$$

By expanding this it can easily be shown that if $\mathbf{f}_i$ and $\mathbf{f}_j$ are uncorrelated, then their covariance equals zero.

The *correlation coefficient* r_{ij} of two random variables $\mathbf{f}_i$ and $\mathbf{f}_j$ is defined as

$$r_{ij} = C_{ij}/\sigma_{f_i}\sigma_{f_j} \tag{86}$$

where the σ's were defined in (70).

Exercise 6. Given n random variables $\mathbf{f}_1, \mathbf{f}_2, ..., \mathbf{f}_n$ with $\sigma_{f_i}^2 = \sigma^2$, $i = 1, 2, ..., n$, let us define a random variable $\mathbf{f}$ as

$$\mathbf{f} = (\mathbf{f}_1 + \mathbf{f}_2 + \cdots + \mathbf{f}_n)/n$$

If $\mathbf{f}_1, \mathbf{f}_2, ..., \mathbf{f}_n$ are uncorrelated, show that the variance σ_f^2 of $\mathbf{f}$ is given by

$$\sigma_f^2 = \sigma^2/n \quad \blacksquare \tag{87}$$

The n random variables $\mathbf{f}_1, \mathbf{f}_2, ..., \mathbf{f}_n$ are called *orthogonal* if

$$E\{\mathbf{f}_i\mathbf{f}_j\} = 0 \qquad \text{for all } i, j \text{ with } i \neq j \tag{88}$$

Note that uncorrelated random variables that have zero mean are orthogonal.

2.3.6 Functions of Random Variables

Let n random variables $\mathbf{g}_1, \mathbf{g}_2, ..., \mathbf{g}_n$ be functions of the random variables $\mathbf{f}_1, \mathbf{f}_2, ..., \mathbf{f}_n$:

$$\mathbf{g}_1 = \mathscr{L}_1(\mathbf{f}_1, \mathbf{f}_2, ..., \mathbf{f}_n)$$
$$\vdots \tag{89}$$
$$\mathbf{g}_n = \mathscr{L}_n(\mathbf{f}_1, \mathbf{f}_2, ..., \mathbf{f}_n)$$

Let us denote the joint density function of the random variables $\mathbf{g}_1, \mathbf{g}_2, ..., \mathbf{g}_n$ by $p_{g_1, ..., g_n}(y_1, y_2, ..., y_n)$; that is,

$$p_{g_1, ..., g_n}(y_1, y_2, ..., y_n) = \frac{\partial^n \mathscr{P}\{\mathbf{g}_1 \leqslant y_1, \mathbf{g}_2 \leqslant y_2, ..., \mathbf{g}_n \leqslant y_n\}}{\partial y_1 \, \partial y_2 \, \cdots \, \partial y_n}$$

Our aim is to express the relationship between the joint density functions

$$p_{g_1, ..., g_n}(y_1, y_2, ..., y_n) \qquad \text{and} \qquad p_{f_1, ..., f_n}(z_1, z_2, ..., z_n)$$

To determine $p_{g_1, ..., g_n}(y_1, y_2, ..., y_n)$ for a given set of numbers $y_1, y_2, ..., y_n$, we solve the following set of simultaneous equations:

$$\mathscr{L}_1(z_1, z_2, ..., z_n) = y_1$$
$$\mathscr{L}_2(z_1, z_2, ..., z_n) = y_2$$
$$\vdots \tag{90}$$
$$\mathscr{L}_n(z_1, z_2, ..., z_n) = y_n$$

Let this system have a single real solution $z_1, z_2, ..., z_n$; then it can be shown that

$$p_{g_1, ..., g_n}(y_1, y_2, ..., y_n) = \frac{p_{f_1, ..., f_n}(z_1, z_2, ..., z_n)}{|J(z_1, z_2, ..., z_n)|} \tag{91}$$

where J, called the *Jacobian* of transformation (80), is given by

$$J(z_1, z_2, ..., z_n) = \begin{vmatrix} \dfrac{\partial \mathscr{L}_1}{\partial z_1} & \dfrac{\partial \mathscr{L}_1}{\partial z_2} & \cdots & \dfrac{\partial \mathscr{L}_1}{\partial z_n} \\ \vdots & \vdots & \vdots & \vdots \\ \dfrac{\partial \mathscr{L}_n}{\partial z_1} & \dfrac{\partial \mathscr{L}_n}{\partial z_2} & \cdots & \dfrac{\partial \mathscr{L}_n}{\partial z_n} \end{vmatrix} \tag{92}$$

If Eqs. (90) have more than one solution, then we add in the right-hand side (91) the corresponding expressions resulting from all the solutions. For a proof of (91), see, for example, Papoulis [9].

2.4 RANDOM FIELDS

2.4.1 Definition of a Random Field

In Section 2.3.4, we discussed sets of random variables over the set Ω. We will now generalize this discussion in the following manner. Let us define a one-parameter family of functions $\mathbf{f}_s(\omega_i)$ over the set of all outcomes $\Omega = \{\omega_1, \omega_2, ...\}$ of an experiment, where the parameter $s \in I$ and I is an interval on the real axis or a region of a multidimensional Euclidean space. *Note that for each value of s we have a function defined over the set Ω.* Also, note that for each value of ω_i, $\mathbf{f}_s(\omega_i)$ is a function of s over the region I.

When I is one-dimensional and a collection of discrete points, e.g., $I = \{1, 2, ..., n\}$, our family of functions is just a set of n random variables as defined in Section 2.3.4.

This discussion indicates that there are two ways of looking at $\mathbf{f}_s(\omega_i)$, $\omega_i \in \Omega$, $s \in I$. They are as follows:

(i) $\mathbf{f}_s(\omega_i)$ is clearly a family of random variables, each member of the family being generated by a value of s.

(ii) $\mathbf{f}_s(\omega_i)$ can also be looked on as a family of functions of s, each member of this family corresponding to an outcome ω_i.

When I is one-dimensional, the family of functions $\mathbf{f}_s(\omega_i)$ is called a *stochastic process*. When the dimensionality of I is two or greater, the family of functions $\mathbf{f}_s(\omega_i)$ is called a *random field*. In what follows, we shall concentrate on random fields with I two-dimensional.

Let I be the xy-plane, so that s is a point in the xy-plane, and s can be represented either by its coordinates or by its position vector $\vec{r}$. The random field $\mathbf{f}_s(\omega_i)$, which can now be expressed as $\mathbf{f}_{\vec{r}}(\omega_i)$, will henceforth be denoted by $\mathbf{f}(\vec{r}, \omega_i)$. For a given value of $\vec{r}$, $\mathbf{f}(\vec{r}, \omega_i)$ is a random variable, while for a given outcome ω_i, $\mathbf{f}(\vec{r}, \omega_i)$ is a function over the xy-plane.

In Fig. 8, we have given an example of a random field $\mathbf{f}(\vec{r}, \omega_i)$ with $\Omega = \{\omega_1, \omega_2, \omega_3\}$. We will remind the reader that the ω_i's are the outcomes of the underlying experiment. The underlying experiment could, for example, be the selection of a picture from a collection. The outcome ω_i corresponds to the selection of the ith picture.

It is seen that with $\vec{r} = OA$ in Fig. 8, $\mathbf{f}(\vec{r}, \omega_i)$ is a function of ω_i. Its value for ω_1 equals 2, for ω_2 its value is 4, and for ω_3 it is 3. So we see that for a fixed $\vec{r}$, $\mathbf{f}(\vec{r}, \omega_i)$ is a function of ω_i and is, therefore, a random variable. For a fixed ω_i, however, $\mathbf{f}(\vec{r}, \omega_i)$ is a two-dimensional function (picture) in the xy-plane.

The random field $\mathbf{f}(\vec{r}, \omega_i)$ is a random variable for a specific value of $\vec{r}$. In general, this random variable will not have the same statistical properties for all values of $\vec{r}$. In other words, the distribution and density functions for the random variable $\mathbf{f}(\vec{r}, \omega_i)$ will depend on the value of $\vec{r}$ that is chosen.

Let

$$P_f(z; \vec{r}) = \mathscr{P}\{\mathbf{f}(\vec{r}, \omega_i) \leqslant z\} \tag{93}$$

Clearly, $P_f(z; \vec{r})$ is the distribution function for the random variable $\mathbf{f}(\vec{r}, \omega_i)$ at the point $\vec{r}$ in the xy-plane. The density function at the point $\vec{r}$ would then be given by

$$p_f(z; \vec{r}) = \partial P_f(z; \vec{r})/\partial z \tag{94}$$

Henceforth, we will denote $\mathbf{f}(\vec{r}, \omega_i)$ by $\mathbf{f}(\vec{r})$ (or $\mathbf{f}(x, y)$), it being understood that this represents a family of two-dimensional functions, each function corresponding to an outcome ω_i.

Given points $\vec{r}_1, \vec{r}_2, \ldots, \vec{r}_n$ in the xy-plane, we have n random variables $\mathbf{f}(\vec{r}_1), \mathbf{f}(\vec{r}_2), \ldots, \mathbf{f}(\vec{r}_n)$. The joint distribution and density functions of these random variables are given by

$$P_f(z_1, z_2, \ldots, z_n; \vec{r}_1, \vec{r}_2, \ldots, \vec{r}_n) = \mathscr{P}\{\mathbf{f}(\vec{r}_1) \leqslant z_1, \ldots, \mathbf{f}(\vec{r}_n) \leqslant z_n\} \tag{95}$$

and

$$p_f(z_1, \ldots, z_n; \vec{r}_1, \ldots, \vec{r}_n) = \frac{\partial^n P_f(z_1, \ldots, z_n; \vec{r}_1, \ldots, \vec{r}_n)}{\partial z_1 \cdots \partial z_n} \tag{96}$$

$P_f(z_1, \ldots, z_n; \vec{r}_1, \ldots, \vec{r}_n)$ and $p_f(z_1, \ldots, z_n; \vec{r}_1, \ldots, \vec{r}_n)$ are called the nth-order distribution and density functions, respectively, of the random field $\mathbf{f}(\vec{r})$.

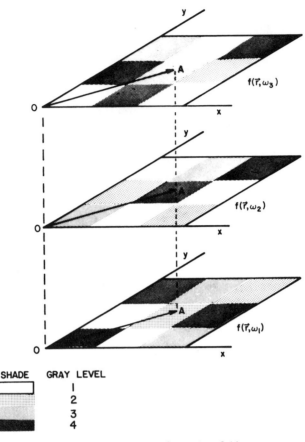

SHADE	GRAY LEVEL
	1
	2
	3
	4

Fig. 8 An example of a random field.

2.4.2 Mean, Autocorrelation, Autocovariance[§]

The random field $\mathbf{f}(\vec{r})$ is a random variable for a given $\vec{r}$. Since, in general, the density function of this random variable depends on the value of $\vec{r}$ that is chosen, its expected value must also be a function of $\vec{r}$. If $\mu_f(\vec{r})$ denotes this expectation, then by (68)

$$\mu_f(\vec{r}) = E\{\mathbf{f}(\vec{r})\} = \int_{-\infty}^{\infty} z p_f(z; \vec{r}) \, dz \tag{97}$$

This expectation is called the *mean* of the random field $\mathbf{f}$ at $\vec{r}$.

[§] A random field may be real or complex. Since in this book we will only be concerned with real random fields, the definitions given here and elsewhere apply only for that case, unless otherwise mentioned.

The *autocorrelation* $R(\vec{r}_1, \vec{r}_2)$ of a random field $\mathbf{f}(\vec{r})$ is defined as the expected value of the product of the two random variables $\mathbf{f}(\vec{r}_1)$ and $\mathbf{f}(\vec{r}_2)$ and by using (82) is shown to be given by

$$R_{ff}(\vec{r}_1, \vec{r}_2) = E\{\mathbf{f}(\vec{r}_1)\mathbf{f}(\vec{r}_2)\} = \int\limits_{-\infty}^{\infty}\!\!\int z_1 z_2 \, p_f(z_1, z_2; \vec{r}_1, \vec{r}_2) \, dz_1 \, dz_2 \quad (98)$$

The *autocovariance* $C(\vec{r}_1, \vec{r}_2)$ of a random field $\mathbf{f}(\vec{r})$ is defined as

$$C_{ff}(\vec{r}_1, \vec{r}_2) = E\{[\mathbf{f}(\vec{r}_1) - \mu_f(\vec{r}_1)][\mathbf{f}(\vec{r}_2) - \mu_f(\vec{r}_2)]\}$$

$$= R_{ff}(\vec{r}_1, \vec{r}_2) - \mu_f(\vec{r}_1)\mu_f(\vec{r}_2) \quad (99)$$

The *cross correlation* of two real random fields is defined by

$$R_{fg}(\vec{r}_1, \vec{r}_2) = E\{\mathbf{f}(\vec{r}_1)\,\mathbf{g}(\vec{r}_2)\} \quad (100)$$

and their *cross covariance* by

$$C_{fg}(\vec{r}_1, \vec{r}_2) = E\{[\mathbf{f}(\vec{r}_1) - \mu_f(\vec{r}_1)][\mathbf{g}(\vec{r}_2) - \mu_g(\vec{r}_2)]\}$$

$$= R_{fg}(\vec{r}_1, \vec{r}_2) - \mu_f(\vec{r}_1)\mu_g(\vec{r}_2) \quad (101)$$

Two random fields $\mathbf{f}(\vec{r})$ and $\mathbf{g}(\vec{r})$ are called *uncorrelated* if for any $\vec{r}_1$ and $\vec{r}_2$

$$C_{fg}(\vec{r}_1, \vec{r}_2) = 0$$

which is equivalent to

$$E\{\mathbf{f}(\vec{r}_1)\,\mathbf{g}(\vec{r}_2)\} = E\{\mathbf{f}(\vec{r}_1)\}\,E\{\mathbf{g}(\vec{r}_2)\} \quad (102)$$

They are called *orthogonal* if for any $\vec{r}_1$ and $\vec{r}_2$

$$R_{fg}(\vec{r}_1, \vec{r}_2) = 0 \quad (103)$$

We say that the random fields $\mathbf{f}(\vec{r})$ and $\mathbf{g}(\vec{r})$ are *independent* if the set

$$\mathbf{f}(\vec{r}_1), \mathbf{f}(\vec{r}_2), ..., \mathbf{f}(\vec{r}_n)$$

is independent of the set

$$\mathbf{g}(\vec{r}_1'), \mathbf{g}(\vec{r}_2'), ..., \mathbf{g}(\vec{r}_m') \quad (104)$$

for any $\vec{r}_1, \vec{r}_2, ..., \vec{r}_n, \vec{r}_1', \vec{r}_2', ..., \vec{r}_m'$, as defined in (83b).

2.4.3 Stationary or Homogeneous Random Fields

A random field is called *stationary* or *homogeneous* [12] if its expected value $\mu(\vec{r})$ is independent of position $\vec{r}$, that is, if

$$\mu_f(\vec{r}) = \mu = \text{constant independent of } \vec{r} \quad (105)$$

and if its autocorrelation function is translation invariant, that is, if

$$R_{ff}(\vec{r}_1, \vec{r}_2) = E\{\mathbf{f}(\vec{r}_1)\mathbf{f}(\vec{r}_2)\} = E\{\mathbf{f}(\vec{r}_1 + \vec{r}_0)\mathbf{f}(\vec{r}_2 + \vec{r}_0)\}$$
$$= R_{ff}(\vec{r}_1 + \vec{r}_0, \vec{r}_2 + \vec{r}_0) \qquad (106)$$

for all $\vec{r}_1, \vec{r}_2$, and $\vec{r}_0$ in the xy-plane. Setting $\vec{r}_0 = -\vec{r}_2$ in (106), we see that the correlation function

$$R_{ff}(\vec{r}_1, \vec{r}_2) = R_{ff}(\vec{r}_1 - \vec{r}_2, 0) \equiv R_{ff}(\vec{r}_1 - \vec{r}_2) \qquad (107)$$

depends only on the difference vector $(\vec{r}_1 - \vec{r}_2)$. Since $E\{\mathbf{f}(\vec{r}_1)\mathbf{f}(\vec{r}_2)\} = E\{\mathbf{f}(\vec{r}_2)\mathbf{f}(\vec{r}_1)\}$ implies $R_{ff}(\vec{r}_1, \vec{r}_2) = R_{ff}(\vec{r}_2, \vec{r}_1)$, therefore, in the homogeneous case we may conclude that

$$R_{ff}(\vec{r}_1 - \vec{r}_2) = R_{ff}(\vec{r}_2 - \vec{r}_1) \qquad (108)$$

If x_1, y_1 and x_2, y_2 denote the coordinates of the position vectors $\vec{r}_1$ and $\vec{r}_2$, respectively, then (109) can be expressed as

$$R_{ff}(x_1, y_1, x_2, y_2) = R_{ff}(x_1 - x_2, y_1 - y_2) = R_{ff}(x_2 - x_1, y_2 - y_1) \qquad (109)$$

If we use α and β to denote the difference coordinates $x_1 - x_2$ and $y_1 - y_2$, respectively, (100) can be expressed as

$$R_{ff}(x_1, y_1, x_2, y_2) = R_{ff}(\alpha, \beta) = R_{ff}(-\alpha, -\beta)$$

Clearly, then, for a real homogeneous random field the autocorrelation function is given by

$$R_{ff}(\alpha, \beta) = E\{\mathbf{f}(x+\alpha, y+\beta)\mathbf{f}(x, y)\} \qquad (110a)$$

We see that, in general, the autocorrelation function of a random field is a function of four variables. For homogeneous random fields, however, it is a function of only two variables α and β. Also, it is invariant with respect to 180° rotation. The autocorrelation function may, of course, possess a higher symmetry than this. For example, $R_{ff}(\alpha, \beta)$ may be invariant with respect to all rotations. In this case, the autocorrelation is a function of only one variable, that is, the Euclidean distance $|\vec{r}_1 - \vec{r}_2| = \sqrt{\alpha^2 + \beta^2}$. Random fields with this property are called *homogeneous and isotropic* random fields.

Similar conclusions can be drawn about the cross-correlation function $R_{fg}(x_1, y_1, x_2, y_2)$ defined in (100). Two random fields are called *jointly homogeneous* if this function depends on only $x_1 - x_2$ and $y_1 - y_2$. In other words for two real random fields that are jointly homogeneous, the cross-correlation function is given by

$$R_{fg}(\alpha, \beta) = E\{\mathbf{f}(x+\alpha, y+\beta)\mathbf{g}(x, y)\} \qquad (110b)$$

The concept of homogeneous random fields is a generalization of one-dimensional wide-sense stationary stochastic processes to higher dimensions. In fact homogeneous random fields are also sometimes referred to as "wide-sense stationary random processes or fields."

2.4.4 Spectral Density

The *spectral density* $S_{ff}(u, v)$ of a homogeneous random field $\mathbf{f}(\vec{r})$ is the Fourier transform of its autocorrelation

$$S_{ff}(u, v) = \int\int_{-\infty}^{\infty} R_{ff}(\alpha, \beta) \exp[-j2\pi(\alpha u + \beta v)] \, d\alpha \, d\beta \qquad (111a)$$

Similarly, the *cross spectral density* of two homogeneous random fields $\mathbf{f}$ and $\mathbf{g}$ is the Fourier transform of their cross correlation

$$S_{fg}(u, v) = \int\int_{-\infty}^{\infty} R_{fg}(\alpha, \beta) \exp[-j2\pi(\alpha u + \beta v)] \, d\alpha \, d\beta \qquad (111b)$$

If we use $\vec{w}$ to denote a vector in the uv-plane, and $\vec{r}$ a vector in the $\alpha\beta$-plane,[§] we will sometimes find it more convenient to write (111a) as

$$S_{ff}(\vec{w}) = \int_{\alpha\beta\text{-plane}} R_{ff}(\vec{r}) \exp(-j2\pi\vec{r}\cdot\vec{w}) \, d\vec{r} \qquad (112)$$

From (111a), $R_{ff}(\alpha, \beta)$ is the inverse Fourier transform of $S(u, v)$ and is given by

$$R_{ff}(\alpha, \beta) = \int\int_{-\infty}^{\infty} S_{ff}(u, v) \exp[+j2\pi(\alpha u + \beta v)] \, du \, dv \qquad (113)$$

In the more compact notation, this can be rewritten as

$$R_{ff}(\vec{r}) = \int_{uv\text{-plane}} S_{ff}(\vec{w}) \exp(+j2\pi\vec{r}\cdot\vec{w}) \, d\vec{w} \qquad (114)$$

With $\alpha = \beta = 0$, (113) gives

$$\int_{-\infty}^{\infty} \int_{-\infty}^{\infty} S_{ff}(u, v) \, du \, dv = R_{ff}(0, 0) = E\{[\mathbf{f}(r)]^2\} \geqslant 0 \qquad (115)$$

2.4.5 Linear Operations on Random Fields

In Section 2.1.2, we showed that a linear shift-invariant operation on a picture $f(x, y)$ can be expressed as a convolution of $f(x, y)$ with a point spread

[§] The context should make it clear whether $\vec{r}$ is a vector in the xy-plane or in the $\alpha\beta$-plane.

function $h(x, y)$. Let us now consider the action of such a linear operation having point spread function $h(x, y)$ on a homogeneous random field $\mathbf{f}(\vec{r})$, which henceforth will be written as $\mathbf{f}(x, y)$. Since a random field is a family of two-dimensional functions defined over the xy-plane, the result of such an operation can be expressed as

$$\mathbf{g}(x, y) = \int\int_{-\infty}^{\infty} \mathbf{f}(x-\alpha, y-\beta) h(\alpha, \beta) \, d\alpha \, d\beta \tag{116}$$

Clearly, (116) is a family of equations, one for each member in the family of functions represented by $\mathbf{f}(x, y)$. Each member of $\mathbf{f}(x, y)$ on the right-hand side of (116) gives rise to a function of x and y; the family of these functions is the random field $\mathbf{g}(x, y)$. If $\mathbf{f}$ is homogeneous, it can be verified that $\mathbf{g}$ is also.

We will now present a theorem on the relationship between the spectral densities of the "input" $\mathbf{f}(x, y)$ and the "output" $\mathbf{g}(x, y)$ in (116).

Theorem. Let $S_{ff}(u, v)$ and $S_{gg}(u, v)$ denote the spectral densities of the homogeneous random fields $\mathbf{f}(x, y)$ and $\mathbf{g}(x, y)$, respectively. If $\mathbf{g}$ is derived from $\mathbf{f}$ by (116), then

$$S_{gg}(u, v) = S_{ff}(u, v) |H(u, v)|^2 \tag{117}$$

where $H(u, v)$ is the Fourier transform of the point spread function $h(x, y)$.

Proof: From (116), we can write

$$\mathbf{g}(x+a, y+b) = \int\int_{-\infty}^{\infty} \mathbf{f}(x+a-\alpha, y+b-\beta) h(\alpha, \beta) \, d\alpha \, d\beta$$

Multiplying both sides by $\mathbf{g}(x, y)$, taking the expectation, interchanging the order of integration and expectation, and using (110a) and (110b), we obtain

$$R_{gg}(a, b) = \int\int_{-\infty}^{\infty} R_{fg}(a-\alpha, b-\beta) h(\alpha, \beta) \, d\alpha \, d\beta$$

Therefore, symbolically,

$$R_{gg}(\alpha, \beta) = R_{fg}(\alpha, \beta) * h(\alpha, \beta) \tag{118}$$

Similarly, by multiplying both sides of (116) by $\mathbf{f}(x+a, y+b)$ and taking the expectation, one can show that

$$R_{fg}(a, b) = \int\int_{-\infty}^{\infty} R_{ff}(a+\alpha, b+\beta) h(\alpha, \beta) \, d\alpha \, d\beta$$

which by a transformation of variables $\alpha = -\alpha'$ and $\beta = -\beta'$ can easily be shown to be a convolution of $R_{ff}(\alpha, \beta)$ and $h(-\alpha, -\beta)$. Therefore,

$$R_{fg}(\alpha, \beta) = R_{ff}(\alpha, \beta) * h(-\alpha, -\beta) \tag{119}$$

Substituting (119) in (118), we obtain

$$R_{gg}(\alpha, \beta) = R_{ff}(\alpha, \beta) * h(-\alpha, -\beta) * h(\alpha, \beta) \tag{120}$$

Since the Fourier transform of $h(-\alpha, -\beta)$ equals $H^*(u, v)$, we obtain (117) from Eq. (120) and the convolution theorem as given by (23a). This completes the proof of the theorem. ∎

In our derivation of (117), **f** and **g** were assumed to be real random fields. The theorem is easily shown to be true for complex random fields, also. In the complex case, the autocorrelation is defined as $E\{\mathbf{f}(r_1)\mathbf{f}^*(r_2)\}$.

Exercise 7.   The random fields **f** and **g** are related as

$$\mathbf{g}(x, y) = \iint \mathbf{f}(x-\alpha, y-\beta)\, h(\alpha, \beta)\, d\alpha\, d\beta + \mathbf{v}(x, y)$$

where the random field $\mathbf{v}(x, y)$ represents additive noise. If **f**, **g** and **v** are homogeneous random fields and if **f** and **v** have zero means and are uncorrelated, show that

$$S_{gg}(u, v) = S_{ff}(u, v)|H(u, v)|^2 + S_{vv}(u, v) \quad ∎ \tag{121}$$

2.4.6   Ergodicity

In this subsection, we will discuss spatial and ensemble averages and bring out the connection between the definition of autocorrelation as introduced in Section 2.4.2 and the definition of autocorrelation as introduced in Section 2.1.4 for deterministic functions. *In what follows, we will be concerned only with homogeneous random fields.*

Expressions (97) and (98) for the mean and autocorrelation are called *ensemble averages*. Let us first consider (97). Some thought shows that (97) is equivalent to repeating the underlying experiment a large number of times, and for every performance, observing the outcome ω_i, sampling the corresponding two-dimensional function from the family $\mathbf{f}(\bar{r})$ at the position $\bar{r}$, and averaging the values so obtained.

Let us define a spatial average as

$$\mathbf{E} = \lim_{S \to \infty} \frac{1}{S} \iint_{\mathscr{S}} \mathbf{f}(x, y)\, dx\, dy \tag{122}$$

where $\mathscr{S}$ is a bounded region of the xy-plane, S is the area of $\mathscr{S}$, and by $\lim_{S \to \infty}$ is meant a limiting process which tends to include the entire xy-plane.

Equation (122) represents a family of equations. Each member of the family of functions represented by the random field $\mathbf{f}(x, y)$ when substituted on the right-hand side in (122) yields a number. The collection of these numbers, denoted by $\mathbf{E}$, is a function over the set Ω of outcomes. Therefore, $\mathbf{E}$ is a random variable.

Suppose the random variable $\mathbf{E}$ is such that its value is the same for all the outcomes ω_i, i.e., that $\mathbf{E}$ is equal to a constant. If this constant is equal to the mean μ (see Eq. (105)), the random field is called *ergodic with respect to the mean*.

Note that if a collection of pictures is a random field that is ergodic with respect to the mean, the mean value of the random field can be obtained simply by spatially averaging any one of the pictures in the collection.

To see that definition (98) for the autocorrelation is an ensemble average, we note that this definition is equivalent to performing the underlying experiment a large number of times; and for every performance, observing the outcome ω_i, sampling the associated two-dimensional function (from the family $\mathbf{f}(x, y)$) at points (x_1, y_1) and (x_2, y_2), determining the product of these two samples, and averaging the result so obtained.

Let us now define the following spatial average for a homogeneous random field:

$$\mathbf{R}(\alpha, \beta) = \lim_{S \to \infty} \frac{1}{S} \int \int_{\mathcal{S}} \mathbf{f}(x, y) \mathbf{f}(x+\alpha, y+\beta) \, dx \, dy \qquad (123)$$

Clearly $\mathbf{R}(\alpha, \beta)$ is a random variable. If this random variable is equal to a constant for each (α, β) and if this constant value is equal to $R_{ff}(\alpha, \beta)$, then the random field is called *ergodic with respect to autocorrelation*.

If a collection of pictures is ergodic with respect to autocorrelation, then the autocorrelation function $R_{ff}(\alpha, \beta)$ can be obtained simply by performing the integration on the right-hand side in (123) for *any* picture in the collection. For a more general discussion of ergodicity, see, for example, [12].

2.4.7   The Orthogonality Principle in Linear Mean-Square Estimation

Suppose we wish to construct an estimate for a random variable $\mathbf{s}$ in terms of a linear combination of other variables $\mathbf{x}_1, \mathbf{x}_2, \ldots, \mathbf{x}_N$. The estimate, denoted by $\hat{\mathbf{s}}$, may then be expressed as

$$\hat{\mathbf{s}} = a_1 \mathbf{x}_1 + a_2 \mathbf{x}_2 + \cdots + a_N \mathbf{x}_N \qquad (124)$$

The constants a_1 through a_N are chosen so as to minimize some measure of error between the true values of the random variable $\mathbf{s}$ and its estimate $\hat{\mathbf{s}}$. A commonly used criterion is the mean-square error defined as

$$e = E\{[\mathbf{s} - \hat{\mathbf{s}}]^2\} \qquad (125)$$

By substituting (124) in this equation, differentiating e with respect to the a_i's and setting each derivative equal to zero, we can show that

$$E\{(\mathbf{s} - \hat{\mathbf{s}})\mathbf{x}_i\} = 0, \qquad i = 1, 2, \ldots, N \tag{126}$$

These results are known as the orthogonality principle in linear mean-square estimation. The principle says that the error $\mathbf{s} - \hat{\mathbf{s}}$ must be statistically orthogonal to all the random variables used in estimation.

In deriving the above principle, no assumptions were made about the mean values of the random variables. If they are all zero, the estimate in (124) would indeed result in the least estimation error. For the case of non-zero-mean random variables, one can further reduce the estimation error by adding a constant to the right-hand side in (124):

$$\hat{\mathbf{s}} = \sum_{i=1}^{N} a_i \mathbf{x}_i + b \tag{127}$$

It can be shown that for optimum estimation the orthogonality conditions in (126) are still satisfied, which leads to N equations for $N + 1$ unknowns in (127). An additional equation is given by

$$E[\mathbf{s} - \hat{\mathbf{s}}] = 0 \tag{128}$$

For proof of this, the reader is referred to [9, Chap. 11].

2.5   VECTOR SPACE REPRESENTATION OF IMAGES

Consider a sampled image $f(m, n)$ with $m = 1, 2, \ldots, N$ and $n = 1, 2, \ldots, N$. It is most naturally represented as an $N \times N$ matrix. However, there is nothing to prevent us from considering the given image as a vector in an N^2-dimensional space, each pixel corresponding to a separate dimension. Since such a vector representation will be used in Chapters 5 and 7, we will discuss it in some detail here. We will use $[f]$ to denote the $N \times N$ matrix whose (m, n)th element is $f(m, n)$. Although our discussion will be limited to square image matrices, it may easily be generalized to the rectangular case.

Given the image matrix

$$[f] = \begin{bmatrix} f(1, 1) & f(1, 2) & \cdots & f(1, N) \\ f(2, 1) & & \cdots & \\ f(3, 1) & & \cdots & \\ \vdots & & & \\ f(N, 1) & \cdots & \cdots & f(N, N) \end{bmatrix} \tag{129}$$

a common way to generate the vector representation is by *column scanning* the matrix. This entails concatenating one column after another as shown below:

$$
\vec{f} = \begin{bmatrix} f(1,1) \\ f(2,1) \\ \vdots \\ f(N,1) \\ f(1,2) \\ \vdots \\ f(N,2) \\ \vdots \\ f(N,N) \end{bmatrix} \begin{array}{l} \left.\rule{0pt}{30pt}\right\} \text{1st col. of } [f] \\[10pt] \left.\rule{0pt}{20pt}\right\} \text{2nd col. of } [f] \\[6pt] \vdots \\[4pt] \left.\rule{0pt}{6pt}\right\} \text{Nth col. of } [f] \end{array}
\tag{130}
$$

which results in an N^2-dimensional vector $\vec{f}$.

Pratt [10] has shown that one may write down an algebraic relationship between $[f]$ and $\vec{f}$. To illustrate this, an N element long vector $\vec{v}_n$ and an $N^2 \times N$ matrix $[A_n]$ are first defined as follows:

$$
\vec{v}_n = \begin{bmatrix} 0 \\ 0 \\ \vdots \\ 0 \\ 1 \\ 0 \\ 0 \\ \vdots \\ 0 \end{bmatrix} \begin{array}{l} \text{1st element} \\ \text{2nd element} \\[4pt] \\ n-1 \\ n \\ n+1 \\ \\ \\ N \end{array}
\tag{131}
$$

$$
\overset{\leftarrow N \rightarrow}{}
$$

$$
[A_n] = N^2 \begin{bmatrix} [0] \\ [0] \\ \vdots \\ [0] \\ [I] \\ [0] \\ \vdots \\ [0] \end{bmatrix} \begin{array}{l} \text{1st submatrix} \\ \text{2nd submatrix} \\[4pt] \\ n-1 \\ n \\ n+1 \\ \\ N \end{array}
\tag{132}
$$

By substituting (124) in this equation, differentiating e with respect to the a_i's and setting each derivative equal to zero, we can show that

$$E\{(\mathbf{s} - \hat{\mathbf{s}})\mathbf{x}_i\} = 0, \qquad i = 1, 2, \ldots, N \tag{126}$$

These results are known as the orthogonality principle in linear mean-square estimation. The principle says that the error $\mathbf{s} - \hat{\mathbf{s}}$ must be statistically orthogonal to all the random variables used in estimation.

In deriving the above principle, no assumptions were made about the mean values of the random variables. If they are all zero, the estimate in (124) would indeed result in the least estimation error. For the case of non–zero-mean random variables, one can further reduce the estimation error by adding a constant to the right-hand side in (124):

$$\hat{\mathbf{s}} = \sum_{i=1}^{N} a_i \mathbf{x}_i + b \tag{127}$$

It can be shown that for optimum estimation the orthogonality conditions in (126) are still satisfied, which leads to N equations for $N + 1$ unknowns in (127). An additional equation is given by

$$E[\mathbf{s} - \hat{\mathbf{s}}] = 0 \tag{128}$$

For proof of this, the reader is referred to [9, Chap. 11].

2.5 VECTOR SPACE REPRESENTATION OF IMAGES

Consider a sampled image $f(m, n)$ with $m = 1, 2, \ldots, N$ and $n = 1, 2, \ldots, N$. It is most naturally represented as an $N \times N$ matrix. However, there is nothing to prevent us from considering the given image as a vector in an N^2-dimensional space, each pixel corresponding to a separate dimension. Since such a vector representation will be used in Chapters 5 and 7, we will discuss it in some detail here. We will use $[f]$ to denote the $N \times N$ matrix whose (m, n)th element is $f(m, n)$. Although our discussion will be limited to square image matrices, it may easily be generalized to the rectangular case.

Given the image matrix

$$[f] = \begin{bmatrix} f(1, 1) & f(1, 2) & \cdots & f(1, N) \\ f(2, 1) & & \cdots & \\ f(3, 1) & & \cdots & \\ \vdots & & & \\ f(N, 1) & \cdots & \cdots & f(N, N) \end{bmatrix} \tag{129}$$

a common way to generate the vector representation is by *column scanning* the matrix. This entails concatenating one column after another as shown below:

$$
\vec{f} = \begin{bmatrix} f(1, 1) \\ f(2, 1) \\ \vdots \\ f(N, 1) \\ f(1, 2) \\ \vdots \\ f(N, 2) \\ \vdots \\ f(N, N) \end{bmatrix} \begin{array}{l} \left. \vphantom{\begin{matrix}a\\a\\a\\a\end{matrix}} \right\} \text{1st col. of } [f] \\[1em] \left. \vphantom{\begin{matrix}a\\a\\a\end{matrix}} \right\} \text{2nd col. of } [f] \\[1em] \vdots \\[1em] \left. \vphantom{a} \right\} \text{Nth col. of } [f] \end{array} \tag{130}
$$

which results in an N^2-dimensional vector $\vec{f}$.

Pratt [10] has shown that one may write down an algebraic relationship between $[f]$ and $\vec{f}$. To illustrate this, an N element long vector $\vec{v}_n$ and an $N^2 \times N$ matrix $[A_n]$ are first defined as follows:

$$
\vec{v}_n = \begin{bmatrix} 0 \\ 0 \\ \vdots \\ 0 \\ 1 \\ 0 \\ 0 \\ \vdots \\ 0 \end{bmatrix} \begin{array}{l} \text{1st element} \\ \text{2nd element} \\ \\ n - 1 \\ n \\ n + 1 \\ \\ \\ N \end{array} \tag{131}
$$

$$
[A_n] = N^2 \begin{bmatrix} [0] \\ [0] \\ \vdots \\ [0] \\ [I] \\ [0] \\ \vdots \\ [0] \end{bmatrix} \begin{array}{l} \text{1st submatrix} \\ \text{2nd submatrix} \\ \\ n - 1 \\ n \\ n + 1 \\ \\ N \end{array} \tag{132}
$$

with $\leftarrow N \rightarrow$ across the top of $[A_n]$.

Note that in the $N^2 \times N$ matrix $[A_n]$ each submatrix is of size $N \times N$. $[I]$ is the identity matrix:

$$[I] = \begin{bmatrix} 1 & & & \varnothing \\ & \cdot & & \\ & & \cdot & \\ & & & \cdot \\ \varnothing & & & 1 \end{bmatrix} \tag{133}$$

and $[0]$ is a matrix with all its elements equal to zero.

It may be seen by direct examination that

$$[f]\vec{v}_n = \vec{f}_n \tag{134}$$

where $\vec{f}_n$ is the nth column of $[f]$. Also,

$$[A_n]\vec{f}_n = \begin{bmatrix} [0]\vec{f}_n \\ \vdots \\ [0]\vec{f}_n \\ \vdots \\ [I]\vec{f}_n \\ [0]\vec{f}_n \\ \vdots \\ [0]\vec{f}_n \end{bmatrix} = \begin{bmatrix} \vec{0} \\ \vec{0} \\ \vec{0} \\ \vec{0} \\ \vec{f}_n \\ \vec{0} \\ \vec{0} \\ \vec{0} \end{bmatrix} \tag{135}$$

where $\vec{0}$ denotes an N-element-long zero vector. Therefore, the operation $[A_n][f]\vec{v}_n$ merely places the nth column of $[f]$ at its appropriate place in the vector $\vec{f}$. Hence

$$\vec{f} = \sum_{n=1}^{N} [A_n][f]\vec{v}_n \tag{136}$$

It may similarly be shown that

$$[f] = \sum_{n=1}^{N} [A_n]^t \vec{f} \vec{v}_n^t \tag{137}$$

We will now discuss the matrix representation of linear transformations of image data. *A linear transform of a data string can always be represented as a matrix–vector product.* When a sampled image is expressed as a vector, the same should hold true. In other words, for any linear transformation, the result of which is an output image $[g]$ (represented by $\vec{g}$ in vector form), it should be possible to construct a matrix $[T]$ such that

$$\vec{g} = [T]\vec{f} \tag{138}$$

In general, the sizes of $[g]$ and $[f]$ will be different. We will assume that $[g]$ is $M \times M$ and $[f]$ is $N \times N$. Therefore, $[T]$ is a $M^2 \times N^2$ matrix.

On the other hand, in the series representation a linear transformation of the image $f(m, n)$ is, in its most general sense, expressed as

$$g(p, q) = \sum_{m=1}^{N} \sum_{n=1}^{N} h(p, q, m, n) f(m, n), \quad p = 1, 2, \ldots, M, \quad q = 1, 2, \ldots, M$$

(139)

Consider the special, and frequently encountered, case when the linear transformation is separable in its row and column dependencies. Now the function $h(p, q, m, n)$ takes the form

$$h(p, q, m, n) = h_c(p, m) h_r(q, n)$$

(140)

which, when substituted in (139), results in

$$g(p, q) = \sum_{m=1}^{N} \sum_{n=1}^{N} h_c(p, m) f(m, n) h_r(q, n)$$

(141)

We will use $[h_c]$ to denote the $M \times N$ matrix whose (p, m)th element is $h_c(p, m)$. Similarly, $[h_r]$ will denote the $M \times N$ array $h_r(q, n)$. With this notation, (141) is more compactly expressed as

$$[g] = [h_c][f][h_r]^t$$

(142)

In order to see the relationship between the matrix $[T]$ in (138) and the matrices $[h_c]$ and $[h_r]$ here, let us examine (141) for the first element of $\bar{g}$. We have

$$(\bar{g})_{1\text{st element}} = g(1, 1) = \sum_{m=1}^{N} \sum_{n=1}^{N} h_c(1, m) f(m, n) h_r(1, n)$$

$$= h_r(1, 1) \sum_{m=1}^{N} h_c(1, m) f(m, 1) + h_r(1, 2) \sum_{m=1}^{N} h_c(1, m) f(m, 2)$$

$$+ \cdots + h_r(1, N) \sum_{m=1}^{N} h_c(1, m) f(m, N)$$

(143)

The expanded summation shown here suggests the following construction for the $[T]$ matrix:

$$[T] = \begin{bmatrix} h_r(1, 1)[h_c] & h_r(1, 2)[h_c] & h_r(1, N)[h_c] \\ \vdots & \vdots & \vdots \\ h_r(N, 1)[h_c] & \cdots & h_r(N, N)[h_c] \end{bmatrix}$$

(144)

Using the definition of left direct product of two matrices given in Section 2.2.2, we can write

$$[T] = [h_c] \otimes [h_r] \tag{145}$$

REFERENCES

1. G. Alexists, "Convergence Problems of Orthogonal Series," p. 62. Pergamon, New York, 1961.
2. H. C. Andrews, "Computer Techniques in Image Processing." Academic Press, New York, 1970.
3. R. N. Bracewell, "The Fourier Transform and Its Applications." McGraw-Hill, New York, 1968.
4. I. J. Good, The interaction algorithm and practical Fourier series, *J. Roy. Statist. Soc. Ser. B* **20**, 1958, 361–372; **22**, 1960, 372–375.
5. J. W. Goodman, "Introduction to Fourier Optics." McGraw-Hill, New York, 1968.
6. A. Haar, Zur theorie der orthogonalen funktionensysteme, *Math. Ann.* **69**, 1910, 331–371.
7. M. J. Lighthill, "Introduction to Fourier Analysis and Generalized Functions." Cambridge Univ. Press, London and New York, 1960.
8. A. Papoulis, "The Fourier Integral and Its Applications." McGraw-Hill, New York, 1962.
9. A. Papoulis, "Probability, Random Variables, and Stochastic Processes." McGraw-Hill, New York, 1965.
10. W. K. Pratt, Vector space formulation of two-dimensional signal processing operations, *Comput. Graphics Image Processing* **4**, 1975, 1–24.
11. C. Watari, A generalization of Haar functions, *Tohoku Math. J.* **8**, 1956, 286–290.
12. E. Wong, "Stochastic Processes in Information and Dynamical Systems." McGraw-Hill, New York, 1971.
13. Special issues of *IEEE Trans. Audio Electroacoust.* on fast Fourier transforms, **AE-15**, June 1967; **AE-17**, June 1969.

Chapter 3

Visual Perception

Knowledge about the human visual system (VS) can be very useful to the designer and user of picture-processing techniques. In particular, one must know something about subjective picture quality, and about the fidelity of a picture to an original scene, in designing systems for picture digitization or coding, or for image enhancement, when the pictures are intended for viewing by humans. (Picture quality will be discussed in greater detail in Section 6.1.) Similarly, in analyzing the structure of a picture for purposes of picture description, one wants to extract picture parts that correspond to those seen by humans, and to describe them in terms corresponding to those used by humans.

The subject of visual perception is very broad and complex; the present chapter cannot do more than briefly introduce a few basic topics. For more detailed overviews, including quantitative data, see, e.g., Graham [4], Cornsweet [3], and Zusne [8]. Many important topics will not even be touched on here; for example, the ways in which perceptual abilities are acquired (perceptual learning), or the way in which one adapts to perceptual distortions. We shall not discuss the anatomy and physiology of the VS, but rather shall treat it from the "black box" standpoint of perception psychology.

An important point to keep in mind when studying the VS is that it cannot be treated simply as a special type of image digitization and transmission system. To regard it as such is to commit the "homunculus fallacy"; when an image has been transmitted by the eye to the brain, there is no "little man" inside the brain to look at it! The input to the VS may be an image, but the output which it furnishes to the higher brain centers must be something quite different. This fact has many implications as regards the perception of even the simplest stimuli, as we shall see in the course of this chapter.

3.1 BRIGHTNESS AND CONTRAST

In this and the next section we discuss the visual perception of simple stimuli such as spots, edges, and bars of light. Perception of color, texture, form, etc., will be discussed in later sections.

The ability to detect a bright spot or flash depends not only on such properties as the brightness, size, and duration of the spot, but also on the brightness of the background against which the spot appears. There is, of course, an absolute threshold—at the quantum level—below which detection is impossible (see also Section 3.7); but more generally, there is a contrast threshold—a "*just noticeable difference*" between spot and background.

In general, detection thresholds depend on the previous pattern of illumination (in space and time); this dependence is called *adaptation*. When there has been no previous illumination for a long period (of the order of an hour or more), there is complete "dark adaptation," and thresholds are at their lowest. Vision under conditions of dark adaptation is called *scotopic*, and is characterized by reduced ability to perceive colors; under light adaptation, vision is called *photopic*. Detection thresholds also depend on position of the stimulus relative to the visual axis (i.e., the direction in which the eye is turned), being generally lower at the periphery. There are adaptation-like effects that depend on *subsequent* illumination (up to about 0.1 sec); the contrast threshold rises even before perception of a light flash. Such time-dependent phenomena are known as *metacontrast* effects.

If the background illumination I is uniform and extensive (in space and time), the threshold "just noticeable difference" ΔI in illumination is approximately proportional to I over a wide range; this relationship is known as *Weber's law*. Thus the higher I, the higher must ΔI be for detectability. One can say that the VS has a logarithmic response to brightness, since detectability depends on the ratio, rather than the difference, between I and $I + \Delta I$.

The *apparent brightness* of a stimulus also depends on adaptation; in addition, it is a nonlinear function of the intensity of the stimulus. In general, the apparent magnitude of a perceived stimulus can be approximated by a power function of intensity. It should also be pointed out that the VS is much

Fig. 1   Simultaneous contrast. (From Cornsweet [3], p. 279, Fig. 11.7.)

less accurate at judging the magnitude of a single stimulus than it is at determining which of two stimuli is greater in magnitude; there is much less
accuracy for absolute judgments than for relative judgments.

Apparent brightness depends strongly on the *local* background intensity.
In Fig. 1, the small squares all have equal intensities, but they appear quite
different in brightness, because their backgrounds have widely different
intensities. This phenomenon is called *simultaneous contrast*. If the contrast
ratio of an object to its background remains constant, the apparent brightness
of the object can remain constant over a wide range of luminances (i.e.,
actual intensities) of the object and its background; this phenomenon is
called *brightness constancy*.

It must be emphasized that the definition of "background" in this connection is not always straightforward. Thus in Fig. 2, making a small "cut"
in the gray ring causes its two halves to be seen as "belonging to" the white and
black backgrounds, respectively, so that they have different apparent brightnesses. In Fig. 3, the upper gray triangle is seen as belonging to the black
cross, but the lower one is not; hence the upper one is contrasted with the
cross, and so looks lighter than the lower one (which is contrasted with the
white background), even though the latter has more black in its vicinity.

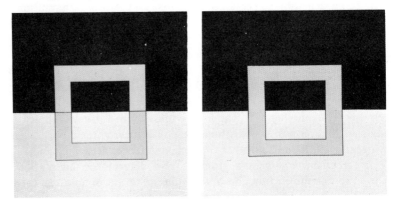

Fig. 2   The Benussi ring.

Fig. 3 The Benary cross. (From J. Beck, "Surface Color Perception," p. 44, Plate 2. Cornell University Press, Ithaca, New York, 1972.)

3.2 ACUITY AND CONTOUR

When visual stimuli have complex space or time patterns, it becomes more difficult to predict their detectability. Such predictions would be relatively easy if the VS were linear, i.e., if the effect of a composite stimulus were the sum of the effects of the parts. There would then, for example, be a simple tradeoff between the intensity, size, and duration of a stimulus, e.g., one could compensate for a decrease in intensity by increasing area or duration. (Within restricted ranges of size and time, such tradeoffs do exist.) It is frequently assumed that the VS is in fact linear once an initial logarithmic transformation (Section 3.1) has been performed.

If linearity is assumed, it becomes straightforward to predict the response of the VS to various types of patterned stimuli, provided that we know its responses to certain simple patterns such as points, lines, edges, or sinusoids (i.e., its point, line, or edge spread function, or its modulation transfer function; see Section 6.1.1). The response to sinusoids, in particular, has been extensively measured. For a wide range of background luminances, this response has a bandpass characteristic, being greatest in the vicinity of 5 to 10 cycles per degree (of angle subtended by the stimulus at the eye), and falling off at both lower and higher frequencies. This characteristic is demonstrated in Fig. 4, where the spatial frequency increases to the right while the contrast increases upward; the curve along which the pattern is just visible represents the modulation transfer function of the VS.

The ability of the VS to detect fine spatial detail is known as *acuity*. It should be pointed out that acuity not only depends on background luminance, etc., as just discussed, but also varies greatly with the position of the stimulus. It is greatest within about a degree of the visual axis, but falls off very rapidly toward the periphery of the visual field. This can be demonstrated by fixing one's eyes on the middle of a row of books, and trying to read the titles of the books some distance away from the point of fixation, without moving the eyes.

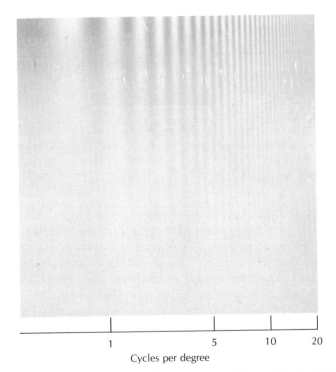

Cycles per degree

Fig. 4   Sinusoidally modulated pattern. (From Cornsweet [3], p. 343, Fig. 12.21; photograph made by F. W. Campbell and J. G. Robson.)

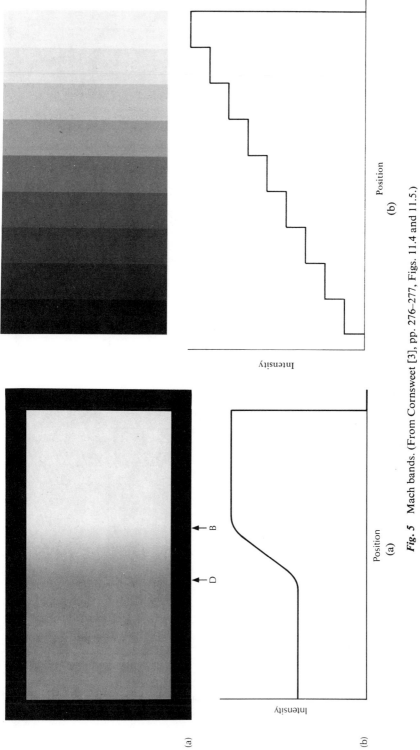

Fig. 5 Mach bands. (From Cornsweet [3], pp. 276–277, Figs. 11.4 and 11.5.)

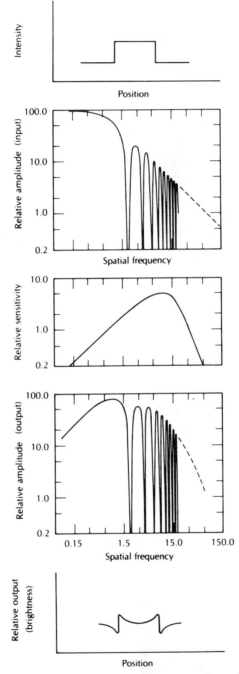

Fig. 6 Response of the visual system to a steplike pattern. (From Cornsweet [3], p. 346, Fig. 12.24.)

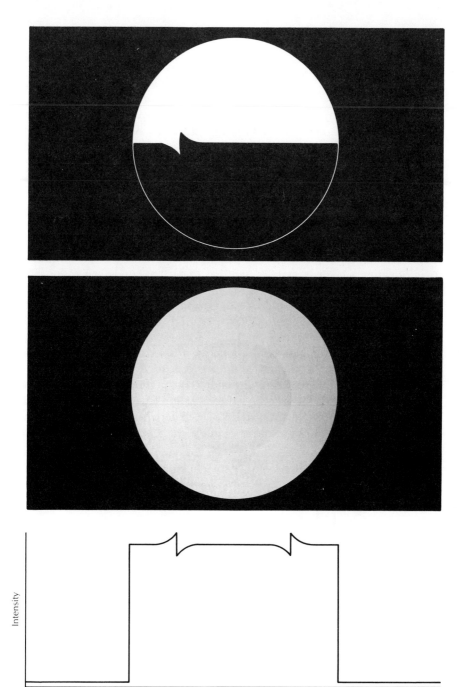

(a)

(b)

Intensity

(c)   Position

Fig. 7 "Filling in" of regions from their edges. (From Cornsweet [3], p. 273, Fig. 11.2.) When the disk shown in part (a) is spun rapidly about its center, the brightness cross section through the center is as shown in part (c), but what one sees is shown in the photograph in part (b).

The response of the VS to abrupt changes in luminance ("edges" or "contours") displays "overshoots" known as *Mach bands* (Fig. 5), which have the effect of enhancing or deblurring the edges. Such overshoot responses are, in fact, predicted if one multiplies the spatial frequency spectrum of a steplike function by the modulation transfer function of the VS (Fig. 6). The VS also seems to "fill in" the apparent brightness in the interior of a region based on that at the region's edges (perhaps at the frequency for which the response is strongest). This is demonstrated in Fig. 7, where the two regions have the same luminance except near their common edge, but each of them appears to have a different uniform brightness. This phenomenon can take place even when there are gaps in the edges (Fig. 8); the contours appear to be interpolated across the gaps. The insensitivity of the VS to low spatial frequency information when edges are present has important consequences for picture compression and enhancement (see Chapters 5 and 6).

Contours and simple patterns such as spots, lines, or bars produce adaptation and contrast effects on the perception of other contours, including "backward masking" effects (analogous to metacontrast), in which the perceptibility of a visual stimulus is reduced if a second stimulus is presented immediately afterwards. Many of these effects are dependent on the *slant* or *size* of the contours involved. For example, adaptation to bars of a particular orientation θ raises the detection threshold for bars oriented at θ but does not affect the threshold for bars in very different orientations, e.g., those perpendicular to θ. As another example, a background of (or previous

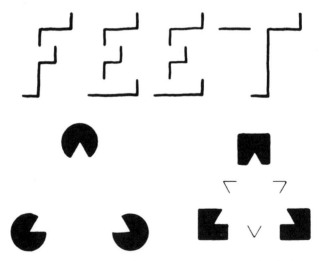

Fig. 8 "Filling in" from edges having gaps. (From S. Coren, Subjective contours and apparent depth, *Psych. Rev.* **79**, 1972, 359–367, Figs. 2A, 3, 8A.)

Fig. 9 Zollner illusion. (From Luckiesh [7], p. 77, Fig. 37.) The vertical bars appear to
be slanted, due to the presence of the many short oblique crossbars.

exposure to) many bars in a given orientation θ tends to cause a single bar
to be perceived as more nearly perpendicular to θ than it actually is (Fig. 9).
Analogous phenomena hold for bar width or spot size (Fig. 10). For another
approach to explaining these "illusions" of size and slant, see Section 3.5.
A large collection of illusions is given by Luckiesh [7].

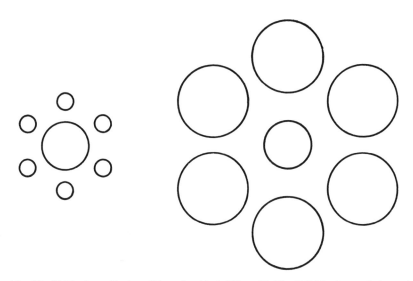

Fig. 10 Ebbinghaus illusion. (From Luckiesh [7], p. 56, Fig. 17.) The inner circle on the
left looks larger than the one on the right.

3.3   COLOR

Up to now we have ignored the *wavelength* of the light which produces the visual stimulus. As this wavelength varies, the perceived *color* (or, more precisely, *hue*) of the light changes, from red (corresponding to the longest visible wavelength) through orange, yellow, green, and blue to violet. Mixtures of wavelengths also give rise to perceived hues, some of which (e.g., purple) cannot be obtained from any single wavelength. "White" (or gray) light can also be obtained by mixing colored lights. In fact, any perceivable hue can be obtained by mixing three colors (e.g., a red, a green, and a blue) in appropriate proportions. Visual detection thresholds are color dependent; the VS is more sensitive to green than to red or blue.

The appearance of a colored spot of light can be described in terms of its brightness, its hue, and its *saturation*. This last can be thought of as related to the degree to which a hue is "undiluted" by white light; for example, pink is an unsaturated red.

Many of the adaptation, contrast, and constancy phenomena described in Sections 3.1 and 3.2 also hold for color. Adaptation to, or contrast with, a particular hue distorts the perception of other hues; for example, gray seen after green, or seen against a green background, looks purplish. Some of these effects are slant specific, e.g., after viewing vertical green bars, vertical gray bars look purplish, but horizontal ones do not. There seem to be important differences, however, between hue and brightness; for example, abrupt changes in hue do not always produce sharp contours when brightness is constant.

3.4   PATTERN AND TEXTURE

The visual field is not perceived as an array of independent picture points; it is usually seen as consisting of a relatively small number of regions, e.g., objects on a background. Only a few of the possible subsets of the visual field can be perceived as regions. For example, a region must be, at least partially, surrrounded by edges (i.e., abrupt changes in luminance); if it is not, one cannot see it as an individual entity (Fig. 11). Moreover, not all possible combinations of edges can be perceived as defining regions or objects. The *Gestalt laws of organization* describe those groupings or patterns which are most naturally seen as units.

The *law of similarity* states that similar entities tend to group together (Fig. 12). Here "similar" seems to be definable in terms of a small set of entity properties such as brightness, color, slope, and size. According to the *law of proximity*, closely clustered entities tend to group (Fig. 13). By the

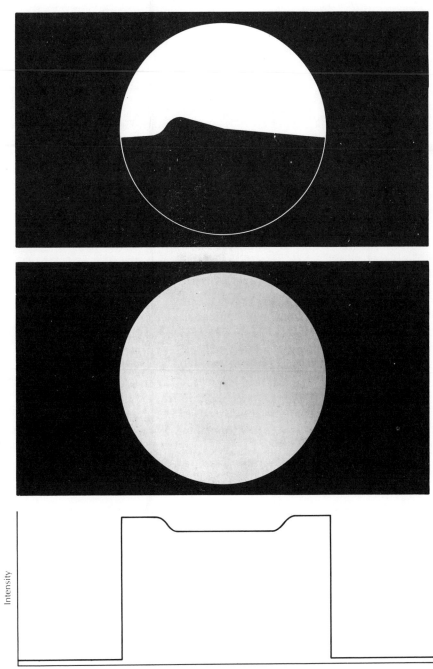

(a)

(b)

(c)

Intensity

Position

Fig. 11 A region cannot be seen as an entity if it has *no* edges. (From Cornsweet [3], p. 275, Fig. 11.3.) Compare Fig. 7.

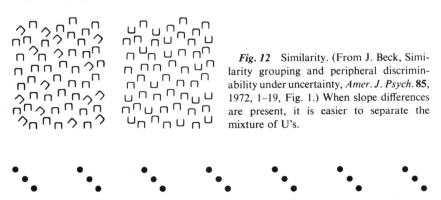

Fig. 12   Similarity. (From J. Beck, Similarity grouping and peripheral discriminability under uncertainty, *Amer. J. Psych.* **85**, 1972, 1–19, Fig. 1.) When slope differences are present, it is easier to separate the mixture of U's.

Fig. 13   Proximity. (From M. Wertheimer, Principles of perceptual organization, *in* "Readings in Perception," D. C. Beardslee and M. Wertheimer (eds.), p. 122. Van Nostrand-Reinhold, Princeton, New Jersey, 1958.) We see the dots grouped in 3's, not (e.g.) in horizontal rows.

law of good continuation, when curves cross or branch, parts that smoothly continue one another are seen as belonging together (Fig. 14); while by the *law of closure*, closed figures tend to be seen as units (Fig. 15). Groupings which violate the laws are difficult to see as units, even if they constitute familiar objects; one can realize intellectually that Fig. 16 contains an "M" and a "W," but one does not readily "see" them there.

When a visual field is seen as composed of regions, not all of these regions can be seen as "objects" at the same time. For example, in Fig. 17, one can see either the two profiles or the vase, but not both at once. In general, only the region on one side of an edge is seen, at a given time, as a "figure" that has

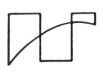

Fig. 14   Good continuation. (From M. Wertheimer, Principles of perceptual organization, *in* "Readings in Perception," D. C. Beardslee and M. Wertheimer (eds.), p. 130, Fig. 23. Van Nostrand-Reinhold, Princeton, New Jersey, 1958.) We see a rectangular wave and a smooth curve, not three closed regions.

Fig. 15   Closure. (From M. Wertheimer, Principles of perceptual organization, *in* "Readings in Perception," D. C. Beardslee and M. Wertheimer (eds.), p. 130, Fig. 25. Van Nostrand-Reinhold, Princeton, New Jersey, 1958.) We see two touching closed regions, not a curve that crosses itself.

Fig. 16 Hidden figures. (After M. Wertheimer, Principles of perceptual organization, *in* "Readings in Perception," D. C. Beardslee and M. Wertheimer (eds.), p. 134, Fig. 39. Van Nostrand-Reinhold, Princeton, New Jersey, 1958.) This is not easily seen as a "W" on top of an "M".

Fig. 17 Rubin vase. (From Hochberg [6], p. 84, Fig. 5-8.) This can be seen either as a vase or as two faces.

a shape; the region on the other side is then seen as a shapeless "ground," which usually appears to extend behind the figure. If one of the two regions is brighter, or smaller in size, or more symmetrical, or bounded (i.e., "closed"), it is generally easier to see as the figure, but one can also see it as the ground by making a conscious effort.

   The properties that are important in producing similarity grouping are also important in the perception of *visual textures.* These are complex visual patterns composed of entities, or subpatterns, that have characteristic brightnesses, colors, slopes, sizes, etc. Thus a texture can be regarded as a similarity grouping. The local subpattern properties give rise to the perceived lightness, directionality, coarseness, etc., of the texture as a whole. For a large collection of examples of textures, see Brodatz [1].

3.5   SHAPE AND SPACE

In determining which arrangements of parts in a scene are seen as figures, *simplicity* seems to play an important role [6]. In Fig. 14, for example, the preferred grouping is the simpler one (a smooth curve and a rectangular wave, not three irregular closed figures); similar remarks apply to Figs. 15 and 16. One can attempt to formulate this criterion of simplicity in terms of *information theory*: The grouping that can be specified using the least information is the preferred figure. Here the specification might be formulated in terms of the numbers of (unequal) lines, angles, line crossings, etc., in the grouping. For a review of this and other applications of information theory to pattern perception see Corcoran [2]. It should be emphasized, however, that a single information measure cannot capture all aspects of shape perception. The shape of a figure is a highly multidimensional concept—shapes can be compact, elongated, or dispersed; smooth or jagged; etc.

The image formed by the eye is two-dimensional; many different arrangements of objects in three-dimensional space could give rise to the same image. The VS uses a variety of "cues" to reduce or eliminate this ambiguity. Here again, many of these cues can be regarded as expressing principles of simplicity. Thus the larger of two similar objects may be seen as nearer—perhaps because, by judging the objects to be at different distances, one can assume them to be congruent, which simplifies the description of the scene. More generally, if texture coarseness decreases in a given direction, one can see the textured objects as uniformly textured but receding in that direction. If object A appears partly to hide object B, object A is seen as nearer; this too may be because the visible portion of object B has a relatively complex shape, which can be simplified by imagining a suitable "completion" of B in back of A. Converging lines can be seen as receding, perhaps because this allows one to regard them as parallel; and in general, objects drawn in perspective are easy to see as three-dimensional, because this makes their shapes simpler or more familiar (e.g., Fig. 18).

When the VS treats size changes as distance changes, or shape changes as perspective changes, it is said to be displaying *size and shape constancy*. Many of the illusions involving slant and size (see Section 3.2) can also be interpreted along these lines. Similar interpretations can be given for the cues that involve blur (interpreted as due to atmospheric effects on the image of a distant object) and shadow (interpreted in terms of the scene lit from above and behind, as by sunlight).

The following are some other important cues to three-dimensional depth. When the eyes or head are moved, the relative motions of parts of a scene give clues to their relative distances (if one makes the simplifying assumption that the parts themselves have not moved!); this cue is called *motion parallax*.

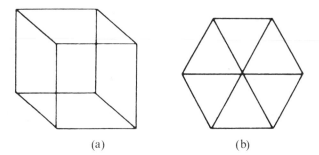

(a)   (b)

Fig. 18 Kopfermann cubes. (From Hochberg [6], p. 87, Fig. 5-10.) When we see (a) as three-dimensional, its description becomes simpler, since its lines now can be regarded as all being of equal length.

Comparison of the images seen by the two eyes also gives a distance cue, called *binocular parallax*; the distance to an object is related to the amount of shift required to bring its two images into registration. Here too, of course, one is making a simplifying assumption, namely, that one has correctly identified the two images as images of the same object. Finally, for a relatively close object, the eyes may have to focus ("accommodate") or to turn inward ("converge") in order to see it sharply, and the degrees to which these actions are necessary also provide depth measures.

When the VS has chosen a particular three-dimensional interpretation of a scene, it tends to ignore any cues that are inconsistent with the chosen interpretation, or to reinterpret these cues in other ways even when this is inconsistent with normal experience. For example, if a room is built in a trapezoidal shape, it will appear rectangular when seen (with one eye) from the proper viewpoint, and people moving around in it will appear to change size.

3.6 DURATION AND MOTION

As indicated in Section 3.1, the response of the VS to a stimulus depends on temporal, as well as spatial factors. In this connection, it is useful to study the response of the VS to simple temporal patterns, e.g., to impulses ("flashes") or to modulated ("flickering") illumination. As was the case with spatial patterns, there is a tendency for this response to fall off at both the high and low ends of the frequency spectrum: totally unchanging patterns (provided they are immobile relative to the eye) tend to fade, while patterns that change too rapidly "fuse" and appear to be unchanging. It should be stressed that the spatial and temporal characteristics of the VS are interdependent; the response to a flickering pattern depends in a complex way on its spatial and temporal frequencies.

When part of the visual image is displaced, e.g., if a light is turned off, and another light is turned on after a short enough time, one perceives a single light moving continuously from the first position to the second. As in Section 3.5, one can regard this perception as a "simple" interpretation of the stimulus, in which the succession of distinct images can be accounted for by assuming that a single object is in motion. In this connection, if a collection of parts move in unison, one tends to see them as a single figure; this is the Gestalt *law of common fate*. If an object changes size or shape as well as position, and it is possible to account for this in terms of translational and rotational motions in three dimensions, one tends to perceive such motions.

Some of the adaptation effects described in Sections 3.1 and 3.2 are motion-specific. For example, after prolonged viewing of a downward-moving pattern, stationary patterns appear to move upward (the "waterfall effect"); and the detection threshold for downward-moving patterns is raised, but that for upward-moving patterns is not.

3.7   DETECTION AND RECOGNITION

The processes of detecting, classifying, and recognizing a visual (or any other) stimulus can be analyzed from the standpoint of *statistical decision theory*. The observer can be thought of as estimating the prior and posterior probabilities that the stimulus was actually present, and then using some criterion (e.g., thresholding a likelihood ratio) to make his decision. His choice of this criterion determines the probabilities of his missing an actual stimulus (false dismissal), and of reporting a stimulus when none was actually present (false alarm). The tradeoff between these probabilities, as a function of the criterion used, is called the observer's "receiver operating character-istic" (ROC). From the decision-theoretic standpoint, one should speak not only of a detection "threshold," but also of detection criteria. For a review of this topic see Green and Swets [5].

Perceptual decision criteria are influenced by many factors besides the physical nature of the stimulus. Expectation or "perceptual set" plays an important role; in particular, it affects the estimation of prior probabilities. It also affects how ambiguous figures are perceived; for example, prior viewing of the young woman in Fig. 19a makes it less likely that the old woman will be seen in Fig. 19b, and conversely. "Response biases," e.g., estimates of the values of hits and the costs of misses, also enter into the formulation of decision criteria.

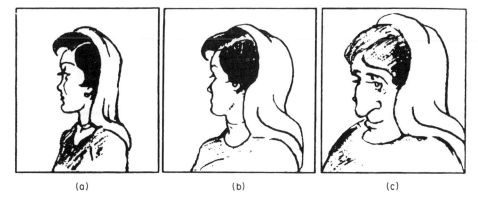

(a)   (b)   (c)

Fig. 19 Ambiguous face. (From Hochberg [6], p. 70, Fig. 4-28.) The center face can be seen as resembling either the one on the left or the one on the right.

Visual detection and recognition tasks, particularly the latter, involve not only the VS, but memory processes as well. The stored information that might be involved in recognition, say, of a shape or pattern, could be of a variety of types, ranging from a "template" of the pattern (or perhaps of an idealized prototype), to a set of features or measurements that characterize the pattern, or a structural description based on such features. As we shall see in Chapter 12, the use of features makes it possible to formulate invariant descriptions of the pattern, i.e., descriptions that do not change when the pattern varies— at least, to limited degrees—in brightness, color, position, orientation, or size. The transformations, however, under which a pattern is still easily recognized are hard to characterize. For example, recognition is impaired by change of the three-dimensional reference frame, or by reversal of figure and ground, even though the pattern itself remains exactly the same.

Little is known about the nature of the features that the VS may use for recognition, although some clues can be obtained from the neurophysiology of the VS, as well as from studies of the movements that the eye makes when it examines patterns. One can also raise many interesting questions about the manner in which the information used for recognition is extracted from the observed pattern, and the manner in which the stored information is retrieved (e.g., are these processes serial or parallel?); see Corcoran [2] for a review of this topic.

REFERENCES

1. P. Brodatz, "Textures." Dover, New York, 1966.
2. D. W. J. Corcoran, "Pattern Recognition." Penguin, Baltimore, Maryland, 1971.
3. T. N. Cornsweet, "Visual Perception." Academic Press, New York, 1970.

4. C. H. Graham *et al.* (eds.), "Vision and Visual Perception." Wiley, New York, 1965.
5. D. M. Green and J. A. Swets, "Signal Detection Theory and Psychophysics." Wiley, New York, 1966.
6. J. Hochberg, "Perception." Prentice-Hall, Englewood Cliffs, New Jersey, 1964.
7. M. Luckiesh, "Visual Illusions." Dover, New York, 1965.
8. L. Zusne, "Visual Perception of Form." Academic Press, New York, 1970.

Chapter 4

Digitization

Pictures can, in general, be considered continuous functions, the gray level being a continuous function of position in the picture. Before such a picture can be processed by a digital computer or, in many cases, transmitted over a channel, it needs to be digitized.

In its ordinary sense, digitization consists of sampling the gray level in the picture at an $M \times N$ array of points. Since the gray level at these points may take any value in a continuous range, for digital processing the gray level needs to be quantized. By this we mean that we divide the range of gray level into K intervals, and require the gray level at any point to take on only one of these values. In order for the picture reproduced from these numbers to be a "good" reproduction of the original, M, N, and K have to be large. Ordinarily, the finer the sampling and quantization, the better the reproduced picture. Nothing is gained, however, by increasing M, N, and K beyond the spatial and gray scale resolution capabilities of the receiver.

In a more general sense, the aim of sampling is to represent a continuous picture by a finite string or array of numbers, called *samples*. The only constraint on these numbers is that it should be possible to reconstruct a picture from them. There may be small errors involved in the reconstruction provided that these errors do not cause any impairment in the representation of the scene with respect to the spatial and gray scale resolution capabilities of the receiver.

In the next two sections, we will discuss two different approaches to picture sampling. In the first approach, the samples are the values of the picture function (gray levels) at a discrete array of points, and we discuss the constraints that a picture must satisfy for this type of sampling to be adequate. In the second approach, the picture function is expanded in terms of orthonormal functions, and the coefficients of expansion are the samples.

4.1   SAMPLING USING AN ARRAY OF POINTS

We will now present the theory of a sampling technique in which the samples are the gray levels of the picture at an array of points. Before we expose the reader to such sampling of pictures, we will first consider the case of a one-dimensional signal. This is to facilitate the presentation of the well-known Whittaker–Kotelnikov–Shannon theorem. A two-dimensional analog of the theorem will then be presented.

4.1.1   One-Dimensional Functions

Let us consider a one-dimensional function $f(t)$, which we seek to represent by samples $f(kT)$, where k takes on integer values from $-\infty$ to $+\infty$ and T is the sampling period. Evidently the validity of the representation depends on whether it is possible to reconstruct the function from its samples.

One way to reconstruct the original $f(t)$ from the samples $f(kT)$ would be to interpolate suitably between the samples. Following the classic paper of Peterson and Middleton [13], this can be done using an interpolation function $g(t)$ as follows:

$$f(t) = \sum_{k=-\infty}^{\infty} f(kT)\, g(t-kT) \tag{1}$$

In other words, the contribution that the sample $f(kT)$ makes to the reconstruction at time t is weighted by the factor $g(t-kT)$ which is the interpolation function $g(t)$ displaced by time kT along the t-axis. We will now assume that f and g are Fourier transformable.

By Eq. (6) of Chapter 2, we can write

$$f(kT)\, g(t-kT) = \int_{-\infty}^{\infty} f(\tau)\, g(t-\tau)\, \delta(\tau-kT)\, d\tau \tag{2}$$

Substituting in (1) and inverting the order of summation and integration, we obtain

$$f(t) = \int_{-\infty}^{\infty} f(\tau)\, g(t-\tau) \left(\sum_{k=-\infty}^{\infty} \delta(\tau-kT) \right) d\tau \tag{3}$$

The function in the large parentheses is periodic with period T, and can, therefore, be represented by a Fourier series of the form

$$\sum_{k=-\infty}^{\infty} \delta(\tau - kT) = \sum_{n=-\infty}^{\infty} a_n \exp\left(+j\frac{2\pi n}{T}\tau\right) \tag{4}$$

where the coefficients a_n of the Fourier expansion are given by

$$a_n = \frac{1}{T}\int_{-T/2}^{T/2} \left(\sum_{k=-\infty}^{\infty}\delta(\tau - kT)\right)\exp\left(-j\frac{2\pi n}{T}\tau\right)d\tau$$

$$= \frac{1}{T}\int_{-T/2}^{T/2}\delta(\tau)\exp\left(-j\frac{2\pi n}{T}\tau\right)d\tau$$

since only the $k = 0$ term of the sum is nonzero in the range of integration. By Eq. (6) of Chapter 2, it follows that

$$a_n = 1/T \qquad \text{for all} \quad n \tag{5}$$

Substituting (4) and (5) in (3), we can write

$$f(t) = \sum_{n=-\infty}^{\infty}\int_{-\infty}^{\infty}\left[f(\tau)\exp\left(+j\frac{2\pi n}{T}\tau\right)\right]\left(\frac{g(t-\tau)}{T}\right)d\tau \tag{6}$$

Each term in the summation is a convolution of the functions

$$f(t)\exp\left(+j\frac{2\pi nt}{T}\right) \qquad \text{and} \qquad \frac{g(t)}{T} \tag{7}$$

By the convolution property of Fourier transforms as given by Eq. (23a) of Chapter 2, the Fourier transform of each term in the summation in (6) is the product of the Fourier transforms of these two functions. Let $F(\omega)$ and $G(\omega)$ denote the Fourier transforms of $f(t)$ and $g(t)$, respectively. Then using the one-dimensional analog of property (21b) in Chapter 2, the Fourier transforms of the two functions in (7) are $F(\omega - (2\pi n/T))$ and $G(\omega)/T$, respectively. Taking the Fourier transform of both sides of (6), we obtain

$$F(\omega) = \frac{G(\omega)}{T}\sum_{n=-\infty}^{\infty}F\left(\omega - \frac{2\pi n}{T}\right) \tag{8}$$

Since the steps taken in deriving (8) from (1) are all reversible, (8) is a *necessary and sufficient* condition for the exact reconstructability of $f(t)$ from its samples $f(kT)$ using (1). We shall now formulate sufficient conditions on G and T in order for reconstructability to hold.

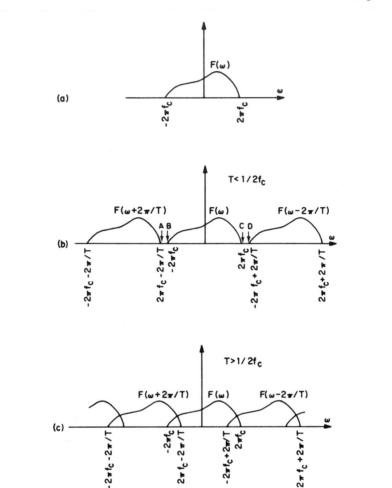

Fig. 1   (a) $F(\omega)$ for a one-dimensional bandlimited function. (b) Nonoverlapping copies of $F(\omega)$. (c) Overlapping copies of $F(\omega)$.

Now $F(\omega-(2\pi n/T))$ is just $F(\omega)$ shifted by $2\pi n/T$. Suppose that $f(t)$ is bandlimited, i.e., that $F(\omega) = 0$ for $|\omega| \geqslant 2\pi f_c$, say, as in Fig. 1a. If $T \leqslant 1/2f_c$, then the shifted copies of $F(\omega)$ are far enough apart that no two of them can have nonzero values at any one point, as shown in Fig. 1b. For such an F, if we take

$$G(\omega) = \begin{cases} T, & |\omega| < 2\pi f_c \\ 0, & \text{otherwise} \end{cases}$$

then (8) is immediately satisfied, since on the right-hand side the unshifted copy of $F(\omega)$ has weight 1, while all the other copies have weight 0. Since this G is a rect function, its inverse Fourier transform g is a sinc function; in fact, we have

$$g(t) = \frac{1}{2\pi} \int_{-2\pi f_c}^{2\pi f_c} T e^{j\omega t} \, d\omega = \frac{\sin 2\pi f_c t}{\pi t / T} \tag{9}$$

Thus if $T = 1/2f_c$, we have $g(t) = \text{sinc}(2\pi f_c t)$.

If overlap of the copies is allowed, i.e., $T > 1/2f_c$, as in Fig. 1c, and f is still permitted to be any function limited in frequency by $2\pi f_c$, no $G(\omega)$ will satisfy (8) for all possible F. On the other hand, if $T < 1/2f_c$, we have some flexibility in defining G. In fact, there exist intervals for which $F(\omega - (2\pi n/T)) = 0$ for all n, and in these intervals, G can be chosen arbitrarily. Thus for $T < 1/2f_c$, our solution (9) for $g(t)$ is no longer unique.

The preceding discussion has established the Whittaker–Kotelnikov–Shannon theorem:

Theorem. If the Fourier transform of a function $f(t)$ vanishes for $|\omega| \geqslant 2\pi f_c$, then $f(t)$ can be exactly reconstructed from samples of its values taken $1/2f_c$ apart or closer.

4.1.2   Sampling Lattices and Reciprocal Lattices

To extend the theory of sampling just given to two dimensions, we need to define sampling lattices in the picture plane and reciprocal lattices in the spatial frequency plane.

Consider two vectors $\vec{r}_1$ and $\vec{r}_2$ in the picture plane (Figs. 2a and 2b). We will call them *basis vectors*. A sampling lattice is a periodic arrangement of points in the xy-plane, where the points are defined by the position vectors $\vec{r}_{mn}$ given by

$$\vec{r}_{mn} = m\vec{r}_1 + n\vec{r}_2, \qquad m \text{ and } n = 0, \pm 1, \pm 2, \ldots \tag{10}$$

In Figs. 2a and 2b we have shown two examples of sampling lattices.

The reciprocal basis vectors $\vec{w}_1$ and $\vec{w}_2$ in the uv-plane are uniquely derived from the basis vectors $\vec{r}_1$ and $\vec{r}_2$ by

$$\vec{r}_i \cdot \vec{w}_j = \begin{cases} 0, & i \neq j \\ 1, & i = j \end{cases} \tag{11}$$

By the previous definition, the vector $\vec{w}_1$ is perpendicular to $\vec{r}_2$. If θ is the angle between $\vec{r}_1$ and $\vec{r}_2$, it is easy to show that the magnitude of $\vec{w}_1$ is

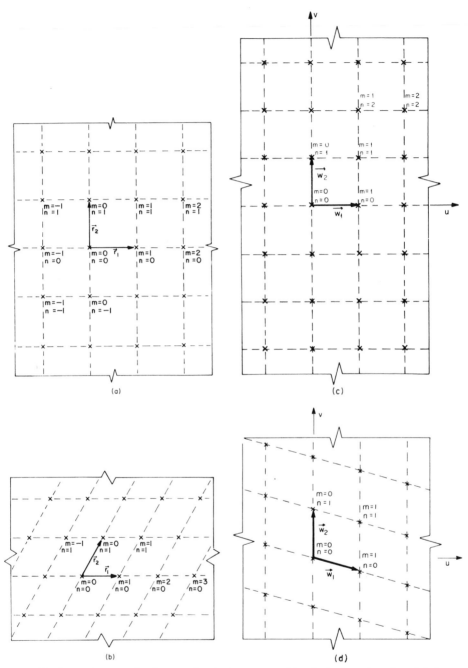

Fig. 2 (a) An example of a sampling lattice generated by the basis vectors $\vec{r}_1$ and $\vec{r}_2$ in the xy-plane. The sampling lattice is a two-dimensional periodic array of points marked x. (b) Another example of a sampling lattice in the xy-plane. (c) Reciprocal lattice in the spatial frequency plane for the sampling lattice in (a). Note that $\vec{w}_1$ and $\vec{w}_2$ are uniquely related to $\vec{r}_1$ and $\vec{r}_2$ in (a). (d) Reciprocal lattice for the sampling lattice in (b).

$1/|\vec{r}_1| \sin \theta$. Similarly, $\vec{w}_2$ is perpendicular to $\vec{r}_1$ and its magnitude is equal to $1/|\vec{r}_2| \sin \theta$.

The reciprocal basis vectors $\vec{w}_1$ and $\vec{w}_2$ define a reciprocal lattice in the uv-plane. The reciprocal lattice is a periodic arrangement of points in the uv-plane, where the points are defined by the position vectors $\vec{w}_{mn}$ given by

$$\vec{w}_{mn} = m\vec{w}_1 + n\vec{w}_2, \qquad m \text{ and } n = 0, \pm 1, \pm 2, \ldots \qquad (12)$$

Figures 2c and 2d are reciprocal lattices for the sampling lattices in Figs. 2a and 2b, respectively.

4.1.3   Sampling of Pictures Using a Sampling Lattice

We will now extend the preceding theory to two-dimensional functions defined over the xy-plane. We assume that these functions are Fourier transformable, and denote the transform of $f(x, y)$ by $F(u, v)$. For convenience in presentation in this subsection, we will denote $f(x, y)$ and $F(u, v)$ by $f(\vec{r})$ and $F(\vec{w})$, respectively. Here $\vec{r}$ is a position vector in the picture plane with coordinates (x, y) while $\vec{w}$ is a position vector in the spatial frequency plane with coordinates (u, v). Then by (12) of Chapter 2

$$F(\vec{w}) = F(u, v) = \int \int f(x, y) \exp[-j2\pi(xu + yv)] \, dx \, dy$$

$$= \int f(\vec{r}) \exp(-j2\pi\vec{w} \cdot \vec{r}) \, d\vec{r}$$

We will now assume that $f(x, y)$ is spatial frequency limited. By this we mean that $F(u, v)$ is zero outside a bounded region in the spatial frequency plane. We wish to represent the function $f(\vec{r})$ by its samples $f(\vec{r}_{mn})$ where $\vec{r}_{mn}$ are the points on a sampling lattice as defined in the preceding subsection. Evidently, the samples $f(\vec{r}_{mn})$ are a valid representation provided it is possible to reconstruct $f(\vec{r})$ from these samples. As in the one-dimensional case, we will use this reconstructability condition to derive constraints which should be satisfied by $f(\vec{r})$ so that it may be represented by its samples.

One way to reconstruct the original $f(\vec{r})$ from its samples $f(\vec{r}_{mn})$ would be to interpolate suitably between sampling points. Following the treatment for the one-dimensional case, this can be done by using a suitable interpolation function $g(\vec{r})$ such that $f(\vec{r})$ may be expanded as a linear function of its samples $f(\vec{r}_{mn})$:

$$f(\vec{r}) = \sum_m \sum_n f(\vec{r}_{mn}) \, g(\vec{r} - \vec{r}_{mn}) \qquad (13)$$

Here $f(\vec{r}_{mn})\, g(\vec{r} - \vec{r}_{mn})$ is the contribution of the sample $f(\vec{r}_{mn})$ to the reconstruction at the point $\vec{r}$. Employing steps similar to those used in deriving (8) from (1), we arrive at the result (for a detailed derivation see [13])

$$F(\vec{w}) = \frac{G(\vec{w})}{Q} \sum_p \sum_q F(\vec{w} - \vec{w}_{pq}) \tag{14}$$

where the set of points $\vec{w}_{pq}$ is the reciprocal lattice corresponding to the sampling lattice $\vec{r}_{mn}$ as defined by (11) and (12). In (14), $G(\vec{w})$ is the Fourier transform of $g(\vec{r})$, and Q the area of the parallelogram formed by the vectors $\vec{r}_1$ and $\vec{r}_2$.

Assume that $f(\vec{r})$ is a spatial frequency-limited function so that $F(\vec{w})$ looks like Fig. 3a. For a given choice of $\vec{w}_1$ and $\vec{w}_2$, the functions $F(\vec{w} - \vec{w}_{pq})$ for various values of p and q are shown in Fig. 3b. It is clear from Fig. 3b that the equality in Eq. (14) will be satisfied if the choice of $\vec{w}_1$ and $\vec{w}_2$ (which determine $\vec{r}_1$ and r_2, hence the sampling strategy in the xy-plane) is such that $F(\vec{w} - \vec{w}_{pq})$ for different integral values of p and q do not overlap. The interpolation function $g(\vec{r})$ can then be chosen such that its Fourier transform $G(\vec{w})$ equals the constant Q over the region of the uv-plane over which $F(\vec{w})$ is nonzero, and is zero wherever $F(\vec{w} + \vec{w}_{pq})$, $p \neq 0$, $q \neq 0$, are nonvanishing; the value of $G(\vec{w})$ being arbitrary over that portion of the uv-plane that is not covered by $F(\vec{w})$ or its periodic images. It is clear that if the domain of $F(\vec{w})$ is irregularly shaped, then, even for the choice of $\vec{w}_1$ and $\vec{w}_2$ that permits closest packing of the repetitive spectra in the uv-plane, there may always be regions where $G(\vec{w})$ may take arbitrary values. Therefore, even for such a case the interpolation function may not be uniquely determined. This is certainly a basic difference between one- and two-dimensional sampling by this technique. The discussion presented here leads to the following theorem:

Theorem.   A function $f(\vec{r})$ whose Fourier transform $F(\vec{w})$ vanishes over all but a bounded region of spatial frequency space can be everywhere reproduced from its values taken over a lattice of points $(m\vec{r}_1 + n\vec{r}_2)$, $m, n = 0, \pm 1, \pm 2, \ldots$, provided the vectors $\vec{r}_1$ and $\vec{r}_2$ are small enough to ensure nonoverlapping of the spectrum $F(\vec{w})$ with its images on a periodic lattice of points $(p\vec{w}_1 + q\vec{w}_2)$, $p, q = 0, \pm 1, \pm 2, \ldots$, with $\vec{r}_i \cdot \vec{w}_j = 0$ for $i \neq j$, and $\vec{r}_i \cdot \vec{w}_i = 1$ for $i, j = 1$ and 2.

4.1.4   Generalization to Random Fields

The preceding subsection presented a technique for sampling a single bandlimited picture. In other words, given a bandlimited picture, one can determine the sampling strategy in the picture plane and the interpolation function such that the picture can be reconstructed without error from the samples.

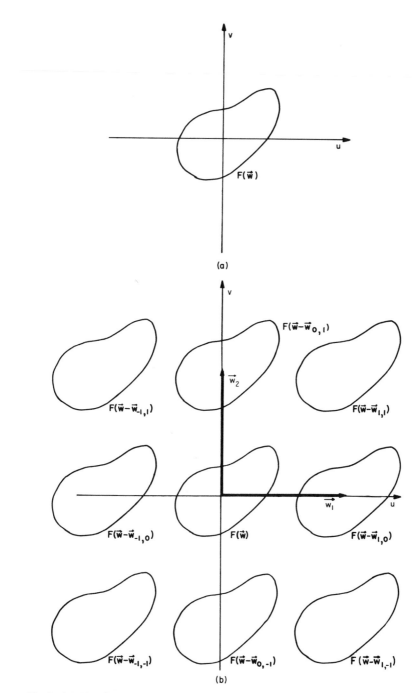

Fig. 3 (a) $F(\vec{w})$ for a two-dimensional bandlimited function $f(x, y)$. (b) Nonoverlapping copies of $F(u, v)$.

Now we pose the following question: How can one determine a sampling strategy and the interpolation function for a *family* or a *class* of pictures? Evidently, the sampling procedures and the interpolation function should now depend on the average or statistical properties of the pictures in the family.

In Section 2.4.1, a family of pictures was called a *random field*. Therefore, we now turn our attention to reformulating the previously introduced sampling techniques for random fields. We will assume the given random field to be homogeneous. If we use the notation $\mathbf{f}(\vec{r})$ to denote the random field, then its autocorrelation function is given by [Eqs. (98), (106), and (110a) of Chapter 2]

$$R_{ff}(\vec{r}_1, \vec{r}_2) = E\{\mathbf{f}(\vec{r}_1)\mathbf{f}(\vec{r}_2)\} = R_{ff}(\vec{r}_1 - \vec{r}_2) = R_{ff}(\vec{r}_2 - \vec{r}_1) \qquad (15)$$

In keeping with the sampling technique introduced in the preceding subsections, we desire to represent each picture in the random field $\mathbf{f}(\vec{r})$ by samples that are values of the gray level at a set of periodic sampling points $\vec{r}_{mn}$ generated by basis vectors $\vec{r}_1$ and $\vec{r}_2$ as in (10). To be able to reconstruct each picture in the random field from its samples, we seek an expansion of form (13), that is,

$$\mathbf{f}(\vec{r}) = \sum_m \sum_n \mathbf{f}(\vec{r}_{mn})\, g(\vec{r} - \vec{r}_{mn}) \qquad (16)$$

This is a family of equations, one for each picture in the collection represented by the random field $\mathbf{f}(\vec{r})$.

Unless the interpolation function $g(\vec{r})$ is of an appropriate form and the random field $\mathbf{f}(\vec{r})$ satisfies certain constraints, the equality in (16) will not be satisfied. To determine such a $g(\vec{r})$ and such constraints, we will proceed as follows. In the absence of any *a priori* knowledge of the correct $g(\vec{r})$ in (16), we first seek an optimum function $g(\vec{r})$ such that the linear combination of the periodic samples of $\mathbf{f}(\vec{r})$ as given by

$$\mathbf{f}_e(\vec{r}) = \sum_m \sum_n \mathbf{f}(\vec{r}_{mn})\, g(\vec{r} - \vec{r}_{mn}) \qquad (17)$$

results in the minimization of the ensemble average error as given by

$$e = E\{(\mathbf{f}(\vec{r}) - \mathbf{f}_e(\vec{r}))^2\} \qquad (18)$$

Substituting (17) in (18) and making use of (15), we obtain

$$e = R_{ff}(0) - 2\sum_m \sum_n R_{ff}(\vec{r} - \vec{r}_{mn})\, g(\vec{r} - \vec{r}_{mn})$$
$$+ \sum_m \sum_n \sum_p \sum_q R_{ff}(\vec{r}_{mn} - \vec{r}_{pq})\, g(\vec{r} - \vec{r}_{mn})\, g(\vec{r} - \vec{r}_{pq}) \qquad (19)$$

To determine g which minimizes e at every $\vec{r}$, we assume an arbitrary variation $\varepsilon g'(\vec{r})$ in $g(\vec{r})$ where ε is a real number and $g'(\vec{r})$ an arbitrary function of $\vec{r}$, such that the function $g(\vec{r}) + \varepsilon g'(\vec{r})$ is "close" to the function $g(\vec{r})$. In Eq. (19), we replace $g(\vec{r})$ by $g(\vec{r}) + \varepsilon g'(\vec{r})$. Now if $g(\vec{r})$ is the optimum function we are after, then the derivative $\partial e/\partial \varepsilon$ must be equal to zero at $\varepsilon = 0$ for any $g'(\vec{r})$ (so long as the preceding conditions are satisfied).

If we substitute $g(\vec{r}) + \varepsilon g'(\vec{r})$ for $g(\vec{r})$ in (19), determine the derivative $\partial e/\partial \varepsilon$, substitute $\varepsilon = 0$ in the expression for $\partial e/\partial \varepsilon$, and equate the resulting expression to zero, we obtain

$$\sum_m \sum_n R_{ff}(\vec{r} - \vec{r}_{mn}) \, g'(\vec{r} - \vec{r}_{mn}) = \sum_m \sum_n \sum_p \sum_q R_{ff}(\vec{r}_{mn} - \vec{r}_{pq}) \, g(\vec{r} - \vec{r}_{mn}) \, g'(\vec{r} - \vec{r}_{pq})$$

(20)

which is a condition for $g(\vec{r})$ to be the optimum interpolation function. This equation can be rewritten as

$$\sum_p \sum_q \left\{ R_{ff}(\vec{r} - \vec{r}_{pq}) - \sum_m \sum_n R_{ff}(\vec{r}_{mn} - \vec{r}_{pq}) \, g(\vec{r} - \vec{r}_{mn}) \right\} g'(\vec{r} - \vec{r}_{pq}) = 0 \quad (21)$$

If (21) is to be satisfied for any $g'(r)$, the expression within the curly brackets must vanish for all $\vec{r}_{pq}$. In particular for $\vec{r}_{pq} = 0$ we have

$$R_{ff}(\vec{r}) = \sum_m \sum_n R_{ff}(\vec{r}_{mn}) \, g(\vec{r} - \vec{r}_{mn}) \tag{22}$$

In light of Eq. (13), we can give the following interpretation to this condition: The optimum interpolation function $g(\vec{r})$ for the random field $\mathbf{f}(\vec{r})$ is one that exactly reproduces the nonrandom autocorrelation function $R_{ff}(\vec{r})$ from its samples. Since (22) is identical in form to (13), Fourier-transforming both sides leads to an equation similar to (14), that is,

$$S_{ff}(\vec{w}) = \frac{G(\vec{w})}{Q} \sum_p \sum_q S_{ff}(\vec{w} - \vec{w}_{pq}) \tag{23}$$

where $S_{ff}(\vec{w})$ is the spectral density of the process (see Eq. (103) of Chapter 2) and where $G(\vec{w})$ is the Fourier transform of $g(\vec{r})$. The constant Q and the periodic points $\vec{w}_{pq}$ in the uv-plane are related to the vectors $\vec{r}_1$ and $\vec{r}_2$ as in (14). By arguments identical to those in Section 4.1.3, (23) is satisfied if we choose the reciprocal vectors $\vec{w}_1$ and $\vec{w}_2$ in the uv-plane such that the $S_{ff}(\vec{w} - \vec{w}_{pq})$, for different integral values of p and q, do not overlap. Also, the interpolation function $g(\vec{r})$ should be such that its Fourier transform $G(\vec{w})$ equals the constant Q over the region of the uv-plane over which $S_{ff}(\vec{w})$ is nonzero. Its value is arbitrary over that portion of the uv-plane that is not covered by $S_{ff}(\vec{w})$ or its periodic images, and it is zero elsewhere. Note that since $R_{ff}(\vec{r})$ is real and is symmetric with respect to $180°$ rotation, $S_{ff}(\vec{w})$, $G(\vec{w})$, and $g(\vec{r})$ are all real and possess the same symmetry.

We have shown that the sampling strategy and $g(\vec{r})$ as dictated by (22) minimize the mean square error e as given by (18). We will now show that for bandlimited random fields ($S_{ff}(\vec{w}) = 0$ outside a finite region $\mathcal{S}$ in the uv-plane) this error is indeed zero.

Substituting (22) in (19), we have for the minimum mean-square error

$$e = R_{ff}(0) - \sum_m \sum_n R_{ff}(\vec{r} - \vec{r}_{mn})\, g(\vec{r} - \vec{r}_{mn}) \tag{24}$$

which can be expressed as

$$e = R_{ff}(0) - \int R_{ff}(\vec{r}')\, g(\vec{r}') \left\{ \sum_m \sum_n \delta(\vec{r}' - \vec{r} + \vec{r}_{mn}) \right\} d\vec{r}' \tag{25}$$

We will now examine the two terms on the right-hand side separately. From Eq. (104) of Chapter 2, the first term is

$$R_{ff}(0) = \int S_{ff}(\vec{w})\, d\vec{w} \tag{26}$$

As regards the second term, the Fourier transform of the product $R_{ff}(\vec{r}')\, g(\vec{r}')$ is given by

$$\int_{uv\text{-plane}} S_{ff}(\vec{w} - \vec{s})\, G(\vec{s})\, d\vec{s} \tag{27}$$

by the convolution property of the Fourier transform (Eq. (23a) of Chapter 2), while the Fourier transform of $\sum_m \sum_n \delta(\vec{r}' - \vec{r} + \vec{r}_{mn})$ is given by

$$\frac{1}{Q}\left(\sum_m \sum_n \delta(\vec{w} + \vec{w}_{mn}) \exp(-j2\pi\vec{w}\cdot\vec{r}) \right) \tag{28}$$

using Exercise 4 and Eq. (21a) of Chapter 2, where Q and $\vec{w}_{mn}$ are the same as in (23). By using Parseval's theorem as given by Eq. (24) of Chapter 2, Eqs. (27) and (28) lead to the following result:

$$\int R_{ff}(\vec{r}')\, g(\vec{r}') \left\{ \sum_m \sum_n \delta(\vec{r}' - \vec{r} + \vec{r}_{mn}) \right\} d\vec{r}'$$

$$= \frac{1}{Q}\int_{uv\text{-plane}} \left\{ \int_{uv\text{-plane}} S_{ff}(\vec{w} - \vec{s})\, G(\vec{s})\, d\vec{s} \right\}$$

$$\times \sum_m \sum_n \delta(\vec{w} + \vec{w}_{mn}) \exp(+j2\pi\vec{w}\cdot\vec{r})\, d\vec{w}$$

$$= \int_{uv\text{-plane}} \frac{G(\vec{s})}{Q} \sum_m \sum_n \exp(+j2\pi\vec{r}\cdot\vec{w}_{mn})\, S_{ff}(\vec{s} - \vec{w}_{mn})\, d\vec{s} \tag{29}$$

Substituting (26) and (29) in (25), we obtain

$$e = \int_{uv\text{-plane}} \left[S_{ff}(\vec{w}) - \frac{G(\vec{w})}{Q} \sum_{m} \sum_{n} \exp(j2\pi\vec{r}\cdot\vec{w}_{mn}) S_{ff}(\vec{w}-\vec{w}_{mn}) \right] d\vec{w}$$

(30)

If $G(\vec{w})$ and $\vec{w}_{mn}$ are chosen to satisfy (23) by the method previously described, it is easy to see that then the expression within the brackets in (30) is zero, making the sampling error e equal to zero for the bandlimited process.

4.1.5 Aliasing Problems in Picture Sampling

To best illustrate the concept of aliasing, let us consider the following two experiments:

Experiment 1. Consider a sampling lattice generated by basis vectors $\vec{r}_1$ and $\vec{r}_2$ in Fig. 2a. The reciprocal vectors $\vec{w}_1$ and $\vec{w}_2$ in the frequency plane for this sampling lattice are those given by Fig. 2c. Let us assume that this sampling lattice is used for sampling a picture $f(\vec{r})$ whose Fourier transform $F(\vec{w})$ is nonzero only within the dashed rectangle shown in Fig. 4. Also, to satisfy the conditions on the interpolation function $g(\vec{r})$ as given in Section 4.1.3, let $G(\vec{w})$ be equal to the constant Q within the dashed region and zero outside. (Note that the dashed rectangle is such that it does not overlap with

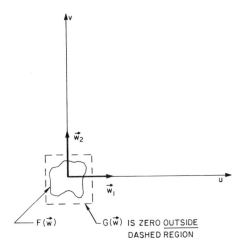

Fig. 4 The sampling lattice obtained from the choice of $\vec{w}_1$ and $\vec{w}_2$ shown here would lead to error-free reproduction of all pictures whose Fourier transforms are zero outside the dashed rectangle.

its own periodic images, such as those in Fig. 3, on the reciprocal lattice.) The sampling lattice and the function $g(\vec{r})$ just described would result in error-free reproduction from samples of all pictures that have Fourier transform zero outside the dashed rectangle in Fig. 4. ■

Experiment 2. Now let us apply the sampling lattice and the interpolation function in Experiment 1 to the picture in Fig. 5 which is described by

$$f(\vec{r}) = \cos 2\pi(\vec{w}_0 \cdot \vec{r})$$

and which has Fourier transform given by (Chapter 2, Exercise 3)

$$F(\vec{w}) = \tfrac{1}{2}[\delta(\vec{w} - \vec{w}_0) + \delta(\vec{w} + \vec{w}_0)]$$

The Fourier transform of the picture consists of two impulses in the spatial frequency plane, one at $\vec{w}_0$ and the other at $-\vec{w}_0$, as shown in Fig. 6a. Note that the periodicity of the sinusoidal pattern is such that the points $\vec{w}_0$ and $-\vec{w}_0$ fall outside the dashed rectangle.

Fig. 5 $\cos 2\pi(\vec{w}_0 \cdot \vec{r})$.

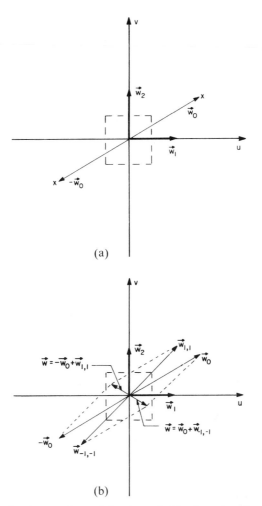

Fig. 6 (a) The Fourier transform of the picture in Fig. 5 consists of two impulses in the uv-plane, one at $\vec{w}_0$ and the other at $-\vec{w}_0$. (b) The Fourier transform of the picture reconstructed from the samples of the picture in Fig. 5 consists of two impulses, one at $\vec{w} = \vec{w}_0 + \vec{w}_{-1, -1}$ and the other at $\vec{w} = -\vec{w}_0 + \vec{w}_{1,1}$.

Let us now attempt to reconstruct the picture in this experiment from its samples by using the interpolation formula in Eq. (13). The Fourier transform of the reconstructed picture is given by the right-hand side of (14), that is,

$$\frac{G(\vec{w})}{Q} \sum_m \sum_n F(\vec{w} - \vec{w}_{mn}) \tag{31}$$

which, after substituting the expression for $F(\vec{w})$, becomes

$$\frac{G(\vec{w})}{2Q} \sum_m \sum_n [\delta(\vec{w} - \vec{w}_{mn} - \vec{w}_0) + \delta(\vec{w} - \vec{w}_{mn} + \vec{w}_0)]$$

Since $G(\vec{w})$ is nonzero (and equal to Q) only inside the dashed rectangle in Fig. 6a, it follows from the geometrical considerations in this particular case that the preceding expression has only two nonzero terms given by

$$\tfrac{1}{2}[\delta(\vec{w} - (\vec{w}_0 + w_{-1,-1})) + \delta(\vec{w} + (\vec{w}_0 - \vec{w}_{1,1}))]$$

In other words, the Fourier transform of the reconstructed picture has two impulses, one at $\vec{w} = \vec{w}_0 + \vec{w}_{-1,-1}$, and the other at $\vec{w} = -\vec{w}_0 + \vec{w}_{1,1}$. This is shown in Fig. 6b. The reconstructed picture is the inverse Fourier transform of the previous expression and is given by

$$\cos 2\pi[(\vec{w}_0 - \vec{w}_{1,1}) \cdot \vec{r}]$$

which would look like the picture in Fig. 7.

Fig. 7 The reconstructed picture from the samples of the picture in Fig. 5. Note the change in frequency and orientation.

Thus we see that the picture in Fig. 5 after it is sampled and reconstructed can look like the picture in Fig. 7. Note that the original periodic pattern in Fig. 5 appears at a different frequency and orientation in Fig. 7, hence the name *aliasing* for this effect. The frequency $\vec{w}_0 - \vec{w}_{1,1}$ [$(\vec{w}_0 - \vec{w}_{mn})$ in a more general case] is called the *aliased spatial frequency*. ▌

In the preceding discussion on aliasing, we examined a picture with a pattern at a single spatial frequency $\vec{w}_0$ and it gave rise to a single aliased frequency $\vec{w}_0 - \vec{w}_{1,1}$. In practice, depending on the reciprocal vectors $\vec{w}_1$ and $\vec{w}_2$ and the region over which $G(\vec{w})$ is nonzero, a pattern at a frequency $\vec{w}_0$ may, in the reconstructed picture, give rise to a number of aliased frequencies $\vec{w}_0 + \vec{w}_{mn}$ for various m and n. The presence of these aliased frequencies in pictures reconstructed from their samples gives rise to what are called *Moiré patterns*.

Moiré patterns can best be illustrated by using Moiré pattern transparencies. Figure 8a is a rectangular grid transparency. When this transparency is placed on a picture, the light points serve as sampling points. Figure 8b is the transparency of a bar pattern. The transparency in Fig. 8a is placed on top of the bar pattern transparency in Fig. 8b with the bar pattern slightly rotated in a clockwise direction with respect to the vertical direction of the sampling transparency. Figure 8c is a photograph of the transparencies on a light table. In this figure the low-frequency rotated Moiré pattern is quite evident.

A picture must contain periodic structures and their relationship to the geometry of the sampling lattice must be just right for Moiré patterns to occur. In practice, one does not very often run into pictures with strong periodic components. Cases that do arise include pictures of plowed fields, streets in high-altitude photographs of urban areas, ocean wave patterns, and wind patterns in sand.

For pictures with continuous spectra, aliasing can cause another kind of problem whose effects are less dramatic and more difficult to interpret. We will illustrate this by the following example.

In the preceding discussion, it was pointed out that if a picture $f(\vec{r})$ is sampled by the sampling lattice in Experiment 1 and if its Fourier transform $F(\vec{w})$ is zero outside the dashed rectangle in the uv-plane in Fig. 4, then it can be reconstructed without error from its samples. Now consider a case where the same sampling lattice is used for a picture whose Fourier transform is nonzero over a much larger region, as in Fig. 9a. After the picture is sampled, we reconstruct it using the same interpolation function as in Experiment 1, i.e., $G(\vec{w})$ is equal to Q within the dashed rectangle in Fig. 9a and zero outside. The Fourier transform of the reconstructed picture is again given by (31), which we rewrite here as

$$F(\vec{w}) + \sum_{m \neq 0} \sum_{n \neq 0} F(\vec{w} - \vec{w}_{mn})$$

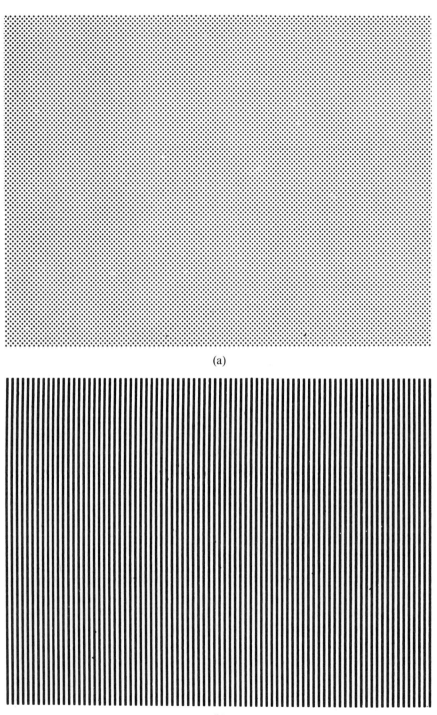

(a)

(b)

(c)

Fig. 8 (a) A rectangular grid transparency. When this transparency is placed on a picture, the light points serve as sampling points. (b) Bar pattern picture. (c) This figure illustrates the Moiré pattern caused by sampling the bar pattern in (b). (From [9].)

for $\vec{w}$ within the dotted rectangle. Of course, the entire expression, hence the Fourier transform of the reconstructed picture, is zero outside the dotted rectangle (because $G(\vec{w})$ is zero there). Some of the terms in the previous expression are pictorially illustrated in Fig. 9b. In this particular example, because of the geometry of the various regions these three terms are the only ones making a nonzero contribution to the Fourier transform of the reconstructed picture.

Note that those frequencies in the original picture that are outside of the region over which $G(\vec{w})$ is nonzero are irretrievably lost in reconstruction, leading to a loss of resolution. Within this region the transform is modified, leading to distortion. In the example under consideration, the frequencies in $F(\vec{w})$ outside the rectangle are lost to the reconstructed picture, and the frequencies within the rectangle are modified in regions A and B (Fig. 9b) by the periodic images of $F(\vec{w})$ on the reciprocal lattice. Figures 10a and 10b illustrate the aliasing effect just discussed. Notice the loss in resolution and other distortions.

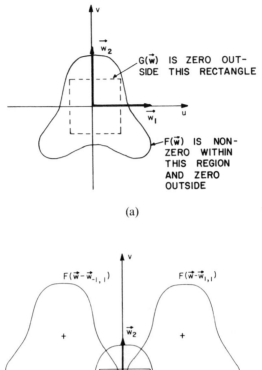

(a)

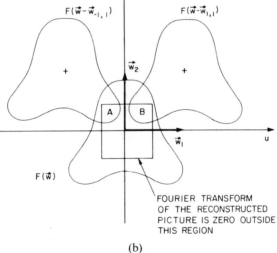

(b)

Fig. 9 (a) The sampling lattice in Experiment 1 is used to sample a picture whose Fourier transform is nonzero over a larger region than would lead to error-free reconstruction. (b) Three of the terms in Eq. (31) are pictorially illustrated here for $F(\vec{w})$ shown in Fig. 9a. These three terms correspond to (m, n) equal to $(0, 0)$, $(1, -1)$, and $(1, 1)$.

Fig. 10a   Photographic print of a picture before sampling.

Fig. 10b Picture of Fig. 10a after sampling and reconstruction. (Courtesy Perkin-Elmer Corp. These pictures appear in the book cited in [9].)

4.2   SAMPLING USING ORTHONORMAL FUNCTIONS

The aim of sampling is to represent a picture by a finite string or array of numbers. As long as it is possible to reconstruct a picture from these numbers, the samples need not correspond to gray levels on a sampling lattice in the picture plane. In this section, we will show that if we expand a picture function in terms of a set of orthonormal functions, we may take the coefficients of the expansion as the picture samples.

4.2.1   Orthonormal Expansions

Let $f(x, y)$ be a real function defined over a region $\mathscr{S}$ of the xy-plane. The function $f(x, y)$ is assumed to be square integrable:

$$\iint_{\mathscr{S}} [f(x, y)]^2 \, dx \, dy < \infty \tag{32}$$

Suppose we are given a set of square integrable functions $\varphi_{mn}(x, y)$, $m = 0, 1, 2, \ldots; n = 0, 1, 2, \ldots$ defined over the same region $\mathscr{S}$.[§] The set of functions is called *orthogonal* if

$$\iint \varphi_{mn}(x, y)\, \varphi_{pq}^*(x, y) \, dx \, dy = 0 \tag{33}$$

for $m \neq p$ or $n \neq q, m, n, p, q = 0, 1, 2, \ldots$. If in addition to (33) the following property holds

$$\iint_{\mathscr{S}} |\varphi_{mn}(x, y)|^2 \, dx \, dy = 1, \qquad m, n = 0, 1, 2, \ldots \tag{34}$$

then the set of functions is called *orthonormal*. The functions φ_{mn} may be either real- or complex-valued.

Exercise 1.   Show that over the rectangle defined by $-A/2 \leqslant x \leqslant A/2$, $-B/2 \leqslant y \leqslant B/2$, the functions

$$\varphi_{mn}(x, y) = \frac{1}{\sqrt{AB}} \exp\left[j2\pi \left(\frac{mx}{A} + \frac{ny}{B} \right) \right], \qquad m, n = 0, 1, 2, \ldots$$

form an orthornormal set.   ▮

[§] The need for using two indices for labeling the member functions in the set may not be quite evident now, and in fact, is not necessary for the development of the formal theory of orthonormal expansions in two dimensions. As will be shown presently, however, it makes the presentation of some of the practical two-dimensional sampling techniques using orthonormal expansions more convenient.

We now wish to approximate the function $f(x, y)$ at all points within $\mathscr{S}$ by a sum of the form

$$\sum_{m=0}^{M-1} \sum_{n=0}^{N-1} a_{mn} \varphi_{mn}(x, y) \tag{35}$$

in such a way that the mean-square error

$$e_{MN}^2 = \int \int_{\mathscr{S}} \left| f(x, y) - \sum_{m=0}^{M-1} \sum_{n=0}^{N-1} a_{mn} \varphi_{mn}(x, y) \right|^2 dx\, dy \tag{36}$$

is minimized. The subscript MN in e_{MN}^2 is indicative of there being MN terms in the summation in (35). The following theorem addresses itself to this problem:

Theorem.   The constants a_{mn} that minimize e_{MN}^2 are given by

$$a_{mn} = \int \int_{\mathscr{S}} f(x, y) \varphi_{mn}^*(x, y)\, dx\, dy \tag{37}$$

Proof: We will prove the theorem by showing that if the constants a_{mn} are given by (37), then for any arbitrary selection b_{mn} of constants

$$\int \int_{\mathscr{S}} \left| f(x, y) - \sum_{m=0}^{M-1} \sum_{n=0}^{N-1} a_{mn} \varphi_{mn}(x, y) \right|^2 dx\, dy$$

$$\leq \int \int_{\mathscr{S}} \left| f(x, y) - \sum_{m=0}^{M-1} \sum_{n=0}^{N-1} b_{mn} \varphi_{mn}(x, y) \right|^2 dx\, dy \tag{38}$$

The right-hand side of (38) can be written as

$$\int \int_{\mathscr{S}} \left| f(x, y) - \sum_{m=0}^{M-1} \sum_{n=0}^{N-1} b_{mn} \varphi_{mn}(x, y) \right|^2 dx\, dy$$

$$= \int \int_{\mathscr{S}} \left| f(x, y) - \sum_{m=0}^{M-1} \sum_{n=0}^{N-1} a_{mn} \varphi_{mn}(x, y) \right.$$

$$\left. + \sum_{m=0}^{M-1} \sum_{n=0}^{N-1} (a_{mn} - b_{mn}) \varphi_{mn}(x, y) \right|^2 dx\, dy$$

$$= \int \int_{\mathscr{S}} \left| f(x, y) - \sum_{m=0}^{M-1} \sum_{n=0}^{N-1} a_{mn} \varphi_{mn}(x, y) \right|^2 dx\, dy + \sum_{m=0}^{M-1} \sum_{n=0}^{N-1} |a_{mn} - b_{mn}|^2 \tag{39}$$

In arriving at the second equality in (39), we made use of (33), (34), and (37). The nonnegative nature of the terms in the second equality in (39) proves (38) and, hence, the theorem.   ∎

We can now pose the following question: Does approximation (35) to $f(x, y)$ become increasingly accurate as the number of terms in (35) is increased? The dependence of the mean-square error e_{MN}^2 on M and N depends on the nature of the orthonormal functions.

An orthonormal set of functions, $\varphi_{mn}(x, y)$, $m = 0, 1, 2, \ldots$; $n = 0, 1, 2, \ldots$; is called *complete* if for every square integrable function f we have

$$\lim_{M \to \infty, N \to \infty} e_{MN}^2 = 0 \tag{40}$$

— that is, if the mean-square error in approximating $f(x, y)$ by (35) approaches zero as the number of terms in (35) approaches infinity. Henceforth, we will be concerned with complete orthonormal sets of functions only. A complete orthonormal set of functions is also called an *orthonormal basis*.

Summarizing the preceding discussion, we can say that given an orthonormal basis $\varphi_{mn}(x, y)$, $m = 0, 1, 2, \ldots$; $n = 0, 1, 2, \ldots$; defined over a region $\mathscr{S}$ of the xy-plane, then any function $f(x, y)$, square integrable over $\mathscr{S}$, can be expanded as

$$f(x, y) = \sum_{m=0}^{\infty} \sum_{n=0}^{\infty} a_{mn} \varphi_{mn}(x, y) \tag{41a}$$

where

$$a_{mn} = \int\!\!\int_{\mathscr{S}} f(x, y) \varphi_{mn}^*(x, y) \, dx \, dy \tag{41b}$$

Of course, this expansion is valid only over the region $\mathscr{S}$ of the xy-plane.

Equations (41) have important practical implications. For example, suppose that in a communication link an orthonormal set of functions is available at both the transmitting and the receiving ends. Say that it is desired to transmit a picture $f(x, y)$. Then by (41) we need transmit the coefficients a_{mn} only, since by (41a) they can be used to reconstruct the picture at the receiving end. At the transmitting end the a_{mn} are obtained from $f(x, y)$ by using (41b). In practice, of course, one would transmit only a finite number of a_{mn}, even though, in general, an infinite number of them would be required for an error-free reconstruction of the picture at the receiving end. The orthonormal functions are usually ordered so that higher-order terms contribute to the fine detail in a picture and neglecting them may lead to a loss of resolution. Nothing is gained, however, by increasing M and N beyond the spatial resolution capabilities of the observer or the user at the receiving end.

Since a picture $f(x, y)$ can be represented by and reconstructed from the coefficients a_{mn}, we can call these coefficients "samples of the picture." Given a picture and an orthonormal set of functions defined over the same region of the xy-plane, these samples may be obtained by using (41b).

4.2.2   Sampling of a Random Field Using Orthonormal Expansions

If we sample a *single* picture $f(x, y)$ using an orthonormal basis, and retain only $M \times N$ samples, then the error in reconstructing the picture from these samples is given by (36).

We would now like to determine the following: Given a random field, i.e., an ensemble or a class of pictures (television pictures, for example), if we use an orthonormal basis to sample each picture in the class and retain only $M \times N$ samples for each picture, then what is the error e_{MN}^2 when averaged over all the pictures in the class? Can e_{MN}^2 when averaged over all the pictures be expressed as a function of the statistical properties of the class? We want to study the dependence of the average e_{MN}^2 on the statistical properties of the given random field. In what follows we will assume the random field to be real and homogeneous.

Let $\mathbf{f}(x, y)$ again denote a real homogeneous random field with auto-correlation function $R_{ff}(\alpha, \beta)$. Relationships (41) for the random field $\mathbf{f}(x, y)$ can be expressed as

$$\mathbf{f}(x, y) = \sum_{m=0}^{\infty} \sum_{n=0}^{\infty} \mathbf{a}_{mn} \, \varphi_{mn}(x, y) \tag{42a}$$

at all points (x, y) within $\mathscr{S}$. In (42a)

$$\mathbf{a}_{mn} = \int\!\!\int_{\mathscr{S}} \mathbf{f}(x, y) \, \varphi_{mn}^*(x, y) \, dx \, dy, \qquad m, n = 0, 1, 2, \dots \tag{42b}$$

Note that each $\mathbf{a}_{mn}$ is now a random variable. This is because (42b) is actually a family of equations, one for each picture in the random field. The value of each $\mathbf{a}_{mn}$ will depend on which picture is selected. Similarly, (42a) represents a family of equations and can be used to reconstruct each picture in the random field from its samples.[§]

If only $M \times N$ samples are retained for every picture in the random field, then upon reconstruction of a picture from its samples, there will be a mean-square error e_{MN}^2, as defined in the preceding subsection. This mean-square error when averaged over all the pictures in the random field is called the

---

[§] For mathematical precision, a more correct interpretation of the equality in (42a) is as follows. As the number of terms on the right-hand side in (42a) approaches infinity, the summation converges to $\mathbf{f}(x, y)$ in some sense. For example, in Section 4.2.3 for the case of Fourier sampling, the convergence is in the mean-square sense, i.e.,

$$E\left\{ \left| \mathbf{f}(x, y) - \sum_{m=0}^{M-1} \sum_{n=0}^{N-1} \mathbf{a}_{mn} \, \varphi_{mn}(x, y) \right|^2 \right\}_{\substack{M \to \infty \\ N \to \infty}} = 0$$

sampling error for the random field $\mathbf{f}(\vec{r})$ and will be denoted by ε_{MN}^2. From (36) ε_{MN}^2 is given by

$$\varepsilon_{MN}^2 = E\left\{\int\int_{\mathscr{S}} \left| \mathbf{f}(x, y) - \sum_{m=0}^{M-1}\sum_{n=0}^{N-1} a_{mn} \varphi_{mn}(x, y) \right|^2 dx\, dy \right\} \tag{43}$$

By making use of (42b), this equation can easily be shown to reduce to

$$\varepsilon_{MN}^2 = E\left\{\int\int_{\mathscr{S}} [\mathbf{f}(x, y)]^2 \, dx\, dy - \sum_{m=0}^{M-1}\sum_{n=0}^{N-1} |a_{mn}|^2 \right\} \tag{44}$$

Substituting (42b) in (44), we obtain for the sampling error

$$\varepsilon_{MN}^2 = E\left\{\int\int_{\mathscr{S}} [\mathbf{f}(x, y)]^2 \, dx\, dy - \sum_{m=0}^{M-1}\sum_{n=0}^{N-1} \left| \int\int_{\mathscr{S}} \mathbf{f}(x, y)\, \varphi_{mn}^*(x, y)\, dx\, dy \right|^2 \right\}$$

$$= E\left\{\int\int_{\mathscr{S}} [\mathbf{f}(x, y)]^2 \, dx\, dy - \sum_{m=0}^{M-1}\sum_{n=0}^{N-1} \int\int_{\mathscr{S}}\int\int_{\mathscr{S}} \mathbf{f}(x, y)\mathbf{f}(x', y') \right.$$

$$\left. \times \varphi_{mn}^*(x, y)\, \varphi_{mn}(x', y')\, dx\, dy\, dx'\, dy' \right\} \tag{45}$$

The operation of expectation in (45) is ensemble averaging, while the integrations in (45) involve spatial averaging (see Section 2.4.6 for the difference). Since both operations are linear, the order in which they occur can be interchanged. Interchanging their order in (45) and making use of the definition of the autocorrelation $R_{ff}(\alpha, \beta)$ in Section 2.4.3, we can write

$$\varepsilon_{MN}^2 = SR_{ff}(0,0) - \sum_{m=0}^{M-1}\sum_{n=0}^{N-1} \int\int_{\mathscr{S}}\int\int_{\mathscr{S}} R_{ff}(x-x', y-y')$$

$$\times \varphi_{mn}^*(x, y)\, \varphi_{mn}(x', y')\, dx\, dy\, dx'\, dy' \tag{46}$$

which expresses the dependence of the mean-square error as averaged over all the pictures in the ensemble on the statistical properties of the ensemble with S as the area of the region $\mathscr{S}$ in the xy-plane.

At this point a few words about the autocorrelation function $R_{ff}(\alpha, \beta)$ are in order. Under the assumption that a class of pictures form a homogeneous random field, the autocorrelation function $R_{ff}(\alpha, \beta)$ is often assumed to be of the form

$$R_{ff}(\alpha, \beta) = [R_{ff}(0,0) - \eta^2] \exp[-c_1|\alpha| - c_2|\beta|] + \eta^2 \tag{47}$$

where c_1 and c_2 are positive constants and where, by the definition of the autocorrelation in Section 2.4.3,

$$R_{ff}(0,0) = E\{[\mathbf{f}(x, y)]^2\} \quad \text{and} \quad \eta = E\{\mathbf{f}(x, y)\}$$

We will remind the reader that for a homogeneous random field, the mean value η of the gray level in the picture is a constant independent of position. Note that the autocorrelation function in (47) can be used to model pictures with different amounts of correlation in the horizontal and vertical directions by choosing different values of c_1 and c_2.

4.2.3 Examples of Sampling Using Orthonormal Expansions: Fourier Sampling

Suppose that the region in the xy-plane over which the pictures are to be sampled is a rectangle with sides A and B, and that over this region the orthonormal basis functions are of the form

$$\varphi_{mn}(x, y) = \frac{1}{\sqrt{AB}} \exp\left[+j2\pi\left(\frac{m}{A}x + \frac{n}{B}y\right)\right] \tag{48}$$

The sampling defined in this way is called *Fourier sampling*.

The Fourier samples of a picture $f(x, y)$ are obtained by substituting (48) in (41b):

$$a_{mn} = \frac{1}{\sqrt{AB}} \int_{-B/2}^{B/2} \int_{-A/2}^{A/2} f(x, y) \exp\left[-j2\pi\left(\frac{m}{A}x + \frac{n}{B}y\right)\right] dx\, dy \tag{49}$$

where we have assumed the origin to be at the center of the picture. By making use of the Fourier transform relationship in Eq. (12) of Chapter 2, (49) can be written as

$$a_{mn} = \frac{1}{\sqrt{AB}} F\left(\frac{m}{A}, \frac{n}{B}\right) \tag{50}$$

where $F(m/A, n/B)$ is the value of the Fourier transform $F(u, v)$ of the picture at $u = m/A$ and $v = n/B$.

We will now briefly describe an optical method of computing the Fourier samples a_{mn} of a picture. In Fig. 11 we have marked two planes, the xy-plane in front of a thin lens, and the $x'y'$-plane behind the lens. Each plane is one focal length d_0 away from the lens. A transparency $f(x, y)$ is placed in the xy-plane in front of the lens and a parallel beam of coherent light passed through it. Let $U(x', y')$ denote the light distribution in the focal plane behind the lens. $U(x', y')$ is given by (see Chapter 5 of Goodman [4])

$$U(x', y') = \frac{1}{j\lambda d_0} \int\!\!\!\int_{-\infty}^{\infty} f(x, y) \exp\left[-j\frac{2\pi}{\lambda d_0}(xx' + yy')\right] dx\, dy \tag{51}$$

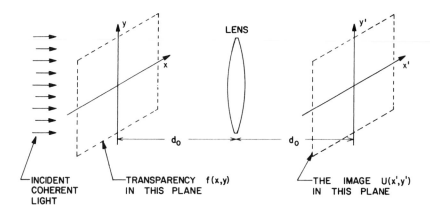

Fig. 11 If a two-dimensional transparency with transmittance $f(x, y)$ is placed in the xy-plane, then the light distribution behind the lens in the $x'y'$-plane is proportional to the Fourier transform of $f(x, y)$. Both planes are one focal length d_0 away from the lens.

where λ is the wavelength of the light used and d_0 the focal length of the lens. By Eq. (12) of Chapter 2, (51) can be written as

$$U(x', y') = \frac{1}{j\lambda d_0} F\left(\frac{x'}{\lambda d_0}, \frac{y'}{\lambda d_0}\right)$$ (52)

In other words, except for a constant, the light distribution in the image at the point (x', y') is equal to the value of the Fourier transform $F(u, v)$ at $u = x'/\lambda d_0$ and $v = y'/\lambda d_0$. Thus the Fourier transform of a picture $f(x, y)$ may be obtained optically; it is represented by the light distribution, both in amplitude and phase, in the focal plane behind the lens. If a photographic plate is placed in the $x'y'$-plane, it will record only the intensity given by $|U(x', y')|^2$, which is proportional to the power spectrum of $f(x, y)$; the phase information is lost. Ordinary photographic methods are unable to record phase, although techniques such as holographic methods are capable of doing so.

Combining (50) and (52), we obtain

$$a_{mn} = \frac{j\lambda d_0}{\sqrt{AB}} U\left(\frac{m\lambda d_0}{A}, \frac{n\lambda d_0}{B}\right)$$ (53)

This shows that the Fourier sample a_{mn} is given by the light level at the point $x' = m\lambda d_0/A$, $y' = n\lambda d_0/B$ in the $x'y'$-plane in Fig. 11.

In the rest of our discussion of Fourier sampling we will extend the general result for the sampling error as given by Eq. (46) to the particular case of

Fourier sampling for the autocorrelation function given by (47). For simplicity we will assume the random field to be zero mean, i.e., $\eta = 0$ in (47). It is a simple matter to extend the results to the case of nonzero η. Substituting (47) with $\eta = 0$ and (48) in (46), we obtain

$$\varepsilon_{MN}^2 = ABR_{ff}(0,0) - \frac{R_{ff}(0,0)}{AB}$$

$$\times \sum_{m=0}^{M-1} \sum_{n=0}^{N-1} \int\int_{\mathscr{S}} \int\int_{\mathscr{S}} \exp(-c_1|x-x'|-c_2|y-y'|)$$

$$\times \exp\left[j2\pi\left(\frac{m}{A}x + \frac{n}{B}y\right)\right] \exp\left[-j2\pi\left(\frac{m}{A}x' + \frac{n}{B}y'\right)\right] dx\,dy\,dx'\,dy'$$

$$= ABR_{ff}(0,0) - \frac{R_{ff}(0,0)}{AB} \sum_{m=0}^{M-1} \sum_{n=0}^{N-1} \left\{ \int_{-A/2}^{A/2} \int_{-A/2}^{A/2} \exp(-c_1|x-x'|) \right.$$

$$\times \exp\frac{j2\pi mx}{A} \exp\frac{-j2\pi mx'}{A}\,dx\,dx' \right\} \left\{ \int_{-B/2}^{B/2} \int_{-B/2}^{B/2} \exp(-c_2|y-y'|) \right.$$

$$\times \exp\frac{j2\pi ny}{B} \exp\frac{-j2\pi ny'}{B}\,dy\,dy' \Bigg\}$$

$$= ABR_{ff}(0,0)\left[1 - \sum_{m=0}^{M-1} \sum_{n=0}^{N-1} \left\{ \frac{2c_1 A}{(c_1 A)^2 + (2\pi m)^2} \right.\right.$$

$$+ \frac{2[\exp(-c_1 A)-1][(c_1 A)^2-(2\pi m)^2]}{[(c_1 A)^2 + (2\pi m)^2]^2} \right\} \left\{ \frac{2c_2 B}{(c_2 B)^2 + (2\pi n)^2} \right.$$

$$+ \frac{2[\exp(-c_2 B)-1][(c_2 B)^2-(2\pi n)^2]}{[(c_2 B)^2 + (2\pi n)^2]^2} \Bigg\} \Bigg] \tag{54}$$

For given values of M and N, the normalized sampling error $\varepsilon_{MN}^2/ABR_{ff}(0,0)$ depends on $c_1 A$ and $c_2 B$ only. If we assume $M = N$ in (54), we obtain an expression for $\varepsilon_{N^2}^2/ABR_{ff}(0,0)$ which is the normalized sampling error using N^2 Fourier samples. In Fig. 12, the middle curve corresponds to $\varepsilon_{N^2}^2/ABR_{ff}(0,0)$ for Fourier sampling with $c_1 A = c_2 B = 1$. Under the conditions assumed, this curve indicates how rapidly the sampling error decreases as the number of samples is increased.

Standard Sampling

We now consider a sampling technique in which each sample is obtained by averaging a small portion of the picture. Let the region in the xy-plane over

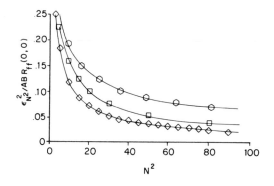

Fig. 12 Normalized sampling error for a random field using Fourier ⊡, standard ⊙, and optimum ◇ sampling techniques as a function of the number of samples N^2. (From [6].)

which the pictures are defined be again a rectangle with sides A and B. Over this region we define the orthonormal basis functions as

$$\varphi_{mn}(x, y) = \sqrt{\frac{MN}{AB}} \quad \begin{cases} \dfrac{mA}{M} \leq x < \dfrac{(m+1)\,\mathring{A}}{M} \\[2mm] \dfrac{nB}{N} \leq y < \dfrac{(n+1)\,B}{N} \end{cases}$$

$$= 0 \quad \text{elsewhere}, \quad \begin{aligned} m &= 0, 1, \ldots, M-1 \\ n &= 0, 1, \ldots, N-1 \end{aligned} \quad (55)$$

where we have assumed the origin to coincide with the lower left corner of the rectangle. In other words, the picture area is divided into MN rectangular regions, and each $\varphi_{mn}(x, y)$ is constant over one of these regions and zero elsewhere. For example, if $M = 8$ and $N = 6$, the set of orthonormal functions generated by the previous definition would have 48 members. As an illustration the member $\varphi_{3,2}(x, y)$ of this set is shown in Fig. 13.

By substituting (55) in (41b), we obtain for the samples

$$a_{mn} = \sqrt{MN/AB} \int_{nB/N}^{(n+1)\,B/N} \int_{mA/M}^{(m+1)A/M} f(x, y) \, dx \, dy \qquad (56)$$

It is seen that except for a constant factor, a_{mn} is the average gray level of the picture over the area where φ_{mn} is nonzero.

We will now extend the general result for the sampling error for a random field as given by (46) to the case of standard sampling. We will again assume a zero mean real homogeneous random field with the autocorrelation function

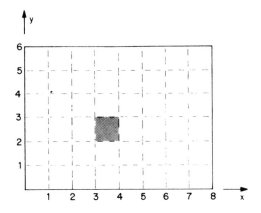

Fig. 13 An example of an orthonormal function used in standard sampling. The function $\varphi_{3,2}(x, y)$ shown here belongs to the orthonormal set generated by Eq. (55) with $M = 8$ and $N = 6$.

given by (47) with $\eta = 0$. Substituting (55) and (47) with $\eta = 0$ in (46), we obtain for the sampling error

$$\varepsilon_{MN}^2 = ABR_{ff}(0,0) - \frac{MN}{AB}$$

$$\times R_{ff}(0,0) \sum_{m=0}^{M-1} \sum_{n=0}^{N-1} \int_{nB/N}^{(n+1)B/N} \int_{mA/M}^{(m+1)A/M} \int_{nB/N}^{(n+1)B/N}$$

$$\times \int_{mA/M}^{(m+1)A/M} \exp(-c_1|x-x'|-c_2|y-y'|) \, dx \, dy \, dx' \, dy'$$

$$= ABR_{ff}(0,0) - \frac{MN}{AB} R_{ff}(0,0) \sum_{m=0}^{M-1} \sum_{n=0}^{N-1} \left\{ \int_{mA/M}^{(m+1)A/M} \int_{mA/M}^{(m+1)A/M} \right.$$

$$\times \left. \exp(-c_1|x - x'|) \, dx \, dx' \right\}$$

$$\times \left\{ \int_{nB/N}^{(n+1)B/N} \int_{nB/N}^{(n+1)B/N} \exp(-c_2|y-y'|) \, dy \, dy' \right\}$$

$$= ABR_{ff}(0,0) \left[1 - \frac{4MN}{(c_1 A)(c_2 B)} \left\{ 1 + \frac{M}{c_1 A} \left[\exp\left(\frac{-c_1 A}{M}\right) - 1 \right] \right\} \right.$$

$$\times \left. \left\{ 1 + \frac{N}{c_2 B} \left[\exp\left(\frac{-c_2 B}{N}\right) - 1 \right] \right\} \right] \tag{57}$$

For a given number of samples MN, the normalized sampling error $\varepsilon_{MN}^2/ABR_{ff}(0,0)$ depends on $c_1 A$ and $c_2 B$ only. If we assume $M = N$ in (57), we obtain the normalized sampling error using N^2 samples. In Fig. 12 the top curve corresponds to the normalized sampling error for this case. It is clear from the figure that for a given number of samples, Fourier sampling is more efficient than standard sampling.

4.2.4 Optimal Sampling

Optimal sampling of a random field defined over a region $\mathscr{S}$ of the xy-plane is achieved by that set of orthonormal functions $\varphi_{mn}(x, y)$ which for every M and N yields the minimum value for the sampling error ε_{MN}^2. Since the first term in (46) is independent of the choice of the orthonormal basis, ε_{MN}^2 is minimized when the second term, i.e., the nonnegative quantity

$$\sum_{m=0}^{M-1} \sum_{n=0}^{N-1} \int_{-B/2}^{B/2} \int_{-A/2}^{A/2} \int_{-B/2}^{B/2} \int_{-A/2}^{A/2} R_{ff}(x-x', y-y')\, \varphi_{mn}^*(x, y)$$
$$\times\, \varphi_{mn}(x', y')\, dx\, dy\, dx'\, dy' \tag{58}$$

is maximized. In (58) we have assumed the region $\mathscr{S}$ to consist of a rectangle with sides A and B, the origin of the xy-plane coinciding with the center of the rectangle.

The assumption of homogeneity of the random field that is incorporated in this equation is not necessary for the present section. For the general case, which includes inhomogeneous random fields, $R_{ff}(x-x', y-y')$ in (46) can be replaced by the more general $R_{ff}(x, y, x', y')$ and (58) can then be written as

$$\sum_{m=0}^{M-1} \sum_{n=0}^{N-1} \int_{-B/2}^{B/2} \int_{-A/2}^{A/2} \int_{-B/2}^{B/2} \int_{-A/2}^{A/2} R_{ff}(x, y, x', y')\, \varphi_{mn}^*(x, y)$$
$$\times\, \varphi_{mn}(x', y')\, dx\, dy\, dx'\, dy' \tag{59}$$

The problem then is to find functions $\varphi_{mn}(x, y)$ that for a given $R_{ff}(x, y, x', y')$ maximize (59) subject to the orthonormality condition

$$\int_{-B/2}^{B/2} \int_{-A/2}^{A/2} \varphi_{mn}(x, y)\, \varphi_{pq}^*(x, y)\, dx\, dy = \begin{cases} 0, & m \neq p \quad \text{or} \quad n \neq q \\ 1, & m = p \quad \text{and} \quad n = q \end{cases} \tag{60}$$

A straightforward extension of the theory given by Brown [2] to the case of two dimensions shows that the functions $\varphi_{mn}(x, y)$ that maximize (59) subject to the orthonormality conditions (60) are the solutions of the following integral equation:

$$\int_{-B/2}^{B/2} \int_{-A/2}^{A/2} R_{ff}(x, y, x', y')\, \varphi(x', y')\, dx'\, dy' = \gamma \varphi(x, y) \tag{61}$$

Questions pertaining to the existence of the solutions of (61) and their dependence on the form of $R_{ff}(x, y, x', y')$ belong to the study of integral equations [18] and will not be pursued here. Suffice it to say that for continuous $R_{ff}(x, y, x', y')$ the integral equation in (61) has nonzero solutions $\varphi_{mn}(x, y)$ (eigenfunctions) for certain values γ_{mn} of γ (eigenvalues).

Since the orthonormal functions $\varphi_{mn}(x, y)$ that we seek are a solution of (61) for certain values γ_{mn} of γ, the functions $\varphi_{mn}(x, y)$ and the corresponding eigenvalues must satisfy

$$\int_{-B/2}^{B/2} \int_{-A/2}^{A/2} R_{ff}(x, y, x', y')\, \varphi_{mn}(x', y')\, dx'\, dy' = \gamma_{mn}\, \varphi_{mn}(x, y) \qquad (62)$$

Substituting (62) in (59) and making use of the orthonormality relationship in (60), (59) reduces to

$$\sum_{m=0}^{M-1} \sum_{n=0}^{N-1} \gamma_{mn} \qquad (63)$$

The sampling error for the case of optimal sampling is then obtained by substituting (63) for the double summation in (46), giving[§]

$$\varepsilon_{MN}^2 = ABR_{ff}(0, 0, 0, 0) - \sum_{m=0}^{M-1} \sum_{n=0}^{N-1} \gamma_{mn} \qquad (64)$$

Often the autocorrelation function can be considered to be separable in its x and y dependence, i.e.,

$$R_{ff}(x, y, x', y') = R'(x, x')\, R''(y, y') \qquad (65)$$

One example of such a separable autocorrelation function is given by Eq. (47) with $\alpha = x - x'$, $\beta = y - y'$ for the case where $\eta = 0$. For separable autocorrelation functions as in (65), one may look for solutions $\varphi(x, y)$ of (61) that are also separable in their x and y dependence. The function $\varphi(x, y)$ in (61) can then be expressed as

$$\varphi(x, y) = \varphi'(x)\, \varphi''(y) \qquad (66)$$

Substituting (65) and (66) in (61), the integral equation can be decomposed into two one-dimensional integral equations:

$$\int_{-A/2}^{A/2} R'(x, x')\, \varphi'(x')\, dx' = \gamma'\varphi'(x) \qquad (67a)$$

$$\int_{-B/2}^{B/2} R''(y, y')\, \varphi''(y')\, dy' = \gamma''\varphi''(y) \qquad (67b)$$

[§] While for the case of homogeneous random fields, the value of the autocorrelation function at the origin can be denoted by $R_{ff}(0, 0)$, for the more general case the autocorrelation function $R_{ff}(x, y, x', y')$ is a function of four variables, and its value at the origin must be denoted by $R_{ff}(0, 0, 0, 0)$.

where we have expressed γ in (61) as a product $\gamma'\gamma''$. The integral equation (67a) has solutions $\varphi_m'(x)$ for certain values γ_m' of γ'. Similarly, (67b) has solutions $\varphi_n''(y)$ for certain values γ_n'' of γ''. The orthonormal functions over the region $\mathscr{S}$ of the xy-plane are then given by the products

$$\varphi_{mn}(x, y) = \varphi_m'(x) \varphi_n''(y) \tag{68}$$

and to each function $\varphi_{mn}(x, y)$ there corresponds an eigenvalue

$$\gamma_{mn} = \gamma_m'\gamma_n'' \tag{69}$$

An important question presents itself at this point. How should the orthonormal functions $\varphi_{mn}(x, y)$ and the corresponding eigenvalues γ_{mn} be ranked? In other words, we would like to know, of all $\varphi_{mn}(x, y)$ and the corresponding γ_{mn}, which one should be assigned the indices $m = 0$, $n = 0$; which one $m = 0$, $n = 1$; and so on. Let us first consider the case of separable autocorrelation functions, that is, when the eigenfunctions and eigenvalues are obtained by solving (67a) and (67b). In order that the sampling error ε_{MN}^2 in (64) be a minimum for $M = 1$, $N = 1$ (only one sample), it is clear that the indices $m = 0$, $n = 0$ should be assigned to that solution that results in the largest product $\gamma_m'\gamma_n''$. Once γ_0' and γ_0'' have been picked, the indices $m = 0$, $n = 1$ should be assigned to that solution to which corresponds the largest number $\gamma_0'\gamma_n''$ except for $\gamma_0'\gamma_0''$. The process of ranking can be continued in this way.

For random fields for which the autocorrelation function is not separable, the use of double indices for the orthonormal functions is really meaningless (see footnote on p. 93). The solutions of (61) and their corresponding eigenvalues can now be labeled by a single index. In this case there will be a single summation on the right-hand side in (64). By making use of the equation corresponding to (64) in this case and by the arguments regarding minimization of ε_{MN}^2 presented previously, it is easy to see that the solution with the largest eigenvalue will get the first rank, the solution with the next largest value will be ranked second, and so on.

So far we have indicated that given a random field one can, in general, find an optimum set of orthonormal functions that minimize the sampling error by solving (61) [or (67a) and (67b) for the special case of a separable autocorrelation function]. There exist useful situations in which closed form solutions to these integral equations can be obtained. One such case is when the autocorrelation function is of the form given by (47) with $\eta = 0$. In this case, the solutions to both (67a) and (67b) can be obtained by solving the integral equation

$$\int_{-T}^{T} k(s, t) \varphi(t) \, dt = \gamma\varphi(s) \tag{70}$$

where T equals $A/2$ for (67a) and $B/2$ for (67b), and where

$$k(s,t) = k_0 e^{-c|s-t|} \tag{71}$$

c being equal to c_1 for (67a) and c_2 for (67b). We can arbitrarily set $k_0 = \sqrt{R(0,0)}$ for both the cases.

The theoretical techniques for solving (70) with $k(s,t)$ given by (71) can be found in many places in the literature (see, for example, pp. 186–190 of [19]). In Fig. 12, the bottom curve corresponds to the case in which the sampling error was calculated by first solving (70) with $k(s,t)$ given by (71), writing down the corresponding solutions for (67a) and (67b), substituting these solutions and their corresponding eigenvalues in (68) and (69) to generate the orthonormal functions $\varphi_{mn}(x,y)$ and their corresponding eigenvalues γ_{mn}, ranking the solutions and their eigenvalues by the method just discussed, and finally substituting the eigenvalues in (64). The values of c_1 and c_2 were chosen such that $c_1 A = c_2 B = 1$. As expected, this procedure results in minimum error sampling of the random field. This optimality, however, is gained at the expense of considerable complexity in implementation of this technique.

The orthonormal functions obtained by the method indicated in this section are called *Karhunen–Loève* (K–L) *functions*, and the sampling procedure that uses these functions is referred to as *Karhunen–Loève sampling*.

4.3 QUANTIZATION OF PICTURE SAMPLES

In digital processing the picture samples must be quantized. This means that the range of values of the samples must be divided into intervals and all the values within an interval must be represented by a single level. In order that a picture reconstructed from the quantized samples be acceptable, it may sometimes be necessary to use 100 or more quantizing levels. When the samples are obtained by using an array of points as in Section 4.1 or standard sampling as in Section 4.2.3, a fine degree of quantization is particularly important for samples taken in regions of a picture across which the gray level changes slowly. In this situation large parts of these regions will be quantized to constant grey levels, while between these parts, there will be curves along which there is an abrupt gray level jump. These curves will tend to appear as conspicuous "false contours" cutting across the regions and may make the quantized approximation to the original picture unacceptable since they define spurious "objects" which may compete with or conceal the real objects shown in the picture. In Fig. 14a we have shown a picture reconstructed from samples that were quantized to 16 discrete levels. The original picture

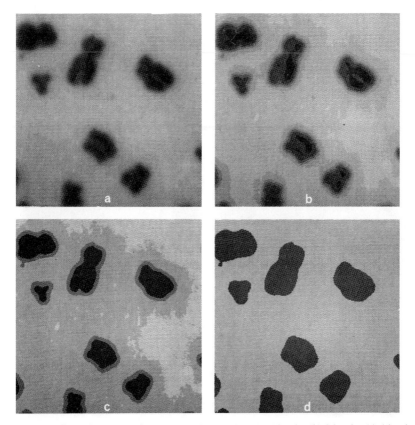

Fig. 14   Effect of using too few quantization levels: (a) 16 levels; (b) 8 levels; (c) 4 levels; and (d) 2 levels.

was sampled on a 128×128 square array of points. In the reconstructed pictures in Figs. 14b–14d, the samples were quantized to 8, 4, and 2 levels, respectively.

As in the case of sampling, it is usually simplest to choose quantization levels that are evenly spaced, but unequally spaced levels may sometimes be preferable. For example, suppose that the sample values in a certain range occur frequently, while the others occur rarely. In such a case one might wish to use quantization levels that are finely spaced inside this range and coarsely spaced outside it; this increases the average accuracy of the quantization without increasing the number of levels. This method, known as "tapered quantization," is illustrated in Fig. 15.

In the next section we will present the theory of optimum quantization. It will be seen that this theory legitimizes the reasons given here for tapering the quantization scale.

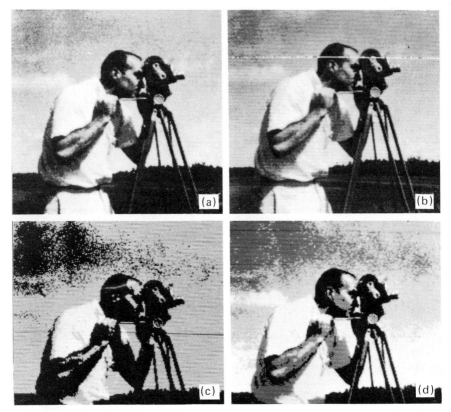

Fig. 15 Tapered quantization: A picture of a cameraman is shown here quantized to (a) 16 equally spaced levels; (b) 16 tapered levels; (c) 4 equally spaced levels; and (d) 4 tapered levels. (From [8].)

4.3.1 Optimal Quantization

Let the range of values of the samples be represented by the line $H_1 H_2$ in Fig. 16. We wish to quantize the samples to K discrete levels, represented in Fig. 16 by $q_1, q_2, ..., q_K$. These are the output levels of the quantizer. Now let the input intervals be represented by the decision levels $z_1, z_2, ..., z_{K+1}$. This means that if a sample at the input to the quantizer has a value anywhere between z_K and z_{K+1} it is assigned the value q_K at the output.

Let δ_q^2 denote the mean-square quantization error between the input and the output of the quantizer for a given choice of the output levels $q_1, q_2, ..., q_K$, and the input intervals as represented by the decision levels $z_1, z_2, ..., z_{K+1}$.

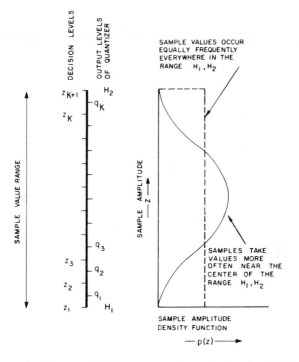

Fig. 16 If a sample takes any value between z_K and z_{K+1}, it is assigned a fixed value q_K at the output of the quantizer. $p(z)$ is the sample value probability density function.

Thus $\delta_q^{\,2}$ is given by

$$\delta_q^{\,2} = \sum_{k=1}^{K} \int_{z_k}^{z_{k+1}} (z - q_k)^2 p(z)\, dz \tag{72}$$

where $p(z)$ is the probability density function for the input sample value which is represented by the continuous variable z. Equation (72) is obtained by applying Eq. (60) of Chapter 2 to each of the input intervals.

For a given number K of output levels, we would now like to determine the output levels (q_k's) and the decision levels (z_k's) such that the mean-square quantization error $\delta_q^{\,2}$ is a minimum. If we wish to minimize $\delta_q^{\,2}$ for a given K, we can derive the necessary conditions by partially differentiating $\delta_q^{\,2}$ with respect to the z_k's and q_k's and setting the derivatives equal to zero:

$$\frac{\partial}{\partial z_k} \delta_q^{\,2} = (z_k - q_{k-1})^2 p(z_k) - (z_k - q_k)^2 p(z_k) = 0, \qquad k = 2, 3, \ldots, K \tag{73}$$

$$\frac{\partial}{\partial q_k} \delta_q^{\,2} = -2 \int_{z_k}^{z_{k+1}} (z - q_k)\, p(z)\, dz = 0, \qquad k = 1, 2, \ldots, K \tag{74}$$

Note that in (73) we have, for obvious reasons, not differentiated with respect to z_1 and z_{k+1}. These are the fixed end points of the sample amplitude range at the input.

From (73), for $p(z_k)$ not equal to zero, we obtain

$$z_k = (q_{k-1} + q_k)/2, \qquad k = 2, 3, \ldots, K \tag{75}$$

while (74) implies

$$q_k = \int_{z_k}^{z_{k+1}} z p(z)\, dz \bigg/ \int_{z_k}^{z_{k+1}} p(z)\, dz, \qquad k = 1, 2, \ldots, K \tag{76}$$

We see that for an optimum quantizer the decision levels (z_k's) are located halfway between the output levels (q_k's), while each q_k is the centroid of the portion of $p(z)$ between z_k and z_{k+1}.

If the sample values occur equally frequently everywhere in the range $H_1 H_2$ in Fig. 16, then the sample values are uniformly distributed over the range $H_1 H_2$ and $p(z)$ is equal to some constant. In this case, (75) and (76) reduce to

$$z_k = (q_{k-1} + q_k)/2, \qquad k = 2, 3, \ldots, K$$
$$q_k = (z_k + z_{k+1})/2, \qquad k = 1, 2, \ldots, K$$

The two equations are simultaneously satisfied provided the decision levels as well as the output levels are equally spaced, with the output levels midway between the decision levels and vice versa. This is called "uniform quantization."

If the sample values occur more frequently in some part of the range $H_1 H_2$ in Fig. 16, then the density function $p(z)$ is not equal to a constant and the solutions of (75) and (76) become more complex.

Given the sample value density function $p(z)$ and the end values z_1 and z_{K+1}, a method of solving (75) and (76) is as follows. Pick q_1, then calculate the succeeding z_k's and q_k's by using (75) and (76). If the calculated value of the last output level q_K is the centroid of the area between z_K and z_{K+1}, then the calculated z_k's and q_k's represent the correct solution. If q_K is not the appropriate centroid, the calculation must be repeated with a different choice of q_1. The search for the correct value of q_1 can be systematized so as to yield the correct solutions in a short time. Max [11] employed this procedure to calculate the decision levels (z_k's) and the output levels (q_k's) for the optimum quantizer for the case when the sample value has Gaussian density [$p(z) = (1/\sqrt{2\pi}) \exp(-z^2/2)$] with zero mean and unit variance, and when the end values z_1 and z_{K+1} of the input range are given by $z_1 = -\infty$ and $z_{K+1} = +\infty$, with the restriction that $z_{(K/2)+1} = 0$ for K even, and $q_{(K+1)/2} = 0$ for K odd. This procedure yields symmetric results. In Table 1 we have shown the results

TABLE 1

Optimum Quantization for $K = 16^a$ [11]

Decision levels	Output levels	Decision levels	Output levels
$z_1 = -\infty$	$q_1 = -2.733$	$z_{10} = 0.2582$	$q_{10} = 0.3881$
$z_2 = -2.401$	$q_2 = -2.069$	$z_{11} = 0.5224$	$q_{11} = 0.6568$
$z_3 = -1.844$	$q_3 = -1.618$	$z_{12} = 0.7996$	$q_{12} = 0.9424$
$z_4 = -1.437$	$q_4 = -1.256$	$z_{13} = 1.099$	$q_{13} = 1.256$
$z_5 = -1.099$	$q_5 = -0.9424$	$z_{14} = 1.437$	$q_{14} = 1.618$
$z_6 = -0.7996$	$q_6 = -0.6568$	$z_{15} = 1.844$	$q_{15} = 2.069$
$z_7 = -0.5224$	$q_7 = -0.3881$	$z_{16} = 2.401$	$q_{16} = 2.733$
$z_8 = -0.2582$	$q_8 = -0.1284$	$z_{17} = \infty$	
$z_9 = 0.0$	$q_9 = 0.1284$		

$^a p(z) = (1/\sqrt{2\pi}) \exp(-z^2/2)$, $z_1 = -\infty$, $z_{K+1} = \infty$.

of such a computation for $K = 16$. Note that the levels tend to be closer near the center of the scale, where $p(z)$ takes its maximum value, so that the sample values occur more frequently there.

Nonuniform quantization is usually accomplished by *companding* [16]. This involves passing each sample through a nonlinear device called a "compressor" and then uniformly quantizing the output of the compressor. Of course, now the quantized samples must pass through the inverse of the compressor, called the "expander," before reconstruction of the picture.

4.3.2 Sampling, Quantization, and Picture Detail

Let a picture be sampled on a rectangular array of $M \times N$ points, so that it is represented by $M \times N$ samples. Let the samples be quantized to K levels. If $K = 2^b$ and if the natural binary code is used to transform the quantized samples into binary words, then each sample is represented by a b-bit binary word. Therefore, the total number of bits necessary to represent the picture is $M \times N \times b$.

The following question now arises: For a given total number of bits, how should one choose the values for N, M, and b in order that the reconstruction error is a minimum? In this section it will be shown that the proper choice of N, M, and b strongly depends on picture detail. We will not endeavor to present any systematic techniques for determining the optimum values of N, M, and b, for a given total number of bits, since such techniques do not yet exist.

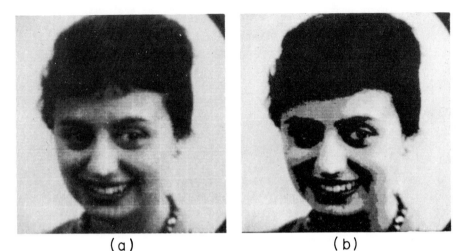

(a)   (b)

Fig. 17 Tradeoff between sampling and quantization. (a) Picture of a face, 128 × 128 samples, 64 quantization levels. (b) Same picture as in (a), 256 × 256 samples, 16 quantization levels. (From [7].)

Figure 17 shows two pictures of a face reconstructed with different values of N, M, and b but with the same total number of bits. It is clear that the picture in Fig. 17a is more pleasing (esthetically) than the picture in Fig. 17b, even though the former has lower spatial resolution. Similar results for a picture of a crowd are presented in Fig. 18a and in Fig. 18b. This example yields a result opposite to that for the picture of the face; here the picture with a higher spatial resolution and lower gray scale resolution is preferable to the picture with lower spatial resolution and higher gray scale resolution.

In a recent study the pictures of the face and the crowd, as shown in Figs. 17 and 18, were represented by $N \times N$ samples and the samples quantized into 2^b levels for different values of N and b. The reconstructed pictures were ranked by observers according to their subjective quality. The results were plotted in the form of isopreference curves (solid curves) in the Nb-plane (Fig. 19). [Each point in the Nb-plane represents a picture with $N \times N$ samples and 2^b quantization levels]. The points on an isopreference curve represent pictures of the same quality as judged by the observers. Results for the face are shown in Fig. 19a while those for the crowd are in Fig. 19b. It is seen that the isopreference curves depend markedly on the picture types and differ greatly from the curves for constant total number of bits (the dashed lines in the figure).

The discussion and the examples presented point to the following im-

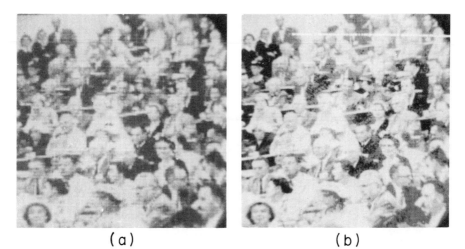

(a)   **(b)**

Fig. 18 Tradeoff between sampling and quantization. (a) Picture of a crowd, 128 × 128 samples, 64 quantization levels. (b) Same picture as in (a), 256 × 256 samples, 16 quantization levels. (From [7].)

portant observation: In a slowly changing scene it is important to have fine quantization, but the sampling can be coarse; while in a scene with a large amount of detail, it is necessary to sample finely, but quantization can be coarse.

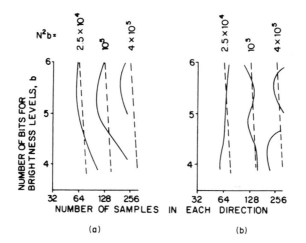

Fig. 19 Isopreference curves (a) for the pictures in Fig. 17, (b) for the pictures in Fig. 18. The dashed lines are the lines of constant total number of bits required to represent a picture. (From [7].)

4.4 BIBLIOGRAPHICAL NOTES

The theory of sampling using a periodic lattice of points in two or more dimensions was given in a classic paper by Peterson and Middleton [13]. The case of a rectangular sampling lattice has also been treated by Bracewell [1].

In Section 4.1 it was shown that a two-dimensional function can be reproduced exactly from its samples taken over a suitable sampling lattice, provided the function is bandlimited, i.e., its Fourier transform (power spectrum for the case of random fields) vanishes outside some region in the frequency plane. The question now arises: Suppose a function $f(x, y)$ is not bandlimited, is there any possible advantage in smoothing or filtering the function before sampling? The answer, discussed in the paper by Peterson and Middleton, is yes, and it is shown that prefiltering may lead to minimization of aliasing problems. Moiré patterns in sampled images were discussed in a now classic paper by Mertz and Grey [12]. A more recent treatment of the effects of aliasing in two-dimensional sampling has been given by Legault [9].

There is considerable literature on the orthonormal expansion of functions. Readers with a mathematical inclination may find the book by Davis [3] enjoyable. Sampling of random fields using orthonormal expansions is a generalization to two dimensions of the one-dimensional theory that is given in the book by Van Trees [19]. The theory of optimum sampling is based on the treatment for the one-dimensional case given by Brown [2]. The results for the sampling error using Fourier, standard, and optimum sampling are to be found in Habibi and Wintz [6].

The theory of optimum quantization was given by Max [11]. Optimum quantization for constant output entropy, rather than constant number of output levels, has been discussed by Wood [20] based on an approximation to Max's results given by Roe [15]. Nonuniform quantization through the use of a nonlinear gain characteristic followed by uniform quantization has been described by Smith [16]. The false contours that result from using too few quantization levels can be "broken up" by adding an irregular "dither" to the grey level prior to quantization; see Roberts [14] and Lippel [10]. The effects of using too few quantization levels can also be minimized by using optimally designed pre- and postfilters around the quantizer; see Graham [5].

A picture that is reconstructed from samples contains, in general, both sampling and quantization errors. A consequence of the analysis given by Totty and Clark [17] is that if a picture is sampled using orthogonal basis functions, the total mean square error between the original picture and the reconstructed picture is equal to the sum of the mean-square sampling error and the mean-square quantization error for any quantization process.

The subjective tradeoff between sampling and quantization has been discussed by Huang [7].

REFERENCES

1. R. N. Bracewell, Two-dimensional aerial smoothing in radio astronomy, *Aust. J. Phys.* **9**, 1956, 297–314.
2. J. L. Brown, Mean square truncation error in series expansion of random functions, *J. SIAM* **8**, 1960, 28–32.
3. P. Davis, "Interpolation and Approximation." Ginn (Blaisdell), Waltham, Massachusetts, 1966.
4. J. W. Goodman, "Introduction to Fourier Optics." McGraw-Hill, New York, 1968.
5. D. N. Graham, Optimal Filtering to Reduce Quantization Noise, Master of Science Thesis, Dep. Elec. Eng, Massachusetts Inst. of Technol., Cambridge, Massachusetts, June 1966.
6. A. Habibi and P. A. Wintz, Image coding by linear transformation and block quantization, *IEEE Trans. Comm. Technol.* **COM-19**, 1971, 50–62, 1971.
7. T. S. Huang, O. J. Tretiak, B. Prasada, and Y. Yamaguchi, Design considerations in PCM transmission of low resolution monochrome still pictures, *Proc. IEEE* **55**, 1967, 331–335.
8. T. S. Huang, PCM picture transmission, *IEEE Spectrum* **2**, 1965, 57–63.
9. R. Legault, The aliasing problems in two-dimensional sampled imagery, *in* "Perception of Displayed Information" (L. M. Biberman, ed.). Plenum Press, New York, 1973.
10. B. Lippel, Effect of dither on luminance quantization of pictures, *IEEE Trans. Comm. Technol.* COM-19, 1971, 879–888.
11. J. Max, Quantizing for minimum distortion, *IRE Trans. Informat. Theory* **IT-6**, 1960, 7–12.
12. P. Mertz and F. Grey, A theory of scanning and its relation to the characteristics of the transmitted signal in telephotography and television, *BSTJ* **13**, 1934, 464–515.
13. D. P. Peterson and D. Middleton, Sampling and reconstruction of wave-number-limited functions in n-dimensional Euclidean spaces, *Informat. Contr.* **5**, 1962, 279–323.
14. L. G. Roberts, Picture coding using pseudo-random noise, *IRE Trans. Informat. Theory* **IT-8**, 1962, 145–154.
15. G. M. Roe, Quantizing for minimum distortion, *IEEE Trans. Informat. Theory* **IT-10**, 1964, 384–385.
16. B. Smith, Instantaneous companding of quantized signals, *BSTJ* **36**, 1957, 653–709.
17. R. E. Totty and G. C. Clark, Reconstruction error in waveform transmission, *IRE Trans. Informat. Theory* **IT-13**, 1967, 336–338.
18. F. G. Tricomi, "Integral Equations." Wiley (Interscience), New York, 1957.
19. H. L. Van Trees, "Detection, Estimation, and Modulation Theory," Part 1. Wiley, New York, 1968.
20. R. C. Wood, On optimum quantization, *IEEE Trans. Informat. Theory* **IT-15**, 1969, 248–252.

Chapter 5

Compression

Suppose we intend to transmit a picture over a channel or store it in an electronic device. For given gray scale and spatial resolution capabilities of a receiver or a user, the aim of picture compression is to represent the picture by as few bits as possible for the purpose of transmission or storage. Consider, for example, a 5×5 cm photograph with a resolution of 50 μm in all directions. Let us assume that the signal-to-noise ratio in the photograph is such that one can extract 256 ($=2^8$) gray levels from the photograph. (By this we mean that the standard deviation of the noise fluctuations is approximately $\frac{1}{256}$ of the maximum range of gray scale in the photograph.) If fixed-length binary code words are used, then the gray level at each resolution element in the photograph can be represented by a binary word 8 bits long. It would, therefore, take 8×10^6 bits to store or transmit this picture in a "distortion free" form.

If the spatial and gray scale resolution of the receiver (or the user) are inferior to those of the original picture, then one can take liberties with the sampling and quantization of the picture and thereby represent it by a reduced number of bits. This means that now a certain amount of distortion is permitted between the original picture and the version that can be reproduced from the binary data. This leads us to the following questions: For a given amount and type of distortion, what techniques would allow us to represent the picture by a reduced number of bits? For a given amount of distortion, is there a minimum number of bits that are needed to represent the picture? The first question is answered in the following sections where we discuss various two-dimensional picture-compression techniques that (at the cost of a small amount of distortion, often unnoticeable) significantly economize on the number of bits required for a picture. The second question is answered by the rate-distortion function, which will be discussed in conceptual terms at the end of the chapter.

Suppose the given picture is to be received by a system the spatial and gray scale resolution of which exceeds or at least matches those of the picture. It must then be possible to reproduce the picture faithfully from the digital data. For the picture just described this would require 8×10^6 bits. A question that now arises is: Can we represent the picture in this example by less than 8×10^6 bits and still be able to reproduce it faithfully? If some gray levels occur more often than others, then the answer is yes, if we use shorter binary words for gray levels that occur more often. Some of the more commonly used techniques for doing this are discussed in Section 5.7.

5.1 TRANSFORM COMPRESSION

In this section we will first justify qualitatively that in picture compression one needs to represent a picture by uncorrelated data, and we will present some reversible linear transformations that achieve this. The data must then be ranked according to degree of significance of their contribution to both the information content and the subjective quality of the picture. Once such a ranking is achieved then those elements of the data that are unimportant from the point of view of the gray scale and spatial resolution capability of the receiver can be neglected. This makes possible a major degree of picture compression.

5.1.1 Karhunen–Loève Compression: The Continuous Case

As a rather trivial but conceptually illustrative example of picture compression, consider the case where we know *a priori* that all the pictures in a collection are sinusoidal patterns. If we sampled the pictures on a fine grid and quantized the resulting samples, we would need a large number of bits to represent each picture. On the other hand, the only information we need to extract from these pictures in order to reproduce them without distortion consists of the spatial frequency, the orientation, the amplitude, and the phase (with respect to a fixed origin, which could be the center of the pictures) of the sinusoidal pattern in each picture. The total number of bits required for this is relatively small, resulting in data compression.

The simple example just presented has several important features. The reason why data compression was achieved ·in this example is that the gray levels at all points in each picture are highly correlated. By this we mean that the gray levels at all points in a picture can be predicted from the level at any one point in the same picture given the spatial frequency, the phase, the orientation, and the amplitude. Note, also, that the data (spatial frequency, orientation, amplitude, and phase) that are used to represent a picture and from which the picture can be reproduced are uncorrelated. For example, a picture with a given spatial frequency may have any phase, any amplitude, and any orientation.

This discussion leads us to a basic idea in picture compression. One attempts to represent a picture by uncorrelated data because then each element of the data is a unique property of the picture—unique in the sense that it cannot be predicted (at least from the point of view of linear mean square estimation theories) from the rest of the data. The example just discussed was of a rather restricted nature because of our *a priori* knowledge that the pictures were sinusoidal patterns. For a more general class of pictures, when an attempt is made to represent each picture by uncorrelated data, the number of bits required for the uncorrelated data may be quite large. In such a case the elements of the uncorrelated data should be ranked in order of their importance. When this is done, the higher-order terms may, for example, represent high spatial resolution effects in the picture. If the receiver or user of the picture has limited spatial resolution capability, these high-resolution terms may as well be deleted from the data. In fact, as we will see presently, such deletions from the uncorrelated data contribute significantly to picture compression.

For a restricted class of pictures such as in the previous example, it is easy to find a set of uncorrelated parameters that represent a picture and from which it can be reproduced. For a more general class of pictures, the problem becomes more difficult. In Chapter 4, we discussed various techniques for representing pictures by samples. One technique involved expanding a picture in terms of a family of orthonormal functions and taking the coefficients of expansion as picture samples. In what follows we will seek a set of orthonormal functions that result in uncorrelated samples for a given class of pictures (a random field $\mathbf{f}(x, y)$) defined in terms of its autocorrelation function $R(\vec{r}_1, \vec{r}_2)$ (see Eq. (89) of Chapter 2).§ We recall that if (x, y) and (x', y') denote the co-

___

§ In this chapter, since we will be concerned with only one random field at a time, the autocorrelation function of a homogeneous random field $\mathbf{f}(r)$ will be denoted by $R(\alpha,\beta)$ instead of $R_{ff}(\alpha,\beta)$.

ordinates of the position vectors $\vec{r}_1$ and $\vec{r}_2$, respectively, then $R(\vec{r}_1, \vec{r}_2)$ can also be expressed as $R(x, y, x', y')$. If the random field $\mathbf{f}(\vec{r})$ is homogeneous, then the autocorrelation function becomes a function of only two variables and can be expressed as $R(x - x', y - y')$ as discussed in Section 2.4.3.

The problem of obtaining uncorrelated samples from a picture is answered by the following theorem:

Theorem (Karhunen–Loève transformation for continuous pictures). Let $-A/2 \leqslant x \leqslant A/2$, $-B/2 \leqslant y \leqslant B/2$ define a region $\mathscr{S}$ of the xy-plane. Let $\varphi_{mn}(x, y)$ be a complete family of orthonormal functions defined over the region $\mathscr{S}$. A random field $\mathbf{f}(x, y)$ may then be expanded in region $\mathscr{S}$ as follows [see Eqs. (42a) and (42b) of Chapter 4]:

$$\mathbf{f}(x, y) = \sum_{m=0}^{\infty} \sum_{n=0}^{\infty} \mathbf{a}_{mn} \varphi_{mn}(x, y) \tag{1}$$

where the summation on the right-hand side converges to $f(x, y)$ in some sense and where

$$\mathbf{a}_{mn} = \int_{-B/2}^{B/2} \int_{-A/2}^{A/2} \mathbf{f}(x, y)\, \varphi_{mn}^*(x, y)\, dx\, dy \tag{2}$$

For zero-mean random fields the functions $\varphi_{mn}(x, y)$ that result in uncorrelated samples $\mathbf{a}_{mn}$ must satisfy the following integral equation:

$$\int_{-B/2}^{B/2} \int_{-A/2}^{A/2} R(x, y, x', y')\, \varphi_{mn}(x', y')\, dx'\, dy' = \gamma_{mn} \varphi_{mn}(x, y) \tag{3}$$

for $-A/2 \leqslant x \leqslant A/2$, $-B/2 \leqslant y \leqslant B/2$, where

$$\gamma_{mn} = E\{|\mathbf{a}_{mn}|^2\} \tag{4}$$

Proof: We do not want to eliminate the possibility that the desired orthonormal functions $\varphi_{mn}(x, y)$ may be complex. An examination of (2) reveals that even for real random fields $\mathbf{a}_{mn}$ can be complex. Uncorrelatedness for complex random variables $\mathbf{a}_{mn}$ means

$$E\{\mathbf{a}_{mn}\mathbf{a}_{ij}^*\} = E\{\mathbf{a}_{mn}\} E\{\mathbf{a}_{ij}^*\}, \qquad m \neq i \quad \text{or} \quad n \neq j \tag{5}$$

If we take the expectation of both sides of (2) and use the assumption that the random field $\mathbf{f}(x, y)$ has zero mean, we obtain

$$E\{\mathbf{a}_{mn}\} = \int_{-B/2}^{B/2} \int_{-A/2}^{A/2} E\{\mathbf{f}(x, y)\}\, \varphi_{mn}^*(x, y)\, dx\, dy$$

$$= 0 \qquad \text{for} \quad m, n = 0, 1, 2, 3, \ldots \tag{6}$$

Thus for a zero-mean random field the samples also have zero mean. Substituting (6) in (5), the uncorrelatedness of the $\mathbf{a}_{mn}$ implies that

$$E\{\mathbf{a}_{mn}\mathbf{a}_{ij}^*\} = 0, \qquad m \neq i \quad \text{or} \quad n \neq j \tag{7}$$

To prove the theorem, we must now show that the functions $\varphi_{mn}(x, y)$ that yield samples satisfying (7) must be solutions of the integral equation (3). Multiplying both sides of (1) by $\mathbf{a}_{ij}^*$, we obtain

$$\mathbf{f}(x, y)\,\mathbf{a}_{ij}^* = \sum_{m=1}^{\infty} \sum_{n=1}^{\infty} \mathbf{a}_{mn}\,\mathbf{a}_{ij}^*\,\varphi_{mn}(x, y) \tag{8}$$

Taking the expectation of both sides and making use of the linearity of expectation and Eq. (7), we obtain

$$E\{\mathbf{f}(x, y)\,\mathbf{a}_{ij}^*\} = E\{|\mathbf{a}_{ij}|^2\}\,\varphi_{ij}(x, y) \tag{9}$$

The complex conjugate of (2) can be rewritten as

$$\mathbf{a}_{ij}^* = \int_{-B/2}^{B/2} \int_{-A/2}^{A/2} \mathbf{f}(x', y')\,\varphi_{ij}(x', y')\,dx'\,dy' \tag{10}$$

where we have made use of the fact that the random field is real.[§] Multiplying both sides of (10) by $\mathbf{f}(x, y)$ and taking the expectation, we obtain

$$E\{\mathbf{f}(x, y)\,\mathbf{a}_{ij}^*\} = \int_{-B/2}^{B/2} \int_{-A/2}^{A/2} R(x, y, x', y')\,\varphi_{ij}(x', y')\,dx'\,dy' \tag{11}$$

where we have made use of the definition of the autocorrelation function. Comparing (9) and (11), we see that $\varphi_{ij}(x, y)$ must satisfy

$$\int_{-B/2}^{B/2} \int_{-A/2}^{A/2} R(x, y, x', y')\,\varphi_{ij}(x', y')\,dx'\,dy' = E\{|\mathbf{a}_{ij}|^2\}\,\varphi_{ij}(x, y) \tag{12}$$

which proves the theorem. ∎

Exercise 1.   Prove the converse to the previous theorem, that is, given a set of orthonormal functions that are the solutions of the integral equation (3), then if a zero-mean random field is expanded in terms of these orthonormal functions, the coefficients of expansion are uncorrelated. ∎

By comparing Eq. (61) of Chapter 4 with (3) we see that the orthonormal functions that give uncorrelated samples also minimize the sampling error.

Thus far we have seen how we may represent a continuous picture by uncorrelated data. This method could perhaps be implemented in hardware, but this has never been done. A more realistic approach, however, is first to digitize the picture by sampling it on a fine sampling lattice (see Section

[§] The assumption of real random fields is not necessary to the theorem provided one makes use of the definition of autocorrelation for complex fields, which is $R(x, y, x', y') = E\{\mathbf{f}(x, y)\,\mathbf{f}^*(x', y')\}$.

4.1.3) and then use a digital computer to transform the samples into un-correlated data. We will now address ourselves to this problem.

5.1.2 Karhunen–Loève Compression: The Discrete Case

Let a picture belonging to a random field $f(x, y)$ be sampled on an $N \times N$ square sampling lattice. We assume that N is large enough not to create any aliasing problems (see Section 4.1.5). The samples thus obtained may be denoted by $f(m, n)$, where m and n both take integer values from 0 through $N - 1$. The matrix having elements $f(m, n)$ will be denoted by $[f]$. Our aim at this point is to find a reversible transformation such that the elements of the transform are uncorrelated. The transformation must be reversible because we want to be able to reconstruct $[f]$ from the uncorrelated data.

By the discussion in Section 2.2, given two $N \times N$ deterministic nonsingular matrices $[P]$ and $[Q]$, we can transform the matrix $[f]$ into another matrix $[F]$ by

$$[F] = [P][f][Q] \tag{13}$$

The inverse transform is given by (Eq. (33) of Chapter 2)

$$[f] = [P]^{-1}[F][Q]^{-1} \tag{14}$$

Let us denote the matrix $[P]^{-1}$ by $[P']$ and $[Q]^{-1}$ by $[Q']$; then (14) may be written in an expanded form as

$$f(m, n) = \sum_{u=0}^{N-1} \sum_{v=0}^{N-1} F(u, v) P'(m, u) Q'(v, n) \tag{15}$$

for $m = 0, \ldots, N-1$, $n = 0, \ldots, N-1$. Some thought indicates that (15) may be rewritten as

$$[f] = \sum_{u=0}^{N-1} \sum_{v=0}^{N-1} [\varphi^{(u, v)}] F(u, v) \tag{16}$$

where $[\varphi^{(u, v)}]$ is an $N \times N$ matrix whose (m, n)th element is $P'(m, u) Q'(v, n)$.

As an example of the representation in (16), note that a comparison of Eq. (40) of Chapter 2 with (15) reveals that for the discrete Fourier transform the (m, n)th element of this matrix $[\varphi^{(u, v)}]$ is

$$\exp\left[j2\pi \left(\frac{mu}{M} + \frac{nv}{N} \right) \right]$$

For the rest of this section we consider an $N \times N$ matrix to be a vector in an N^2-dimensional space. The first component of this vector for the matrix $[\varphi]$ is $\varphi(0, 0)$; the second component is $\varphi(0, 1); \ldots$; the Nth component

$\varphi(0, N-1)$; the $(N+1)$st component $\varphi(1,0)$; the $(N+2)$nd component $\varphi(1,1), \ldots$; and finally the N^2th component $\varphi(N-1, N-1)$. One now has a framework for defining the dot product of two matrices. By the definition of dot product in a complex vector space, the dot product of two $N \times N$ matrices $[\varphi]$ and $[\Gamma]$ is equal to

$$[\varphi] \cdot [\Gamma] = \sum_{m=0}^{N-1} \sum_{n=0}^{N-1} \varphi(m, n) \, \Gamma^*(m, n) \qquad (17)$$

where $\Gamma^*(m, n)$ is the complex conjugate of the element $\Gamma(m, n)$ of the matrix $[\Gamma]$. Note that the dot product of two matrices is a single number, real or complex.

Going back to (16), we have a set of N^2 matrices $[\varphi^{(u, v)}]$. These matrices form an orthonormal set provided[§]

$$[\varphi^{(u, v)}] \cdot [\varphi^{(r, s)}] = \begin{cases} 0, & u \neq r \quad \text{or} \quad v \neq s \\ 1, & u = r \quad \text{and} \quad v = s \end{cases} \qquad (18)$$

Assume for a moment that the matrices $[\varphi^{(u, v)}]$ in (16) are indeed orthonormal; then multiplying (in the sense of the dot product) both sides by $[\varphi^{(r, s)}]$ and making use of (18), we obtain

$$[\mathbf{f}] \cdot [\varphi^{(r, s)}] = \mathbf{F}(r, s) \qquad (19)$$

Summarizing the previous discussion: given a set of N^2 orthonormal matrices $[\varphi^{(u, v)}]$, we may expand an aribtrary $N \times N$ matrix $[\mathbf{f}]$ as

$$[\mathbf{f}] = \sum_{u=0}^{N-1} \sum_{v=0}^{N-1} \mathbf{F}(u, v) [\varphi^{(u, v)}] \qquad (20a)$$

where the coefficients of expansion $\mathbf{F}(u, v)$ are given by

$$\mathbf{F}(u, v) = [\mathbf{f}] \cdot [\varphi^{(u, v)}], \qquad u = 0, 1, 2, \ldots, N-1, \quad v = 0, 1, 2, \ldots, N-1 \qquad (20b)$$

Equations (20a) and (20b) provide a conceptually convenient framework for transforming a matrix $[\mathbf{f}]$ into another matrix $[\mathbf{F}]$. Of course, given $[\mathbf{F}]$, we may recover $[\mathbf{f}]$ by using (20a), so that the transformation is reversible.

The orthonormal expansion in (1) for the continuous case may be compared to that in (20) for the discrete case. Note that the expansion in (20) involves a finite number of terms only.

[§] Note that in an N^2-dimensional space, we cannot have more than N^2 matrices (defined as vectors in this space) that are mutually orthogonal.

Theorem (Karhunen–Loève transformation for discrete pictures). Let $R(m, n, p, q)$ be the autocorrelation function of $[\mathbf{f}]$, that is,

$$R(m, n, p, q) = E\{\mathbf{f}(m, n)\mathbf{f}(p, q)\} \tag{21}$$

For zero-mean random fields, the orthonormal matrices $[\varphi^{(u, v)}]$ that result in uncorrelated $\mathbf{F}(u, v)$ in (20) satisfy the equation

$$\sum_{p=0}^{N-1} \sum_{q=0}^{N-1} R(m, n, p, q)\, \varphi^{(u, v)}(p, q) = \gamma_{uv}\, \varphi^{(u, v)}(m, n) \tag{22}$$

where $\varphi^{(u, v)}(p, q)$ and $\varphi^{(u, v)}(m, n)$ are the (p, q)th and the (m, n)th elements, respectively, of the matrix $[\varphi^{(u, v)}]$, and where

$$\gamma_{uv} = E\{|\mathbf{F}(u, v)|^2\} \tag{23}$$

The matrices $[\varphi^{(u, v)}]$ are called the *eigenmatrices* or the *basis matrices* of $R(m, n, p, q)$.

Proof: By making use of the definition of the dot product in (17), (20b) can be written as

$$\mathbf{F}(u, v) = \sum_{m=0}^{N-1} \sum_{n=0}^{N-1} \mathbf{f}(m, n)\, \varphi^{(u, v)*}(m, n) \tag{24}$$

Taking the expectation of both sides, we obtain

$$E\{\mathbf{F}(u, v)\} = \sum_{m=0}^{N-1} \sum_{n-0}^{N-1} E\{\mathbf{f}(m, n)\}\, \varphi^{(u, v)*}(m, n)$$

For a zero-mean random field $E\{\mathbf{f}(m, n)\} = 0$. Substituting this in the preceding equation, we have

$$E\{\mathbf{F}(u, v)\} = 0, \qquad u = 0, 1, ..., N - 1, \quad v = 0, 1, ..., N - 1 \tag{25}$$

Now suppose that the $\mathbf{F}(u, v)$ are uncorrelated. We want to retain the possibility that $\mathbf{F}(u, v)$ may be complex even for real random fields. Uncorrelatedness of $\mathbf{F}(u, v)$, therefore, means (see (5))

$$E\{\mathbf{F}(u, v)\,\mathbf{F}^*(u', v')\} = E\{\mathbf{F}(u, v)\}\, E\{\mathbf{F}^*(u', v')\}, \qquad u \neq u' \quad \text{or} \quad v \neq v'$$

which by (25) reduces to

$$E\{\mathbf{F}(u, v)\,\mathbf{F}^*(u', v')\} = 0, \qquad u \neq u' \quad \text{or} \quad v \neq v' \tag{26}$$

Now (20a) can be written as

$$\mathbf{f}(m, n) = \sum_{u=0}^{N-1} \sum_{v=0}^{N-1} \mathbf{F}(u, v)\, \varphi^{(u, v)}(m, n) \tag{27}$$

for $m = 0, ..., N-1$, $n = 0, ..., N-1$. Multiplying both sides by $\mathbf{F}^*(u', v')$, taking expectation, and making use of (26), we obtain

$$E\{\mathbf{f}(m, n)\mathbf{F}^*(u', v')\} = E\{|\mathbf{F}(u', v')|^2\}\varphi^{(u', v')}(m, n) \qquad (28)$$

On the other hand, from (24), we have

$$\mathbf{F}^*(u', v') = \sum_{p=0}^{N-1} \sum_{q=0}^{N-1} \mathbf{f}(p, q)\, \varphi^{(u', v')}(p, q) \qquad (29)$$

where we have assumed the random field $[\mathbf{f}]$ to be real (the footnote on p. 120 also applies here). Multiplying both sides of (29) by $\mathbf{f}(m, n)$, taking the expectation, and using (21), we obtain

$$E\{\mathbf{f}(m, n)\, \mathbf{F}^*(u', v')\} = \sum_{p=0}^{N-1} \sum_{q=0}^{N-1} R(m, n, p, q)\, \varphi^{(u', v')}(p, q) \qquad (30)$$

Comparing (28) with (30), we see that the basis matrices $[\varphi^{(u, v)}]$ must satisfy (22) and (23), which proves the theorem. ∎

We thus see that the basis matrices $[\varphi^{(u, v)}]$ that yield an uncorrelated representation of a picture matrix $[\mathbf{f}]$ are a solution of Eq. (22). By a slight change in notation, (22) can be put in a more convenient form for the purpose of solution on a digital computer. The trick is to represent a two-dimensional array of numbers by a one-dimensional string of numbers by replacing indices of matrix elements by a single index as shown in Table 1. With this change

TABLE 1

Double indices of matrix elements	Equivalent single index
$0, 0$	0
$0, 1$	1
$0, 2$	2
$\vdots$	$\vdots$
$0, N-1$	$N-1$
$1, 0$	N
$1, 1$	$N+1$
$\vdots$	$\vdots$
$1, N-1$	$2N-1$
$2, 0$	$2N$
$2, 1$	$2N+1$
$\vdots$	$\vdots$
$N-1, N-2$	N^2-2
$N-1, N-1$	N^2-1

in notation, the picture matrix $[\mathbf{f}]$ will become a one-dimensional string denoted by a vector $\tilde{\mathbf{f}}$:

$$
\begin{bmatrix}
\mathbf{f}(0,0) & \mathbf{f}(0,1) & \cdots & \mathbf{f}(0,N-1) \\
\vdots & \vdots & \vdots & \vdots \\
\mathbf{f}(N-1,0) & \mathbf{f}(N-1,1) & \cdots & \mathbf{f}(N-1,N-1)
\end{bmatrix}
\Rightarrow
\begin{bmatrix}
\mathbf{f}_0 \\
\mathbf{f}_1 \\
\vdots \\
\mathbf{f}_{N-1} \\
\mathbf{f}_N \\
\mathbf{f}_{N+1} \\
\vdots \\
\mathbf{f}_{N^2-1}
\end{bmatrix}
$$

and the orthonormal matrices can also be represented by equivalent one-dimensional strings as

$$
\begin{bmatrix}
\varphi^{(u,v)}(0,0) & \cdots & \varphi^{(u,v)}(0,N-1) \\
\vdots & \vdots & \vdots \\
\varphi^{(u,v)}(N-1,0) & \cdots & \varphi^{(u,v)}(N-1,N-1)
\end{bmatrix}
\Rightarrow
\begin{bmatrix}
\varphi_0^{\,s} \\
\vdots \\
\varphi_{N-1}^{\,s} \\
\varphi_N^{\,s} \\
\vdots \\
\varphi_{N^2-1}^{\,s}
\end{bmatrix}
$$

where s is the equivalent index in the new notation of the double index (u,v). In the new notation, $R(m,n,p,q)$ will become an $N^2 \times N^2$ matrix $R(i,j)$, where i is the equivalent index of (m,n) and j the equivalent of (p,q). In order to avoid confusion between this $R(i,j)$ and the two-dimensional autocorrelation function $R(\alpha,\beta)$ of a homogeneous random field, we will denote $R(i,j)$ as obtained from $R(m,n,p,q)$ (by change in index notation) by $K(i,j)$. Evidently,

$$K(i,j) = E\{\mathbf{f}_i\mathbf{f}_j\}, \qquad i = 0, 1, \ldots, N^2 - 1, \quad j = 0, 1, \ldots, N^2 - 1 \tag{31}$$

where $\mathbf{f}_i$ and $\mathbf{f}_j$ are the ith and the jth components, respectively, of the picture matrix $[\mathbf{f}]$ in its string representation.

It is easy to see that in this notation (22) can be written as

$$\sum_{j=0}^{N^2-1} K(i,j)\varphi_j^{\,s} = \gamma_s\varphi_i^{\,s}, \qquad i = 0, 1, \ldots, N^2 - 1 \tag{32}$$

or equivalently,

$$
\begin{bmatrix}
K(0,0) & K(0,1) & \cdots & K(0,N^2-1) \\
K(1,0) & K(1,1) & \cdots & K(1,N^2-1) \\
\vdots & \vdots & \cdots & \vdots \\
K(N^2-1,0) & K(N^2-1,1) & \cdots & K(N^2-1,N^2-1)
\end{bmatrix}
\begin{bmatrix}
\varphi_0^s \\
\varphi_1^s \\
\vdots \\
\varphi_{N^2-1}^s
\end{bmatrix}
= \gamma_s
\begin{bmatrix}
\varphi_0^s \\
\varphi_1^s \\
\vdots \\
\varphi_{N^2-1}^s
\end{bmatrix}
$$

$$(33)$$

Therefore, each vector $\vec{\varphi}^s = [\varphi_0^s, \varphi_1^s, \ldots, \varphi_{N^2-1}^s]$ is transformed into a scalar multiple of itself when it is multiplied by the matrix $[K]$. The vectors $\vec{\varphi}^s$, $s = 0, 1, \ldots, N^2 - 1$ are called the *eigenvectors* of the matrix $[K]$. To each eigenvector φ^s there corresponds an eigenvalue γ_s. Techniques for obtaining eigenvectors and eigenvalues of a matrix are well known in the theory of linear transformations; see, for example, the book by Carnahan *et al.* [8]. These methods require inverting the matrix $[K]$ which is $N^2 \times N^2$. Even for small N, this requires a large number of computations.

5.1.3   Karhunen–Loève Compression: Application to Pictures

We will now present an example of picture compression using the concepts previously discussed. For this example we will use the picture in Fig. 1. This

Fig. 1   The picture of the cameraman is a 256×256 matrix each element of which is an 8-bit number. (From [93].)

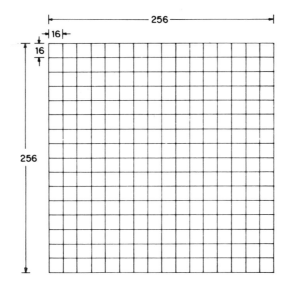

Fig. 2 Partitioning of a 256 × 256 picture into 256 16 × 16 subpictures.

picture is a 256 × 256 matrix each element of which is an 8-bit number. There-fore, the total number of bits required to represent the picture is $2^8 \times 2^8 \times 2^3 = 2^{19}$. Let us partition this picture into 256 16 × 16 subpictures for convenience in numerical implementation (Fig. 2). Each subpicture may now be trans-formed into uncorrelated coefficients by first finding the eigenvectors and the corresponding eigenvalues of the $[K]$ matrix, which is 256 × 256. Note that for a homogeneous random field $[K]$ would be the same for each subpicture. Even for subpictures of this small size, finding the eigenvectors and the eigenvalues of the $[K]$ matrix is computationally expensive since it involves inverting a 256 × 256 matrix. For the example under discussion, a slightly different approach as now described was used.

The autocorrelation of Fig. 1 (in zero-mean form) can be modeled by (see Habibi and Wintz [30])

$$R(x, y, x', y') \simeq \exp[-0.125|x-x'| - 0.249|y-y'|] \qquad (34)$$

In Section 4.2.4 we indicated that the analytical solutions of (3) for this auto-correlation function are known. Let these solutions for an arbitrary sub-picture (which we take to be centered at the origin) be $\varphi_{uv}(x, y)$, where u and v take positive integer values. These solutions may be ranked either on the basis of eigenvalues as discussed in Section 4.2.4 or on the basis of sequency. The sequency of a zero-mean picture in any given direction is defined as half the average number of sign changes per unit distance in that direction.

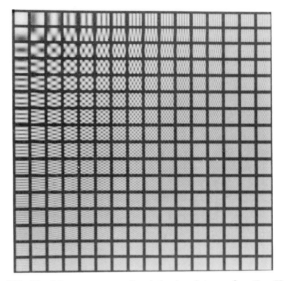

Fig. 3 The 256 16×16 sequency ordered basis pictures for the Karhunen–Loève transformation. (From [93].)

If each of the orthonormal functions $\varphi_{uv}(x, y)$ is sampled on a 16×16 grid and the resulting matrix denoted by $[\varphi^{(u, v)}]$, it is clear that we will have a set of matrices that are "approximately" orthonormal, i.e., (18) will not hold exactly. The finer the sampling of the orthonormal functions $\varphi_{uv}(x, y)$, the more accurately orthonormal the corresponding matrices $[\varphi^{(u, v)}]$ will be. In Fig. 3 we have shown 256 sequency ordered 16×16 matrices $[\varphi^{(u, v)}]$ for the autocorrelation function of (34). Note that since the matrices are sequency ordered, the matrix $[\varphi^{(0,0)}]$, which is at the top left corner in Fig. 3, has no variations; the matrix $[\varphi^{(0, 1)}]$, which is second from the left in the top row, has no sign changes in one direction but has one sign change in the other; and so on.

Once the matrices $[\varphi^{(u, v)}]$ are determined, the uncorrelated coefficients $F(u, v)$ for each subpicture can be found by using (20b). Of course, the coefficients $F(u, v)$ will not be completely uncorrelated because the matrices $[\varphi^{(u, v)}]$ are not exactly orthonormal; however, the correlations between them should be much less than those between the 256 picture elements in each 16×16 subpicture. It follows from (20b) that for each subpicture there will be 256 coefficients $F(u, v)$. The subpicture may be reconstructed from these coefficients by using (20a).

Each $F(u, v)$ is a coefficient in the orthonormal expansion in (20a). Since, as we see in Fig. 3, the matrices $[\varphi^{(u, v)}]$ with higher values of u and v have

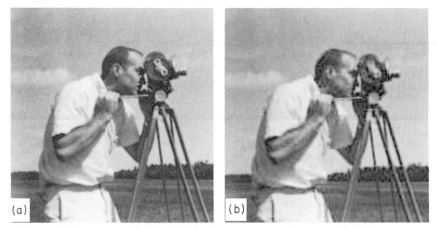

Fig. 4 (a) Reconstructed picture obtained by retaining the first 128 of the 256 Karhunen–Loève coefficients for each of the subpictures of Fig. 1. (b) Reconstructed picture obtained by retaining the first 64 of the 256 Karhunen–Loève coefficients for each of the subpictures. (From [93].)

more rapid variations in their elements, the coefficients for larger u and v represent the higher spatial resolution effects in each 16×16 subpicture. It is clear that if the spatial resolution capabilities of the receiver or the user of these pictures are limited, we need retain only those $F(u, v)$ that are compatible with this resolution—contributing, thereby, to data compression.

Suppose that we retain only the first 128 out of the 256 $F(u, v)$ for each subpicture. These 128 coefficients are chosen on the basis of their ranking by the eigenvalues γ_{uv}. (As mentioned earlier, the ranking achieved in this fashion is roughly the same as that based on sequency considerations.) If we use (20a) to reconstruct each subpicture from the 128 coefficients for that subpicture, the overall reconstructed picture is as shown in Fig. 4a. We see that half the coefficients for each subpicture can be disregarded with no visible degradation in picture quality. In the reconstruction in Fig. 4b where only 64 out of the 256 coefficients $F(u, v)$ for each subpicture were retained, the spatial resolution is lower. This is revealed by a careful examination of the camera and other edges in the picture.

After each subpicture has been transformed into uncorrelated coefficients, the coefficients must be quantized and binary code words assigned to the quantized coefficients. Before we can discuss quantization, however, the following property of the coefficients becomes important. Note that most of each subpicture is covered with slowly varying gray levels. Therefore, the largest contribution comes from those coefficients that represent slow

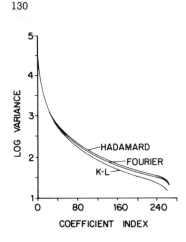

Fig. 5 The variance of the coefficients $\mathbf{F}(u,v)$ as obtained by averaging $|\mathbf{F}(u,v)^2|$ over all the subpictures of Fig. 1. Note that $E\{\mathbf{F}(u,v)\} = 0$ for zero-mean pictures. (From [93].)

variations. This means that when the coefficients $\mathbf{F}(u,v)$ are sequency ranked, those with small u and v will have large magnitudes. This is also true when the coefficients $\mathbf{F}(u,v)$ are ranked on the basis of the eigenvalues γ_{uv} of the corresponding orthonormal matrices $[\varphi^{(u,v)}]$. This is because by Eqs. (23) and (25), for a zero-mean picture the expected value of each $\mathbf{F}(u,v)$ is zero, but the variance of $\mathbf{F}(u,v)$ is equal to the eigenvalue γ_{uv}. This implies that if γ_{uv} is large for a given u and v, then the corresponding $\mathbf{F}(u,v)$ generally has large magnitude. In Fig. 5 we have plotted the variance of the $\mathbf{F}(u,v)$ as obtained by averaging each $|\mathbf{F}(u,v)|^2$ over all the subpictures. In this figure, the coefficients have been ranked by the magnitudes of their associated eigenvalues. Note that the vertical scale is logarithmic.

Since the variances of the coefficients vary widely, as illustrated in Fig. 5, it would be inefficient to use the same quantizer for all the coefficients. That is, if the quantizer output levels are adjusted to span the expected range of the coefficient with the largest variance, then the coefficients with smaller variances will fall in smaller ranges with the result that most of the quantizer levels will not be used. One can get around this difficulty by first normalizing each coefficient by dividing it by its standard deviation and then quantizing the normalized coefficients. Note that the normalized coefficients have unit variance.

Returning to the example under discussion, let us assume that we retain 128 out of 256 coefficients for each subpicture. If we normalize each coefficient by its variance and quantize the resulting normalized coefficients to 16 levels (4 bits), the total number of bits required to represent the picture is $256 \times 128 \times 4$ ($= 2^{17}$). Since we have 256×256 ($= 2^{16}$) picture elements in Fig. 1, the number of bits averages out to be 2 bits per picture element. Note that the direct representation of the picture, in which each picture element

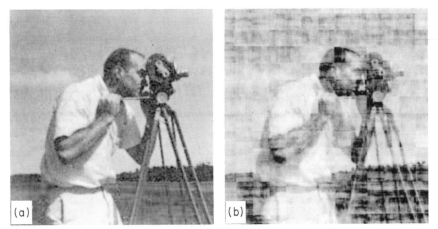

Fig. 6 (a) Reconstructed picture obtained by quantizing each of the 128 Karhunen–Loève coefficients of the picture in Fig. 4a to 16 levels (4 bits). Note that with this representation the picture shown here needs 2 bits per picture element on the average as compared to 8 bits per picture element in Fig. 1. (b) Same as (a), but quantizing to only 4 levels. (From [93].)

was coded separately, required 8 bits per picture element. Therefore, we have a compression ratio of 4. To examine the quality of the picture for this compression ratio, the 128 coefficients for each subpicture must be denormalized by multiplying them by their standard deviations. Each subpicture can then be reconstructed by using (20a) and inserted into its proper place in the reconstructed picture. The result is shown in Fig. 6a.

We can try to increase the compression ratio by quantizing each of the retained coefficients to only 4 levels (2 bits), yielding a compression ratio of 8 (1 bit per picture element). The resulting reconstruction is shown in Fig. 6b. Note the degradation in picture quality.

One can achieve a greater degree of compression for the same quality of reconstructed pictures by nonuniform quantization as discussed in Section 4.3.1. The optimal quantization scheme described there would minimize the mean square quantization error for each coefficient taken singly; it would have to be applied to each coefficient individually. Quantization strategies for minimizing the total mean square quantization error for all the retained coefficients have been discussed by Huang and Schultheiss [42]. In the context of picture compression these methods have been briefly discussed by Wintz [93]. Even though these methods result in higher compression efficiencies, their disadvantages lie in the problems inherent in handling binary words of unequal length.

5.2   FAST IMPLEMENTATION OF KL COMPRESSION

For Karhunen–Loève compression the calculation of the basis matrices for general covariance functions can require matrix inversions, which are often of large order for image data. Even after the basis matrices have been determined, the calculation of the transform coefficients can still be computationally burdensome. For example, if the representation in (20b) is used, the calculation of each transform coefficient will take N^2 multiplications yielding a total of N^4 multiplications for all the N^2 coefficients.

One can avoid the calculation of the basis matrices, if the autocorrelation function of the image is of the form $E[f(m, n)f(p, q)] = \rho_1^{|m-p|}\rho_2^{|n-q|}$, which is the same as $e^{-\alpha|m-p|}e^{-\beta|n-q|}$, where ρ_1, ρ_2, α, and β are constants, the former two being less than unity. Since this autocorrelation function is separable, from the discussion in Section 4.2.4, it follows that the basis matrix $\varphi^{(u,\,v)}(m,\,n)$ may be expressed in the separable form $\varphi^{(u)}(m) \cdot \varphi^{(v)}(n)$, where $\varphi^{(u)}(m)$ is the eigenvector of the matrix $R(m, p)$ given by

$$R(m, p) = \rho^{|m-p|}, \qquad m, p = 0, 1, 2, \ldots, N - 1 \tag{35}$$

where we have assumed for convenience that $\rho = \rho_1 = \rho_2$. The eigenvectors and the eigenvalues of this matrix can be theoretically derived [29] and are given by

$$\varphi^{(u)}(m) = \sqrt{\frac{2}{N + \gamma_u}}\, \sin\left[\omega_u\left(m - \frac{N - 1}{2}\right) + \frac{u + 1}{2}\,\pi\right],$$
$$m = 0, 1, \ldots, N - 1 \tag{36}$$

for $u = 0, 1, \ldots, N - 1$, where the eigenvalues γ_u are given by

$$\gamma_u = \frac{1 - \rho^2}{1 - 2\rho \cos \omega_u + \rho^2} \tag{37}$$

In both (36) and (37), the ω_u's are the N roots of the transcendental equation

$$\tan N\omega = \frac{(1 - \rho^2) \sin \omega}{\cos \omega - 2\rho + \rho^2 \cos \omega} \tag{38}$$

Note that although this transcendental equation has an infinite number of roots, those that differ by multiples of 2π will lead to identical eigenvalues and eigenvectors. It may easily be shown (by sketching $\tan N\omega$, $\sin \omega$, and $\cos \omega$ curves) that in the interval $0 \leqslant \omega < 2\pi$ the transcendental equation has $2N$ roots. However, if $\omega = \theta$ is a root, then so is $2\pi - \theta$, and they both lead to the same eigenvalues and eigenvectors. Therefore, only the N roots in the interval $0 \leqslant \omega < \pi$ lead to N linearly independent eigenvectors and their corresponding eigenvalues.

Using (36), one can write for the Karhunen–Loève basis matrices

$$\varphi^{(u,\,v)}(m,\,n) = \frac{2}{\sqrt{(N + \gamma_u)(N + \gamma_v)}} \sin\left[\omega_u\left(m - \frac{N-1}{2}\right) + \frac{u+1}{2}\,\pi\right]$$

$$\times \sin\left[\omega_v\left(n - \frac{N-1}{2}\right) + \frac{v+1}{2}\,\pi\right],$$

$$m,\,n = 0,\,1,\,\ldots,\,N-1, \qquad (39)$$

for $u,\,v = 0,\,1,\,\ldots,\,N-1$. Using (20b), one may now calculate the transform coefficients.

When the autocorrelation function is of the form $\rho_1^{|m-p|}\rho_2^{|n-q|}$, the above approach is direct and perfectly valid, however, using (20b), it would still take N^4 multiplications to compute all the transform coefficients. Jain [44] has shown that for the case of this autocorrelation function, the image boundary pixels, if they are known, may be used to modify the rest of the image in such a way as to possess a Karhunen–Loève transform that can be implemented using fast Fourier transform algorithms or the more recently developed fast sine transform algorithm.

Jain's fast implementation is derived from the interpolative representation for images. Before we discuss such a representation for images, we will first discuss the one-dimensional case to establish the fundamental notions involved.

5.2.1 Interpolative Data Representation

First a brief statement about the notation. In this and the next subsection our images will be $(N + 2) \times (N + 2)$ matrices as opposed to $N \times N$. Similarly, when we are discussing only the one-dimensional case, our data vector will be $N + 2$ elements long, as opposed to N. This will make the indexing somewhat easier when we show how the boundary elements are used to modify the rest of the data for generating the fast implementations of the Karhunen–Loève compression.

The one-dimensional case

It is well known [68, Chap. 11] that if the autocorrelation matrix $R(m,\,n)$ of a zero-mean data vector $\mathbf{f}(0),\,\mathbf{f}(1),\,\ldots,\,\mathbf{f}(N+1)$, is given by

$$R_f(m,\,n) = E\{\mathbf{f}(m)\mathbf{f}(n)\} = \rho^{|m-n|} \qquad (40)$$

where ρ is a constant less than unity, then the data can be described by the following first-order difference equation:

$$\mathbf{f}(m) - \rho\mathbf{f}(m-1) = \xi(m), \qquad m = 1,\,2,\,\ldots,\,N+1 \qquad (41)$$

The residuals $\xi(m)$ form an uncorrelated zero-mean sequence possessing the following autocorrelation:

$$R_\xi(m, n) = E\{\xi(m)\xi(n)\} = (1 - \rho^2)\delta_{mn} \tag{42}$$

where δ_{mn} is the Kronecker delta (δ_{mn} equals unity when $m = n$, and equals zero otherwise). The autocorrelation in (40) implies that the variance of the random variables $\mathbf{f}(m)$, which is given by $R_f(m, m)$, is unity. The assumptions of zero mean and unity variance merely simplify the presentation of the theory, and are otherwise nonessential to the theory that follows. Note that the constant ρ describes the adjacent elements' correlation in the data. Also, note that in (41) $\xi(0)$ equals $\mathbf{f}(0)$.

When the data have the properties described above, it is often called a wide-sense Markov random process. A wide-sense Markov process is usually defined by the following statements: The linear mean-square estimate of $\mathbf{f}(m)$ in terms of all the preceding elements $\mathbf{f}(0), \mathbf{f}(1), \ldots, \mathbf{f}(m-1)$ is the same as the linear estimate of $\mathbf{f}(m)$ in terms of $\mathbf{f}(m-1)$ only. In other words, let $\hat{\mathbf{f}}(m)$ be the following linear mean-square estimate of $\mathbf{f}(m)$:

$$\hat{\mathbf{f}}(m) = \sum_{j=1}^{m} b_j \mathbf{f}(m - j) \tag{43}$$

If we use the orthogonality principle (see Chapter 2) to determine the coefficients (b_j's), the result is

$$\hat{\mathbf{f}}(m) = \rho \mathbf{f}(m - 1) \tag{44}$$

Therefore in (41) the residual $\xi(m)$ may be interpreted as the estimation error for the mth element.

Not so well known is the fact that the sequence $\mathbf{f}(0), \mathbf{f}(1), \ldots, \mathbf{f}(N+1)$ may also be given an interpolative (a two-sided difference equation) representation. In order to derive such a representation we will proceed as follows. Let $\hat{\mathbf{f}}(m)$ be the linear mean-square estimate of $\mathbf{f}(m)$ in terms of all the other elements in the finite data sequence. The estimate may be expressed as

$$\hat{\mathbf{f}}(m) = \sum_{j=1}^{N-m+1} a_j \mathbf{f}(m + j) + \sum_{k=1}^{m} b_k \mathbf{f}(m - k) \tag{45}$$

The orthogonality principle presented in Chapter 2 says that in order to minimize the estimation error the coefficients (a_j's and b_k's) must satisfy the following orthogonality conditions:

$$E\{(\mathbf{f}(m) - \hat{\mathbf{f}}(m))\mathbf{f}(i)\} = 0 \qquad \text{for} \quad i = 0, 1, \ldots, m - 1$$
$$\text{and} \quad m + 1, m + 2, \ldots, N + 1 \tag{46}$$

Substituting (45) in (46), we get

$$\rho^{|m-i|} - \sum_{j=1}^{N-m+1} a_j \rho^{|m+j-i|} - \sum_{k=1}^{m} b_k \rho^{|m-k-i|} = 0 \qquad \text{for} \quad i = 0, 1, \ldots, m-1$$

$$\text{and} \quad m+1, m+2, \ldots, N+1 \qquad (47)$$

Let us first consider the set of orthogonality conditions for $i \leqslant m-1$. Equation (47) may now be written as

$$\rho^{m-i} - \sum_{j=1}^{N-m+1} a_j \rho^{m+j-i} - \sum_{k=1}^{m} b_k \rho^{|m-k-i|} = 0 \qquad (48)$$

If we replace the index i by $i+1$ (assuming, of course, that $i+1 \leqslant m-1$) we get

$$\rho^{m-i-1} - \sum_{j=1}^{N-m+1} a_j \rho^{m+j-i-1} - \sum_{k=1}^{m} b_k \rho^{|m-k-i-1|} \qquad (49)$$

Multiplying (49) by ρ and subtracting the result from (48),

$$\sum_{k=1}^{m} b_k [\rho^{|m-k-i|} - \rho\rho^{|m-k-i-1|}] = 0 \qquad (50)$$

Now let us consider a specific value for i, $i = 0$, in (50):

$$\sum_{k=1}^{m} b_k [\rho^{|m-k|} - \rho\rho^{|m-k-1|}] = 0$$

which when expressed in the form

$$\sum_{k=1}^{m-1} b_k [\rho^{m-k} - \rho\rho^{m-1-k}] + b_m [1 - \rho^2] = 0 \qquad (51)$$

gives us the result

$$b_m = 0 \qquad (52)$$

because the difference inside the first brackets in (51) is zero for all k from 1 through $m-1$.

By writing (50) for $i = 1$ and utilizing (52), one can easily show that $b_{m-1} = 0$. When this algebraic calculation is repeated for all the permissible values of i in (50), which are $i = 0, 1, 2, \ldots, m-2$, the following is established:

$$b_m = b_{m-1} = b_{m-2} = \cdots = b_2 = 0 \qquad (53)$$

By using the orthogonality conditions in (47) for $i \geqslant m+1$, one can similarly show that

$$a_2 = a_3 = a_4 = \cdots = a_{N-m+1} = 0 \qquad (54)$$

When (53) and (54) are substituted in (48), we get

$$a_1\rho + b_1\rho^{-1} = 1 \tag{55}$$

Similarly, when (53) and (54) are substituted in the equation that corresponds to (48) for the case $i \geqslant m + 1$, we get

$$a_1\rho^{-1} + b_1\rho = 1 \tag{56}$$

The solution of (55) and (56) is

$$a_1 = b_1 = \frac{\rho}{1 + \rho^2} \tag{57}$$

The solution in (53), (54), and (57) for the coefficients is valid only at the interior points of the data sequence, since the data elements at both ends only have neighbors on one side. For $\mathbf{f}(0)$, the linear estimation reduces to

$$\hat{\mathbf{f}}(0) = \sum_{j=1}^{N-1} a_j \mathbf{f}(i)$$

and for $\mathbf{f}(N + 1)$, it is

$$\hat{\mathbf{f}}(N + 1) = \sum_{k=1}^{N+1} b_k \mathbf{f}(N + 1 - k)$$

The application of the orthogonality principle as before results in the following solution:

$$a_2 = a_3 = \cdots = a_{N+1} = 0$$
$$b_2 = b_3 = \cdots = b_{N+1} = 0 \tag{58}$$
$$a_1 = b_1 = \rho$$

Equations (45)–(58) lead to the following two-sided difference equation representation for the data:

$$\mathbf{f}(m) = \frac{\rho}{1 + \rho^2} [\mathbf{f}(m - 1) + \mathbf{f}(m + 1)] + v(m), \quad 1 \leqslant m \leqslant N$$
$$\mathbf{f}(0) = \rho\mathbf{f}(1) + v(0) \tag{59}$$
$$\mathbf{f}(N + 1) = \rho\mathbf{f}(N) + v(N + 1)$$

where $v(i)$ is the estimation error at the ith data element. Note that a very important difference exists between the "residual" $v(i)$ here and the residuals in (41). While the $\xi(i)$ are uncorrelated, the $v(i)$ possess pairwise correlations:

$$
E[v(i)v(j)] = \begin{cases}
\dfrac{1 - \rho^2}{1 + \rho^2}, & i = j \\[3mm]
-\rho \dfrac{1 - \rho^2}{(1 + \rho^2)^2}, & |i - j| = 1 \\[3mm]
0, & \text{otherwise}
\end{cases}
\tag{60a}
$$

for i and j equal to $1, 2, \ldots, N$. The correlation properties of the end residuals are described by

$$
E[v^2(0)] = E[v^2(N + 1)] = (1 - \rho^2)
$$

$$
E[v(0)v(1)] = E[v(N)v(N + 1)] = -\rho \frac{1 - \rho^2}{1 + \rho^2}
$$

and

$$
E[v(0)v(i)] = E[v(j)v(N + 1)] = 0 \quad \text{for} \quad i > 1 \quad \text{and} \quad j < N \tag{60b}
$$

The correlation in (60a) and (60b) may be derived by substituting the expressions for $v(i)$ in terms of $f(i)$ [as given by 59)] and then using (40).

In discussing the fast implementation of the Karhunen–Loève transform, we will be primarily interested in the correlation properties of the partial sequence $\vec{v}^t = (v(1), v(2), \ldots, v(N))$, which excludes $v(0)$ and $v(N + 1)$ from the set of all residuals in (59). Let $[R_{v,p}]$ denote the correlation matrix of this partial sequence, i.e., $R_{v,p}(m, n) = E\{v(m)v(n)\}$ (the subscript p stands for partial). The matrix structure of $[R_{v,p}]$ obtained from (60a) is displayed below:

$$
[R_{v,p}] = E\{vv^t\} = \beta
\begin{bmatrix}
1 & -\alpha & & & & & \\
-\alpha & 1 & -\alpha & & & & \\
& -\alpha & 1 & -\alpha & & & \\
& & & \cdots & & & \\
& & & \cdots & & & \\
& & & \cdots & & & \\
& & & & -\alpha & 1 & -\alpha \\
& & & & & -\alpha & 1
\end{bmatrix}
\tag{61}
$$

where the constants α and β are given by

$$\alpha = \frac{\rho}{1 + \rho^2}, \qquad \beta = \frac{1 - \rho^2}{1 + \rho^2} \qquad (62)$$

Let $[Q]$ denote the following $N \times N$ symmetric tridiagonal Toeplitz matrix[§]

$$[Q] = \begin{bmatrix} 1 & -\alpha & & & & & \\ -\alpha & 1 & -\alpha & & & & \\ & -\alpha & 1 & -\alpha & & & \\ & & & \cdots & & & \\ & & & \cdots & & & \\ & & & \cdots & & & \\ & & & & -\alpha & 1 & -\alpha \\ & & & & & -\alpha & 1 \end{bmatrix} \qquad (63)$$

In terms of $[Q]$, $[R_{v,p}]$ is expressed as

$$[R_{v, p}] = \beta[Q] \qquad (64)$$

Before ending this subsection we would like to mention a few important properties of the matrix $[Q]$. Recall that an N-element vector $\vec{\varphi}_i$ is an eigenvector of the $N \times N$ matrix $[Q]$ provided it satisfies the relationship

$$[Q]\vec{\varphi}_i = \gamma_i \vec{\varphi}_i \qquad (65)$$

where γ_i is a scalar number, called the eigenvalue, associated with the eigenvector $\vec{\varphi}_i$. A nonsingular real symmetric $N \times N$ matrix has N distinct eigenvectors, hence the subscript i on $\vec{\varphi}$. The eigenvectors and their corresponding eigenvalues for the matrix $[Q]$ are given by

$$\varphi_i(m) = \sqrt{\frac{2}{N + 1}} \sin \frac{im\pi}{N + 1}, \qquad i = 1, 2, \ldots, N, \qquad m = 1, 2, \ldots, N \quad (66a)$$

where $\varphi_i(m)$ is the mth element of $\vec{\varphi}_i$, and

$$\gamma_i = 1 - 2\alpha \cos \frac{i\pi}{N + 1}, \qquad i = 1, 2, \ldots, N \qquad (66b)$$

To derive (66a) and (66b), $[Q]$ is first expressed as

$$[Q] = [I] - \alpha[P] \qquad (67)$$

[§] An $N \times N$ matrix $[R]$ is of Toeplitz form provided $R(m,n) = R(p,q)$ whenever $m - n = p - q$. In other words, all the elements on the principal diagonal are identical; and also, all elements on each diagonal line parallel to the principal diagonal are identical. The correlation matrix in (35) is also of Toeplitz form.

where $[I]$ is the identity matrix, and $[P]$ is given by

$$[P] = \begin{bmatrix} 0 & 1 & & & & & \\ 1 & 0 & 1 & & & & \\ & 1 & 0 & & & & \\ & & & \cdots & & & \\ & & & & \cdots & & \\ & & & & & \cdots & \\ & & & & & & 1 \\ & & & & & 1 & 0 \end{bmatrix} \begin{matrix} \\ \\ \\ N \\ \\ \\ \\ \end{matrix} \qquad (68)$$

Since every vector is an eigenvector of $[I]$, it should be clear from (67) that we only need to find the eigenvectors of $[P]$. Let $\vec{\varphi}_i'$ and γ_i' be the eigenvectors and their corresponding eigenvalues for $[P]$. Then from (67) we have

$$\vec{\varphi}_i = \vec{\varphi}_i'$$

and

$$\gamma_i = (1 - \alpha\gamma_i') \qquad (69)$$

Now consider for a moment an N-element vector $\vec{h}$ given by

$$h(m) = \sin\frac{km\pi}{N+1}, \qquad m = 1, 2, \ldots, N \qquad (70)$$

where k is any arbitrary nonzero positive integer. By substitution one may now show that

$$[P]\vec{h} = \begin{bmatrix} \sin\dfrac{k2\pi}{N+1} \\[2ex] \sin\dfrac{k\pi}{N+1} + \sin\dfrac{k3\pi}{N+1} \\[2ex] \sin\dfrac{k2\pi}{N+1} + \sin\dfrac{k4\pi}{N+1} \\[2ex] \vdots \\[2ex] \sin\dfrac{k(N-1)\pi}{N+1} \end{bmatrix} \qquad (71)$$

By using trigonometric identities such as

$$\sin A + \sin B = 2 \sin \frac{A + B}{2} \cos \frac{A - B}{2}$$

$$\sin 2A = 2 \sin A \cos A$$

and

$$\sin \frac{k(N - 1)\pi}{N + 1} = \sin \frac{k(N + 1)\pi}{N + 1} + \sin \frac{k(N - 1)\pi}{N + 1}$$

we can show that (71) reduces to

$$[P]\vec{h} = 2\left(\cos \frac{k\pi}{N + 1}\right)\vec{h} \tag{72}$$

which shows that $\vec{h}$ is an eigenvector of $[P]$, and that $2 \cos k\pi/(N + 1)$ is its eigenvalue. Clearly, if $\vec{h}$ is an eigenvector so is $c\vec{h}$ for any arbitrary constant c. The value of c is chosen as to make the length of $c\vec{h}$ equal to unity. The length of $\vec{h}$ is given by[§]

$$\|\vec{h}\| = \left[\sum_{m=1}^{N} \sin^2 \frac{mk\pi}{N + 1}\right]^{1/2} = \left[\frac{N}{2} - \frac{1}{2}\sum_{m=1}^{N} \cos \frac{2mk\pi}{N + 1}\right]^{1/2} = \sqrt{\frac{N + 1}{2}} \tag{73}$$

[§] Here we have used the fact that $\sum_{m=1}^{N} \cos 2mk\pi/(N + 1) = -1$. This may be shown as follows. Let

$$S = \sum_{m=1}^{N} \exp\left(j \frac{2mk\pi}{N + 1}\right) \tag{i}$$

Then

$$S \exp\left(j \frac{2k\pi}{N + 1}\right) = \sum_{m=1}^{N} \exp\left(j \frac{2(m + 1)k\pi}{N + 1}\right) \tag{ii}$$

Subtracting (ii) from (i), we get

$$S = \exp\left(j \frac{2k\pi}{N + 1}\right) \frac{\left[1 - \exp\left(j \frac{2Nk\pi}{N + 1}\right)\right]}{\left[1 - \exp\left(j \frac{2k\pi}{N + 1}\right)\right]} = \exp\left(j \frac{(N + 1)k\pi}{N + 1}\right) \frac{\sin \dfrac{Nk\pi}{N + 1}}{\sin \dfrac{k\pi}{N + 1}}$$

$$= (-1)^k \frac{\sin \dfrac{(N + 1 - 1)k\pi}{N + 1}}{\sin \dfrac{k\pi}{N + 1}} = (-1)^k \frac{(-1)(-1)^k \sin \dfrac{k\pi}{N + 1}}{\sin \dfrac{k\pi}{N + 1}}$$

$$= -1$$

Therefore, the constant c is given by $\sqrt{2/(N+1)}$. Since $c\vec{h}$ is orthonormal-ized, since the value of the integer k in the definition of $\vec{h}$ is arbitrary, and since for $k = 1, 2, \ldots, N$ we have N distinct versions of $\vec{h}$, the eigenvectors $\vec{\varphi}$ are given by

$$\varphi_i(m) = \sqrt{\frac{2}{N+1}} \sin \frac{im\pi}{N+1}, \qquad i = 1, 2, \ldots, N \tag{74}$$

where we have used (69), (70), and (73). From (72), the ith eigenvalue of $[P]$ is given by

$$\gamma_i' = 2 \cos \frac{i\pi}{N+1} \tag{75}$$

Substituting in (69), we get the eigenvalues of $[Q]$:

$$\gamma_i = 1 - 2 \cos \frac{i\pi}{N+1}, \qquad i = 1, 2, \ldots, N \tag{76}$$

This completes our discussion on the interpolative representation of the first-order Markov data.

The two-dimensional case

Consider an $(N+2) \times (N+2)$ discrete zero-mean random field $\mathbf{f}(m, n)$. In the two-dimensional interpolative representation, which would corre-spond to (45) for the one-dimensional case, we now construct a linear mean-square estimate of $\mathbf{f}(m, n)$ in terms of all the other pixels:

$$\hat{\mathbf{f}}(m, n) = \sum_{k, l \neq (0, 0)} \sum a(k, l)\mathbf{f}(m - k, n - l) \tag{77}$$

In this estimate, the ordered pairs (k, l) take all the integer values, except $(0, 0)$, such that both $m - k$ and $n - l$ are in the range 0 through $N + 1$.

We will now assume that the autocorrelation of the random field is given by

$$R_f(m, k; n, l) = E\{\mathbf{f}(m, n)\mathbf{f}(k, l)\} = \rho^{|m-k|}\rho^{|n-l|} \tag{78}$$

This form of the autocorrelation implies that the variance of the random variable $\mathbf{f}(m, n)$ is unity. The form in (78) also implies that the image has identical correlation properties along both the horizontal and the vertical directions. The assumptions of zero mean, unity variance, and the correla-tion properties being identical in both the horizontal and the vertical direc-tions are not essential to the theory that follows. However, they do make the presentation easier. Also, note that the constant ρ, which is less than unity, is the correlation between pixels that are adjacent to each other horizontally or vertically.

In order to minimize the mean-square error between $\mathbf{f}(m, n)$ and $\hat{\mathbf{f}}(m, n)$, the coefficients $a(k, l)$ must satisfy the following orthogonality conditions:

$$E\left[\mathbf{f}(m, n) - \sum_{(k, l) \neq (0, 0)} \sum a(k, l)\mathbf{f}(m - k, n - l)\right]\mathbf{f}(i, j) = 0$$

$$i \text{ and } j = 0, 1, 2, \ldots, N + 1, \qquad (i, j) \neq (m, n) \qquad (79)$$

Substituting (78) in (79), we get

$$\rho^{|m - i|}\rho^{|n - j|} - \sum_{(k, l) \neq (0, 0)} \sum a(k, l)\rho^{|m - k - i|}\rho^{|n - l - j|} = 0$$

$$i \text{ and } j = 0, 1, 2, \ldots, N + 1, \qquad (i, j) \neq (m, n) \qquad (80)$$

Proceeding in a manner analogous to the one-dimensional case, one can show that when (m, n) is one of the interior pixels (i.e., it is not on the boundary), the coefficients $a(k, l)$ are given by

$$a(1, 0) = a(0, 1) = a(-1, 0) = a(0, -1) = \alpha$$

and

$$a(1, 1) = a(1, -1) = a(-1, 1) = a(-1, -1) = \alpha^2 \qquad (81)$$

where $\alpha = \rho(1 + \rho^2)$. Therefore, an interior pixel may be represented by the following:

$$\mathbf{f}(m, n) = \alpha[\mathbf{f}(m + 1, n) + \mathbf{f}(m, n + 1) + \mathbf{f}(m, n - 1) + \mathbf{f}(m - 1, n)]$$
$$+ \alpha^2[\mathbf{f}(m + 1, n + 1) + \mathbf{f}(m + 1, n - 1) + \mathbf{f}(m - 1, n + 1)$$
$$+ \mathbf{f}(m - 1, n - 1)] + \mathbf{v}(m, n) \qquad (82)$$

where we have used (77) and (81), and where $\mathbf{v}(m, n)$ is the estimation error $\mathbf{f}(m, n) - \hat{\mathbf{f}}(m, n)$. As was first shown by Jain [44], Eq. (82) can be rearranged and expressed as follows:

$$\mathbf{f}(m, n) - \alpha[\mathbf{f}(m + 1, n) + \mathbf{f}(m - 1, n)] = \mathbf{g}(m, n) \qquad (83a)$$

where the array $\mathbf{g}(m, n)$ satisfies

$$\mathbf{g}(m, n) - \alpha[\mathbf{g}(m, n + 1) + \mathbf{g}(m, n - 1)] = \mathbf{v}(m, n) \qquad (83b)$$

If (83a) is substituted in (83b), the resulting difference equation is identical to (82).

Using (82) and (78), one can write for the correlation properties of $\mathbf{v}(m, n)$

$$E[\mathbf{v}(m, n)\mathbf{v}(k, l)] \begin{cases} = \beta^2, & m = k \text{ and } n = l \\ = -\alpha\beta^2, & |m - k| = 1 \text{ and } n = l \quad \text{or} \\ & m = k \text{ and } |n - l| = 1 \\ = \alpha^2\beta^2, & |m - k| = 1 \text{ and } |n - l| = 1 \\ = 0, & \text{otherwise} \end{cases}$$

where the indices m, n, k and l range from 1 through N and where

$$\beta = \frac{1 - \rho^2}{1 + \rho^2} \tag{84}$$

Since the indices m, n, k, and l do not take either of the values 0 or $N + 1$, this correlation function does not apply to boundary pixels. Using Kronecker deltas the above correlation function can be very compactly expressed as

$$E[\mathbf{v}(m, n)\mathbf{v}(k, l)] = \beta^2(\delta_{mk} - \alpha\delta_{m+1,k} - \alpha\delta_{m-1,k})$$
$$\times (\delta_{nl} - \alpha\delta_{n+1,l} - \alpha\delta_{n-1,l}) \tag{85}$$

The rest of this subsection will be devoted to developing a matrix representation for the correlation function in (84). For this purpose, we note that for the residuals in the same row, m is equal to k. Therefore from (85)

$$E[\mathbf{v}(m, n)\mathbf{v}(m, l)] = \beta^2(\delta_{nl} - \alpha\delta_{n+1,l} - \alpha\delta_{n-1,l}) \tag{86a}$$

For the residuals that are in the same column the index n equals l, and we get from (85)

$$E[\mathbf{v}(m, n)\mathbf{v}(k, n)] = \beta^2(\delta_{mk} - \alpha\delta_{m+1,k} - \alpha\delta_{m-1,k}) \tag{86b}$$

Since (86a) is independent of the row index m, it states that the correlation function of all the rows (excluding the topmost and the bottommost) is the same, and it also gives us the nature of this function. Equation (86b) gives us similar information about the columns, except that now the leftmost and the rightmost columns are excluded. Therefore, the correlation function in (85) is *separable* in its row and column dependences.

Defining two discrete functions as

$$R_{\text{row}}(n, l) = \beta(\delta_{nl} - \alpha\delta_{n+1,l} - \alpha\delta_{n-1,l}) \tag{87a}$$

and

$$R_{\text{col}}(m, k) = \beta(\delta_{mk} - \alpha\delta_{m+1,k} - \alpha\delta_{m-1,k}) \tag{87b}$$

the row and column correlation functions in (86a) and (86b) may be expressed as

$$E[\mathbf{v}(m, n)\mathbf{v}(m, l)] = R_{\text{col}}(m, m)R_{\text{row}}(n, l)$$

and

$$E[\mathbf{v}(m, n)\mathbf{v}(k, n)] = R_{\text{row}}(n, n)R_{\text{col}}(m, k) \tag{88}$$

The general correlation function of (85) can be expressed as

$$E[\mathbf{v}(m, n)\mathbf{v}(k, l)] = R_{\text{col}}(m, k)R_{\text{row}}(n, l) \tag{89}$$

Comparing (87) with (83), we can write

$$[R_{row}] = [R_{col}] = \beta[Q] \tag{90}$$

where $[R_{row}]$ and $[R_{col}]$ are $N \times N$ matrices consisting of the elements $R_{row}(n, l)$ and $R_{col}(m, k)$, respectively.

Suppose now we construct a one-dimensional $N^2 \times 1$ vector $\vec{v}$ by column scanning the matrix $v(m, n)$. The first N elements of $\vec{v}$ constitute the first column of $v(m, n)$, the next N elements the second column, and so on:

$$\vec{v} = \begin{bmatrix} v(1, 1) \\ v(2, 1) \\ \vdots \\ v(N, 1) \\ v(1, 2) \\ v(2, 2) \\ \vdots \\ v(N, 2) \\ v(1, 3) \\ \vdots \\ v(N, N) \end{bmatrix} \tag{91}$$

It may now be shown by direct substitution of (89) in the following expectation that

$$E[\vec{v}\vec{v}^t] = [R_{col}] \otimes [R_{row}] \tag{92}$$

where $\otimes$ denotes the left direct product of the matrices as defined in Section 2.2.2. Using (90), we get

$$E[\vec{v}\vec{v}^t] = \beta^2[Q] \otimes [Q] \tag{93}$$

5.2.2 The Fast Implementation

We will first discuss the one-dimensional case to bring forth the essence of the ideas involved, and then present the extension to the two-dimensional case, The implentations presented are originally due to Jain [43].

The one-dimensional case

The fast implementation assumes that the end elements of the data sequence $f(0), f(1), \ldots, f(N + 1)$, are known. That is,

$$f(0) = c \quad \text{and} \quad f(N + 1) = d \tag{94}$$

where c and d are known constants. The rest of the data elements are described by the first difference equation in (59), which may also be expressed as follows:

$$[Q]\vec{f} = \vec{v} + \vec{b} \tag{95}$$

where the N-element-long $\vec{f}$ and $\vec{v}$ are the data and residual vectors *without the end elements*:

$$\vec{f} = \begin{bmatrix} f(1) \\ f(2) \\ \vdots \\ f(N) \end{bmatrix}, \qquad \vec{v} = \begin{bmatrix} v(1) \\ v(2) \\ \vdots \\ v(N) \end{bmatrix} \tag{96}$$

The vector $\vec{b}$ in (95) is needed to account for the contribution of $f(0)$ and $f(N + 1)$ to $f(1)$ and $f(N)$, respectively. The elements of $\vec{b}$ are given by

$$\begin{aligned} b(1) &= \alpha c \\ b(N) &= \alpha d \\ b(k) &= 0, \qquad 2 \leqslant k \leqslant N - 1 \end{aligned} \tag{97}$$

We will now define a new N element vector $\vec{s}$ as follows:

$$\vec{s} = [Q]^{-1}\vec{v} \tag{98}$$

From (95), $\vec{s}$ may be obtained from a given data string by

$$\vec{s} = \vec{f} - [Q]^{-1}\vec{b} \tag{99}$$

By using (98), the mean value of $\vec{s}$ is given by

$$E\{\vec{s}\} = [Q]^{-1}E\{\vec{v}\} = 0 \tag{100}$$

since it follows trivially from (59) that the $E\{\vec{v}\}$ is zero when $f(0)$, $f(1)$, ..., $f(N + 1)$ belong to a zero-mean random process. The correlation matrix of $\vec{s}$ is given by

$$[R_s] = E\{\vec{s}\vec{s}^t\} = [Q]^{-1}E\{\vec{v}\vec{v}^t\}[Q]^{-1^t} \tag{101}$$

where again we have used (98). Using (61), we can write

$$[R_s] = \beta[Q]^{-1} \tag{102}$$

where we have used the fact that the correlation matrix is always symmetric. The eigenvector $\vec{\varphi}_i$ and the eigenvalues γ_i of $[Q]$ are given by (66a) and (66b), respectively. It is easy to show[§] that $\vec{\varphi}_i$ for $i = 1, 2, \ldots, N$ are also the eigenvectors of $[Q]^{-1}$; however, the eigenvalues are now given by $1/\gamma_i$.

Let $\vec{S}$ be the Karhunen–Loève transform of $\vec{s}$. The ith element of $\vec{S}$ can be obtained by using (66a):

$$\mathbf{S}(i) = \vec{s} \cdot \vec{\varphi}_i = \sqrt{\frac{2}{N+1}} \sum_{m=1}^{N} \mathbf{s}(m) \sin \frac{im\pi}{N+1}, \qquad i = 1, 2, \ldots, N \quad (103)$$

For computer implementation we will augment $\vec{s}$ as follows: $s(0) = 0$ and $s(m) = 0$ for $m \geqslant N + 1$. Equation (103) may now be written as

$$\mathbf{S}(i) = 2 \frac{1}{\sqrt{2N+2}} \sum_{m=1}^{2N+1} \mathbf{s}(m) \sin\left(im \frac{2\pi}{2N+2}\right)$$

$$= 2 \operatorname{Im}\{\text{DFT of } \mathbf{s}(m)\} \qquad \text{for} \quad i = 1, 2, \ldots, N \quad (104)$$

where Im stands for imaginary. Of course, the DFT (discrete Fourier transform) in (104) can be implemented by using an FFT algorithm. It is also possible [95] to write a fast algorithm for directly performing the sine transformation of (103).

The preceding discussion implies the following fast procedure for Karhunen–Loève compression:

Step 1. From the end points $\mathbf{f}(0) = c$ and $\mathbf{f}(N+1) = d$ compute $[Q]^{-1}\vec{b}$. We will now show that this computation may be efficiently performed by using an FFT algorithm. Let $[\Phi]$ be the $N \times N$ matrix whose ith column is the N-element vector $\vec{\varphi}_i$ given by (66a). We just showed that $\vec{\varphi}_i$ and $1/\gamma_i$ are the eigenvectors and eigenvalues, respectively, of $[Q]^{-1}$. In terms of $[\Phi]$, the second equation of the footnote below may be written as

$$[Q]^{-1}[\Phi] = [\Phi] \operatorname{diag}[1/\gamma_1, 1/\gamma_2, \ldots, 1/\gamma_N] \quad (105)$$

where $\operatorname{diag}[1/\gamma_1, \ldots, 1/\gamma_N]$ is an $N \times N$ diagonal matrix. Therefore,

$$[Q]^{-1} = [\Phi] \operatorname{diag}[1/\gamma_1, \ldots, 1/\gamma_N][\Phi]^{\mathrm{t}} \quad (106)$$

The term $[Q]^{-1}\vec{b}$ may now be expressed as

$$[Q]^{-1}\vec{b} = [\Phi] \operatorname{diag}[1/\gamma_1, \ldots, 1/\gamma_N][\Phi]^{\mathrm{t}}\vec{b} \quad (107)$$

[§] The eigenvectors $\vec{\varphi}_i$ and eigenvalues γ_i satisfy the following relationship:

$$[Q]\vec{\varphi}_i = \gamma_i\vec{\varphi}_i, \qquad i = 1, 2, \ldots, N$$

Multiplying both sides from the left by $[Q]^{-1}$, we get

$$[Q]^{-1}\vec{\varphi}_i = \frac{1}{\gamma_i}\vec{\varphi}_i, \qquad i = 1, 2, \ldots, N$$

which shows that the $\vec{\varphi}_i$ are also the eigenvectors of $[Q]^{-1}$, but the eigenvalues are now $1/\gamma_i$.

Using (66a), we find that the ith element of the vector $[\Phi]^t \vec{b}$ is given by

$$\sum_{m=1}^{N} b(m) \sqrt{\frac{2}{N+1}} \sin \frac{im\pi}{N+1} = \sqrt{\frac{2}{N+1}} \alpha[c - (-1)^i d] \sin \frac{i\pi}{N+1} \qquad (108)$$

where we have used (97). Substituting this and (66a) in (107), we get for the nth element of $[Q]^{-1} \vec{b}$

$$\frac{2\alpha}{N+1} \sum_{i=1}^{N} \left\{ \frac{1}{\gamma_i} [c - (-1)^i d] \sin \frac{i\pi}{N+1} \right\} \sin \frac{ni\pi}{N+1}, \qquad n = 1, 2, \ldots, N$$

$$(109)$$

As was the case with (103), the operation here may again be expressed as a DFT summation by padding with zeroes the data vector whose elements are given by the expression inside the curly braces in (109). The DFT summation may then be computed by using an FFT algorithm.

Step 2. The N element vector $[Q]^{-1} \vec{b}$ computed by the preceding step is subtracted from the vector $\vec{f}$ to yield $\vec{s}$ as required by (99). Note that $\vec{f}$ is N elements long and consists of $(f(1), f(2), \ldots, f(N))$, which is the original data without the end elements $f(0)$ and $f(N + 1)$. The Karhunen–Loève transform of $\vec{s}$ is calculated by using (104).

Step 3. The rest of the steps are the same as in direct Karhunen–Loève compression as discussed in Section 5.1.3, except that now we have to retain the information about the end elements $f(0)$ and $f(N + 1)$, since they would be needed in reconstructing the original data from the coefficients $S(m)$ by using the reverse of the two steps outlined above. These two data elements may also be compressed separately by using a 2×2 Karhunen–Loève transform, or they may be transmitted directly. In any event, most of the compression will generally be achieved by first ranking the $S(i)$ by the sizes of their corresponding eigenvalues and discarding those that correspond to the smallest eigenvalues.

The two-dimensional case

We will now present the fast implementation for $(N + 2) \times (N + 2)$ images whose autocorrelation function is given by (78).

Note that (83a) may be interpreted as the $[Q]$ matrix operating on the nth column of the interior $N \times N$ image $f(m, n)$, $m, n = 1, 2, \ldots, N$, the result being the nth column of the $N \times N$ matrix of the $g(m, n)$. Equation (83a) may be more compactly expressed as

$$[Q][f] = [g] + \alpha[B_1] \qquad (110)$$

where $[\mathbf{f}]$ is the matrix of the interior pixels, i.e., $\mathbf{f}(m, n)$ with $m, n = 1$, $2, \ldots, N$, and, similarly, $[\mathbf{g}]$ is the $N \times N$ matrix of $\mathbf{g}(m, n)$. The second term on the right-hand side in (110) is required because from (83a) the topmost and the bottommost rows of $[\mathbf{g}]$ contain the top and the bottom boundary elements of $\mathbf{f}(m, n)$, i.e., those $\mathbf{f}(m, n)$ for which m or n is either 0 or $N + 1$. Since these boundary elements are not supplied by $[\mathbf{f}]$, we need $\alpha[B_1]$, where the matrix $[B_1]$ is given by

$$[B_1] = \begin{bmatrix} \mathbf{f}(0, 1) & \mathbf{f}(0, 2) & \cdots & \mathbf{f}(0, N) \\ \vdots & \vdots & & \vdots \\ \mathbf{f}(N + 1, 1) & \mathbf{f}(N + 1, 2) & \cdots & \mathbf{f}(N + 1, N) \end{bmatrix} \updownarrow N$$

$$\xleftarrow{\hspace{3cm} N \hspace{3cm}}\rightarrow$$

Similarly, (83b) can be expressed more compactly as

$$[\mathbf{g}][Q] = [\mathbf{v}] + \alpha[Q][B_2] + \alpha^2[B_3] \tag{111}$$

where

$$[B_2] = \begin{bmatrix} \mathbf{f}(1, 0) & 0 & 0 & 0 & 0 & \mathbf{f}(1, N + 1) \\ \mathbf{f}(2, 0) & 0 & 0 & 0 & 0 & \mathbf{f}(2, N + 1) \\ \mathbf{f}(3, 0) & 0 & 0 & 0 & 0 & \mathbf{f}(3, N + 1) \\ \vdots & & & & & \vdots \\ \mathbf{f}(N, 0) & 0 & 0 & 0 & 0 & \mathbf{f}(N, N + 1) \end{bmatrix} \updownarrow N \tag{112}$$

$$\xleftarrow{\hspace{3cm} N \hspace{3cm}}\rightarrow$$

and

$$[B_3] = \begin{bmatrix} \mathbf{f}(0, 0) & 0 & 0 & 0 & 0 & \mathbf{f}(0, N + 1) \\ 0 & 0 & & 0 & 0 & 0 \\ 0 & & & & & \\ \vdots & & & & & \vdots \\ 0 & 0 & & 0 & 0 & \\ 0 & 0 & & 0 & 0 & 0 \\ \mathbf{f}(N + 1, 0) & 0 & & 0 & 0 & \mathbf{f}(N + 1, N + 1) \end{bmatrix} \tag{113}$$

From (110) and (111), we get

$$[Q][\mathbf{f}][Q] = [\mathbf{v}] + [B] \tag{114}$$

where

$$[B] = \alpha[B_1][Q] + \alpha[Q][B_2] + \alpha^2[B_3] \tag{115}$$

Note that the $N \times N$ matrix $[B]$ depends only on those pixels that are on the border of the image.

We will define a new $N \times N$ matrix $[\mathbf{h}]$ as follows:

$$[\mathbf{h}] = [Q]^{-1}[\mathbf{v}][Q]^{-1} \tag{116}$$

From (114) this matrix may be obtained from the image data by using the following relationships:

$$[\mathbf{h}] = [\mathbf{f}] - [Q]^{-1}[B][Q]^{-1} \tag{117}$$

We will show that the Karhunen–Loève transform of $[\mathbf{h}]$ possesses a fast implementation. In order to do so we first note that

$$E\{[\mathbf{h}]\} = 0 \tag{118}$$

where we have used (116), and the fact that if the image belongs to a zero-mean random field, (82) implies that $E\{[\mathbf{v}]\} = 0$. We now construct a vector $\vec{\mathbf{h}}$ by column scanning the $N \times N$ matrix $[\mathbf{h}]$ [as was done in constructing the vector $\vec{\mathbf{v}}$ from $[\mathbf{v}]$ in (91)]. In terms of the vectors $\vec{\mathbf{h}}$ and $\vec{\mathbf{v}}$, (116) may be expressed as (see Chapter 2)

$$\vec{\mathbf{h}} = ([Q]^{-1} \otimes [Q]^{-1})\vec{\mathbf{v}} \tag{119}$$

where $\otimes$ denotes the left direct product of two $N \times N$ matrices. The correlation matrix for $\vec{\mathbf{h}}$ is given by

$$[R_{\mathbf{h}}] = E\{\vec{\mathbf{h}}\vec{\mathbf{h}}^t\} = E\{([Q]^{-1} \otimes [Q]^{-1})\vec{\mathbf{v}}\vec{\mathbf{v}}^t([Q]^{-1} \otimes [Q]^{-1})^t\} \tag{120}$$

where we have used (119). Substituting (93) in (120) and using the fact that

$$[Q]^{-1} \otimes [Q]^{-1} = ([Q] \otimes [Q])^{-1}$$

we get

$$[R_{\mathbf{h}}] = \beta^2[Q]^{-1} \otimes [Q]^{-1} \tag{121}$$

where we have also used the fact that since $[Q]$ is a symmetric matrix, so are $[Q]^{-1}$ and $([Q]^{-1} \otimes [Q]^{-1})$.

In (65) we defined $\vec{\varphi}_i$, $i = 1, 2, \ldots, N$, as the eigenvectors of $[Q]$. In the footnote on p. 146 we showed that the $\vec{\varphi}_i$ are also the eigenvectors of $[Q]^{-1}$. The latter relationship was compactly expressed in Eq. (105), which we repeat here for convenience:

$$[Q]^{-1}[\Phi] = [\Phi][\Gamma] \tag{122}$$

where $[\Gamma]$ is an $N \times N$ diagonal matrix whose elements are given by $1/\gamma_1$, $1/\gamma_2, \ldots, 1/\gamma_N$. Therefore, from (122)

$$[Q]^{-1} = [\Phi][\Gamma][\Phi] \tag{123}$$

where we have used the fact that $[\Phi]$ is a symmetric orthogonal matrix which implies $[\Phi]^{-1} = [\Phi]$.

Equation (123) is used to obtain the following result:

$$[Q]^{-1} \otimes [Q]^{-1} = ([\Phi][\Gamma][\Phi]) \otimes ([\Phi][\Gamma][\Phi])$$
$$= ([\Phi] \otimes [\Phi])(([\Gamma][\Phi] \otimes [\Gamma][\Phi])) \tag{124}$$

where we have used the identity

$$([A][B]) \otimes ([C][D]) = ([A] \otimes [C])([B] \otimes [D])$$

Using the same identity again for the second left direct product in (124), we get

$$[Q]^{-1} \otimes [Q]^{-1} = ([\Phi] \otimes [\Phi])([\Gamma] \otimes [\Gamma])([\Phi] \otimes [\Phi]) \tag{125}$$

which shows that the matrix of the eigenvectors of $[Q]^{-1} \otimes [Q]^{-1}$ is given by $[\Phi] \otimes [\Phi]$, since $[\Gamma] \otimes [\Gamma]$ is an $N^2 \times N^2$ diagonal matrix.

Let $\vec{H}$ be the Karhunen–Loève transform of the modified data vector $\vec{h}$. If $\vec{\Psi}_m$ is the mth eigenvector of $[Q]^{-1} \otimes [Q]^{-1}$ (i.e., the N^2 elements of $\vec{\Psi}_m$ constitute the mth column of $[\Phi] \otimes [\Phi]$), then the mth element of $\vec{H}$ is given by

$$H(m) = \vec{h} \cdot \vec{\Psi}_m = \vec{\Psi}_m^t \vec{h} \tag{126}$$

or, equivalently,

$$\vec{H} = ([\Phi] \otimes [\Phi])\vec{h} \tag{127}$$

where again we have used the symmetry of $[\Phi] \otimes [\Phi]$. If $[H]$ is a matrix whose column scanned vector is given by $\vec{H}$, then (127) implies the following relationship between $[H]$ and $[h]$ (see Chapter 2):

$$[H] = [\Phi][h][\Phi] \tag{128}$$

In expanded notation this may be written as

$$H(u, v) = \frac{2}{N+1} \sum_{m=1}^{N} \sum_{n=1}^{N} h(m, n) \sin \frac{\pi u m}{N+1} \sin \frac{\pi v n}{N+1} \tag{129}$$

which, as in the one-dimensional case, can easily be implemented using an FFT algorithm.

5.3   FOURIER, HADAMARD, AND COSINE TRANSFORM COMPRESSION

The Fourier transform of a discrete picture is defined in Section 2.2.1. If it is rewritten in forms (20a) and (20b), it is easy to show that the basis matrices $[\varphi^{(u, v)}]$ for the Fourier transformation are given by

$$\varphi^{(u, v)}(m, n) = \frac{1}{N} \exp\left[\frac{j2\pi}{N}(mu + nv)\right] \tag{130}$$

where the factor $1/N$ is needed for the purpose of the normalization condition in (18) and where m and n designate the mth column and nth row, respectively, of the basis matrix $[\varphi^{(u, v)}]$.

The Fourier transformation is suboptimum in the sense that the coefficients $F(u, v)$ are not uncorrelated. It can be shown, however, that it is asymptotically equivalent to the Karhunen–Loève transform [29]. As N in (130) approaches infinity, the Fourier coefficients $F(u, v)$ tend to become uncorrelated. This indicates that if the picture size is greater than the distances over which significant correlations between picture elements exist, the performance of the Fourier transform in a picture compression scheme should not be very different from that of the Karhunen–Loève transform.

For an example of Fourier compression, we will again consider the discrete picture in Fig. 1. As in the preceding case this picture was divided into 256 16×16 subpictures for convenience in numerical implementation. Upon Fourier transformation, each subpicture was transformed into 256 Fourier coefficients. The variance of each coefficient $F(u, v)$ was estimated by averaging $|F(u, v)|^2$ over all the subpictures. The 256 complex Fourier coefficients in each subpicture were ranked on the basis of their variances (Fig. 5) and only the highest ranking 128 were retained in each subpicture. Since the picture is real, of the original 256 complex coefficients, only 128 are distinct. It follows that of the 128 retained complex coefficients only 64 complex coefficients should be distinct. Of course, these 64 complex coefficients amount to representing a subpicture by 128 real coefficients.

When each subpicture is reconstructed from its 128 Fourier coefficients by using (20a) and (130), the result is as shown in Fig. 7a. If only 64 coefficients

Fig. 7 (a) Reconstructed picture obtained by retaining the first 128 of the 256 Fourier coefficients for each of the subpictures of Fig. 1. (b) Same as (a), but using only 64 coefficients. (From [93].)

are retained for each subpicture, the reconstructed picture looks like Fig. 7b. Note that the reconstructions in Figs. 7a and 7b are similar to those in Figs. 4a and 4b, respectively, for the case of Karhunen–Loève compression. The next step is to normalize each of the retained coefficients by its variance (for the same reasons as before) and quantize the normalized coefficients. When a uniform quantizer is used and the output levels of the quantizer are represented by equal length binary code words, the results are very similar to those shown in Figs. 6a and 6b.

From a computational standpoint, an even more efficient transform is the Hadamard transform described in Section 2.2.2. The Hadamard matrix is composed of $+1$'s and -1's only. Therefore, computation of a Hadamard transform does not require multiplications. For an $N \times N$ picture, the Hadamard transform coefficients can be calculated with a number of additions or subtractions proportional to $N^2 \log_2 N$. Of course, like the Fourier coefficients, the Hadamard transform coefficients are not completely uncorrelated, but they are more uncorrelated than the picture elements.

When the Hadamard transformation given by Eqs. (52) of Chapter 2 is expressed in the form described by Eqs. (20a) and (20b), the basis matrices are given by (see Pratt *et al.* [71])

$$\varphi^{(u,v)}(m,n) = (1/N)(-1)^{b(u,v,m,n)} \tag{131}$$

for N a power of 2, where $1/N$ is needed for the normalization condition in (18). Here

$$b(u,v,m,n) = \sum_{h=0}^{\log_2 N - 1} [b_h(u)b_h(v) + b_h(m)b_h(n)] \tag{132}$$

where $b_h(\cdot)$ is the hth bit in the binary representation of $(\cdot)$. This result is valid only when the Hadamard matrices in Eqs. (61) of Chapter 2 are symmetric, as they are if Eqs. (55) and (56) there are employed in constructing them. When (131) is substituted in (20b), and if we use (17), we obtain

$$F(u,v) = (1/N) \sum_{m=0}^{N-1} \sum_{n=0}^{N-1} f(m,n) \cdot (-1)^{b(u,v,m,n)} \tag{133}$$

In Fig. 8 we have shown 256 Hadamard basis matrices, $[\varphi^{(u,v)}]$, each 16×16, for $u = 0, 1, \ldots, 15$ and $v = 0, 1, \ldots, 15$.

As an example of Hadamard compression, each 16×16 subpicture of Fig. 1 was transformed into 256 Hadamard coefficients $F(u,v)$. The variance of each of these coefficients was estimated by averaging each $|F(u,v)|^2$ over all the subpictures. The coefficients in each subpicture were then ranked according to their variances (Fig. 5) and only the first 128 retained. When we reconstruct each subpicture from the retained 128 coefficients by using (20a) and (131), the result is as shown in Fig. 9a. As in the Karhunen–Loève and Fourier

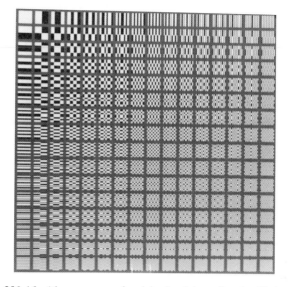

Fig. 8 The 256 16×16 sequency ordered basis pictures for the Hadamard transformation. (From [93].)

Fig. 9 (a) Reconstructed picture obtained by retaining the first 128 of the 256 Hadamard coefficients for each of the subpictures of Fig. 1. (b) Same as (a), but using only 64 coefficients. (From [93].)

cases, deleting half the coefficients in each subpicture does not result in any visible degradation of the picture. If, however, we retain only the first 64 coefficients for each subpicture, the reconstruction looks like Fig. 9b and a certain loss in spatial resolution is apparent. If in each of the two cases the retained Hadamard coefficients are normalized, quantized, and equal length binary code words are assigned to the output of the quantizer, then for the same quantization strategy the results are very similar to those in the cases of Karhunen–Loève and Fourier compression.

Discrete cosine transform compression

We will now describe the image transform that has attracted the most attention in recent years. The discrete cosine transform of an N-element data vector is defined by

$$F(u) = \frac{2c(u)}{N} \sum_{m=0}^{N-1} f(m) \cos \frac{(2m+1)u\pi}{2N}, \qquad u = 0, 1, \ldots, N-1 \quad (134)$$

where

$$c(u) = \frac{1}{\sqrt{2}}, \qquad \text{for} \quad u = 0$$

$$= 1, \qquad \text{for} \quad u = 1, \ldots, N-1 \quad (135)$$

The inverse transform is given by

$$f(m) = \sum_{u=0}^{N-1} c(u)F(u) \cos \frac{(2m+1)u\pi}{2N}, \qquad m = 0, 1, \ldots, N-1 \quad (136)$$

The two-dimensional discrete cosine transform is given by

$$F(u, v) = \frac{4c(u, v)}{N^2} \sum_{m=0}^{N-1} \sum_{n=0}^{N-1} f(m, n) \cos \frac{(2m+1)u\pi}{2N} \cos \frac{(2n+1)v\pi}{2N},$$

$$u, v = 0, 1, \ldots, N-1 \quad (137)$$

where

$$c(u, v) = \tfrac{1}{2} \qquad \text{for} \quad u = v = 0$$

$$= 1 \qquad \text{for} \quad u, v = 1, 2, \ldots, N-1 \quad (138)$$

The inverse of (137) is

$$f(m, n) = \sum_{u=0}^{N-1} \sum_{v=0}^{N-1} c(u, v)F(u, v) \cos \frac{(2m+1)u\pi}{2N} \cos \frac{(2n+1)v\pi}{2N},$$

$$m, n = 0, 1, \ldots, N-1 \quad (139)$$

The discrete cosine transform may be implemented by using a double sized fast Fourier algorithm. To show this, consider the one-dimensional transform in (134). We first zero-pad the data to make it $2N$ elements long:

$$f_p(m) = f(m), \qquad m = 0, 1, \ldots, N - 1$$
$$= 0, \qquad m = N, N + 1, \ldots, 2N - 1 \qquad (140)$$

We can rewrite (134) as

$$F(u) = \frac{2c(u)}{N} \operatorname{Re}\left\{\exp\left(j\frac{\pi u}{2N}\right) \sum_{m=0}^{2N-1} f_p(m) \exp\left(jum\frac{2\pi}{2N}\right)\right\},$$
$$u = 0, 1, \ldots, N - 1 \qquad (141)$$

The summation is clearly a $2N$-element discrete Fourier transform, which may be implented with an FFT algorithm.

As was shown recently by Chen et al. [10], it is also possible to directly write a fast algorithm for the cosine transform. This algorithm, which requires that $N = 2^m$ for some $m \geq 2$, needs only real operations on a set of N points. This algorithm is faster than the FFT based approach.

For most practical images, of all the different transform techniques, the discrete cosine transform comes closest to the Karhunen–Loève transform in its energy compaction properties. This is illustrated in Fig. 10, where for the image in Fig. 10a, Fig. 10b shows the integrated mean-square error as a function of the number of retained coefficients for different types of transforms. Figure 10c shows the mean-square error as a function of block size. For Fig. 10c the image in Fig. 10a was divided into $M \times M$ blocks, each block was transformed and then only the 25% of the coefficients with the largest variances were retained. Then the pixel by pixel error was computed between the original block and the reconstruction from the retained coefficients.

This superior energy compaction property is in keeping with the observation, first made by Ahmed et al. [2], that for ρ (defined in Section 5.2) in the neighborhood of 0.9 for a first-order Markov process, the basis vectors of the Karhunen–Loève transformation closely resemble those of the discrete cosine transform.

In addition to its better energy compaction, the discrete cosine transform possesses another interesting advantage over the discrete Fourier transform. For ease in implementation an $N \times N$ image is usually segmented into $M \times M$ blocks for image coding with $M \ll N$. Consider only one of these blocks. When the discrete Fourier transform of the block is taken, there is an implied assumption (induced by the underlying theory) that this block replicates over the entire two-dimensional plane containing the image. In

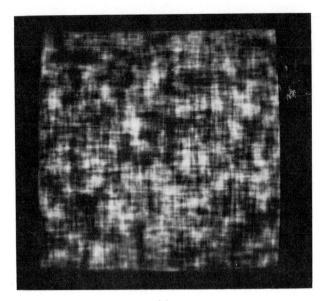

(a)

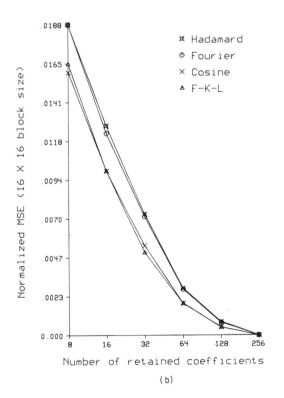

(b)

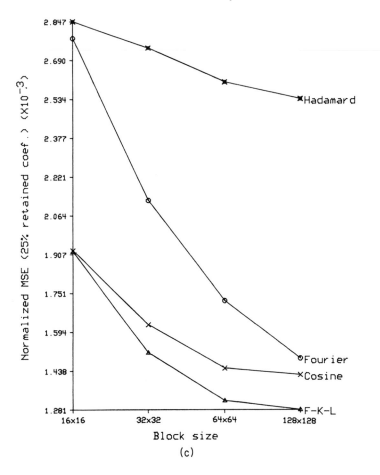

Fig. 10   For the image in (a), shown in (b) is the integrated-mean-square error as a function of the number of retained coefficients. The synthesized Markov process image in (a) is a matrix of 256 × 256 pixels. This matrix was divided into 256 16 × 16 submatrices. Each 16 × 16 sub-matrix was transformed yielding 256 coefficients. The 256 coefficients were ranked according to their variance and only a certain number of the highest variance coefficients retained. Integrated-mean-square error was found by integrating the squared difference between the original 16 × 16 blocks and the 16 × 16 blocks reconstituted from the retained coefficients. (c) Shown here is the integrated-mean-square error as a function of block size. For each block size, only 25% of the coefficients with the largest variances were retained.

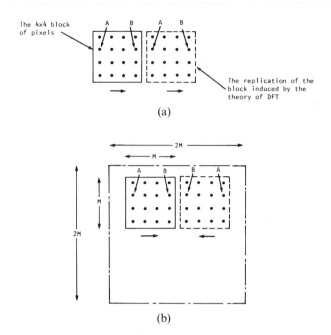

Fig. 11 (a) Suppose we take the DFT of the 4 × 4 block of pixels shown within the solid box; the theory of this transformation will cause this block to be perceived as belonging to a periodically repeating pattern. The dashed block is one such repetition. Therefore, pixel *B* will be perceived to be followed by pixel *A*. (b) The periodicities imposed by the structure of the discrete cosine transform are different. If the original block is 4 × 4 (as shown by the solid box), then what is repeated is an 8 × 8 pattern. Within this larger 8 × 8 block, the four 4 × 4 blocks are mirror images of each other at the adjoining boundaries. Therefore, pixel *B* will be perceived to be followed by the same pixel.

Fig. 11a we have shown a 4 × 4 block of pixels. In Fourier transformation the pixel *B* on the right border will be perceived by the algorithm to be *followed* by the pixel *A*, which is actually on the left border. If the gray levels at *A* and *B* are very different, in any reconstruction of the block from only a partial number of Fourier coefficients, the Gibbs phenomenon will result in both *A* and *B* taking on erroneous values. Depending upon the number of Fourier coefficients retained, the reconstructed values at *A* and *B* will both generally be somewhere half-way between the original values there. This phenomenon, referred to as the *blocking artifact*, tends to make the block boundaries very visible in Fourier compression, especially when the compression ratio is large. For attempts at reducing this artifact the reader is referred to [3].

The discrete cosine transform, on the other hand, does not suffer from the above-mentioned artifact. While the Fourier theory implies the replication of the $M \times M$ blocks, the discrete cosine transform theory imposes this replication on "hypothetical" $2M \times 2M$ blocks that are related to the original $M \times M$ blocks through mirror symmetries. The consequence of this mirror symmetry is illustrated in Fig. 11b where we have shown that pixel B is followed by itself, eliminating the discontinuity. This causes a considerable reduction in the blocking artifact.[§]

Before we terminate this section we would like to make a few comments about the choice of block size in transform compression. Transform coding is easier to implement if small sized blocks are used. However, as emphasized at the outset in this chapter, it is important that the transform coefficients be as decorrelated as possible. Although an appropriate transform procedure will decorrelate the coefficients within the same block, there are always some correlations between the coefficients among the neighboring blocks. This is caused by the fact that for any two continuous blocks, the pixels in each block near the common boundary will be correlated with one another. Generally, the larger the blocks the smaller the correlations between interblock coefficients. Another important consideration that has an important bearing on block size is adaptivity, a subject not discussed here due to space limitations. In adaptive transform coding, one first classifies each block into three or four classes depending upon their activity level, a measure derived from the "non-dc" transform coefficients. Each class has its own procedure for coefficient quantization and the allocation of bits to the quantized levels. In an adaptive scheme one has to remember the identity of each block, which for four classes would require two bits per block. These are called overhead bits. The smaller the block size, the larger the contribution of the overhead bits on a per pixel basis.

An example of discrete cosine transform image compression is shown in Fig. 12. The 256×256 image of Fig. 12a was divided into 16×16 blocks. Only the 128 transform coefficients with the largest variances were retained for each block. (The variance of each coefficient was estimated by taking the ensemble average over all the blocks.) The retained coefficients were normalized by their standard deviations and quantized by a 16-level uniform quantizer, yielding an overall compressed data rate of 2 bits/pixel. The image reconstructed from the compressed data is shown in Fig. 12b.

[§] The mirror symmetry imposed by the discrete cosine transform is also responsible for its superior energy compaction properties. The imposition of the mirror symmetry on the data can easily be shown by using (136) to prove that $f(-m + 1) = f(m)$.

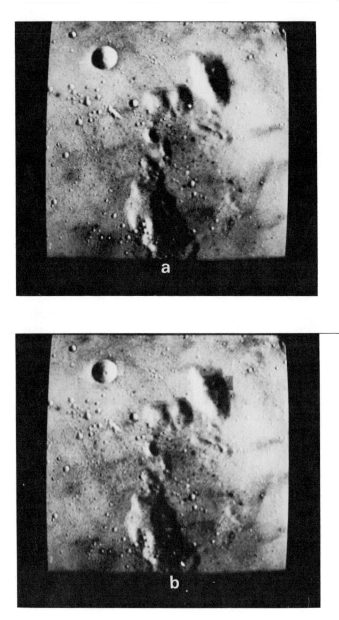

Fig. 12 An example of image compression using discrete cosine transforms is shown here. The 256 × 2568 bits/pixel image in (a) was divided into 16 × 16 blocks. Only the 128 transform coefficients with the largest variances were retained in each block. The quantizer used was a 16-level uniform quantizer, yielding a compressed data rate of 2 bits/pixel. The reconstructed image at this data rate is shown in (b).

5.4 BIT ALLOCATION IN TRANSFORM COMPRESSION

In our discussion so far, each transform coefficient was normalized by its standard deviation, then the same quantizer was used for all the normalized coefficients, and finally equal length binary code words were used for representing the quantizer output. With this approach to bit allocation, 8-bit/pixel image data can usually be compressed to 2 bits/pixel without excessive visual degradation of the image.

The above approach to bit assignment, although easy to implement, is not optimal for two reasons, and higher compression ratios can be obtained by using the alternative strategies described in this section. First, this method results in the same mean-square quantization error for all the normalized coefficients; however, when at the receiver these quantized normalized coefficients are multiplied back by their standard deviations, the mean-square error of each coefficient becomes proportional to its variance. In other words, the coefficients with larger variances, which are relatively more important in the final reconstruction, suffer from larger quantization errors.

The second objection to using the same quantizer for all the coefficients is based on the informational value of different coefficients. Since each transform coefficient is a linear combination of pixels in a block, by the central limit theorem as the number of these pixels becomes large, the coefficients should tend to become Gaussian distributed.[§] [This conclusion does not apply to the dc coefficient, whose first-order statistical properties are better modeled by a Rayleigh density function. This is due to the fact that images being nonnegative always have nonnegative dc coefficients.] Rate-distortion theory (see Section 5.9) says that if a Gaussian random variable has a variance equal to σ^2, and if mean-square-error distortion equal to D is acceptable in our "perception" of the random variable, then we need to represent the random variables with only $\frac{1}{2}\log_2(\sigma^2/D)$ bits. [To be more precise, the random variable *cannot* be represented by less than $\frac{1}{2}\log_2(\sigma^2/D)$ bits if it is to be reproduced with mean-square-error distortion not exceeding D.] Therefore, one can say that for any given level of distortion in our perception of a Gaussian random variable, its informational content is directly proportional to $\log_2 \sigma^2$. This might lead us to the intuitive conclusion that since the number of bits assigned to a coefficient is indicative of its contribution to the overall informational representation of the image, this number should be made proportional to the logarithm of the coefficient variance.

[§] The conditions under which this is true are discussed in [21, 22, 70].

We will show that the above conclusion is borne out if the bit assignments are made by minimizing the total mean-square quantization error (or its average) for all the coefficients. Let $\mathbf{f}(m, n)$, $m, n = 0, 1, 2, \ldots, M - 1$ be the pixels in a $M \times M$ block of the image, and let $\mathbf{F}(u, v)$, $u, v = 0, 1, 2, \ldots, M - 1$ be its unitary transform, such as the ones we have discussed so far. Also, let $\mathbf{F}_q(u, v)$ represent the quantized values of the coefficients and $\mathbf{f}_q(m, n)$ the block reconstructed from the quantized coefficients. The average mean-square error between the original block and its reconstruction is given by

$$D = \frac{1}{M^2} E \sum_{m=0}^{M-1} \sum_{n=0}^{M-1} [\mathbf{f}(m, n) - \mathbf{f}_q(m, n)]^2 \tag{142}$$

By the distance preserving property of unitary transforms, this expression may be written as[§]

$$D = \frac{1}{M^2} E \sum_{u=0}^{M-1} \sum_{v=0}^{M-1} [\mathbf{F}(u, v) - \mathbf{F}_q(u, v))]^2 \tag{143}$$

where we have assumed that as in the case of Karhunen–Loève or discrete cosine transformations, the coefficients $\mathbf{F}(u, v)$ are real numbers.

Let $\sigma^2(u, v)$ be the variance of the (u, v)th transform coefficient. Then clearly $\mathbf{F}(u, v)/\sigma(u, v)$ is a random variable with unit variance. Now suppose the quantizer for the (u, v)th coefficient was designed on the basis of a unit variance input. Let $d_{u, v}(b_{u, v})$ be the mean-square quantization error of this quantizer when $b_{u, v}$ bits are used to represent its output levels (we will assume equal length binary code words, therefore $b_{u, v}$ bits translate into $2^{b_{u, v}}$ quantization levels). The mean-square quantization error for $\mathbf{F}(u, v)$ itself will be equal to $\sigma^2(u, v)d_{u, v}(b_{u, v})$. [Note that in practice it is not necessary to divide $\mathbf{F}(u, v)$ by $\sigma(u, v)$ prior to quantization. Multiplication of the output levels of the unit–input variance quantizer by $\sigma(u, v)$ would yield directly the quantizer for $\mathbf{F}(u, v)$. In other words, $\sigma(u, v)$ is simply a scale factor.] Since the expected value of the right-hand side in (143) is by definition the mean-square quantization error for that coefficient, we therefore have

$$E[\mathbf{F}(u, v) - \mathbf{F}_q(u, v)]^2 = \sigma^2(u, v)d_{u, v}(b_{u, v}) \tag{144}$$

[§]To illustrate this distance preserving property consider the one-dimensional case. Let $\vec{\mathbf{f}}$ be a real data vector, $\vec{\mathbf{F}}$ its transform, and $[P]$ a unitary transformation matrix. Then $\vec{\mathbf{F}} = [P]\vec{\mathbf{f}}$. Since $[P]$ is unitary, we have $[P]^{-1} = [P]^{*t}$. We can now write

$$\sum_{m=0}^{M-1} [\mathbf{f}(m) - \mathbf{f}_q(m)]^2 = (\vec{\mathbf{f}} - \vec{\mathbf{f}}_q)^t(\vec{\mathbf{f}} - \vec{\mathbf{f}}_q) = (\vec{\mathbf{f}} - \vec{\mathbf{f}}_q)^{*t}(\vec{\mathbf{f}} - \vec{\mathbf{f}}_q)$$

$$= (\vec{\mathbf{F}} - \vec{\mathbf{F}}_q)^{*t}[P]^{-1*t}[P]^{-1}(\vec{\mathbf{F}} - \vec{\mathbf{F}}_q) = (\vec{\mathbf{F}} - \vec{\mathbf{F}}_q)^{*t}(\vec{\mathbf{F}} - \vec{\mathbf{F}}_q)$$

$$= \sum_{u=0}^{M-1} |\mathbf{F}(u) - \mathbf{F}_q(u)|^2$$

The average of the total quantization error for the whole block may now be written as

$$D = \frac{1}{M} \sum_{u=0}^{M-1} \sum_{v=0}^{M-1} \sigma^2(u, v) d_{u,v}(b_{u,v}) \qquad (145)$$

The bit assignments, $b_{u,v}$, must be made in such a way as to minimize D subject to the following constraint:

$$\sum_{u=0}^{M-1} \sum_{v=0}^{M-1} b_{u,v} = m^2 b_{\text{aver}} \qquad (146)$$

where b_{aver} is the average number of bits per pixel we want to use for the block. In nonadaptive compression, b_{aver} will be the same for all the blocks. On the other hand, in adaptive compression we may form three or four categories of blocks on the basis of their activity levels, as measured by their non-dc transform coefficients, and assign a different b_{aver} to each category. Going back to the case of nonadaptive compression, we should mention that the final compressed data rate will be slightly greater than b_{aver} bits/ pixel, because one also has to transmit *one* $M \times M$ bit assignment matrix to the receiver, which adds to the total number of bits required to represent the image. The bit assignment matrix consists of the elements $b_{u,v}$, $u, v = 0, 1, 2, \ldots, M - 1$. One may also have to transmit one $M \times M$ matrix of coefficient variances in order to help the receiver determine what numerical values to associate with different quantization levels for each coefficient.

In almost all the approaches that have been developed for the minimization of (145) subject to the constraint in (146), empirical expressions are used for the distortion $d_{u,v}(b_{u,v})$. For example, in their work on block quantization, Huang and Schultheiss [42], using the Max optimum nonuniform quantizer of Section 4.3.1 and equal length binary code words to represent the output levels, have assumed

$$d_{u,v}(b_{u,v}) = K \exp(-2b_{u,v} \ln 2) \qquad (147)$$

This expression was empirically obtained by examining the numerical result [in Ref. 11 of Chap. 4] for the dependence of the mean-square quantization error on the number of output levels. In (147) the value of K, which is a constant independent of $b_{u,v}$, does not have to be known for computing the bit assignments, since it gets lumped with the Lagrange multiplier in the solution to the constrained minimization problem. Huang and Schultheiss [42] have obtained the following result:

$$b_{u,v} = b_{\text{aver}} + \tfrac{1}{2} \log_2 \sigma_{u,v}^2 - \frac{1}{2M^2} \sum_{u=0}^{M-1} \sum_{v=0}^{M-1} \log_2 \sigma_{u,v}^2 \qquad (148)$$

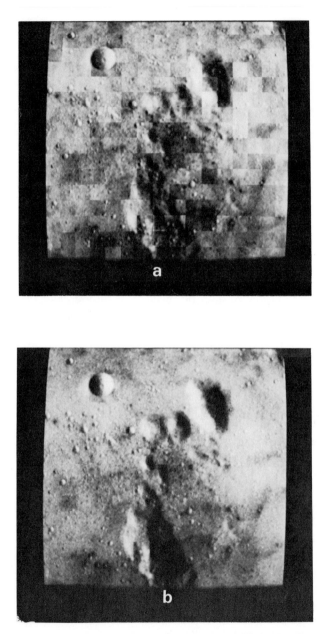

Fig. 13   (a) Same as Fig. 12b except that now only a 4-level uniform quantizer is used on the retained coefficients leading to a compressed data rate of 1 bit/pixel. (b) Shown here is the result of block quantization for the compressed data rate of 1 bit/pixel. Equation (150) was used to calculate the number of bits used for each coefficient. Improvements over (a) are obvious.

For the case of optimum uniform quantizers and again equal length binary code words to represent the output levels, Wintz and Kurtenbach [94] have assumed

$$d_{u,v}(b_{u,v}) = \exp(-\tfrac{1}{2}b_{u,v} \ln 10) \tag{149}$$

an expression obtained empirically as before. Substituting (149) in (145), and carrying out the constrained minimization, they have obtained the following result:

$$b_{u,v} = b_{\text{aver}} + \frac{2}{\ln 10} \left[\ln \sigma_{u,v}^2 - \frac{1}{M^2} \sum_{u=0}^{M-1} \sum_{v=0}^{M-1} \ln \sigma_{u,v}^2 \right] \tag{150}$$

Both (148) and (150) may result in noninteger values for $b_{u,v}$, in which case they are rounded to the nearest integer. After such rounding off, it is possible that the condition in (146) may not be satisfied. In that event, the bit assignments are modified more or less arbitrarily until the condition is satisfied. Before ending this section we would like to mention that the constrained minimization in (145) and (146) can also be carried out by using integer programming algorithms originally due to Fox [19]. Some image compression results using bit assignments calculated in this manner can be found in [45].

In Fig. 13a we have shown the compressed image at 1 bit/pixel when all the transform coefficients are normalized by their standard deviations, and then the same 2-bit quantizer used on all the normalized coefficients. For each 16×16 block only the 128 coefficients with the largest variances were retained. Figure 13b shows the result obtained at the same data rate of 1 bit/pixel when the bit assignments are calculated by using (150). It is clear that the latter technique makes much more efficient use of bits and results in an image of significantly better subjective quality.

5.5 PREDICTIVE COMPRESSION

As pointed out earlier, the first step in picture compression is to represent a picture by uncorrelated data. We proved in Section 5.1 that of all the linear orthogonal transformations, the Karhunen–Loève transformation achieves this result. If we do not limit ourselves to linear orthogonal transformations, there are other techniques that achieve the same result. One such technique that has the advantage of easy implementation is predictive compression, which we will now discuss.

Let a digitized picture be represented by the matrix $[\mathbf{f}]$. Let $\mathbf{f}(m, n)$ be the element of this matrix that is in the mth column and the nth row (Fig. 14).

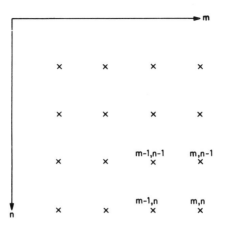

Fig. 14   The points $(m-1, n)$, $(m-1, n-1)$, and $(m, n-1)$ are used to form the estimate at the point (m, n). Note the direction of increasing m and n.

Let $R(m, n, p, q)$ be the autocorrelation function of the real random field to which the picture belongs, i.e.,

$$R(m, n, p, q) = E\{\mathbf{f}(m, n)\mathbf{f}(p, q)\} \tag{151}$$

Because the picture elements $\mathbf{f}(m, n)$ are correlated, it is possible to derive an estimate or prediction $\hat{\mathbf{f}}(m, n)$ for a given element $\mathbf{f}(m, n)$ in terms of the rest of the picture elements. The difference $\mathbf{f}(m, n) - \hat{\mathbf{f}}(m, n)$ is the estimation error $\mathbf{e}(m, n)$ for that picture element and will be called the *differential signal*. Since the prediction $\hat{\mathbf{f}}(m, n)$ is directly dependent on the correlations between $\mathbf{f}(m, n)$ and the rest of the picture, it is reasonable that the sequence of random variables formed by the differential signal $\mathbf{e}(m, n)$ should be less correlated than the elements in the original picture.

It is known that the best estimate $\hat{\mathbf{f}}(m, n)$ (best in the sense that it minimizes the mean-square estimation error) is in general a nonlinear function of the picture elements that are used to form the estimate [67]. Often, for reasons of mathematical tractability, the additional constraint of linearity is imposed on the form of the estimate. In such cases the estimate obtained is the best *linear* estimate.

We will further assume that as the picture is scanned row by row from top to bottom, only the three nearest neighboring elements that have already been scanned are used to form the linear estimate for a picture element $\mathbf{f}(m, n)$ (Fig. 14). In other words, $\hat{\mathbf{f}}(m, n)$ is of the following form:

$$\hat{\mathbf{f}}(m, n) = a_1 \mathbf{f}(m-1, n) + a_2 \mathbf{f}(m-1, n-1) + a_3 \mathbf{f}(m, n-1) \tag{152}$$

where the unknowns a_1, a_2, and a_3 are such that the mean-square estimation error

$$E\{[\mathbf{f}(m, n) - \hat{\mathbf{f}}(m, n)]^2\} \tag{153}$$

is minimized. Substituting (152) in (153), differentiating the resulting expression with respect to a_1, a_2, and a_3 separately, equating each derivative to zero, and using (151), we obtain the following three equations:

$$a_1 R(m-1, n, m-1, n) + a_2 R(m-1, n-1, m-1, n)$$
$$+ a_3 R(m, n-1, m-1, n) = R(m, n, m-1, n)$$

$$a_1 R(m-1, n, m-1, n-1) + a_2 R(m-1, n-1, m-1, n-1) \tag{154}$$
$$+ a_3 R(m, n-1, m-1, n-1) = R(m, n, m-1, n-1)$$

$$a_1 R(m-1, n, m, n-1) + a_2 R(m-1, n-1, m, n-1)$$
$$+ a_3 R(m, n-1, m, n-1) = R(m, n, m, n-1)$$

which can be solved for a_1, a_2, and a_3. If we further assume that the random field $\mathbf{f}$ is homogeneous, has zero mean, and has autocorrelation function given by Eq. (47) of Chapter 4 (with $\eta = 0$), these equations reduce to

$$a_1 R(0, 0) + a_2 R(0, 1) + a_3 R(1, 1) = R(1, 0)$$
$$a_1 R(0, 1) + a_2 R(0, 0) + a_3 R(1, 0) = R(1, 1) \tag{155}$$
$$a_1 R(1, 1) + a_2 R(1, 0) + a_3 R(0, 0) = R(0, 1)$$

where

$$R(\alpha, \beta) = R(0, 0) \exp(-c_1 |\alpha| - c_2 |\beta|) \tag{156}$$

Note that for this autocorrelation function $R(1, 1) = R(1, 0) R(0, 1) / R(0, 0)$. Using this relationship and solving (155) for a_1, a_2, and a_3, we obtain

$$a_1 = R(1, 0)/R(0, 0), \qquad a_2 = -R(1, 1)/R(0, 0), \qquad a_3 = R(0, 1)/R(0, 0) \tag{157}$$

The differential signal $\mathbf{e}(m, n)$ at each picture element is given by

$$\mathbf{e}(m, n) = \mathbf{f}(m, n) - \hat{\mathbf{f}}(m, n)$$
$$= \mathbf{f}(m, n) - [a_1 \mathbf{f}(m-1, n) + a_2 \mathbf{f}(m-1, n-1) + a_3 \mathbf{f}(m, n-1)] \tag{158}$$

It is clear that if the random field $\mathbf{f}$ has zero mean, then

$$E\{\mathbf{e}(m, n)\} = 0 \tag{159}$$

Therefore, the variance of the differential signal at every point is given by

$$E\{\mathbf{e}^2(m, n)\} = E\{[\mathbf{f}(m, n) - (a_1 \mathbf{f}(m-1, n) + a_2 \mathbf{f}(m-1, n-1)$$
$$+ a_3 \mathbf{f}(m, n-1))]^2\} \tag{160}$$

By expanding the right-hand side of (160) and making use of (155), it can be shown that

$$E\{e^2(m,n)\} = R(0,0) - [a_1 R(1,0) + a_2 R(1,1) + a_3 R(0,1)] \quad (161)$$

Since **f** is homogeneous, the variance of each element is the same, namely $R(0,0)$. Moreover (156) implies that $R(1,0)$, $R(0,1)$, and $R(1,1)$ cannot be greater than $R(0,0)$. By substituting the values of a_1, a_2, and a_3 from (157) in (161), it is thus seen that the variance of the differential data $e(m,n)$ is less than the variance of the picture elements $f(m,n)$.

By substituting the values of a_1, a_2, and a_3 from (157) in (158) it can be shown that for zero-mean random fields with autocorrelation function given by (156), the following result holds:

$$E\{e(m,n)e(p,q)\} = 0, \qquad m \neq p \quad \text{or} \quad n \neq q \quad (162)$$

i.e., the differential data $e(m,n)$ are uncorrelated.

It is clear that if the gray levels in a picture are known on the topmost row and the leftmost column (Fig. 14), the entire picture can be reconstructed from the differential data $e(m,n)$.

Figure 15a shows a system that generates the differential data $e(m,n)$ from the digitized picture. The picture is scanned row by row and the picture elements introduced serially into the adder at top left in the figure. Since in practice one would like to have the differential data quantized, in Fig. 15b we have shown the system with a quantizer in the feedback loop. The output of the system is now equal to e_{mn} + quantization error. In Fig. 15c we have shown the decoder which reconverts the differential data back into the picture. Of course, the reconstructed picture is now corrupted by the effects of the noise introduced by the quantizer in Fig. 15b. At the end of this section we briefly discuss some aspects of the distortions caused by the quantizer.

It should be evident in a qualitative sense that the differential data for a picture represent a "smaller amount of information" than the gray levels in the original digitized picture. This is because pictures generally contain areas of almost constant or slowly varying gray levels, and in these regions $e(m,n)$ is very small. When these differences are small enough to be undetectable by the user of the pictures, they may be approximated by zero. In fact that is one of the results achieved by the quantizer which we will discuss later in the section.

If the autocorrelation function cannot be modeled by (156), then one may need a larger number of picture elements for estimation in order for the differential data to be uncorrelated completely. In practice, however, the number of picture elements required for considerable decorrelation is usually very small. As an example consider the picture in Fig. 16a. The picture was sampled on a 208×250 matrix. Suppose the picture is scanned line by line

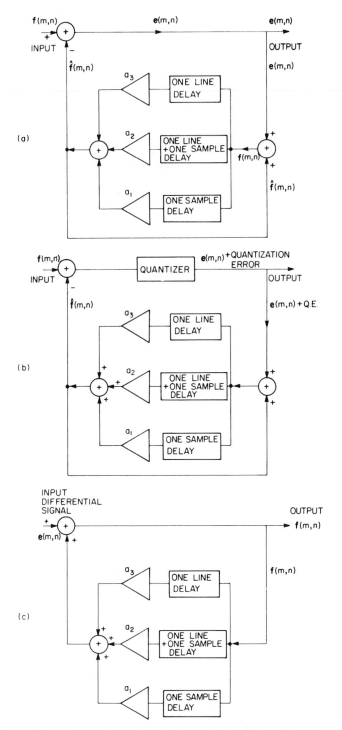

Fig. 15 (a) Block diagram of a system that generates the differential signal $e(m, n)$. (b) System in Fig. 15a with a quantizer in the feedback loop. (c) Block diagram of a system that reconstructs the picture from the differential data.

(a)

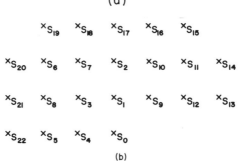

(b)

Fig. 16 (a) Picture used for obtaining the results shown in Figs. 17–19. (From Habibi [31].) (b) As the picture is scanned row by row, S_0 represents the current sample, S_1 the sample one line above, and so on as shown in the figure.

starting at the top. At a given instant in time, let S_0 represent the current sample, S_1 the sample one line above, and so on as shown in Fig. 16b. Let $R_s(i, j)$ denote the expectation $E\{S_i S_j\}$. We have used the subscript s in $R_s(i, j)$ to avoid confusion with the autocorrelation $R(\alpha, \beta)$ of a homogeneous random field.

A linear estimate $\hat{S}_0$ of the current sample S_0 in terms of the samples $S_1, S_2, \ldots, S_n$ has the form

$$\hat{S}_0 = a_1 S_1 + a_2 S_2 + \cdots + a_n S_n \tag{163}$$

TABLE 2

Correlations between S_0 and S_i for the picture in Fig. 16a [31]

Correlations	Interlaced	Noninterlaced
$R_s(0, 1)$	0.9771	0.9866
$R_s(0, 2)$	0.9534	0.9771
$R_s(0, 3)$	0.9479	0.9570
$R_s(0, 4)$	0.9648	0.9648
$R_s(0, 5)$	0.9026	0.9026
$R_s(0, 6)$	0.8679	0.8901
$R_s(0, 7)$	0.9197	0.9479
$R_s(0, 8)$	0.8901	0.8981
$R_s(0, 9)$	0.9483	0.9573
$R_s(0, 10)$	0.9193	0.9483
$R_s(0, 11)$	0.7569	0.8927
$R_s(0, 12)$	0.7120	0.8997
$R_s(0, 13)$	0.8416	0.8463
$R_s(0, 14)$	0.8254	0.8416
$R_s(0, 15)$	0.8421	0.8828
$R_s(0, 16)$	0.8866	0.9338
$R_s(0, 17)$	0.9079	0.9591
$R_s(0, 18)$	0.8878	0.9337
$R_s(0, 19)$	0.8406	0.8800
$R_s(0, 20)$	0.8186	0.8371
$R_s(0, 21)$	0.8371	0.8439
$R_s(0, 22)$	0.8478	0.8478

where $a_1, a_2, ..., a_n$ are such that the mean-square estimation error $E\{(S_0 - \hat{S}_0)^2\}$ is minimized. By using steps identical to those employed in arriving at (154) it can be shown that the mean-square estimation error is minimized provided $a_1, a_2, ..., a_n$ are a solution of the following n simultaneous equations:

$$R_s(0, i) = \sum_{j=1}^{n} a_j R_s(i, j), \qquad i = 1, 2, ..., n \qquad (164)$$

Table 2 shows the values of $R_s(0, i)$ as obtained by spatially averaging the products $S_0 S_i$ over the entire picture, after the digitized picture in Fig. 16a is normalized by first subtracting the mean from each picture element and then dividing by the standard deviation, which makes $R_s(0, 0) = 1$. If ergodicity conditions were satisfied, the $R_s(0, i)$, as calculated by this spatial averaging, would equal the ensemble averages.

If the random field is homogeneous, the other $R_s(i, j)$'s can be simply determined from the $R_s(0, i)$'s. For example, from the definition of homogeneous random fields (Section 2.4.3) and Fig. 16b, it is clear that $R_s(1, 7)$ must be

TABLE 3

A List of Numerical Values of the Coefficients a_i Used for Each Predictor [31]

Predictor:	1st order horizontal	1st order vertical	2nd order	3rd order	4th order	6th order	12th order	18th order	22nd order
a_1	0.965	0.977	0.617	0.826	0.897	0.855	0.664	0.648	0.630
a_2			0.379		-0.059	-0.057	-0.073	-0.063	-0.081
a_3				-0.594	-0.574	-0.534	-0.460	-0.446	-0.429
a_4				0.746	0.729	0.827	0.834	0.831	0.865
a_5						-0.108	-0.135	-0.131	-0.261
a_6						0.006	0.002	0.008	0.006
a_7							0.021	0.037	0.035
a_8							-0.001	-0.011	0.139
a_9							0.117	0.142	0.002
a_{10}							0.051	-0.005	-0.124
a_{11}							-0.125	-0.107	0.069
a_{12}							0.096	0.048	0.029
a_{13}								0.041	0.006
a_{14}								0.001	-0.049
a_{15}								-0.057	0.123
a_{16}								0.112	-0.076
a_{17}								-0.040	0.071
a_{18}								-0.014	-0.086
a_{19}									0.061
a_{20}									-0.086
a_{21}									0.129
a_{22}									0.016

equal to $R_s(0,3)$. Thus from the information in Table 2, one can compute the constants a_i in (164)

The predictive compression system will be said to employ a first-order horizontal predictor if only the picture element S_4 is used for estimation in (163). This means that the summation on the right-hand side in (163) has only one term $a_4 S_4$. The predictor will be called first-order vertical if only S_1 is used to estimate S_0. In a second-order predictor S_1 and S_4 are used for estimation, while in a third-order predictor S_1, S_3, and S_4 are used for estimation. For $n > 3$, the nth-order predictor uses $S_1, S_2, ..., S_n$ for estimation.

Table 3 lists the numerical values of the constants a_i that each predictor employs. These values were obtained by solving (164) for each predictor. Figure 17 shows the mean-square estimation error obtained for each predictor by averaging $e^2(m, n)$ over all the picture elements in Fig. 16a. These curves show a significant reduction in estimation error when the number of points used in prediction is increased to 3, and no significant reduction past this point. Of course, the results in Table 3 and Fig. 17 are valid only for the picture in Fig. 16a.

Figure 18 shows the histogram of the differential signal $e(m, n)$ in the case of a third-order predictor for the picture in Fig. 16a after it is normalized

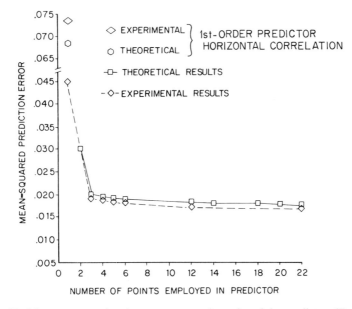

Fig. 17 Mean-square estimation error versus the order of the predictor. (From [31].) For the first-order predictor using horizontal correlation the experimental ($\Diamond$) and theoretical ($\bigcirc$) points are also shown.

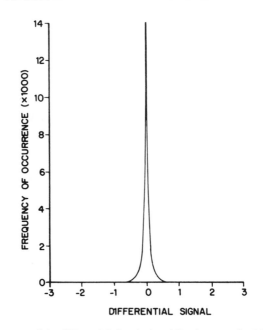

Fig. 18   Histogram of the differential signal $e(m, n)$ for the case of a third-order predictor for the picture in Fig. 16a after it is normalized (zero mean and unit variance). (From [31].)

(zero mean and unit variance). Except for a normalization factor, this histogram is an estimate of the density function of the differential data. With such a highly peaked density function, it is clear by the arguments presented in Section 4.3.1 that the differential data would be best quantized by a non-uniform quantizer. Given the histogram in Fig. 18, the output levels of this nonuniform quantizer can be calculated using the formulas in Section 4.3.1.

Nonuniform quantization of the differential data can also be justified on the basis of properties of the human visual system. In Section 4.3.2 we indicated that in a slowly changing region it is important to have fine quantization. The differential signals will be small in such regions, so it is necessary that the quantization levels be more densely packed. This is achieved by the non-uniform quantizer.

The result of 3-bit compression of the picture in Fig. 1, using the concepts previously presented, is shown in Fig. 19a. (In this and the other results in Fig. 19, only the first-order predictor using the nearest horizontal neighbor on the left was used.) By 3-bit predictive compression we mean that the number of bits required for the reconstruction in Fig. 19a is on the average 3 bits per picture element. Equal length binary code words were used for the output

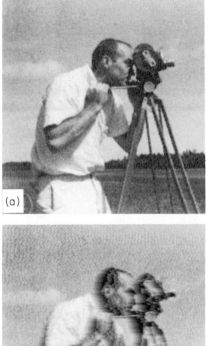

Fig. 19 (a) Result of 3-bit predictive compression of Fig. 1. The first-order predictor was used and the differential data quantized to 8 levels (3 bits). Note that this picture needs 3 bits per picture element, as compared to 8 bits per picture element in Fig. 1. (b) Reconstruction for 2-bit predictive compression. (c) Reconstruction for 1-bit predictive compression.

levels of the nonuniform quantizer so that for a 3-bit predictive compression system the quantizer has 8 output levels. Figures 19b and 19c, respectively, show the reconstructions for 2-bit and 1-bit predictive compression systems, again using equal length binary code words for the output levels of the quantizer.

The degree of compression achieved by a predictive compression system can be increased by using variable-length binary code words for the output levels of the quantizer. This is because the probabilities of occurrence of the various output levels of the quantizer are not the same, and the levels which occur more often can be assigned shorter code words. These variable length codes can be derived on the basis of information-theoretic concepts and will not be discussed here. In picture transmission, however, their use requires buffer storage.

We conclude this section by briefly describing several types of visual impairments in a picture that are unique to predictive compression. These include slope overload noise, edge busyness, granularity noise, and contouring noise [5, 59].

At sharp transitions in a picture, the error $e(m, n)$ is usually very large. If it is larger than the greatest quantizer step, the system is said to be in "slope overload." The result is that an abrupt transition may appear smeared, since when the system gets into slope overload, it may take several samples to recover. A nonuniform quantizer may be designed with large outer steps to force quick recovery. If, however, the quantizer structure is too coarse and the sampling is not synchronized with horizontal scanning, vertical edges may have a jagged appearance and may flicker and look "busy." This is known as "edge busyness."

Granularity noise and contouring noise are associated with flat regions or regions with gently sloping gray levels. (As mentioned in Section 4.3.2, the visual detectability of noise is greatest in such a region.) Granularity noise is caused in flat regions by the output of the quantizer oscillating back and forth between the smallest output levels. This oscillation depends on the picture noise in the regions and the past history of the predictor. In gently sloping regions these random oscillations do not occur. Instead, the quantizer output continues to increase in uniform steps in the direction of the slope. If, however, the sampling interval multiplied by any one of the quantizer steps is not equal to the rate of change of brightness level, then periodic corrections become necessary. If the step used to make these corrections is too large, the resulting overshoots give rise to visible contouring patterns called "contouring noise."

5.6 BLOCK TRUNCATION COMPRESSION

Recently a new image compression technique was proposed by Delp and Mitchell [16], Mitchell *et al.* [60], and Kishimoto *et al.* [48], whose performance is comparable to the adaptive cosine transform coding of Chen and Smith [9] for compressed data rates in the neighbourhood of 1.5 bits/pixel, but which possesses a much simpler hardware implementation. This technique has been called block truncation coding, because an $N \times N$ image is first divided into blocks of $M \times M$ pixels with $M \ll N$, and then the digital representation of each pixel in a block is truncated to one bit by thresholding and moment preserving selection of binary levels. Of course, in addition to the one bit that has to be transmitted for each pixel, one also has to send information that would help the receiver recreate the moment preserving binary levels that go with the one-bit representation.

Pixel gray levels represented symbolically

f_1	f_2	f_3	f_4
f_5	f_6	f_7	f_8
f_9	f_{10}	f_{11}	f_{12}
f_{13}	f_{14}	f_{15}	f_{16}

B	B	A	A
A	B	B	B
A	A	A	B
A	A	A	B

1	1	0	0
0	1	1	1
0	0	0	1
0	0	0	1

An actual example with numerical values

121	114	56	47
37	200	247	255
16	0	12	169
43	5	7	251

204	204	17	17
17	204	204	204
17	17	17	204
17	17	17	204

1	1	0	0
0	1	1	1
0	0	0	1
0	0	0	1

(a)　　　　　　　　　(b)　　　　　　　　　(c)

Fig. 20 (a) A 4 × 4 block of pixels. (b) Its two-level representation. The two levels are such that the first two moments of the pixel block are preserved. (c) Binary representation of (b).

In order to present the basic idea behind block truncation coding, we have shown symbolically in Fig. 20a a 4 × 4 block of pixels from an image, with pixel gray levels given by $f_1, f_2, \ldots$. We first calculate the sample mean, $\bar{f}$, of the block pixels:

$$\bar{f} = \frac{1}{m} \sum_{i=1}^{m} f_i \tag{165}$$

where $m = M^2$ is the total number of pixels in the block (in our case 16). To generate the moment preserving binary representation, we compare each pixel gray level with $\bar{f}$. If $f_i < \bar{f}$, we set it equal to A, while if $f_i \geq \bar{f}$, we set it equal to B, leading to the binary representation in Fig. 20b. The levels A and B are calculated in such a way that the first and the second moments of the block pixels are preserved.

While the first moment of the original block pixels is given by (165), the second moment is

$$\overline{f^2} = \frac{1}{m} \sum_{i=1}^{m} f_i^2 \tag{166}$$

If q is the number of pixels with $f_i \geq \bar{f}$, the first and the second moments of the binary representation in Fig. 20b are given by

$$\frac{1}{m} [(m - q)A + qB] \tag{167}$$

and

$$\frac{1}{m}\left[(m - q)A^2 + qB^2\right] \tag{168}$$

respectively.

In order to preserve the first two moments, we equate (167) with (165), and (168) with (166). When the resulting two equations are solved for A and B, the result is

$$A = \bar{f} - \bar{\sigma}\sqrt{\frac{q}{m - q}}$$

and   (169)

$$B = \bar{f} + \bar{\sigma}\sqrt{\frac{m - q}{q}}$$

(a)

Fig. 21   The 512 × 512 8 bit/pixel image shown in (a) was compressed to 1.63 bits/pixel. The reconstructed image from the compressed data is shown in (b). (From [16].)

(b)

Fig. 21 (*Continued*)

where

$$\bar{\sigma} = \sqrt{\bar{f^2} - (\bar{f})^2} \tag{170}$$

The information that the transmitter sends to the receiver for each block consists of the bit plane in Fig. 20c derived from the binary representation in Fig. 20b, and the values of $\bar{f}$ and $\bar{\sigma}$. The receiver recreates the binary representation of Fig. 20b. Of course, the difference between the original block in Fig. 20a and its binary representation at the receiver is the error incurred in image compression by this method. Suppose the original image has 8-bit pixels. If we represent both $\bar{f}$ and $\bar{\sigma}$ by 8 bits each, then the total number of overhead bits required for each block is 16. Adding to these the 16 bits required for the bit plane of Fig. 20c, we get a compressed data rate of 2 bits/pixel when the block size is 4 × 4.

If it is desired to achieve data rates of less than 2 bits/pixel, one may assign fewer bits to $\bar{f}$ and $\bar{\sigma}$. Delp and Mitchell [16] have shown that for 8 bit/pixel images if $\bar{f}$ and $\bar{\sigma}$ are represented by only 6 and 4 bits, respectively, no noticeable degradation is introduced in the reconstructed images. This results in a data rate of 1.63 bits/pixel. Utilizing this approach, shown in Fig. 21b is a compressed image at the data rate of 1.63 bits/pixel. The original version of this image shown in Fig. 21a is 512 × 512 at 8 bits/pixel. One could also try to increase the compression by increasing the block size, since then the same number of overhead bits required for $\bar{f}$ and $\bar{\sigma}$ would be distributed among a larger number of pixels; however, this would generally result in a "blocky" appearance in the reconstructed image. When the block size is

Fig. 22 The "blockiness" artifact is not readily visible when compressed images are displayed without magnification. It can, however, be illustrated with magnification, as is shown here for the "northwest" segment of the airport in Fig. 21b. (From [16].)

4×4, the "blocky" appearance is not readily visible when the image reconstructed from the compressed data is displayed with no magnification. This artifact can be made more apparent with magnification, as is illustrated in Fig. 22 for the "northwest" segment of the airport in Fig. 21b.

5.7 ERROR-FREE COMPRESSION

In many applications, such as computerized tomography and LANDSAT imagery, where an enormous amount of image data is constantly produced for archival storage, legal and other reasons usually dictate that no information be lost during the process of image compression. Although with error-free techniques the degree of compression achieved is usually very small (between 2 and 3 for most images), the resulting savings in the physical space required might still be very large (i.e., half the number of warehouses if the images are compressed by a factor of 2).

Error-free compression is based on the idea that since not all the gray levels in an image occur equally often, by assigning shorter binary code words to the more frequently occurring gray levels one can achieve compression over the case when all the levels are represented by equal length code words. If we assign equal length binary code words to an image with K gray levels, the code word size for each sample is $\log_2 K$ bits (for simplicity, we will assume that K is a power of 2). Now suppose an error-free compression scheme using unequal binary code words results, on the average, in R bits per image sample. The degree of compression achieved is $(\log_2 K)/R$.

Let us denote the gray levels by $f_1, f_2, \ldots, f_K$; and let the probability of the gray level f_i be given by $\text{Prob}(f_i) = p_i$. As will be discussed in greater detail in Section 5.9, we may associate an entropy, H, with these gray levels, which is given by

$$H = -\sum_{i=1}^{K} p_i \log p_i \qquad (171)$$

One can show [6, 20, 46] that if the data samples are independent of each other, the number R defined above cannot be less than H. In other words, in this case the entropy is the lower bound on the average length of the binary code words used.

To achieve the lower bound the following procedure is generally employed: (1) from the given image one first generates a representation, the elements of which are much less dependent upon one another than the samples in the original image; (2) unequal binary code words are assigned to the elements of this representation by a technique originally due to Huffman.

The first step in the above procedure is often accomplished by subtracting from each pixel one or more of its neighbors. One may use either

$$\xi(m, n) = f(m, n) - f(m, n - 1) \tag{172}$$

or

$$\xi(m, n) = f(m, n) - f(m - 1, n) - f(m, n - 1) + f(m - 1, n - 1) \tag{173}$$

and show that the $\xi(m, n)$'s are much less dependent upon one another than the original pixels ($f(m, n)$'s).

The above difference equations differ from similar equations in Section 5.5 because no coefficients have been used to multiply the neighbors of the pixel $f(m, n)$. The multiplying coefficients in Section 5.5 are almost always fractions, since they are obtained by dividing the image autocorrelation function for a certain lag by the autocorrelation for zero lag. On the other hand, since we are dealing with quantized pixels, the $f(m, n)$'s can all be represented by integers. If, for the sake of achieving optimality, we were to multiply these integers by fractional coefficients, the resulting $\xi(m, n)$'s would become non-integers and would have to be requantized. The errors caused by this requantization would defeat the original aim, which was to achieve error-free compression of the original digitized data as represented by the $f(m, n)$'s. Therefore the $\xi(m, n)$'s may be more dependent upon one another than the $e(m, n)$'s in Section 5.5, but the former do not need any further quantization and consequently the pixels ($f(m, n)$'s) can be recovered exactly from them.

In Fig. 23 we have shown an image, which is a matrix of 256×256 elements, each element a 12-bit number. In Fig. 24a we have shown the values of the normalized autocorrelation function of this image. In Figs. 24b and 24c we have shown the normalized autocorrelations for the $\xi(m, n)$'s obtained by using (172) and (173), respectively. We see that relative to the original pixels, the $\xi(m, n)$'s are considerably more decorrelated and, therefore, less dependent upon one another.

After the representation of an image by its equivalent $\xi(m, n)$'s, the next step is to assign a binary code word to each possible value of $\xi(m, n)$. The assignment is made in such a way that, on the average, the length of a code word in bits is as close as possible to the entropy of the $\xi(m, n)$'s. A commonly used technique for achieving this is Huffman coding, which will be described next.

5.7.1 Huffman Codes

Suppose that the pixels in the original image are quantized to K gray levels. If the approximately decorrelated represenation is achieved by using

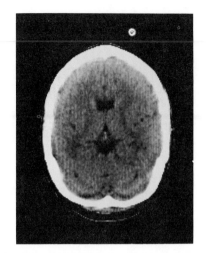

Fig. 23 Shown here is a 256 × 256 12-bit image used for lossless compression studies.

(172), the resulting $\xi(m, n)$'s will have $2K$ possible distinct values. On the other hand, if (173) is used, there will be a total of $4K$ values for $\xi(m, n)$. The different possible values of $\xi(m, n)$ are called *source symbols*.

To illustrate how the Huffman code is constructed, consider an example where $\xi(m, n)$ can take only eight possible values, $q_1, q_2, \ldots, q_8$, whose probabilities are given by

$$
\begin{array}{ll}
p_1 = p\{q_1\} = 0.4 & p_5 = p\{q_5\} = 0.12 \\
p_2 = p\{q_2\} = 0.08 & p_6 = p\{q_6\} = 0.08 \\
p_3 = p\{q_3\} = 0.08 & p_7 = p\{q_7\} = 0.04 \\
p_4 = p\{q_4\} = 0.2 & p_8 = p\{q_8\} = 0
\end{array}
\tag{174}
$$

where p_i is the probability of the ith source symbol. [In practice, these probabilities may be estimated by calculating the histogram of the $\xi(m, n)$'s.] The following procedure is now used:

Step 1: Search the list of probabilities for the two levels with the lowest probabilities. In our example, these are levels 7 and 8 with probabilities 0.04 and 0, respectively.

Step 2: Add the two lowest probabilities together. Form a new list that includes all the probabilities not affected in Step 1, plus the sum generated there. The new list has one less element.

Step 3: Go back to Step 1 and repeat the procedure until the list contains only one element.

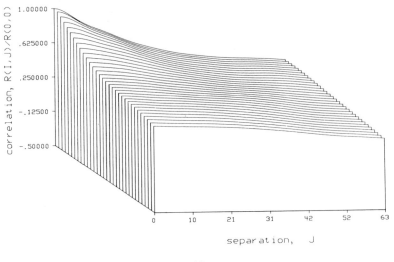

(a)

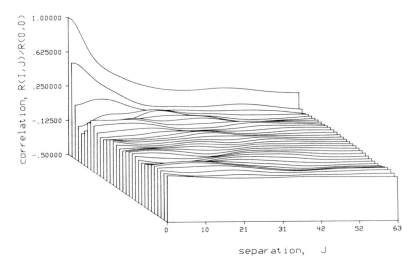

(b)

Fig. 24 (a) Normalized autocorrelation function of the image in Fig. 23. (b) Normalized autocorrelation function for the residuals obtained by using(172). (c) Normalized autocorrelation function for the residuals obtained by using Eq. (173).

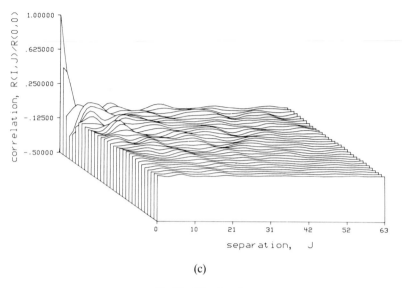

(c)

Fig. 24 (*Continued*)

In Fig. 25 the execution of Step 1 and Step 2 constitutes a round. For example, the list of probabilities after the first round contains only 7 probabilities, and so on.

Figure 25 has been redrawn in Fig. 26 to make it look more like a tree. The code words are generated by starting at the root and assigning a 1 to one branch and a 0 to the other. Similar branch assignments are made at each node of the tree. The code word for a given level of $\xi(m, n)$ is now obtained by tracing the path from the root of the tree to that level and forming a string of the 1's and 0's encountered.

The entropy of the $\xi(m, n)$'s is obtained by using (171) and (174):

$$H = -[0.4 \log_2 0.4 + 3(0.08 \log_2 0.08) + 0.2 \log_2 0.2 + 0.12 \log_2 0.12$$

$$+ 0.04 \log_2 0.04]$$

$$= 2.42 \text{ bits} \tag{175}$$

Compare this with the average length, R, of the code words

$$R = 1 \times 0.4 + 3 \times 4 \times 0.08 + 3 \times 0.2 + 3 \times 0.12 + 5 \times 0.04 = 2.52 \text{ bits}$$

$$\tag{176}$$

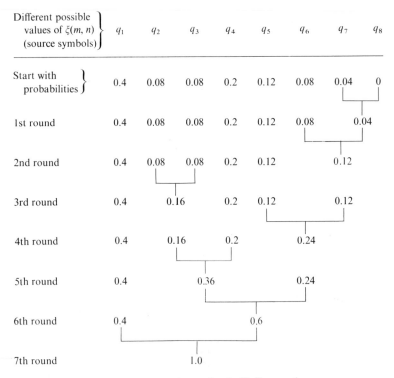

Fig. 25 Building the tree for the Huffman code.

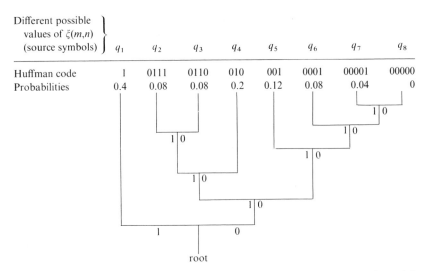

Fig. 26 The tree generated in Fig. 25 is shown here more clearly. This tree is used for determining the code words for the source symbols.

	Entry number	List of probabilities	Left branch	Right branch
	1	0.4	—	—
	2	0.08	—	—
Initial	3	0.08	—	—
entries	4	0.2	—	—
in the	5	0.12	—	—
list	6	0.08	—	—
	7	0.04	—	—
	8	0	—	—
	9	0.04	7	8
	10	0.12	6	9
	11	0.16	2	3
	12	0.24	5	10
	13	0.36	4	11
	14	0.6	12	13
	15	1.0	1	14

Fig. 27 Computer representation of the tree structure of Fig. 26.

If we had not used the statistical information about $\xi(m, n)$, we would probably have used a 3-bit natural binary code (i.e., 000, 001, 010, 011, ...). In this case R would be equal to 3 bits.

The procedure given above for constructing a Huffman code can be efficiently implemented by the following algorithm. Using the preceding example, we first construct a list of probabilities with eight entries as shown in Fig. 27. These probabilities are the same as in (174). We now search this list for the two smallest probabilities; the sum of these is appended to the list as a ninth entry. The identities (entry numbers) of the summands are recorded in the left- and right-branch columns. In the example here, the ninth entry was obtained by adding the seventh and the eighth entries, so we record 7 in the left-branch column and 8 in the right-branch column. Excluding the seventh and the eighth entries, we now search the new list for the smallest two probabilities, which are the sixth and the ninth entries. (Instead of the sixth, we could also have chosen the second or the third entries.) We sum these two probabilities and make the sum our tenth entry in the list. The numbers 6 and 9 are entered under the left-branch and the right-branch columns, respectively. This process is repeated until we have an entry with unity probability (Fig. 27), which corresponds to the root of the tree in Fig. 26.

Binary code words are generated by starting at the last entry in the final list of probabilities and assigning a 1 to the left branch and a 0 to the right branch. In Fig. 27 the last entry number is 15; therefore, we assign a 1 to the entry number 1 and a 0 to the entry number 14. Since the entry number 1 has no left or right branches, the binary code word corresponding to this entry is simply 1. On the other hand, the entry number 14 does have branches, so we assign 1 to the entry number 14 and 0 to the entry number 13. This process is continued until we again reach an entry with no left or right branches; then the string of 1's and 0's encountered in tracing the path from the root to that entry gives us its code word.

A Huffman code is a *uniquely decodable code*, because a string of binary digits can de decoded in only one way. Going back to the example we have been discussing, suppose that the binary pattern for the first three $\xi(m, n)$'s in an image corresponds to 0110100001. Examining this bit stream from the left, we notice that neither 0, 01, nor 011 corresponds to any possible value of $\xi(m, n)$ in Fig. 24. However, 0110 corresponds to q_3. Therefore, the first sample is equal to q_3, and there is no ambiguity about that, since 0110 is not a prefix of any other code word.[§] The next bit in the bit stream is 1, which corresponds to q_1. Therefore, the next sample is unambiguously q_1, because 1 is not a prefix of any other code word. Examining the rest of the bits, we note that 0, 00, 000, or 0000 do not correspond to any of the possible values of $\xi(m, n)$. However, 00001 corresponds to q_7, therefore the third sample is equal to q_7.

5.7.2 Huffman Shift Code

Huffman coding described in the preceding subsection suffers from one disadvantage. Consider the 256 × 256 image of Fig. 24, in which each pixel is represented by a 12-bit equal length binary code word. Therefore, the image pixels can have 4096 levels. If we derive a decorrelated representation of this by using (172), the resulting $\xi(m, n)$ can have 8192 levels, which is a very large number of source symbols. If we use the preceding algorithm to generate the Huffman code the resulting library will be very long, since it will have to contain the code words for each of the 8192 source symbols. This difficulty is further exacerbated by the fact that the code words corresponding to the very infrequently occurring source symbols will be very long. The majority of the source symbols do occur very infrequently, as is illustrated in Fig. 28b by the histogram of the $\xi(m, n)$'s for the image of Fig. 23. For comparison, Fig. 28a shows the histogram of the gray levels in the original image of Fig. 23.

[§] All codes with this prefix property are uniquely decodable. However, one can design uniquely decodable codes that do not have the prefix property. For further discussion on this, see, for example, Gallagher [20].

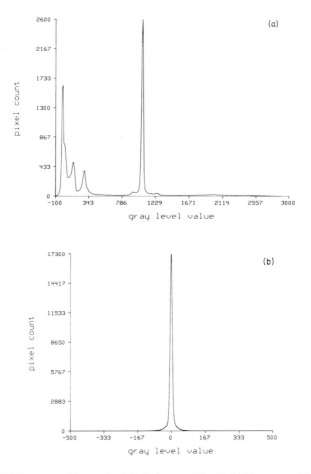

Fig. 28   (a) Histogram of the gray levels in the image of Fig. 23. (b) Histogram of the residuals, $\xi(m,n)$'s, calculated by using (172) for the image of Fig. 23. Although the horizontal axis shown here extends only from -500 to $+500$, there are residuals occurring *very* infrequently over a *much* wider range. The total range spanned by the residuals is 8192!

By making a small sacrifice in the degree of compression achieved, Huffman coding can be modified in such a way as to make large code-word libraries unnecessary [25]. The code words resulting from one such modification, to be described below, are called Huffman shift codes. Although the shift codes are not optimal, they are much easier to work with because a large number of source symbols can be encoded using a small number of code words. The price paid, in terms of the loss of optimality, is in most cases very small.

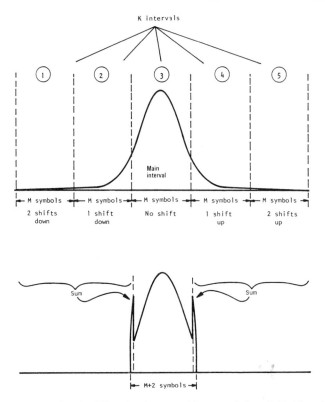

Fig. 29 For generating the shift code, the source histogram is first divided into *L* intervals, with each interval containing *M* symbols. This step is illustrated in the upper half of the figure. (The center interval here is the main interval.) We now add the probabilities of all the symbols on the right of the main interval, and assign the resulting probability to a hypothetical symbol immediately to the right of the main interval. A similar hypothetical symbol is created on the left of the main interval. Creation of these hypothetical symbols (used as shift-up and shift-down words) is illustrated in the lower half of the figure.

To generate a shift code, the histogram of Fig. 28b is divided into *L* intervals (Fig. 29), with each interval containing *M* source symbols (we are assuming that the total number of source symbols is divisible by *L*). For the purpose of generating the shift code, we add the probabilities of all the symbols that are on the right of the main interval, and assign this probability to a hypothetical symbol immediately on the right of the main interval. We similarly create a hypothetical symbol on the left of the main interval (Fig. 29).

A Huffman code is now constructed for the *M* + 2 symbols in Fig. 29 by using the algorithm in the preceding subsection. The code word for the first symbol is used as a *shift-down word*, and the code word for the $(M + 2)$nd symbol as a *shift-up word*. The shift-down and shift-up words have the following functions.

Counting the symbols from the left-hand boundary of each interval, suppose we want to find the code word for the mth symbol in the main interval; then we directly use the Huffman code for the $(m + 1)$st symbol generated for the symbols of Fig. 29. Now suppose we want the code word for the mth symbol in the first interval immediately to the right of the main interval; the code word is given by the shift-up code word followed by the code word for the mth symbol in the main interval. Generalizing, the code word for the mth symbol in the Jth interval to the right of the main is given by J repetitions of the shift-up code word followed by the code word for the mth symbol in the main. The shift-down code words are similarly used for the intervals on the left of the main interval.

The choice of M, which also determines L, depends upon how much penalty one wants to pay by way of losing some compression. For most images M can be as small as 16 without any significant degradation in the degree of data compression. Suppose we choose $M = 14$ (which implies we are using 16 distinct code words, two being the shift words) for the histogram of Fig. 28b which corresponds to the image in Fig. 23. As shown in Table 4, the image data can be compressed to 6.75 bits pixel; this corresponds to a data volume reduction of 44%. If on the other hand we had used the Huffman code directly for all the 8192 source symbols, we would have compressed the data to 6.09 bits/pixel, a 49% data volume reduction. Clearly, the price paid for the convenience of shift codes can be very small.

TABLE 4

Comparison of Bit Rate (in Bits/Pixel) Achieved with Huffman Shift Coding and Huffman Coding

		Bit rate achieved in bits/pixel	Data volume reduction (%)
Huffman shift coding	8 code words	8.18	32
	16 code words	6.75	44
	32 code words	6.40	47
	64 code words	6.32	47
	128 code words	6.22	48
Huffman coding	8192 code words	6.11	49
Entropy		6.09	49

5.8 MORE ON COMPRESSION TECHNIQUES

Both the transform and the predictive compression techniques have advantages and disadvantages. If the aim of picture compression is to reduce the data transfer rate in a transmission system, then the susceptibility of a compression technique to channel noise becomes an important consideration. The transform compression techniques are less vulnerable to channel noise than the predictive compression techniques. This is because if a transform coefficient is incorrectly received at the receiving end, its effect on the reconstructed picture is distributed all over the picture, making it less objectionable from a human visual standpoint. On the other hand, in a predictive compression technique, erroneous reception of an element of the differential data will result in incorrect reproduction of a picture element, and because of the predictor at the receiver, this error will propagate to neighboring picture elements [5]. This creates quite an unpleasant effect in the reconstructed picture. Other advantages of transform compression techniques include their lesser sensitivity to variations from one picture to another and their superior coding performance at lower bit rates. One of the major advantages of predictive compression techniques is the ease and the economy with which they can be implemented in hardware. Recently there have been attempts at combining the attractive features of both transform and predictive compression techniques [33, 34].

We will now briefly mention some other methods that have been suggested for picture compression. For details see the references that are cited.

For pictures in which the number of possible gray levels is small and which are composed of only a few regions each having a constant gray level, an efficient method of compression is contour coding. This involves tracing the contours or boundaries between the constant gray level regions and sending only that information to the receiver which would enable it to reproduce these contours. In the context of picture compression, Wilkins and Wintz [91] give an algorithm for tracing these contours.

Another method of compression for pictures composed of few regions each having constant or slowly varying gray level is run-length coding [12, 26, 77]. Here raster scanning of the picture followed by quantization will give rise to a relatively small number of "runs" of constant gray level, and the picture can be encoded by specifying the lengths (or, equivalently, the positions) of these runs.

Another method of picture compression separates a picture into "highs" and "lows" [27, 82]. The "lows" picture is obtained by low-pass spatial filtering of the picture. This results in essentially an out-of-focus picture with no sharp edges. By the two-dimensional sampling theorem in Section 4.1.3, this "lows" picture can be represented by many fewer samples than would have been needed for the original picture. The "highs" signal is obtained by taking either the gradient or the Laplacian of the picture (Sections 6.3.1 and 6.3.2) and consists of essentially the edges in the picture. A two-dimensional high-frequency picture (also called the "synthetic highs") can be synthesized from this edge information. This high-frequency information, when combined with the "lows" picture, gives back essentially the original picture. The "highs" picture may be efficiently transmitted by contour coding the edge information [27].

Roberts [76] has suggested a pseudorandom noise modulation technique for picture compression. If a continuous picture is sampled at an array of points, the samples usually need to be quantized to between 16 and 256 gray levels depending on the requirements of the user of the picture. For example, the digitized picture in Fig. 1 was sampled at a 256×256 array of points and each sample represented by 8 bits (256 levels of gray). If an attempt is made to reduce the number of bits by making the quantization too coarse, the result is the appearance of artificial discontinuities (false contours) in the picture. These discontinuities are a result of the quantization noise, which is correlated with the picture samples. If uncorrelated random noise of the same rms value as the quantization noise is added to the original continuous picture, these discontinuities do not appear. Roberts used this observation in his pseudorandom noise modulation technique in which noise of uniform amplitude distribution, and peak-to-peak value equal to one quantum step, is added to the picture samples before quantization, and identical noise is subtracted at the receiver. The result looks like an unquantized output, in which random noise of the same rms value has replaced the quantization noise. Usable pictures are produced at 2 bits per picture element, fair ones at 3 bits, and good ones at 4 bits. Roberts' system also has excellent performance in the presence of channel noise.

5.9 THE RATE-DISTORTION FUNCTION

An important question was raised at the beginning of this chapter: If the user or receiver of pictures belonging to a certain class is willing to accept an average amount of distortion D, then what is the least average number of bits required to represent pictures in that class? The answer to this question is, in principle, provided by the rate-distortion function $R(D)$.

We must first decide just what we mean by distortion. The mean-square error measure of distortion has been extensively used in the past primarily because of its mathematical tractability. The fact that this type of measure is a poor criterion is clear from an observation we made in the last section. We indicated there that if a picture is quantized too coarsely, artificial contours appear in the picture, but if uncorrelated noise of the same rms value as the quantization noise is added to the original picture, the objectionable artificial contours do not appear. This means that for a given amount of mean-square error between a picture and its reconstruction, the quality of the reconstructed picture depends on other factors, such as the nature of the correlations between the errors and the gray levels, and the context of the errors.

Specification of a distortion measure that is both physically meaningful and analytically tractable constitutes one of the major difficulties in our ability to use the rate-distortion function. Another source of difficulty is the fact that the computation of the rate-distortion function requires a detailed knowledge of the statistics of the random field to which the pictures belong. Even if these statistics could be determined in practice, their form may render the computation of any results a formidable if not an impossible task. Up to this time the performance achieved by various data compression systems has been compared with absolute bounds derived from rate-distortion theory only in relatively simple cases [7, 15, 32, 34, 49, 77, 83, 84]. Attempts are currently being made to extend the theory to the highly redundant, non-stationary sources and subtle distortion criteria often encountered in practice.

In spite of the previously mentioned limitations, rate-distortion theory does provide, from a conceptual standpoint, a theoretical framework that deals directly, in quantitative terms, with the concept of redundancy and its reduction to achieve data compression. For these reasons, we have included here a very brief introduction to rate-distortion theory, and have discussed its applications to pictorial data in conceptual terms. The theory is extensively discussed in the books by Berger [7], Gallager [20], and Jelinek [46]. We will first introduce some relevant information-theoretic concepts.

5.9.1   Some Information-Theoretic Concepts

Assume that a source X can produce any of the m possible symbols belonging to a set $A_m = \{a_1, a_2, ..., a_m\}$. It is customary to call this set the "alphabet." Let the probability of the event that the source will produce a_j be $\mathscr{P}(a_j)$; then the $\mathscr{P}(a_j)$, $j = 1, \ldots, m$, satisy the condition

$$\sum_{j=1}^{m} \mathscr{P}(a_j) = 1 \tag{177}$$

Let φ be a function defined over the alphabet. Suppose that the source operates over a long period of time, and for every a_i produced by the source, the corresponding $\varphi(a_i)$ is recorded. Then the mean or expected value of φ is given by (see Section 2.3.2)

$$E\{\varphi\} = \sum_{j=1}^{m} \varphi(a_j)\mathscr{P}(a_j) \tag{178}$$

Suppose now that we are told that the source has produced the symbol a_i; we can then ask how much information $I(a_i)$ we have received.[§] Let us suppose that the amount of information associated with the symbol a_i is a continuous function of the probability $\mathscr{P}(a_i)$. Equivalently, we can assume that this information is a continuous function of the logarithm of $\mathscr{P}(a_i)$:

$$I(a_i) = h(\log \mathscr{P}(a_i)) \tag{179}$$

Let us further assume that if two independent symbols a_i and a_j are both produced, then the resulting information is the sum $I(a_i)+I(a_j)$. Now the probability of receiving both a_i and a_j, when they are independent, is $\mathscr{P}(a_i)\cdot\mathscr{P}(a_j)$; thus the log of this probability is

$$\log(\mathscr{P}(a_i)\cdot\mathscr{P}(a_j)) = \log(\mathscr{P}(a_i)) + \log(\mathscr{P}(a_j)) \tag{180}$$

We thus have

$$h(\log(\mathscr{P}(a_i))+\log(\mathscr{P}(a_j))) = I(a_i) + I(a_j)$$
$$= h(\log \mathscr{P}(a_i)) + h(\log \mathscr{P}(a_j)) \tag{181}$$

In other words, h is an additive function of $\log\mathscr{P}(a_i)$. Now it can be shown that the only continuous additive functions are the linear homogeneous functions, i.e., we have

$$h(\log(\mathscr{P}(a_i))) = c \cdot \log \mathscr{P}(a_i) \tag{182}$$

Here c should be a negative constant, since $\log(\mathscr{P}(a_i))$ is negative, and we naturally want I to be positive. Since changing the base to which the log is taken is equivalent to multiplication by a positive constant, we can set $c = -1$ without loss of generality, obtaining

$$I(a_i) = -\log \mathscr{P}(a_i) \tag{183}$$

This result can be further justified along the following lines. Suppose $\mathscr{P}(a_j) = 1$ for some particular value of j, which means the source will always produce only that a_j. Now if we are told that the source has produced that particular a_j, then we really have not received any information because we

---

[§] The symbol I was used in Section 2.4.1 to denote an interval. Here it is used as a measure of information. Also, the symbols a_i were used in Section 5.2 to denote prediction coefficients; here they represent the output states of an information source. We hope this will not cause any confusion.

knew *a priori* what the source was going to produce. Equation (183) thus very correctly tells us that if $\mathscr{P}(a_j) = 1$, then $I(a_j) = 0$.

The base of the logarithm in (183) determines the information unit. The unit of information for base e logarithms is called a *nat*, while that for base 2 logarithms is called a *bit*.

The function $I(a_i)$ defined in (183) is called the *self-information*. The expected value of self-information is called the *entropy* of the source X and by (178) is given by

$$H(X) = -\sum_{j=1}^{m} \mathscr{P}(a_j) \log \mathscr{P}(a_j) \tag{184}$$

Clearly, $H(X)$ is a measure of the average amount of information one receives upon being told what symbol the source X has produced. Alternatively, $H(X)$ may be interpreted as a measure of the average *a priori* uncertainty regarding the source output.

Exercise 2. What are the entropies in bits in the following cases?

(i) $\mathscr{P}(a_1) = \mathscr{P}(a_2) = \mathscr{P}(a_3) = \mathscr{P}(a_4) = \frac{1}{4}$;
(ii) $\mathscr{P}(a_1) = \frac{1}{2}$, $\mathscr{P}(a_2) = \frac{1}{4}$, $\mathscr{P}(a_3) = \frac{1}{8}$, $\mathscr{P}(a_4) = \frac{1}{8}$. ∎

Exercise 3. Prove that the entropy of the ensemble of four messages is greatest when $\mathscr{P}(a_1) = \mathscr{P}(a_2) = \mathscr{P}(a_3) = \mathscr{P}(a_4)$. ∎

Now suppose that the source outputs a_j are transmitted over a noisy channel. Let the output of the receiver Y be represented by the alphabet $B_n = \{b_1, b_2, ..., b_n\}$. One may define probabilities $\mathscr{P}(a_j, b_k)$ on the product space $A_m \times B_n$ consisting of all ordered pairs (a_j, b_k). Here $\mathscr{P}(a_j, b_k)$ is the probability that the source output is a_j while the receiver output is b_k. Associated with $\mathscr{P}(a_j, b_k)$ are the probabilities

$$\mathscr{P}(a_j) = \sum_{k=1}^{n} \mathscr{P}(a_j, b_k) \tag{185}$$

and

$$\mathscr{Q}(b_k) = \sum_{j=1}^{m} \mathscr{P}(a_j, b_k) \tag{186}$$

and the conditional probabilities

$$\mathscr{P}(a_j | b_k) = \mathscr{P}(a_j, b_k) / \mathscr{Q}(b_k) \tag{187}$$

$$\mathscr{Q}(b_k | a_j) = \mathscr{P}(a_j, b_k) / \mathscr{P}(a_j) \tag{188}$$

where $\mathscr{Q}(b_k)$ is the probability that the receiver output is b_k; it is analogous to $\mathscr{P}(a_j)$ at the source output. $\mathscr{P}(a_j | b_k)$ is the probability of the source output being a_j given that the receiver output is b_k, and $\mathcal{Q}(b_k|a_j)$ the probability of the receiver output being b_k given that the source output was a_j.

One can now define *conditional self-information* $I(\cdot|\cdot)$ as

$$I(a_j|b_k) = -\log \mathcal{P}(a_j|b_k) \tag{189}$$

The number $I(a_j|b_k)$ measures the information one receives upon being told that the source has produced a_j if one already knows that the receiver has produced b_k. The conditional self-information

$$I(b_k|a_j) = -\log \mathcal{Q}(b_k|a_j) \tag{190}$$

has a similar interpretation.

Another important, perhaps the most important, measure of information is the *mutual information*, which is specified by the relation

$$I(a_j; b_k) = I(a_j) - I(a_j|b_k) \tag{191}$$

Clearly, $I(a_j; b_k)$ is the difference between the amount of information that the occurrence of a_j at the source output conveys to someone who is ignorant of what is happening at the receiver, and that which it conveys to someone who already knows that b_k has occurred at the receiver output. By using (183)–(191), the mutual information may be expressed as

$$I(a_j; b_k) = \log \mathcal{P}(a_j|b_k)/\mathcal{P}(a_j) \tag{192}$$

$$= \log \mathcal{Q}(b_k|a_j)/\mathcal{Q}(b_k) \tag{193}$$

$$= \log \mathcal{P}(a_j, b_k)/\mathcal{P}(a_j)\mathcal{Q}(b_k) \tag{194}$$

Note that it follows from these equations that

$$I(a_j; b_k) = I(b_k; a_j) \tag{195}$$

Just as entropy was defined to be the average value of self-information, one can define the *conditional entropy* as the average value of conditional self-information. If $H(X|Y)$ and $H(Y|X)$ denote the conditional entropies for the source X and the receiver Y, then

$$H(X|Y) = -\sum_{j,k} \mathcal{P}(a_j, b_k) \log \mathcal{P}(a_j|b_k) \tag{196}$$

$$H(Y|X) = -\sum_{j,k} \mathcal{P}(a_j, b_k) \log \mathcal{Q}(b_k|a_j) \tag{197}$$

The conditional entropy $H(X|Y)$ is the average information conveyed about the source by a specified receiver output. $H(X|Y)$ can also be considered to be a measure of average uncertainty regarding which symbol the source has produced after the symbol produced by the receiver has been specified. $H(Y|X)$ has a similar interpretation.

The expected value of (191) (or, equivalently, (194)) is called the *average mutual information* between the source X and the receiver Y and is denoted by $I_A(X;Y)$. Thus

$$H(X;Y) = \sum_{j,k} \mathscr{P}(a_j,b_k) \log \frac{\mathscr{P}(a_j,b_k)}{\mathscr{P}(a_j)\mathscr{Q}(b_k)} \qquad (198)$$

This expression for $H(X;Y)$ may also be written, using (184), (185), (187), and (196), as

$$H(X;Y) = H(X) - H(X|Y) \qquad (199)$$

which indicates that the average mutual information may be considered to be the average *a priori* uncertainty about the source output minus the uncertainty that remains after the receiver output is specified.

It should be clear that the conditional probabilities $\mathscr{P}(a_j|b_k)$ completely specify the channel with respect to the behavior of the receiver and the source. It is also clear that $H(X|Y)$ is the average information (in bits or nats per symbol) that is lost in going from the source to the receiver and, therefore, is related to the noise in the channel. In an ideal system, this would be zero and the average mutual information would then be equal to the average source information $H(X)$. In this case the information flowing from the source to the receiver is $H(X)$ bits or nats per source symbol. If $H(X|Y)$ is not zero, then the average information per symbol that is flowing from the source to the receiver must be equal to the average information per symbol $H(X)$ that is being produced at the source minus the average information per symbol that is being lost in the channel as given by $H(X|Y)$. Hence, by (199), $H(X;Y)$ is really the rate of information transfer (in bits or nats per symbol) through the channel. From this discussion the following definition for the *channel capacity* C seems justified:

$$C = \max H(X;Y) \qquad (200)$$

where the maximum is taken with respect to all possible choices of input distribution $\mathscr{P}(a_j)$.

5.9.2 The Rate-Distortion Function

Let us assume that the information is produced by a discrete memoryless source. By this we mean that the successive symbols generated by the source are independent and identically distributed, i.e., $\mathscr{P}(a_j)$ does not depend on time. Next, we assume the channel to be a discrete memoryless channel, which means that the channel processes successive letters of an input word (i.e., an input sequence of symbols) independently of one another. Note that a channel is characterized by the set of conditional probabilities $\mathcal{Q}(b_k|a_j)$. We will denote this set by $\mathcal{Q}_C$. Then

$$\mathcal{Q}_C = \left\{ \mathcal{Q}(b_k|a_j) \middle| \begin{array}{l} k = 1, 2, ..., n \\ j = 1, 2, ..., m \end{array} \right\} \tag{201}$$

Now let us consider the problem of reconstructing the output of the source to within a certain accuracy at the receiving end of the channel. To determine whether or not the required accuracy has been achieved, we need a quantitative measure of the distortion that may exist between the source output and the channel output at the receiver. Let us assume that there is given for this purpose a nonnegative matrix $\rho(a_j, b_k)$ that specifies the penalty charged for reproducing the source symbol a_j by the symbol b_k. We will use ρ as our distortion measure. The expected value of the distortion depends on the $\mathcal{Q}(b_k|a_j)$, so we denote it by

$$d(\mathcal{Q}_C) = \sum_{j,k} \rho(a_j, b_k) \mathscr{P}(a_j, b_k)$$

$$= \sum_{j,k} \rho(a_j, b_k) \mathscr{P}(a_j) \mathcal{Q}(b_k|a_j) \tag{202}$$

Here $d(\mathcal{Q}_C)$ is the average distortion associated with the channel. A channel is said to be *D-admissible* if $d(\mathcal{Q}_C) \leqslant D$ for all possible choices of the $\mathscr{P}(a_j)$. The set of all D-admissible conditional probability assignments is denoted by

$$\mathcal{Q}_D = \{\mathcal{Q}_C | d(\mathcal{Q}_C) \leqslant D\} \tag{203}$$

Each conditional probability assignment gives rise not only to an average distortion $d(\mathcal{Q}_C)$ but also to an average mutual information

$$H(X;Y) = \sum_{j,k} \mathscr{P}(a_j) \mathcal{Q}(b_k|a_j) \log \frac{\mathcal{Q}(b_k|a_j)}{\mathcal{Q}(b_k)} \tag{204}$$

We define the rate-distortion function $R(D)$ as

$$R(D) = \min_{\mathcal{Q}_C \in \mathcal{Q}_D} H(X;Y) \tag{205}$$

for the distortion measure $\rho(a_j, b_k)$. $R(D)$ is measured in nats (or bits) per source symbol.

Note that in order to determine the channel capacity, the mutual information is maximized with respect to the source distribution, while on the other hand the rate-distortion function requires minimization with respect to the channel conditional probabilities $\mathcal{Q}(b_k|a_j)$.

As was mentioned before, $H(X;Y)$ is the rate of information transfer (in bits or nats per source symbol) from the source to the receiver. Thus by (205), $R(D)$ is the minimum rate at which information about the source must be supplied to the user in order that the user may reproduce it with a prescribed fidelity. It is this interpretation of the rate-distortion function that makes it of considerable practical importance.

The rate-distortion function $R(D)$ can be shown to have the following properties:

1. $R(D)$ is not defined for $D < 0$.
2. There exists a $D_{max} \geqslant 0$ given by

$$D_{max} = \min_{k} \sum_{j} \mathscr{P}(a_j) \rho(a_j, b_k)$$

such that $R(D) = 0$ for $D \geqslant D_{max}$.

3. $R(D)$ is positive, strictly decreasing, and continuous for $0 < D < D_{max}$.
4. $R(D)$ is convex, that is, for all D' and D'' and all λ with $0 \leqslant \lambda \leqslant 1$ we have

$$R(\lambda D' + (1 - \lambda) D'') \leqslant \lambda R(D') + (1 - \lambda) R(D'').$$

Proofs of these properties can be found in Berger [7]. These properties indicate that an $R(D)$ curve in general must look like Fig. 30.

It should be emphasized that the concepts of the source, the channel, and the receiver in the preceding sections are purely formal and the existence of a communication link is not necessarily implied. For example, when we deal with a picture digitizer, the source can be identified with the original picture, the receiver with the user of the quantized samples, and the channel with the sampler and the quantizer. (Of course, in this case since the source is continuous, one would have to extend the rate-distortion function to the continuous case.) In this case the rate-distortion function gives the minimum rate at which information must be extracted from the original picture by the

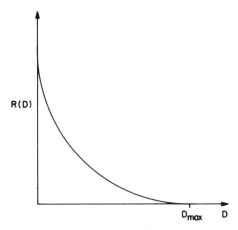

Fig. 30 A typical $R(D)$ curve.

sampler–quantizer so that the user may reconstruct the picture within a pre-specified distortion.

The rate-distortion function developed here does lend itself, at least conceptually, to the case of digitized pictures. Suppose that a picture has been "adequately" sampled and quantized. Let the picture be composed of $M \times N$ elements, the brightness level at each element taking on one of 2^B values. Given this picture, our aim is to represent it by the least number of bits such that one could reproduce the original within a certain prespecified distortion.

Following the excellent philosophical discussion by Landau and Slepian [51], one way to apply the rate-distortion function to the previously mentioned problem is to regard each symbol a_i of the set A_m as an entire picture. The set A_m is finite because there can only be $2^{B \times M \times N}$ pictures. The distortion measure $\rho(a_j, b_k)$ now expresses the penalty charged for reproducing the picture a_j as a_k. Conceptually such a measure exists, but we know little of it. We would have to prescribe such a measure for $2^{2B \times N \times M}$ pairs of pictures. To appreciate the magnitude of this number, consider the typical values $N = M = 256, B = 8; 2^{B \times N \times M} = 2^{524288}$. Also, to compute the rate distortion function, one would have to know the probability distribution over the $2^{B \times N \times M}$ pictures, since not all pictures in such an ensemble will occur equally often. For example, if we are dealing with television, then pictures in which the brightness level changes chaotically from one extreme to another extreme, from one picture element to another picture element should never occur. It is clear, however, that to determine such a probability distribution function for such a large number of pictures would be an impossibly difficult task. If these practical difficulties did not exist, one could use this interpretation of the alphabet and the distortion measure and use the rate-distortion function to determine the minimum number of bits per picture for a given distortion in reproduction.

A more tractable application of rate-distortion theory to our problem might come from regarding the symbols a_j of the alphabet A_m as the gray levels of picture elements. The distortion matrix $\rho(a_j, b_k)$ now measures the penalty charged for reproducing the gray level a_j as b_k. In light of Section 4.3.2, it is clear that such a distortion measure would be excessively local in nature, because the human eye does not view a picture element independently of its context. As was pointed out there, the eye is more tolerant to distortion of a picture element in a region of high detail, but rather sensitive in a region where the gray level changes slowly.

It is clear that any meaningful results from rate-distortion theory for picture compression must await proper formulation of the distortion measure and adequate statistical description of pictures. Both these topics are of current research interest. Some recent results, under simplifying assumptions, appear in [37, 58, 79, 86].

5.10 BIBLIOGRAPHICAL NOTES

Pictures as they are usually produced by a source have more detail and resolution than the observer can utilize. The phrase "redundant information" is often used to denote the information in a picture that may not be intelligible to the observer. The picture compression schemes discussed in the first six sections of this chapter are, therefore, called redundancy reduction techniques. Another commonly used name for these methods is source encoding, although this name is slightly more general in the sense that it includes techniques (cf. Section 5.7) derived from information theory that reconstruct a digitized picture perfectly but still reduce the number of bits required by making use of the statistics of the gray levels [40, 75]. Some investigations have been directed at determining various statistics of pictures [50, 65, 81].

In a picture transmission system, a source encoder would, in general, be followed by a channel encoder at the transmitting end. While the aim of the source encoder may be to remove the source redundancy, the job of the channel encoder is to insert controlled redundancy to combat channel noise. An excellent discussion of this point is found in [7].

The Karhunen–Loève transformation [56] is also called the "method of principal components" [39]. A number of investigators have studied the application of linear orthogonal transformations in picture compression [2, 3, 10, 11, 17, 30, 31, 42, 51, 71, 73, 85, 93]. Most of these contributions involve the application of the Karhunen–Loève, Fourier, Hadamard, Haar, slant, and cosine transforms. Among the various transforms, the discrete cosine transform is perhaps the most widely used at this time. This active interest in discrete cosine transforms was triggered by the result of Ahmed *et al.* [2], who showed that for an adjacent element correlation coefficient equal to 0.9, the basis functions of the discrete cosine transform closely resemble those of the Karhunen–Loève transform, provided the data can be modeled as a first-order Markov process. This was followed by the work of Jain, who showed that when, using the boundary elements, a first-order Markov process is suitably modified, the Karhunen–Loève transform of the result can always be found by using the discrete sine transform [44]. More recently, Kitajima [48] has introduced the "symmetric cosine transform" and shown that if one takes this transform of the data multiplied by a suitable window, the resuting coefficients become decorrelated for large data lengths.

Although the discrete cosine and sine transform of an N point sequence can be implented using a $2N$ point FFT algorithm, there has also been considerable interest recently in the development of algorithms that implement them directly. Chen *et al.* [10] has used matrix factorization to derive a special algorithm to compute the discrete cosine transform of a signal when N is a power of 2, resulting in a saving of $\frac{1}{2}$ over methods based on FFT algorithms. More recently, Narasimha and Peterson [61] and Makhoul [57] have developed methods in which the N element data sequence is rearranged in such a way that only an N-point FFT algorithm is required to compute the discrete cosine transform. Makhoul [57] has also given the extension of this technique to the two-dimensional case. The reader is also referred to the number theoretic based approaches, which are valid for any N, given by Tseng and Miller [88] and Wagh and Ganesh [89].

The bit allocation schemes discussed in Section 5.4 are also called block quantization. At the most fundamental level, block quantization deals with jointly quantizing the elements of an N-dimensional data vector. The joint quantization is achieved by partitioning the N-dimensional space into M regions, M being the number of output vectors of the block quantizer. In Chapter 4 we presented Max's derivation for optimum quantization of a one-dimensional random variable. Gersho [23] has recently extended this to the block quantization of vector data under the assumption that the number of quantized output vectors is very large.

Predictive compression systems, more commonly known as differential pulse code modulation (DPCM), are primarily based on an invention by Cutler [14]. In his original patent in 1952, Cutler used one or more integrators to perform the prediction function. From a theoretical standpoint, predictive compression has its roots in Wiener's theory of optimum linear prediction [90]. Graham [28] applied this theory to the system described by Cutler. O'Neal [66, 67] has analyzed DPCM and delta modulation (DPCM with only two quantizing levels) using one-dimensional prediction. Millard and Maunsell [59] and Abbott [1] describe DPCM for the Picturephone system. Persuasive arguments in favor of using two-dimensional prediction have been presented by Connor et al. [13] and Habibi [31]. Connor et al. showed that two-dimensional prediction resulted in dramatic improvements in the rendition of vertical edges. Application of DPCM to encoding of television signals has also been discussed by Limb and Mounts [53] and Estournet [18]. The noise characteristics of DPCM systems in slope overload have been investigated by Protonotarios [74]. The effect of channel errors has been studied by Arguello et al. [5].

Both transform and predictive compression techniques have their advantages and limitations. Recently there have been attempts at combining the attractive features of both [33, 34]. In the Karhunen–Loève transformation, one uses an orthogonal operator to transform a picture into uncorrelated data. Habibi and Hershel [32] have shown that if one instead uses a lower triangular operator, one can obtain a generalized DPCM system that reduces to simple DPCM for Markov data.

In general, pictures are not homogeneous. Areas of soft texture can lie adjacent to flat areas or contrasting areas. In Section 4.4 we have indicated that the visual response to noise changes markedly between these areas. In view of this, greater compression efficiencies can be achieved if the parameters of a compression algorithm are changed according to the local characteristics of the picture. Such adaptive compression techniques have been investigated by Anderson and Huang [3], Tasto and Wintz [85], Hayes [38], Limb [52], and Chen and Smith [9].

Other topics that were not covered in this chapter or were only briefly mentioned include compression of color images [11, 24, 54, 72], compression of graphics [41, 100], run length coding [12, 26, 77], the methods of "highs" and "lows" [27, 82], and interframe coding [35, 55, 62].

We have by no means been exhaustive in listing the references. The picture compression bibliography of Wilkins and Wintz [92] lists some 600 items. The reader's attention is also directed to the several special issues of IEEE journals [96–100] and to the recent review paper by Netravali [64] dealing with picture compression.

REFERENCES

1. R. P. Abbott, A differential pulse code modulation coded for video telephony using four bits per sample, *IEEE Trans. Commun. Technol.* **COM-19**, 1971, 907–912.
2. N. Ahmed, T. Natarajan, and K. R. Rao, Discrete cosine transform, *IEEE Trans. Comput.* **C-23**, 1974, 90–93.
3. G. B. Anderson and T. S. Huang, Picture bandwidth compression by piecewise Fourier transformation, *IEEE Trans. Commun. Technol.* **COM-19**, 1971, 133–140.
4. H. C. Andrews, Some unitary transformations in pattern recognition and image processing, *in* "Information Processing 71," pp. 155–160. North-Holland Publ., Amsterdam, 1972.
5. R. J. Arguello, H. R. Sellner, and J. A. Stuller, The effect of channel errors in the differential pulse-code modulation transmission of sampled imagery, *IEEE Trans. Commun. Technol.* **COM-19**, 1971, 926–933.
6. R. Ash, "Information Theory." Wiley, New York, 1965.
7. T. Berger, "Rate Distortion Theory: A Mathematical Basis for Data Compression." Prentice-Hall, Englewood Cliffs, New Jersey, 1971.
8. B. Carnahan, H. A. Luther, and J. O. Wilkes, "Applied Numerical Methods." Wiley, New York, 1969.
9. W. Chen and C. H. Smith, Adaptive coding of monochrome and color images, *IEEE Trans. Commun.* **COM-25**, 1977, 1285–1292.
10. W. Chen, C. H. Smith, and S. Fralick, A fast computational algorithm for the discrete cosine transform, *IEEE Trans. Commun.* **COM-25**, 1977, 1285–1291.
11. W. H. Chen and W. K. Pratt, Color Image Coding with the Slant Transform, *Proc. 1973 Symp. Appl. Walsh Functions* pp. 155–161, April 1973.
12. C. Cherry, M. H. Kubba, D. E. Pearson, and M. P. Barton, An experimental study of the possible bandwidth compression of visual image signals, *Proc. IEEE* **51**, 1963, 1507–1517.
13. D. J. Connor, R. F. W. Pease, and W. G. Scholes, Television coding using two dimensional spatial prediction, *BSTJ* **50**, 1971, 1049–1061.

14. C. C. Cutler, Differential Quantization of Communication Signals, Patent No. 2,605,361, July 29, 1952.

15. L. D. Davisson, Rate distortion theory and application, *Proc. IEEE* **60**, 1972, 800–808.

16. E. J. Delp and O. R. Mitchell, Image truncation using block truncation coding, *IEEE Trans. Commun.* **COM-27**, 1979, 1335–1342.

17. H. Enomoto and K. Shibata, Orthogonal transform coding system for television signals, *Television J. Inst. TV Eng. Japan* **24**, 1970, 99–108; also in *Proc. 1971 Symp. Appl. Walsh Functions* pp. 11–17, April 1971.

18. D. Estournet, Compression d'information de signaux d'images par les systeme differential codes, *Onde Elec.* **49**, 1969, 858–867.

19. B. Fox, Discrete optimization via marginal analysis, *Management Sci.* November 1966, 201–216.

20. R. G. Gallager, "Information Theory and Reliable Communication." Wiley, New York, 1968.

21. N. C. Gallagher and B. Liu, Statistical properties of the Fourier transform of random phase diffusers, *Optik* **42**, 1976, 65–86.

22. N. C. Gallagher, Jr., Quantizing schemes for the discrete Fourier transform of a random time series, *IEEE Trans. Informat. Theory* **IT-24**, 1978, 156–164.

23. A. Gersho, Asymptotically optimal block quantization, *IEEE Trans. Informat. Theory* **IT-25**, 1979, 373–380.

24. L. S. Golding and R. Garlow, Frequency interleaved sampling of a color television signal, *IEEE Trans. Comm. Technol.* **COM-19**, 1971, 972–979.

25. R. C. Gonzalez and P. A. Wintz, "Digital Image Processing." Addison-Wesley, Reading, Massachusetts, 1977.

26. G. G. Gouriet, Bandwidth compression of television signals, *IEE Proc. (London)* **104B**, 1957, 256–272.

27. D. N. Graham, Image transmission by two-dimensional contour coding, *Proc. IEEE* **55**, 1967, 336–346.

28. R. E. Graham, Predictive quantizing of television signals, *IRE Wescon Convent. Record* Pt. 4, 1958, 147–156.

29. V. Grenander and G. Szego, "Toeplitz Forms and their Applications." Springer-Verlag, Berlin and New York, 1969.

30. A. Habibi and P. A. Wintz, Image coding by linear transformation and block quantization, *IEEE Trans. Commun. Technol.* **COM-19**, 1971, 50–62.

31. A. Habibi, Comparison of *n*th-order DPCM encoder with linear transformation and block quantization techniques, *IEEE Trans. Commun. Technol.* **COM-19**, 1971, 948–956.

32. A. Habibi and R. S. Hershel, A unified representation of differential pulse code modulation (DPCM) and transform coding systems, *IEEE Trans. Commun.* **COM-22**, 1974, 292–296.

33. A. Habibi and G. S. Robinson, A survey of digital coding, *Computer* 7, 1974, 22–34.

34. A. Habibi, Hybrid coding of pictorial data, *IEEE Trans. Commun.* **COM-22**, 1974, 614–621.

35. B. G. Haskell, F. W. Mounts, and T. C. Candy, Interframe coding of videotelephone pictures, *Proc. IEEE* **60**, 1972, 792–800.

36. B. G. Haskell, P. L. Gordon, R. L. Schmidt, and J. V. Scattaglia, Interframe coding of 525-line, monochrome television at 1.5 M bits/sec, *IEEE Trans. Commun.* **COM-25**, 1977, 1339–1348.

37. J. F. Hayes, A. Habibi, and P. A. Wintz, Rate distortion function for a Gaussian source model of images, *IEEE Trans. Informat. Theory* **IT-16**, 1970, 507–508.

38. J. F. Hayes, Experimental results on picture bandwidth compression, *Proc. UMR-Mervin J. Kelly Commun. Conf.* Univ. of Missouri, Rolla, Rolla, Missouri, Oct. 1970.

39. H. Hotelling, Analysis of a complex of statistical variables into principal components, *Educ. Psychol.* **24**, 1933, 417–441, 498–520.

40. T. S. Huang, Digital picture coding, *Proc. Nat. Electron. Conf.* 1966, 793–797.

41. T. S. Huang, Coding of two-tone images, *IEEE Trans. Commun.* **COM-25**, 1977, 1406–1424.

42. T. T. Y. Huang and P. M. Schultheiss, Block quantization of correlated Gaussian random variables, *IRE Trans. Commun. Syst.* **CS-11**, 1963, 289–296.

43. A. K. Jain, Image coding via a nearest neighbors image model, *IEEE Trans. Commun.* **COM-23**, 1975, 318–331.

44. A. K. Jain, A fast Karhunen–Loeve transform for a class of random processes, *IEEE Trans. Commun.* **COM-24**, 1976, 1023–1029.

45. A. K. Jain and S. H. Wang, Stochastic Image Models and Hybrid Coding, unpublished.

46. F. Jelinek, "Probabilistic Information Theory," Chapter 11. McGraw-Hill, New York, 1968.

47. T. Kishimoto, E. Mitsuya, and K. Hoshida, A method of still picture coding by using statistical properties, *Nat. Conf. Inst. Electron. Commun. Eng., Japan* No. 974 (March 1978).

48. H. Kitajima, A symmetric cosine transform, *IEEE Trans. Comput.* **C-29**, 1980, 317–323.

49. A. N. Kolmogorov, On the Shannon theory of information transmission in the case of continuous signals, *IRE Trans. Informat. Theory* **IT-2**, 1956, 102–108.

50. E. R. Kretzmer, Statistics of television signals, *BSTJ* **31**, 1952, 751–763.

51. H. J. Landau and D. Slepian, Some computer experiments in picture processing for bandwidth reduction, *BSTJ* **50**, 1971, 1525–1540.

52. J. O. Limb, Adaptive encoding of picture signals, *Symp. Picture Bandwidth Compression*, Massachusetts Inst. Technol., Cambridge, Massachusetts, April 1969.

53. J. O. Limb and F. W. Mounts, Digital differential quantizer for television, *BSTJ* **48**, 1969, 2583–2599.

54. J. O. Limb, C. B. Rubinstein, and K. A. Walsh, Digital coding of color picturephone signals by element-differential quantization, *IEEE Trans. Commun. Technol.* **COM-19**, 1971, 992–1006.

55. J. O. Limb, Buffering of data generated by the coding of moving images, *BSTJ* **51**, 1972, 239–261.

56. M. Loève, Fonctions aleatoires de seconde ordre, *in* "Processus Stochastiques et Mouvement Brownien" (P. Levy, ed.). Hermann, Paris, 1948.

57. J. Makhoul, A fast cosine transform in one and two dimensions, *IEEE Trans. Acoust. Speech Signal Processing* **ASSP-28**, 1980, 27–34.

58. J. L. Mannos and D. J. Sakrison, The effect of a visual fidelity criterion on the encoding of images, *IEEE Trans. Informat. Theory* **IT-20**, 1974, 525–536.

59. J. B. Millard and H. I. Maunsell, Digital encoding of the video signal, *BSTJ* **50**, 1971, 459–497.

60. O. R. Mitchell, E. J. Delp, and S. J. Carlton, Block truncation coding: a new approach to image compression, *Conf. Record, IEEE Internat. Conf. Commun.* **I**, June 1978, 12B.1.1–12B.1.4.

61. M. J. Narasimha and A. M. Peterson, On the computation of the discrete cosine transform, *IEEE Trans. Commun.* **COM-26**, 1978, 934–946.

62. T. R. Natarajan and N. Ahmed, On interframe transform coding, *IEEE Trans. Commun.* **COM-25**, 1977, 1323–1329.

63. A. N. Netravali, On quantizers for DPCM coding of picture signals, *IEEE Trans. Informat. Theory* **IT-23**, 1977, 360–370.

64. A. N. Netravali and J. O. Limb, Picture coding: A review, *Proc. IEEE* **68**, 1980, 366–406.

65. A. Nishikawa, R. J. Massa, and J. C. Mott-Smith, Area properties of television pictures, *IEEE Trans. Informat. Theory* **IT-11**, 1965, 348–352.

66. J. B. O'Neal, Jr., Delta modulation quantizing noise analytical and computer simulation results for Gaussian and TV input signals, *BSTJ* **45**, 1966, 117–142.

67. J. B. O'Neal, Jr., Predictive quantizing (differential pulse code modulation) for the transmission of television signals, *BSTJ* **45**, 1966, 689–722.

68. A. Papoulis, "Probability, Random Variables and Stochastic Processes." McGraw-Hill, New York, 1971.

69. J. Pearl, Basis-restricted transformations and performance measures for spectral representations, *IEEE Trans. Informat. Theory* **IT-17**, 1971, 751–752.

70. W. A. Pearlman, Quantization Error Bounds for Computer-Generated Holograms, Tech. Rep. #6503-1. Stanford Univ. Information Systems Laboratory, 1974.

71. W. K. Pratt, J. Kane, and H. C. Andrews, Hadamard transform image coding, *Proc. IEEE* **57**, 1969, 58–68.

72. W. K. Pratt, Spatial transform coding of color images, *IEEE Trans. Commun. Technol.* **COM-19**, 1971, 980–992.

73. W. K. Pratt, L. R. Welch, and W. Chen, Slant transform for image coding, *IEEE Trans. Commun.* **COM-22**, 1974, 1075–1093.

74. E. N. Protonotarios, Slope overload noise in differential pulse code modulation systems, *BSTJ* **46**, 1966, 689–721.

75. R. F. Rice and J. R. Plaunt, Adaptive variable-length coding for efficient compression of spacecraft television data, *IEEE Trans. Commun. Technol.* **COM-19**, 1971, 889–897.

76. L. G. Roberts, Picture coding using pseudo-random noise, *IRE Trans. Informat. Theory* **IT-8**, 1962, 145–154.

77. A. H. Robinson and C. Cherry, Results of prototype television bandwidth compression scheme, *Proc. IEEE* **55**, 1967, 356–564.

78. J. A. Roese, Hybrid transform predictive image coding, *in* "Image Transmission Techniques" (W. K. Pratt, ed.). Academic Press, New York, 1979.

79. D. J. Sakrison and V. R. Algazi, Comparison of line-by-line and two-dimensional encoding of random images, *IEEE Trans. Informat. Theory* **IT-17**, 1971, 386–398.

80. D. K. Sarma and A. N. Netravali, Design of quantizers for DPCM coding of picture signals, *IEEE Trans. Commun.* **COM-25**, 1977, 1267–1274.

81. W. F. Schreiber, The measurement of third order probability distributions of television signals, *IRE Trans. Informat. Theory* **IT-2**, 1956, 94–105.

82. W. F. Schreiber, C. F. Knapp, and N. D. Synthetic highs, an experimental TV bandwidth reduction system, *J. Soc. Motion Picture TV Eng.* **68**, 1959, 525–537.

83. C. E. Shannon, "The Mathematical Theory of Communication." Univ. of Illinois Press, Urbana, Illinois, 1949.

84. C. E. Shannon, Coding theorems for a discrete source with a fidelity criterion, *IRE Nat. Conv. Record* Pt. 4, 1959, 142–163.

85. M. Tasto and P. A. Wintz, Image coding by adaptive block quantization, *IEEE Trans. Commun. Technol.* **COM-19,** 1971, 50–60.

86. M. Tasto and P. A. Wintz, A bound on the rate-distortion function and application to images, *IEEE Trans. Informat. Theory* **IT-18**, 1972, 150–159.

87. A. G. Tescher, Transform image coding, *in* "Image Transmission Techniques" (W. K. Pratt, ed.). Academic Press, New York, 1979.

88. B. D. Tseng and W. C. Miller, On computing the discrete cosine transform, *IEEE Trans. Comput.* **C-27**, 1978, 966–968.

89. M. D. Wagh and H. Ganesh, A new algorithm for the discrete cosine transform of arbitrary number of points, *IEEE Trans. Comput.* **C-29**, 1980, 269–277.

90. N. Wiener, "Extrapolation, Interpolation and Smoothing of Stationary Time Series." MIT Press, Cambridge, Massachusetts, 1949.

91. L. C. Wilkins and P. A. Wintz, A Contour Tracing Algorithm for Data Compression for Two-Dimensional Data, Tech. Rep. No. TR-EE-69-3, School of Elec. Eng., Purdue Univ., West Lafayette, Indiana, Sept. 1970.

92. L. C. Wilkins and P. A. Wintz, Bibliography on data compression, picture properties and picture coding, *IEEE Trans. Informat. Theory* **IT-17**, 1971, 180–199.

93. P. A. Wintz, Transform picture coding, *Proc. IEEE* **60**, 1972, 809–820.

94. P. A. Wintz and A. J. Kurtenbach, Waveform error control in PCM telemetry, *IEEE Trans. Informat. Theory* **IT-14**, 1968, 650–661.

95. P. Yip and K. R. Rao, A fast computational algorithm for the discrete sine transform, *IEEE Trans. Commun.* **COM-28**, 1980, 304–307.

96. *Proc. IEEE.* (Special issue on redundancy reduction) **55**, 1967.

97. *IEEE Trans. Commun. Technol.* (Special issue on signal processing for digital communication) **COM-19**, 1971.

98. *Proc. IEEE.* (Special issue on digital picture processing) **60**, 1972.

99. *IEEE Trans. Commun.* (Special issue on image bandwidth compression) **COM-25**, 1977.

100. *Proc. IEEE* (Special issue on digital encoding of graphics) **68**, July 1980.

Chapter 6

Enhancement

Whenever a picture is converted from one form to another, e.g., imaged, copied, scanned, transmitted, or displayed, the "quality" of the output picture may be lower than that of the input. This chapter reviews methods of evaluating picture quality, and of "enhancing" low-quality pictures.

Many enhancement techniques are designed to compensate for the effects of a specific (known or estimated) degradation process. This approach, generally known as *image restoration*, makes extensive use of filtering theory; it will be treated in Chapter 7.

In the present chapter, a more elementary class of image-enhancement methods will be discussed. These include methods of modifying the gray scale (e.g., increasing contrast), deblurring, and smoothing or removing noise. In these methods, little or no attempt is made to estimate the actual degradation process that has operated on the picture. These methods, however, do take into account certain general properties of picture degradations. For example, increasing the contrast is a reasonable enhancement operation, since degradation usually attenuates the picture signal; debiurring is reasonable, since degradation usually blurs, and the original picture or object is assumed to have been sharp; and smoothing is reasonable, since degradation usually introduces noise, and the original is assumed to have been piecewise smooth.

We may also use these enhancement methods to make the picture more acceptable to, and more effectively usable by, its user. For example, when a picture contains "false contours" due to inadequate quantization (see Section 4.3), their presence may mask important information, which becomes more readily visible when we smooth out the contours. In general, we can use enhancement techniques to suppress selected features of a picture, or to emphasize such features at the expense of other features. From this viewpoint, enhancement can be regarded as selective emphasis and suppression of information in the picture, with the aim of increasing the picture's usefulness.

The enhancement methods described in this chapter are all quite basic and simple. In practical situations, one must often experiment extensively in order to find an effective method. In the absence of knowledge about how the given picture was actually degraded, it is difficult to predict in advance how effective a particular method will be. It is often necessary to use combinations of methods, or to use "tunable" methods whose parameters vary from place to place in the picture, depending on the local context. The techniques described in this chapter provide elementary examples, and can also be used as building blocks in the design of more complex techniques.

6.1 QUALITY

The "quality" of a picture depends on the purpose for which the picture is intended. The picture may be intended for casual human viewing, as in the case of a TV image, or it may be needed for precise, quantitative measurement of some sort. The types and degrees of degradation that would be objectionable or acceptable might be quite different in these two cases. In this section we will deal primarily with objective quality criteria, not with criteria that involve subjective evaluation.

There are many ways of measuring the "fidelity" of a picture $g(x, y)$ to its original $f(x, y)$. One class of such methods uses simple measures of the similarity or difference between f and g. For example, a widely used difference measure is the mean-square deviation $\iint (f - g)^2 \, dx \, dy$. Note that this type of measure cannot distinguish between a few large deviations and many small ones. One can, of course, also use measures such as the mean absolute deviation $\iint |f - g| \, dx \, dy$, the maximum absolute deviation $\max |f - g|$, or various measures of the correlation between f and g (see Section 9.4). If one wishes to evaluate the picture transformation process that took f into g, and not just the individual picture g, one should use averages of such measures, taken over ensembles of input f's. A collection of such measures is reviewed in Levi [27].

The picture transformation process that takes f into g can be quite arbitrary. It certainly need not be linear, and it may not even be deterministic—i.e., it may be "noisy." Over limited ranges of values, however, one can often assume, to a good approximation, that the transformation consists of a linear operation combined additively with signal-independent noise. We shall further assume here that the linear operation is shift invariant (see Section 2.1.2). As we have seen, such an operation is a convolution, i.e., is of the form

$$g(x, y) = \int \int h(x - x', y - y') f(x', y') \, dx' \, dy' = h * f$$

If we also take the noise into account, we have

$$g = h * f + v$$

where $v(x, y)$ is assumed to be uncorrelated with $h * f$.

In Sections 6.1.1–6.1.3, we review some of the standard methods of evaluating a (deterministic) picture transformation, in terms of its effects on various simple f's, such as bright points or lines, sinusoidal bar patterns, etc. In Section 6.1.4, we briefly discuss various types of pictorial noise.

6.1.1 Spread and Transfer Functions

As mentioned in Section 2.1.1, the output of a picture-to-picture transformation $\mathcal{O}$ for a point source input $\delta(x, y)$ (essentially: a bright point centered on a dark background) is called the *point spread function* (PSF) of $\mathcal{O}$. If $\mathcal{O}$ is linear and shift invariant, knowledge of its point spread function determines its effect on any arbitrary input f, since f can be regarded as a linear combination of shifted δ's. As we have seen in Section 2.1, if $\mathcal{O}(f) = h * f$, then the PSF of $\mathcal{O}$ is just $h * \delta = h$.

The PSF can be regarded as a measure of the degradation caused by $\mathcal{O}$, since it describes the blurred output that is obtained when a sharp point is input. In fact, when we convolve h with f, we are simply blurring f by weighted averaging at every point, where the weighting is described by the function h. Note that $\mathcal{O}$ may also involve an overall attenuation (or intensification) of its input. In fact, if the input is a constant c, the output is $h * c = c \int \int h(x, y) \, dx \, dy$. Thus $\int \int h$ is a measure of the overall attenuation produced by $\mathcal{O}$.

Other "spread functions" of $\mathcal{O}$ can also be used to derive quality measures. Two important examples are the *line spread function* (LSF) and the *edge spread function* (ESF); these are the outputs obtained when the input is a bright straight line, or an abrupt step in brightness (a straight "edge"). Note that if $\mathcal{O}$ is not isotropic (i.e., if its point spread function does not have central symmetry), then the LSF and ESF will depend on the orientation of the given line or edge.

More precisely, we can define the LSF as follows: Let $\delta(x)$ be a one-dimensional delta function, defined analogously to $\delta(x, y)$ in Section 2.1.1.

Then $\delta(x)$ has the sifting property $\int g(x)\delta(x-\alpha)\,dx = g(\alpha)$. We can regard $\delta(x)$ as a function of two variables, x and y, which is independent of y. From this viewpoint, $\delta(x)$ can be regarded as a *line source* along the y-axis. The line spread function (for this direction) is then

$$h_l(x, y) \equiv \int\int h(x-x', y-y')\delta(x')\,dx'\,dy'$$

Using the sifting property of $\delta(x)$, this becomes

$$\int\left[\int h(x-x', y-y')\delta(x')\,dx'\right]dy' = \int h(x, y-y')\,dy'$$

Since we can change the variable of integration from y' to $y-y'$, we see that $h_l(x, y)$ can also be written as $\int h(x, y)\,dy$. Note that this is a function of x alone, and could be denoted by $h_l(x)$. We have also shown that the LSF for a line source in the y-direction is just the integral of the PSF with respect to y, i.e., $h_l = \int h\,dy$. In general, the LSF for a line source in a given direction θ is just the integral of the PSF taken in that direction.

Exercise 1.   The function $\delta(x)$ can also be expressed as $\int_{-\infty}^{\infty}\delta(x, y)\,dy$. Use this expression to give another proof that $h_l = \int h\,dy$, based on the sifting property of the two-dimensional delta function. ∎

An edge source (along the y-axis, say) can be defined as a unit step function

$$s(x, y) = \begin{cases} 0, & x < 0 \\ 1, & x \geqslant 0 \end{cases} \qquad \text{for} \quad \text{all} \ y$$

The corresponding ESF is then

$$h_e(x, y) \equiv \int\int h(x-x', y-y')s(x', y')\,dx'\,dy'$$

It can be seen that $s(x, y) = \int_{-\infty}^{x}\delta(x')\,dx'$, and it follows that the ESF is the indefinite integral, with respect to x, of the LSF; this will be proved in Section 7.1.2. Similarly, the ESF in any direction is the indefinite integral of the corresponding LSF in that direction; or, equivalently, the LSF is the derivative of the ESF.

The Fourier transform $H(u, v)$ of the PSF $h(x, y)$ is called the *optical transfer function* (OTF), or sometimes just the *transfer function*. Its amplitude and phase are called the *modulation transfer function* (MTF) and *phase transfer function* (PTF), respectively. If we denote these functions by $M(u, v)$ and $\Phi(u, v)$, we have

$$H(u, v) = M(u, v)\,e^{j\Phi(u, v)}$$

If the PSF is isotropic, then so is the OTF (Section 2.1.3, Exercise 2). In this case the MTF (and PTF and OTF) become functions of a single variable $\sqrt{u^2+v^2}$, and can be plotted in the form of "MTF curves." We shall see in Section 7.1.2 that the one-dimensional Fourier transform of the LSF, for a line source in a given direction θ, is equal to a cross section of the OTF along a line through the origin with slope $\theta+\frac{1}{2}\pi$; if the OTF is isotropic, all these cross sections are identical.

Just as the PSF, LSF, and ESF are the outputs that result from point, line, and edge sources, respectively, so the OTF specifies the outputs that result from sinusoidal bar pattern inputs (Section 2.1.3) having all possible positions, orientations, and spatial frequencies. To see this, consider the input

$$A + B\cos(2\pi ux')$$

which is a sinusoidal bar pattern with the bars running parallel to the y'-axis. The resulting output is

$$A\int\int h(x-x',y-y')\,dx'\,dy' + B\int\int h(x-x',y-y')\cos(2\pi ux')\,dx'\,dy'$$

in which the first term is a constant times A (see the second paragraph of this section). As for the second term, we can integrate $h(x-x',y-y')$ with respect to y' to obtain the LSF $h_l(x-x')$. The second term thus becomes

$$B\int h_l(x-x')\cos(2\pi ux')\,dx'$$

Letting $x-x'=z$, this can be rewritten as

$$B\int h_l(z)\cos 2\pi u(x-z)\,dz = B\left[\cos 2\pi ux\int h_l(z)\cos 2\pi uz\,dz \right.$$
$$\left. +\sin 2\pi ux\int h_l(z)\sin 2\pi uz\,dz\right]$$

in which the two integrals are, respectively, the real and imaginary parts of the one-dimensional Fourier transform of $h_l(z) = h_l(x-x')$. By the preceding paragraph, this transform is just the cross section of the OTF H along the u-axis, and we can write this cross section as

$$H(u,0) = C(u,0) + jS(u,0) = M(u,0)e^{j\Phi(u,0)}$$

where

$$M(u,0) = \sqrt{C^2(u,0)+S^2(u,0)}, \qquad \Phi(u,0) = \tan^{-1}[S(u,0)/C(u,0)]$$

In this notation, the previously mentioned second term becomes

$$B[\cos 2\pi ux\cdot C(u,0)+\sin 2\pi ux\cdot S(u,0)] = BM(u,0)\cos[2\pi ux-\Phi(u,0)]$$

Thus we see that if the input is a sinusoidal bar pattern $A + B\cos(2\pi ux')$, then the output is a sinusoidal bar pattern in the same direction (here: bars parallel to the y-axis), and with the same spatial frequency u, but with amplitude multiplied by $M(u,0)$ and phase shifted by $\Phi(u,0)$. In general, for a bar pattern having spatial frequency components (u,v), we would multiply the amplitude by $M(u,v)$ and shift the phase by $\Phi(u,v)$; the details are left as an exercise to the reader. Thus the OTF allows us to determine directly the amplitudes and phases of the outputs that result from arbitrary sinusoidal bar pattern inputs.

6.1.2 An Example: Unweighted Averaging

A basic example of a linear shift-invariant picture degradation is unweighted averaging: the gray level at each point (x, y) of the output picture is the average of the gray levels in the input picture over a neighborhood of (x, y). Let $\mathscr{A}$ denote this neighborhood when the point in question is the origin, and let A be the area of $\mathscr{A}$. Then the unweighted averaging operation has point spread function h given by

$$h(x, y) = \begin{cases} 1/A & \text{for } (x, y) \text{ in } \mathscr{A} \\ 0 & \text{otherwise} \end{cases}$$

Note that $\iint h = \iint_{\mathscr{A}} h = (1/A)\iint_{\mathscr{A}} 1 = 1$, as should be expected since the averaging operation involves no overall attenuation or intensification.

Suppose, in particular, that $\mathscr{A}$ is the square $|x| \leqslant 1/2n$, $|y| \leqslant 1/2n$. Thus h is just the function $n^2 \operatorname{rect}(nx, ny)$ of Section 2.1.1, which has value n^2 inside $\mathscr{A}$ and 0 outside. For this h, the LSF for a line source in the x-direction is given by

$$h_l(y) = \int h(x, y)\, dx = \int_{-1/2n}^{1/2n} n^2\, dx = \begin{cases} n & \text{for } |y| \leqslant 1/2n \\ 0 & \text{otherwise} \end{cases}$$

For other directions, the LSF can be computed analogously; note that it is not simply a rotation of this function.

The corresponding cross section of the MTF, for sinusoidal bar patterns in the x-direction, is obtained from the one-dimensional Fourier transform of $h_l(y)$, which is readily (see Section 2.1.3, Exercise 1)

$$F(u, v) = \frac{\sin(\pi v/n)}{\pi v/n} = \operatorname{sinc}\left(\frac{v}{n}\right) \qquad \text{for all } u$$

Since this transform is real, its modulus is just its absolute value, while its phase is identically zero. Thus the MTF is $|\operatorname{sinc}(v/n)|$, so that the output of our unweighted averaging operation for the input $A + B\cos(2\pi vy)$ is

$A + B |\text{sinc}(v/n)| \cos(2\pi v y)$. Analogous results can be obtained for other directions.

It should be pointed out that $|\text{sinc}(v/n)|$ does not decrease monotonically with increasing spatial frequency v. In fact, this function does decrease to zero as v increases to n, but it then increases again; it has zeros at integer multiples of n, separated by peaks which become smaller and smaller as v increases. This corresponds to the fact that when the sinusoidal bar frequency is an exact multiple of n, the averaging neighborhood covers an integer number of periods of the bar pattern, thus yielding a constant value of the average at any point. When the frequency is higher or lower, however, the average fluctuates from point to point, and the sinusoidal modulation is still visible. (On the fact that the modulation is visible even when the frequency gets higher, see the discussion of pseudoresolution in Section 6.1.3.)

Unweighted averaging over a circular, rather than square, neighborhood will produce isotropic spread and transfer functions, but the MTF will still oscillate, rather than decreasing monotonically. One can obtain a monotonically decreasing MTF by performing suitably weighted averaging. For example, if the averaging in the y-direction is weighted as $\text{sinc}(y/n)$, the MTF for sinusoidal bars parallel to the x-axis will be (see Section 2.1.3) $n \text{ rect}(nv)$, which is "flat" for $|v| \leqslant n/2$ and then cuts off sharply to zero. Note that this averaging operation may produce negative values in the output "picture," since it involves both positive and negative weights. Such an MTF could be achieved approximately, but not exactly, if a finite averaging neighborhood were used. On the other hand, such an MTF can be very easily obtained by operating in the spatial frequency domain rather than in the space domain— namely, by taking the Fourier transform F of the given picture f; suppressing all but the low spatial frequencies from F [i.e., multiplying F by $n \text{ rect}(nv)$]; and then taking the inverse transform.

6.1.3 Resolution and Acutance

Classically, image quality has often been measured in terms of the output resulting from simple input patterns such as steps and bars. One such measure is *resolution* or *resolving power*, which describes the distinguishability of small, close objects, such as the sets of bars on a resolution chart, in the output. If the bar width is b units, and the spaces are equal to the widths, then we have $1/2b$ "line pairs" (bar + space = pair) per unit distance. The resolution, informally, is the greatest number of input line pairs per unit distance such that, on the output, we can still count the bars correctly.

To illustrate the meaning of this definition, consider the unweighted averaging operation discussed in Section 6.1.2, where we assume that the bars are parallel to (say) the x-axis and are much longer than they are wide. If there are fewer than n line pairs per unit distance (i.e., $1/2b < n$), averaging over a square of side $1/n$ does not totally average out the bars, and correct counting should still be possible. In fact, it is easily verified that after averaging, the cross section of the bars still has peaks at the centers of the bars and troughs at the centers of the spaces. On the other hand, if $1/2b = n$, so that the averaging neighborhood size is exactly equal to the period of the bar pattern, then for any position of the neighborhood, the value of the average is constant, and the bars can no longer be "resolved."

It is important to observe that if the averaging neighborhood is still bigger, i.e., if $1/2b > n$, the averaged image once again contains a bar pattern. For example, suppose that $1/n = 3b$, so that the neighborhood is as wide as two bars and a space, or two spaces and a bar. In this case, when the neighborhood is centered at the center of a bar, we are averaging one bar and two spaces, giving an average gray level of $\frac{1}{3}$ (assuming the bars to be 1 and the spaces 0). On the other hand, when it is centered at the center of a space, we have the average of one space and two bars, or $\frac{2}{3}$. Thus here again we see bars in the output picture; but they are in the wrong places! Moreover, we will not be able to count them correctly; if the original pattern contained k bars, we will obtain peak gray levels at the centers of the $k-1$ spaces between these bars, so that we will count $k-1$ instead of k.

The phenomenon described in the preceding paragraph is known as *spurious resolution* or *pseudoresolution*. It is illustrated in Fig. 1, where a bar pattern (Fig. 1a) has been averaged using square neighborhoods of sides 3, 5, 7, 9, and 11; the resulting outputs are shown in Figs. 1b–1f, respectively. Note that in (e) and (f) the bar counts are no longer reliable.

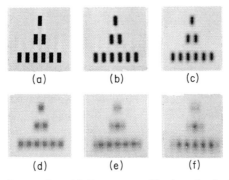

Fig. 1 Unweighted averaging. (a) Bar pattern (the bar size is 4×10 points). (b)–(f) Results of averaging (a) using square neighborhoods of sides 3, 5, 7, 9, and 11. Note the spurious resolution in (e) and (f).

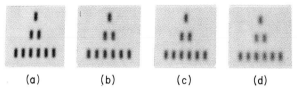

(a)   (b)   (c)   (d)

Fig. 2   Weighted averaging by iterated unweighted averaging. (a) Result of averaging
Fig. 1b, using a square neighborhood of side 3; in other words, 3 × 3 averaging has now
been performed twice in succession on Fig. 1a. (b)–(d) Results of averaging (a)–(c) in the
same way—i.e., Fig. 1a has now been averaged 3, 4, and 5 times.

Exercise 2.   Explicitly calculate the cross section of the averaged bar pattern as a function of bar size, averaging window size, and position.   ∎

Centrally weighted averaging preserves resolution over a much greater
range of neighborhood sizes than does unweighted averaging. An example is
provided by Fig. 2, which shows the results of *iterated* 3 × 3 averaging applied
to the same bar pattern used in Fig. 1.

Exercise 3.   Show that if we perform unweighted averaging m times, each
time using a $(2k+1) \times (2k+1)$ neighborhood, the result is a weighted average
over a $(2mk+1) \times (2mk+1)$ neighborhood, with the weights decreasing expo-
nentially from the center. The weights can be explicitly expressed in terms of
binomial coefficients.   ∎

Another useful class of image quality measures relates to the average
steepness of an edge in the output picture that results from a perfect step
edge in the input. We recall that the output edge cross section is described
by the ESF, which is the indefinite integral of the LSF, as indicated in Section
6.1.1. If we denote this function by $h_e(y)$ (for an edge along the x-axis), then
we can measure its average steepness by an expression of the form

$$\frac{1}{h_e(b)-h_e(a)} \int_a^b \left(\frac{dh_e}{dy}\right)^2 dy \quad \text{or} \quad \int_a^b h_l(y)^2\, dy \Big/ \int_a^b h_l(y)\, dy$$

where $h_l(y)$ is the LSF, and where a, b are points at or near the top and bottom
of the output edge, respectively. This expression is known as *acutance*; it has
been shown experimentally to correlate well with subjective judgments of edge
sharpness.

As a simple illustration of this concept, we again consider the case of
unweighted averaging. For an edge along the x-axis, say, having value 0 for
$y \le 0$ and 1 for $y > 0$, the ESF corresponding to an averaging neighborhood
of size $1/n$ is readily

$$h_e(y) = \begin{cases} 0 & \text{for } y \le -1/2n \\ ny + \tfrac{1}{2} & \text{for } -1/2n \le y \le 1/2n \\ 1 & \text{for } y \ge 1/2n \end{cases}$$

Thus $dh_e/dy = h_l(y) = n$ for $|y| \leqslant 1/2n$, and 0 elsewhere, as found in Section 6.1.2. If we take $a = -1/2n$, $b = 1/2n$, the acutance becomes

$$1/(1-0) \int_{-1/2n}^{1/2n} n^2 \, dy = n^2 \cdot (1/n) = n$$

which is inversely proportional to the size of the averaging neighborhood.

Exercise 4. Compute the acutance for the case of a circular averaging neighborhood of diameter $1/n$. ∎

In the unweighted averaging case, acutance and resolution are numerically equal; an averaging neighborhood size of $1/n$ yields a resolution of (up to) n line pairs per unit length, and an acutance of n. In general, however, acutance and resolution can have very different values. In fact, acutance can be low while resolution is high, and vice versa. Suppose, for example, that the point spread function, in cross section, consists of a broad plateau surmounted by a sharp peak. Because of the plateau, edges become very blurred, so that the acutance will be low. On the other hand, bars should remain resolvable as long as their period is larger than the width of the peak.

Exercise 5. Treat the case of "pyramidally" weighted averaging, in which the weights decline linearly from the center of the square averaging neighborhood to its edges. In particular, determine the spread and transfer functions and the acutance. ∎

6.1.4 Noise

Pictures are subject to many different types of noise. Some of these are independent of the picture signal, but others are not; some are uncorrelated from point to point, while others are "coherent." In the following paragraphs we give a few examples of commonly encountered kinds of noise.

When a picture is transmitted, *channel noise* is introduced whose value is generally independent of the strength of the picture signal. The situation is similar when a picture is scanned by a vidicon television camera. In these cases, we can write $g = f + v$, where the noise v and input picture f are uncorrelated.

A simple illustration of the effects of picture-independent noise is shown in Fig. 3. Here the bars have constant gray level, say s, and the spaces have gray level r. In Fig. 3, each point has its gray level incremented or decremented by an amount z, randomly chosen to lie in the range $|z| \leqslant \theta(s-r)$, for various values of θ. Note that even when the range of noise levels exceeds the difference between the bars and the background, the bars are still visible.

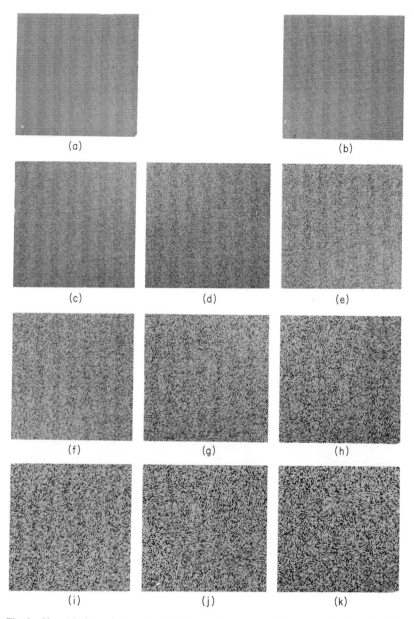

Fig. 3 Signal-independent noise. (a) Bar pattern; spaces have gray level *r*, bars have gray level *s*. (b)–(k) Results of incrementing or decrementing the gray level of each point in (a) by an amount *z*, randomly chosen in the range $|z| \leqslant \theta(s-r)$, for $\theta = 1, 2, ..., 10$.

The problem of estimating the true gray levels of a picture when noise is present will be discussed in Section 7.5. Such estimates require some degree of knowledge about the statistics of the picture and of the noise. If we know that the nonnoisy picture contains a large region of constant gray level, we can get some insight into the noise statistics by analyzing the gray level fluctuations in the corresponding region of the noisy picture. For example, if we assume the noise to have a Gaussian distribution with zero mean, its standard deviation is just the standard deviation of these fluctuations. We can also estimate the noise autocorrelation and power spectrum (assuming ergodicity) by measuring the autocorrelation and power spectrum of the noisy picture over the given region.

In many cases the noise level does depend on that of the picture signal; this is true, for example, when a picture is scanned by a flying-spot scanner. If the noise is proportional to the signal, i.e., $g = f + v_1 f$, we have $g = f(1 + v_1) = fv$ (say), so that we can regard this situation as one where we have uncorrelated noise that is multiplicative rather than additive. A simple example is the coherent "noise" in a television picture due to the presence of the TV raster lines; here v is a bar pattern that has maxima on the raster lines and zeros between them. (For methods of removing such noise patterns, see Section 6.4.1.) A less trivial example is *photographic graininess*, which arises from the fact that photographic images are formed from clumps of developed "grains" in the emulsion.

Noise proportional to the signal is illustrated in Fig. 4, which is analogous to Fig. 3 except that the noise ranges for points on the bars and on the spaces are proportional to s and r, respectively. Note that the bars are somewhat less visible in this case.

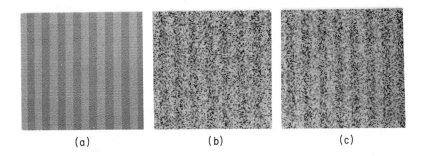

(a)   (b)   (c)

Fig. 4 Signal-dependent noise. (a) Bar pattern having two gray levels, r and s. (b) Result of adding noise to (a) as in Fig. 3, except that the noise ranges for the spaces and bars are proportional to r and s, respectively. (c) Result of using the average of the two noise ranges of (b) at every point of (a); here the noise is no longer signal dependent. The bars are more clearly visible, because the noise range for the spaces is not a subinterval of the range for the bars, as it was in (b).

An important type of noise in digital pictures is *quantization noise* (or quantization error), which is the difference between a quantized picture and its original. In Section 4.3.1 we saw how, for a given probability density of gray levels, this error could be minimized by suitable choice of the quantization levels.

One often wants to convert a picture that contains shades of gray into a "black and white" picture by thresholding it (see Section 10.1). The resulting output picture can be regarded as consisting of black "objects" on a white "background," or vice versa. If the original objects were too noisy, the black regions may contain scattered white points, and the white regions scattered black points. This condition is known as *salt-and-pepper noise*. More generally, we can apply this term to any situation in which scattered points of a picture are markedly darker or lighter than their immediate surroundings.

Two simple examples of salt-and-pepper noise are given in Figs. 5 and 6. Figure 5 shows a black-and-white bar pattern in which a fraction p of the black points have been changed to white and vice versa, where

$$p = 0, 0.1, 0.2, 0.3, 0.4, 0.5$$

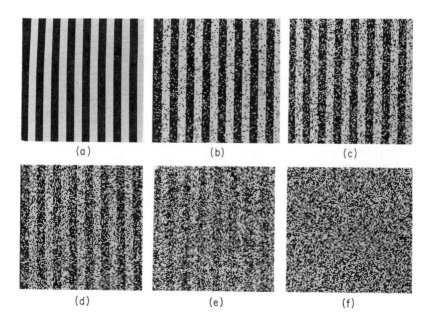

(a)   (b)   (c)

(d)   (e)   (f)

Fig. 5 Salt-and-pepper noise. (a) Black-and-white bar pattern. (b)–(f) Results of changing fraction p of the black points of (a) to white, and vice versa, for $p = 0.1, 0.2, 0.3, 0.4,$ and 0.5.

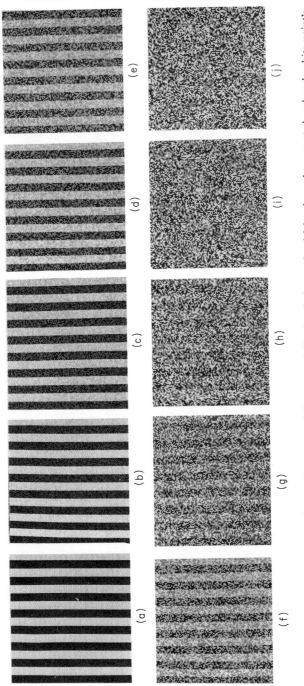

Fig. 6 Gray salt-and-pepper noise. In the pattern of Fig. 5a, each black point's gray level b has been decremented and each white point's level w has been incremented by a random amount z in the range $0 \leqslant z \leqslant \theta(b - w)$, where $\theta = 0.1, 0.2, \ldots, 0.9, 1.0$ in parts (a)–(j), respectively.

in Figs. 5a–5f, respectively. In Fig. 6, each black point has had its gray level decremented, and each white point has had its level incremented, by a random amount z in the range $0 \leqslant z \leqslant \theta(b-w)$, where $b = $ black, $w = $ white, and $\theta = 0.1, 0.2, \ldots, 0.9, 1$ in Figs. 6a–6j, respectively. A method of removing salt-and-pepper noise is described in Section 6.4.1.

Noise may depend not only on the gray level of the picture at the given point, but also on the levels at nearby points. This is so for many of the examples previously mentioned—e.g., for the flying-spot scanner, since the spot size is finite; and for photographic grain, since the clumping is influenced by local conditions. An interesting artificial example is *random walk noise*, where the picture is degraded by interchanging the gray levels of randomly chosen pairs of nearby points.

As we have seen in Chapters 4 and 5, a picture is often processed by applying an invertible transformation to it (e.g., taking its Fourier transform), operating on the transform, and then applying the inverse transformation to obtain the desired processed picture as output. Errors (or noise) may be introduced by the operations in the transform domain, and it is important to analyze the effects of these errors on the output picture.

If picture-independent noise is added to the Fourier transform of a picture, the reconstructed picture will also contain independent noise, which by Parseval's theorem (Section 2.1.4) will have the same power. A similar result holds if noise is added to the power spectrum of the picture. Noise in the phase of the Fourier transform has more complicated effects. One can estimate the output noise autocorrelation in this case in terms of that of the ideal output picture; for the details, the reader is referred to Anderson and Huang [2], where the case of multiplicative noise in the Fourier domain is also treated.

Quantization noise in the Fourier domain is a case of special interest, since the range of values in the Fourier transform of a picture is generally much greater than that in the picture itself, with most of the power being found at low spatial frequencies. This makes it especially important to use unequally spaced quantization levels (see Section 4.3.1) when quantizing a Fourier transform. Errors in quantizing the phase of the transform tend to have much worse effects on the reconstructed picture than do errors in quantizing the amplitude.

6.2 GRAY SCALE MODIFICATION

A simple but surprisingly powerful class of enhancement operations involves modifying the gray scale of the given picture. Two types of such operations will be discussed here. The first is *gray level correction*, which modifies the gray levels of the individual picture points so as to compensate for uneven "exposure" when the picture was originally recorded. The second type is *gray scale transformation*, which has the aim of changing the gray scale in a uniform way throughout the picture, or perhaps throughout some region of the picture, usually in order to increase contrast and thereby make details of the picture more easily visible. An important special case of this is *histogram modification*, in which a gray scale transformation is used to give the picture a specified distribution of gray levels.

6.2.1 Gray Level Correction

A picture recording system should map object brightness into picture gray level in a monotonic fashion, and this mapping should ideally be the same at every point of the picture. In practice, however, the mapping often varies from point to point. For example, light passing along the axis of an optical system is generally attenuated less than light that passes through the system obliquely. Thus when an image is formed by the system, the parts of the image far from the axis will be attenuated relative to the parts near the axis; this phenomenon is called "vignetting." As another example, the photocathode of a vidicon may not be equally sensitive at all points; thus in a picture obtained using the vidicon, equal gray levels may not correspond to equally bright points in the scene.

If we can determine the nonuniform "exposure mapping" that produced a given picture, it is then straightforward to correct the picture, by changing the gray level of each point, to achieve the effect of a uniform mapping. Specifically, suppose that we describe the nonuniform mapping by an expression of the form

$$g(x, y) = e(x, y) f(x, y)$$

where $f(x, y)$ is the ideal gray level that should have resulted at picture point (x, y) had the "exposure" been uniform [i.e., $f(x, y)$ is the desired monotonic function of the object brightness at the object point corresponding to (x, y)], and $g(x, y)$ is the actual gray level at point (x, y), due to the nonuniform mapping. To determine the function $e(x, y)$, we can calibrate the picture recording system by taking a picture of a uniform field of known brightness. For such a field, f is a known constant, call it c. If $g_c(x, y)$ is the picture of the uniform field, we have $e(x, y) = g_c(x, y)/c$. Once we know $e(x, y)$, we can correct any picture $g(x, y)$ obtained by the system (as long as the calibration does not change!), since

$$f(x, y) = g(x, y)/e(x, y) = cg(x, y)/g_c(x, y)$$

In any practical gray scale, the range $[z_1, z_K]$ of gray levels used is limited by the dynamic ranges of the available display devices. The correction operation just described may give rise to gray levels outside the allowable range. One way of handling this situation is simply to change any gray level less than z_1 to z_1, and any level greater than z_K to z_K. Another possibility is to shrink and/or shift the scale of the corrected gray levels until it falls within the allowable range. (Methods of doing this will be described in Section 6.2.3.) It should also be noted that even if the uncorrected gray levels were quantized to a discrete set of values $z_1, ..., z_K$, the corrected levels—even though they lie in the range $[z_1, z_K]$—need not have these discrete values. Thus gray level correction of a quantized picture must be followed by requantization. Similar remarks apply to gray scale transformations; in general, they may result in new gray levels that lie outside the allowable range or that require requantization.

6.2.2   Analysis of Illumination Effects

In Section 6.2.1 we were concerned with the mapping from scene brightness to picture gray level. The scene brightness itself is the result of several factors, including the illumination and reflectivity of the scene, both of which may vary from point to point. In this section we discuss the factors that give rise to the scene brightness and how to distinguish their effects.

When a ray of light is incident on a surface from a given direction, it gives rise to reflected rays which, in general, may have arbitrary directions. It is convenient to relate the directions of the incident ray I and the reflected rays R to the direction of the normal N to the surface at the given point P. Let θ_I and θ_R be the angles that I and R make with N; and let φ_I and φ_R be the slopes of the projections of I and R onto the tangent plane at P, with respect to some given coordinate system in that plane. In general, the fraction of the incident ray that is reflected in any given direction depends on θ_I, φ_I, θ_R, and φ_R, as well as on the wavelength λ of the light. This fraction is called the *reflectivity* of the surface at P, and may be denoted by $r(\theta_I, \varphi_I, \theta_R, \varphi_R, \lambda)$.

Let $I(\lambda)$ be the spectral composition of the light source, i.e., its intensity as a function of wavelength. Then the intensity of the reflected light in a given direction R resulting from an incident ray in direction I is $r(\theta_I, \varphi_I, \theta_R, \theta_R, \lambda)I(\lambda)$. Let $S(\lambda)$ be the spectral sensitivity of the detector, i.e., its response as a function of wavelength. Then its total response to the reflected ray R is given by

$$\int r(\theta_I, \varphi_I, \theta_R, \varphi_R, \lambda)I(\lambda)S(\lambda)\, d\lambda$$

We will ignore the dependence on λ from now on, and assume that r is a function of the θ's and φ's only.

In certain special cases, the reflected intensity depends on the θ's and φ's in very simple ways. In perfect *specular reflection*, it is zero except in one direction R that lies in the same plane as I and N, and such that $\theta_R = \theta_I$. In perfect *diffuse reflection*, the reflected intensity depends only on $\cos \theta_I$; this type of reflection is sometimes called *Lambertian*. Reflection from real surfaces can often be regarded as a mixture of these two types.

In order to determine the incident light intensity at a point P of the scene, we must know the locations and characteristics of light sources that are present. (Note that there may be several light sources present, e.g., the sun and the sky, in outdoor scenes; light fixtures and windows, in indoor scenes.) In general, the light emitted by a given point Q of a light source (at a given wavelength) may vary with direction. Moreover, the light emitted in a given (small) solid angle spreads out with the square of the distance from Q; thus the resulting light intensity at a point P in a given direction from Q falls off with the square of the distance from Q. To find the total incident intensity at P, we must integrate this intensity over all light source points Q. This does not take into account light that reaches P after reflection from other parts of the scene. We should also take into account the fact that P may be in shadow, i.e., the light rays from some source points to P may be blocked by other parts of the scene. Note that in order to accurately compute the effects of these factors, we need a complete three-dimensional model of the scene. On methods of deriving three-dimensional information about a scene from pictures, see the Appendix to Chapter 12.

In summary, the light incident on any point P of a scene depends on the nature and positions of the light sources relative to P, as well as on how this light is reflected toward or occluded from P by other parts of the scene. The light reflected from P in any given direction R depends on the angular relationships between that direction and the incident light rays. This reflected light determines the brightness of P as viewed from direction R. The brightness does not depend strongly on the distance of the observer from P. To see this, note first that the light reflected from P in a small solid angle centered at R spreads out as the square of the distance from P, so that its intensity should fall off with the square of this distance. However, we are not actually measuring the reflected light from the point P, but rather from a small "resolution cell" of the scene located at and around P; and the area of this cell grows with the square of the distance from P. Thus the apparent brightness of the scene at P as seen from direction R is, at least approximately, independent of distance.

Given an array of gray levels representing scene brightnesses as seen from a given observation point, one might like to know what combination of illumination, slope, and reflectivity gave rise to each brightness value. As we have seen, this combination is very underdetermined. Nevertheless, we can sometimes obtain clues as to the relative roles of these factors. For example, suppose that the illumination, reflectivity, slope, and range are all piecewise smooth functions, i.e., they vary slowly except for a few abrupt discontinuities. Such discontinuities will usally produce brightness discontinuities, i.e., edges. Moreover, it may be possible to deduce what type of discontinuity gave rise to a given edge by analyzing the brightness values in the vicinity of that edge, since these values may behave differently at discontinuities in illumination (shadow edges), in range (occluding edges), in slope (facet edges), and in reflectivity. The problem of deriving a set of "intrinsic images," i.e., arrays of illumination, reflectivity ("albedo"), slope, and range values, from a given array of brightness values is discussed by Barrow and Tenenbaum in [4].

In special cases it becomes much easier to analyze the effects of illumination and reflectivity on the observed brightness values. For example, suppose that the scene is relatively flat, so that slope effects are negligible; this is approximately true, e.g., in the case of terrain viewed from a sufficiently high altitude. This assumption also eliminates the problems of multiple reflections and shadows. Suppose further that the incident light is roughly parallel; this is approximately true for sunlight. If we are viewing the scene through a relatively narrow angle, the directions from our observation point to the points of the scene are also roughly parallel. Hence we can ignore the dependence of reflectivity on the angles of incidence and reflection, and consider only its variation from point to point due to changes in the composition of the reflecting surface. In this case, if the incident light intensity at $P = (x, y)$ is $I(x, y)$, and the reflectivity (for the given angles of incidence and reflection) at P is $R(x, y)$, we have the trivial relationship

$$f(x, y) = I(x, y)R(x, y)$$

where $f(x, y)$ is the brightness observed at (x, y). Thus if $I(x, y)$ is constant, the brightness is proportional to the reflectivity.

It often happens that $I(x, y)$ varies slowly across the scene, whereas $R(x, y)$ can fluctuate or change abruptly. (In any case, the angular relationship between the incident direction and the direction of view does vary slowly, while the surface composition fluctuates.) Thus we can try to compensate for the effects of varying illumination by eliminating gradual brightness changes while preserving abrupt ones. Horn [17] describes a method of doing this by applying a Laplacian operator to remove ramplike variations while preserving edge information, and then applying an "inverse Laplacian" operator to construct a piecewise constant function having the given edges. Stockham [43] uses high-emphasis spatial frequency filtering in conjunction with a logarithmic transformation to reduce illumination effects; this approach is briefly discussed at the end of Section 6.3.3.

6.2.3 Gray Scale Transformation

We next consider gray scale transformations that are the same at every point of the picture (or a region), rather than varying from point to point. Such a transformation can be expressed as a mapping from the given gray scale z into a transformed gray scale z', i.e.,

$$z' = t(z)$$

We shall assume that in both the old and new gray scales, the allowable range of gray levels is the same, i.e., $z_1 \leqslant z \leqslant z_K$ and $z_1 \leqslant z' \leqslant z_K$. We can now discuss how to design gray scale transformations that have enhancing effects, e.g., that increase contrast.

It is easy to increase the contrast of a picture if the picture does not occupy its full allowable gray level range. (This can happen if the picture recording device used had a smaller dynamic range than $[z_1, z_K]$, or if the picture was originally "underexposed.") Suppose that, in the given picture f, we have $a \leqslant z = f(x, y) \leqslant b$ for all x, y, where $[a, b]$ is a subinterval of $[z_1, z_K]$. Let

$$z' = \frac{z_K - z_1}{b - a}(z - a) + z_1 = \frac{z_K - z_1}{b - a} z + \frac{z_1 b - z_K a}{b - a}$$

This simple linear gray scale transformation stretches and shifts the gray scale to occupy the full range $[z_1, z_K]$.

A similar approach can be used if *most* of the gray levels of the given picture lie in the subrange $[a, b]$. In this case, we can use the transformation

$$z' = \begin{cases} \dfrac{z_K - z_1}{b - a}(z - a) + z_1 & \text{for} \quad a \leqslant z \leqslant b \\[2mm] z_1 & \text{for} \quad z < a \\[1mm] z_K & \text{for} \quad z > b \end{cases}$$

This piecewise linear transformation stretches the $[a, b]$ interval of the original gray scale; but it *compresses* the intervals $[z_1, a]$ and $[b, z_K]$—in fact, it collapses them to single points. This may be tolerable, however, if very few points have gray levels in these intervals, so that little information is lost when we compress.

More generally, we can stretch selected regions of the gray scale, at the cost of compressing other regions, if we want to bring out detail in the stretched regions, and we do not care about loss of information in the compressed

regions. As a simple example, suppose that the gray scale range is [0, 30];
then the transformation

$$z' = \begin{cases} z/2 & \text{for} \quad z \leqslant 10 \\ 2z - 15 & \text{for} \quad 10 \leqslant z \leqslant 20 \\ (z/2) + 15 & \text{for} \quad 20 \leqslant z \leqslant 30 \end{cases}$$

compresses the gray scale by a factor of 2 in the ranges $[0, 10]$ and $[20, 30]$
(on the original), while expanding it by a factor of 2 in the range $[10, 20]$.

Exercise 6. Give the equations for the transformation that stretches gray
scale range $[0, 10]$ into $[0, 15]$, shifts range $[10, 20]$ to $[15, 25]$, and compresses range $[20, 30]$ into $[25, 30]$. ∎

The gray scale transformations that we use can, of course, be smooth
rather than piecewise linear. We can implement any desired mathematical
transformation $z' = t(z)$—quadratic, logarithmic, or completely arbitrary—
subject only to the restriction that the results lie in the allowable range
$[z_1, z_K]$—i.e., that $z_1 \leqslant t(z) \leqslant z_K$ for all $z_1 \leqslant z \leqslant z_K$. This can always be
achieved by incorporating a suitable shift and scale factor into the trans-
formation. We can do this as follows: given any $t(z)$, let $t_1 = \min t(z)$ and
$t_K = \max t(z)$ for $z_1 \leqslant z \leqslant z_K$. Then the modified transformation t' defined by

$$t'(z) = \frac{z_K - z_1}{t_K - t_1} [t(z) - t_1] + z_1$$

satisfies $z_1 \leqslant t'(z) \leqslant z_K$ for all $z_1 \leqslant z \leqslant z_K$.

Exercise 7. Give the equations for a transformation t for which $t(z)$ is a
linear function of $\log z$ over the range $10 \leqslant z \leqslant 100$. ∎

Two simple examples of contrast-stretching gray scale transformations are
shown in Figs. 7 and 8. The graph of such a transformation, $t(z)$ as a function
of z, is a useful aid in visualizing the effect of t. In ranges where this graph has

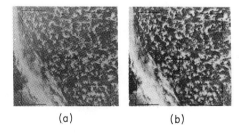

(a)   (b)

Fig. 7 Contrast stretching. (a) "Underexposed" picture (all gray levels in middle half of
range). (b) Result of stretching the gray scale of (a) by a factor of 2.

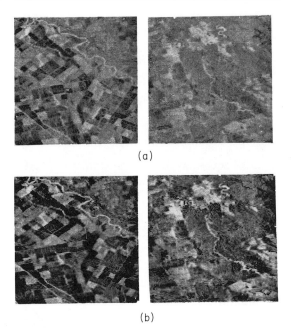

(a)

(b)

Fig. 8 Partial contrast stretching. (a) Input pictures. (b) Result of stretching the middle third of part (a)'s gray scale by a factor of 2 while compressing the upper and lower thirds by a factor of 2.

slope <1, contrast is compressed, while slope >1 implies that contrast is stretched. (Exercise: Draw this graph for the transformation of Exercise 6.)

The examples of transformations considered up to now have all been monotonic [i.e., $z' \leqslant z''$ implies $t(z') \leqslant t(z'')$] and continuous. It is sometimes of interest, however, to consider nonmonotonic discontinuous transformations in which different ranges of input gray levels are mapped into the same range of output levels. As a simple example, if the input range is $[0, 30]$, the discontinuous transformation

$$t(z) = \begin{cases} 3z, & 0 \leqslant z \leqslant 10 \\ 3(z-10), & 10 < z \leqslant 20 \\ 3(z-20), & 20 < z \leqslant 30 \end{cases}$$

maps each third of this range into $[0, 30]$. Within these subranges, we have threefold contrast stretching; but as we cross from one range to another, strong false contours are introduced, as illustrated in Fig. 9.§

---

§ Another important "contrast-stretching" technique is to map the gray levels of a picture into *colors*—e.g., low levels into shades of red; higher ones into orange shades; still higher ones into yellow, and so on. This can greatly enhance the visibility of detail in the picture, because the eye is more sensitive to differences in hue than it is to differences in brightness.

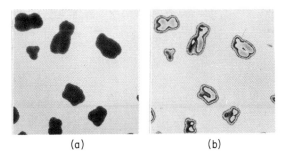

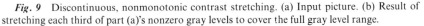

Fig. 9   Discontinuous, nonmonotonic contrast stretching. (a) Input picture. (b) Result of stretching each third of part (a)'s nonzero gray levels to cover the full gray level range.

This discussion has treated the input gray scale as though it were continuous rather than quantized. If it is, in fact, quantized, say to the K discrete values $z_1, ..., z_K$, then any gray scale transformation t can only produce K discrete output values $t(z_1), ..., t(z_K)$, some of which may be equal.[§] Nevertheless, contrast stretching can be advantageous, since it enables us to space (some of) the output values farther apart, so that they become more clearly distinguishable. In a well-designed gray scale, consecutive levels z_i, z_{i+1} should not be easily distinguishable; in fact, if they were, we could never get the impression of continuously varying gray levels in a picture. Thus detail that is not sharply delineated in the input is enhanced in the output when we spread the gray levels. Note, however, that once the levels have been spread far enough apart to become easily distinguishable, there is little to be gained in spreading them still farther apart, since all the available information (in the gray level range that has been stretched) has already been brought out. Note also that in ranges where the gray scale is compressed, information is lost, since when we requantize, several input levels may be mapped into the same output level.

If a picture's gray scale has been distorted by a known gray scale transformation $z' = t(z)$, the distortion can in principle be corrected by applying the inverse transformation $z = t^{-1}(z')$. For example, this approach can be used to correct for the effects of nonlinearities in the gray scales of display devices, or of recording media such as photographic film. In practice, of course, implementation of t^{-1} may be subject to the difficulties previously discussed.

6.2.4   Histogram Modification

Given a picture f, let $p_f(z)$ denote the relative frequency with which gray level z occurs in f, for all z in the gray level range $[z_1, z_K]$ of f. The graph of

§ See, however, Section 6.2.4, where we discuss how to map a single input gray level into more than one output level.

$p_f(z)$ as a function of z, normalized so that $\int_{z_1}^{z_K} p_f(z)\, dz$ is equal to the area of f, is called the *histogram* of f. If f is quantized, and has gray levels $z_1, \ldots, z_K$, its histogram can be represented as a bar graph having K bars. As we shall see in Chapters 10 and 12, the histogram of f can provide useful information about how to segment f into parts, and it also serves as a basis for measuring certain textural properties of f. Note that for any $z_1 \leqslant a \leqslant b \leqslant z_K$, the integral $\int_a^b p_f(z)_f$ measures how heavily the gray scale range $[a, b]$ is populated, i.e., what fraction of f's points have their gray levels in that range.

In this section we describe how to transform a picture's gray scale so as to give the picture a specified histogram $q(z)$. The following are some cases where this type of transformation might be required:

(a)   If we want to quantize a picture f to K discrete levels in such a way as to minimize quantization error (Section 4.3.1), the K levels should be spaced close together in heavily populated regions of f's gray scale, but they can be farther apart in sparse regions. One way of doing this is to pick the levels at the midpoints between the successive K-tiles of f's histogram; this means that when we quantize, just one Kth of the points of f will be quantized to each of the levels. This "tapered" quantization scheme thus transforms f's histogram into a "flat" bar graph in which all the bars have equal height.

(b)   Suppose that we want to compare two pictures f_1 and f_2 in order to (say) detect differences between them. If the pictures were obtained under different lighting conditions, we must somehow compensate for this, since otherwise they will have different gray levels at every point even if they are pictures of the same scene. One way to carry out this compensation might be to transform the gray scale of f_1 so that its histogram matches that of f_2, or to transform both pictures so that they have some standard histogram. (On picture matching see Chapter 9.)

(c)   We often want to measure certain properties of a picture f in order to classify or describe it. If these properties depend on the gray levels that are present in f, their values will be sensitive to the lighting conditions under which f was obtained. This sensitivity can be reduced by "normalizing" f so that it has some standard histogram. (This topic is discussed further in Sections 12.1.1 and 12.1.5.)

Our treatment of the histogram modification problem will deal only with the case of a *digital* picture f, say, having MN points, and quantized to K levels $z_1, \ldots, z_K$. Let level z_i have p_i points; thus the height of the ith bar in f's histogram is proportional to p_i, and $\sum_{i=1}^{K} p_i = MN$. Let the number of points having level z_i in the desired histogram be q_i, where $\sum_{i=1}^{K} q_i = MN$.

In order to transform the p histogram into the q histogram, we proceed as follows: Suppose that

$$\sum_{i=1}^{k_1 - 1} p_i \leqslant q_1 < \sum_{i=1}^{k_1} p_i$$

This means that the number of points in f that have gray levels $z_1, ..., z_{k_1-1}$ is at most q_1. Evidently, all of these points should be given gray level z_1 in the transformed picture f'. In addition, if there are fewer than q_1 of these points, some of the points of f that have gray level z_{k_1} should also be given gray level z_1 in f'. (One can choose these points randomly, or one can make their choice depend on the gray levels of their neighboring points—e.g., use points having low average neighborhood gray levels first.)

Next, let

$$\sum_{i=1}^{k_2-1} p_i \leqslant q_1 + q_2 < \sum_{i=1}^{k_2} p_i$$

This tells us which points of f should be given gray level z_2 in f', namely,

(a)   all points of gray level z_{k_1} that were not given level z_1 in f' (provided that $k_2 > k_1$; if $k_2 = k_1$, we must further subdivide the points that have level z_{k_1});

(b)   all points of gray levels $z_{k_1+1}, ..., z_{k_2-1}$;

(c)   if the left-hand inequality is strict, also some points of gray level z_{k_2} (which must be chosen as in the preceding paragraph).

The procedure is similar for the succeeding output gray levels $z_3, ..., z_K$. The general case for output level z_h is

$$\sum_{i=1}^{k_h-1} p_i \leqslant \sum_{i=1}^{h} q_i < \sum_{i=1}^{k_h} p_i$$

Note that for the last output level z_K we have $\sum_{i=1}^{K} p_i = \sum_{i=1}^{K} q_i = MN$, so that we always end with no points left over.

As a simple example, suppose $K = 8$ and that the p's and q's are given by

i	1	2	3	4	5	6	7	8
p_i	1	7	21	35	35	21	7	1
q_i	16	16	16	16	16	16	16	16

The first few steps of the computation are as follows:

(1) $p_1 + p_2 = 8 < q_1 = 16 < p_1 + p_2 + p_3 = 29$—i.e., $k_1 = 3$. Thus all points of f having levels z_1 and z_2, as well as 8 of the 21 points having level z_3, get level z_1 in f'.

(2) $p_1 + p_2 + p_3 = 29 < q_1 + q_2 = 32 < p_1 + p_2 + p_3 + p_4 = 64$. Here $k_2 = 4$; thus the remaining 13 points of f that had level z_3, as well as 3 of the 35 points having level z_4, get level z_2 in f'.

(3) $p_1+p_2+p_3 = 29 < q_1+q_2+q_3 = 48 < p_1+p_2+p_3+p_4 = 64$. Here $k_3 = k_2 = 4$, and we must further subdivide level z_4 of f—namely, 16 of its remaining points get level z_3 in f'.

Exercise 8. Finish this example. ▮

Two versions of the histogram modification process are illustrated in Fig. 10; the output histogram is flat in both cases. In one version, when a gray level of f has to be subdivided, the points are chosen randomly. In the second version, the choices depend on average neighborhood gray level, as previously described. (In case of a tie in average neighborhood gray level, random choice is used; but this happens much less frequently than in the first version.) Not surprisingly, the first method appears to give somewhat noisier results. In general, the results will be noisy when we subdivide a gray level z such that f contains large regions having constant level z. (Imagine what would happen if f were half black and half white, and we tried to force all levels to occur equally often!)

As Fig. 10 shows, when a picture's histogram is transformed so that all gray levels occur equally often, the result tends to have higher contrast. In other words, performing this histogram "flattening" or "equalization" transformation not only "normalizes" the picture, as discussed earlier, but also tends to enhance it. This is because when we flatten the histogram, the points in densely populated regions of the gray scale are forced to occupy a larger number of gray levels, so that these regions of the gray scale are stretched. At the same time, points in sparse regions of the scale are forced to occupy fewer levels, so that these regions are compressed; but the stretched regions are more populous than the compressed regions, so that the overall effect is one of contrast enhancement. It may also be noted that, of all pictures having a given size and a given number of gray levels, pictures having flat histograms contain the greatest amount of information in the sense of Section 5.9.1. Of course, we are assuming here that there is no special significance to the information in the sparsely populated gray level ranges, so that compressing them is not harmful.

Histogram flattening is sometimes too harsh a transformation, since it may map large ranges of gray levels at the ends of the gray scale into a single level. It may be preferable to produce a histogram that still falls off somewhat at the ends of the scale, rather than a flat one. On "histogram hyperbolization" and its advantages see Frei [12], and compare Hummel [21].

When a histogram has several peaks, corresponding to several densely populated gray level ranges separated by sparsely populated ranges (i.e., valleys), we may want to perform a rather different type of transformation on its histogram; for example, we may want to turn each peak into a spike, so

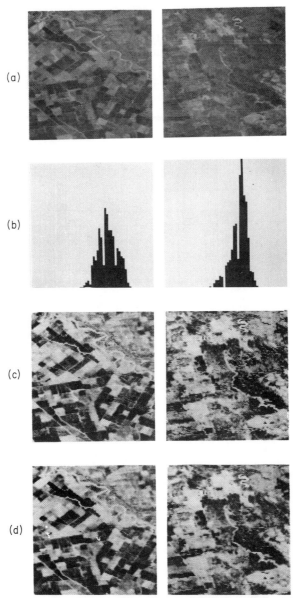

Fig. 10 Histogram flattening. (a) Input pictures. (b) Histograms for (a). (c) Results of transforming (a)'s gray scales so that they have flat histograms. When a gray level is subdivided, the decisions as to which points get which new levels are made randomly. (d) Same as (c), except that when a gray level is subdivided, the new level assigned to a point depends on the average gray level of the point's four horizontal and vertical neighbors (see text). The results are less noisy than in (c).

that each gray level subpopulation maps into a single level, and the inter-
mediate gray levels are eliminated. To do this properly, we must partition
the gray scale into ranges, each containing one peak; it is then trivial to
map the gray levels in each range into a single level. On methods of selecting
gray level "thresholds" (e.g., at valley bottoms) so as to separate histogram
peaks, see Section 10.1. Alternatively, we can use an iterative process in

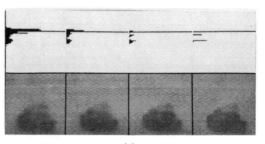

(a)

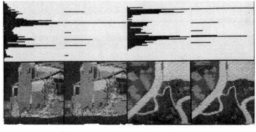

(b)   (c)

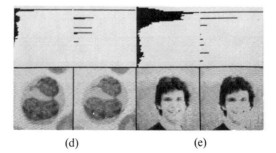

(d)   (e)

Fig. 11 Iterative histogram peak sharpening. (a) Iterations 0, 1, 2, 4 of the sharpening
process applied to an infrared image of a tank. (b)–(e) Original (left) and iteration 4 of the
sharpening process for pictures of a house, terrain, a blood cell, and a face.

which the count in each histogram bin is incremented or decremented in proportion to its differences from the counts in the neighboring bins, so that large counts grow at the expense of smaller counts. When this is done, the peaks grow into spikes and the valleys are wiped out, as illustrated in Fig. 11. For further details on this iterative approach see Davis and Rosenfeld [9] and Peleg [37].

As the examples in Figs. 10 and 11 show, histogram transformations seem to preserve the appearance of the picture. However, it should be realized that this is not automatically guaranteed, since there are no constraints on the transformation to limit how much the picture can change. A more sophisticated approach would be to try to construct a new picture that is as close as possible to the original one, but that has a histogram as close as possible to the desired one. On this constrained optimization approach to histogram transformation see Hummel [22]. On the computationally efficient implementation of histogram transformations see Chang and Wong [7].

It is sometimes advantageous to apply histogram transformations to a picture on a local basis, e.g., to divide the picture into windows, and transform the gray scale in each window so as to give it a flat histogram (or a histogram with a given standard deviation, perhaps). If this is done for a set of nonoverlapping windows, it will give rise to discontinuities at the window borders, where different gray scale transformations meet. Rather, it should be done for windows that overlap, and the computed transformation for each window should be applied only to the center part of that window; the transformations for successive (=maximally overlapping) windows will then be closely similar, so that the discontinuities are less likely to be visible.

6.3 SHARPENING

As pointed out in Section 6.1.1, picture degradation generally involves blurring, the extent of which is described by the spread function of the degradation operation. In this section we discuss some simple methods for counteracting blur by "crispening" or "sharpening" the picture. Methods of deblurring based on estimation of the blur will be treated in Chapter 7.

Blurring is an averaging, or integration, operation; this suggests that we may be able to sharpen by performing differentiation operations. Blurring also weakens high spatial frequencies more than low ones; this suggests that pictures can be sharpened by emphasizing their high spatial frequencies. Differentiation operations are discussed in Section 6.3.1, and a particularly useful class of these operations, the "Laplacians," are treated in Section 6.3.2. High-emphasis spatial frequency filtering is treated in Section 6.3.3.

When a picture is noisy as well as blurred, differentiation and high-emphasis filtering cannot be used indiscriminately to sharpen it, since the noise generally involves high rates of change of gray level, and it usually becomes stronger than the picture signal at high frequencies. These methods should be restricted, if possible, to frequency ranges where the picture is stronger than the noise. Alternatively, one should attempt to remove or reduce the noise before attempting to sharpen the picture. Methods of noise removal and reduction are treated in Section 6.4.

6.3.1 Differentiation

Any partial derivative operator $D = \partial^n/\partial x^k \, \partial y^{n-k}$ is a linear operator; it follows that any linear combination of D's is also a linear operator. Any arbitrary combination of D's is a local operator, since its value for a picture f at a point (x, y) depends only on the values of f in any small neighborhood of (x, y). This implies that such operators are all shift invariant. We assume in this section that all the derivatives of f exist and are continuous.

It is of particular interest to construct derivative operators that are *isotropic*, i.e., rotation invariant (in the sense that rotating f and then applying the operator gives the same result as applying the operator to f and rotating the output). We want our operators to be isotropic because we want to sharpen blurred features, such as edges and lines, that run in any direction. It can be shown that

(a)   An isotropic linear derivative operator can involve only derivatives of even orders.

(b)   In an arbitrary isotropic derivative operator, derivatives of odd orders can occur only raised to even powers.

We shall now illustrate, by a simple example, how isotropic derivative operators can be constructed. A rotation is defined by the coordinate transformation equations

$$x = x' \cos \theta - y' \sin \theta, \qquad y = x' \sin \theta + y' \cos \theta$$

where (x, y) are the unrotated and (x', y') are the rotated coordinates. The first partial derivatives of a picture f in the (x', y') system are given, in terms of its first partials in the (x, y) system, by

$$\frac{\partial f}{\partial x'} = \frac{\partial f}{\partial x}\frac{\partial x}{\partial x'} + \frac{\partial f}{\partial y}\frac{\partial y}{\partial x'} = \frac{\partial f}{\partial x}\cos \theta + \frac{\partial f}{\partial y}\sin \theta$$

$$\frac{\partial f}{\partial y'} = \frac{\partial f}{\partial x}\frac{\partial x}{\partial y'} + \frac{\partial f}{\partial y}\frac{\partial y}{\partial y'} = -\frac{\partial f}{\partial x}\sin \theta + \frac{\partial f}{\partial y}\cos \theta$$

These partial derivatives themselves are thus not rotation invariant; but the sum of their squares is invariant, since we readily have

$$\left(\frac{\partial f}{\partial x'}\right)^2 + \left(\frac{\partial f}{\partial y'}\right)^2 = \left(\frac{\partial f}{\partial x}\right)^2 + \left(\frac{\partial f}{\partial y}\right)^2$$

Assertion (b) suggests that this sum of squares is of the simplest possible form for an isotropic derivative operator (ignoring degenerate operators that involve no derivatives at all!), since it uses only first-order derivatives raised to the smallest possible even power.

Exercise 9. Prove that the *Laplacian* operator $(\partial^2/\partial x^2)+(\partial^2/\partial y^2)$ is rotation invariant. (By assertion (a) this has the simplest possible form for a nondegenerate linear isotropic derivative operator, since it uses only derivatives of the smallest possible even order.) ▌

As the previous equations show, the partial derivative of a picture f in an arbitrary direction (e.g., $\partial f/\partial x'$) is a linear combination of its partial derivatives in the x- and y-directions. In fact, given the derivatives in any two non-collinear directions, not necessarily perpendicular to each other, we can express the derivative in any other direction as a linear combination of them.

We can find the direction in which the partial derivative of f has maximum value by differentiating $\partial f/\partial x'$ with respect to θ, setting the result equal to zero, and solving for θ. This gives us

$$-\frac{\partial f}{\partial x}\sin\theta + \frac{\partial f}{\partial y}\cos\theta = 0$$

so that the desired direction is

$$\theta_n = \tan^{-1}\left(\frac{\partial f}{\partial y}\Big/\frac{\partial f}{\partial x}\right)$$

Note that $\theta_n + \pi$ is also a solution; in one of these directions, $\partial f/\partial x'$ is a maximum, while in the other direction it is a minimum, since it has equal magnitude but opposite sign, i.e., $\partial f/\partial(-x') = -\partial f/\partial x'$. For this θ_n we have

$$\cos\theta_n = \frac{1}{\sqrt{1+\tan^2\theta_n}} = \frac{\partial f}{\partial x}\Big/\sqrt{\left(\frac{\partial f}{\partial x}\right)^2 + \left(\frac{\partial f}{\partial y}\right)^2}$$

$$\sin\theta_n = \sqrt{1-\cos^2\theta_n} = \frac{\partial f}{\partial y}\Big/\sqrt{\left(\frac{\partial f}{\partial x}\right)^2 + \left(\frac{\partial f}{\partial y}\right)^2}$$

Thus the maximum value of $\partial f/\partial x'$ is given by

$$\frac{\partial f}{\partial x}\cos\theta_n + \frac{\partial f}{\partial y}\sin\theta_n = +\sqrt{\left(\frac{\partial f}{\partial x}\right)^2 + \left(\frac{\partial f}{\partial y}\right)^2}$$

The vector whose magnitude is $\sqrt{(\partial f/\partial x)^2 + (\partial f/\partial y)^2}$, and whose direction is θ_n (or $\theta_n + \pi$, whichever gives the positive partial derivative) is called the *gradient* of f. As we saw previously the magnitude of the gradient is a rotation-invariant derivative operator. The gradient, and some of its generalizations, are discussed further in Section 10.2, where we deal with edge detection operations.

Exercise 10. Prove that the partial derivative of f is zero in the direction θ_t perpendicular to θ_n. ∎

Exercise 11. Prove that the magnitude of the gradient is equal to $\sqrt{(\partial f/\partial \alpha)^2 + (\partial f/\partial \beta)^2}$, where α and β are any two perpendicular directions. ∎

For digital pictures, we must use differences rather than derivatives. The first differences in the x- and y-directions are

$$\Delta_x f(i, j) \equiv f(i, j) - f(i-1, j)$$
$$\Delta_y f(i, j) \equiv f(i, j) - f(i, j-1)$$

First differences in other directions can be defined as linear combinations of the x- and y-differences, e.g., as

$$\Delta_\theta f(i, j) = \Delta_x f(i, j) \cos \theta + \Delta_y f(i, j) \sin \theta$$

Using this definition, the maximum directional difference, which we call the *digital gradient*, has magnitude and direction

$$\sqrt{(\Delta_x f)^2 + (\Delta_y f)^2} \qquad \text{and} \qquad \tan^{-1}(\Delta_y f / \Delta_x f)$$

respectively. (Several other definitions of the digital gradient will be given in Section 10.2.)

Exercise 12. What happens to the magnitude of the digital gradient under rotation of the digital picture (see Section 9.3)? ∎

The higher difference operators can be defined by repeated first differencing, e.g.,

$$\Delta_x^2 f(i, j) \equiv \Delta_x f(i+1, j) - \Delta_x f(i, j)$$
$$= [f(i+1, j) - f(i, j)] - [f(i, j) - f(i-1, j)]$$
$$= f(i+1, j) + f(i-1, j) - 2f(i, j)$$

and similarly

$$\Delta_y^2 f(i, j) = f(i, j+1) + f(i, j-1) - 2f(i, j)$$

We have used these definitions [rather than, e.g., $\Delta_x f(i, j) - \Delta_x f(i-1, j)$] because they are symmetric with respect to (i, j). We could have also used symmetrical first differences, i.e.,

$$\Delta_x f(i, j) = f(i+1, j) - f(i-1, j)$$

and

$$\Delta_y f(i, j) = f(i, j+1) - f(i, j-1)$$

but we did not do so because they ignore the gray level at (i, j) itself.

6.3.2   The Laplacian

The *Laplacian* is the linear derivative operator

$$\nabla^2 f \equiv \frac{\partial^2 f}{\partial x^2} + \frac{\partial^2 f}{\partial y^2}$$

As indicated in Exercise 9, it is rotation invariant.

To see the relevance of the Laplacian to picture sharpening, suppose that the blur in the picture is a result of a diffusion process that satisfies the well-known partial differential equation

$$\partial g/\partial t = k \nabla^2 g$$

where g is a function of x, y, and t (time), and $k > 0$ is a constant. At $t = 0$, $g(x, y, 0)$ is the unblurred picture $f(x, y)$; at some $t = \tau > 0$, we have the observed blurred picture $g(x, y, \tau)$. If we expand $g(x, y, t)$ in a Taylor series around $t = \tau$, we have

$$g(x, y, 0) = g(x, y, \tau) - \tau \frac{\partial g}{\partial t}(x, y, \tau) + \frac{\tau^2}{2} \frac{\partial^2 g}{\partial t^2}(x, y, \tau) - \cdots$$

If we ignore the quadratic and higher-order terms, and substitute f for $g(x, y, 0)$ and $k \nabla^2 g$ for $\partial g/\partial t$, this gives us

$$f = g - k\tau \nabla^2 g$$

Thus, to a first approximation, we can restore the unblurred picture f by subtracting from g a positive multiple of its Laplacian. (Higher-order approximations based on the Taylor series expansion could also be used, if desired.)

Diffusion is not necessarily an appropriate model for picture blur; but the foregoing at least makes it plausible that we can achieve sharpening by a subtractive combination of the picture and its Laplacian. Other rationales for the relevance of the Laplacian to picture sharpening will be given later. It should be mentioned that according to the diffusion model, a point source blurs into a spot with a Gaussian distribution of brightness whose variance is proportional to $k\tau$; we can thus estimate $k\tau$ by fitting a Gaussian to the point spread function.

Several modifications to this Laplacian method have been proposed, with the aim of reducing noise sensitivity. One suggestion is to use, instead of the Laplacian, the second partial derivative in the gradient direction θ_n. A further refinement is to use a linear combination of the second partial derivatives in the two perpendicular directions θ_n and θ_t. This last scheme can be designed to smooth the picture in the direction along an edge at the same time that it deblurs the edge (see also Section 6.4.3).

For a digital picture, the discrete analog of the Laplacian is

$$\nabla^2 f(i,j) \equiv \Delta_x^2 f(i,j) + \Delta_y^2 f(i,j)$$

$$= [f(i+1,j) + f(i-1,j) + f(i,j+1) + f(i,j-1)] - 4f(i,j)$$

Note that this is proportional, by the factor $-\frac{1}{5}$, to

$$f(i,j) - \tfrac{1}{5}[f(i+1,j) + f(i-1,j) + f(i,j) + f(i,j+1) + f(i,j-1)]$$

which is the difference between the gray level $f(i,j)$ and the average gray level in a neighborhood of (i,j), where the neighborhood consists of (i,j) and its four horizontal and vertical neighbors. Thus we see that the digital Laplacian of a picture f is obtained, up to a constant factor, by subtracting a blurred (i.e., averaged) version of f from f itself.

Alternative digital "Laplacians" can be defined by using different neighborhoods (e.g., the 3×3 neighborhood consisting of (i,j) and its 8 horizontal, vertical, and diagonal neighbors), or by using a weighted average over the neighborhood. One could also combine the original and blurred pictures nonlinearly, e.g., divide by the blurred picture instead of subtracting it. The operation of subtracting a blurred version of a picture from the original picture (e.g., adding a blurred negative to a sharp positive) is a well-known one in photography, where it is called "unsharp masking."

The effect of the digital Laplacian on a picture can be understood by considering a simple one-dimensional example. Suppose that the $1 \times n$ digital "picture" f contains the sequence of gray levels

$$\ldots, 0, \quad 0, \quad 0, \quad 1, \quad 2, \quad 3, \quad 4, \quad 5, \quad 5, \quad 5, \quad 5, \quad 5,$$

$$5, \quad 6, \quad 6, \quad 6, \quad 6, \quad 6, \quad 6, \quad 3, \quad 3, \quad 3, \quad 3, \ldots$$

It is easily verified that $\Delta_x^2 f$ at these points has the values

$$\ldots, 0, \quad 0, \quad 1, \quad 0, \quad 0, \quad 0, \quad 0, \quad -1, \quad 0, \quad 0, \quad 0, \quad 0,$$

$$1, \quad -1, \quad 0, \quad 0, \quad 0, \quad 0, \quad -3, \quad 3, \quad 0, \quad 0, \quad 0, \ldots$$

Note that this is zero on flat intervals or ramps, as is appropriate for a second difference operator; and it is nonzero at the top and bottom of a ramp, and just on each side of a step. (The use of the Laplacian as an edge detector will be discussed in Section 10.2.1b.) If we subtract $\Delta_x^2 f$ from f, point by point, we obtain

$$..., 0, \quad 0, \quad -1, \quad 1, \quad 2, \quad 3, \quad 4, \quad 6, \quad 5, \quad 5, \quad 5, \quad 5,$$
$$4, \quad 7, \quad 6, \quad 6, \quad 6, \quad 6, \quad 9, \quad 0, \quad 3, \quad 3, \quad 3, ...$$

We have now created gray level "undershoots" at the bottom of the ramp and on the low sides of the edges, and "overshoots" at the ramp top and on the high sides of the edges. This has the effect of increasing the average ramp steepness, and of increasing the contrast just at the edges. Thus we have confirmed, in this case, that subtracting the Laplacian from the picture should have a deblurring effect.

In two dimensions, $f(i, j) - \nabla^2 f(i, j)$ is

$$5f(i, j) - [f(i+1, j) + f(i-1, j) + f(i, j+1) + f(i, j-1)]$$

Readily, we have $f - \nabla^2 f = f$ when (i, j) is in the middle of a ramp or flat region. If (i, j) is just at the bottom of a ramp, or on the low side of an edge, so that some of the neighbors' gray levels are higher than $f(i, j)$, while none are lower, we have $(f - \nabla^2 f) < f$ at (i, j), which produces an undershoot. Similarly, at the top of a ramp or on the high side of an edge, none of the neighbors' gray levels are higher than $f(i, j)$, and some are lower, so that $(f - \nabla^2 f) > f$ at (i, j), producing an overshoot. A simple two-dimensional example illustrating these phenomena is shown in Fig. 12; some real cases are shown in Fig. 13.

We can obtain further insight into why subtracting a digital picture's Laplacian from the picture should have a deblurring effect by considering one last example. Suppose that the original picture f was blurred by adding to the gray level of each point a small fraction ε of the sum of its four neighbors' levels, yielding the blurred picture g in which

$$g(i, j) = f(i, j) + \varepsilon s(i, j)$$

(a)   (b)

Fig. 12 Results of subtracting the Laplacian from the original picture in some simple cases. (a) Original pictures (ramp and bar). (b) Pictures minus Laplacians.

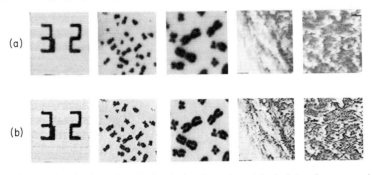

Fig. 13   Results of subtracting the Laplacian from the original picture in some real cases.
(a) Original pictures. (b) Pictures minus Laplacians (negative values have been set to 0, and
values beyond the end of the gray scale have been set to the highest gray level).

where $s(i,j) = f(i+1,j) + f(i-1,j) + f(i,j+1) + f(i,j-1)$. Let us subtract
from g a multiple (by θ, say) of its Laplacian, obtaining

$$(1+4\theta)\,g(i,j) - \theta[g(i+1,j) + g(i-1,j) + g(i,j+1) + g(i,j-1)]$$

If we substitute for the g's in this expression, we obtain

$$(1+4\theta)\,f(i,j) + (1+4\theta)\,\varepsilon s(i,j)$$

$$- \theta s(i,j) - \theta\varepsilon[s(i+1,j) + s(i-1,j) + s(i,j+1) + s(i,j-1)]$$

Let us choose θ so that the coefficient of $s(i,j)$, which is $(1+4\theta)\,\varepsilon - \theta$, vanishes;
this requires $\theta = \varepsilon/(1-4\varepsilon)$. If ε is sufficiently small, we can ignore terms of
order ε^2; in particular, we can ignore the last term, which is a multiple of
$\theta\varepsilon \doteq \varepsilon^2$. Hence

$$g(i,j) - \frac{\varepsilon\,\nabla^2 g(i,j)}{1-4\varepsilon} \doteq \left(1 + \frac{4\varepsilon}{1-4\varepsilon}\right) f(i,j)$$

Thus by subtracting a suitable multiple of g's Laplacian from g, we have
approximately restored the unblurred f.

Exercise 13 [48].   In optical microscopy, let f_k be the cross section of the
specimen at depth k. When we focus on that cross section, the image g_k that we
obtain is degraded by the presence of blurred images of neighboring cross
sections, say $g_k \doteq f_k + \varepsilon(\bar{f}_{k+1} + \bar{f}_{k-1})$, where the overbars denote local averaging. Show how f_k can be restored, to a first approximation, by subtracting a
suitable multiple of $(\bar{g}_{k+1} + \bar{g}_{k-1})$ from g_k. ∎

6.3.3 High-Emphasis Filtering

The effects of derivative operators in sharpening a picture can also be interpreted from a spatial frequency standpoint. Since the derivative of $\sin nx$ is $n \cos nx$, we see that the higher the spatial frequency of a sinusoidal pattern, the higher the amplitude of its derivative is. Thus differentiation strengthens high spatial frequencies more than it does low ones. (Conversely, the integral of $\cos nx$ is $(1/n) \sin nx$, so that integration weakens high frequencies more than it does low ones.)

The effect of subtracting a Laplacian from a picture can be explained along similar lines. As we saw in Section 6.3.2,

$$f(i, j) - \nabla^2 f(i, j) = f(i, j) + 5\{f(i, j) - \tfrac{1}{5}[f(i + 1, j) + f(i - 1, j) \\ + f(i, j) + f(i, j + 1) + f(i, j - 1)]\}$$

Here the second term is proportional to the difference between the original picture f and a blurred version of f, call it $\bar{f}$. Now in $\bar{f}$, high spatial frequencies have been weakened more than low ones. Hence when we subtract $\bar{f}$ from f, since the Fourier transform is a linear operator, the low frequencies in f are more or less cancelled out, while the high frequencies remain relatively intact. Thus, when we add a multiple of $f - \bar{f}$ to f, we are boosting the high frequencies, while leaving the low ones relatively unaffected.

These qualitative remarks can help to justify the use of Laplacians and other derivative operators to sharpen pictures. These methods should, however, be considered only in the absence of knowledge about the blur that is to be corrected. When such knowledge is available, restoration techniques such as inverse filtering (Section 7.2) should be used instead. In such techniques, the degree of emphasis on the high frequencies, as a function of frequency, is chosen so as to just compensate for the weakening caused by the blurring. If noise is present in addition to the blur, however, frequencies at which the noise is strong should not be emphasized. Typically, a high-emphasis filtering operation designed for blur compensation has a transfer function which increases with increasing spatial frequency, up to the point where noise would begin to dominate; it then drops off, more or less abruptly, to zero. The form of the dropoff can be designed to simulate some familiar type of transfer function; this helps avoid artifacts in the sharpened picture. A good example of the type of enhancement that can be achieved by this type of filtering is shown in Fig. 14.

By the convolution theorem (Section 2.1.4), convolving a picture g with some function h gives the same result as multiplying the Fourier transform G of g by the Fourier transform H of h, and then taking the inverse transform.

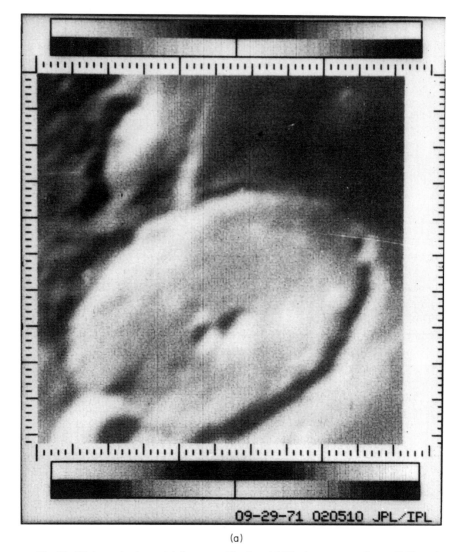

(a)

Fig. 14 High-emphasis spatial frequency filtering. (a) The lunar crater Gassendi blurred by atmospheric turbulence. (b) Results of high-emphasis filtering. (From [35].)

We also saw in Section 2.1.2 that any shift-invariant linear operation is a convolution operation. Analogous results hold for discrete convolutions, using the discrete Fourier transform (Section 2.2.1). Now the digital Laplacian ∇^2 is a shift-invariant linear operation; in fact, applying it to a picture g is

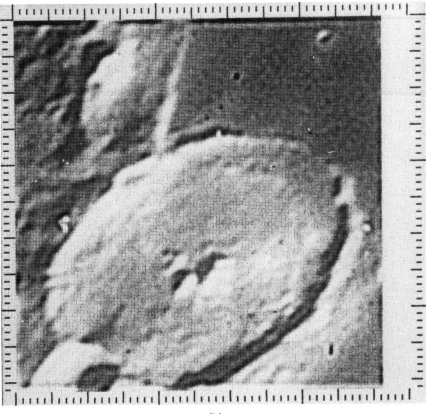

(b)

Fig. 14 (*Continued*)

the same as convolving g with the array h_L defined by

$$
\begin{array}{ccc}
 & 1 & \\
1 & -4 & 1 \\
 & 1 &
\end{array}
$$

in which all points not shown have value 0. Similarly, computing $g - \nabla^2 g$ is the same as convolving g with h_D, defined by

$$
\begin{array}{ccc}
 & -1 & \\
-1 & 5 & -1 \\
 & -1 &
\end{array}
$$

(a)

Fig. 15 (a) High-emphasis filtering using a logarithmic transformation. (b) Results of
filtering. (From [43].)

These space-domain convolution operations can also be performed in the
frequency domain, by multiplying the discrete Fourier transform H_L (or H_D)
by G and then inverse transforming.

Exercise 14. Compute the discrete Fourier transform of the array h_D
(which you may assume to be $N \times N$). ∎

Conversely, given any frequency-domain high-emphasis filter H, we can
apply it to a picture g in two ways: multiply g's Fourier transform G by H
and inverse transform; or convolve g with the inverse Fourier transform h of

(b)

Fig. 15 (*Continued*)

H. The h's obtained in this way will generally have both positive and negative values, but $|h|$ will drop off rapidly from a central peak; thus a good approximation to the desired filtering can be obtained using only a small piece of h surrounding the peak. In the digital case, we can still obtain reasonable results if we take this piece to be as small as 3×3; the resulting truncated h generally resembles the $g - \nabla^2 g$ operator, having a positive peak symmetrically surrounded by smaller negative values, whose magnitudes add up to about 1 less than the value at the peak.

Exercise 15. Compute the h that corresponds to the one-dimensional high-emphasis filter H for which $H(n) = |n| + 1$, $-3 \leqslant n \leqslant 4$ (i.e., $N = 8$). ∎

High-emphasis filtering in conjunction with a logarithmic transformation of the gray scale can sometimes be used to reduce shading effects, due to varying illumination, in a picture without degrading the detail in the picture. As indicated at the end of Section 6.2.2, a simplified model for the picture gray level is $f(x, y) = I(x, y)R(x, y)$, where I and R are illumination and reflectivity, and where I is primarily composed of low spatial frequencies. We cannot reduce the effects of I on f by simply boosting the high frequencies, since I and R are combined multiplicatively, rather than additively. However, if we take logs of both sides, we have $\log f = \log I + \log R$, an additive combination; we can then apply high-emphasis filtering, in either the Fourier or space domain, to decrease the contribution of $\log I$, and then take antilogs to obtain a filtered version of f. An example of such processing is shown in Fig. 15. This type of processing is called *homomorphic filtering* because the log operation transforms multiplication into addition ($\log ab = \log a + \log b$), and is thus a homorphism from the multiplicative group of positive real numbers into the additive group of real numbers.

6.4 SMOOTHING

As we saw in Section 6.1.4, many types of noise can be present in a picture. In this section we describe some simple methods of noise removal, or more generally, of making a picture "smoother." Optimal estimation of a picture that has been degraded by noise will be treated in Section 7.5.

The basic difficulty with noise removal and smoothing techniques is that, if applied indiscriminately, they tend to blur the picture, which is usually objectionable. In particular, one usually wants to avoid blurring sharp edges or lines that occur in the picture. Our main concern in this section will be with methods which permit smoothing without introducing undesirable blurring.

A general approach to picture smoothing would be to define a cost function φ for evaluating the various possible smoothings $\hat{f}$ of a given noisy picture g. This φ should depend both on the irregularity of $\hat{f}$ and on the discrepancy between $\hat{f}$ and g. For example, φ could be a weighted integral over the picture of $(\partial\hat{f}/\partial x)^2 + (\partial\hat{f}/\partial y)^2 + (\hat{f}-g)^2$; the first two terms give the mean magnitude of the gradient of $\hat{f}$, while the third term is the mean squared difference between $\hat{f}$ and g. The weighting function in the integral should be defined so that φ is sensitive to noisy fluctuations in $\hat{f}$, but not to high values of $\hat{f}$'s gradient that are due to the presence of sharp long edges or lines, which are presumably not noise. Given φ, one can attempt to find a smoothed f that minimizes it; if we used a discrete version of φ, defined as a sum over the points of the digital pictures $\hat{f}$ and g, this minimization can be done, in principle, using mathe-

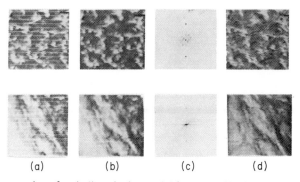

(a)   (b)   (c)   (d)

Fig. 16 Suppression of periodic noise by spatial frequency filtering. (a) Original pictures. (b) Results of removing the lines by interpolation (each point on a line is replaced by the average of the points above and below). (c) Power spectra; note high-value points corresponding to spectrum of lines. (d) Results of removing small neighborhoods of these high-value points and reconstructing the pictures.

matical programming techniques. In practice, however, since the number of variables in this global optimization problem is very large, it may be too difficult to find the optimum $\hat{f}$ in this way unless the picture g is small. The nonoptimal techniques described in this section involve only local processing of g, and should thus be much simpler computationally.

6.4.1 Noise Removal

If the noise occurs in known positions in the picture, or if we are able to distinguish the noise from the rest of the picture, it becomes relatively easy to remove the noise without bad effects on other parts of the picture, since we can operate only on the noise, leaving the rest of the picture intact.

As a simple example, suppose that a periodic line pattern v has been added to the picture f, as in Fig. 16a. We can remove the lines, without affecting the rest of the picture, by changing the gray level of each line point to the average of the levels of neighboring picture points. The results of line removal by this type of "interpolation" are shown in Fig. 16b. Alternatively, we can remove the lines by operating in the Fourier domain. If we take the Fourier transform of the noisy picture $f + v$, we obtain the sum $F + N$ of the transforms of f and v (see Fig. 16c). Now the Fourier transform N of the line pattern v has all its energy concentrated at a set of small spots along a line perpendicular to the direction of the lines. If we suppress these spots from the transform (zero them out, or remove them by interpolation), and then take the inverse transform, we obtain a smoothed picture in which v has been deleted, while f is relatively unaffected, as shown in Fig. 16d.

(a)   (b)   (c)   (d)   (e)

Fig. 17   Suppression of "salt-and-pepper" noise by selective local averaging. (a) Noisy picture. (b) Results of blurring (a)—each point replaced by the average of its eight neighbors. (c)–(e) Results of doing the replacement only for points that differ by at least three gray levels from k of their neighbors for $k = 8, 7, 6$.

Exercise 16.   Describe how to remove a line pattern which has been combined multiplicatively, rather than additively, with a picture (i.e., fv rather than $f + v$). ∎

It should be pointed out that interpolation to replace the removed noise is easy when the noise is fine (isolated points, thin lines, etc.), so that each noise point has nonnoise neighboring points. When the noise is coarse (large artifacts, wide bars, etc.) it becomes much harder to replace it inconspicuously.

Another case in which noise removal is relatively easy is when the noise consists of isolated points that contrast with their neighbors (e.g., "salt-and-pepper" noise). Here we can attempt to detect noise points by comparing each point's gray level z with the levels z_i of its neighbors. If z is substantially larger (or smaller) than all, or nearly all, of the z_i, we can classify it as a noise point, and remove it by interpolation, i.e., replace z by the average of the z_i. An example of noise removal by this method is shown in Fig. 17.

The method just described has several parameters that can be adjusted to suit the characteristics of the noise that is to be detected. These parameters include the neighborhood size, the threshold amount Δ by which z and the z_i must differ ("substantially"), and the number k of z_i from which z must differ ("nearly all"). The parameter Δ might be defined as some multiple of the estimated standard deviation σ of the noise; as pointed out in Section 6.1.4, we can estimate σ by measuring the standard deviation of gray level over a region that we believe to be constant in the nonnoisy picture. (We assume here that the noise has zero mean.) The choice of parameter k is important in discriminating between noise points and points that lie on edges or lines; the latter type of point will differ from some of its neighbors, but should not differ from "nearly all" of them.

A simplified version of this method, which is often proposed, is to compare z to the average of the z_i (i.e., to examine the value of the digital Laplacian at the given point), rather than to the z_i individually. This approach, however, would be less able to distinguish isolated points from points on edges or lines, since the value of the Laplacian at a low-contrast isolated point can be the same as its value on a medium-contrast line or a high-contrast edge, as we will see in Section 10.2.1b. Simplification of the method is possible, however, when the given picture is two-valued ("black and white"). Here we can detect noise points by counting the number of their neighbors from which they differ. A black point that has too many ("nearly all") white neighbors can be changed from black to white, and vice versa. (Replacement by averaging would not be appropriate here, since we want the cleaned picture to remain two-valued.)

As just described the method makes a forced-choice decision as to whether or not the given point is a noise point. If we decide that the point is noise, we change z to the average of the z_i; in other words, in choosing the new gray level for the point, we pay no attention to its old level. On the other hand, if we decide that the point is not noise, we do not change z at all, i.e., we pay no further attention to its neighbors' levels. A more general approach would be to make a "fuzzy" decision about the point, say that it has probability p of being a noise point. We could then give the point a new gray level which would be a weighted average of z and the z_i's, e.g., $(1-p)z + p \sum z_i/k$. If p is high, so that the point is highly likely to be a noise point, this formula gives high weight to the neighborhood average and low weight to the point's old gray level; while if p is low, the opposite is true. This idea will be discussed further in Section 6.4.3.

Smoothing methods based on weighted averages of neighbors, or on averaging with selected neighbors, are also treated in Section 6.4.3. These methods attempt to give greater weight to neighbors that belong to the same region as the given point. Note that even if all the neighbors belong to the same region, one still might want to give them unequal weights, depending on their distances from the given point, and on the correlation properties of the signal and the noise. In particular, one might want to determine a gray level for the given point by fitting some type of surface to the gray levels of the neighboring points.

Noise removal methods can also be used to remove false contours from a picture that has been quantized too coarsely (Section 4.3). One way to do this is to blur the picture and requantize the resulting averages to a more closely spaced set of levels; but to avoid blurring real edges, the averaging is not done at points where the gray level changes by more than one quantization step. Another idea is to add noise, of magnitude less than one quantization step, to the picture, again using a more closely spaced set of levels; this method, which is basically the Roberts compression technique of Section 5.8, breaks up the false contours by trading quantization noise for salt-and-pepper noise.

6.4.2   Averaging

The smoothing methods described in the preceding section depend on first distinguishing noise from nonnoise in the picture, then removing the noise and "mending" the picture by interpolation. In this section, we discuss another class of smoothing methods which do not depend on identification and removal of the noise. Instead, these methods weaken the noise by applying some type of averaging to the picture. Since averaging blurs the picture, these methods too must be applied with care, to avoid degrading sharp detail such as lines or edges.

To see why averaging can weaken noise, suppose that the noise values at each point are independent samples chosen from a distribution having mean 0 and standard deviation σ. Suppose also that we are averaging over a set of picture points whose nonnoisy gray levels are $z_1, \ldots, z_n$, and let the noise values at these points be $w_1, \ldots, w_n$. Then in the average, $(z_1 + \cdots + z_n)/n + (w_1 + \cdots + w_n)/n$, the second term can be regarded (see Section 2.3.5, Exercise 6) as a sample of a random variable with mean 0 and standard deviation $\sigma/\sqrt{n}$. Thus by averaging, we have reduced the amplitude of the noise fluctuations.

We can perform the averaging without any danger of blurring when we are given several independently noisy copies $f_i(x, y)$ of a picture, e.g., several grainy photographs, or several "snowy" TV frames, of the same scene, where the noise values of the copies at a given point are all independent. In this case, we can reduce the noise by pointwise averaging the copies, obtaining the new picture f defined by

$$f(x, y) = (1/n) \sum_{i=1}^{n} f_i(x, y)$$

An example of smoothing by averaging of independent copies is shown in Fig. 18.

The method of pointwise averaging can also be used when the picture to be smoothed is symmetric or periodic (except for the noise). Specifically, let P be a pattern or region that occurs several times on the picture; let $P_1, \ldots, P_n$ be the noisy instances of P. If we average these instances pointwise, we obtain a less noisy version $\bar{P}$ of P, and we can replace each of the P_i's by $\bar{P}$ to obtain a smoother picture.

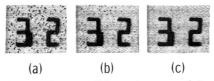

(a)   (b)   (c)

Fig. 18   Smoothing by averaging over different instances of the noise. (a)–(c) Averages of 2, 4, and 8 independently noisy versions of Fig. 17a.

If we only have a single noisy picture available, we can attempt to reduce the noise level by *local* averaging, i.e., we give each point a new gray level which is the average of the original gray levels in some neighborhood of the point (including the point itself). This is relatively straightforward if the noise is finer grained than the smallest picture detail of interest; it should then be possible, by averaging over a small neighborhood of every point, to reduce the noise while keeping the blur at a negligible, or at least tolerable, level. Alternatively, we may be able to remove the noise by suppressing or deemphasizing high spatial frequencies—or equivalently, emphasizing low spatial frequencies—in the picture's Fourier transform. This last approach has been successfully used to remove film-grain noise from photographs.

If the given picture is two-valued, noise that is smaller than the picture detail can be removed by a process of shrinking and reexpanding. For example, suppose that we change all black points to white if they have any white neighbors, and then change all white points to black if they have any black neighbors. The first step shrinks all black regions, while the second step reexpands them; but a black object that is two points wide or less will disappear completely at the first step, so that the second step cannot restore it. Thus this process deletes not only isolated points, but also thin lines. Other uses of shrinking and expanding operations will be discussed in Sections 11.2.1, 11.3.2, and 11.3.4.

The size of the neighborhood that should be used in local averaging depends on the degree of noise reduction that is desired; as pointed out earlier, averaging n points should reduce the standard deviation of the noise by a factor of $\sqrt{n}$. If the noise is signal dependent, one may want to use a different neighborhood size at each point, depending on the average picture gray level in the vicinity of that point, in order to obtain a uniform reduced noise level throughout the picture. One way of obtaining such variable-sized neighborhoods is to calculate the sums of the gray levels in a series of expanding neighborhoods of a point, and stop expanding when the sum reaches a preset threshold. The resulting neighborhood will be large if the gray levels in the vicinity are generally low, and vice versa. The average gray level over the neighborhood is then inversely proportional to the neighborhood's area, since the sum of gray levels over the neighborhood is a constant. A variable-neighborhood averaging method of this type has been used to smooth "quantum-limited" pictures, which consist of clusters of dots; here the neighborhood size at a point was determined by expanding the neighborhood until it contained a preset number of dots.

6.4.3 Selective and Weighted Averaging

Averaging could be used to smooth a picture without blurring it if we could perform the averaging only at selected points, or average only with selected neighbors, in such a way that we never average across edges, lines, etc. In the following paragraphs we describe a number of averaging schemes that tend to avoid averaging over edges.

The simplest idea of this type is to apply an edge (or line) detection operator to the picture (see Sections 10.2 and 10.3), and average only at points where such features are not present. In a sense, this is the opposite of the method used in Fig. 17, where we averaged (or rather, replaced a point by the average of its neighbors) only at points that differed substantially from most of their neighbors. Here we would have to use an edge or line detector that does not respond to isolated points, since we do want to average at such points. Note that if we do not average at edges and lines, noise that is adjacent to them will not be weakened; but since noise is generally less conspicuous when it is located near such features, this may not be a serious objection.

As a more refined idea, when an edge (or line) is present, we can take a directional average, involving only those neighbors that lie in the direction along the edge; while if noise is present, we average with all the neighbors [14]. This should prevent averaging across edges, while still permitting a small amount of averaging at ($=$along) edges. The process can be iterated to provide an increased amount of averaging at each point, while still avoiding averages that cross edges. Figure 19b shows the results of four iterations of a method of this type, applied to the noisy picture shown in Fig. 19a (obtained by adding Gaussian noise of mean 0 and standard deviation 8 to the nonnoisy version). This method used a set of edge detection masks in four orientations (see Section 10.2.2a); if the range of their values at a given point exceeds a given threshold t, here taken to be 3, the point is replaced by the average of its two neighbors in the direction of minimum edge value, while otherwise the point is replaced by the average of its eight neighbors. These results are not very sensitive to the choice of t; see [8] for further details. A variation on this method, using only two edge masks to estimate the direction along the edge, and averaging with the two neighbors in this direction if the estimated gradient magnitude exceeds t, yields blurrier results, as seen in Fig. 19c. For comparison, Fig. 19d shows the method of Fig. 17 applied to the same picture (a point is replaced by the average of its neighbors if it differs from at least six of them by at least 3); this too yields blurrier results.

The method of Figs. 19b and 19c, use averages of either two neighbors or eight, depending on whether it is decided that an edge is present. An alternative idea is to use a weighted average of the neighbors, where the weights assigned to the neighbors in a given direction depend on our confidence that there is an edge through the given point in that direction. (The details of how the weights might be chosen are somewhat complicated, and will not be given here; see [8, 26].) The results of applying two methods of this type

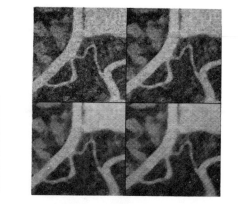

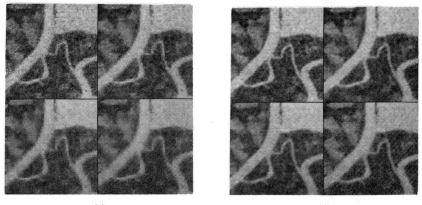

Fig. 19 Smoothing by averaging along edges. (a) Original picture (portion of a LANDSAT image), and result of adding Gaussian noise ($\mu = 0$, $\sigma = 8$ on a gray scale of 0–63). (b) Result of averaging two neighbors along the edge if an edge is present, and all neighbors otherwise (four iterations). (c) Analogous to (b), but using a simpler method of determining the edge direction. (d) Result of iterated averaging only at points differing from at least six of their neighbors by at least 3; see also Fig. 17.

to the same picture are shown in Figs. 20a and 20b; the results appear to be better than those of Fig. 19.

There are other selective averaging schemes which do not explicitly decide whether an edge is present, or determine edge confidences in given directions; rather, these schemes choose neighbors that seem likely to

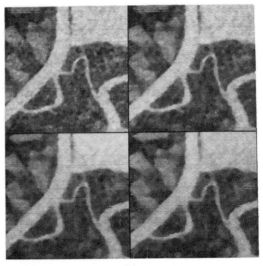

(a)

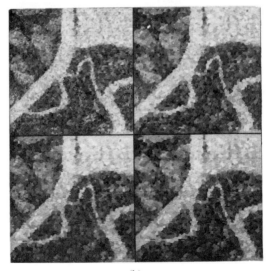

(b)

Fig. 20 Smoothing by iterated weighted averaging, designed to give greater weight to neighbors in the directions along edges (two methods; four iterations of each).

belong to the same region as the given point, based on various simple criteria. The following are some examples of schemes of this type:

(a) Examine a set of neighborhoods that lie on various sides of the point, e.g., if the neighbors of point M are

A B C D E
F G H I J
K L M N O
P Q R S T
U V W X Y

we might use the neighborhoods

A B C	C D E	G H I	K L M		M N O
F G H,	H I J,	L M N,	P Q R,	and	R S T
K L M	M N O	Q R S	U V W		W X Y

Measure the gray level variability over each neighborhood, and replace the point by the average of the neighborhood that has lowest variability. Evidently, this neighborhood is most likely to lie entirely within a uniform region of the picture, so that averaging over it is least likely to blur an edge. For examples of such methods see [8, 31, 45].

(b) Alternatively, we can subdivide the neighborhood of the point in various ways, and choose the half-neighborhood whose average gray level is closest to that of the point; or we can use the half whose average differs the most from that of the other half. (Compare the Kirsch edge detection operation in Section 10.2.2a.) Results using these two methods are shown in Figs. 21a and 21b; the second method seems to be very good. These examples used a 3×3 neighborhood, and divided the eight neighbors into consecutive groups of five and three; see [42] for the details.

(c) A simpler idea is to use the average of the, e.g., five neighbors whose gray levels are closest to that of the given point, whether or not they are consecutive [10]. This also yields good results, as seen from Fig. 21c.

(d) As still another alternative, we can use the average of those neighbors whose rates of change of gray level are lower than that of the given point; if the point is adjacent to an edge, these neighbors should be the ones that are interior to the region containing the point [10]. Here again, the results are good, as shown in Fig. 21d.

In all of these schemes, rather than choose a (half-) neighborhood or a set of neighbors, we can weight the neighbors appropriately, e.g., we can weight each neighbor in accordance with how close its gray level is to that of the given point, or how low its rate of change is. However, such weighting

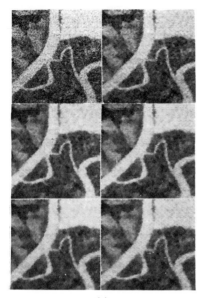

(a)

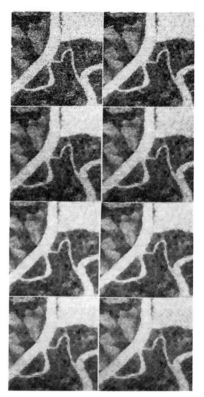

(c)

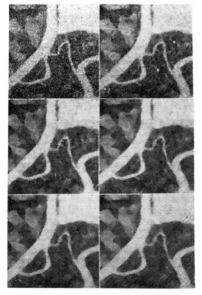

(b)

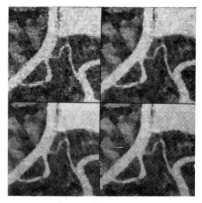

(d)

Fig. 21 Smoothing by selective averaging. (a) Result of averaging each point with its five consecutive neighbors whose average is closest to the value of the point (five iterations). (b) Analogous, but using the five neighbors whose average differs the most from that of the remaining three neighbors. (c) Result of averaging each point with its five neighbors whose values are closest to its own (seven iterations). (d) Result of averaging the neighbors whose rates of change of gray level are lower than that of the point (four iterations).

schemes do not seem to give as good results as simply choosing a best set of neighbors and ignoring the others [42].

One can also use hybrid methods in which, e.g., we do one kind of averaging if the neighborhood is highly variable, and another if it is not [42, 47]; but these do not seem to have any great advantage over the simpler methods. Rather than use a fixed neighborhood of each point, one might attempt to "grow" a neighborhood that does not cross any edges — in other words, to apply region growing methods (Section 10.4.2) to the given picture, perhaps for a limited number of iterations, and then take averages over the resulting regions [41].

6.4.4 Median Filtering and Min/Max Filtering

A powerful smoothing technique that does not blur edges is *median filtering*, in which we replace the value at a point by the median of the values in a neighborhood of the point. To see how this works, we first consider a simple one-dimensional example. Let the input values be

$$0\ 0\ 0\ 6\ 0\ 0\ 1\ 2\ 1\ 0\ 1\ 2\ 1\ 0\ 2\ 4\ 2\ 0\ 2\ 4\ 2\ 0\ 0\ 1\ 2\ 3\ 4\ 4\ 4\ 4\ 4\ 0\ 0\ 0$$

Suppose we replace the value at each point by the mean of the point and its two neighbors, i.e., we take a length-3 running average of the input string. The result is

$$0\ 2\ 2\ 2\tfrac{1}{3}\ 1\tfrac{4}{3}\ 1\tfrac{2}{3}\ 1\tfrac{4}{3}\ 1\ 1\ 2\tfrac{8}{3}\ 2\tfrac{4}{3}\ 2\tfrac{8}{3}\ 2\tfrac{2}{3}\tfrac{1}{3}\ 1\ 2\ 3\tfrac{11}{3}\ 4\ 4\ 4\tfrac{8}{3}\tfrac{4}{3}\ 0$$

We see that this process blurs noise spikes (the 6 becomes three 2's); weakens oscillations, but does not smooth them out completely (e.g., 0 1 2 1 0 1 2 1 0 becomes $1\tfrac{4}{3}\ 1\tfrac{2}{3}\ 1\tfrac{4}{3}\ 1$); and blurs both ramp and step edges (0 1 2 3 4 becomes $\tfrac{1}{3}\ 1\ 2\ 3\tfrac{11}{3}$; 4 4 4 0 0 0 becomes $4\ 4\tfrac{8}{3}\tfrac{4}{3}\ 0\ 0$). On the other hand, let us replace the value at each point by the median of the point and its two neighbors; if their values are a, b, c, where $a \leqslant b \leqslant c$, this median is simply b. This yields

$$0\ 0\ 0\ 0\ 1\ 1\ 1\ 1\ 1\ 1\ 1\ 1\ 2\ 2\ 2\ 2\ 2\ 2\ 0\ 0\ 1\ 2\ 3\ 4\ 4\ 4\ 4\ 0\ 0$$

Here the noise spike is eliminated, the oscillations are flattened, and the ramp and step edges are exactly preserved.

Similarly, to perform two-dimensional median filtering at a point, we sort the values of the point and its neighbors in order of size, and use the middle value as the new value at the point, e.g., for a 3×3 neighborhood, we use the fifth largest value. Since median filtering does not blur edges, it can be iterated. An example of the results of iterated 3×3 median filtering is shown in Fig. 22a.

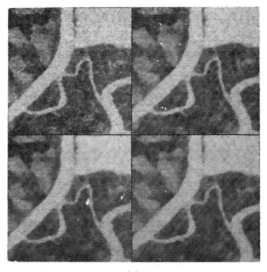

(a)

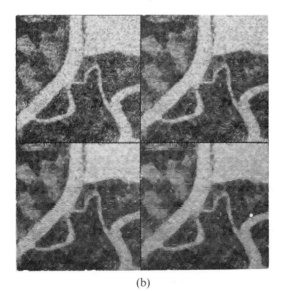

(b)

Fig. 22   (a) Four iterations of median filtering. (b) Four iterations of mode filtering.

A problem with two-dimensional median filtering is that it destroys thin lines as well as isolated points, and it also "clips" corners; to see this, consider the examples

$$
\begin{array}{ccc}
\ldots0 & 1 & 0\ldots \\
\ldots0 & 1 & 0\ldots \\
\ldots0 & 1 & 0\ldots
\end{array}
\quad\text{and}\quad
\begin{array}{cccc}
\ldots0 & 0 & 0 & 0\ldots \\
\ldots1 & 1 & 0 & 0\ldots \\
\ldots1 & 1 & 0 & 0\ldots
\end{array}
$$

We can preserve horizontal and vertical lines or corners by using, e.g., a cross-shaped filtering neighborhood such as

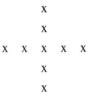

in which the value of the center "x" is replaced by the fifth largest of the xs' values; but this does not help for diagonally oriented lines or corners. Thus median filtering is best applied to pictures that do not contain thin curves or sharp corners.

To perform median filtering at every point of a picture, it is not necessary to sort the values for every neighborhood. Once they have been sorted for the first neighborhood, we can handle successive neighborhoods by deleting those on the trailing edge and merging in those on the leading edge. Another way of reducing the computational cost of computing the median is to compute medians for a set of subneighborhoods and then take the median of these medians (e.g., for a 3×3 neighborhood, take the median of the three values on each row, then the median of these); this does not give the true median, but it may be an acceptable approximation.

One can also compute order statistics other than the median in the neighborhood of a point. Taking neighborhood min or max is a generalization of shrinking or expanding the 1's in a two-valued picture (see Section 11.2.1c) [32]. Suppose that a picture contains small high-valued blemishes on a low-valued background (or vice versa). If we perform several iterations of a local min operation, they will vanish, but large high-valued regions will also shrink; to restore these to the proper size, we perform the same number of iterations of local max. To remove low-valued blemishes on a high-valued background, similarly, we use iterated local max followed by iterated local min. An example of a picture that has been smoothed in this way is shown in Fig. 23. Alternatively, one could first threshold the picture and then use iterated shrinking and expanding, as in Section 11.2.1c. This

(a)

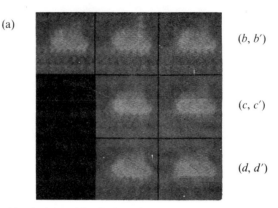

(b, b')

(c, c')

(d, d')

Fig. 23 Smoothing by iterated local min and max operations. (a) Original (infrared image of a tank). (b,b′) min followed by max. (c,c′) Two mins followed by two maxes. (d,d′) Three mins followed by three maxes. In (b,c,d) the mins and maxes are taken over the point and its four horizontal and vertical neighbors; in (b′,c′,d′), the diagonal neighbors are also used.

yields exactly the same result as using iterated min and max and then thresholding; in fact, the local min and max (as well as the other order statistics) commute with any monotonic transformation of the gray scale, and in particular, with thresholding. Thus using local min and max gives the same results as shrinking and expanding for all possible thresholds.

Rather than taking the lowest, highest, or middle ranking values in a neighborhood, one can take the value having any desired rank.[§] An alternative idea is to take the *mode* of the neighborhood, i.e., the value that occurs most often. As Fig. 22b shows, when we iterate this "mode filtering" operation, the noise is smoothed out, but the picture becomes strongly mottled.

6.5 BIBLIOGRAPHICAL NOTES

For general reviews of image quality and enhancement see Linfoot [28], Huang [20], Levi [27], McCamy [30], Prewitt [40], and Biberman [5]. Two discussions of the use of visual system models in the design of image-processing systems, particularly as regards the nonlinear brightness response of the eye and its dependence on spatial and temporal frequency, are Budrikis [6] and Stockham [43]. Illumination effects have been extensively treated by Horn [17–19]. On histogram modification see Hall *et al.* [15], Troy *et al.*

[§] In a two-valued picture, using the neighboring value that has a specified rank means that, e.g., we can change 0's to 1's if they have more than a specified number of 1's as neighbors, etc.

[46], and Haralick *et al.* [16]; see also the references on tapered and optimum quantization in Section 4.4.

Much work on image enhancement, including both gray scale and geometric correction techniques, as well as filtering techniques for sharpening and smoothing, has been done at NASA's Jet Propulsion Laboratory; see, e.g., O'Handley and Green [35].

The use of derivative operations for sharpening a picture is very old (e.g., Goldmark and Hollywood [13]; Kovasznay and Joseph [24, 25]). A more recent review by Prewitt [40] also discusses Laplacians and their modifications (those based on the second derivative in the gradient direction are due to Gabor). Transfer function modification by high-emphasis filtering is also a classical technique; for a recent discussion see Arguello *et al.* [3]. Regarding filtering based on a logarithmic transformation, see Oppenheim *et al.* [36] and Stockham [43]. On the use of derivative operations for edge and line detection see Sections 10.2 and 10.3.

A global approach to smoothing, using mathematical programming, is discussed by Martelli and Montanari [29]. Techniques for removing "salt-and-pepper" noise (in the two-valued case) are described by Dinneen [11]. On smoothing by averaging multiple copies of an image see Kohler and Howell [23]. The application to symmetric objects is given by Agrawal *et al.* [1] and Norman [34]. For early work on smoothing of film-grain noise see Thiry [44]. Regarding averaging in the absence of, or along, edges and lines, see Graham [14]; for a generalization to texture edges see Newman and Dirilten [33]. Variable-neighborhood averaging is discussed by Pizer and Vetter [38, 39] for the case of quantum-limited pictures; they also describe methods of deblurring such pictures by shifting dots in the direction for which local dot density is increasing fastest.

REFERENCES

1. H. O. Agrawal, J. W. Kent, and D. M. MacKay, Rotation technique in electron microscopy of viruses, *Science* **148**, 1965, 638–640.
2. G. B. Anderson and T. S. Huang, Frequency-domain image errors, *Pattern Recognit.* **3**, 1961, 185–196.
3. R. J. Arguello, H. R. Sellner, and J. Z. Stuller, Transfer function compensation of sampled imagery, *IEEE Trans. Comput.* **C-21**, 1972, 812–818.
4. H. G. Barrow and J. M. Tenenbaum, Recovering intrinsic scene characteristics from images, *in* "Computer Vision Systems" (A. R. Hanson and E. M. Riseman, eds.), pp. 3–26. Academic Press, New York, 1978.
5. L. M. Biberman (ed.), "Perception of Displayed Information." Plenum Press, New York, 1973.
6. Z. L. Budrikis, Visual fidelity criterion and modeling, *Proc. IEEE* **60**, 1972, 771–779.
7. S. K. Chang and Y. W. Wong, Optimal histogram matching by monotone gray level transformation, *Comm. ACM* **21**, 1978, 835–840.

8.   J. P. Davenport, A comparison of noise cleaning techniques, Computer Science Technical
     Rep. 689, Univ. of Maryland, College Park, Maryland, September 1978.
9.   L. S. Davis and A. Rosenfeld, Iterative histogram modification. *IEEE Trans. Systems Man
     Cybernet.* **8**, 1978, 300–302.
10. L. S. Davis and A. Rosenfeld, Noise cleaning by interated local averaging, *IEEE Trans.
     Systems Man Cybernet.* **8**, 1978, 705–710.
11. G. P. Dinneen, Programming pattern recognition, *Proc. Western Joint Comput. Conf.*,
     1955, 94–100.
12. W. Frei, Image enhancement by histogram hyperbolization, *Comput. Graphics Image
     Processing* **6**, 1977, 286–294.
13. P. C. Goldmark and J. M. Hollywood, A new technique for improving the sharpness of
     television pictures, *Proc. IRE* **39**, 1951, 1314–1322.
14. R. E. Graham, Snow removal—a noise-stripping process for picture signals, *IRE Trans.
     Informat. Theory* **IT-8**, 1962, 129–144.
15. E. L. Hall, R. P. Kruger, S. J. Dwyer, III, D. L. Hall, R. W. McLaren, and G. S. Lodwick,
     A survey of preprocessing and feature extraction techniques for radiographic images,
     IEEE Trans. Comput. **C-20**, 1971, 1032–1044.
16. R. M. Haralick, K. Shanmugam, and I. Dinstein, Textural features for image classifica-
     tion, *IEEE Trans. Systems Man Cybernet.* **SMC-3**, 1973, 610–621.
17. B. K. P. Horn, Determining lightness from an image, *Comput. Graphics Image Processing*
     3, 1974, 277–299.
18. B. K. P. Horn, Obtaining shape from shading information, *in* "The Psychology of Com-
     puter Vision" (P. H. Winston, ed.), pp. 115–155. McGraw-Hill, New York, 1975.
19. B. K. P. Horn, Understanding image intensities, *Artificial Intelligence* **8**, 1977, 201–231.
20. T. S. Huang, Image enhancement: a review, *Opto-Electronics* **1**, 1969, 49–59.
21. R. Hummel, Histogram modification techniques, *Comput. Graphics Image Processing* **4**,
     1975, 209–224.
22. R. Hummel, Image enhancement by histogram transformation, *Comput. Graphics Image
     Processing* **6**, 1977, 184–195.
23. R. Kohler and H. Howell, Photographic image enhancement by superimposition of
     multiple images, *Photogr. Sci. Eng.* **7**, 1963, 241–245.
24. L. S. G. Kovasznay and H. M. Joseph, Processing of two-dimensional patterns by scan-
     ning techniques, *Science* **118**, 1953, 475–477.
25. L. S. G. Kovasznay and H. M. Joseph, Image processing, *Proc. IRE* **43**, 1955, 560–570.
26. A. Lev, S. W. Zucker, and A. Rosenfeld, Iterative enhancement of noisy images, *IEEE
     Trans. Systems Man Cybernet.* **7**, 1977, 435–442.
27. L. Levi, On image evaluation and enhancement, *Opt. Acta* **17**, 1970, 59–76.
28. E. H. Linfoot, "Fourier Methods in Optical Image Evaluation." Focal Press, New York,
     1964.
29. A. Martelli and U. Montanari, Optimal smoothing in picture processing: an application
     to fingerprints, *Proc. IFIP Congr.* **71** (1971), Booklet TA-2, 86-90.
30. C. S. McCamy, The evaluation and manipulation of photographic images, *in* "Picture
     Processing and Psychopictorics" (B. S. Lipkin and A. Rosenfeld, eds.), pp. 57–74. Academic
     Press, New York, 1970.
31. M. Nagao and T. Matsuyama, Edge preserving smoothing, *Comput. Graphics Image
     Processing* **9**, 1979, 394–407.
32. Y. Nakagawa and A. Rosenfeld, A note on the use of local min and max operations in
     digital picture processing, *IEEE Trans. Systems Man Cybernet.* **8**, 1978, 632–635.
33. T. G. Newman and H. Dirilten, A nonlinear transformation for digital picture processing,
     IEEE Trans. Comput. **C-22**, 1973, 869–873.

34. R. S. Norman, Rotation technique in radially symmetric electron micrographs: mathematical analysis, *Science* **152**, 1966, 1238–1239.

35. D. A. O'Handley and W. B. Green, Recent developments in digital image processing at the Image Processing Laboratory at the Jet Propulsion Laboratory, *Proc. IEEE* **60**, 1972, 821–828.

36. A. V. Oppenheim, R. W. Schafer, and T. G. Stockham, Jr., Nonlinear filtering of multiplied and convolved signals, *Proc. IEEE* **56**, 1968, 1264–1291.

37. S. Peleg, Iterative histogram modification, 2, *IEEE Trans. Systems Man Cybernet.* **8**, 1978, 555–556.

38. S. M. Pizer and H. G. Vetter, Perception and processing of medical radio-isotope scans, *in* "Pictorial Pattern Recognition" (G. C. Cheng *et al.*, eds.), pp. 147–156. Thompson, Washington, D.C., 1968.

39. S. M. Pizer and H. G. Vetter, Processing quantum-limited images, *in* "Picture Processing and Psychopictorics" (B. S. Lipkin and A. Rosenfeld, eds.), pp. 165–176. Academic Press, New York, 1970.

40. J. M. S. Prewitt, Object enhancement and extraction, *in* "Picture Processing and Psychopictorics" (B. S. Lipkin and A. Rosenfeld, eds.), pp. 75–149. Academic Press, New York, 1970.

41. P. G. Roetling, Image enhancement by noise suppression, *J. Opt. Soc. Amer.* **60**, 1970, 867–869.

42. A. Scher, F. R. D. Velasco, and A. Rosenfeld, Some new image smoothing techniques, *IEEE Trans. Systems Man Cybernet.* **10**, 1980, 153–158.

43. T. G. Stockham, Jr., Image processing in the context of a visual model, *Proc. IEEE* **60**, 1972, 828–842.

44. H. Thiry, Some qualitative and quantitative results on spatial filtering of granularity, *Appl. Opt.* **3**, 1964, 39–43.

45. F. Tomita and S. Tsuji, Extraction of multiple regions by smoothing in selective neighborhoods, *IEEE Trans. Systems Man Cybernet.* **7**, 1977, 107–109.

46. E. B. Troy, E. S. Deutsch, and A. Rosenfeld, Gray-level manipulation experiments for texture analysis, *IEEE Trans. Systems Man Cybernet.* **SMC-3**, 1973, 91–98.

47. H. J. Trussell, A fast algorithm for noise smoothing based on a subjective criterion, *IEEE Trans. Systems Man Cybernet.* **7**, 1977, 677–678.

48. M. Weinstein and K. R. Castleman, Reconstructing 3-D specimens from 2-D section images, *in* "Quantitative Imagery in the Biomedical Sciences" (R. E. Herron, ed.), pp. 131–137. S.P.I.E., Redondo Beach, California, 1972.

Chapter 7

Restoration

Picture restoration deals with images that have been recorded in the presence of one or more sources of degradation. There are many sources of degradation in imaging systems. Some types of degradation affect only the gray levels of the individual picture points, without introducing spatial blur; these are sometimes called *point degradations*. Other types which do involve blur are called *spatial degradations*. Still other types involve chromatic or temporal effects. In this chapter, we will only be concerned with point and spatial degradations. Such degradations occur in a variety of applications. In aerial reconnaissance, astronomy, and remote sensing the pictures one obtains are degraded by atmospheric turbulence, aberrations of the optical system, and relative motion between the camera and the object. Electron micrographs are often degraded by the spherical aberration of the electron lens. Medical radiographic images are of low resolution and contrast due to the nature of x-ray imaging systems.

Given an ideal picture $f(x, y)$ and the corresponding degraded picture $g(x, y)$, we will assume that g and f are related by

$$g(x, y) = \int \int h(x, y, x', y') f(x', y') \, dx' \, dy' + v(x, y) \tag{1}$$

where $h(x, y, x', y')$ is the degradation function and $v(x, y)$ the random noise that may be present in the output picture. Evidently, in the absence of noise the degraded image of a point source described by $f(x', y') = \delta(x' - \alpha, y' - \beta)$

would be given by $h(x, y, \alpha, \beta)$; this can be seen by substitution in (1). Therefore, $h(x, y, \alpha, \beta)$ is a point spread function which, in general, is dependent
on the position (α, β) of the point in the ideal picture.

The assumption that the observed picture $g(x, y)$ is a linear function of the
ideal picture $f(x, y)$ as in (1) is approximately correct only over a small
dynamic range of gray levels. For example, in a photographic system what is
recorded is usually a nonlinear function of $f(x, y)$. If, however, the nonlinear
characteristic (H–D curve for photographic emulsions [28]) of the film is
known, it can be used to recover $f(x, y)$ from what is recorded on the film
over a large dynamic range of gray levels (see Section 6.2.2).

The assumption that noise is additive is also subject to criticism (see Section
6.1.4). Many noise sources may be individually modeled as additive. When,
however, additive noise is followed by a nonlinear transformation, its effect on
the function $g(x, y)$ can be assumed additive only over a small dynamic
range. Nevertheless, because the assumption of the additivity of noise makes
the problem mathematically tractable, it is common to most work on picture
restoration. In some cases multiplicative noise can be converted into an
additive form by applying a logarithmic transformation to $g(x, y)$ (see reference [43] in Section 6.5).

If, except for translation, the degraded image of a point is independent of
the position of the point, then the point spread function (PSF) takes the form
$h(x - x', y - y')$ and (1) becomes

$$g(x, y) = \int \int h(x - x', y - y') f(x', y') \, dx' \, dy' + v(x, y) \qquad (2)$$

In this case the degradation is termed *shift invariant* (Section 2.1.2). In this
chapter, we will further restrict ourselves to pictures that have suffered this
type of degradation.

In the absence of noise, Eq. (2) becomes

$$g(x, y) = \int \int h(x - x', y - y') f(x', y') \, dx' \, dy' \qquad \qquad \cdot \quad (3)$$

Fourier transforming both sides, and using the convolution theorem [Eq.
(23a) of Chapter 2], we obtain

$$G(u, v) = H(u, v) F(u, v) \qquad (4)$$

where $G(u, v)$, $F(u, v)$, and $H(u, v)$ are, respectively, the Fourier transforms of
$g(x, y), f(x, y)$ and $h(x, y)$. The function $H(u, v)$ is the transfer function of the
system that transforms the ideal picture $f(x, y)$ into the degraded picture
$g(x, y)$.

7.1 THE *A PRIORI* KNOWLEDGE REQUIRED IN RESTORATION

From a mathematical standpoint, given the model described by (2) and the degraded picture $g(x, y)$, the aim of picture restoration is to make as good an estimate as possible of the original picture or scene $f(x, y)$. Evidently, any such estimation procedure must require some form of knowledge concerning the degradation function $h(x, y)$ in (2). In some cases, the physical phenomenon underlying the degradation can be used to determine $h(x, y)$. Examples of this approach are given in Section 7.1.1. In other situations, it may be possible to determine $h(x, y)$ from the degraded picture itself, e.g., when it is known *a priori* that a certain portion of the degraded picture is the image of a point, line, or edge in the original picture, as described in Section 7.1.2. Section 7.1.3 briefly discusses the *a priori* information about noise that is needed for restoration.

Recently some restoration techniques have been suggested in which some form of *a priori* knowledge is used to place constraints on the solution of the restoration algorithm. For example, the constraint that the solution be a nonnegative function is directly or indirectly implied in the various schemes that have been suggested to date [24, 25, 64, 80].

7.1.1 PSF's of Some Specific Degradations

We first consider the degradation due to diffraction in spatially incoherent optical imaging systems that are diffraction limited. If the exit pupil is denoted by a function as

$$P_e(x, y) = \begin{cases} 1 & \text{for} \quad (x, y) \text{ in the pupil} \\ 0 & \text{otherwise} \end{cases}$$

then the transfer function of the system is given by

$$H(u, v) = \int_{-\infty}^{\infty} \int_{-\infty}^{\infty} P_e(\xi, \eta) \, P_e(\xi - \lambda D_i u, \eta - \lambda D_i v) \, d\xi \, d\eta$$

where λ is the wavelength of the light used and D_i the distance from the exit pupil to the image plane. For a derivation of this result see [28].

Next let us consider the degradation caused in photography by relative motion between the camera and the scene. Let us further assume that the image is invariant in time except for the motion. If the relative motion is approximately the same as would be produced by motion of the recording film in its plane, then, as we will show, the degradation can be modeled by (3). The total exposure at any point of the film can be obtained by integrating the instantaneous exposures over the time interval during which the shutter is open. We will assume that the shutter requires negligible time to change from closed to open and vice versa. If $\alpha(t)$ and $\beta(t)$ are, respectively, the x- and y-components of the displacement, we have

$$g(x, y) = \int_{-T/2}^{T/2} f(x-\alpha(t), y-\beta(t))\, dt \tag{5}$$

where T is the duration of the exposure, for convenience assumed to be from $-T/2$ to $T/2$. Fourier transforming both sides of (5), we obtain

$$
\begin{aligned}
G(u, v) &= \int dx \int dy\, \exp[-j2\pi(ux+vy)] \int_{-T/2}^{T/2} dt\, f(x-\alpha(t), y-\beta(t)) \\
&= \int_{-T/2}^{T/2} dt \int dx \int dy\, f(x-\alpha(t), y-\beta(t))\, \exp[-j2\pi(ux+vy)]
\end{aligned}
$$

By using the transformation

$$x - \alpha(t) = \xi, \qquad y - \beta(t) = \eta$$

the preceding equation can be expressed as

$$
\begin{aligned}
G(u, v) &= \int_{-T/2}^{T/2} dt \int d\xi\, d\eta\, f(\xi, \eta) \\
&\qquad \times \exp[-j2\pi(u\xi+v\eta)]\, \exp[-j2\pi(\alpha(t)u+\beta(t)v)] \\
&= F(u, v) \int_{-T/2}^{T/2} \exp[-j2\pi(u\alpha(t)+v\beta(t))]\, dt \\
&\equiv F(u, v)\, H(u, v) \tag{6}
\end{aligned}
$$

which proves that the degradation can be modeled by (4) or equivalently (3). We see that the transfer function $H(u, v)$ of this degradation is given by

$$H(u, v) = \int_{-T/2}^{T/2} \exp[-j2\pi(u\alpha(t)+v\beta(t))]\, dt \tag{7}$$

For example, if the motion is uniform in the x-direction with velocity V, then

$$\alpha(t) = Vt, \qquad \beta(t) = 0 \tag{8}$$

Substituting (8) in (7), we obtain for this case

$$H(u, v) = (\sin \pi uVT)/\pi uV = T\operatorname{sinc}(uVT) \tag{9}$$

The PSF, $h(x, y)$, may be obtained by inverse Fourier transforming (9); it is $(1/V^2T)\operatorname{rect}(x/VT)$ (see Exercise 1 in Section 2.1.3).

Another case in which the PSF can be inferred from the underlying physical process is that of atmospheric turbulence. Hufnagel and Stanley [45] have shown that for long exposures the transfer function $H(u,v)$ may be approximated by $\exp[-c(u^2+v^2)^{5/6}]$, where c is a constant depending on the nature of the turbulence. For short exposures, however, the problem becomes more difficult and the transfer function, which can still be assumed to be position invariant provided the angle subtended by the object on the film is small, becomes probabilistic [21, 22, 45, 46, 63].

7.1.2 *a Posteriori* Determination of the PSF

If the degradation is of an unknown nature or if the phenomenon underlying the degradation is too complex for the analytical determination of $h(x,y)$, the only possible alternative is to estimate it from the degraded picture itself. For example, if there is any reason to believe that the original scene contains a sharp point, then the image of that point in the degraded picture is the PSF. This would be the case in an astronomical picture, where the image of a faint star could be used as an estimate of the PSF.

If the original scene contains sharp lines, then it is sometimes possible to determine $h(x,y)$ from the images of these lines. To show how it can be done, let us assume an ideal line source parallel to the x-axis in the original scene. We saw in Section 6.1.1 that the image of such a line source, denoted by $h_l(y)$, is related to the PSF by

$$h_l(y) = \int_{-\infty}^{\infty} h(x,y)\,dx \tag{10}$$

In other words the image of a line source is constant in the direction along the line, and its dependence on the perpendicular direction is given by integrating the PSF along the line. It is clear that if the PSF is not circularly symmetric, then the image of a line source depends on the orientation of the line.

Let the Fourier transform of $h_l(y)$ be $H_l(v)$; then

$$H_l(v) = \int_{-\infty}^{\infty} h_l(y)\,e^{-j2\pi vy}\,dy \tag{11}$$

Now

$$H(u,v) = \int\!\!\int_{-\infty}^{\infty} h(x,y)\exp[-j2\pi(ux+vy)]\,dx\,dy$$

If we substitute $u=0$ in this equation and use (10) and (11), we obtain

$$H(0,v) = \int_{-\infty}^{\infty}\left[\int_{-\infty}^{\infty} h(x,y)\,dx\right]e^{-j2\pi vy}\,dy = H_l(v) \tag{12}$$

This shows that if the image of a line parallel to the x-axis is Fourier transformed, the result gives the values of the transfer function $H(u,v)$ along the

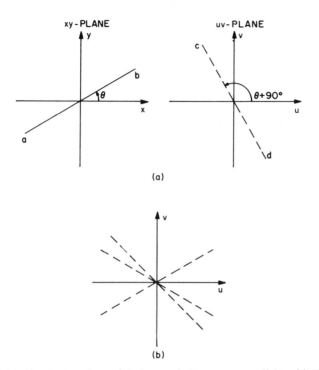

Fig. 1 (a) The Fourier transform of the image of a line source parallel to *ab* in the *xy*-plane yields the values of the transfer function $H(u, v)$ along the line *cd* in the *uv*-plane. (b) If the original scene contains lines at various orientations, then from the images of these lines the values of $H(u, v)$ can be determined along radial lines such as those shown here.

line $u = 0$ in the *uv*-plane. Similarly, it can be shown that the Fourier transform of the image of a line oriented at an angle θ to the *x*-axis furnishes in the *uv*-plane the values of $H(u, v)$ along a line of slope $\theta + 90°$. This result is illustrated in Fig. 1. Therefore, if a scene that has been photographed contains lines at various orientations $\theta_1, \theta_2, ..., \theta_n$, then from the photograph of such a scene we can derive the values of $H(u, v)$ along radial lines through the origin at slopes $\theta_1 + 90°$, $\theta_2 + 90°$, ..., $\theta_n + 90°$.

If there is reason to believe that the PSF is circularly symmetric, then $H(u, v)$ is also circularly symmetric (Section 2.1.3, Exercise 2), so that it needs only to be known along one radial line for it to be known everywhere. If no such *a priori* knowledge is available, $H(u, v)$ would, in general, have to be known along many closely spaced radial lines. If the *uv*-plane can be covered sufficiently densely with such lines, we can construct a close approximation to $H(u, v)$, and $h(x, y)$ can then be obtained by simple Fourier inversion. This computation usually requires $H(u, v)$ to be interpolated on a rectangular lattice of points from the values on the radial lines, which can be a source of error.

The problem of determining the PSF from the images of lines at various orientations is identical to the problem of reconstructing objects from their projections. The method that was previously discussed is only one of many that can be used. Two other methods which have proved popular are the algebraic reconstruction technique and the convolution method, the latter being the fastest and most accurate from the computational standpoint. More on these methods can be found in Chapter 8.

Usually the original scene will not contain sharp points or lines. It is quite likely, however, that it will contain sharp edges. We will now show that the derivative of the image of an edge is equal to the image of a line source parallel to the edge.

Let us consider an ideal edge along the x-axis. Such an edge can be mathematically represented by $S(y)$, where $S(y)$ is a unit step function which is equal to 0 for $y < 0$ and to 1 for $y \geqslant 0$. Let $h_e(x, y)$ be the image of this edge; then

$$h_e(x, y) = \int\int_{-\infty}^{\infty} h(x-x', y-y') S(y') \, dx' \, dy'$$

$$= \int\int_{-\infty}^{\infty} h(x', y') S(y-y') \, dx' \, dy'$$

Since the image of the edge parallel to the x-axis is independent of x, we will write $h_e(y)$ instead of $h_e(x, y)$; thus

$$h_e(y) = \int\int_{-\infty}^{\infty} h(x', y') S(y-y') \, dx' \, dy'$$

Taking the partial derivative of both sides with respect to y and interchanging the order of the integral and derivative operators on the right-hand side, we obtain[§]

$$\frac{\partial h_e(y)}{\partial y} = \int\int_{-\infty}^{\infty} h(x', y') \frac{\partial}{\partial y} S(y-y') \, dx' \, dy'$$

$$= \int\int_{-\infty}^{\infty} h(x', y') \delta(y-y') \, dx' \, dy' = \int_{-\infty}^{\infty} h(x', y) \, dx' \qquad (13)$$

[§] We use here the fact that the derivative of a step function is a δ function. This can be justified by noting that the step is a limit of an increasingly steep ramp function of the form

$$\ldots \underline{\hspace{0.3cm}/^{\overline{}}} \cdots$$

and the derivative of such a ramp function is a rect function; the limit of such rect functions is a delta function.

By comparing (10) and (13), we see that

$$h_l(y) = \partial h_e(y)/\partial y \tag{14}$$

In other words, the image of a line is the derivative of the image of an edge parallel to the line. Therefore, if a picture contains edges in various orientations, then the methods previously discussed can be used to determine the PSF from the derivatives of the images of these edges. A major obstacle to determining the PSF in this way from a photograph is film grain noise which strongly affects the values of the derivative. A number of investigations have been devoted to the effects of noise and methods for overcoming it [7, 9, 10, 33, 55, 57, 67, 83, 108].

Exercise 1.   The operator $\partial/\partial y$ is linear and shift invariant. Prove that its transfer function is $2\pi jv$. *Hint:*

$$\frac{\partial}{\partial y} f(x, y) = \frac{\partial}{\partial y} \left[\int_{-\infty}^{\infty} F(u, v) \exp[j2\pi(ux + vy)] \, du \, dv \right] \quad \blacksquare$$

There is yet another method [44] for estimating the transfer function $H(u, v)$ from the degraded picture itself. Let the degraded picture be divided into n regions, all identical in size. Let the gray level in each region be given by $g_i(x, y)$, $i = 1, 2, ..., n$. Let $f_i(x, y)$ be the gray level in the corresponding region in the undegraded picture. Let us assume that the portion of the plane in which the PSF of the degradation has values significantly different from zero is small compared to the size of the regions. Then, ignoring edge effects, we have

$$g_i(x, y) = \int\int_{-\infty}^{\infty} h(x - x', y - y') f_i(x', y') \, dx' \, dy', \qquad i = 1, 2, ..., n$$

Taking the Fourier transform of both sides, we obtain

$$G_i(u, v) = H(u, v) F_i(u, v), \qquad i = 1, 2, ..., n$$

Taking the product over i gives

$$\prod_{i=1}^{n} G_i(u, v) = \left[\prod_{i=1}^{n} F_i(u, v) \right] H^n(u, v)$$

or

$$H(u, v) = \left[\prod_{i=1}^{n} G_i(u, v) \right]^{1/n} \bigg/ \left[\prod_{i=1}^{n} F_i(u, v) \right]^{1/n} \tag{15}$$

The logarithm of the denominator on the right-hand side of (15) is

$$(1/n) \sum_{i=1}^{n} \ln F_i(u, v)$$

which is the average of the logarithms of the Fourier transforms of the f_i's. If we assume that an average of a large number of $\ln F_i(u, v)$'s tends to be approximately constant, then the denominator in (15) is essentially constant, so that (15) determines $H(u, v)$ up to a multiplicative constant. More realistically, if we write

$$\ln F_i(u, v) = \ln |F_i(u, v)| + \varphi_i(u, v)$$

where $\varphi_i(u, v)$ is the phase of $F_i(u, v)$, then it may be reasonable to assume that the average of the φ_i's is approximately constant, but we still need to know something about the average of $\ln |F_i(u, v)|$ in order to obtain $H(u, v)$ from (15). The reader is referred to [14, 59, 68, 95] for ways to approximate the average of $\ln F_i(u, v)$, and also for techniques that specifically estimate either the phase of the original image or of the transfer function.

7.1.3 Noise in Restoration

To restore a picture in the presence of noise, in addition to a knowledge of the PSF, one needs to know (at least in theory) both the statistical properties of the noise and how it is correlated with the picture. In practice the most common assumptions about noise are that it is white, i.e., its spectral density is constant, and that it is uncorrelated with the picture. Both these assumptions can be seriously questioned. The concept of white noise is a mathematical abstraction, but it is a convenient, though somewhat inaccurate, model provided the noise bandwidth (i.e., the region of the spatial frequency plane where the noise spectrum has values significantly different from zero) is much larger than the picture bandwidth. As far as the picture and noise being uncorrelated is concerned, there are many examples where this is not true, e.g., in the case of film grain noise [20, 42, 72] or in the case of quantum-limited images, such as x-ray and nuclear scan pictures in medicine. Other examples of signal-dependent noise are given in Section 6.1.4. On methods of restoring quantum-limited images see references [38, 39] in Chapter 6.

Different restoration techniques require different amounts of *a priori* information about the noise. For example, the restoration filter derived in Section 7.3, based on Wiener theory, requires the characterization of the noise process in terms of its spectral density. On the other hand, for the constrained deconvolution procedure discussed in Section 7.5, only the variance of the noise need be known.

7.2 INVERSE FILTERING

Assume that the degraded picture $g(x, y)$ and original $f(x, y)$ obey model (3); then, in the absence of noise, the Fourier transforms of $g(x, y)$, $f(x, y)$, and the PSF, $h(x, y)$, satisfy Eq. (4), repeated here for convenience:

$$G(u, v) = H(u, v) F(u, v)$$

or equivalently,

$$F(u,v) = G(u,v)/H(u,v) \tag{16}$$

This implies that if $H(u,v)$ is known, we can restore $f(x,y)$ by multiplying the Fourier transform $G(u,v)$ of the degraded picture by $1/H(u,v)$ and then inverse Fourier transforming. In other words, the filter transfer function is $1/H(u,v)$.

A number of problems arise when one attempts to make practical use of (16). There may be points or regions in the uv-plane where $H(u,v) = 0$. In the absence of noise, the transform $G(u,v)$ of the degraded image would also be zero at these frequencies, leading to indeterminate ratios. So we see that even in the absence of noise, it is, in general, impossible to reconstruct $f(x,y)$ exactly if $H(u,v)$ has zeros in the uv-plane. (One notes, however, that if $H(u,v)$ has at most a countably infinite number of zeros, then $f(x,y)$ is, in principle, perfectly recoverable. That is because the inverse Fourier transform of $G(u,v)/H(u,v)$ is merely an integration process, to which any single frequency component contributes no area.) In the presence of noise, the zeros of $G(u,v)$ and $H(u,v)$ will not coincide. Therefore, in the neighborhoods of zeros of $H(u,v)$, the division in (16) would result in very large values. In fact, when noise is present we have

$$G(u,v) = H(u,v)F(u,v) + N(u,v)$$

where $N(u,v)$ is the Fourier transform of $v(x,y)$, so that applying the restoring filter gives

$$\frac{G(u,v)}{H(u,v)} = F(u,v) + \frac{N(u,v)}{H(u,v)} \tag{17}$$

In the neighborhood of zeros of $H(u,v)$, it may take on values much smaller than those of $N(u,v)$. Thus the term $N(u,v)/H(u,v)$ may have much larger magnitude than $F(u,v)$ in such a neighborhood. The inverse transform of $G(u,v)/H(u,v)$ will then be strongly influenced by these large terms, and will no longer resemble $f(x,y)$. Instead, it will contain many rapid noiselike variations, and will not be a meaningful restoration of $f(x,y)$.

Since the right-hand side of (16) cannot normally be evaluated numerically because of the zeros of $H(u,v)$, a compromise must be made. Often the most that one can do is to restore only those frequencies in the uv-plane where the signal-to-noise ratio is high. This means that in practice the inverse filter is not $1/H(u,v)$ but some other function of u and v; let us call it $M(u,v)$. Of course, if $H(u,v)$ has no zeros and noise is not present we have

$$M(u,v) = 1/H(u,v)$$

The degradation (including noise) and the restoration operation can be represented in Fig. 2. The overall transfer function of both the degradation

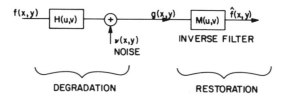

Fig. 2 Schematic representation of the degradation of a picture $f(x, y)$ by transfer function $H(u, v)$ and noise $v(x, y)$, and the restoration of the degraded picture by transfer function $M(u, v)$.

and the restoration is given by the product $H(u, v) M(u, v)$. If $\hat{f}(x, y)$ represents the restored picture and $\hat{F}(u, v)$ its Fourier transform, then

$$\hat{F}(u, v) = (H(u, v) M(u, v)) F(u, v) \tag{18}$$

Sometimes $H(u, v)$ is referred to as the "input transfer function," $M(u, v)$ as the "processing transfer function," and $H(u, v) M(u, v)$ as the "output transfer function."

There is considerable arbitrariness in the selection of $M(u, v)$. For example, for the case of motion blur discussed in Section 7.1.1 the function $H(u, v)$ is equal to $(\sin \pi V T u)/\pi V u$. This function, which only depends on u, is shown in Fig. 3a. Two choices of $M(u, v)$ discussed by Harris [35] are shown in Figs. 3b and 3d. The restoration corresponding to Fig. 3b consists of multiplying each frequency component by a constant times the frequency and also performing a 90° phase shift at all frequencies ($\Delta\theta = \pi/2$ in Fig. 3b). This restoring filter is mathematically described by $M(u, v) = \pi V u e^{j\pi/2}$. It can be shown that applying this filter is equivalent to differentiation in the x-direction (in the xy-plane); see Exercise 1. The output transfer function corresponding to $M(u, v)$ in Fig. 3b is shown in Fig. 3c and is of the form $\sin \pi V T u$. This is a rather extreme departure from the flat spectrum associated with ideal restoration, and very poor restoration might be expected. An examination of the PSF associated with the output transfer function, however, reveals that this method can give satisfactory results if the displacement caused by the motion is greater than the dimensions of the objects in the picture. The other choice of the restoration filter shown is in Fig. 3d; it is mathematically described by $M(u, v) = V u \pi \sin \pi V T u$. The output transfer function for this filter is shown in Fig. 3e.

Note that in both of the preceding cases the restoration filter places very little weight on those parts of the spectrum of the degraded image that are in the neighborhood of zeros of $H(u, v)$. In the vicinity of these points the signal-to-noise ratio is likely to be very low. It must be mentioned at this point that for the case of motion degradation previously discussed, it is possible under

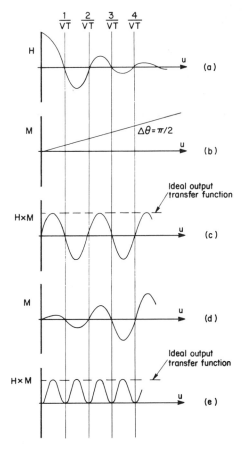

Fig. 3 (a) $H(u,v)$ for the degradation caused by uniform motion at velocity V in the x-direction. T is the exposure time. Note that $H(u,v)$ is independent of v. (b) A choice of $M(u,v)$ for the restoration filter. $M(u,v)$ also depends on u only. (c) The resulting "output transfer function" $H(u,v)\,M(u,v)$. (d) Another choice for the restoration filter $M(u,v)$. (e) The output transfer function $H(u,v)\,M(u,v)$ for the restoration filter in (d). (From [35].)

certain conditions (which include the absence of noise) to recover $f(x,y)$ perfectly from $g(x,y)$, in spite of the fact that $H(u,v)$ is zero at some points. A method for doing this is described by Slepian [91]. A variation of this technique in the presence of noise has been given by Cutrona and Hall [17]; see also Sondhi [94].

In many cases the magnitude of $H(u,v)$ drops rapidly with distance from the origin in the uv-plane. The transform $N(u,v)$ of the noise, on the other hand, while it will not in practice have constant magnitude (see Section 7.1.3), is likely to drop off much less rapidly. Thus as we get far from the origin, the

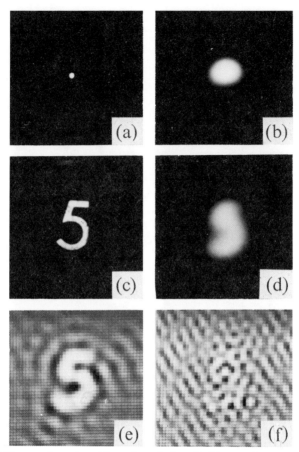

Fig. 4 (a) Picture of a point without degradation. (b) Picture of a point with degradation. This picture is approximately the PSF of the degradation. (c) Picture of the numeral 5
undegraded. (d) "5" degraded. (e) "5" restored by using Eq. (16) with division being done
only for spatial frequencies below 2 cycles/mm. (f) Result of doing the division for spatial
frequencies up to 3 cycles/mm. (From B. L. McGlamery, Restoration of turbulence degraded images, *J. Opt. Soc. Amer.* **57**, 1967, 295.)

quotient $N(u, v)/H(u, v)$ in (17) will become large, while (for most pictures)
$F(u, v)$ will become small. This suggests that if we do not want the noise to
dominate when we apply an inverse restoring filter $1/H(u, v)$, we should apply
this filter only in a neighborhood of the origin; in other words, we should use
a restoring filter of the form

$$M(u, v) = \begin{cases} 1/H(u, v), & u^2 + v^2 \leqslant w_0{}^2 \\ 1, & u^2 + v^2 > w_0{}^2 \end{cases}$$

for some w_0. Of course, w_0 should be chosen so as to exclude the zeros of $H(u, v)$ from the neighborhood. An example of restoration done in this way is shown in Figs. 4a–4e. The neighborhood used in Fig. 4e is small enough to avoid the zeros of $H(u, v)$, so that the restoration is fairly good. When a larger neighborhood is used, the results become very poor, as shown in Fig. 4f.

7.3   LEAST SQUARES FILTERING

One way to avoid arbitrariness in inverse filtering is to find a restoration $\hat{f}(x, y)$ of the picture $f(x, y)$ that minimizes some measure of the difference between $\hat{f}(x, y)$ and $f(x, y)$. If the restored pictures are meant for a human observer, this measure should in some manner incorporate the properties of the human visual system as discussed in Chapter 3. Such properties, however, are very hard to describe mathematically and therefore cannot be incorporated into any simple optimization procedure. One measure that has been extensively used on account of its mathematical simplicity is the mean-squared error. In this section we shall derive a restoration filter that minimizes (in a statistical sense) the mean-squared error between the original picture $f(x, y)$ and its restoration $\hat{f}(x, y)$. This filter is called the *least squares filter* or the *Wiener filter*.

Let the undegraded picture, the corresponding degraded picture, and the noise belong to the random fields $\mathbf{f}(\vec{r})$, $\mathbf{g}(\vec{r})$, and $\mathbf{v}(\vec{r})$, respectively, where $\vec{r}$ is the position vector in the xy-plane. Then in line with the model for degradation described by (2), the following relationship holds:

$$\mathbf{g}(\vec{r}) = \int \int h(\vec{r} - \vec{r}')\mathbf{f}(\vec{r}') \, d\vec{r}' + \mathbf{v}(\vec{r}) \tag{19}$$

where $d\vec{r}'$ represents the area element $dx' \, dy'$ in the xy-plane and $h(\vec{r})$ is the point spread function of the degradation. As with the equations involving random fields in Section 2.4, (19) is a family of equations, one for each picture in the ensemble represented by the random field $\mathbf{f}(\vec{r})$.

In (19), $\mathbf{v}(\vec{r})$ is not known exactly, although its statistical properties are assumed to be known. Hence, given $\mathbf{g}(\vec{r})$, (19) cannot be exactly solved for $\mathbf{f}(\vec{r})$. What we will do here is find an $\hat{\mathbf{f}}(\vec{r})$ such that the mean-square error

$$e^2 = E\{[\mathbf{f}(\vec{r}) - \hat{\mathbf{f}}(\vec{r})]^2\} \tag{20}$$

is minimized. $\hat{\mathbf{f}}(\vec{r})$ will be called the *least squares estimate* of $\mathbf{f}(\vec{r})$ given $\mathbf{g}(\vec{r})$.

It is well known that if no restrictions are placed on the solution to the preceding problem, the least squares estimate $\hat{\mathbf{f}}(\vec{r})$ turns out to be the conditional expectation of $\mathbf{f}(\vec{r})$ given $\mathbf{g}(\vec{r})$ (Ref. [9] of Chapter 2, p. 388). This is in general a nonlinear function of the gray levels $\mathbf{g}(\vec{r})$. Moreover, for its evaluation one needs the joint probability density over the random fields $\mathbf{f}(\vec{r})$ and $\mathbf{g}(\vec{r})$, making the method complicated from an analytical as well as practical standpoint.

The problem becomes mathematically tractable if one minimizes (20) subject to the constraint that the estimate $\hat{\mathbf{f}}(r)$ be a linear function of the gray levels in $\mathbf{g}(\vec{r})$. Such an estimate is called the *linear least squares estimate.* Evidently, in general, such an estimate does not absolutely minimize (20), but of all the linear estimates it yields the smallest value for e^2. There is one case in which the optimum nonlinear estimate is the same as the linear least squares estimate, namely when the random fields $\mathbf{f}(\vec{r})$, $\mathbf{g}(\vec{r})$, and $\mathbf{v}(\vec{r})$ in addition to being homogeneous are jointly Gaussian, an assumption that is not generally valid for pictorial data.

If the estimate $\hat{\mathbf{f}}(\vec{r})$ is to be a linear function of the $\mathbf{g}(\vec{r})$, it can be expressed as

$$\hat{\mathbf{f}}(\vec{r}) = \int\int m(\vec{r}, \vec{r}')\mathbf{g}(\vec{r}')\, d\vec{r}' \tag{21}$$

where the yet to be determined function $m(\vec{r}, \vec{r}')$ is the weight to be given to the gray level in the degraded picture at the point $\vec{r}'$ for the computation of $\hat{\mathbf{f}}$ at $\vec{r}$. It is not hard to see that if all the random fields involved are homogeneous, this weighting function should only depend on $\vec{r} - \vec{r}'$ (reference [9] of Chapter 2, p. 403). Therefore, in such a case (21) can be written as

$$\hat{\mathbf{f}}(\vec{r}) = \int\int m(\vec{r} - \vec{r}')\mathbf{g}(\vec{r}')\, d\vec{r}' \tag{22}$$

Substituting (22) in (20), we obtain

$$e^2 = E\left\{\left[\mathbf{f}(\vec{r}) - \int\int m(\vec{r} - \vec{r}')\mathbf{g}(\vec{r}')\, d\vec{r}'\right]^2\right\} \tag{23}$$

Our aim is to find a function $m(\vec{r})$, which is the point spread function of the restoration filter, such that (23) is minimized. We will now show that a function satisfying

$$E\left\{\left[\mathbf{f}(\vec{r}) - \int\int m(\vec{r} - \vec{r}')\mathbf{g}(\vec{r}')\, d\vec{r}'\right]\mathbf{g}(\vec{s})\right\} = 0 \tag{24}$$

for all position vectors $\vec{r}$ and $\vec{s}$ in the xy-plane will minimize (23). In order to prove this result, we will show that any other choice for the restoration filter would result in a mean-square error larger than that given by (23) with $m(\vec{r})$ satisfying (24). To show this, let $m(\vec{r})$ be a function that does satisfy (24). Then for any other choice $m'(\vec{r})$ for the PSF of the restoration filter the mean-square error is given by

$$e'^2 = E\left\{\left[\mathbf{f}(\vec{r}) - \int\int m'(\vec{r} - \vec{r}')\mathbf{g}(\vec{r}')\, d\vec{r}'\right]^2\right\} \tag{25}$$

We will now show that (25) is minimized when $m'(\vec{r})$ is equal to $m(\vec{r})$. Equation (25) can be written as

$$E\left\{\left[\mathbf{f}(\vec{r}) - \int\int m(\vec{r}-\vec{r}')\mathbf{g}(\vec{r}')\,d\vec{r}' + \int\int [m(\vec{r}-\vec{r}') - m'(\vec{r}-\vec{r}')]\mathbf{g}(\vec{r}')\,d\vec{r}'\right]^2\right\}$$

which can be expressed as

$$e^2 + E\left\{\int\int [m(\vec{r}-\vec{r}') - m'(\vec{r}-\vec{r}')]\mathbf{g}(\vec{r}')\,d\vec{r}'\right\}^2$$

$$+ 2E\left\{\left[\mathbf{f}(\vec{r}) - \int\int m(\vec{r}-\vec{r}')\mathbf{g}(\vec{r}')\,d\vec{r}'\right]\right.$$

$$\left. \times \left[\int\int (m(\vec{r}-\vec{r}') - m'(\vec{r}-\vec{r}'))\mathbf{g}(\vec{r}')\,d\vec{r}'\right]\right\} \tag{26}$$

In this expression, the middle term is always nonnegative. The last term in (26) is a product of two expressions, each involving integration with respect to $\vec{r}'$. Changing the variable of integration in the second of these expressions from $\vec{r}'$ to $\vec{s}$, and interchanging the order of integration and expectation, (26) can be written as

$$e^2 + \text{a nonnegative number} + 2\int\int E\left\{\left[\mathbf{f}(\vec{r}) - \int\int m(\vec{r}-\vec{r}')\right.\right.$$

$$\left.\left. \times \mathbf{g}(\vec{r}')\,d\vec{r}'\right]\mathbf{g}(\vec{s})\right\}[m(\vec{r}-\vec{s}) - m'(\vec{r}-\vec{s})]\,d\vec{s} \tag{27}$$

Since $m(\vec{r})$ satisfies (24), the third term in (27) is zero. Therefore, (27) becomes

$$e^2 + \text{a nonnegative number} \tag{28}$$

so that $e'^2 \geq e^2$. In other words, the mean-square error for an arbitrary m is always at least as great as that for an m that satisfies (24). Thus an m that satisfies (24) will give (23) its minimum possible value. It can be shown that the converse is also true, that is, an m that minimizes (23) must also satisfy (24).

Equation (24) can be written as

$$\int\int m(\vec{r}-\vec{r}')\,E\{\mathbf{g}(\vec{r}')\mathbf{g}(\vec{s})\}\,d\vec{r}' = E\{\mathbf{f}(\vec{r})\mathbf{g}(\vec{s})\} \tag{29}$$

for every $\vec{r}$ and $\vec{s}$ in the xy-plane. Making use of the definitions of the auto-correlation and cross-correlation of a random field (see Eqs. (98) and (100) of Chapter 2), (29) can be written as

$$\int\int m(\vec{r}-\vec{r}')\,R_{gg}(\vec{r}',\vec{s})\,d\vec{r}' = R_{fg}(\vec{r},\vec{s}) \tag{30}$$

for all position vectors $\vec{r}$ and $\vec{s}$ in the xy-plane. Since the random fields have been assumed to be homogeneous, the autocorrelation function $R_{gg}(\vec{r}', \vec{s})$ and the cross-correlation function $R_{fg}(\vec{r}, \vec{s})$ can be expressed as $R_{gg}(\vec{r}' - \vec{s})$ and $R_{fg}(\vec{r} - \vec{s})$, respectively (see Section 2.4.3). Thus (30) becomes

$$\int \int m(\vec{r} - \vec{r}')\, R_{gg}(\vec{r}' - \vec{s})\, d\vec{r}' \;=\; R_{fg}(\vec{r} - \vec{s}) \tag{31}$$

for every $\vec{r}$ and $\vec{s}$ in the xy-plane. Letting $\vec{r}' - \vec{s} = \vec{i}$ and $\vec{r} - \vec{s} = \vec{\tau}$, we obtain

$$\int \int m(\vec{\tau} - \vec{i})\, R_{gg}(\vec{i})\, d\vec{i} \;=\; R_{fg}(\vec{\tau}) \tag{32}$$

for all position vectors $\vec{\tau}$ in the xy-plane, where $d\vec{i}$ represents an elemental area $dx\,dy$. If we denote the coordinates of $\vec{i}$ by (x, y) and of $\vec{\tau}$ by (α, β), we can write (32) as

$$\int_{-\infty}^{\infty} \int_{-\infty}^{\infty} m(\alpha - x,\, \beta - y)\, R_{gg}(x, y)\, dx\, dy \;=\; R_{fg}(\alpha, \beta),$$
$$-\infty < \alpha < \infty, \quad -\infty < \beta < \infty \tag{33}$$

As mentioned before, $m(x, y)$ is the point spread function of the restoration filter, and its Fourier transform $M(u, v)$ is the transfer function. If we take the Fourier transform of both sides of (33), then by the convolution theorem (Eq. (23) of Chapter 2), we have, using Eqs. (111a) and (111b) of Chapter 2,

$$M(u, v)\, S_{gg}(u, v) \;=\; S_{fg}(u, v)$$

or

$$M(u, v) \;=\; S_{fg}(u, v)/S_{gg}(u, v) \tag{34}$$

where $S_{gg}(u, v)$ is the spectral density of the degraded picture $\mathbf{g}(x, y)$, and $S_{fg}(u, v)$ is the cross spectral density of the degraded and undegraded pictures.

It is clear from (34) that, in general, the derivation of the least squares restoration filter $M(u, v)$ requires a knowledge of the cross-correlation statistics between the undegraded and degraded pictures. The filter takes a simpler form for the case where the pictures $\mathbf{f}(\vec{r})$ and noise $\mathbf{v}(\vec{r})$ are uncorrelated and where either $\mathbf{f}(\vec{r})$ or $\mathbf{v}(\vec{r})$ has zero mean, so that

$$E\{\mathbf{f}(\vec{r})\,\mathbf{v}(\vec{r})\} \;=\; E\{\mathbf{f}(\vec{r})\}\, E\{\mathbf{v}(\vec{r})\} \;=\; 0 \tag{35}$$

For such a case

$$R_{fg}(\vec{r}, \vec{s}) \;=\; E\{\mathbf{f}(\vec{r})\,\mathbf{g}(\vec{s})\} \;=\; \int \int h(\vec{s} - \vec{r}')\, E\{\mathbf{f}(\vec{r})\,\mathbf{f}(\vec{r}')\}\, d\vec{r}' \tag{36}$$

where we have made use of (19) and (35). Making use of the homogeneity of the random fields and the definition of the autocorrelation function, we obtain

$$R_{fg}(\vec{r} - \vec{s}) \;=\; \int \int h(\vec{s} - \vec{r}')\, R_{ff}(\vec{r} - \vec{r}')\, d\vec{r}' \tag{37}$$

By using transformations similar to those employed in deriving (32) from (31), (37) can be written as

$$R_{fg}(\hat{i}) = \int \int h(\bar{\tau} - \hat{i}) R_{ff}(\bar{\tau}) \, d\bar{\tau} \qquad (38)$$

where $\hat{i}$ and $\bar{\tau}$ are position vectors in the xy-plane and $d\bar{\tau}$ is the elemental area $dx \, dy$. If (x, y) and (α, β) are the coordinates of $\hat{i}$ and $\bar{\tau}$, respectively, we can write (38) as

$$R_{fg}(x, y) = \int_{-\infty}^{\infty} \int_{-\infty}^{\infty} h(\alpha - x, \beta - y) R_{ff}(\alpha, \beta) \, d\alpha \, d\beta \qquad (39)$$

The right-hand side in (39) is the cross correlation of the two deterministic (and real) functions $h(\alpha, \beta)$ and $R_{ff}(\alpha, \beta)$. The Fourier transform of this cross correlation is given by Eq. (27) of Chapter 2. Therefore, Fourier transforming both sides of (39), we obtain

$$S_{fg}(u, v) = H^*(u, v) S_{ff}(u, v) \qquad (40)$$

Also, when (35) is true, $S_{gg}(u, v)$ is given by Eq. (121) of Chapter 2:

$$S_{gg}(u, v) = S_{ff}(u, v) |H(u, v)|^2 + S_{vv}(u, v)$$

where $S_{vv}(u, v)$ is the spectral density of the noise.

Substituting Eq. (121) of Chapter 2 and (40) in (34), we obtain for the restoration filter

$$M(u, v) = \frac{H^*(u, v) S_{ff}(u, v)}{S_{ff}(u, v) |H(u, v)|^2 + S_{vv}(u, v)} \qquad (41a)$$

$$= \frac{1}{H(u, v)} \frac{|H(u, v)|^2}{|H(u, v)|^2 + [S_{vv}(u, v)/S_{ff}(u, v)]} \qquad (41b)$$

Note that in the absence of noise $S_{vv} = 0$, so that (41b) reduces to the ideal inverse filter $1/H(u, v)$. We thus see that the term in square brackets in (41b) can be regarded as a "modification" function which smooths $1/H(u, v)$ in order to provide optimum restoration (in the mean-square sense) in the presence of noise.

Often the noise can be assumed to be spectrally white, i.e., $S_{vv}(u, v) = a$ constant. This assumption is approximately correct if $S_{ff}(u, v)$ falls off much faster in the uv-plane than $S_{vv}(u, v)$. The constant value of $S_{vv}(u, v)$ can be estimated by considering it to be equal to $S_{vv}(0, 0)$, which is equal to

$$S_{vv}(0, 0) = \int_{-\infty}^{\infty} \int_{-\infty}^{\infty} R_{vv}(x, y) \, dx \, dy \qquad (42)$$

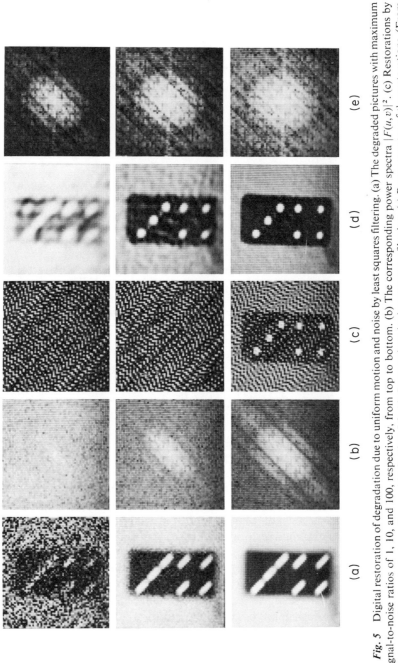

Fig. 5 Digital restoration of degradation due to uniform motion and noise by least squares filtering. (a) The degraded pictures with maximum signal-to-noise ratios of 1, 10, and 100, respectively, from top to bottom. (b) The corresponding power spectra $|F(u,v)|^2$. (c) Restorations by the inverse filtering technique discussed in Section 7.2. (d) Restorations by least squares filtering. (e) Power spectra of the restorations. (From [36].)

where we have used Eq. (111a) from Chapter 2. If the noise process is ergodic (Section 2.4.6), $R_{vv}(x, y)$ can be determined by applying Eq. (28) of Chapter 2 to a picture containing noise only, i.e., to an output picture $g(x, y)$ obtained when the input picture $f(x, y)$ is zero.

If no statistical properties of the random processes involved are known, it is not uncommon to approximate (41) by

$$M(u, v) = \frac{1}{H(u, v)} \frac{|H(u, v)|^2}{|H(u, v)|^2 + \Gamma}$$

where Γ, the noise-to-signal power density ratio, is approximated by a suitable constant. The value of this constant evidently reflects some *a priori* knowledge about the relative magnitudes of signal and noise power in the picture. The optimality of this form of the restoration filter is open to question and superior restoration may be achieved by other techniques [12].

Figure 5, due to Harris [36], illustrates least squares restoration of motion degraded pictures. The results are compared with those obtained by simple inverse filtering as discussed in Section 7.2.

7.4 LEAST SQUARES FILTERING: THE DISCRETE CASE

When a derivation like the one in the preceding section is carried out for discrete data, although fundamentally one arrives at very similar results for the restoration filter, one does run into some interesting conceptual differences that have an important bearing on how the optimum filter may be digitally implemented. *For example, one can now show that transforms, other than the Fourier transform, may be used for the implementation of the optimum filter.* The choice of the transform may be influenced by computational considerations.

Since our aim here is only to bring out the conceptual differences between the continuous and the discrete cases, we will only consider the one-dimensional case in the following.

Let $\mathbf{f}(j)$, $h(j)$, and $\mathbf{g}(j)$ represent, respectively, the ideal data, the blurring function, and the observed data. We will assume that the sequences $\mathbf{f}(j)$, $h(j)$ and $\mathbf{g}(j)$ contain sufficient zero padding so that they will all be considered of the same length, P. (This zero-padding procedure will be explained in detail in Section 7.5.2.) In the presence of observation noise, the general linear relationship between $\mathbf{f}(j)$ and $\mathbf{g}(j)$ may be expressed by (see also Section 7.5.1)

$$\vec{\mathbf{g}} = [\mathfrak{H}_e]\vec{\mathbf{f}} + \vec{\mathbf{v}} \tag{43}$$

where $[\mathfrak{H}_e]$ is the $P \times P$ "blurring" matrix. As will be shown in Section 7.5.1, for the case of position-invariant degradation the elements of the matrix $[\mathfrak{H}_e]$ can be expressed in terms of a one-dimensional function $h(j)$ as follows:

$$[\mathfrak{H}_e] = \begin{bmatrix} h(0) & h(P-1) & h(P-2) & \cdots & h(1) \\ h(1) & h(0) & h(P-1) & \cdots & h(2) \\ \vdots & \vdots & \vdots & & \\ h(P-1) & h(P-2) & h(P-3) & \cdots & h(0) \end{bmatrix} \qquad (44)$$

Since we wish to derive the restoration filter in the transform domain, we will assume that the observed data, $\overset{\star}{\mathbf{g}}$, is subjected to the operations shown in Fig. 6. $[A]$ is a nonsingular $P \times P$ transformation matrix and $[M]$ is the $P \times P$ restoration filter matrix in the transform domain. We will show that for many commonly used transforms, such as the discrete Fourier transform, the matrix $[M]$ has nonzero off-diagonal terms. Since the off-diagonal terms of $[M]$ imply that the spectral components of the observed data are combined to produce a spectral component of the restored signal, this represents a major point of departure from the continuous case. For the continuous case, each spectral component of the observed data is multiplied by a scalar constant $M(u, v)$, given by (41), to obtain the corresponding spectral component of the restored signal. (For this reason, the operations in Fig. 6 are also called vector filtering.)

Let $\vec{\mathbf{G}}$ denote the P-element transform of the random data vector $\overset{\star}{\mathbf{g}}$:

$$\vec{\mathbf{G}} = [A]\overset{\star}{\mathbf{g}} \qquad (45)$$

and let $\overset{\star}{\hat{\mathbf{f}}}$ denote the least squares estimate of $\vec{\mathbf{f}}$. From Fig. 6

$$\overset{\star}{\hat{\mathbf{f}}} = [A]^{-1}[M][A]\overset{\star}{\mathbf{g}} \qquad (46)$$

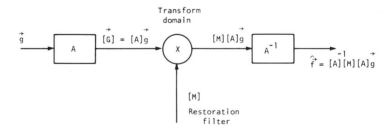

Fig. 6   Schematic representation of the restoration of the observed data $\vec{\mathbf{g}}$. $[A]$ is the transform operator and $[M]$ the restoration operator.

For a given choice of the transformation matrix $[A]$, we want to compute the restoration filter matrix $[M]$ such that the mean-square error e^2 given by

$$e^2 = \text{Trace } E\{(\vec{\mathbf{f}} - \hat{\vec{\mathbf{f}}})(\vec{\mathbf{f}} - \hat{\vec{\mathbf{f}}})^t\} \tag{47}$$

is minimized. This minimization may be carried out by taking partial derivatives of e^2 with respect to the elements of the matrix $[M]$, and setting them equal to zero. However, the same results may be more easily derived by using the orthogonality principle (see Section 2.4.7), which basically says that the difference between the true value of a random variable and its linear estimate must be statistically orthogonal to all the random variables that are used to construct that linear estimate. Therefore, the difference $\vec{\mathbf{f}} - \hat{\vec{\mathbf{f}}}$ must also be statistically orthogonal to $\hat{\vec{\mathbf{f}}}$. That is,

$$E\{(\vec{\mathbf{f}} - \hat{\vec{\mathbf{f}}})\hat{\vec{\mathbf{f}}}^t\} = 0 \tag{48}$$

and, of course, when (48) is satisfied, it follows from (47) that

$$e^2 = \text{Trace } E\{(\vec{\mathbf{f}} - \hat{\vec{\mathbf{f}}})\vec{\mathbf{f}}^t\} \tag{49}$$

Before proceeding further with the derivation of the filter, we need to define some correlation matrices and their transforms. The autocorrelation matrices of the discrete random processes $\vec{\mathbf{f}}$, $\vec{\mathbf{g}}$, and $\vec{\mathbf{v}}$ will be denoted by $[R_{ff}][R_{gg}]$ and $[R_{vv}]$, respectively:

$$[R_{ff}] = E\{\vec{\mathbf{f}}\vec{\mathbf{f}}^t\} \tag{50}$$

$$[R_{gg}] = E\{\vec{\mathbf{g}}\vec{\mathbf{g}}^t\} \tag{51}$$

$$[R_{vv}] = E\{\vec{\mathbf{v}}\vec{\mathbf{v}}^t\} \tag{52}$$

The cross-correlation matrix between $\vec{\mathbf{f}}$ and $\vec{\mathbf{g}}$ will be denoted by

$$[R_{fg}] = E\{\vec{\mathbf{f}}\vec{\mathbf{g}}^t\} \tag{53}$$

If all the random processes are stationary, the matrices $[R_{ff}]$, $[R_{gg}]$, and $[R_{vv}]$ will reduce to the Toeplitz form. Also, if the $\vec{\mathbf{f}}$ and $\vec{\mathbf{g}}$ processes are jointly stationary, the matrix $[R_{fg}]$ will also be Toeplitz.

$[S_{ff}]$, $[S_{gg}]$, and $[S_{vv}]$ will denote the transforms of the respective correlation matrices and will be defined as follows[§]:

$$[S_{ff}] = [A][R_{ff}][A]^{-1} \tag{54}$$

$$[S_{gg}] = [A][R_{gg}][A]^{-1} \tag{55}$$

$$[S_{vv}] = [A][R_{vv}][A]^{-1} \tag{56}$$

[§] If $[A]$ is a unitary transform, which means that $[A]^{*t} = [A]^{-1}$, then one can easily show that $[S_{ff}] = E\{\vec{\mathbf{F}}\vec{\mathbf{F}}^{*t}\}$, where $\vec{\mathbf{F}}$ is the transform of $\vec{\mathbf{f}}$, i.e., $\vec{\mathbf{F}} = [A]\vec{\mathbf{f}}$.

Note that these definitions are general since the assumption of stationarity of the signals is *not* required. These definitions also correspond to Papoulis's definitions [75, Chap. 12] of the transforms of the correlation functions of continuous nonstationary signals.

To derive the optimum restoration filter, we substitute (46) in the orthogonality conditions of (48):

$$E\{(\vec{\mathbf{f}} - [A]^{-1}[M][A]\vec{\mathbf{g}})([A]^{-1}[M][A]\vec{\mathbf{g}})^t\} = 0 \qquad (57)$$

which reduces to

$$E\{(\vec{\mathbf{f}} - [A]^{-1}[M][A]\vec{\mathbf{g}})\vec{\mathbf{g}}^t\} = 0 \qquad (58)$$

since $[A]^{-1}[M][A]$, which is the space (or time) domain representation of the filter, cannot be identically zero. In Fig. 6, all the operations between the input and the output may be lumped together and represented by a single matrix equal to $[A]^{-1}[M][A]$. In terms of the correlation matrices defined in (50)–(53), Eq. (58) can be expressed as

$$[R_{fg}] = [A]^{-1}[M][A][R_{gg}] \qquad (59)$$

Using (43) and assuming that the ideal signal $\vec{\mathbf{f}}$ and the $\vec{\mathbf{v}}$ are uncorrelated, one can show the following:

$$[R_{gg}] = [\mathfrak{H}_e][R_{ff}][\mathfrak{H}_e]^t + [R_{vv}] \qquad (60)$$

$$[R_{fg}] = [R_{ff}][\mathfrak{H}_e]^t \qquad (61)$$

Substituting these equalities in (59), we get the following expression for the restoration filter matrix:

$$[M] = [A][R_{ff}][\mathfrak{H}_e]^t([\mathfrak{H}_e][R_{ff}][\mathfrak{H}_e]^t + [R_{vv}])^{-1}[A]^{-1} \qquad (62)$$

To bring out the similarities between this expression and the result in (41) for the continuous case, we will reexpress (62) as

$$[M] = [A][R_{ff}][A]^{-1}[A][\mathfrak{H}_e]^t[A]^{-1}([A][\mathfrak{H}_e][A]^{-1}[A][R_{ff}][A]^{-1}$$
$$\times [A][\mathfrak{H}_e]^t[A]^{-1} + [A][R_{vv}][A]^{-1})^{-1} \qquad (63)$$

Let $[H]$ and $[H]'$ denote the following transforms of $[\mathfrak{H}_e]$ and $[\mathfrak{H}_e]^t$, respectively:

$$[H] = [A][\mathfrak{H}_e][A]^{-1} \qquad (64)$$

$$[H]' = [A][\mathfrak{H}_e]^t[A]^{-1} \qquad (65)$$

Substituting these two definitions and (54)–(56) in (63), we get

$$[M] = [S_{ff}][H]'([H][S_{ff}][H]' + [S_{vv}])^{-1} \qquad (66)$$

When $[A]$ is unitary

$$[H]' = [H]^{*t} \tag{67}$$

Therefore, in this case

$$[M] = [S_{ff}][H]^{*t}([H][S_{ff}][H]^{*t} + [S_{vv}])^{-1} \tag{68}$$

Comparing (68) with (41a), it is evident that the spectral density $S_{ff}(u)$ for the continuous case is analogous to the transform $[S_{ff}]$, which is equal to $[A][R_{ff}][A]^{-1}$, for the discrete case. Note that in contradistinction to the continuous case of the preceding section, the discrete case discussed here is not limited by the assumption of stationarity. (Although, surely it should be possible to derive a least squares filter for the nonstationary continuous case also.) Similarly, $S_{vv}(u)$ for the continuous case is analogous to $[A][R_{vv}][A]^{-1}$ here.

While the restoration filter matrix obviously depends upon the choice of the transformation matrix $[A]$, we will now show that the minimum mean-square error has no such dependence. Substituting (46) in (49), we can write for the mean-square error

$$e^2 = \text{Trace}\{[R_{ff}] - [A]^{-1}[M][A][\mathfrak{H}_e][R_{ff}]\} \tag{69}$$

Using the optimum value of $[M]$ given by (62), we get

$$e^2 = \text{Trace}\{[R_{ff}] - [R_{ff}][\mathfrak{H}_e]'([\mathfrak{H}_e][R_{ff}][\mathfrak{H}_e]' + [R_{vv}])^{-1}[\mathfrak{H}_e][R_{ff}]\} \tag{70}$$

which is independent of $[A]$. That the minimum mean-square error is independent of the transformation used is perhaps intuitively clear. The parameter e^2 is basically the square of the perpendicular distance from $\vec{\mathbf{f}}$ to the subspace spanned by the random variables $\mathbf{g}(j)$. Since a non-singular transformation may be interpreted as a rotation of the coordinates followed by their expansion or contraction, and, also, since the inverse transformation behaves in exactly the opposite sense, the perpendicular distance between $\vec{\mathbf{f}}$ and the space spanned by $\mathbf{g}(j)$'s should remain unchanged.

We will now consider the case when the degradation to the ideal signal only consists of the additive noise. Since in this case $[\mathfrak{H}_e] = [I]$, the expressions derived previously may be simplified by using this equality. The restoration filter matrix of (68) reduces to

$$[M] = [S_{ff}]([S_{ff}] + [S_{vv}])^{-1} \tag{71}$$

since when $[\mathfrak{H}_e] = [I]$, the transform $[H]$ is also equal to the identity matrix. The expression in (70) for the mean-square error reduces to

$$e^2 = \text{Trace}\{[R_{ff}] - [R_{ff}]([R_{ff}] + [R_{vv}])^{-1}[R_{ff}]\} \tag{72}$$

By utilizing the property that $\text{Trace}([P][Q]) = \text{Trace}([Q][P])$, this expression may be reduced to a more familiar form as follows:

$$
\begin{aligned}
e^2 &= \text{Trace}\{[R_{ff}] - [R_{ff}]([R_{ff}] + [R_{vv}])^{-1}[R_{ff}]\} \\
&= \text{Trace}\{[R_{ff}] - [R_{ff}][R_{ff}]([R_{ff}] + [R_{vv}])^{-1}\} \\
&= \text{Trace}\{([R_{ff}] - [R_{ff}][R_{ff}]([R_{ff}] + [R_{vv}])^{-1})([R_{ff}] + [R_{vv}]) \\
&\quad \times ([R_{ff}] + [R_{vv}])^{-1}\} \\
&= \text{Trace}\{[R_{ff}][R_{vv}]([R_{ff}] + [R_{vv}])^{-1}\}
\end{aligned}
\tag{73}
$$

which is a result originally derived by Pratt [79], although using a slightly different approach.

It is clear from both (69) and (71) that for large data vectors, the generation of the filter matrix can be difficult since the inversion of a large-order matrix would be required. In some cases, however, it may be possible to get around this difficulty by exploiting the properties of the structure of the autocorrelation matrices. One such case is that in which the only degradation is additive stationary white noise. In this case, the restoration filter matrix is given by (71) with $[R_{vv}]$ being equal to

$$
[R_{vv}] =
\begin{bmatrix}
\sigma_v^2 & & & \\
& \sigma_v^2 & & \varnothing \\
& & \ddots & \\
\varnothing & & & \sigma_v^2
\end{bmatrix}
\tag{74}
$$

where σ_v^2 is the variance of each noise random variable (assumed to be zero mean). Let the matrix consisting of the eigenvectors of $[R_{ff}]$ be denoted by $[e_f]$. By definition, $[R_{ff}]$ is diagonalized by $[e_f]$:

$$
[e_f]^{-1}[R_{ff}][e_f] =
\begin{bmatrix}
\lambda_f(1) & & & \\
& \lambda_f(2) & & \varnothing \\
& & \ddots & \\
\varnothing & & & \lambda_f(P)
\end{bmatrix}
\tag{75}
$$

where $\lambda_f(i)$ is the ith eigenvalue of the matrix $[R_{ff}]$. Equations (74) and (75) may be combined as follows:

$$
\begin{aligned}
&[e_f]^{-1}([R_{ff}] + [R_{vv}])[e_f] \\
&\quad =
\begin{bmatrix}
\lambda_f(1) + \sigma^{2v} & & & \\
& \lambda_f(2) + \sigma_v^2 & & \varnothing \\
& & \ddots & \\
\varnothing & & & \lambda_f(P) + \sigma_v^2
\end{bmatrix}
\end{aligned}
\tag{76}
$$

This equation may be recast in the following form:

$$([R_{ff}] + [R_{vv}])^{-1} = [e_f] \begin{bmatrix} \dfrac{1}{\lambda_f(1) + \sigma_v^2} & & \varnothing \\ & \ddots & \\ \varnothing & & \dfrac{1}{\lambda_f(P) + \sigma_v^2} \end{bmatrix} [e_f]^{-1} \quad (77)$$

Using this equation together with (54) and (56), we can write

$$([S_{ff}] + [S_{vv}])^{-1} = [A]([R_{ff}] + [R_{vv}])^{-1}[A]^{-1}$$

$$= [A][e_f] \begin{bmatrix} \dfrac{1}{\lambda_f(1) + \sigma_v^2} & & \varnothing \\ & \ddots & \\ \varnothing & & \dfrac{1}{\lambda_f(P) + \sigma_v^2} \end{bmatrix} [e_f]^{-1}[A]^{-1} \quad (78)$$

which, using (71), leads to the following result:

$$[M] = [A][R_{ff}][e_f] \begin{bmatrix} \dfrac{1}{\lambda_f(1) + \sigma_v^2} & & \varnothing \\ & \ddots & \\ \varnothing & & \dfrac{1}{\lambda_f(P) + \sigma_v^2} \end{bmatrix} [e_f]^{-1}[A]^{-1} \quad (79)$$

Since $[e_f]$ is the matrix of eigenvectors of a real symmetric matrix (all auto-correlation matrices defined here are real symmetric), it can always be chosen to be orthogonal [71, p. 306]. Hence $[e_f]^{-1} = [e_f]^t$. Also, since the transformation matrix $[A]$ is chosen by the user, presumably its inverse is also known. Of course, if $[A]$ is unitary, such as Fourier, Hadamard, Karhunen–Loève, etc., then $[A]^{-1} = [A]^{*t}$. Therefore, in contrast to (71), the expression for the filter matrix in (79) is more convenient for large data sizes, since it does not require inversion of large-sized matrices. Finally, note that if $[A]$ is chosen to be the Karhunen–Loève transform, $[A] = [e_f]^t$. In this case the expression in (79) further simplifies to

$$[M] = \begin{bmatrix} \dfrac{\lambda_f(1)}{\lambda_f(1) + \sigma_v^2} & & \varnothing \\ & \ddots & \\ \varnothing & & \dfrac{\lambda_f(P)}{\lambda_f(P) + \sigma_v^2} \end{bmatrix} \quad (80)$$

7.5 CONSTRAINED DECONVOLUTION

In the Wiener or the least squares restoration filter derived in the preceding section, the following basic assumptions were made: that the undegraded picture and the noise belonged to homogeneous random fields and that their power spectra were known. In many situations one may not have *a priori* knowledge to this extent.

If all that is known (aside from the nature of the degradation) is the variance of the noise, then the method to be described in this section is applicable. This method was first formulated by Phillips [78] and later refined by Twomey [102, 103] in the one-dimensional case. The two-dimensional case of pictures can, in principle, be reduced to a one-dimensional problem and then solved by the method of Phillips and Twomey. The actual implementation, however, is made difficult by the large size of the matrices involved. Hunt [47–49], recognizing the special structure of degradation operators, successfully solved this problem of implementation.

7.5.1 The One-Dimensional Case

We first present the method in the one-dimensional case. For this case the equation corresponding to (2) is

$$g(x) = \int_0^x h(x-x')\, f(x')\, dx' + v(x) \tag{81}$$

where $g(x)$ is the degraded signal, $h(x)$ the point spread function (known as the impulse response in the one-dimensional case), $f(x)$ the ideal signal, and $v(x)$ the uncertainty in the measurement of $g(x)$. Note that $v(x)$ is a deterministic function like the other functions in (81), the difference being that it is only known in terms of its averages; this will be explained in greater detail later. In (81) we are also assuming that the signals are zero outside finite intervals, and that the origin of the coordinates is positioned such that

$$f(x) = 0 \qquad \text{except for } 0 \leqslant x \leqslant A$$

$$h(x) = 0 \qquad \text{except for } 0 \leqslant x \leqslant B$$

where these definitions imply that

$$g(x) \quad \text{and} \quad v(x) = 0 \qquad \text{except} \quad \text{for } 0 \leqslant x \leqslant A + B$$

Of course, within the finite intervals previously defined there may be points where any of the four functions takes zero value.

The discrete approximation to (81) can be expressed as

$$g(p) = \sum_{i=0}^{p} h(p-i) f(i) + v(p) \qquad \text{for} \quad p = 0, 1, \ldots, M + J - 2$$

(82)

where we have assumed that there are M numbers in the sequence $f(i)$, and J in the sequence $h(i)$, so that there are $M+J-1$ numbers in the sequence $g(p)$. Evidently, the number of terms in each of the sequences depends on the sampling interval Δx. It is known that if the noise $v(p)$ is ignored in (82) and straightforward matrix inversion techniques are used to solve for $f(i)$ given $g(p)$, the solutions become more accurate as the sampling interval Δx becomes smaller, but eventually they begin to get worse. The solutions begin to get worse sooner, the larger the magnitude of the noise $v(x)$, since this is the uncertainty in the knowledge of the true value of $g(x)$.

Equation (82) can be written in the matrix form

$$\vec{g} = [\mathfrak{H}] \vec{f} + \vec{v}$$

(83)

where $\vec{g}$, $\vec{f}$, and $\vec{v}$ are vectors composed, respectively, of the sequences $g(p)$, $f(i)$, and $v(p)$; and $[\mathfrak{H}]$ is a matrix whose (p, i)th element is

$$\mathfrak{H}(p,i) = \begin{cases} h(p-i) & \text{if} \quad 0 \leqslant p - i \leqslant J - 1 \\ 0 & \text{otherwise} \end{cases}$$

(84)

for $p = 0, 1, \ldots, M + J - 2$ and $i = 0, 1, \ldots, M - 1$. For example, if $M = 3$ and $J = 2$, the $[\mathfrak{H}]$ matrix looks like

$$\begin{bmatrix} h(0) & 0 & 0 \\ h(1) & h(0) & 0 \\ 0 & h(1) & h(0) \\ 0 & 0 & h(1) \end{bmatrix}$$

We shall not assume that the function $v(p)$ is known but only that some of its statistical or average properties are known. In particular we shall assume that

$$\vec{v}^{t}\vec{v} = \sum_{p=0}^{M+J-2} v^2(p) = \varepsilon$$

(85)

a known constant, where the superscript t indicates the transpose. Note that if $v(p)$ has zero mean, i.e., $\sum_{p=0}^{M+J-2} v(p) \simeq 0$, then

$$\varepsilon \simeq (M+J-1)\sigma_v^2$$

where σ_v^2 is the variance of v. (In picture restoration the variance of noise can be estimated either from those regions of the picture that are almost constant in brightness or from the physical processes responsible for the noise in the measurement of $\vec{g}$.)

We can now formulate the restoration problem as follows: Given $\vec{g}$, $[\mathfrak{H}]$, and ε we want to find an estimate $\hat{\vec{f}}$ of $\vec{f}$ such that the "residual" $g - [\mathfrak{H}]\hat{\vec{f}}$ has the same average properties as $\vec{v}$. In particular, the residual must satisfy

$$(\vec{g} - [\mathfrak{H}]\hat{\vec{f}})^t(\vec{g} - [\mathfrak{H}]\hat{\vec{f}}) = \varepsilon \qquad (86)$$

There may exist many functions $\hat{\vec{f}}$ such that (86) is satisfied. Of all such $\hat{\vec{f}}$ some other constraint must be used to select the "optimum" solution. Such a constraint must have some *a priori* plausibility. For example, if the original undegraded signals $\vec{f}$ are known to be smooth functions, then the additional constraint could be the minimization of a roughness measure such as the second derivative. The numerical approximation to the second-order derivative at a point i is

$$\hat{f}(i+1) - 2\hat{f}(i) + \hat{f}(i-1)$$

Therefore, the criterion for the selection of the optimum solution can be expressed as

$$\text{minimize}\left\{ \sum_{i=-1}^{M} (\hat{f}(i+1) - 2\hat{f}(i) + \hat{f}(i-1))^2 \right\} \qquad (87)$$

It can easily be verified that in matrix notation (87) can be expressed as

$$\text{minimize}\{\hat{\vec{f}}^t[C]^t[C]\hat{\vec{f}}\} \qquad (88)$$

where

$$[C] = \begin{bmatrix} 1 & & & & & & & & \\ -2 & 1 & & & & & & & \\ 1 & -2 & 1 & & & & & & \\ & 1 & -2 & 1 & & & & & \\ & & 1 & -2 & & & & & \\ & & & 1 & & & & & \\ & & & & \ddots & & & & \\ & & & & & 1 & & & \\ & & & & & -2 & 1 & & \\ & & & & & 1 & -2 & 1 & \\ & & & & & & 1 & -2 & \\ & & & & & & & 1 & \end{bmatrix} \qquad (89)$$

is an $(M+2) \times M$ matrix.

The restoration problem then is to find the $\hat{f}$ that minimizes (88) subject to constraint (86).§ The required solution can be obtained by the method of Lagrange multipliers. If λ is the Lagrange multiplier, the required solution must satisfy the system of linear equations

$$\frac{\partial}{\partial \hat{f}(i)} \{\lambda(\hat{g} - [\mathfrak{H}]\hat{f})^t(\hat{g} - [\mathfrak{H}]\hat{f}) + \hat{f}^t[C]^t[C]\hat{f}\} = 0, \quad i = 0, 1, \dots, M-1$$

(90)

This system, together with (86), yields $M+1$ equations for the $M+1$ unknowns $\hat{f}(0), \dots, \hat{f}(M-1)$ and λ. The reader may verify that if we perform the differentiations indicated in (90), we obtain a set of equations that can be combined into the single matrix equation¶

$$\lambda([\mathfrak{H}]^t[\mathfrak{H}]\hat{f} - [\mathfrak{H}]^t\hat{g}) + [C]^t[C]\hat{f} = 0$$

(91)

which immediately gives the required solution

$$\hat{f} = ([\mathfrak{H}]^t[\mathfrak{H}] + \gamma[C]^t[C])^{-1}[\mathfrak{H}]^t\hat{g}$$

(92)

where $\gamma = 1/\lambda$.

The value of the parameter γ in (92) can be determined iteratively as follows. One chooses a value for γ, computes $\hat{f}$ using (92), and computes the residual

$$([\mathfrak{H}]\hat{f} - \hat{g})^t([\mathfrak{H}]\hat{f} - \hat{g})$$

(93)

If the value of γ is correct, then by (86) the residual should equal the known constant ε. If the computed value of (93) exceeds ε, γ is decreased; if the value is less than ε, it is increased. This is based on the fact that by substituting (92) in (93) ε can be shown to be a monotonically increasing function of γ [49].

7.5.2 Formulation in Terms of Circulant Matrices

The two-dimensional problem of picture restoration can be reduced to the one-dimensional case and then solved by the method in Section 7.5.1. In this case, however, M may take very large values, on the order of 40,000. Since the size of the matrix $\mathfrak{H}$ is greater than $M \times M$, it is clear that the matrix inversion in (92) can, in practice, prove to be very difficult and time consuming. In what follows, we will show that this difficulty in implementation can be circumvented

---

§ The corresponding problem in the continuous case would be to find $\hat{f}$ that minimizes $\int |\nabla^2 f|^2 \, dx$ subject to the constraint $\int (g - h * f)^2 \, dx = \varepsilon$, where $\varepsilon = \int v^2 (x) \, dx$ is a known constant.

¶ On taking derivatives of matrix equations, see, for example, Section 3.1 of "Estimation Theory" by R. Deutsch, Prentice-Hall, Englewood Cliffs, New Jersey, 1965.

by making use of the properties of circulant matrices. This was first pointed out by Hunt [48].

We first need to express (82) or (83) in a slightly different form. For an integer $P \geqslant M+J-1$, we form new extended sequences $f_e(i)$, $g_e(i)$, $h_e(i)$, and $v_e(i)$ by padding the original sequences with zeros as follows:

$$f_e(i) = \begin{cases} f(i) & \text{for} \quad 0 \leqslant i \leqslant M-1 \\ 0 & \text{for} \quad M \leqslant i \leqslant P-1 \end{cases}$$

$$h_e(i) = \begin{cases} h(i) & \text{for} \quad 0 \leqslant i \leqslant J-1 \\ 0 & \text{for} \quad J \leqslant i \leqslant P-1 \end{cases}$$

$$g_e(i) = \begin{cases} g(i) & \text{for} \quad 0 \leqslant i \leqslant M+J-2 \\ 0 & \text{for} \quad M+J-1 \leqslant i \leqslant P-1 \end{cases} \quad (94)$$

$$v_e(i) = \begin{cases} v(i) & \text{for} \quad 0 \leqslant i \leqslant M+J-2 \\ 0 & \text{for} \quad M+J-1 \leqslant i \leqslant P-1 \end{cases}$$

Note that all the extended sequences are of the same length P.

Now let us construct a matrix $[\mathfrak{H}_e]$ as follows:

$$[\mathfrak{H}_e] = \begin{bmatrix} h_e(0) & h_e(P-1) & h_e(P-2) & \cdots & h_e(1) \\ h_e(1) & h_e(0) & h_e(P-1) & \cdots & h_e(2) \\ \vdots & \vdots & \vdots & & \vdots \\ h_e(P-1) & h_e(P-2) & h_e(P-3) & \cdots & h_e(0) \end{bmatrix} \quad (95)$$

It can easily be seen by substitution from (94) that with $[\mathfrak{H}_e]$ defined as above, the expression

$$\vec{g}_e = [\mathfrak{H}_e]\vec{f}_e + \vec{v}_e \quad (96)$$

is identical to (83) if $P \geqslant M+J-1$.

The structure of the matrix in (95) is of particular importance. Note that each row can be obtained by cyclically shifting the row immediately above one position to the right. The rightmost element of the row immediately above now appears in the leftmost position. Matrices such as this are called *circulant matrices*.

Expression (88) which we want to minimize can be expressed in an equivalent form involving only circulant matrices. For example, if we want to minimize the second derivative, $[C]$ is given by (89). Let the sequence $c(i)$ be $1, -2, 1$. The extended sequence $c_e(i)$ is then given by

$$c_e(i) = \begin{cases} c(i) & \text{for} \quad 0 \leqslant i \leqslant 2 \\ 0 & \text{for} \quad 3 \leqslant i \leqslant P-1 \end{cases}$$

A matrix $[C_e]$ is formed from the extended sequence $c_e(i)$ in exactly the same manner as $[\mathfrak{H}_e]$ is formed from $h_e(i)$, and expression (88) is rewritten as

$$\text{minimize } \hat{\vec{f}}_e{}'[C_e]'[C_e]\hat{\vec{f}}_e \tag{97}$$

It can be verified that the expression in the brackets in (97) is equal to the corresponding expression in (88) for $P \geqslant M+J-2$.

Writing the constraint (87) as

$$v_e{}'v_e = \text{known constant } \varepsilon \tag{98}$$

it is clear from the preceding subsection that the solution of (97) subject to this constraint is given by

$$\hat{\vec{f}}_e = ([\mathfrak{H}_e]'[\mathfrak{H}_e] + \gamma[C_e]'[C_e])^{-1}([\mathfrak{H}_e]'\vec{g}_e) \tag{99}$$

One final word about the value of P. We mentioned previously that for the convolution in (96) to be identical to that in (83), P can be any integer provided $P \geqslant M+J-1$. In other words, sufficient numbers of zeros must be inserted in the extended sequences to eliminate the "wrap-around" effect caused by $[\mathfrak{H}_e]$ being circulant. Now if we look at (99), there is a double convolution involved in it. This becomes apparent if we write it in the form

$$[\mathfrak{H}_e]'[\mathfrak{H}_e]\hat{\vec{f}}_e + \gamma[C_e]'[C_e]\hat{\vec{f}}_e = [\mathfrak{H}_e]'\vec{g}_e$$

since $[\mathfrak{H}_e]$ operating on $\hat{\vec{f}}_e$ is a convolution, and $[\mathfrak{H}_e]'$ operating on $[\mathfrak{H}_e]\hat{\vec{f}}_e$ is another convolution. To prevent the "wrap-around" effect in the first convolution, a sufficient number of zeros must be inserted in the extended sequence $\hat{\vec{f}}_e$ so that the minimum value of P is $M+J-1$. To prevent the "wrap-around" caused by the second convolution, the number of zeros must be further increased by $J-1$. (Note that J is the length of the sequence $h(j)$.) Therefore, for solution (99) to be identical to (92), P must have the lower bound

$$P \geqslant M + 2J - 2 \tag{100}$$

This can also be verified by direct substitution.

Now let us define $\lambda_h(k)$, $\lambda_c(k)$, and a vector $\vec{w}_k$ as follows:

$$\lambda_h(k) = h_e(0) + h_e(P-1) \exp\left(j\frac{2\pi}{P}k\right) + h_e(P-2) \exp\left(j\frac{2\pi}{P}2k\right)$$

$$+ \cdots + h_e(1) \exp\left(j\frac{2\pi}{P}(P-1)k\right) \tag{101a}$$

$$\lambda_c(k) = c_e(0) + c_e(P-1) \exp\left(j\frac{2\pi}{P}k\right) + c_e(P-2) \exp\left(j\frac{2\pi}{P}2k\right)$$

$$+ \cdots + c_e(1) \exp\left(j\frac{2\pi}{P}(P-1)k\right) \tag{101b}$$

$$\vec{w}_k = \begin{bmatrix} 1 \\ \exp\left(j\dfrac{2\pi}{P}k\right) \\ \exp\left(j\dfrac{2\pi}{P}2k\right) \\ \vdots \\ \exp\left(j\dfrac{2\pi}{P}(P-1)k\right) \end{bmatrix}, \qquad k = 0, 1, \ldots, P-1 \tag{101c}$$

It can be directly verified that

$$[\mathfrak{H}_e]\,\vec{w}_k = \lambda_h(k)\,\vec{w}_k, \qquad k = 0, 1, \ldots, P-1 \tag{102}$$

In other words, the vectors $\vec{w}_k$ are the eigenvectors of the circulant matrix $[\mathfrak{H}_e]$, and the $\lambda_k(k)$'s are the corresponding eigenvalues. Similarly, $\vec{w}_k$ and $\lambda_c(k)$ are the eigenvectors and the corresponding eigenvalues of the circulant matrix $[C_e]$.

Let $[W]$ denote the matrix formed by the column vectors $\vec{w}_k$:

$$[W] = [\vec{w}_0, \vec{w}_1, \ldots, \vec{w}_{P-1}]$$

The (i, k) element of $[W]$ is obviously

$$W(i, k) = \exp\left(j\frac{2\pi}{P}ik\right) \tag{103}$$

It is easily seen that the inverse matrix $[W]^{-1}$ has the form

$$W^{-1}(i, k) = \frac{1}{P}\exp\left(-j\frac{2\pi}{P}ik\right) \tag{104}$$

Let $[D_h]$ and $[D_c]$ be $P \times P$ diagonal matrices whose elements are given by

$$D_h(k, k) = \lambda_h(k) \tag{105}$$

and

$$D_c(k, k) = \lambda_c(k) \tag{106}$$

Equations (102) can be written in a combined matrix form as

$$[\mathfrak{H}_e][W] = [W][D_h]$$

so that multiplying both sides on the right by $[W]^{-1}$, we have

$$[\mathfrak{H}_e] = [W][D_h][W]^{-1} \tag{107}$$

Similarly, we have

$$[C_e] = [W][D_c][W]^{-1} \tag{108}$$

By taking the transpose of both sides of (107) and (108) and making use of the fact that $[\mathfrak{H}_e]$ and $[C_e]$ are real matrices, we obtain[§]

$$[\mathfrak{H}_e]^t = [W][D_h]*[W]^{-1} \tag{109}$$

$$[C_e]^t = [W][D_c]*[W]^{-1} \tag{110}$$

Substituing (105), (106), (109), and (110) in (99), we can express the result as

$$[[D_h]*[D_h] + \gamma[D_c]*[D_c]][[W]^{-1}\hat{\vec{f}}_e] = [D_h]*([W]^{-1}\vec{g}_e) \tag{111}$$

Note that $\hat{\vec{f}}_e$ is a vector of length P, and from (103),

$$([W]^{-1}\hat{\vec{f}}_e)_u = \frac{1}{P}\sum_{i=0}^{P-1} \hat{f}_e(i) \exp\left(-j\frac{2\pi}{P}ui\right), \qquad u = 0, 1, \ldots, P - 1 \tag{112}$$

where $([W]^{-1}\hat{\vec{f}}_e)_u$ is the uth element in the vector $([W]^{-1}\hat{\vec{f}}_e)$. The right-hand side of (112) is identical to the discrete Fourier transform (DFT) of the sequence $\hat{f}_e(i)$ (see Eq. (37) of Chapter 2 for the two-dimensional definition). If we denote the DFT of the sequence $\hat{f}_e(i)$ by $\hat{F}(u)$, we can write

$$([W]^{-1}\hat{\vec{f}}_e)_u = \hat{F}(u) \tag{113}$$

Similarly,

$$([W]^{-1}\vec{g}_e)_u = G(u), \qquad u = 0, 1, \ldots, P - 1 \tag{114}$$

[§] For example, by taking the transpose of both sides of (107) we obtain

$$[\mathfrak{H}_e]^t = ([W]^{-1})^t[D_h][W]^t$$

where we have made use of the fact that $[D_h]$ is a diagonal matrix. Since $[W]^{-1}$ and $[W]$ are symmetrical matrices, we have

$$[\mathfrak{H}_e]^t = [W]^{-1}[D_h][W]$$

Taking the complex conjugate of both sides, we obtain

$$[\mathfrak{H}_e]^t = ([W]^{-1})*[D_h]*([W])*$$

where we have used the fact that $[\mathfrak{H}_e]$ is a real matrix. From (104) it is clear that

$$([W]^{-1})* = (1/P)[W] \quad \text{and} \quad [W]* = P[W]^{-1}$$

from which (109) follows.

where $G(u)$ is the DFT of the sequence $g_e(i)$. By using the definitions of $\lambda_h(k)$ and $\lambda_c(k)$ in (101), it is equally easy to show that

$$D_h(u, u) = PH(u) \tag{115}$$

and

$$D_c(u, u) = PC(u), \qquad u = 0, 1, \ldots, P - 1 \tag{116}$$

where $H(u)$ and $C(u)$ are the DFT's of the sequences $h_e(i)$ and $c_e(i)$, respectively.

Substituting (113)–(116) in (111), it can be verified that we obtain the following result in the frequency domain:

$$P^2(|H(u)|^2 + \gamma|C(u)|^2)\hat{F}(u) = PH^*(u)G(u)$$

which immediately gives

$$\hat{F}(u) = \frac{H^*(u)G(u)}{P(|H(u)|^2 + \gamma|C(u)|^2)}, \qquad u = 0, 1, \ldots, P - 1 \tag{117}$$

If we let $M(u)$ denote the restoration filter, (117) gives us the result

$$M(u) = \frac{H^*(u)}{P(|H(u)|^2 + \gamma|C(u)|^2)} \tag{118}$$

Since fast discrete Fourier transform algorithms are available on most computers, (117) should be much easier and less time consuming to implement then (92) or (99).

7.5.3   Application to Pictures

Although one can use an approach similar to that in the preceding subsection [49], it is much easier to derive the constrained least squares filter for images directly in the frequency domain. In what follows we will present the two-dimensional derivation of Dines and Kak [18].

The two-dimensional convolution between an ideal $M \times N$ image $f(m, n)$ and a $J \times K$ point spread function $h(m, n)$ is expressed as

$$g(p, q) = \sum_{k=0}^{P-1} \sum_{l=0}^{Q-1} h(p - k, q - l)f(k, l) + v(p, q),$$

$$p = 0, 1, \ldots, P - 1, \quad q = 0, 1, \ldots, Q - 1 \tag{119}$$

where we have assumed that all the arrays have been appropriately padded with zeros, as in (94), so that the convolution may be considered to be circular. Therefore, $P > M + J - 1$ and $Q > N + K - 1$. We will have more to say later in this subsection about the correct choices for P and Q. In (119), $p - k$ and $q - l$ take integer values modulo P and Q, respectively.

The constraint equation that corresponds to (85) for the two-dimensional case is

$$\sum_{p=0}^{P-1}\sum_{q=0}^{Q-1} v^2(p, q) = \varepsilon \text{ (a known constant)} \tag{120}$$

where $v(p, q)$ is zero whenever p or q exceed $M + J - 1$ or $N + K - 1$, respectively.

We now seek an estimate $\hat{f}(m, n)$ of the original image that would satisfy (119) subject to the summation constraint in (120). Since this constraint can be satisfied by many functions, we select one that minimizes some property of the image. This property is expressed in terms of the energy content in a filtered version of the estimated image. Specifically,

$$\text{minimize}\left\{\sum_{p=0}^{P-1}\sum_{q=0}^{Q-1} [l(p, q) * \hat{f}(p, q)]^2\right\} \tag{121}$$

where $*$ denotes circular convolution, and $l(m, n)$ is a constraint array which we are free to select. For example, if we wish to obtain a "smooth" estimate then $l(m, n)$ can be chosen as the Laplacian operator:

$$[l] = \left.\begin{bmatrix} \begin{array}{ccc:c} 0 & 1 & 0 & \\ 1 & -4 & 1 & \varnothing \\ 0 & 1 & 0 & \\ \hdashline & \varnothing & & \varnothing \end{array} \end{bmatrix}\right\updownarrow P \tag{122}$$

$$\xleftarrow{\hspace{1.5cm}} Q \xrightarrow{\hspace{1.5cm}}$$

Note that the zero padding of the basic submatrix shown within the dashed line ensures circular convolution in (121). Equation (121) here corresponds to the smoothness criterion in (87) for the one-dimensional case. In expanded notation, the choice of $[l]$ in (122) leads to the following minimization:

$$\text{minimize}\{\sum\sum[\hat{f}(p - 1, q) + \hat{f}(p, q - 1)$$
$$+ \hat{f}(p + 1, q) + \hat{f}(p, q + 1) - 4\hat{f}(p, q)]^2\} \tag{123}$$

The desired estimate $\hat{f}(m, n)$ can be obtained by formulating the problem in the frequency domain. By using the definition of the discrete Fourier transform in Section 2.2.1, and the discrete version of Parseval's theorem as given in Section 2.2, Eqs. (119)–(121) can be expressed in the frequency domain as

$$G(p, q) = PQ\hat{F}(p, q)H(p, q) + E(p, q) \tag{124}$$

$$PQ \sum_{p=0}^{P-1} \sum_{q=0}^{Q-1} |E(p, q)|^2 = \varepsilon \tag{125}$$

$$\text{minimize } P^3Q^3 \sum_{p=0}^{P-1} \sum_{q=0}^{Q-1} |L(p, q)\hat{F}(p, q)|^2 \tag{126}$$

$$\text{subject to } PQ \sum_{p=0}^{P-1} \sum_{q=0}^{Q-1} |G(p, q) - PQ\hat{F}(p, q)H(p, q)|^2 = \varepsilon \tag{127}$$

where $G(p, q)$, $\hat{F}(p, q)$, $H(p, q)$ and $E(p, q)$ are the DFT's of $g(p, q), \hat{f}(p, q)$, $h(p, q)$, and $v(p, q)$, respectively. In order to obtain (124), f was replaced by $\hat{f}$ prior to Fourier transformation of both sides of (119). Equation (127) is merely a restatement of (125), obtained by using (124).

The minimization in (126) can be carried out using Lagrange multipliers. We find $\hat{F}(p, q)$ that minimizes the following functional

$$U = \sum_{p=0}^{P-1} \sum_{q=0}^{Q-1} P^3Q^3 |L(p, q)\hat{F}(p, q)|^2 + \lambda PQ|G(p, q) - PQ\hat{F}(p, q)H(p, q)|^2 \tag{128}$$

where λ is a Lagrange multiplier. Since in general $\hat{F}(k, l)$ is complex, we write

$$\hat{F}(k, l) = A(p, q) + jB(p, q) \tag{129}$$

Substituting (129) in (128), differentiating first with respect to $A(p, q)$ and then with respect to $B(p, q)$, we get

$$\frac{\partial U}{\partial A(p, q)} = P^3Q^32|L(p, q)|^2A(p, q) + 2\lambda P^3Q^3|H(p, q)|^2A(p, q)$$

$$- \lambda P^2Q^2[G(p, q)H^*(p, q) + G^*(p, q)H(p, q)] \tag{130}$$

$$\frac{\partial U}{\partial B(p, q)} = P^3Q^32|L(p, q)|^2B(p, q) + 2\lambda P^3Q^3|H(p, q)|^2B(p, q)$$

$$+ j\lambda P^2Q^2[G(p, q)H^*(p, q) - G^*(p, q)H(p, q)]$$

$$p = 0, 1, \ldots, P - 1, \quad q = 0, 1, \ldots, Q - 1 \tag{131}$$

At the minimum, each of the $2PQ$ derivatives in (130) and (131) must equal zero. From this we get

$$A(p, q) = \frac{1}{PQ} \frac{\lambda \, \text{Re}\{G(p, q)H^*(p, q)\}}{|L(p, q)|^2 + \lambda |H(p, q)|^2} \tag{132}$$

$$B(p, q) = \frac{1}{PQ} \frac{\lambda \, \text{Im}\{G(p, q)H^*(p, q)\}}{|L(p, q)|^2 + \lambda |H(p, q)|^2} \tag{133}$$

where $\text{Re}\{\cdot\}$ and $\text{Im}\{\cdot\}$ denote the real and the imaginary parts, respectively, and $*$ denotes the complex conjugate. From (129), (132), and (133), we obtain

$$\hat{F}(p, q) = \frac{1}{PQ} \frac{H^*(p, q)G(p, q)}{v|L(p, q)|^2 + |H(p, q)|^2} \tag{134}$$

where $v = 1/\lambda$. Therefore, the restoration filter denoted by $M(p, q)$ is given by

$$M(p, q) = \frac{1}{PQ} \frac{H^*(p, q)}{v|L(p, q)|^2 + |H(p, q)|^2} \tag{135}$$

The Lagrange multiplier λ (or $v = 1/\lambda$) must be chosen to satisfy the constraint in (127). Substituting the expression for the estimate (134) in (127), we obtain an expression in the frequency domain that must be satisfied by v:

$$PQ \sum_{p=0}^{P-1} \sum_{q=0}^{Q-1} \frac{v^2 |G(p, q)|^2 |L(p, q)|^4}{[v|L(p, q)|^2 + |H(p, q)|^2]^2} = \varepsilon \tag{136}$$

In order to determine v for the restoration filter, one must solve (136) by an iterative procedure. The manner in which this can be done will be discussed later in this subsection.

We have yet to show the condition under which the filter of (135) results in a minimum rather than a maximum for the functional U. From the calculus of several variables [58] we have the following sufficient condition to guarantee a minimum:

$$\sum_{p=0}^{P-1} \sum_{q=0}^{Q-1} \left\{ \frac{\partial^2 U}{\partial A^2(p, q)} \cos^2 \alpha(p, q) + \frac{\partial^2 U}{\partial B^2(p, q)} \cos^2 \beta(p, q) \right.$$

$$\left. + \text{ all cross partial derivative of order 2} \right\} > 0 \tag{137}$$

for all $\alpha(p, q)$ and $\beta(p, q)$ such that $0 \leqslant \alpha(p, q), \beta(p, q) \leqslant 2\pi$.

In (137), $\cos \alpha(p, q)$ and $\cos \beta(p, q)$ are the direction cosines of a vector that is located in the tangential hyperplane at the minimum in the $2PQ$-dimensional space spanned by the $A(p, q)$'s and $B(p, q)$'s. From (130) and (131), we get

$$\frac{\partial^2 U}{\partial A^2(p, q)} = 2P^3 Q^3 [|L(p, q)|^2 + \lambda |H(p, q)|^2] \tag{138}$$

and

$$\frac{\partial^2 U}{\partial B^2(p, q)} = 2P^3 Q^3 [|L(p, q)|^2 + \lambda |H(p, q)|^2] \tag{139}$$

Since in our case all the cross partials of order 2 are zero, the condition in (137) can be expressed as

$$\sum_{p=0}^{P-1} \sum_{q=0}^{Q-1} [|L(p, q)|^2 + \lambda |H(p, q)|^2][\cos^2 \alpha(p, q) + \cos^2 \beta(p, q)] > 0 \tag{140}$$

Since this strict inequality must hold with each direction cosine taking any value in the range $(-1, +1)$ we must have

$$|L(p, q)|^2 + \lambda |H(p, q)|^2 > 0, \qquad p = 0, 1, \ldots, P-1, \quad q = 0, 1, \ldots, Q-1 \tag{141}$$

Therefore, the Lagrange multiplier must satisfy

$$\lambda > -\frac{|L(p, q)|^2}{|H(p, q)|^2} \tag{142}$$

for all $p = 0, 1, \ldots, P-1$ and $q = 0, 1, \ldots, Q-1$. Equivalently

$$\lambda > -\min_{p, q} \frac{|L(p, q)|^2}{|H(p, q)|^2} = \lambda_{\min} \tag{143}$$

The implication of (143) is that negative values for the Lagrange multiplier are possible in the optimum filter realization. The lower bound in (143) depends upon the ratio of the power spectra of the constraint sequence $l(m, n)$ and the degradation $h(m, n)$. In the case of smoothness constraints such as those given by (122), $|L(0, 0)|^2$ is zero. So if $|H(0, 0)| \neq 0$, (143) predicts that $\lambda > 0$. Thus, ν, the reciprocal of λ, must also be nonnegative. This is an assumption that has been made by many workers in the area [48, 49, 78, 102, 103].

In order to determine the circumstances which may lead to a negative value for ν, the error relationship in (136) will be explored in greater detail. It will be more convenient to work with the original Lagrange multiplier

$\lambda = 1/v$. When viewed as a function λ, the total error energy given by (136) becomes

$$\rho(\lambda) = PQ \sum_{p=0}^{P-1} \sum_{q=0}^{Q-1} \frac{|G(p, q)|^2 |L(p, q)|^4}{\{|L(p, q)|^2 + \lambda |H(p, q)|^2\}^2} \tag{144}$$

which leads to

$$\frac{\partial \rho(\lambda)}{\partial \lambda} = -PQ \sum_{p=0}^{P-1} \sum_{q=0}^{Q-1} \frac{|G(p, q)|^2 |L(p, q)|^4 |H(p, q)|^2}{\{|L(p, q)|^2 + \lambda |H(p, q)|^2\}^3} \tag{145}$$

Using the lower bound on λ given by (143), we can see from (145) that

$$\frac{\partial \rho(\lambda)}{\partial \lambda} < 0 \qquad \text{for} \quad \lambda > \lambda_{\min} \tag{146}$$

Therefore, the total error energy is a monotonically decreasing function of λ. In order to gain further insights into the behavior of the error energy as a function of λ, we can evaluate $\rho(\lambda)$ for some particular values of the argument. As λ approaches zero, (144) yields

$$\rho(0) = PQ \sum_{p=0}^{P-1} \sum_{q=0}^{Q-1} |G(p, q)|^2 \tag{147}$$

Therefore, as $\lambda \to 0$, the error energy approaches the energy in the observed image. If λ is allowed to approach infinity ($v \to 0$), then

$$\lim_{\lambda \to \infty} \rho(\lambda) = 0 \tag{148}$$

From (145)–(148), we can sketch a typical $\rho(\lambda)$ versus λ curve as in Fig. 7. We note that the monotonicity property (146) and the condition of (147)

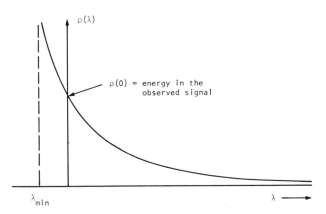

Fig. 7 Typical plot of the noise energy ρ as a function of the Lagrange multiplier λ with $\lambda_{\min}$ defined by Eq. (143).

imply that λ will assume negative values if and only if (i) the negative values are permitted by (143), and (ii) the error energy is greater than the energy in the observed image, i.e.,

$$\varepsilon > PQ \sum_{p=0}^{P-1} \sum_{q=0}^{Q-1} |G(p, q)|^2 \tag{149}$$

The first condition is satisfied if all the frequencies are constrained so that

$$|L(p, q)| \neq 0 \qquad \text{for any } p \text{ and } q \tag{150}$$

The second condition is satisfied when the signal-to-noise ratio in the observed image is less than unity.

We will now make some comments about the practical implementation of the filter. The correct value of λ (or ν) is obtained by numerically evaluating (144) for different λ, and selecting the one for which $\rho(\lambda)$ is equal to the *a priori* known constant ε^2.

Of course, before λ can be calculated using (144) and also before the filter can be implemented, the proper values of P and Q must be determined. These two parameters must be chosen so as to avoid interperiod interference caused by the circular convolutions implied in the frequency domain estimate in (134). The circular convolutions in (134) are more evident when that expression is rewritten as

$$PQ\hat{F}(p, q)\{\nu|L(p, q)|^2 + |H(p, q)|^2\} = H^*(p, q)G(p, q) \tag{151}$$

From the frequency domain multiplications in this expression, it follows that sufficient zero padding must be incorporated (by making P and Q adequately large) such that the circular convolutions in

$$\hat{f}(m, n) * \nu l(m, n) * l(-m, n) + \hat{f}(m, n) * h(m, n) * h(-m, -n)$$
$$= h(-m, -n) * g(m, n) \tag{152}$$

are equal to aperiodic linear convolutions. The left-hand side implies that

$$P \geqslant \text{maximum}[M + 2M_l - 2; M + 2J - 2]$$

and

$$Q \geqslant \text{maximum}[N + 2N_l - 2; N + 2K - 2] \tag{153}$$

where we have assumed that the original image, and therefore $\hat{f}(m, n)$, is of size $M \times N$; $l(m, n)$, prior to zero padding, of size $M_l \times N_l$; and $h(m, n)$ of size $J \times K$.

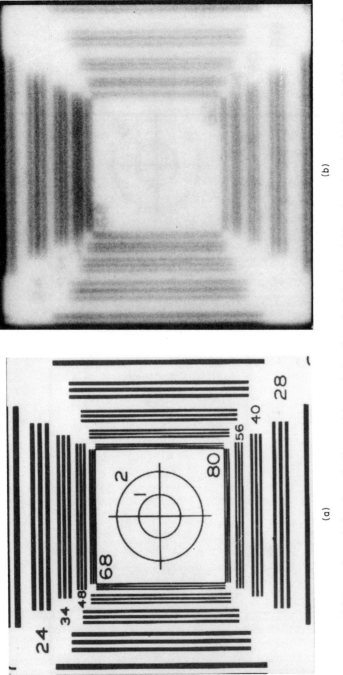

(a)   (b)

Fig. 8   (a) Picture of a resolution chart. (b) Picture of the resolution chart after being degraded by a Gaussian shaped PSF and addition of random noise.

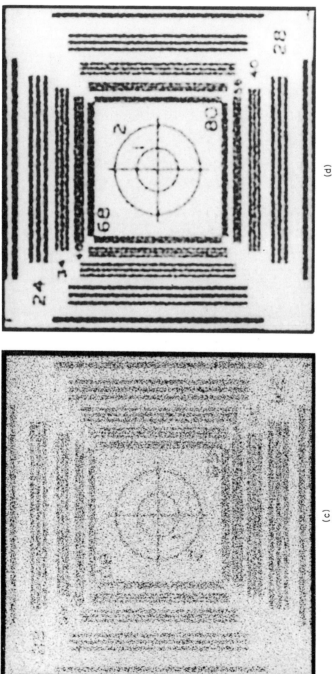

(d)

(c)

Fig. 8 (c) Restoration with $\gamma = 0$. (d) Restoration with the constraint on the residual satisfied. (From [49].)

Finally, a few comments about the restoration filter in (135) are in order. Even though the restoration filter in (135) looks somewhat similar to the Wiener filter in (41b) (which can also be implemented in the discrete case by taking a sufficiently large number of samples in the uv-plane), there are important differences between the two. While the Wiener filter gives the best restoration in an average sense for a family of pictures, the formula here gives an optimum restoration for the one degraded picture that is to be restored. Also, the derivation of the Wiener filter required the basic assumption that the random fields be homogeneous and their spectral densities be known. The filter here, on the other hand, makes no such assumptions. It does, however, require an intelligent choice for the optimality criterion, one particular form of which was given in (121).

One might think that in the formulation presented in this section, since the smoothest solution is being sought, the result should be a restored picture with blurred edges. However, an examination of (120) and (119), which the restored picture $\hat{f}(m, n)$ must satisfy, leads to the conclusion that the degree to which the edges get blurred should to a large extent depend on the magnitude of ε, which is a measure of the uncertainty in the knowledge of the gray levels in the degraded picture.

Figure 8 from Hunt [49] shows an example of restoration by constrained deconvolution. Figure 8a shows a picture of a resolution chart. The chart was digitized on a 450×450 grid and was blurred by a radially symmetric Gaussian shaped point spread function with a standard deviation of approximately 24 samples. To this was added random noise drawn from a uniform distribution on the interval $[0, 0.5]$. The noisy blurred picture is shown in Fig. 8b. Figure 8c shows the restoration with $v = 0$ while Fig. 8d shows the restoration with the constraint on the residual satisfied. Note the improvement in quality over Fig. 8c.

7.6 RECURSIVE FILTERING

We will now introduce a technique of picture restoration in which a picture is represented by a Markov process corrupted by white noise. In this technique an attempt is made to recover the original uncorrupted picture from its degraded version by the method of least squares estimation. The optimum estimate at each point can be expressed in terms of the optimum estimate at the neighboring points and the data at that point. This permits a rapid "on-line" implementation.

In what follows we will first discuss the representation of pictures by wide-sense Markov random fields.

7.6.1 Representation of Pictures by Wide-Sense Markov Random Fields[§]

Let $X_{m,n}$ denote all the points in an L-shaped region of a picture matrix as shown in Fig. 9, that is,

$$X_{m,n} = \{(i,j)\,|\,i < m \quad \text{or} \quad j < n\} \tag{154}$$

Suppose we are given an uncorrupted discrete random field $\mathbf{f}(m,n)$, assumed to be homogeneous, defined on an $M \times N$ array of points. Given that we know the gray levels $\mathbf{f}(i,j)$ at all points within $X_{m,n}$, we want to estimate the gray level at (m,n) with the constraint that this estimate be a linear function of the gray levels in $X_{m,n}$. In other words, if $\hat{\mathbf{f}}(m,n)$ is the optimum estimate for $\mathbf{f}(m,n)$, then

$$\hat{\mathbf{f}}(m,n) = \sum_{\substack{\text{for all } (i,j) \\ \text{such that} \\ (m-i,\,n-j)\,\in\,X_{m,n}}} c_{i,j}\,\mathbf{f}(m-i,\,n-j), \tag{155}$$

where the coefficients $c_{i,j}$ must be determined such that the mean-square estimation error

$$e_{m,n} = E\{[\mathbf{f}(m,n) - \hat{\mathbf{f}}(m,n)]^2\} \tag{156}$$

is minimized; $\hat{\mathbf{f}}(m,n)$ is the "linear least squares estimate of $\mathbf{f}(m,n)$."

Substituting (155) in (156), differentiating with respect to each $c_{i,j}$, and setting each derivative equal to zero, we obtain the following set of simultaneous equations for the unknowns $c_{i,j}$:

$$E\{[\mathbf{f}(m,n) - \hat{\mathbf{f}}(m,n)]\,\mathbf{f}(i,j)\} = 0 \qquad \text{for} \quad \text{all } (i,j) \in X_{m,n} \tag{157}$$

which says that the coefficients $c_{i,j}$ must be such that the estimation error $\mathbf{f}(m,n) - \hat{\mathbf{f}}(m,n)$ is statistically orthogonal to each $\mathbf{f}(i,j)$ that is used to form

---

[§] Markov random fields may be defined as either strict sense or wide sense. The strict-sense Markov fields are defined in terms of conditional distribution functions; and the wide-sense Markov fields are defined directly in terms of least squares estimates. For the case of Gaussian random fields the two definitions are equivalent.

The shape of the region $X_{m,n}$ is the same as that used by Abend et al. [1] for defining strict-sense Markov random fields. They have shown that if a strict-sense Markov random field is defined as one which satisfies

$$p(\mathbf{f}(m,n)\,|\,\text{gray levels at points in } X_{m,n}) = p(\mathbf{f}(m,n)\,|\,\mathbf{f}(m-1,n),\,\mathbf{f}(m-1,n-1),\,\mathbf{f}(m,n-1))$$

where $p(\mathbf{f}(m,n)\,|\,A)$ is the conditional probability density of $\mathbf{f}(m,n)$ given A, then

$$p\left(\mathbf{f}(m,n)\,\left|\,\begin{array}{l}\text{gray levels at all points}\\\text{in the picture matrix}\\\text{except the point } (m,n)\end{array}\right.\right) = p\left(\mathbf{f}(m,n)\,\left|\,\begin{array}{ccc}\mathbf{f}(m-1,n-1) & \mathbf{f}(m,n-1) & \mathbf{f}(m+1,n-1)\\\mathbf{f}(m-1,n) & & \mathbf{f}(m+1,n)\\\mathbf{f}(m-1,n+1) & \mathbf{f}(m,n+1) & \mathbf{f}(m+1,n+1)\end{array}\right.\right)$$

that is, the probability of the gray level at the point (m,n), given the rest of the picture, depends explicitly only on its eight neighbors.

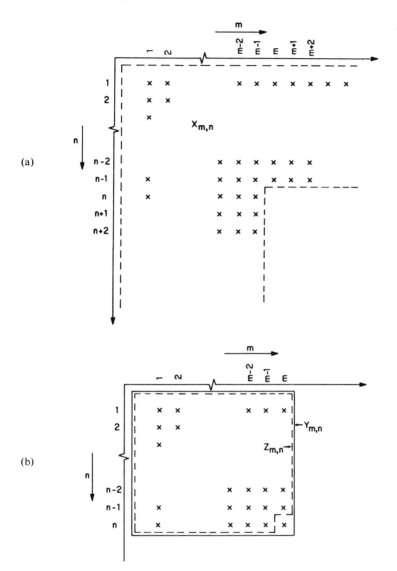

Fig. 9 (a) The L-shaped region formed by the dashed lines is $X_{m,n}$. (b) The regions $Y_{m,n}$ and $Z_{m,n}$.

the linear estimate. This is the orthogonality principle in linear least squares estimation as discussed in Section 2.4.7.

Let D represent the following collection of pairs (i, j):

$$D = \{(0, 1), (1, 1), (1, 0)\} \tag{158}$$

A random field will be called *wide-sense Markov* if the coefficients $c_{i,j}$ in (155) are such that $\hat{\mathbf{f}}$ is of the form

$$\hat{\mathbf{f}}(m, n) = \sum_{(i,j) \in D} c_{i,j} \mathbf{f}(m-i, n-j) \tag{159}$$

That is, the least squares estimate of $\mathbf{f}(m, n)$ in terms of $X_{m,n}$ is the same as that in terms of only the three immediate neighbors on the left and above. (Note the directions of increasing m and n in Fig. 9.)

Substituting (159) in (157) we obtain the following conditions that a wide-sense Markov random field must satisfy:

$$E\left\{\left[\mathbf{f}(m, n) - \sum_{(i,j) \in D} c_{i,j} \mathbf{f}(m-i, n-j)\right] \mathbf{f}(p, q)\right\} = 0 \tag{160}$$

for all $(p, q) \in X_{m,n}$. For a wide-sense Markov field, the coefficients $c_{i,j}$ must be such that (160) is satisfied for all $(p, q) \in X_{m,n}$. In particular, (160) must be satisfied for the following values of (p, q): $(m-1, n)$, $(m-1, n-1)$, and $(m, n-1)$. Substituting these values of (p, q) in (160), we obtain the following equations, which can be solved for $c_{1,0}$, $c_{1,1}$, and $c_{0,1}$:

$$c_{1,0} R_{ff}(0, 0) + c_{1,1} R_{ff}(0, 1) + c_{0,1} R_{ff}(-1, 1) = R_{ff}(-1, 0)$$

$$c_{1,0} R_{ff}(0, 1) + c_{1,1} R_{ff}(0, 0) + c_{0,1} R_{ff}(-1, 0) = R_{ff}(-1, 1) \tag{161}$$

$$c_{1,0} R_{ff}(1, -1) + c_{1,1} R_{ff}(1, 0) + c_{0,1} R_{ff}(0, 0) = R_{ff}(0, -1)$$

where

$$R_{ff}(\alpha, \beta) = E\{\mathbf{f}(m, n) \mathbf{f}(m+\alpha, n+\beta)\} \tag{162}$$

It is clear that a wide-sense Markov random field is described by the following difference equation:

$$\mathbf{f}(m, n) - \sum_{(i,j) \in D} c_{i,j} \mathbf{f}(m-i, n-j) = \xi(m, n)$$

where $\xi(m, n)$ is the difference $\mathbf{f}(m, n) - \hat{\mathbf{f}}(m, n)$ at each point. The difference equation is driven by white noise. By this we mean that $\xi(m, n)$ is an array of uncorrelated random variables. The following theorem addresses itself to this point.

Theorem. A discrete random field $\mathbf{f}(m,n)$ is wide-sense Markov if and only if it satisfies the following difference equation for all points (m,n) with $m > 1$ and $n > 1$:

$$\mathbf{f}(m,n) - \sum_{(i,j)\in D} c_{i,j}\mathbf{f}(m-i,\,n-j) = \xi(m,n) \tag{163}$$

and, for the points on the topmost row and the leftmost columns,

$$\mathbf{f}(1,1) = \xi(1,1) \tag{164a}$$

$$\mathbf{f}(m,1) - \mathscr{A}\mathbf{f}(m-1,1) = \xi(m,1), \qquad m > 1 \tag{164b}$$

$$\mathbf{f}(1,n) - \mathscr{B}\mathbf{f}(1,n-1) = \xi(1,n), \qquad n > 1 \tag{164c}$$

where the $c_{i,j}$ are the solutions of (161), and

$$\mathscr{A} = R_{ff}(1,0)/R_{ff}(0,0), \qquad \mathscr{B} = R_{ff}(0,1)/R_{ff}(0,0) \tag{165}$$

and where $\xi(m,n)$ is a discrete random field of orthogonal random variables, that is,

$$E\{\xi(m,n)\xi(p,q)\} = 0, \qquad m \neq p \quad \text{or} \quad n \neq q \tag{166}$$

For a zero-mean random field the random variables $\xi(m,n)$ are uncorrelated.

Proof: First a few words about Eqs. (164). The difference equation (164b) for points on the topmost row is consistent with (163). In keeping with our definition of a wide-sense Markov random field, we insist that the least squares estimate $\hat{\mathbf{f}}(m,1)$ of $\mathbf{f}(m,1)$ in terms of all the points in $X_{m,1}$ be the same as that in terms of only $\mathbf{f}(m-1,1)$, that is,

$$\hat{\mathbf{f}}(m,1) = \mathscr{A}\mathbf{f}(m-1,1) \tag{167}$$

where, by arguments similar to those leading to (160), the coefficient $\mathscr{A}$ must be such that

$$E\{[\mathbf{f}(m,1) - \mathscr{A}\mathbf{f}(m-1,1)]\mathbf{f}(p,1)\} = 0 \qquad \text{for all } (p,1) \in X_{m,1} \tag{168}$$

With $p = m-1$, this relationship yields

$$\mathscr{A} = R_{ff}(-1,0)/R_{ff}(0,0) = R_{ff}(1,0)/R_{ff}(0,0)$$

Clearly, then,

$$\mathbf{f}(m,1) = \mathscr{A}\mathbf{f}(m-1,1) + \xi(m,1)$$

where $\xi(m,1)$ is the error $\mathbf{f}(m,1) - \hat{\mathbf{f}}(m,1)$.

It can, similarly, be shown that the points on the leftmost column should satisfy the following orthogonality condition:

$$E\{[\mathbf{f}(1,n) - \mathscr{B}\mathbf{f}(1,n-1)]\mathbf{f}(1,q)\} = 0 \qquad \text{for all } (1,q) \in X_{1,q} \tag{169}$$

As for the case of topmost row points, (169) implies that points on the leftmost column should obey (164c).

Coming to the proof of the theorem, let us assume that the field is wide-sense Markov; we then want to show that (166) is true. Note that from (160) [(168) and (169) for points on the top and left boundary] each $\xi(m, n)$ is orthogonal to $\mathbf{f}(p, q)$ for all $(p, q) \in X_{m, n}$. Now $\xi(k, l)$ for any $(k, l) \in X_{m, n}$ is a linear combination of $\mathbf{f}(p, q)$'s in $X_{m, n}$. Therefore, $\xi(m, n)$ must be orthogonal to $\xi(k, l)$ for all $(k, l) \in X_{m, n}$. Since this must be true for every (m, n) in the picture, it follows that

$$E\{\xi(p, q)\xi(m, n)\} = 0, \qquad p \neq m \quad \text{or} \quad q \neq n$$

which is (166).

Conversely, if (166) is true for $\xi(m, n)$ as defined by (163) and (164), then we must show that the field $\mathbf{f}(m, n)$ is wide-sense Markov. We proceed as follows. From (164b) and (164a), $\mathbf{f}(2, 1) = \mathscr{A}\xi(1, 1) + \xi(2, 1)$. Similarly, $\mathbf{f}(1, 2) = \mathscr{B}\xi(1, 1) + \xi(1, 2)$. Substituting these two expressions in (163), we obtain

$$\mathbf{f}(2, 2) = (c_{1,1} + \mathscr{B}c_{1,0} + \mathscr{A}c_{0,1})\xi(1, 1) + c_{1,0}\xi(1, 2) + c_{0,1}\xi(2, 1) + \xi(2, 2)$$

Similarly, any $\mathbf{f}(m, n)$ can be expressed in terms of $\xi(p, q)$'s with $(p, q) \in Y_{m, n}$ defined in Fig. 9b. By (166) this implies that $\mathbf{f}(m, n)$ is orthogonal to any $\xi(k, l)$ for which $k > m$ or $l > n$. From this it follows that the estimation error $\mathbf{f}(k, l) - \hat{\mathbf{f}}(k, l) \; [= \xi(k, l)]$ is orthogonal to all $\mathbf{f}(p, q)$ with $(p, q) \in X_{k, l}$; this, with $\hat{\mathbf{f}}(k, l)$ defined by (159), is exactly (160). Therefore, the random field $\mathbf{f}(m, n)$ is wide-sense Markov.

Note that for a zero-mean random field $\mathbf{f}(m, n)$, (163) and (164) imply that the random variables $\xi(m, n)$ also have zero mean. In this case, therefore, (166) implies that the random variables $\xi(m, n)$ are uncorrelated. ∎

A wide-sense Markov random field obeys the difference equation (163). Now suppose we are given a homogeneous random field, not necessarily wide-sense Markov, whose autocorrelation function is known. We would like to represent this random field by (163) to a good approximation. This can be done by using the known autocorrelation function for $R_{ff}(\alpha, \beta)$ in Eqs. (161) to solve for the $c_{i, j}$'s. Note that if the given random field is not wide-sense Markov, the random variables $\xi(m, n)$ may now not be completely uncorrelated. It is obvious that the degree of correlation among the $\xi(m, n)$ should serve as a measure of the goodness of the representation of the given random field by (163).

Under certain conditions this procedure of modeling a non-wide-sense Markov field by (163) may not be mathematically valid. The modeling is valid only if the autocorrelation function of $\xi(m, n)$ is a positive-definite function; otherwise one has to place further restrictions on the solutions $c_{i, j}$ of (161).

This has been discussed in detail by Woods [105]. In this section we will not be concerned with the validity of the modeling. We will assume that the $c_{i,j}$'s calculated from (161) result in a valid solution and, if not, that these $c_{i,j}$'s are good approximations to those necessary for a valid solution.

Let us assume that the autocorrelation function of a given random field can be approximated by Eq. (47) of Chapter 4. We shall further assume that the random field is normalized in that the mean value of the random field has been subtracted from every picture and each picture has been divided by $\sqrt{R_{ff}(0,0)}$. The autocorrelation function can then be written as

$$R_{ff}(\alpha, \beta) = \exp(-c_1 |\alpha| - c_2 |\beta|) \tag{170}$$

which can also be expressed as

$$R_{ff}(\alpha, \beta) = \rho_{\rm h}^{|\alpha|} \rho_{\rm v}^{|\beta|} \tag{171}$$

where $\rho_{\rm h} = e^{-c_1}$ and $\rho_{\rm v} = e^{-c_2}$ are measures of the horizontal and vertical correlation, respectively. Substituting this $R_{ff}(\alpha, \beta)$ in (161) we obtain the following solution:

$$c_{1,0} = \rho_{\rm h}, \qquad c_{0,1} = \rho_{\rm v}, \qquad c_{1,1} = -\rho_{\rm h}\rho_{\rm v} \tag{172}$$

It can easily be verified that with the $c_{i,j}$'s as given and for the autocorrelation function of (170), the conditions in (160) are exactly satisfied. Therefore, (166) is also exactly satisfied.

7.6.2 Vector–Matrix Formulation of the Wide-Sense Markov Representation

In this section we will present a more general approach, originally due to Stuller and Kurz [99], to finding a difference equation representation for an image. While with the preceding approach one could represent each pixel in terms of the three immediate neighbors to the left and above, plus a random component, the method presented here permits one to express this representation in terms of an arbitrary number of pixels. If the model of the preceding section was found unsuitable for an image (as checked by the $\xi(m\,n)$'s not being white and/or their autocorrelation matrix not being positive definite), one could try the more general model presented here.

Assume that a discrete image, $f(m, n)$, $m, n = 1, 2, \ldots, N$, is raster scanned along an arbitrary path as shown in Fig. 10a. (This includes the common case shown in Fig. 10b, where the scanning is from left to right and top to bottom.) Such a scan will generate a time ordered one-dimensional sequence of pixels that may be represented by a single index. This sequence will be denoted by $\mathbf{f}_1, \mathbf{f}_2, \ldots, \mathbf{f}_{N^2}$, or more briefly, by the N^2-element vector $\dot{\mathbf{f}}$. We

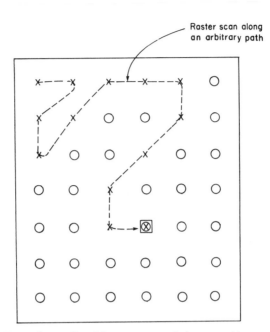

Fig. 10a   A discrete image $f(m, n)$ is raster scanned along an arbitrary path shown by the dashed line.

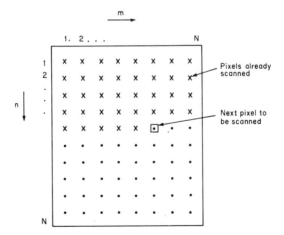

Fig. 10b   The conventional raster scan is shown here, which consists of scanning from left to right and top to bottom.

now seek a representation in which $\mathbf{f}_m$ is expressed as a linear combination of an arbitrary number of pixels from its "past," i.e., from $\mathbf{f}_{m-1}, \mathbf{f}_{m-2}, \ldots, \mathbf{f}_1$, plus a random component consisting of uncorrelated random variables. In vector–matrix form, such a representation may be expressed as

$$\vec{\mathbf{f}} = [L]\vec{\mathbf{f}} + \vec{\xi} \tag{173}$$

where $[L]$ is constrained to be a lower triangular matrix with its principal diagonal equal to zero. We want each element of the vector $([L]\vec{\mathbf{f}})$ to be the linear least squares estimate of the corresponding element of $\vec{\mathbf{f}}$. The random variable ξ_m would then constitute the estimation error for the mth element of $\vec{\mathbf{f}}$. We also constrain the ξ_m's to be white, i.e.,

$$[R_{\xi\xi}] = E\{\vec{\xi}\vec{\xi}^t\} = \sigma_\xi^2[I] \tag{174}$$

where $[R_{\xi\xi}]$ is the autocorrelation matrix; σ_ξ^2 the variance of ξ_m, assumed to be the same for all m; and $[I]$ the identity matrix. The orthogonality principle (see Section 2.4.7) says that the estimation error ξ_m must be orthogonal to all the random variables used in the formation of the estimate. Since the least squares estimate for $\mathbf{f}_m$ is expressed in terms of the random variables $\mathbf{f}_{m-1}, \mathbf{f}_{m-2}, \ldots, \mathbf{f}_1$, the random variable ξ_m must be orthogonal to all of them. This implies that

$$[R_{f\xi}] = E\{\vec{\mathbf{f}}\vec{\xi}^t\} \tag{175}$$

must be a lower triangular matrix. Note that from (173), each $\mathbf{f}_m$ may be expressed as

$$\mathbf{f}_m = \xi_m + \text{linear function of } (\mathbf{f}_{m-1}, \mathbf{f}_{m-2}, \ldots, \mathbf{f}_1) \tag{176}$$

Since each ξ_m is orthogonal to $\mathbf{f}_m, \mathbf{f}_{m-1}, \ldots, \mathbf{f}_1$, it follows that

$$E\{\mathbf{f}_m \xi_m\} = E\{\xi_m^2\} = \sigma_\xi^2 \tag{177}$$

Hence all the elements on the principal diagonal of $[R_{f\xi}]$ are equal to σ_ξ^2. Using (173), we can write

$$[R_{f\xi}] = [B]^{-1}[R_{\xi\xi}] \tag{178}$$

where

$$[B] = [I] - [L] \tag{179}$$

Equation (178) implies that $[B]^{-1}$, if it exists, must have its principal diagonal elements equal to unity. This follows from two facts: (i) the inverse of a lower triangular matrix is also lower triangular; and (ii) the product of two lower triangular matrices is also lower triangular, and the diagonal elements of this product are given by the product of the corresponding diagonal elements of the original two matrices. Since the diagonal elements of $[R_{f\xi}]$ are equal to σ_ξ^2 by (177), and since the diagonal elements of $[R_{\xi\xi}]$ are equal to σ_ξ^2 by definition, our conclusion about the diagonal elements of $[B]^{-1}$ follows.

If the diagonal elements of $[B]^{-1}$ are all unity, so are the diagonal elements of $[B]$. This follows from the fact that the inverse of a lower triangular matrix is also lower triangular; the diagonal elements of the inverse matrix being inverses of the diagonal elements of the original matrix.

So far we have shown that if (173) and (174) are given, and if the mth element of $([L]\vec{f})$ is the least squares estimate of f_m, then $[L]$, if it exists, will have its diagonal elements equal to zero. (This follows from our having shown that the diagonal elements of $[B]$ are equal to unity.) We must now prove that a lower diagonal matrix $[L]$ does indeed exist. To do so, we use (173) and (174) to write

$$[R_{\xi\xi}] = E\{([I] - [L])\vec{f}\vec{f}^{t}([I] - [L])^{t}\} = [B][R_{ff}][B]^{t} \qquad (180)$$

The matrix $[B]$ must therefore satisfy

$$[B][R_{ff}][B]^{t} = \sigma_\xi^2[I] \qquad (181)$$

where we have used (174). It is well known in matrix algebra [71] that if $[R_{ff}]$ is positive definite, then a unique invertible lower triangular $[B]$ does indeed exist that would satisfy (181). The positive definiteness of $[R_{ff}]$, therefore, guarantees the existence of a lower triangular $[L]$. Different computational strategies exist for solving (181) for $[B]$, given an $[R_{ff}]$ [31, 104].

The solution of (181) for a lower triangular $[B]$, therefore, leads to a general wide-sense Markov representation of (173). We will now derive the form of the $[L]$ matrix for the case when the raster scan is from left to right and top to bottom, as shown in Fig. 10b, and when the autocorrelation matrix, $[R_{ff}]$, is separable.

As was also discussed in Section 5.2.1, a random field is considered to have a separable autocorrelation provided

$$R_{ff}(m, n, p, q) = E\{f(m, n)f(p, q)\} = R_{col}(m, p)R_{row}(n, q) \qquad (182)$$

where $[R_{row}]$ and $[R_{col}]$ are each $N \times N$ matrices for an $N \times N$ image. These two matrices have all the properties of covariance matrices, and may be considered to be autocorrelations of one-dimensional stationary Markov sequences, if the original image is also Markov and stationary (homogeneous). We will now assume that $[R_{row}]$ and $[R_{col}]$ are both positive definite and may be considered to be the autocorrelations of one-dimensional wide-sense Markov-k_r and Markov-k_c sequences,[§] respectively.

As was the case in (181), since $[R_{\text{row}}]$ and $[R_{\text{col}}]$ are positive definite, unique invertible lower triangular $[G_r]$ and $[G_c]$ exist such that

$$[G_r][R_{\text{row}}][G_r]^t = \alpha[I]$$

and

$$[G_c][R_{\text{col}}][G_c]^t = \beta[I] \tag{183}$$

where the constants α and β are chosen such that the principal diagonals of both $[G_r]$ and $[G_c]$ are unity.

If $\mathbf{\bar{f}}$ is the N^2-element vector generated by column scanning the image matrix $[\mathbf{f}]$, and $[R_{ff}]$ its autocorrelation matrix, as defined in (50), then it may be shown by substitution that (see Section 2.5 also)

$$[R_{ff}] = [R_{\text{col}}] \otimes [R_{\text{row}}] \tag{184}$$

where $\otimes$ denotes the left direct product.

From (181), we get

$$\sigma_\xi^2 [B]^{-1}([B]^t)^{-1} = [R_{ff}] \tag{185}$$

which, by using the identity $([P][Q])^{-1} = [Q]^{-1}[P]^{-1}$, can be written as

$$(1/\sigma_\xi^2)[B]^t[B] = [R_{ff}]^{-1} \tag{186}$$

Substituting (184) in (186), and using the identity $([P] \otimes [Q])^{-1} = [P]^{-1} \otimes [Q]^{-1}$, we have

$$\frac{1}{\sigma_\xi^2}[B]^t[B] = [R_{\text{col}}]^{-1} \otimes [R_{\text{row}}]^{-1} \tag{187}$$

From (183), we have the following expressions for $[R_{\text{row}}]$ and $[R_{\text{col}}]$:

$$[R_{\text{row}}]^{-1} = \frac{1}{\alpha}[G_r]^t[G_r] \quad \text{and} \quad [R_{\text{col}}]^{-1} = \frac{1}{\beta}[G_c]^t[G_c] \tag{188}$$

Substituting these in (187) and using the identities $([P] \otimes [Q])([R] \otimes [S]) = ([P][R]) \otimes ([Q][S])$ and $[P]^t \otimes [Q]^t = ([P] \otimes [Q])^t$, we get

$$[B] = [G_c] \otimes [G_r] \tag{189}$$

[§] A sequence $\mathbf{x}_1, \mathbf{x}_2, \ldots, \mathbf{x}_N$ is wide-sense Markov-k provided the least squares estimate of $\mathbf{x}_n$ in terms of *all* the previous neighbors is equal to $c_1\mathbf{x}_{n-1} + c_2\mathbf{x}_{n-2} + \cdots + c_k\mathbf{x}_{n-k}$ for some choice of $c_1, c_2, \ldots, c_k$. Therefore, such a sequence may be represented by

$$\mathbf{\bar{x}} = [P]\mathbf{\bar{x}} + \vec{\xi}$$

where $[P]$ is a lower triangular matrix with zero principal diagonal and with the further property that $P(m,n) = P(m - n)$ where $P(m - n) = 0$ for $(m - n) > k$. See also [75, p. 422].

which is true provided σ_ξ^2 is chosen such that

$$\frac{\sigma_\xi^2}{\alpha\beta} = 1 \tag{190}$$

Therefore, the matrix $[L]$, which is related to $[B]$ by (179), is given by

$$[L] = [I] - [G_c] \otimes [G_r] \tag{191}$$

Substituting this expression in (173), and using the vector–matrix conversion formulas in Section 2.5, we can write

$$[\mathbf{f}] = [\mathbf{f}] - [G_c][\mathbf{f}][G_r]^t + [\xi] \tag{192}$$

In the expanded notation, this may be written as

$$\mathbf{f}(m, n) = -\sum_{\substack{p=0 \\ (p,q) \neq (m,n)}}^{N-1} \sum_{q=0}^{N-1} G_c(m, p)\mathbf{f}(p, q)G_r(n, q) + \xi(m, n) \tag{193}$$

where we have used the fact that both $G_c(m, m)$ and $G_r(n, n)$ are equal to unity.

Recognizing that in (193) G_c represents the one-dimensional Markov-k_c property along the columns, and G_r represents a similar property along the rows, by the definition presented in the footnote on page 321, both $[G_c]$ and $[G_r]$ are lower triangular matrices with the properties that $G_c(m, n) = G_c(m - n)$ for $(m - n) < k_c$ when $m > k_c$ and $n > k_c$; and $G_r(m, n) = G_r(m - n)$ for $(m - n) < k_r$ when $m > k_r$ and $n > k_r$. Also, $G_c(m, n) = 0$ for $(m - n) > k_c$, similarly, $G_r(m - n) = 0$ for $(m - n) > k_r$. Using the singly indexed sequence x_{m-n} and y_{m-n} to denote $G_r(m - n)$ and $G_c(m - n)$, respectively, Eq. (193) can be rewritten as

$$\mathbf{f}(m, n) = -\sum_{\substack{p=0 \\ (p,q) \neq (0,0)}}^{k_r} \sum_{q=0}^{k_c} x_p y_p \mathbf{f}(m - p, n - q) + \xi(m, n) \tag{194}$$

for $m > k_r$ and $n > k_c$. This shows that the dependence of $\mathbf{f}(m, n)$ on the previously scanned pixels extends only k_r raster lines upward and k_c columns leftward from (m, n).

7.6.3 An Algorithm for Restoration in the Presence of Additive Noise

We will now present a recursive algorithm for the restoration of images that are degraded by additive noise only. This algorithm was presented in [74] and its generalization to convolutional degradations is given in [73].

We assume that the two-dimensional autocorrelation of the $M \times N$ image random field, $\mathbf{f}(m, n)$, is equal to (or can be approximated by) (170).

We will also assume initially that the mean of this random field is zero, although we will later indicate what modifications must be made for the nonzero case. As was shown in Section 7.6.1, such a random field is modeled by

$$\mathbf{f}(i, j) = \rho_v \mathbf{f}(i - 1, j) + \rho_h \mathbf{f}(i, j - 1) - \rho_v \rho_h \mathbf{f}(i - 1, j - 1) + \xi(i, j) \quad (195)$$

or, equivalently by

$$\mathbf{f}(i, j) - \rho_h \mathbf{f}(i, j - 1) = \rho_v [\mathbf{f}(i - 1, j) - \rho_h \mathbf{f}(i - 1, j - 1)] + \xi(i, j) \quad (196)$$

where ρ_v and ρ_h are the vertical and the horizontal correlation coefficients of the random field, respectively, and $\xi(i, j)$ is an array of zero-mean uncorrelated random variables with variance $\sigma_\varepsilon^2 = (1 - \rho_v^2)(1 - \rho_h^2)$. Let $\vec{\mathbf{S}}(i)$ be a column vector $[\mathbf{f}(i, 1), \mathbf{f}(i, 2), \ldots, \mathbf{f}(i, N)]^t$ and $\vec{\mathbf{\Omega}}(i)$ be a column vector $[\xi(i, 1), \xi(i, 2), \ldots, \xi(i, N)]^t$, where t denotes matrix transpose. Equation (196) can now be written as

$$
\begin{array}{cc}
j\text{th col.} & N\text{th col.} \\
\downarrow & \downarrow
\end{array}
$$

$$[0 \quad 0 \quad \cdots \quad -\rho_h \quad 1 \quad 0 \quad \cdots \quad 0]\vec{\mathbf{S}}(i)$$

$$
\begin{array}{cc}
j\text{th col.} & N\text{th col.} \\
\downarrow & \downarrow
\end{array}
$$

$$= \rho \, [0 \quad \cdots \quad 0 - \rho_h \quad 1 \quad 0 \quad \cdots \quad 0]\vec{\mathbf{S}}(i - 1)$$

$$+ \, [0 \quad \cdots \quad 0 \quad 0 \quad \cdots \quad 1 \quad 0 \quad \cdots \quad 0]\vec{\mathbf{\Omega}}(i)$$

$$
\begin{array}{cc}
\uparrow & \uparrow \\
j\text{th col.} & N\text{th col.} \quad (197)
\end{array}
$$

A vector equation like (197) can be written for each value of $j = 2, 3, \ldots, N$. However, some caution needs to be exercised when $j = 1$. At the left-hand border of the image, i.e., when $j = 1$, Eq. (196) reduces to the following:

$$\mathbf{f}(i, 1) = \rho_v \mathbf{f}(i - 1, 1) + \xi(i, 1), \qquad 1 \leqslant i \leqslant M \quad (198)$$

Equation (198) can be written as

$$
\begin{array}{ccc}
N\text{th col.} & N\text{th col.} & N\text{th col.} \\
\downarrow & \downarrow & \downarrow
\end{array}
$$

$$[1 \quad 0 \quad \cdots \quad 0]\vec{\mathbf{S}}(i) = \rho_v[1 \quad 0 \quad \cdots \quad 0]\vec{\mathbf{S}}(i - 1) + [1 \quad 0 \quad \cdots \quad 0]\vec{\mathbf{\Omega}}(i)$$

$$(199)$$

Equations (199) for $j = 1$ and $N - 1$ equations like (197), one for each value of j between 2 and N, give us N equations that must be satisfied by the N elements of the ith row of the image. All these N equations can be combined into the following vector–matrix form:

$$[A]\vec{S}(i) = \rho_v[A]\vec{S}(i - 1) + [I]\vec{\Omega}(i) \tag{200}$$

where $[A]$ is the $N \times N$ matrix

$$A = \begin{bmatrix} 1 & 0 & & & \cdots & 0 \\ -\rho_h & 1 & 0 & & \cdots & 0 \\ 0 & -\rho_h & 1 & 0 & \cdots & 0 \\ 0 & 0 & -\rho_h & 1 & 0 & \cdots & 0 \\ \vdots & & & & & \vdots \\ 0 & & \cdots & & 0 & -\rho_h & 1 \end{bmatrix} \tag{201}$$

and $[I]$ is the $N \times N$ identity matrix. The first row of $[A]$ is the row vector on the left-hand side of (199). The jth row of $[A]$, for $j = 1, 2, 3, .. , N$, is the row vector obtained by substituting various values of j in the row vector in the left-hand side of (196). The matrix $[A]$ being a lower triangular Toeplitz matrix has linearly independent rows and hence its inverse always exists. Premultiplying by $[A]^{-1}$ on both sides of (196), we get

$$\vec{S}(i) = \rho_v\vec{S}(i - 1) + [A]^{-1}\vec{\Omega}(i) \tag{202}$$

for $i = 1, 2, \ldots, N$. This system of first-order linear N-dimensional vector difference equations coupled with suitable initial conditions describes the image in the domain $\{(i, j) | 1 \leqslant i \leqslant M, 1 \leqslant j \leqslant N\}$. The covariance matrix of the random vectors $\mathbf{S}$ and $\mathbf{\Omega}$ is

$$[C_\xi(k)] = E\{\vec{\Omega}(i)\vec{\Omega}^t(i + k)\} = \sigma_\omega^2[I]\,\Delta(k) \tag{203}$$

where $\Delta(k)$ is the Kronecker delta, i.e., $\Delta(k) = 0$ when $k \neq 0$ and $\Delta(0) = 1$, and

$$[C_s(k)] = E\{\vec{S}(i)\vec{S}^t(i + k)\} = \rho_v^{|k|}[\rho_h^{|p - q|}]_{N \times N} \tag{204}$$

where $[\rho_h^{|p - q|}]_{N \times N}$ is an $N \times N$ symmetric Toeplitz matrix whose (p, q)th element is $\rho_h^{|p - q|}$.

We have modeled the image by a sequence of N-dimensional vectors, $\vec{S}(i)$, that are obtained by passing through a linear system a sequence of zero-mean orthogonal N-dimensional random vectors $\vec{\Omega}(i)$, whose covariance matrix is given by (203). Since $\vec{S}(1) = [A]^{-1}\vec{\Omega}(1)$, one can easily obtain from (202) the following relationship between the output $\vec{S}(i)$ and the input $\vec{\Omega}(i)$ of the linear system:

$$\vec{S}(i) = \sum_{k=1}^{i} \rho_v^{(i-k)}[A]^{-1}\vec{\Omega}(k) \tag{205a}$$

$$= [A]^{-1} \sum_{k=1}^{i} \rho_v^{(i-k)}\vec{\Omega}(k) \tag{205b}$$

Therefore, from (205a), the elements of an image vector $\vec{S}(i)$ are obtained by the discrete convolution of a one-dimensional impulse response $\rho_v^{\ i}$ with the elements of the vector given by the premultiplication of the gain matrix $[A]^{-1}$ with the input vector. In terms of any other known initial conditions $\vec{S}(j), j < 1$, the system output is given by

$$\vec{S}(i) = \rho_v^{(i-j)}\vec{S}(j) + [A]^{-1} \sum_{k=j+1}^{i} \rho_v^{(i-k)}\vec{\Omega}(k) \tag{206}$$

Figure 11 shows the linear system with input and output vectors. In Fig. 11, if the output sequence is obtained from the output sides of the delay units rather than from their input sides, the image vector is given by

$$\vec{S}(i + 1) = \rho_v\vec{S}(i) + [A]^{-1}\vec{\Omega}(i) \tag{207}$$

for $i = 0, 1, \ldots, m - 1$. Equations (202) and (207) are two alternative first-order linear N-dimensional vector difference equations describing the same random field.

As a function of the row index i, the proposed vector model [(202) or (207)] is causal and hence suitable for recursive linear estimation by Kalman filtering. We will now derive this optimum recursive image estimator.

Let the observed image be given by

$$y(i, j) = f(i, j) + v(i, j) \tag{208}$$

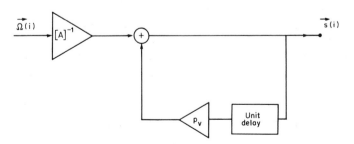

Fig. 11 The linear system that generates the image random field. The input to the system consists of a sequence of white noise vectors.

where $v(i, j)$ is zero-mean white noise of variance σ_v^2. If we arrange all the observations and noise in a row into corresponding vectors, i.e., $\vec{Y}(i) = [y(i, 1), y(i, 2), \ldots, y(i, N)]^t$ and $\vec{e}(i) = [v(i, 1), v(i, 2), \ldots, v(i, N)]^t$, then the sequence of observed vectors can be expressed as

$$\vec{Y}(i) = \vec{S}(i) + \vec{e}(i) \tag{209}$$

for $i = 1, 2, \ldots, M$. $\vec{e}(i)$ is a sequence of zero-mean random vectors with covariance

$$C_v(k) = E\{\vec{e}(i)\vec{e}^t(i + k)\} = \sigma_v^2[I]\,\Delta(k) \tag{210}$$

where Δ is the Kronecker delta defined before.

Given the first-order dynamical model of (207) and (209), a Kalman filter for obtaining the optimum estimates $\vec{S}(k)$ in terms of $\vec{Y}(1), \vec{Y}(2), \ldots, \vec{Y}(k)$ can be easily derived. The resulting derivation involves a considerable amount of algebra that may be found in many texts on estimation theory.(See, e.g., Chapter 4 of [69]. The details of the derivations are also given in [73].) The optimum estimator is described by the following equations:

$$\hat{\vec{S}}(i + 1) = \rho_v\hat{\vec{S}}(i) + [H(i + 1)][\vec{Y}(i + 1) - \rho_v\hat{\vec{S}}(i)] \tag{211a}$$

$$[H(i + 1)] = [Q(i)][[Q(i)] + [C_e]]^{-1} \tag{211b}$$

$$[Q(i + 1)] = \rho_v^2([I] - [H(i + 1)])[Q(i)] + [A]^{-1}[C_\xi][A]^{-1t} \tag{211c}$$

In terms of the covariance matrix $[P(i)]$ of the estimation error vector

$$\vec{\varepsilon}(i) = \vec{S}(i) - \hat{\vec{S}}(i) \tag{212}$$

the matrix $[Q(i)]$ in (211b) and (211c) is

$$[Q(i)] = \rho_v^2[P(i)] + [A]^{-1}[C_\xi][A]^{-1t} \tag{213}$$

The estimator vector is

$$\hat{\vec{S}}(i) = [\hat{f}(i, 1), \hat{f}(i, 2), \ldots, \hat{f}(i, N)]^t \tag{214}$$

where $\hat{f}(i, j)$ is the estimate of the image gray level $f(i, j)$. The term $\rho_v\hat{\vec{S}}(i)$ is the "*a priori* estimate" of $\vec{S}(i + 1)$ before $\vec{Y}(i + 1)$ has been observed and is equal to the one-step predictor of $\vec{S}(i + 1)$. The classical Kalman estimator assumes the process to be zero mean. Since images are, in reality, nonzero mean, (211) has to be modified to be more suitable to image processing (of course, an alternative is to subtract the mean from the observations before filtering and add it back after filtering). To take care of the nonzero mean of images the term $\rho_v\hat{\vec{S}}(i)$ in (211a) should be replaced [2, 73] by

$$\rho_v\hat{\vec{S}}(i) + [A]^{-1}\vec{M} \tag{215}$$

where $\vec{M}$ is the mean of the vector $\vec{\Omega}(i)$.

Fig. 12   The original image "Face."

For a 256×256 picture (i.e., $M = N = 256$), (211) calls for solving all the 256 pixels of a row of the image simultaneously. All the matrices in (211) are, then, 256×256 and all the column vectors are 256×1. Hence computing the coefficient matrix $[H(i)]$ involves multiplication and inversion of 256×256-size matrices, which requires a large amount of computer memory and a long processing time. This would make it virtually impossible to restore an image of this size even in a fairly large computer. One way to get around this difficulty is by segmenting the image into several images each of vertical length M rows but horizontal length N_1 columns, where N_1 is a number such that multiplication and inversion of matrices of size $N_1 \times N_1$ is easily feasible in the available computer. The gain matrices, each of size $N_1 \times N_1$, are computed only for one segment and applied to all the $N_s \, (= N/N_1)$ segments of the image to be filtered.

In experimentally testing the performance of the proposed filter, a 256 $\times$ 256 image of a human face, shown in Fig. 12, was chosen as the original image (uncorrupted by noise). It was corrupted by the addition of a sequence of computer-generated zero-mean uncorrelated Gaussian random variables so as to get a signal-to-noise ratio (SNR)[§] of 10 dB. The noise-degraded image is shown in Fig. 13. The image was divided into 16 segments ($N_s = 16$), each segment being 256 rows by 16 columns in size. Let H_s denote the 16×16 gain matrix for this case. In designing the filter for this segmented image, it was observed that the error covariance matrix $P(i)$ and consequently the gain matrix $H_s(i)$ attained a steady-state value after 75 iterations of (211b) and (211c), beginning the iterations with $i = 1$. To reduce the

---

[§] SNR is defined here as the ratio of the variance of the original image $s(i, j)$ to the variance of the noise $v(i, j)$.

Fig. 13   The image corrupted by additive noise (10-dB SNR).

computer memory requirement, this steady-state value of $[H_s(i)]$ was used as the gain matrix for all $i, i = 1, 2, \ldots, 256$. Thus the filter acquired the form

$$\hat{\vec{S}}(i + 1) = \rho_v \hat{\vec{S}} + [H_s][\vec{Y}(i + 1) - \rho_v \hat{\vec{S}}(i + 1)] \tag{216}$$

where $[H_s]$ is the steady-state gain matrix. The segmented noisy image of Fig. 13 was filtered using (216). The output of the filter is shown in Fig. 14. The artifacts created by segmentation can be noticed in the filtered image. To avoid these artifacts, the filter given by (211) for the whole image was

Fig. 14   The image of Fig. 13 filtered in segments.

modified by approximating the full 256×256 gain matrix $[H]$ by a quasi-Toeplitz matrix possessing a very small number of unique elements. We will now describe this approximation.

Since segmentation leads to artifacts, it is clearly desirable to filter the entire 256×256 image without breaking it up into strips. However, for this one needs to calculate the full 256×256 gain matrix, which is a very difficult and computationally expensive task. We will now point to some empirically observed properties of 16×16 gain matrices. Since these properties are expected to be even more valid for larger gain matrices, the full 256×256 gain matrix will then be approximately constructed using these properties. In order to state these properties, we will first go back to the case of filtering 256×256 images by first segmenting them. Consider the first segment of such an image being estimated by (216). There the vector $\bar{S}(i + 1)$ is a 16×1 column vector $[\mathbf{f}(i + 1, 1), \mathbf{f}(i + 1, 2), \ldots, \mathbf{f}(i + 1, 16)]^t$. Equation (216) can also be written as

$$\hat{\mathbf{f}}(i + 1, j) = \rho_v \hat{\mathbf{f}}(i, j) + \sum_{k=1}^{16} H_s(j, k)[\mathbf{y}(i + 1, k) - \rho_v \hat{\mathbf{f}}(i, k)] \quad (217)$$

where $H_s(j, k)$ are elements of the 16×16 gain matrix H_s.

Examination of the steady-state matrices H_s for different images has revealed the following.

(i)   Elements in the middle rows (around the 8th) approximately obey the following relationship:

$$H_s(j, k) \simeq h(j - k) \quad (218)$$

where h is a function of a single variable.

(ii)   For $|j - k| > 4$, the value of $h(j - k)$ drops off rapidly.

Hence, for j in the neighborhood of 8, (217) may be written as

$$\hat{\mathbf{f}}(i + 1, j) \simeq \rho_v \mathbf{f}(i, j) + \sum_{k=j-4}^{j+4} h(j - k)[\mathbf{y}(i + 1, k) - \rho_v \hat{\mathbf{f}}(i, k)] \quad (219)$$

We expect the previous two observations made on 16×16 gain matrices to be even more valid for the 256×256 versions. In other words, if one were to actually derive the 256×256 gain matrix $[H]$, a large inner portion of it (away from the boundary effects) is expected to conform to the two observations just made. These two observations can, therefore, be used to approximately construct the full 256×256 gain matrix as follows.

(1)   For the top 8 and bottom 8 rows of $[H]$

$$\begin{aligned} H(j, k) &= H_s(j, k), & j &= 1, 2, \ldots, 8 \\ H(257 - j, 257 - k) &= H_s(17 - j, 17 - k), & k &= 1, 2, \ldots, 16 \end{aligned} \quad (220)$$

where $H(j, k)$ are elements of the matrix H. For the rest of the elements in the top 8 and bottom 8 rows, one may use

$$H(j, k) = 0, \qquad j = 1, 2, \dots, 8$$
$$H(257 - j, 257 - k) = 0, \qquad k = 17, 18, \dots, 256 \tag{221}$$

The reason for this is the dropoff property mentioned in (ii) previously.

(2)   For the middle 240 rows of H, if $k > j - 8$,

$$H(j, k) = H(j - 1, k - 1), \qquad j = 9, 10, \dots, 248, \quad k = 1, 2, \dots, 246 \tag{222}$$

However, if $k \leqslant j - 8$,

$$H(j, k) = 0 \tag{223}$$

Note that the previous equation uses observation (1) and propagates (with a unit shift at each stage) the elements of the 8th row down the matrix until the 248th row.

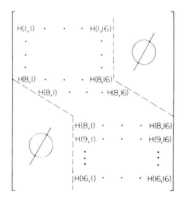

Fig. 15   The 256×256 gain matrix $[H]$ constructed from the 16×16 gain matrix $[H_s]$.

This construction results in a gain matrix that is sparse and has quasi-Toeplitz form, as shown in Fig. 15. Note that this 256×256 gain matrix has the same number of "unique" elements as the smaller 16×16 version.

The 256×256 gain matrix constructed as above was used in the estimator equations (211) to recursively filter 256×256 images. Note that the images no longer need to be segmented. The results of such filtering of the noisy image of Fig. 13 are shown in Fig. 16. The improvements over Fig. 14 are obvious.

Fig. 16 The image of Fig. 13 filtered without segmentation.

7.7 SOME FURTHER RESTORATION METHODS

In this section we will present the theory behind three more restoration techniques. They all have one feature in common: extensive computational requirements. We first discuss the nonlinear technique of the maximum *a posteriori* (MAP) method which has the advantage of taking into account the nonlinearities associated with the image recording process, and allowing the ensemble mean of the image random process to be nonstationary. The maximum entropy method, discussed next, also permits one to take into account the nonlinearities encountered in image recording. It has the additional advantage of guaranteeing positivity in the restored image. Like the MAP technique, the maximum entropy approach is also nonlinear. The third method presented here is linear and shows how one might solve the restoration problem by designing a deconvolving filter whose PSF is constrained to satisfy certain shape requirements.

7.7.1 The Maximum *a Posteriori* Method

Let $\mathbf{g}(x, y)$ be the random field to which the observed image belongs. Also, let $\mathbf{f}(x, y)$ be the random field representing the original undegraded image. Assume for a moment that we know the statistical properties of $\mathbf{f}$ and $\mathbf{g}$, and we can somehow construct the *a posteriori* density function $p(\mathbf{f} \mid \mathbf{g})$ from the observation $\mathbf{g}$. This is the probability density of $\mathbf{f}$ conditioned on knowing a specific degraded image $\mathbf{g}$. Let $\hat{\mathbf{f}}$ be the "value" of $\mathbf{f}$ at which

$p(\mathbf{f}|\mathbf{g})$ (considered as a function of $\mathbf{f}$) takes its largest value. For the given observed image, $\hat{\mathbf{f}}$ represents the most probable value of $\mathbf{f}$. In other words, for the given observed image, $\hat{\mathbf{f}}$ is the most probable original image, and, therefore, is called the *maximum a posteriori* estimate of $\mathbf{f}$.

Just as the least squares estimate in Section 7.3 minimized the cost function consisting of the expected value of $(\mathbf{f} - \hat{\mathbf{f}})^2$, the MAP estimate also satisfies a cost function, and for the reason both are examples of a class of estimates called Bayes estimates. The cost function $(\mathbf{f} - \hat{\mathbf{f}})^2$ that is minimized by the least squares estimate is shown symbolically in Fig. 17a, while Fig. 17b shows the cost function minimized by the MAP estimate, as $\Delta \to 0$. In the cost function of Fig. 17b, the penalty is zero if the estimate is within $\Delta/2$ of the correct value, and for all estimates outside this range the penalty is the same. We should also mention that if the constraint of linearity [such as given by (21)] is not used, the least squares estimate is, in general, the mean of the conditional density $p(\mathbf{f}|\mathbf{g})$ obtained by using (76) of Chap. 2. The reader is referred to [87, pp. 286–298] for proofs of the assertions made here.

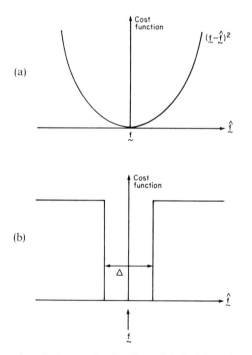

Fig. 17 (a) Shown here is the penalty function minimized by a least squares estimate. (b) The penalty function shown here is minimized by the MAP estimate as $\Delta \to 0$. Vectors are indicated by squiggly underlines in figures and by bold letters in text.

Clearly, then the determination of the MAP estimate requires knowledge of the *a posteriori* density function $p(\mathbf{f} \,|\, \mathbf{g})$. As we will see presently, this not only requires an explicit statement of the relationship between $\mathbf{g}$ and $\mathbf{f}$, but also the probability density functions for $\mathbf{f}$ and the measurement noise in the system. Note that the linear least squares estimates of Sections 7.3 and 7.6 only required knowledge of the correlation functions. The MAP and other estimates described in this section, although more general, also require more statistical information.

The disadvantage of requiring more statistical information is balanced by the fact that the estimates discussed here permit nonlinear relationships to exist between $\mathbf{f}$ and $\mathbf{g}$. As was mentioned in the introduction to this chapter, in a photographic system the recorded values (usually the film optical density) are in general a nonlinear function of the optical intensities incident from the scene. Therefore, a more precise way to write (1) would be

$$g(x, y) = s[\mathbf{b}(x, y)] + \mu(x, y) \tag{224}$$

with

$$\mathbf{b}(x, y) = \int \int h(x, y, x', y')\mathbf{f}(x', y') \, dx' \, dy' \tag{225}$$

where the function s represents the nonlinear transformation of the recording process. One may consider the recorded image, $g(x, y)$, to be the end result of a two-step process: the image formation step which transforms $\mathbf{f}(x, y)$ into $\mathbf{b}(x, y)$, and the nonlinear image recording step which takes us from $\mathbf{b}(x, y)$ to $g(x, y)$. Although both the image formation and the recording processes occur in the continuous domain, for digital processing one may write equivalent discrete relationships for the sampled versions of the functions involved:

$$g(m, n) = s[\mathbf{b}(m, n)] + v(m, n) \tag{226}$$

with

$$\mathbf{b}(m, n) = \sum_i \sum_j h(m, n, i, j)\mathbf{f}(i, j) \tag{227}$$

As before, we let $\vec{\mathbf{g}}$ and $\vec{\mathbf{f}}$ be M^2 and N^2-element-long vectors obtained by column scanning the $M \times M$ matrix $g(m, n)$ and the $N \times N$ matrix $\mathbf{f}(m, n)$, respectively. Let $\vec{\mathbf{b}}$ be the vector obtained similarly from $\mathbf{b}(m, n)$, and $\vec{\mathbf{e}}$ the vector from $v(m, n)$. The above relationships may be written more compactly as

$$\vec{\mathbf{g}} = s(\vec{\mathbf{b}}) + \vec{\mathbf{e}} \tag{228}$$

with

$$\vec{\mathbf{b}} = [\mathfrak{H}]\vec{\mathbf{f}} \tag{229}$$

where [$\mathfrak{H}$] represents the general transformation, not necessarily position invariant, between the elements of $\vec{f}$ and those of $\vec{b}$.

We will now show how the *a posteriori* density function, $p(\vec{f}|\vec{g})$ is determined. From the familiar law relating the joint and conditional densities, we have

$$p(\vec{f}, \vec{g}) = p(\vec{f}|\vec{g})p(\vec{g}) = p(\vec{g}|\vec{f})p(\vec{f}) \tag{230}$$

which leads to

$$p(\vec{f}|\vec{g}) = Kp(\vec{g}|\vec{f})p(\vec{f}) \tag{231}$$

where K is equal to $1/p(\vec{g})$ and may be treated as a constant independent of $\vec{f}$.

Hunt [50] has argued that an appropriate density function to use for the undegraded images is the multivariate Gaussian:

$$p(\vec{f}) = \left[\frac{1}{(2\pi)^{N^2}|[C_{ff}]|}\right]^{1/2} e^{-(1/2)(\vec{f} - \vec{f}_m)^t[C_{ff}]^{-1}(\vec{f} - \vec{f}_m)} \tag{232}$$

where

$$\vec{f}_m = E\{\vec{f}\}$$
$$[C_{ff}] = E\{(\vec{f} - \vec{f}_m)(\vec{f} - \vec{f}_m)^t\} \tag{233}$$

The vector $\vec{f}_m$ is the ensemble mean of $\vec{f}$. The matrix $[C_{ff}]$ is the covariance matrix of $\vec{f}$. Perhaps the most significant point to note here is that $\vec{f}_m$ is not constrained to have all its components equal to the same constant. In other words, different components of $\vec{f}_m$ (i.e., different pixels in the original image) can have different ensemble means associated with them. This implies that the image, when considered as a random field, is now permitted to be nonhomogeneous (nonstationary). This is definitely closer to reality that the often used assumption of homogeneity (stationarity) in much of the analytical work in image processing. To illustrate using Hunt's example [50], consider the ensemble of images consisting of full face photographs of individuals made for driver licenses. Assuming all faces are registered by the photographer to be of approximately the same size and orientation in the image frame, it is clear that the ensemble average for each pixel will be different. It will be approximately zero outside an oval shaped area representing the location of the faces. Within the oval shaped area there will be further structure corresponding to the various features in a human face.

In contrast to the nonuniform ensemble mean, the covariance matrix will be assumed to possess the Toeplitz form that it has for homogeneous random fields. This is tantamount to saying that while different regions in an image may have different average gray levels, the variations from these averages and the correlation properties of these variations are of the same order of magnitude everywhere. This may be somewhat unrealistic especially in regions where the ensemble averages are much smaller than the diagonal elements of $[C_{ff}]$, since the Gaussian assumption would then associate significant probabilities with the gray level being negative (which is clearly impossible). (Note that the diagonal elements of a Toeplitz $[C_{ff}]$ all have the same value, which is equal to the variance of the pixel gray levels.) But still, the combined assumptions of nonstationary mean and stationary correlation properties are much more realistic than the often used assumption of both these parameters being stationary.

In order to compute the MAP estimate by using (231), in addition to $p(\vec{f})$, we also need to know the density function of the noise vector $\vec{e}$. It has been shown [8, 65] that a zero-mean multivariate Gaussian distribution is a good model in both the film and the photoelectronic recording processes. We can therefore write

$$p(\vec{e}) = \left[\frac{1}{(2\pi)^{N^2} |[C_{ee}]|} \right] e^{-(1/2)\vec{e}^{t}[C_{ee}]^{-1}\vec{e}} \tag{234}$$

where $[C_{ee}]$ is the covariance matrix of $\vec{e}$:

$$[C_{ee}] = E\{\vec{e}\vec{e}^{t}\} \tag{235}$$

From (234), one can easily compute the conditional density $p(\vec{g}|\vec{f})$, since with a given $\vec{f}$, the only uncertainty in $\vec{g}$ is caused by the observation noise. From (228), for a specified $\vec{f}$, the variations in $\vec{g}$ are given by $\vec{g} - s(\vec{b})$ and governed by the density function in (234). Therefore,

$$p(\vec{g}|\vec{f}) = \left[\frac{1}{(2\pi)^{N^2} |[C_{ee}]|} \right]^{1/2} e^{-(1/2)(\vec{g}-s(\vec{b}))^{t}[C_{ee}]^{-1}(\vec{g}-s(\vec{b}))} \tag{236}$$

Substituting (232) and (236) in (231), and taking the logarithm of both sides, we get

$$\ln p(\vec{f}|\vec{g}) = \ln K - \tfrac{1}{2}(\vec{f} - \vec{f}_m)^{t}[C_{ff}]^{-1}(\vec{f} - \vec{f}_m) - \tfrac{1}{2}\ln (2\pi)^{N^2}|[C_{ff}]|$$
$$- \tfrac{1}{2}(\vec{g} - s(\vec{b}))^{t}[C_{ee}]^{-1}(\vec{g} - s(\vec{b})) - \tfrac{1}{2}\ln (2\pi)^{N^2}|[C_{ee}]| \tag{237}$$

Since the logarithm is a monotonically increasing function of its argument, the maxima of both $p(\vec{f}|\vec{g})$ and $\ln p(\vec{f}|\vec{g})$ will occur at the same $\vec{f}$. Therefore, the MAP estimate may be found by locating the maximum of the right-hand side in (237). Since the constants in (237) are of no consequence, we may use the following function for *minimization*, since we are also dropping the negative sign:

$$\psi(\vec{f}) = (\vec{f} - \vec{f}_m)^{t}[C_{ff}]^{-1}(\vec{f} - \vec{f}_m) + (\vec{g} - s(\vec{b}))^{t}[C_{ee}]^{-1}(\vec{g} - s(\vec{b})) \tag{238}$$

The gradient of ψ is given by Hunt [50]:

$$\nabla\psi = [C_{ff}]^{-1}(\vec{f} - \vec{f}_m) - [\mathfrak{H}]^t[S_b][C_{ee}]^{-1}(\vec{g} - s([\mathfrak{H}]\vec{f})) \qquad (239)$$

where

$$[S_b] = \begin{bmatrix} \left.\dfrac{\partial s(u)}{\partial u}\right|_{u=b_1} & & & \varnothing \\[2ex] & \left.\dfrac{\partial s(u)}{\partial u}\right|_{u=b_2} & & \\[2ex] & & \ddots & \\[2ex] \varnothing & & & \left.\dfrac{\partial s(u)}{\partial u}\right|_{u=b_{N^2}} \end{bmatrix} \qquad (240)$$

with $\vec{b}$ given by (229). The MAP estimate $\vec{f}$ must satisfy the equation $\nabla\psi = 0$. Therefore, from (239) we get the following nonlinear equation for the estimate:

$$[C_{ff}]^{-1}(\vec{f} - \vec{f}_m) - [\mathfrak{H}]^t[S_b][C_{ee}]^{-1}(\vec{g} - s([\mathfrak{H}]\vec{f})) = 0 \qquad (241)$$

where the partial derivatives in the matrix $[S_b]$ must now be calculated at $\vec{b} = [\mathfrak{H}]\vec{f}$.

Because of the large dimensionality of the problem, for most images of practical interest a direct solution of (241) is computationally almost impossible. However, when $[\mathfrak{H}]$ is assumed to be block Toeplitz (corresponding to the case of a position invariant degradation), and since $[C_{ff}]$ and $[C_{ee}]$ have already been assumed to be block Toeplitz, one can use fast Fourier transforms combined with a procedure such as the steepest descent method for finding the minimum of $\psi(\vec{f})$ in (238). The steepest descent approach is an iterative technique. Let $\vec{f}^{(k)}$ be the approximation to the correct $\vec{f}$ at the kth step. The $(k + 1)$st approximation is then obtained by using

$$\vec{f}^{(k+1)} = \vec{f}^{(k)} + \alpha_k \nabla\psi(\vec{f}^{(k)}) \qquad (242)$$

Although various methods are available for selecting the constant α_k for optimum convergence of the iterations, due to the complexity of the nonlinear functions Hunt [50] recommends the use of a fixed α for all k. This fixed value of α is determined by trial and error. Suppose that for a given choice of α the algorithm diverges after a few steps; then a smaller value of α should be tried the next time. The convergence of the iterations is measured by the magnitude of the gradient, $\|\nabla\psi(\vec{f}^{(k)})\|$. The solution is said to be achieved when

$$\|\nabla\psi(\vec{f}^{(k)})\| < \varepsilon \qquad (243)$$

where ε is chosen as a tolerance on the error in the final gradient. (If the solution achieved were absolutely correct, the gradient would be zero.)

The difficulty in implementing the iterative procedure in (242) lies in having to compute the gradient as given by (239). However, when $[h]$ and $[C_{ff}]$ are Toeplitz (or block Toeplitz) one may construct their circulant approximations. Then, as in Section 7.5, one may use FFT algorithms to compute the matrix–vector products in (239). The reader is referred to [15] and [100] for a comparison of this technique with others.

7.7.2　Maximum Entropy Restoration

First we will answer the question: Why use the maximum entropy criterion for restoration? Note that in the constrained deconvolution method of Section 7.5 we first constructed a roughness measure, which was the sum of the squares of the second derivatives over the image [see Eq. (123)]. The aim there was to minimize this roughness measure subject to satisfying the equality in (120). (If the total energy represented by ε were zero, the roughness measure would not influence the solution, which now would be the correct $f(x, y)$, assuming that h is invertible.) *The important thing to note is that the minimization of the roughness measure exerts a smoothing influence on the solution.*

Clearly, many other roughness measures are possible, whose minimization or maximization would cause a smoothing influence on the restored image. Consider, for example, the function

$$H_f = - \sum_{m=1}^{N} \sum_{n=1}^{N} f(m, n) \ln f(m, n) \tag{244}$$

in which $f(m, n) \ln f(m, n)$ will always exist, since the image gray levels are nonnegative numbers. We will assume that the sum of gray levels

$$\sum_{m=1}^{N} \sum_{n=1}^{N} f(m, n) = f_{\text{sum}} \tag{245}$$

is a known constant. It can be easily show that as $f(i, j)$ and $f(k, l)$ approach each other while f_{sum} stays the same, H_f will increase [24]. To illustrate, assume that $f(i, j) > f(k, l)$; then for the two pixels to approach each other while (245) continues to be satisfied, we may introduce the following changes:

$$\Delta f(i, j) = -\varepsilon, \qquad \Delta f(k, l) = +\varepsilon \tag{246}$$

as $\varepsilon \to 0$. After these changes, let the new summation in (244) be denoted by H_f':

$$H_f' = -\left[\sum_{\substack{m=1 \\ (m,n)\neq(i,j) \\ (m,n)\neq(k,l)}}^{N}\sum_{n=1}^{N} f(m,n)\ln f(m,n)\right] - \{f(i,j)-\varepsilon\}\ln\{f(i,j)-\varepsilon\}$$

$$- \{f(k,l)+\varepsilon\}\ln\{f(k,l)+\varepsilon\} \tag{247}$$

Using the limit

$$\lim_{x\to 0}\ln(1+x) = x \tag{248}$$

Eq. (247) can be reduced to

$$H_f' = H_f + \varepsilon\ln\frac{f(i,j)}{f(k,l)} \tag{249}$$

where, since $\varepsilon \to 0$, terms proportional to ε^2 have been neglected. Since $f(i,j) > f(k,l)$, we see from (249) that the change

$$\Delta H_f = H_f' - H_f > 0 \tag{250}$$

is positive.

The above discussion implies that if there are no other conditions to be satisfied, H_f will take its maximum value when the image is a constant function, which is the smoothest possible case since all the derivatives will now be equal to zero. In a restoration problem, where other conditions also have to be satisfied, H_f should serve as a roughness measure, and its maximization should exert a smoothing influence on the solution. Because the structure of (244) is identical to that of (184) in Chapter 5, the function H is called the entropy of the image. Note, however, that the entropy here is not identical in concept to the entropy in Chapter 5. In that chapter the entropy is defined for a discrete random process and gives its information rate. Here, the entropy is defined for a single deterministic nonnegative function and serves as its roughness measure.

We will now briefly present Frieden's [24] approach to the maximum entropy restoration of images. In this approach one maximizes a weighted sum of the image entropy and the observation noise entropy. Since the noise component at each pixel location may take either positive or negative values, the definition of noise entropy requires some care. The difficulty is gotten around by applying additional *a priori* knowledge into the problem by assuming that a constant B is known such that[§]

$$B = -\text{most negative } v(m,n) \tag{251}$$

[§] In this subsection, the functions $g(x,y)$, $f(x,y)$, and $v(x,y)$ are deterministic. Hence the use of regular (nonboldface) notation.

where $v(m, n)$ is the observation noise at the location (m, n). In practice B may be roughly estimated by setting it equal to $-2\sigma_v$, where σ_v is the standard deviation of the noise. According to Frieden, the quality of the restorations does not depend critically upon B precisely satisfying (251); however, the results are best when (251) is indeed satisfied. We may now define a new nonnegative array

$$v'(m, n) = v(m, n) + B \qquad (252)$$

and the noise entropy as

$$H_v = -\sum_{m=1}^{N} \sum_{n=1}^{N} v'(m, n) \ln v'(m, n) \qquad (253)$$

The restoration problem is solved by maximizing the weighted sum

$$H = H_f + \rho H_v \qquad (254)$$

where the constant ρ is used to emphasize one of H_f and H_v with respect to the other. The larger the ρ, the greater the emphasis on exerting the smoothing influence on noise, relative to the smoothing influence on the image. Frieden [26] recommends a value of $\rho = 20$ as about optimum for a wide range of object and noise situations.

Maximization of (254) is carried out subject to satisfying the equality in (245) and those in (119):

$$g(p, q) = \sum_{m=1}^{N} \sum_{n=1}^{N} h(p - m, q - n) f(m, n) + v'(m, n) - B \qquad (255)$$

We have assumed that the arrays $f(m, n)$, $v(m, n)$, and $g(m, n)$ are all of dimension $N \times N$. [This will be the case provided the original image $f(m, n)$ is considered to be padded with a border of zeros as in Section 7.5.3.] The maximization can be carried out using Lagrange multipliers. We find the $2N^2$ unknowns $f(m, n)$ and $v(m, n)$ that maximize the functional U given by

$$U = H_f + \rho H_v$$

$$+ \sum_{p=1}^{N} \sum_{q=1}^{N} \lambda_{pq} \left\{ \sum_{m=1}^{N} \sum_{n=1}^{N} h(p - m, q - n) f(m, n) + v'(m, n) - B - g(p, q) \right\}$$

$$+ \beta \left\{ \sum_{m=1}^{N} \sum_{n=1}^{N} f(m, n) - f_{\text{sum}} \right\} \qquad (256)$$

where $\lambda_{p, q}$, $p, q = 1, 2, \ldots, N$ and β are the $N^2 + 1$ Lagrange multipliers.

Let $\hat{f}(m, n)$ and $\hat{v}(m, n)$ denote the optimum values of $f(m, n)$ and $v'(m, n)$. Clearly,

$$\left.\frac{\partial U}{\partial f(m, n)}\right|_{f = \hat{f}} = 0$$

$$\left.\frac{\partial U}{\partial v'(m, n)}\right|_{v' = \hat{v}} = 0 \tag{257}$$

Performing these differentiations, we obtain

$$\hat{f}(m, n) = \exp\left(-1 + \beta + \sum_{p=1}^{N} \sum_{q=1}^{N} \lambda_{p, q} h(p - m, q - n)\right) \tag{258}$$

and

$$\hat{v}(m, n) = \exp(-1 + \lambda_{m, n}/\beta) \tag{259}$$

These solutions have to satisfy the conditions given by (245) and (252):

$$\sum_{m=1}^{N} \sum_{n=1}^{N} \hat{f}(m, n) = f_{\text{sum}} \tag{260}$$

and

$$\sum_{m=1}^{N} \sum_{n=1}^{N} h(p - m, q - n)\hat{f}(m, n) + v'(m, n) - B = g(p, q), \, p, q = 1, 2, \ldots, N \tag{261}$$

The restored image $\hat{f}(m, n)$ is obtained by first substituting (258) and (259) in (260) and (261). The resulting $N^2 + 1$ equations are solved for the $N^2 + 1$ unknowns $\lambda_{p, q}$, $p, q = 1, 2, \ldots, N$, and β. These equations are highly non-linear, but, according to Frieden, are always solvable by an $(N^2 + 1)$-dimensional Newton–Raphson method, provided B is large enough.

7.7.3 Deconvolution by Constraining the Shape of the PSF

An entirely different approach to image restoration is as follows: Let $h(x, y)$ be the PSF of the image degradation, and let $m(x, y)$ be the PSF of the restoration filter. The PSF of the combined effect of degradation and the restoration is $h(x, y) * m(x, y)$; we will denote this combined PSF by $c(x, y)$. Then, in the absence of observation noise, $c(x, y)$ should be as close to an impulse as possible in order to achieve perfect restoration. In the presence of observation noise, it is very likely that if $m(x, y)$ is chosen so as to make $h(x, y) * m(x, y)$ close to an impulse, the level of noise in the restored picture may reach unacceptable proportions. Therefore, in this case, a meaningful statement of the restoration problem would be as follows: calculate $m(x, y)$ so as to make $c(x, y)$ as close to an impulse as possible subject to the constraint that the variance of the noise in the restored image does not exceed a predetermined value.

A digital solution to the above problem was recently provided by Chu and McGillem [16]. They have used the following measure of "narrowness" of the composite PSF, $c(x, y)$:

$$r^2 = \frac{\int_{-\infty}^{\infty} \int_{-\infty}^{\infty} w(x, y)c^2(x, y) \, dx \, dy}{\int_{-\infty}^{\infty} \int_{-\infty}^{\infty} c^2(x, y) \, dx \, dy} \tag{262}$$

where the smaller the r^2, the closer the $c(x, y)$ is to an impulse. The weight function $w(x, y)$ is specified as

$$w(x, y) = \begin{cases} 0, & (x, y) \in D \\ 1, & \text{otherwise} \end{cases} \tag{263}$$

where D is a prespecified small neighborhood around the origin in the xy-plane. A weight function of this form associates zero penalty with values of $c(x, y)$ over the domain D, and unit penalty for those portions of $c(x, y)$ that are outside D. That the minimization of the measure r^2 leads to $c(x, y)$ confining most of its energy within the domain D can also be seen by substituting (263) in (262), and rewriting the latter as

$$r^2 = \frac{\int_{-\infty}^{\infty} \int_{-\infty}^{\infty} c^2(x, y) \, dx \, dy - \int\int_{(x, y) \in D} c^2(x, y) \, dx \, dy}{\int_{-\infty}^{\infty} \int_{-N}^{\infty} c^2(x, y) \, dx \, dy} = 1 - \alpha \tag{264}$$

where

$$\alpha = \frac{\int\int_{(x, y) \in D} c^2(x, y) \, dx \, dy}{\int_{-\infty}^{\infty} \int_{-\infty}^{\infty} c^2(x, y) \, dx \, dy} \tag{265}$$

Note that α can only take values between 0 and 1. Minimization of r^2 is equivalent to a maximization of α, which, in turn, amounts to maximizing the energy contained in that part of $c(x, y)$ that is over the domain D. [We should also mention that if we had chosen $w(x, y) = (x^2 + y^2)$ in (262), r^2 would then be the *radius of gyration* of the composite PSF. Many investigators [4, 5, 92, 98] have done a constrained minimization of the radius of gyration (see also [81]).]

Now that we have a measure of the narrowness of the PSF, we need an expression for the variance of noise in the restored image. We will assume that the block diagram of Fig. 18 is an appropriate model for both the degradation and the restoration. The degradation is assumed to take place in

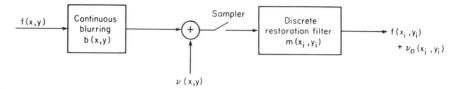

Fig. 18 The model used for degradation and subsequent restoration by constraining the shape of the PSF is shown here.

the continuous domain (as would be the case for optical image formation). The degraded image is given by (2), repeated here for convenience:

$$\mathbf{g}(x, y) = \iint h(x - x', y - y')\mathbf{f}(x', y') \, dx' \, dy' + \mathbf{v}(x, y) \qquad (266)$$

The restoration is achieved by first sampling $g(x, y)$ on an $N \times N$ matrix and convolving the sampled data with a $(2M + 1) \times (2M + 1)$ restoration filter. The samples of the restoration filter will be denoted by $m(x_i, y_j)$ where $i, j = -M, -M + 1, \ldots, 0, \ldots, M$. If the noise at the sampling points in the output image is denoted by $v_o(x_i, y_j)$, we can write the following relationship:

$$\mathbf{v}_o(x_i, y_j) = \mathbf{v}(x_i, y_j) * m(x_i, y_j)$$

$$= \sum_{k=-M}^{M} \sum_{l=-M}^{M} m(x_k, y_l)\mathbf{v}(x_i - x_k, y_j - y_l) \qquad (267)$$

We will assume that the left-hand side above is desired at the sampling points in the interior of the image sufficiently removed from the border, so that for all values of k and l, the $(x_i - x_k, y_j - y_l)$'s fall within the domain of support of $\mathbf{g}(x, y)$. From (267), we can write for the variance σ_o^2 of the noise in the restored image

$$\sigma_o^2 = E\{\mathbf{v}_o^2(x_i, y_j)\} = \sum_{k=-M}^{M} \sum_{l=-M}^{M} \sum_{p=-M}^{M} \sum_{q=-M}^{M} m(x_k, y_l)m(x_p, y_q)$$

$$\times E\{\mathbf{v}(x_i - x_k, y_j - y_l)\mathbf{v}(x_i - x_p, y_j - y_q)\} \qquad (268)$$

If we consider the input noise to be a stationary random process, (268) simplifies to

$$\sigma_o^2 = \sum_{k=-M}^{M} \sum_{l=-M}^{M} \sum_{p=-M}^{M} \sum_{q=-M}^{M} m(x_k, y_l)m(x_p, y_q)R_{vv}(p - k, q - l) \qquad (269)$$

where $R_{vv}(\cdot, \cdot)$ is the autocorrelation function of the random field $\mathbf{v}(x, y)$.

The problem of designing the restoration filter requires minimizing r^2 in (262) subject to the condition that

$$\sigma_o^2 \leqslant \sigma^2 \tag{270}$$

where σ^2 is the user specified upper limit on the output noise variance. Note that the design of the restoration filter requires *a priori* specification of the domain D in (263), of M for the size of the restoration filter, as well as σ^2.

Following Chu and McGillem[16], we will now present a derivation of the filter equations for the one-dimensional case. In this case, Eqs. (262), (263), and (269) reduce to

$$r^2 = \frac{\int_{-\infty}^{\infty} w(x)c^2(x)\,dx}{\int_{-\infty}^{\infty} c^2(x)\,dx} \tag{271}$$

$$w(x) = \begin{cases} 0, & |x| < \dfrac{D}{2} \\ 1, & \text{otherwise} \end{cases} \tag{272}$$

$$\sigma_o^2 = \sum_{k=-M}^{M} \sum_{p=-M}^{M} m(x_k)m(x_p)R_{vv}(p-k) \tag{273}$$

where in (272), D now denotes the width of the interval over which we associate zero penalty with $c(x)$. For the one-dimensional case the degradation model is given by

$$\mathbf{g}(x) = \int h(x-x')\mathbf{f}(x')\,dx' + \mathbf{v}(x) \tag{274}$$

and the restoration is achieved by convolving the sampled function $\mathbf{g}(x_i)$ with a $(2M+1)$-element filter whose samples are denoted by $m(x_i)$. The composite PSF is equal to

$$c(x) = h(x) * m(x) = h(x) * \sum_{i=-M}^{M} m(x_i)\,\delta(x-x_i) = \sum_{i=-M}^{M} m(x_i)h(x-x_i) \tag{275}$$

Substituting (275) in (271), we get

$$r^2 = \frac{\int_{-\infty}^{\infty} w(x) \sum_{i=-M}^{M} \sum_{j=-M}^{M} m(x_i)m(x_j)h(x-x_i)h(x-x_j)\,dx}{\int_{-\infty}^{\infty} \sum_{i=-M}^{M} \sum_{j=-M}^{M} m(x_i)m(x_j)h(x-x_i)h(x-x_j)\,dx} \tag{276}$$

which in vector–matrix notation may be expressed as

$$r^2 = \frac{\vec{m}^t[A]\vec{m}}{\vec{m}^t[B]\vec{m}}$$

(277)

where $\vec{m}$ is a $(2M + 1)$-element column vector composed of $m(x_{-m})$, $m(x_{-m+1})$, ..., $m(x_m)$; $[A]$ is a $(2M + 1) \times (2M + 1)$ matrix whose elements are given by

$$A(i, j) = \int_{-\infty}^{\infty} w(x)h(x - x_i)h(x - x_j)\, dx$$

(278)

$[B]$ is also a $(2M + 1) \times (2M + 1)$ matrix whose elements are given by

$$B(i, j) = \int_{-\infty}^{\infty} h(x - x_i)h(x - x_j)\, dx$$

(279)

The expression (273) for the output noise variance may also be expressed more compactly as

$$\sigma_o^2 = \vec{m}^t[R_{vv}]\vec{m}$$

(280)

Comparing the denominators in (271) and (277), we note that $\vec{m}[B]\vec{m}$ is basically a gain factor, since it is equal to the total energy of the composite PSF. Since this factor has no bearing on the shape of $c(x)$, we might as well set it equal to unity. The calculation of the restoration filter may then be stated as

$$\text{minimize } \vec{m}^t[A]\vec{m}$$

(281a)

$$\text{subject to } \vec{m}^t[B]m = 1$$

(281b)

$$\text{and } \vec{m}^t[R_{vv}]\vec{m} = \sigma^2$$

(281c)

where we have used (270), (277), and (280). As was done earlier in this chapter, to carry out this constrained minimization, we construct a functional U defined by

$$U = \vec{m}^t[A]\vec{m} + \lambda_1(\vec{m}^t[B]\vec{m} - 1) + \lambda_2(\vec{m}^t[R_{vv}]\vec{m} - \sigma^2)$$

(282)

and set its gradient (with respect to $\vec{m}$) equal to zero. The constants λ_1 and λ_2 are the Lagrange multipliers.

The result is

$$[B]^{-1}([A] + \lambda_2[R_{vv}])\vec{m} = \lambda_1\vec{m}$$

(283)

which says that the solution $\vec{m}$ is an eigenvector, and the correct choice of λ_1 the corresponding eigenvalue, of the matrix $[B]^{-1}([A] + \lambda_2[R_{vv}])$. In general, this matrix will possess $(2M + 1)$ eigenvectors and their corresponding eigenvalues. The eigenvector that corresponds to the smallest eigenvalue is chosen for $\vec{m}$ (assuming that a correct choice of λ_2 has already been made). To show this, we rewrite (283) as

$$([A] + \lambda_2[R_{vv}])\vec{m} = \lambda_1[B]\vec{m} \tag{284}$$

Multiplying both sides from the left by $\vec{m}^t$ and using (277), (281b), and (281c), we get

$$r^2 = \lambda_1 - \lambda_2\sigma^2 \tag{285}$$

If our aim is to minimize r^2, this equation shows that if many different values of λ_1 will satisfy (283), we should choose the smallest. The correct $\vec{m}$ will be the eigenvector corresponding to this choice.

Since λ_2 is not known *a priori*, in practice the above procedure may be employed iteratively by first assigning an arbitrary value to λ_2, computing λ_1 and $\vec{m}$, changing λ_2 and repeating the computation to check if the next value of λ_1 is smaller. The reader is referred to [16] for computer simulation results obtained with this technique.

7.8 BIBLIOGRAPHICAL NOTES

In addition to the techniques that have been presented in this chapter for solving Eq. (2), several other approaches are worth noting. Jansson [52–54] has proposed an iterative method for solving (2), which can best be implemented digitally. In a method due to MacAdam [64], Eq. (2) is first converted into a vector–matrix form as in Eq. (43), and the solution is then obtained by dividing the z-transform of the left-hand side by the z-transform of the equivalent one-dimensional impulse response function implied in Eq. (43). The solution is obtained with the constraint that it lie within a certain range (for example, the constraint could be that all samples of the solution be positive). This method suffers from the disadvantage that when the picture matrix is of large size, the computation time may become unreasonably long. It does, however, have the attractive feature that the restored picture can be guaranteed to be positive. The positivity constraint is also implied in the methods proposed by Frieden [24, 25], which use maximum likelihood and maximum entropy algorithms for restoration, as well as those proposed by Richardson [80], which assume that the picture is a two-dimensional probability density function and then use Bayes' theorem for restoration. Frieden [27] has also proposed a restoration technique in which the degraded image is restored by convolving it with a weighted sum of the shifted versions of the point spread function of the degradation. The number of terms in this weighted sum is small, and the weights are calculated by minimizing the sidelobes of the output point spread function. The advantage of this method lies in the small number of mathematical steps required for its implementation. While Frieden's method for the selection of weights tends to minimize the distortion between the original ideal picture and its restored version, it also suffers from increased susceptibility to noise. By using the mathematical methods developed by Backus and Gilbert [5], Saleh [84] has studied possible choices of the superposition weights that effect a compromise between distortion and noise.

The reader has probably noticed that in the restoration solutions derived in this chapter the restored picture does not contain those frequency components at which the transfer function $H(u, v)$ of the degradation has zero values. One would think that if $H(u, v)$ is zero outside a certain bounded region in the frequency plane (as is the case with all optical imaging), then we cannot hope to recover the spectral frequencies in the original $f(x, y)$ that are outside of this bounded region. Actually this is not the case, at least in theory. For all bounded functions $f(x, y)$ the Fourier transform $F(u, v)$ is an analytic function. This means that if $F(u, v)$ is known for a certain range of (u, v), then the techniques of analytic continuation can be used to extend the solution to all (u, v). Harris [34] has discussed several practical methods for carrying out the analytic continuation. From a theoretical standpoint, the method proposed by Slepian and Pollak [89] (see also [44]), which makes use of prolate spheroidal wave functions, is most satisfying. The reason why these techniques for increasing the resolution in the restored picture have not proved popular is because of their extreme susceptibility to noise [13, 23]. In one example [37] it was found that in order to succeed in analytic continuation a noise-to-signal amplitude ratio of $1:1000$ was required.

In Section 7.1.1 we gave some examples of cases in which the point spread function of the degradation can be determined from an understanding of the underlying physical process. To add to those examples, the point spread function of a defocused lens can be calculated, taking into account both geometrical optics and the effects of diffraction [28, 29]. It can be shown that for low spatial frequencies the transfer function calculated on the basis of geometrical optics agrees well with that calculated when diffraction effects are involved [40, 41, 96]. The point spread function due to lens aberration can also be calculated theoretically [6, 25, 66]. Only spherical aberration can be considered to be shift invariant, the others being definitely shift variant.

In Section 7.2.1 we also calculated the point spread function of linear motion degradation. Many investigators have worked on this problem [61, 85, 88, 91, 93]. In our derivation we assumed that the image that is incident on the film is invariant in time except for a displacement of the origin. This is not necessarily true even when the camera moves perpendicularly to the optical axis. For example, the images of objects at different distances from the film move by different amounts, thereby producing a spatially varying blur. Several investigators have also considered the effect of camera shutter operation on the point spread function of motion degradation [39, 76, 88].

In Section 7.2.2 we discussed the problem of determining the point spread function $h(x, y)$ *a posteriori* from the degraded image $g(x, y)$. The method for estimating the transfer function $H(u, v)$ given by Eq. (15) is a result of Stockham's work on the restoration of old Caruso recordings.

In this chapter we have assumed that the point spread function $h(x, y)$, whether it is known *a priori* or estimated *a posteriori*, is a deterministic function. The problem of least squares filtering of pictures with a deterministic PSF was first solved by Helstrom [38]. Slepian [90] has solved the least mean square estimation problem for the case where $h(x, y)$ is stochastic. The optimum filter was found to again be given by Eq. (41), except that H^* and $|H|^2$ are replaced by $E\{H^*\}$ and $E\{|H|^2\}$, where $E\{\ \}$ denotes the ensemble average.

In Section 7.6 we discussed on-line recursive estimation of pictures from noisy observations. A basic assumption was made there that the random field is wide-sense Markov. Specification of the Markov property requires that the "past," the "present," and the "future" be defined. It is, of course, trivial to do so for one-dimensional signals. For pictorial data, however, there is no unique way to specify these. In our definitions of the Markov property the region $X_{m,n}$ is the past, the point (m, n) the present, and the rest of the picture the future. For other ways to specify these regions, see, for example, Jain and Angel [51] and Woods [105]. Woods [106] has also presented techniques for developing recursive Markov models for images using the method of spectral factorization [19]. The reader is also referred to [97, 107] for additional treatments of the problem of recursive linear mean-square prediction and filtering.

In this chapter we considered only degradations that are shift invariant. Many important types of degradations do not, however, fall into this category. The reader is referred to the literature for techniques that can be used to handle shift-variant degradations [30, 43, 60, 62, 82, 85, 86, 101].

REFERENCES

1. K. Abend, T. J. Harley, and L. N. Kanal, Classification of binary random patterns, *IEEE Trans. Informat. Theory* **IT-11**, 1965, 538–544.
2. A. Albert, "Regression and the Moore–Penrose Pseudo-Inverse." Academic Press, New York, 1972.
3. E. S. Angel and A. K. Jain, Restoration of images degraded by spatially varying point spread functions by a conjugate gradient method, *Appl. Opt.* **17**, 1978, 2186–2190.

4. R. Arguello, H. Sellner, and J. A. Stuller, Transfer function compensation of sampled images, *IEEE Trans. Comput.* **C-21**, 1972, 812–818.

5. G. Backus and F. Gilbert, Uniqueness in the inversion of inaccurate gross earth data, *Phil. Trans. Roy. Soc. London Ser. A* **266**, 1970, 123–192.

6. R. Barakat, Numerical results concerning the transfer functions and the total illuminance for optimum balanced fifth-order spherical aberration, *J. Opt. Soc. Amer.* **54**, 1964, 38–44.

7. M. A. Berkovitz, Edge gradient analysis OTF accuracy study, *Proc. SPIE Seminar Modulation Transfer Function*, Boston, Massachusetts, 1968.

8. L. M. Biberman and S. Nudelman, "Photoelectronic Imaging Devices," Vols. 1 and 2. Plenum Press, New York, 1971.

9. E. S. Blackman, Effects of noise on the determination of photographic system modulation transfer function, *Photogr. Sci. Eng.* **12**, 1968, 244–250.

10. E. S. Blackman, Recovery of system transfer functions from noisy photographic records, *Proc. SPIE Seminar Image Information Recovery*, 1969.

11. C. P. C. Bray, Comparative analysis of geometric vs. diffraction heterochromatic lens evaluations using optical transfer function theory, *J. Opt. Soc. Amer.* **55**, 1965, 1136–1138.

12. E. O. Brigham, H. W. Smith, F. X. Bostick, and W. C. Dusterhoeft, An iterative technique for determining inverse filters, *IEEE Trans. Geosci. Electron.* **GE-6**, 1968, 86–96.

13. G. J. Buck and J. J. Gustincic, Resolution limitations of a finite aperture, *IEEE Trans. Antennas Propagat.* **AP-15**, 1967, 376–381.

14. T. M. Cannon, Blind deconvolution of spatially invariant image blurs with phase," *IEEE Trans. Acoust. Speech Signal Processing* **ASSP-24**, 1976, 58–63.

15. T. M. Cannon, H. J. Trussell, and B. R. Hunt, Comparison of image restoration methods, *Appl. Opt.* **17**, 1978, 3384–3390.

16. N. Y. Chu and C. D. McGillem, Image restoration filters based on a 1–0 weighting over the domain of support of the PSF, *IEEE Trans. Acoust. Speech Signal Processing* **ASSP-27**, 1979, 457–464.

17. L. J. Cutrona and W. D. Hall, Some considerations in post-facto blur removal, *in* Evaluation of Motion-Degraded Images, NASA Publ. SP-193, pp. 139–148, December 1968.

18. K. A. Dines and A. C. Kak, Constrained least squares filtering, *IEEE Trans. Acoust. Speech Signal Processing* **ASSP-25,** 1977, 346–350.

19. M. P. Ekstrom and J. W. Woods, Two-dimensional spectral factorization with applications in recursive digital filtering, *IEEE Trans. Acoust. Speech Signal Processing* **ASSP-24,** 1976, 115–128.

20. D. G. Falconer, Image enhancement and film-grain noise, *Opt. Acta* **17**, 1970, 693–705.

21. D. L. Fried, Optical resolution through a randomly inhomogeneous medium for very long and very short exposures, *J. Opt. Soc. Amer.* **56**, 1966, 1372–1379.

22. D. L. Fried, Limiting resolution looking down through the atmosphere, *J. Opt. Soc. Amer.* **56**, 1966, 1380–1384.

23. B. R. Frieden, Bandlimited reconstruction of optical objects and spectra, *J. Opt. Soc. Amer.* **57**, 1967, 1013–1019.

24. B. R. Frieden, Restoring with maximum likelihood and maximum entropy, *J. Opt. Soc. Amer.* **62**, 1972, 511–518.

25. B. R. Frieden and J. J. Burke, Restoring with maximum entropy II: Superresolution of photographs of diffraction-blurred images, *J. Opt. Soc. Amer.* **62**, 1972, 1207–1210.

26. B. R. Frieden, Image enhancement and restoration, *in* "Picture Processing and Digital Filtering" (T. S. Huang, ed.). Springer-Verlag, Berlin and New York, 1975.

27. B. R. Frieden, Image restoration by discrete deconvolution of minimal length, *J. Opt. Soc. Amer.* **64**, 1974, 682–686.

28. J. W. Goodman, "Introduction to Fourier Optics." McGraw-Hill, New York, 1968.

29. J. W. Goodman, Use of a large-aperture optical system as a triple interferometer for removal of atmospheric image degradations, *in* Evaluation of Motion-Degraded Images, NASA Publ. SP-193, pp. 89–93, December 1968.

30. E. M. Granger, Restoration of images degraded by spatially varying smear, *in* Evaluation of Motion-Degraded Images, NASA Publ. SP-193, pp. 161–174, December 1968.

31. E. Guillman, "The Mathematics of Circuit Analysis." Wiley, New York, 1949.

32. A. Habibi, Two-dimensional Bayesian estimate of images, *Proc. IEEE* **60**, 1972, 878–883.

33. H. B. Hammill and C. Holladay, The effect of certain approximations in image quality evaluation from edge traces, *SPIE J.* **8**, 1970, 223–228.

34. J. L. Harris, Diffraction and resolving power, *J. Opt. Soc. Amer.* **54**, 1964, 931–936.

35. J. L. Harris, Sr., Image evaluation and restoration, *J. Opt. Soc. Amer.* **56**, 1966, 569–574.

36. J. L. Harris, Sr., Potential and limitations of techniques for processing linear motion-degraded imagery, *in* Evaluation of Motion-Degraded Images, NASA Publ. SP-193, pp. 131–138, December 1968.

37. J. L. Harris, Information extraction from diffraction limited imagery, *Pattern Recognit.* **2**, 1970, 69–77.

38. C. W. Helstrom, Image restoration by the method of least squares, *J. Opt. Soc. Amer.* **57**, 1967, 297–303.

39. L. O. Hendenberg and W. E. Welander, Experimental transfer characteristics of image motion and air conditions in aerial photography, *Appl. Opt.* **2**, 1963, 379–386.

40. H. H. Hopkins, The frequency response of a defocused optical system, *Proc. Roy. Soc. Ser. A* **231**, 1955, 91–103.

41. H. H. Hopkins, Interferometric methods for the study of diffraction images, *Opt. Acta* **2**, 1955, 23–29.

42. T. S. Huang, Some notes on film grain noise, Restoration of Atmospherically-Degraded Images, NFS Summer Study Rep., Woods Hole, Massachusetts, 1966.

43. T. S. Huang, Digital computer analysis of linear shift-variant systems, *in* Evaluation of Motion-Degraded Images, NASA Publ. SP-193, pp. 83–87, December 1968.

44. T. S. Huang, W. F. Schreiber, and O. J. Tretiak, Image processing, *Proc. IEEE* **59**, 1971, 1586–1609.

45. R. E. Hufnagel and N. R. Stanley, Modulation transfer function associated with image transmission through turbulent media, *J. Opt. Soc. Amer.* **54**, 1964, 52–61.

46. R. E. Hufnagel, An improved model for turbulent atmosphere, Restoration of Atmospherically Degraded Images, NSF Summer Study Rep., Woods Hole, Massachusetts, 1966.

47. B. R. Hunt, A matrix theory proof of the discrete convolution theorem, *IEEE Trans. Audio Electroacoust.* **AU-19**, 1971, 285–288.

48. B. R. Hunt, Deconvolution of linear systems by constrained regression and its relationship to the Wiener theory, *IEEE Trans. Automat. Control.* **AC-17**, 1972, 703–705.

49. B. R. Hunt, The application of constrained least squares estimation to image restoration by digital computer, *IEEE Trans. Comput.* **C-22**, 1973, 805–812.

50. B. R. Hunt, Bayesian methods in nonlinear digital image restoration, *IEEE Trans. Comput.* **C-26**, 1977, 219–229.

51. A. K. Jain and E. Angel, Image restoration, modeling, and reduction of dimensionality, *IEEE Trans. Comput.* **C-23**, 1974, 470–476.

52. P. A. Jansson, R. H. Hunt, and E. K. Plyler, Response function for spectral resolution enhancement, *J. Opt. Soc. Amer.* **58**, 1968, 1665–1666.

53. P. A. Jansson, Method for determining the response function of a high-resolution infrared spectrometer, *J. Opt. Soc. Amer.* **60**, 1970, 184–191.

54. P. A. Jansson, Resolution enhancement of spectra, *J. Opt. Soc. Amer.* **60**, 1970, 596–599.

55. R. A. Jones, An automated technique for deriving MTF's from edge traces, *Photogr. Sci. Eng.* **11**, 1967, 102–106.

56. R. A. Jones, Accuracy test procedure for image evaluation techniques, *Appl. Opt.* **7**, 1968, 133–136.

57. R. A. Jones and E. C. Yeadon, Determination of the spread function from noisy edge scans, *Photogr. Sci. Engr.* **13**, 1969, 200–204.

58. W. Kaplan, "Advanced Calculus." Addison-Wesley, New York, 1959.

59. K. T. Knox, Image retrieval from astronomical speckle patterns, *J. Opt. Soc. Amer.* **66**, 1976, 1236–1239.

60. M. J. Lahart, Local image restoration by a least squares method, *J. Opt. Soc. Amer.* **69**, 1979, 1333–1339.

61. A. W. Lohmann and D. P. Paris, Influence of longitudinal vibrations on image quality, *Appl. Opt.* **4**, 1965, 393–397.

62. A. W. Lohmann and D. P. Paris, Space-variant image formation, *J. Opt. Soc. Amer.* **55**, 1965, 1007–1013.

63. R. F. Lutomirski and H. T. Yura, Modulation-transfer function and phase-structure function of an optical wave in a turbulent medium—1, *J. Opt. Soc. Amer.* **59**, 1969, 999–1000.

64. D. P. MacAdam, Digital image restoration by constrained deconvolution, *J. Opt. Soc. Amer.* **60**, 1970, 1617–1627.

65. C. E. K. Mees, "The Theory of the Photographic Process." Macmillan, New York, 1954.

66. L. Miyamoto, Wave optics and geometrical optics in optical design, *Progr. Opt.* **1**, 1961.

67. J. C. Moldon, High resolution image estimation in a turbulent environment, *Pattern Recognit.* **2**, 1970, 79–90.

68. J. B. Morton and H. C. Andrews, A posteriori method of image restoration, *J. Opt. Soc. Amer.* **69**, 1979, 280–290.

69. N. E. Nahi, "Estimation Theory and Applications." Wiley, New York, 1969.

70. N. E. Nahi, Role of recursive estimation in statistical image enhancement, *Proc. IEEE* **60**, 1972, 872–877.

71. B. Noble and J. W. Daniel, "Applied Linear Algebra," 2nd ed. Prentice Hall, Englewood Cliffs, New Jersey, 1977.

72. E. L. O'Neill, "Introduction to Statistical Optics." Addison-Wesley, Reading, Massachusetts, 1963.

73. D. P. Panda and A. C. Kak, Image Restoration and Enhancement, Tech. Rep. TR-EE 76-17. School of Electrical Engineering, Purdue Univ., W. Lafayette, Indiana, 1976.

74. D. P. Panda and A. C. Kak, Recursive least squares smoothing of noise in images, *IEEE Trans. Acoust. Speech Signal Processing* **ASSP-25**, 1977, 520–524.

75. A. Papoulis, "Probability, Random Variables and Stochastic Processes." McGraw-Hill, New York, 1965.

76. D. P. Paris, Influence of image motion on the resolution of a photographic system—II, *Photogr. Sci. Eng.* **7**, 1963, 233–236.

77. J. Philip, Digital image and spectrum restoration by quadratic programming and by modified Fourier transformation, *IEEE Trans. Patt. Anal. Machine Intelligence* **PAMI-1**, 1979, 385–399.

78. D. L. Phillips, A technique for the numerical solution of certain integral equations of the first kind, *J. ACM* **9**, 1962, 84–97.

79. W. K. Pratt, Generalized Wiener filtering computational techniques, *IEEE Trans. Comput.* **C-21**, 1972, 636–641.

80. W. H. Richardson, Bayesian-based iterative method of image restoration, *J. Opt. Soc. Amer.* **62**, 1972, 55–59.

81. T. E. Riemer and C. D. McGillem, Optimum constrained image restoration filters, *IEEE Trans. Aerospace Electron. Systems*, 1977, 136–146.

82. G. M. Robbins and T. S. Huang, Inverse filtering for linear shift-variant imaging systems, *Proc. IEEE* **60**, 1972, 862–872.

83. P. G. Roetling, R. C. Haas, and R. E. Kinzly, Some practical aspects of measurement and restoration of motion-degraded images, *Proc. NASA/ERC Seminar*, Cambridge, Massachusetts, December, 1968.

84. E. A. Saleh, Trade-off between resolution and noise in restoration by superposition of images, *Appl. Opt.* **13**, 1974, 1833–1838.

85. A. A. Sawchuk, Space-variant image motion degradation and restoration, *Proc. IEEE* **60**, 1972, 854–861.

86. A. A. Sawchuck, Space-variant image restoration by coordinate transformations, *J. Opt. Soc. Amer.* **64**, 1974, 138–144.

87. M. Schwartz and L. Shaw, "Signal Processing: Discrete Spectral Analysis, Detection and Estimation." McGraw-Hill, New York, 1975.

88. R. V. Shack, The influence of image motion and shutter operation on the photographic transfer function, *Appl. Opt.* **3**, 1964, 1171–1181.

89. D. Slepian and H. O. Pollak, Prolate spheroidal wave functions, Fourier analysis and uncertainty—I, *BSTJ* **40**, 1961, 43–63.

90. D. Slepian, Linear least squares filtering of distorted images, *J. Opt. Soc. Amer.* **57**, 1967, 918–922.

91. D. Slepian, Restoration of photographs blurred by image motion, *BSTJ* **46**, 1967, 2353–2362.

92. H. A. Smith, Improvement of the resolution of a linear scanning device, *SIAM J. Appl. Math.* **14**, 1966, 23–40.

93. S. C. Som, Analysis of the effects of linear smear, *J. Opt. Soc. Amer.* **61**, 1971, 859–864.

94. M. M. Sondhi, Image restoration: The removal of spatially invariant degradations, *Proc. IEEE* **60**, 1972, 842–853.

95. G. Stockham, T. M. Cannon, and R. B. Ingebretsen, Blind deconvolution through digital signal processing, *Proc. IEEE* **63**, 1975, 678–692.

96. P. A. Stokseth, Properties of a defocused optical system, *J. Opt. Soc. Amer.* **59**, 1969, 1314–1321.

97. M. G. Strintzis, Dynamic representation and recursive estimation of cyclic and two-dimensional processes. *IEEE Trans. Automat. Control* **AC-23**, 1978, 801–809.

98. J. A. Stuller, An algebraic approach to image restoration filter design, *Comput. Graphics Image Processing* **1**, 1972, 107–122.

99. J. A. Stuller and B. Kurz, Two-dimensional Markov representations of sampled images, *IEEE Trans. Commun.* **COM-24**, 1976, 1148–1152.

100. H. J. Trussell, The relationship between image restoration by the maximum a posteriori method and a maximum entropy method, *IEEE Trans. Acoust. Speech Signal Processing* **ASSP-28**, 1980, 114–117.

101. H. J. Trussell and B. R. Hunt, Image restoration of space-variant blurs by sectional method, *IEEE Trans. Acoust. Speech Signal Processing* **ASSP-26**, 1978, 608–609.

102. S. Twomey, On the numerical solution of Fredholm integral equations of the first kind by the inversion of the linear system produced by quadrature, *J. ACM* **10**, 1963, 97–101.

103. S. Twomey, The application of numerical filtering to the solution of integral equations encountered in indirect sensing measurements, *J. Franklin Inst.* **297**, 1965, 95–109.

104.   A. Whalen, "Detection of Signals in Noise." Academic Press, New York, 1971.
105.   J. W. Woods, Two-dimensional discrete Markovian fields, *IEEE Trans. Informat. Theory* **IT-18**, 1972, 232–240.
106.   J. W. Woods, Markov image modelling, *IEEE Trans. Automat. Control* **AC-23**, 1978, 846–850.
107.   J. W. Woods and C. H. Rademan, Kalman filtering in two dimensions, *IEEE Trans. Informat. Theory* **IT-23**, 1977, 473–482.
108.   E. C. Yeadon, R. A. Jones, and J. T. Kelley, Confidence limits for individual modulation transfer function measurements based upon the phase transfer function, *Photogr. Sci. Eng.* **12**, 1968, 244–250.

Chapter 8

Reconstruction

The problem of digitally reconstructing an image from its projections has become important during the past few years. There are many areas where practical applications of this problem arise. The application that has revolutionized diagnostic radiology is that of computerized tomography where x rays are used to generate the projection data for a cross section of the human body. From the projection data one reconstructs a cross-sectional image depicting with very high resolution the morphological details of the body in that cross section. Other medical applications are in the areas of nuclear medicine and ultrasonic imaging. In nuclear medicine this technique is used to map the distribution of the concentration of a gamma-ray emitting isotope in a given cross section of the body. With ultrasound the aim is similar to that with x rays, i.e., to construct cross-sectional images depicting morphological detail. The problem here is, however, made difficult by the refraction of ultrasound as it propagates through tissue. Nonmedical areas of application where images may be reconstructed from projections include radioastronomy, optical interferometry, electron microscopy, and geophysical exploration.

Mathematically the problem may be stated as follows. Let $f(x, y)$ represent a two-dimensional function. A line running through $f(x, y)$ is called a *ray* (Fig. 1). The integral of $f(x, y)$ along a ray is called a *ray integral* and a set of ray integrals forms a *projection*. A ray integral may be mathematically

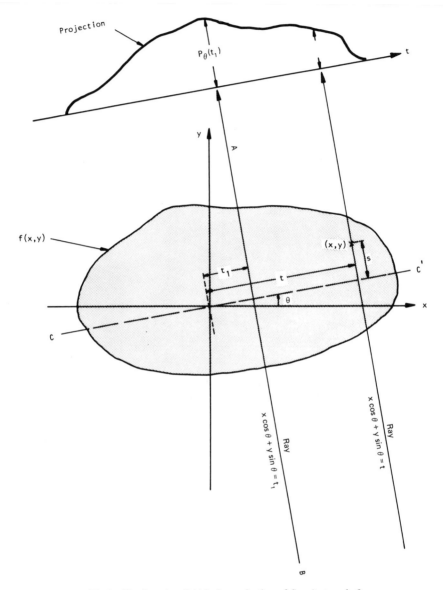

Fig. 1   The function $P_\theta(t)$ is the projection of $f(x, y)$ at angle θ.

defined as follows. The equation of line AB in Fig. 2 is given by

$$x \cos \theta + y \sin \theta = t_1$$

where t_1 is the perpendicular distance of the line from the origin. Clearly the integral of the function $f(x, y)$ along this line may be expressed as

$$P_\theta(t_1) = \int_{\text{ray } AB} f(x, y) \, ds = \int_{-\infty}^{\infty} \int_{-\infty}^{\infty} f(x, y) \, \delta(x \cos \theta + y \sin \theta - t_1) \, dx \, dy \tag{1}$$

The function $P_\theta(t)$ as a function of t (for a given value of θ) defines the parallel projection of $f(x, y)$ for angle θ. The two-dimensional function $P_\theta(t)$ is also called the *Radon transform* of $f(x, y)$. A projection taken along a set of parallel rays is called a *parallel projection*, two examples of which are shown in Fig. 2. One may also generate projections by integrating a function along a set of lines emanating from a point source as shown in Fig. 3. Such projections are called *fan-beam projections*. In this chapter we will be concerned with reconstructing an image $f(x, y)$ from its projections taken at various angles.

Most of the computer simulation results in this chapter will be shown for the image in Fig. 4a. This is the well-known Shepp and Logan [54] "head phantom," so called because of its use in testing the accuracy of reconstruction algorithms for their ability to reconstruct cross sections of the human head with x-ray tomography. (The human head is believed to place the greatest demands on the numerical accuracy and the freedom from artifacts of a reconstruction method.) The image in Fig. 4a is composed of ten ellipses, as illustrated in Fig. 4b. The parameters of these ellipses are given in Table 1.

A major advantage of using an image like Fig. 4a for computer simulation is that now one can write analytical expressions for the projections. The projection of an image composed of a number of ellipses is simply the sum of the projections for each of the ellipses. This follows from the linearity of the Radon transform. We will now present expressions for the projections of a single ellipse. Let $f(x, y)$ be as shown in Fig. 5a, i.e.,

$$f(x, y) = \rho \qquad \text{for } \frac{x^2}{A^2} + \frac{y^2}{B^2} \leq 1 \quad \text{(inside the ellipse)}$$

$$= 0 \qquad \text{otherwise} \qquad \text{(outside the ellipse)} \tag{2}$$

It is easy to show that the projections of such a function are given by

$$P_\theta(t) = \frac{2\rho AB}{a^2(\theta)} \sqrt{a^2(\theta) - t^2} \qquad \text{for } |t| \leq a(\theta)$$

$$= 0 \qquad \text{for } |t| > a(\theta) \tag{3}$$

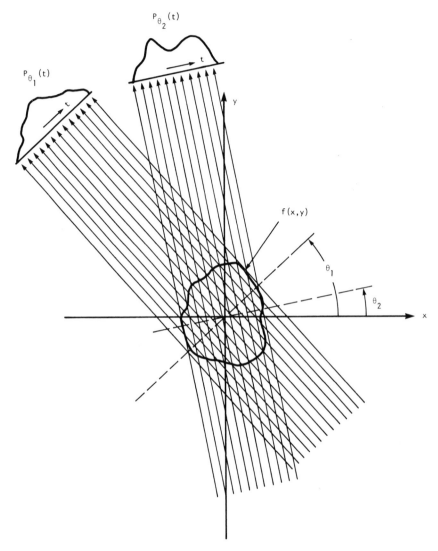

Fig. 2   This figure illustrates parallel projections.

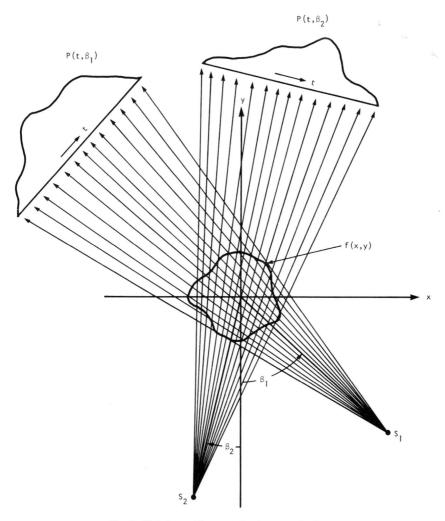

Fig. 3   This figure illustrates fan-beam projections.

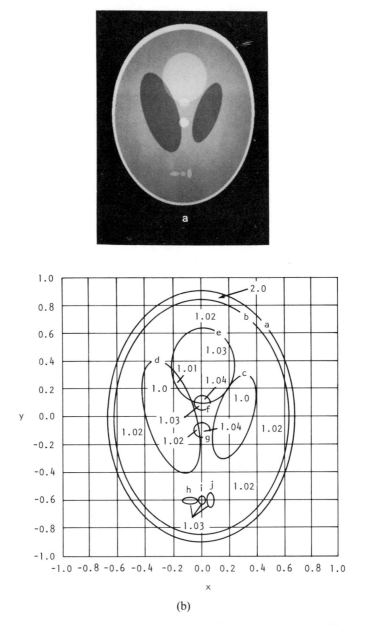

Fig. 4 (a) Shown here is the Shepp and Logan "head phantom" image. The computer simulation results shown in this chapter were generated on this image. (b) The Shepp and Logan phantom is a superposition of 10 ellipses shown here. On a scale of 0 to 2, the various gray levels in the phantom are also shown.

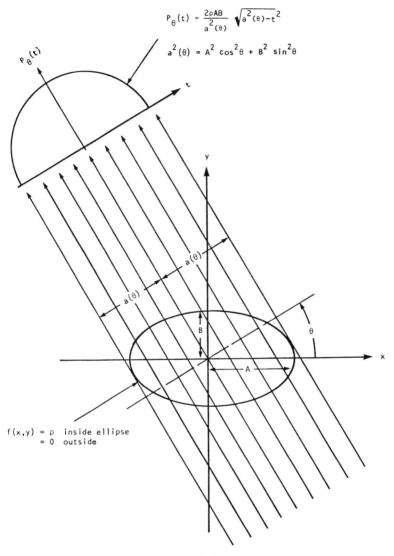

$$P_\theta(t) = \frac{2\rho AB}{a^2(\theta)} \sqrt{a^2(\theta) - t^2}$$

$$a^2(\theta) = A^2 \cos^2\theta + B^2 \sin^2\theta$$

$f(x,y) = \rho$ inside ellipse
         $= 0$ outside

(a)

Fig. 5 (a) This figure illustrates a projection of an ellipse. The gray level in the interior of the ellipse is ρ and zero outside. (b) Shown here is an ellipse with its center located at (x_1, y_1) and its major axis rotated by α.

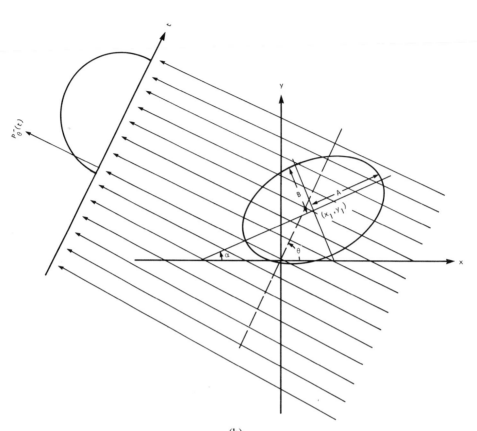

(b)

Fig. 5 (*Continued*)

TABLE 1

The Component Ellipses of the Shepp and Logan Head Phantom are Shown Here[a]

Ellipse	Coordinates of the center	A Major axis	B Minor axis	α Rotation angle	ρ Gray level
a	(0, 0)	0.92	0.69	0	2
b	(0, −0.0184)	0.874	0.6624	0	−0.98
c	(0.22, 0)	0.31	0.11	72°	−0.02
d	(−0.22, 0)	0.41	0.16	108°	−0.02
e	(0, 0.35)	0.25	0.21	0	0.01
f	(0, 0.1)	0.046	0.046	0	0.01
g	(0, −0.1)	0.046	0.046	0	0.01
h	(−0.08, −0.605)	0.046	0.046	0	0.01
i	(0, −0.605)	0.023	0.023	0	0.01
j	(0.06, −0.605)	0.046	0.023	90°	0.01

[a] The rotation angle α (shown in Fig. 5b) is measured counterclockwise from the *x*-axis.

where $a^2(\theta) = A^2 \cos^2 \theta + B^2 \sin^2 \theta$. Note that $a(\theta)$ is equal to the projection half-width as shown in Fig. 5a.

Now consider the ellipse described above centered at (x_1, y_1) and rotated by an angle α as shown in Fig. 5b. Let $P'(\theta, t)$ be the resulting projections. They are related to $P_\theta(t)$ in (3) by

$$P_\theta(t) = P_{\theta - \alpha}(t - s \cos(\gamma - \theta)) \tag{4}$$

where $s = \sqrt{x_1{}^2 + y_1{}^2}$ and $\gamma = \tan^{-1}(y_1/x_1)$.

8.1   METHODS FOR GENERATING PROJECTION DATA

In this section we will show how in various practical applications the projections of a two-dimensional function are generated.

8.1.1   Computerized X-Ray Tomography

Consider a parallel beam of x rays as shown in Fig. 6. Only those photons that are propagating in the direction depicted by the head of the arrow are considered to be a part of the beam. As the beam propagates, photons are continually lost from the beam either because they are deflected (scattered) or because they are absorbed. At each point both these losses are accounted for by a constant known as the linear attenuation coefficient, which is usually denoted by μ. Let N_{in} be the number of incident photons in the time span of a measurement (usually a few milliseconds). Within the same time instant let N_d be the number of photons exiting on side B (Fig. 6). If we assume that all the incident photons have the same energy, the relationship between N_d and N_{in} is given by

$$N_d = N_{in} \exp\left(-\int_{ray} \mu(x, y) \, ds\right) \tag{5}$$

where $\mu(x, y)$ is the linear attenuation coefficient at the point (x, y) and ds is an element of length along the ray. From the above equation

$$\int_{ray} \mu(x, y) \, ds = \ln \frac{N_{in}}{N_d} \tag{6}$$

The left-hand side of (6) is simply a ray integral for a projection of the function $\mu(x, y)$.

A basic assumption, that is always violated, was made above: all the x-ray photons have the same energy. The need for this assumption arises due

$$P_\theta(k\tau) = \int\limits_{\text{ray path AB}} \mu(x, y) \, ds = \ln \frac{N_{in}}{N_d}$$

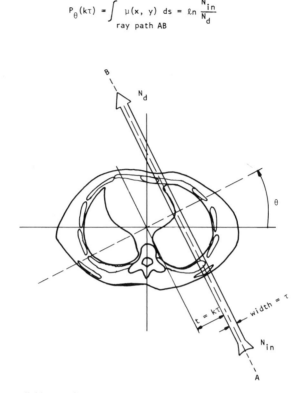

Fig. 6 A parallel beam of x rays propagating through a cross section of the human body.

to the dependence of the linear attenuation coefficient on energy. Since, in practice, the x-ray photons produced by an x-ray tube are never monoenergetic, Eq. (5) fails to be strictly valid as a relationship between the incident and the transmitted intensities. This causes the appearance of what are called polychromaticity artifacts in reconstructed images.

8.1.2   Computerized Emission Tomography

Here the aim is to make cross-sectional images of radioactive isotope distributions in the human body. (An isotope may be administered to a patient in the form of radiopharmaceuticals either by injections or by inhalation.) Radioactive isotopes are characterized by the emission of gamma-ray photons, a product of nuclear decay. Note that gamma-ray photons are indistinguishable from x-ray photons; different terms are used simply to

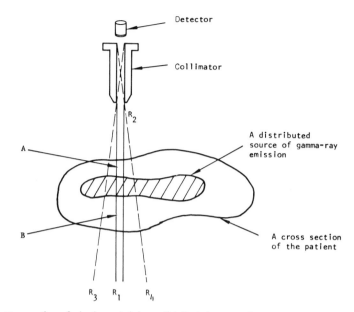

Fig. 7   A cross section of a body containing a distributed source of gamma rays.

indicate their origin. The concentration of an isotope in any cross-section changes with time due to radioactive decay, flow, and biochemical kinetics within the body. This implies that all the data for one cross-sectional image must be collected in a time short compared to the time constant associated with the changing concentration. But then this aspect also gives emission CT its greatest potential and utility in diagnostic medicine, because now by analyzing the images taken at different times for the same cross section one can determine the functional state of various organs in a patient's body.

   Figure 7 shows a cross section of a body with a distributed source of gamma rays in it. A very small, nevertheless macroscopic, element of this source may be considered to be an isotropic source of gamma rays. The number of gamma-ray photons emitted per second by such an element is proportional to the concentration of the source at that point. Assume that the collimator in front of the detector has infinite collimation, which means it accepts only those photons that travel toward it in the ray bundle $R_1 R_2$. (Infinite collimation, in practice, would imply an infinitely long time to make a statistically meaningful observation.) Then clearly the total number of photons recorded by the detector in a "statistically meaningful" time interval is proportional to the total concentration of the emitter in the ray $R_1 R_2$. In other words, it is a ray integral. By moving the detector collimator assembly to an adjacent position laterally, one may determine this integral for another ray parallel to $R_1 R_2$. After one such scan is completed, generating one projection, one may rotate the patient or the detector-collimator assembly and generate other projections. (One may in practice completely eliminate the lateral scans by using an array system.)

8.1.3 Ultrasound Computerized Tomography

With ultrasound one may either do time-of-flight or attenuation tomography. In time-of-flight tomography the reconstructed image represents the refractive-index parameter. The refractive index of a material at a point is defined as

$$n(x, y) = \frac{V_w}{V(x, y)} \tag{7}$$

where V_w and $V(x, y)$ are, respectively, the ultrasonic propagation velocities in water and at the point (x, y) in the material.

Now consider an ultrasonic pulse propagating from A to B in Fig. 8. It can be shown that [34]

$$\int_A^B [1 - n(x, y)] \, ds = -V_w \, T_d \tag{8}$$

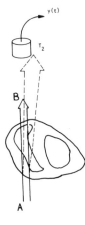

Fig. 8 The ray AB represents the propagation path of an ultrasonic pulse under ideal conditions. The dashed ray is the pictorial depiction of the fact that in actual practice there is always some refraction.

where T_d is the difference between the transit time through the material and the transit time when the material is replaced by water. T_d is positive if the former transit time is longer than the latter. Note that we have expressed the ray integral for $1 - n(x, y)$ rather than $n(x, y)$. To ensure that in the reconstructed image the background values are zero, one usually makes the image for $1 - n(x, y)$. [For a point in water outside the material we have $n(x, y) = 1$, so that $1 - n(x, y) = 0$.]

The ray integral is valid provided in Fig. 8 the ultrasonic beam travels along a straight line from A to B. In medical imaging this assumption is approximately satisfied only for soft-tissue structures. In parts of the body containing bone the severe beam refraction at tissue-bone interfaces makes it impossible to determine the ray integrals with any reasonable accuracy.

One can also make tomograms for the ultrasonic attenuation coefficient. In order to determine the ray integrals of the attenuation coefficient one must examine the spectral composition of the incident and transmitted waveforms [18, 36].

8.1.4 Other Applications

Other applications of image reconstruction from projections are in radio astronomy, electron microscopy, optical interferometry, and in the determination of the point spread functions of image degradations (the last application has already been discussed in Section 7.1.2). In radio astronomy [5, 6] the aim is to reconstruct the "brightness" distribution of a celestial source of radio waves from its strip integral measurement taken with an antenna beam which is much longer than the source is one direction but suitably narrow in the other. In electron microscopy one attempts to reconstruct the molecular structure of complex biomolecules from a series of transmission micrograms taken at various angles [15, 25]. In optical interferometry the aim is to determine (or reconstruct) the refractive index field of an optically transparent medium by measuring changes in optical path lengths of light rays due to their passage through the medium [4, 52, 55].

8.2 THE FOURIER SLICE THEOREM

Fundamental to a number of reconstruction techniques is the Fourier slice theorem. It relates the one-dimensional Fourier transform of a projection of a function $f(x, y)$ to the two-dimensional Fourier transform of $f(x, y)$.

Let $F(u, v)$ be the Fourier transform of the image $f(x, y)$. By definition

$$F(u, v) = \int_{-\infty}^{\infty} \int_{-\infty}^{\infty} f(x, y) e^{-j2\pi(ux + vy)} \, dx \, dy \tag{9}$$

Also let $S_\theta(w)$ be the Fourier transform of the projection $P_\theta(t)$; that is,

$$S_\theta(w) = \int_{-\infty}^{\infty} P_\theta(t) e^{-j2\pi wt} \, dt \tag{10}$$

Let us first consider the values of $F(u, v)$ on the line $v = 0$ in the uv-plane. From (9),

$$F(u, 0) = \int_{-\infty}^{\infty} \int_{-\infty}^{\infty} f(x, y) e^{-j2\pi ux} \, dx \, dy$$

$$= \int_{-\infty}^{\infty} \left[\int_{-\infty}^{\infty} f(x, y) \, dy \right] e^{-j2\pi ux} \, dx$$

$$= \int P_0(t) e^{-j2\pi ut} \, dt = S_0(w) \tag{11}$$

since $\int f(x, y) \, dy$ gives the projection of the image for $\theta = 0$. Also, note that for this projection x and t are the same.

The above result indicates that the values of the Fourier transform $F(u, v)$ on the line defined by $v = 0$ can be obtained by Fourier transforming the vertical projection of the image. This result can be generalized to show that if $F(w, \theta)$ denotes the values of $F(u, v)$ along a line at an angle θ with the u-axis as shown in Fig. 9, and if $S_\theta(w)$ is the Fourier transform of the projection $P_\theta(t)$, then

$$F(w, \theta) = S_\theta(w) \tag{12}$$

This can be proved as follows. Let $f(t, s)$ be the function $f(x, y)$ in the rotated coordinate system (t, s) in Fig. 9. The coordinates (t, s) are related to the (x, y) coordinates by

$$\begin{bmatrix} t \\ s \end{bmatrix} = \begin{bmatrix} \cos\theta & \sin\theta \\ -\sin\theta & \cos\theta \end{bmatrix} \begin{bmatrix} x \\ y \end{bmatrix} \tag{13}$$

Clearly,

$$P_\theta(t) = \int_{-\infty}^{\infty} f(t, s) \, ds \tag{14}$$

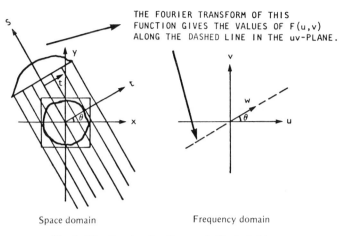

THE FOURIER TRANSFORM OF THIS
FUNCTION GIVES THE VALUES OF $F(u,v)$
ALONG THE DASHED LINE IN THE uv-PLANE.

Space domain   Frequency domain

Fig. 9   The Fourier slice theorem is illustrated here.

Therefore,

$$S_\theta(w) = \int_{-\infty}^{\infty} P_\theta(t)e^{-j2\pi wt}\, dt = \int_{-\infty}^{\infty} \int_{-\infty}^{\infty} f(t, s)\, ds\, e^{-j2\pi wt}\, dt \qquad (15)$$

Transforming the right-hand side of (15) into (x, y) coordinates we get

$$S_\theta(w) = \int_{-\infty}^{\infty} \int_{-\infty}^{\infty} f(x, y)e^{-j2\pi w(x\cos\theta + y\sin\theta)}\, dx\, dy$$

$$= F(u, v) \qquad \text{for} \quad u = w\cos\theta, v = w\sin\theta$$

$$= F(w, \theta)$$

which proves (12). This result is also known as the *projection slice theorem*.

The above result indicates that by taking the projections of an image at angles $\theta_1, \theta_2, \ldots, \theta_k$ and Fourier transforming each of these projections, we can determine the values of $F(u, v)$ on radial lines as shown in Fig. 10. If an infinite number of projections were taken then $F(u, v)$ would be known at all points in the uv-plane. Knowing $F(u, v)$, the image function $f(x, y)$ can be recovered by using the inverse Fourier transform:

$$f(x, y) = \int_{-\infty}^{\infty} \int_{-\infty}^{\infty} F(u, v)e^{j2\pi(ux + vy)}\, du\, dv \qquad (16)$$

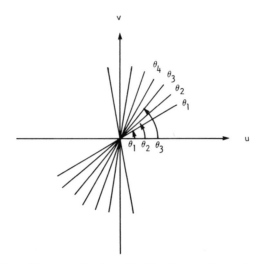

Fig. 10 The figure illustrates that by taking Fourier transforms of projections taken at different angles $\theta_1, \theta_2, \ldots, \theta_N, \ldots$, one can fill up the frequency domain.

If the function $f(x, y)$ is bounded by $-A/2 < x < A/2$ and $-A/2 < y < A/2$, for the purpose of computation (16) can be written as

$$f(x, y) = \frac{1}{A^2} \sum_m \sum_n F\left(\frac{m}{A}, \frac{n}{A}\right) \exp\left[j2\pi\left(\frac{m}{A}x + \frac{n}{A}y\right)\right]$$

$$\text{for} \quad -\frac{A}{2} < x < \frac{A}{2} \quad \text{and} \quad -\frac{A}{2} < y < \frac{A}{2} \quad (17)$$

Since in practice only a finite number of Fourier components will be known, we can write

$$f(x, y) \simeq \frac{1}{A^2} \sum_{m=-N/2}^{N/2} \sum_{n=-N/2}^{N/2} F\left(\frac{m}{A}, \frac{n}{A}\right) \exp\left[j2\pi\left(\frac{m}{A}x + \frac{n}{A}y\right)\right]$$

$$\text{for} \quad -\frac{A}{2} < x < \frac{A}{2} \quad \text{and} \quad -\frac{A}{2} < y < \frac{A}{2} \quad (18)$$

arbitrarily assuming N to be an even integer. It is clear that the spatial resolution in the reconstructed picture is determined by N. Equation (18) can be rapidly implemented by using the fast Fourier transform (FFT) algorithm provided the N^2 Fourier coefficients $F(m/A, n/A)$ are known.

In practice only a finite number of projections of an object can be taken. In that case the function $F(u, v)$ is only known along a finite number of radial lines such as in Fig. 10. In order to be able to use (18) one must then interpolate from these radial points to the points on a square grid. Theoretically, one can exactly determine the N^2 coefficients required in (18) provided as many values of the function $F(u, v)$ are known on some radial lines [15]. This calculation involves solving a large set of simultaneous equations, often leading to unstable solutions. It is more common to determine the values on the square grid by some kind of nearest-neighbor or linear interpolation from the radial points. Since the density of the radial points becomes sparser as one gets farther away from the center, the interpolation error also becomes larger. This implies that there is greater error in the calculation of the high-frequency components in an image than in the low-frequency ones, which results in some image degradation.

8.3 THE FILTERED-BACKPROJECTION ALGORITHM FOR PARALLEL PROJECTION DATA

The algorithm that is currently being used in almost all applications using x rays (or gamma rays) is the filtered-backprojection algorithm. It has been shown to be extremely accurate and amenable to fast implementation. We present it in this section for the case of parallel projection data. Fan projections will be considered in Section 8.6.

8.3.1 Theory

If, as before, (w, θ) are the polar coordinates in the uv-plane, the integral in (16) can be expressed as follows:

$$f(x, y) = \int_0^{2\pi} \int_0^\infty F(w, \theta)e^{j2\pi w(x \cos \theta + y \sin \theta)}w \, dw \, \theta$$

$$= \int_0^\pi \int_0^\infty F(w, \theta)e^{j2\pi w(x \cos \theta + y \sin \theta)}w \, dw \, d\theta$$

$$+ \int_0^\pi \int_0^\infty F(w, \theta + \pi)e^{j2\pi w(x \cos(\theta + \pi) + y \sin(\theta + \pi))}w \, dw \, d\theta$$

Using the property

$$F(w, \theta + \pi) = F(-w, \theta)$$

the above expression for $f(x, y)$ may be written as

$$f(x, y) = \int_0^\pi \left[\int_{-\infty}^\infty F(w, \theta) |w| e^{j2\pi wt} \, dw \right] d\theta$$

$$= \int_0^\pi \left[\int_{-\infty}^\infty S_\theta(w) |w| e^{j2\pi wt} \, dw \right] d\theta \tag{19}$$

where, as noted before,

$$t = x \cos \theta + y \sin \theta$$

and where we have used (12). The integral in (19) may be expressed as

$$f(x, y) = \int_0^\pi Q_\theta(x \cos \theta + y \sin \theta) \, d\theta \tag{20}$$

where

$$Q_\theta(t) = \int_{-\infty}^\infty S_\theta(w) |w| e^{j2\pi wt} \, dw \tag{21}$$

The above formulas for reconstruction say that from each projection $P_\theta(t)$ we first calculate a "filtered projection" $Q_\theta(t)$ by using (21), and then use (20) to reconstruct the function $f(x, y)$.

The parameter w has the dimension of spatial frequency. The integration in (21) must, in principle, be carried out over all the spatial frequencies. In practice the energy contained in the Fourier transform components above a certain frequency is negligible, so for all practical purposes the projections may be considered to be bandlimited. Let W be any frequency greater than the smallest beyond which the spectral energy in all the projections may be ignored. Then by using the sampling theorem, the projection $P_\theta(t)$ can be represented by

$$P_\theta(t) = \sum_{k=-\infty}^\infty P_\theta\left(\frac{k}{2W}\right) \frac{\sin 2\pi W(t - k/2W)}{2\pi W(t - k/2W)} \tag{22}$$

Substituting this in (10), we get

$$S_\theta(w) = \frac{1}{2W} \sum_{k=-\infty}^\infty P_\theta\left(\frac{k}{2W}\right) e^{-2j\pi w(k/2W)} b_W(w) \tag{23}$$

where

$$b_W(w) = 1, \qquad |w| \leqslant W$$

$$= 0, \qquad \text{otherwise}$$

Now if the projection functions are of finite order, which means they can be represented by $N + 1$ samples for some value of N, (23) reduces to

$$S_\theta(w) = \frac{1}{2W} \sum_{k=-N/2}^{N/2} P_\theta\left(\frac{k}{2W}\right) e^{-j2\pi w(k/2W)} b_W(w) \qquad (24)$$

We will arbitrarily assume N to be an even number. Noting that the functions $S_\theta(w)$ are zero outside the interval $(-W, W)$ of the spatial frequency axis, suppose in this interval we desire to know each $S_\theta(w)$ at a set of equi-spaced points given by

$$w = m\frac{2W}{N} \qquad \text{for} \quad m = -\frac{N}{2}, \ldots, 0, \ldots, \frac{N}{2}$$

Substituting these in (24), we get

$$S_\theta\left(m\frac{2W}{N}\right) = \frac{1}{2W} \sum_{k=-N/2}^{N/2} P_\theta\left(\frac{k}{2W}\right) e^{-j2\pi(mk/N)},$$

$$m = -\frac{N}{2}, \ldots, 0, \ldots, \frac{N}{2} \qquad (25)$$

The above equation is the familiar discrete Fourier transform (DFT) relationship and, therefore, can be rapidly evaluated by a fast Fourier transform (FFT) algorithm.

Given the samples of a projection, Eq. (25) gives the samples of its Fourier transform. The next step is to evaluate the "modified projection" $Q_\theta(t)$ digitally. Since the Fourier transforms $S_\theta(w)$ have been assumed to be bandlimited, (21) can be approximated by

$$Q_\theta(t) = \int_{-W}^{W} S_\theta(w)|w|e^{j2\pi wt}\, dw \simeq \frac{2W}{N} \sum_{m=-N/2}^{N/2} S_\theta\left(m\frac{2W}{N}\right)\left|m\frac{2W}{N}\right| e^{j2\pi m(2W/N)t} \qquad (26)$$

provided N is large enough. Again, if we want to determine the projections $Q_\theta(t)$ for only those t at which the projections $P_\theta(t)$ are sampled, we get

$$Q_\theta\left(\frac{k}{2W}\right) \simeq \left(\frac{2W}{N}\right) \sum_{m=-N/2}^{N/2} S_\theta\left(m\frac{2W}{N}\right)\left|m\frac{2W}{N}\right| e^{j2\pi(mk/N)},$$

$$k = -\frac{N}{2}, \ldots, -1, 0, 1, \ldots, \frac{N}{2} \qquad (27a)$$

By the above equation the function $Q_\theta(t)$ at the sampling points of the projection functions is given (approximately) by the inverse DFT of the product

of $S_\theta(m(2W/N))$ and $|m(2W/N)|$. From the standpoint of noise in the re-
constructed image superior results are usually obtained if one multiplies
$S_\theta(2W/N)|m(2W/N)|$ by a function such as a Hamming window [26]:

$$Q_\theta\left(\frac{k}{2W}\right) \simeq \left(\frac{2W}{N}\right) \sum_{n=-N/2}^{N \cdot 2} S_\theta\left(m\frac{2W}{N}\right)\left|m\frac{2W}{N}\right| G\left(m\frac{2W}{N}\right)e^{j2\pi(mk/N)} \quad (27b)$$

where $G(m(2W/N))$ represents the window function used. The purpose of the
window function is to deemphasize high frequencies which in many cases
represent mostly observation noise. By the familiar convolution theorem for
the case of discrete transforms, (27b) can be written as

$$Q_\theta\left(\frac{k}{2W}\right) \simeq \frac{2W}{N} P_\theta\left(\frac{k}{2W}\right) * \varphi\left(\frac{k}{2W}\right) \quad (28)$$

where $*$ denotes circular (periodic) convolution and where $\varphi(k/2W)$ is the
inverse DFT of the discrete function $|m(2W/N)| G(m(2W/N))$, $m = N/2, \ldots,$
$-1, 0, 1, \ldots, N/2$.

Clearly at the sampling points of the projections, the functions $Q_\theta(t)$
may be obtained either in the Fourier domain by using (26), or in the space
domain by using (28). The reconstructed picture $f(x, y)$ may then be obtained by the discrete approximation to the integral in (20), i.e.,

$$\hat{f}(x, y) = \frac{\pi}{K} \sum_{i=1}^{K} Q_{\theta_i}(x \cos \theta_i + y \sin \theta_i) \quad (29)$$

where the K angles θ_i are those for which the projections $P_\theta(t)$ are known.

Equation (29) calls for each filtered projection Q_{θ_i} to be "backprojected."
This can be explained as follows. To every point (x, y) in the image plane
there corresponds a value of $t(=x \cos \theta + y \sin \theta)$ for a given value of θ.
The contribution that Q_{θ_i} makes to the reconstruction at (x, y) depends
upon the value of t for that (x, y). This is further illustrated in Fig. 11. It is
easily seen that for the indicated angle θ_i, the value of $t = (x \cos \theta_i +
y \sin \theta_i)$ is the same for all (x, y) on the line LM. Therefore, the filtered pro-
jection Q_{θ_i} will make the same contribution to the reconstruction at all
these points. From this follows that in reconstruction each function $Q_{\theta_i}(t)$ is
smeared back over the image plane. The sum (multiplied by π/K) of all
such smearings results in the reconstruction image.

Note that the value of $x \cos \theta_i + y \sin \theta_i$ in (29) may not correspond to
one of the values of t for which Q_{θ_i} is determined in (27) or in (28). However,
Q_{θ_i} for such t may be approximated by suitable interpolation; often linear
interpolation is adequate.

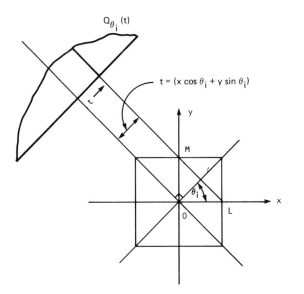

Fig. 11 In reconstruction the filtered projection $Q_{\theta_i}(t)$ makes the same contribution to all points (pixels) on line LM in the xy-plane.

Before concluding this subsection we would like to make two comments about the filtering operation in (21). First, note that (21) may be expressed in the t-domain as

$$Q_\theta(t) = \int P_\theta(\alpha)p(t - \alpha)\, d\alpha \tag{30}$$

where $p(t)$ is nominally the inverse Fourier transform of the $|w|$ function in the frequency domain. Since $|w|$ is not a square integrable function its inverse transform does not exist in an ordinary sense. However, one may examine the inverse Fourier transform of

$$|w|e^{-\varepsilon|w|} \tag{31}$$

as $\varepsilon \to 0$. The inverse Fourier transform of this function, denoted by $p_\varepsilon(t)$, is given by

$$p_\varepsilon(t) = \frac{\varepsilon^2 - (2\pi t)^2}{(\varepsilon^2 + (2\pi t)^2)^2} \tag{32}$$

This function is sketched in Fig. 12. Note that for large t we get $p_\varepsilon(t) \simeq -1/(2\pi t)^2$.

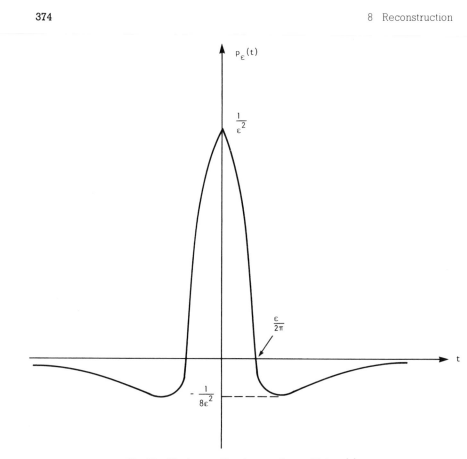

Fig. 12   The inverse Fourier transform of $|w|\,e^{-\varepsilon|w|}$.

Now we present our second comment about (21). This equation may also be written as

$$Q_\theta(t) = \int_{-\infty}^{\infty} j2\pi w S_\theta(w)\left[\frac{-j}{2\pi}\,\mathrm{sgn}(w)\right]e^{j2\pi wt}\,dw \tag{33}$$

where

$$\begin{aligned}
\mathrm{sgn}(w) &= \quad 1 \quad \text{for} \quad w > 0 \\
&= -1 \quad \text{for} \quad w < 0
\end{aligned} \tag{34}$$

By using the standard convolution theorem the above may be expressed as

$$Q_\theta(t) = \{\text{IFT of } j2\pi w S_\theta(w)\} * \left\{\text{IFT of } \frac{-j}{2\pi}\,\mathrm{sgn}(w)\right\} \tag{35}$$

where the symbol $*$ denotes convolution and the abbreviation IFT stands for inverse Fourier transform. The IFT of $j2\pi w S_\theta(w)$ is $(\partial/\partial t)P_\theta(t)$ while the IFT of $-j/2\pi\ \text{sgn}(w)$ is $1/t$. Therefore, the above result may be written as

$$Q_\theta(t) = \frac{1}{2\pi^2 t} * \frac{\partial P_\theta(t)}{\partial t} \tag{36}$$

$$= \text{Hilbert transform of } \frac{\partial P_\theta(t)}{\partial t} \tag{37}$$

Exercise 1.   Show analytically that when the projections of an image are backprojected without filtering, the point spread function of the resulting distortion in the reconstruction is $1/\sqrt{(x^2 + y^2)}$. [Hint: You may assume that $f(x, y) = \delta(x - x', y - y')$. The projections will now be given by $P_\theta(t) = \delta(t - t')$, where $t' = x'\cos\theta + y'\sin\theta$. Noting that $Q_\theta(t) = P_\theta(t)$, use (20) to get the desired result.]   ∎

8.3.2   Computer Implementation of the Algorithm

Let us assume that the projection data is sampled with a sampling interval of τ cm. We will further assume that there is no aliasing, which implies that in the transform domain the projections do not contain any energy outside the frequency interval $(-W, W)$, where

$$W = \frac{1}{2\tau} \quad \text{cycles/cm} \tag{38}$$

Let the sampled projections be represented by $P_\theta(k\tau)$, where k takes integer values. The theory presented in the preceding subsection says that for each sampled projection $P_\theta(k\tau)$ we must generate a filtered $Q_\theta(k\tau)$ by using the periodic (circular) convolution given by (27). Equation (27) is very attractive since it directly conforms to the definitions of the DFT and, if N is decomposable, possesses a fast FFT implementation. However, note that (27) is only valid when the projections are of finite bandwidth and finite order. Since these two assumptions (taken together) are not strictly satisfied, computer processing based on (27) usually leads to interperiod interference artifacts created when an aperiodic convolution [required by Eq. (21)] is implemented as a periodic convolution. This is illustrated in Fig. 13. Figure 13a shows a reconstruction of the image in Fig. 4a from 100 projections and 127 rays in each projection using Eqs. (27) and (29). Equation (27) was implemented with a base 2 FFT algorithm using 128 points. Figure 13b shows the reconstructed values on the horizontal line for $y = -0.605$ (see Fig. 4b). For comparison we have also shown the values on this line in the original image.

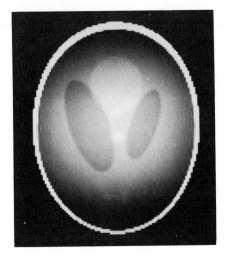

(a)

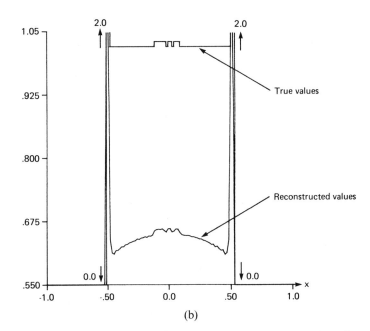

(b)

Fig. 13 (a) This reconstruction of the Shepp and Logan phantom shows the artifacts caused when the projection data are not adequately zero padded prior to FFT based implementation of the filtering operation in the filtered-backprojection algorithm. The dark regions at the top and the bottom of the reconstruction are the most visible of the artifacts here. This 128 × 128 reconstruction was made from 110 projections with 127 rays in each projection, (b) A numerical comparison of the true and the reconstructed values on the $y = -0.605$ line. (For the location of this line see Fig. 5b.) The "dishing" and the dc shift artifacts are quite evident in this comparison. (c) Shown here are the reconstructed values obtained on the $y = -0.605$ line if the 127 rays in each projection are zero-padded to 256 points before using the FFT's. The dishing caused by interperiod interference has disappeared; however, the dc shift still remains.

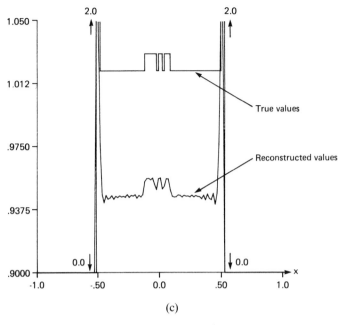

(c)

Fig. 13 (*Continued*)

The comparison illustrated in Fig. 13b shows that reconstruction based on Eqs. (27a) and (29) introduces a slight "dishing" and a dc shift in the image. These artifacts are partly caused by the periodic convolution implied by (27) and partly by the fact that the implementations in (27) "zero out" all the information in the continuous frequency domain in the cell represented by $m = 0$, whereas the theory [Eq. (21)] calls for such "zeroing out" to occur at only *one* frequency, viz., $w = 0$. The contribution to these artifacts by the interperiod interference can be *eliminated* be adequately zero padding the projection data before using the implementations in (27a) or (27b). Zero padding of the projections also reduces, *but never completely eliminates*, the contribution to the artifacts by the zeroing out of the information in the $m = 0$ cell in (27). This is because zero padding in the space domain causes the cell size to get smaller in the frequency domain. (If N_{FFT} points are used for performing the discrete Fourier transform, the size of each sampling cell in the frequency domain is equal to $1/N_{FFT}\tau$.) To illustrate the effect of zero padding, the 127 rays in each projection in the preceding example were padded with 129 zeroes to make the data string 256 elements long. These data were transformed by an FFT algorithm and filtered with a $|w|$ function as before. The $y = -0.605$ line through the reconstruction is shown in Fig. 13c. The dishing distortion is less severe now.

We will now show that the artifacts mentioned above can be eliminated by the following alternative implementation of (21), which does not require the approximation used in the discrete representation of (26). When the highest frequency in the projections is finite [as given by (38)], Eq. (21) may be expressed as

$$Q_\theta(t) = \int_{-\infty}^{\infty} S_\theta(w)H(w)e^{j2\pi wt}\, dw \tag{39}$$

where

$$H(w) = |w|b_W(w) \tag{40}$$

where, again,

$$\begin{aligned} b_W(w) &= 1, & |w| \le W \\ &= 0, & \text{otherwise} \end{aligned}$$

$H(w)$, shown in Fig. 14, represents the transfer function of a filter with which the projections must be processed. The impulse response, $h(t)$, of this filter is given by the inverse Fourier transform of $H(w)$ and is

$$\begin{aligned} h(t) &= \int_{-\infty}^{\infty} H(w)e^{j2\pi wt}\, dw \\ &= \frac{1}{2\tau^2}\frac{\sin 2\pi t/2\tau}{2\pi t/2\tau} - \frac{1}{4\tau^2}\left(\frac{\sin \pi t/2\tau}{\pi t/2\tau}\right)^2 \end{aligned} \tag{41}$$

where we have used (38). Since the projection data are measured with a sampling interval of τ, for digital processing the impulse response need only be known with the same sampling interval. The samples, $h(n\tau)$, of $h(t)$ are given by

$$h(n\tau) = \begin{cases} \dfrac{1}{4\tau^2}, & n = 0 \\[2mm] 0, & n \text{ even} \\[2mm] -\dfrac{1}{n^2\pi^2\tau^2}, & n \text{ odd} \end{cases} \tag{42}$$

This function is shown in Fig. 15.

Since both $P_\theta(t)$ and $h(t)$ are now bandlimited functions, they may be expressed as

$$P_\theta(t) = \sum_{k=-\infty}^{\infty} P_\theta(k\tau)\frac{\sin 2\pi W(t - k\tau)}{2\pi W(t - k\tau)}, \quad h(t) = \sum_{k=-\infty}^{\infty} h(k\tau)\frac{\sin 2\pi W(t - k\tau)}{2\pi W(t - k\tau)} \tag{43}$$

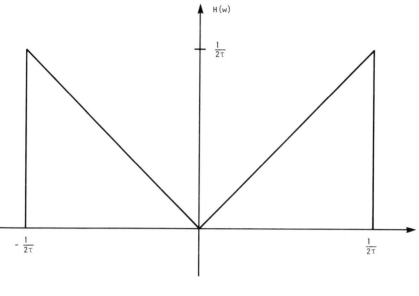

Fig. 14 The transfer function of the filter used on projections that are bandlimited to a frequency $1/2\tau$.

By the convolution theorem (39) can be written as

$$Q_\theta(t) = \int_{-\infty}^{\infty} P_\theta(t')h(t - t') \, dt' \tag{44}$$

Substituting (43) in (44) we get the following result for the values of the filtered projections at the sampling points:

$$Q_\theta(n\tau) = \tau \sum_{k=-\infty}^{\infty} h(n\tau - k\tau)P_\theta(k\tau) \tag{45}$$

In practice each projection is of only finite extent. Suppose that each $P_\theta(k\tau)$ is zero outside the index range $k = 0, 1, \ldots, N - 1$. We may now write the following two equivalent forms of (45):

$$Q_\theta(n\tau) = \tau \sum_{k=0}^{N-1} h(n\tau - k\tau)P_\theta(k\tau), \qquad n = 0, 1, \ldots, N - 1 \tag{46a}$$

or

$$Q_\theta(n\tau) = \tau \sum_{k=-(N-1)}^{N-1} h(k\tau)P_\theta(n\tau - k\tau), \qquad n = 0, 1, \ldots, N - 1 \tag{46b}$$

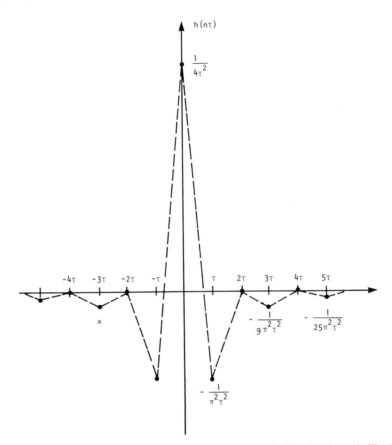

Fig. 15 The unit sample response corresponding to the transfer function shown in Fig. 14.

Equation (46) implies that in order to determine $Q_\theta(n\tau)$ the length of the sequence $h(n\tau)$ used should be from $n = -(N - 1)$ to $n = (N - 1)$. It is important to realize that the results obtained by using (46b) are not identical to those obtained by using (27a). This is because the discrete Fourier transform of the sequence $h(n\tau)$ with n taking values in a finite range [such as when n ranges from $-(N - 1)$ to $(N - 1)$] is not the sequence $|k[(2W)/N]|$. While the latter sequence is zero at $k = 0$, the DFT of $h(n\tau)$ with n ranging from $-(N - 1)$ to $(N - 1)$ is nonzero at this point. This is illustrated in Fig. 16.

The discrete convolution in (46) may be implemented directly on a general purpose computer. However, it is much faster to implement it in the frequency domain using FFT algorithms. [By using specially designed hard-

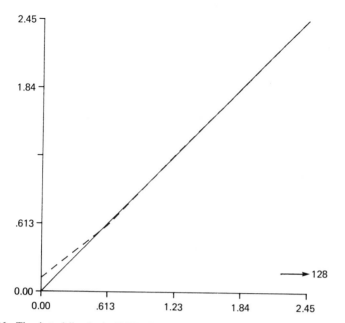

Fig. 16 The dotted line is the DFT of the truncated $h(n\tau)$ sequence. The solid line is the w function.

ware, direct implementation of (46) can be made as fast as or faster than the frequency domain implementation.] For the frequency domain implementation one has to keep in mind the fact that one can now only perform periodic (or circular) convolutions, whereas the convolution required in (46) is aperiodic. To eliminate the interperiod interference artifacts inherent to periodic convolution we pad the projection data with a sufficient number of zeroes. It can easily be shown [32] that if we pad each $P_\theta(k\tau)$ with zeroes so that it is $(2N - 1)$ elements long, we avoid interperiod interference over the N samples of $Q_\theta(k\tau)$. Of course, if one wants to use the base 2 FFT algorithm, which is most often the case, the sequences $P_\theta(k\tau)$ and $h(k\tau)$ have to be zero-padded so that each is $(2N - 1)_2$ elements long, where $(2N - 1)_2$ is the smallest integer that is a power of 2 and that is greater than or equal to $2N - 1$. Therefore, the frequency domain implementation may be expressed as

$$Q_\theta(n\tau) = \tau \times \text{IFFT}\{\text{FFT}(P_\theta(n\tau) \text{ with ZP}) \times \text{FFT}(h(n\tau) \text{ with ZP})\} \quad (47a)$$

where FFT and IFFT denote, respectively, the fast Fourier transform and the inverse fast Fourier transform; and ZP stands for zero padding. One usually obtains surperior reconstructions when some smoothing is also incorporated in Eqs. (46) and (47a). For example, in (47a) smoothing may be implemented

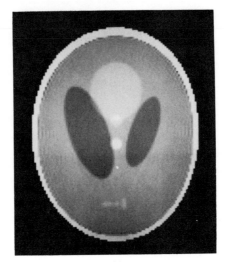

(a)

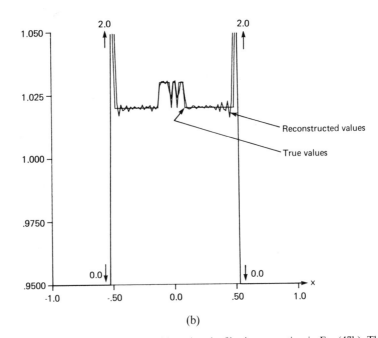

(b)

Fig. 17 (a) Reconstruction obtained by using the filtering operation in Eq. (47b). The 127 rays in the projections were zero padded so that each projection was 256 elements long. The unit sample response $h(n\tau)$ in Eq. (42) was used with n ranging from -128 to $+127$, yielding 256 points for this function. The number of projections used was 100 and the display matrix size 128×128. (b) A numerical comparison on the $y = -0.605$ line of the reconstruction in (a) with the original in Fig. 5a. Note that the dishing and dc shift artifacts so visible in Figs. 13b and 13c have disappeared.

by multiplying the product of the two FFTs by a Hamming window. When such a window is incorporated, (47a) may be written as

$$Q_\theta(n\tau) = \tau \times \text{IFFT}\{\text{FFT}(P_\theta(n\tau) \text{ with ZP}) \times \text{FFT}(h(n\tau) \text{ with ZP})$$

$$\times \text{ smoothing window}\} \qquad (47b)$$

After the filtered projections $Q_\theta(n\tau)$ are determined with the alternative implementation presented here, the rest of the procedure for reconstructing the image is the same as in the preceding subsection. That is, we use (29) for backprojections and their summation. Again, as before, for a given (x, y) and θ_i the argument $x \cos \theta_i + y \sin \theta_i$ may not correspond to one of the $k\tau$ at which Q_{θ_i} is known. This will call for interpolation and, often, linear interpolation is adequate. Sometimes, in order to eliminate the computations required for interpolation, preinterpolation of the functions $Q_\theta(t)$ is also used. In this technique, which can be combined with the computation in (47), prior to backprojection the function $Q_\theta(t)$ is preinterpolated onto 10 to 1000 times the number of points in the projection data. From this dense set of points one simply retains the nearest neighbor to obtain the value of Q_{θ_i} at $x \cos \theta_i + y \sin \theta_i$. A variety of techniques are available for preinterpolation [53]. In one method, prior to performing the IFFT, the *frequency domain function* is padded with a large number of zeros. The inverse transform of this sequence yields the preinterpolated Q_θ. It was recently shown [37] that if the data sequence contains "fractional" frequencies this approach may lead to large errors especially near the beginning and the end of the data sequence. Note that with preinterpolation and with appropriate programming, the backprojection for parallel projection data can be accomplished with virtually no multiplications.

Using the implementation in (47a), Fig. 17b shows the reconstructed values on the line $y = -0.605$ for the image in Fig. 4a. Comparing with Fig. 13d, we see that the dc shift and the dishing have been eliminated. Figure 17a shows the complete reconstruction. The number of rays used in each projection was 127 and the number of projections was 100. To make the convolutions aperiodic the projection data were padded with zeroes to make each projection 256 elements long.

8.4 ALIASING ARTIFACTS IN RECONSTRUCTED IMAGES

Figure 18 shows sixteen reconstructions of an ellipse with various values of K, the number of projections, and N, the number of rays in each projection. The projections for the ellipse were generated by using (3). The gray level inside the ellipse [ρ in Eq. (2)] was 1 and the background 0. To bring out all

Number of projections

K

64   128   256   512

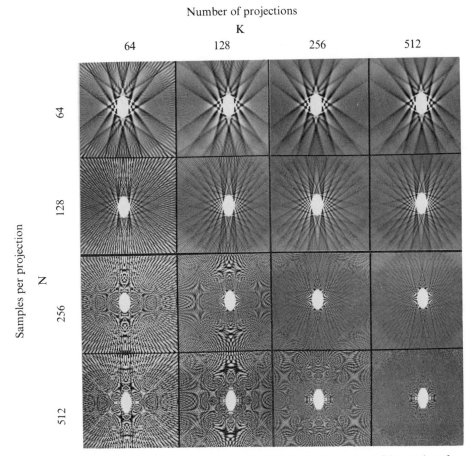

Fig. 18 Sixteen 128 × 128 reconstructions of an ellipse for various values of the number of projections and the number of rays in each projection. The reconstructions were windowed for the purpose of display to bring out the aliasing streaks and Moiré artifacts.

the artifacts the reconstructed images were windowed between 0.1 and −0.1. (In other words, all the gray levels above 0.1 were set at white and all below −0.1 at black.) The images in Fig. 18 are displayed on a 128 × 128 matrix. Figure 19 is a graphical depiction of the reconstructed numerical values on the middle horizontal lines for two of the images in Fig. 18. From Figs. 18 and 19 the following artifacts are evident: Gibbs phenomena, streaks, and Moiré patterns. In this section we will discuss these artifacts and their sources.

We will show that the streaks evident in Fig. 18 for the cases when N is small and K is large are caused by aliasing errors in the projection data.

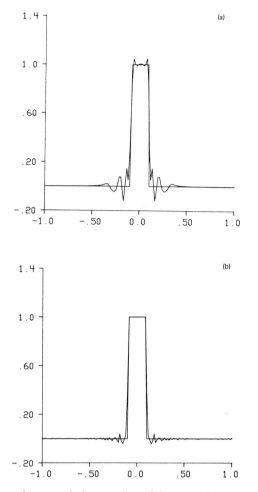

Fig. 19 This figure is a numerical comparison of the true and reconstructed values on the middle horizontal lines in two of the reconstructions in Fig. 18. The jagged lines are the reconstructed values, while the straight lines are the true values: (a) 512 projections with 64 rays in each; (b) 512 projections with 512 rays in each.

Note that a fundamental problem with tomographic images in general is that the objects (in this case an ellipse), and therefore their projections, are not bandlimited. In other words, the bandwidth of the projection data exceeds the highest frequency that can be recorded at a given sampling rate. To illustrate how aliasing errors enter the projection data, assume that the Fourier transform $S_\theta(f)$ of a projection $P_\theta(t)$ looks as shown in Fig. 20a. The bandwidth of this function is B as shown there. Let us choose a sampling

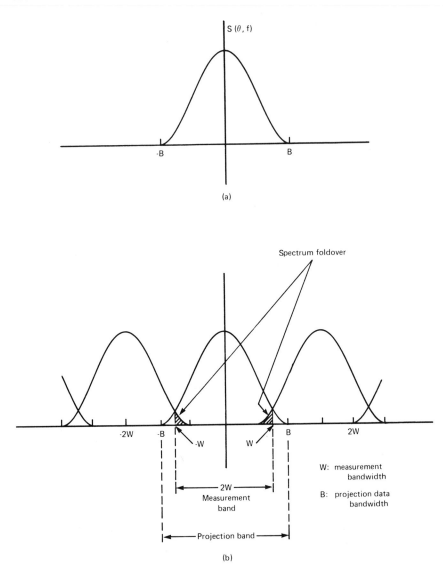

Fig. 20   Depiction of aliasing distortion. (a) $S(\theta, f)$ is the Fourier transform of the true projection at angle θ. (b) The sum of the replications of $S(\theta, f)$ are shown here. The sum of these replications constitutes the Fourier transform of the sampled projection data.

interval τ for sampling the projection. By the discussion in Chapter 4, with this sampling interval we can associate a measurement bandwidth W which is equal to $1/2\tau$. We will assume that $W < B$. By the discussion in Section 4.1.1 it follows that the Fourier transform of the *samples* of the projection will be as shown in Fig. 20b. We see that the information within the measurement band is contaminated by the tails (shaded areas) of the higher and lower replications of the original Fourier transform. This contaminating information constitutes the aliasing errors in the sampled projection data. These contaminating frequencies constitute the aliased spectrum.

Backprojection is a linear process so the final image can be thought of as made up of two functions. One is the image made from the bandlimited projections degraded primarily by the finite number of projections. The second is the image made from the aliased portion of the spectrum in each projection.

The reconstruction corresponding to the aliased spectrum can be seen by itself by subtracting the transforms of the sampled projections from the corresponding theoretical transforms of the original projections. Then if this result is filtered as before (with the bandlimited $|w|$ function) the reconstructed image will be that due to the aliased spectrum. We performed a computer simulation study along these lines for an elliptical object. In order to present the result of this study we first show in Fig. 21a the reconstruction of an ellipse for $N = 64$. (The number of projections was 512 and will remain the same for the discussion here.) We subtracted the transform of each projection for the $N = 64$ case from the corresponding transform for $N = 1024$ case. The latter was assumed to be the true transform because the projections are oversampled (at least in comparison with with the $N = 64$ case). The reconstruction obtained from the difference data is shown in Fig. 21b. Figure 21c is the bandlimited image obtained by subtracting the aliased spectrum image of Fig. 21b from the complete image shown in Fig. 21a. Figure 21c is the reconstruction that would be obtained provided the projection data for the $N = 64$ case were truly bandlimited (i.e., did not suffer from aliasing errors after sampling). The aliased-spectrum reconstruction in Fig. 21b and the absence of streaks in Fig. 21c prove our point that when the number of projections is large, the streaking artifacts are caused by aliasing errors in the projection data.

The thin streaks that are evident in Fig. 18 for the cases of large N and small K (e.g., when $N = 512$ and $K = 64$) are caused by an insufficient number of projections. It is easily shown that when only a small number of filtered projections of a small object are backprojected, the result is a star shaped pattern. This is illustrated in Fig. 22 where in (a) are shown four projections of a point object, in (b) the filtered projections, and in (c) their back-projections.

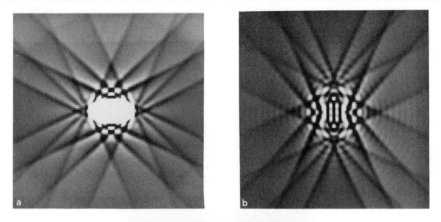

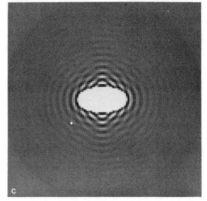

Fig. 21 (a) Reconstruction of an ellipse with 512 projections and 64 rays in each projection. (b) Reconstruction from only the aliased frequencies in each projection. Note that the streaks exactly match those in (a). (c) Image obtained by subtracting (b) from (a). This is the reconstruction that would be obtained, provided the data for the $N = 64$ case were truly bandlimited.

The reader may have noticed that the thin streaks caused by an insufficient number of projections (see, e.g., the image for $N = 512$ and $K = 64$ in Fig. 18) appear broken. This is caused by two-dimensional aliasing due to the display grid being only 128×128. When, say, $N = 512$, the highest frequency in each projection can be 256 cycles per projection length; whereas the highest frequency that can be displayed on the image grid is 64 cycles per image width (or height). The effect of this two-dimensional aliasing is very pronounced in the left three images for the $N = 512$ row and the left two images for the $N = 256$ case in Fig. 12. As mentioned in Chapter 4 the artifacts generated by this two-dimensional aliasing are also called Moiré patterns.

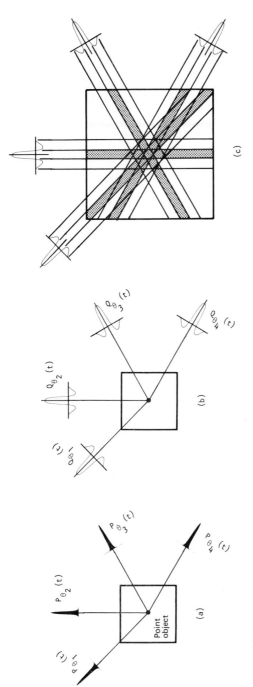

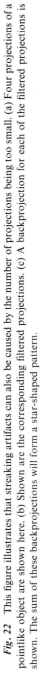

Fig. 22 This figure illustrates that streaking artifacts can also be caused by the number of projections being too small. (a) Four projections of a pointlike object are shown here. (b) Shown are the corresponding filtered projections. (c) A backprojection for each of the filtered projections is shown. The sum of these backprojections will form a star-shaped pattern.

8.5 NOISE IN RECONSTRUCTED IMAGES

8.5.1 The Continuous Case

Consider the case where each projection, $P_\theta(t)$, is corrupted by additive noise $v_\theta(t)$. The measured projections, $P_{\theta_m}(t)$, are now given by

$$P_\theta{}^m(t) = P_\theta(t) + v_\theta(t) \tag{48}$$

We will assume that the noise is a stationary zero-mean random process and that its values are uncorrelated for any two rays in the system. Therefore,

$$E\{v_{\theta_1}(t_1)v_{\theta_2}(t_2)\} = S_0\,\delta(\theta_1 - \theta_2)\,\delta(t_1 - t_2) \tag{49}$$

The reconstruction from the measured projection data is obtained by first filtering each projection:

$$Q_\theta{}^m(t) = \int_{-\infty}^{\infty} S_\theta{}^m(w)|w|G(w)e^{j2\pi wt}\,dw \tag{50}$$

where $S_\theta{}^m(w)$ is the Fourier transform of $P_\theta{}^m(t)$ and $G(w)$ is the smoothing filter used; and then backprojecting the filtered projections:

$$\hat{f}(x, y) = \int_0^\pi Q_\theta{}^m(x\cos\theta + y\sin\theta)\,d\theta \tag{51}$$

where $\hat{f}(x, y)$ is the reconstructed approximation to the original image $f(x, y)$. For the purpose of noise calculations, we substitute (50) in (51) and write

$$\hat{f}(x, y) = \int_0^\pi \int_{-\infty}^{\infty} [S_\theta(w) + E_\theta(w)]|w|G(w)e^{j2\pi w(x\cos\theta + y\sin\theta)}\,dw\,d\theta \tag{52}$$

where, as before, $S_\theta(w)$ is the Fourier transform of the ideal projection $P_\theta(t)$, and $E_\theta(w)$ is the Fourier transform of the additive noise, $v_\theta(t)$. [Here we assume $E_\theta(w)$ exists in some sense. Note that in spite of the infinite integration limits we are only dealing with projections with finite support.] Clearly,

$$E_\theta(w) = \int_{-\infty}^{\infty} v_\theta(t)e^{-j2\pi wt}\,dt \tag{53}$$

from which we can write

$$E\{E_{\theta_1}(w_1)E_{\theta_2}^*(w_2)\} = \int_{-\infty}^{\infty}\int_{-\infty}^{\infty} E\{v_{\theta_1}(t_1)v_{\theta_2}(t_2)\}e^{-j2\pi(w_1t_1 - w_2t_2)}\,dt_1\,dt_2$$

$$= S_0\,\delta(w_1 - w_2)\,\delta(\theta_1 - \theta_2) \tag{54}$$

where we have used (49).

Since $E_\theta(w)$ is random, the reconstructed image given by (52) is also random. The mean value of $\hat{f}(x, y)$ is given by

$$E\{\hat{f}(x, y)\} = \int_0^\pi \int_{-\infty}^\infty [S_\theta(w) + E\{E_\theta(w)\}] |w| G(w) e^{j2\pi w(x \cos \theta + y \sin \theta)} \, dw \, d\theta$$

(55)

Since we are dealing with zero-mean noise, $E\{v_\theta(t)\} = 0$; hence, from (53) we get $E\{E_\theta(w)\} = 0$. Substituting this in (55), we get

$$E\{\hat{f}(x, y)\} = \int_0^\pi \int_{-\infty}^\infty S_\theta(w) |w| G(w) e^{j2\pi w(x \cos \theta + y \sin)} \, dw \, d\theta$$

(56)

The variance of noise at a point (x, y) in the reconstructed image is given by

$$\sigma^2_{\text{recon}}(x, y) = E\{\hat{f}(x, y) - E\{\hat{f}(x, y)\}\}^2$$

(57)

Substituting (52) and (56), we get

$$\sigma^2_{\text{recon}}(x, y) = E\left\{\left[\int_0^\pi \int_{-\infty}^\infty E_\theta(w) |w| G(w) e^{j2\pi w(x \cos \theta + y \sin \theta)} \, dw \, d\theta\right]^2\right\}$$

$$= E\left\{\left[\int_0^\pi \int_{-\infty}^\infty E_\theta(w) |w| G(w) e^{j2\pi w(x \cos \theta + y \sin \theta)} \, dw \, d\theta\right]\right.$$

$$\left. \times \left[\int_0^\pi \int_{-\infty}^\infty E_\theta(w) |w| G(w) e^{j2\pi w(x \cos \theta + y \sin \theta)} \, dw \, d\theta\right]^*\right\}$$

$$= \pi S_0 \int_{-\infty}^\infty |w|^2 |G(w)|^2 \, dw$$

(58)

where we have used (54). Therefore, we may write

$$\frac{\sigma^2_{\text{recon}}}{S_0} = \pi \int_{-\infty}^\infty |w|^2 |G(w)|^2 \, dw$$

(59)

where we have dropped the (x, y) dependence of σ^2_{recon} since it has turned out to be independent of position in the picture plane.

Equation (59) says that in order to reduce the variance of noise in a reconstructed image, the filter function $G(w)$ must be chosen such that the area under the square of $|w| G(w)$ is as small as possible. But note that if there is to be no image distortion $|w| G(w)$ must be as close to $|w|$ as possible. Therefore, the choice of $G(w)$ depends upon the desired tradeoff between image distortion and noise variance.

We will conclude this subsection by presenting a brief description of the spectral density of noise in a reconstructed image. To keep our presentation simple we will assume that the projections consist only of zero-mean white noise, $v_\theta(t)$. The reconstructed image from the noise projections is given by

$$\hat{f}(x, y) = \int_0^\pi \int_{-\infty}^\infty E_\theta(w)|w|G(w)e^{j2\pi w(x\cos\theta + y\sin\theta)} \, dw \, d\theta$$

$$= \int_0^{2\pi} \int_0^\infty E_\theta(w)w \, G(w)e^{j2\pi w(x\cos\theta + y\sin\theta)} \, dw \, d\theta$$

where as before $E_\theta(w)$ is the Fourier transform of $v_\theta(t)$. Let $R(\alpha, \beta)$ be the autocorrelation function of the reconstructed image:

$$R(\alpha, \beta) \equiv E\{\hat{f}(x + \alpha, y + \beta)\hat{f}(x, y)\} = E\{\hat{f}(x + \alpha, y + \beta)\hat{f}^*(x, y)\}$$

$$= S_0 \int_0^{2\pi} d\theta \int_0^\infty dw \, w^2 |G(w)|^2 \, e^{j2\pi w(\alpha\cos\theta + \beta\sin\theta)} \tag{60}$$

From this one can show that the spectral density of the reconstructed noise is dependent only on the distance from the origin in the frequency domain and is given by

$$S_v(w, \theta) = S_0|G(w)|^2 w, \quad w \geqslant 0, \quad 0 < \theta \leqslant 2\pi \tag{61}$$

This may be shown by first expressing the result for the autocorrelation function in polar coordinates:

$$R(r, \varphi) = S_0 \int_0^\pi d\theta \int_0^\infty dw \, w^2 |G(w)|^2 e^{j2\pi wr\cos(\theta - \varphi)} \tag{62}$$

$$= S_0 \int_0^\infty w|G(w)|^2 w J_0(2\pi wr) \, dw \tag{63}$$

and recognizing the Hankel transform relationship (see Chapter 2) between the autocorrelation function and the spectral density.

8.5.2   The Discrete Case

Although the continuous case does bring out the dependence of the noise variance in the reconstructed image on the filter used for the projection data, it is based on a somewhat unrealistic assumption. The assumption of stationarity which led to (49) implies that in any projection the variance of measurement noise for each ray is the same. This is almost never true in practice. The variance of noise is often signal dependent and this has an important bearing on the structure of noise in the reconstructed image.

As an illustration of the case of signal-dependent noise consider x-ray computerized tomography. Let τ be the sampling interval and also the width of the x-ray beam, as shown in Fig. 6. If the width τ of the beam is small enough the integral of the attenuation function $\mu(x, y)$ along the dashed line AB in Fig. 6 is given by (1) and (6):

$$P_\theta(t) \equiv \int_{\text{ray path } AB} \mu(x, y)\, ds = \ln N_{\text{in}} - \ln N_\theta(k\tau) \tag{64}$$

where $N_\theta(k\tau)$ denotes the value of N_d for the ray at location $(\theta, k\tau)$ as shown in the figure. Randomness in the measurement of $P_\theta(t)$ is introduced by statistical fluctuations in $N_\theta(k\tau)$. Note that in practice only $N_\theta(k\tau)$ is measured directly. The value of N_{in} for all rays is inferred by monitoring the x-ray source with a reference detector and from the knowledge of the spatial distribution of emitted x rays. It is usually safe to assume that the reference x-ray flux is large enough so that N_{in} may be considered to be known with negligible error. In the rest of the discussion here we will assume that for each ray-integral measurement N_{in} is a known deterministic constant, while on the other hand the directly measured quantity $N_\theta(k\tau)$ is a random variable. The randomness of $N_\theta(k\tau)$ is statistically described by the Poisson probability function [58]:

$$p\{N_\theta(k\tau)\} = \frac{[\overline{N}_\theta(k\tau)]^{N_\theta(k\tau)}}{N_\theta(k\tau)!}\, e^{-\overline{N}_\theta(k\tau)} \tag{65}$$

where $p\{\cdot\}$ denotes the probability and $\overline{N}_\theta(k\tau)$ the expected value of the measurement:

$$\overline{N}_\theta(k\tau) = E\{N_\theta(k\tau)\} \tag{66}$$

The distribution being Poisson the variance of each measurement is given by

$$\text{variance}\{N_\theta(k\tau)\} = \overline{N}_\theta(k\tau) \tag{67}$$

Because of the randomness in $N_\theta(k\tau)$, the true value of $P_\theta(k\tau)$ will differ from its measured value which will be denoted by $P_\theta^m(k\tau)$. To bring out this distinction we reexpress (64) as follows:

$$P_\theta^m(k\tau) = \ln N_{\text{in}} - \ln N_\theta(k\tau) \tag{68}$$

and

$$P_\theta(k\tau) = \int_{\text{ray}} \mu(x, y)\, ds \tag{69}$$

By interpreting $e^{-P_\theta(k\tau)}$ as the probability that (along a ray such as the one shown in Fig. 6) a photon entering the object from side A will emerge (without scattering or absorption) at side B, one can show that

$$\overline{N}_\theta(k\tau) = N_{\text{in}}\, e^{-P_\theta(k\tau)} \tag{70}$$

We will now assume that all fluctuations (departures from the mean) in $N_\theta(k\tau)$ that have a significant probability of occurrence are much less than the mean. With this assumption and using (64) and (65) it is easily shown that

$$E\{\mathbf{P}_\theta{}^m(k\tau)\} = P_\theta(k\tau) \tag{71}$$

and

$$\text{variance}\{\mathbf{P}_\theta{}^m(k\tau)\} = \frac{1}{\overline{N}_\theta(k\tau)} \tag{72}$$

From the statistical properties of the measured projections, $\mathbf{P}_\theta{}^m(k\tau)$, we will now derive those of the reconstructed image. By combining (29) and (45), the relationship between the reconstruction at a point (x, y) and the *measured* M_{proj} projections is given by

$$\hat{\mathbf{f}}(x, y) = \frac{\pi\tau}{M_{\text{proj}}} \sum_{i=1}^{M_{\text{proj}}} \sum_k \mathbf{P}_{\theta_i}^m(k\tau) h(x\cos\theta_i + y\sin\theta_i - k\tau) \tag{73}$$

Using (71), (72), and (73), we get

$$E\{\hat{\mathbf{f}}(x, y)\} = \frac{\pi\tau}{M_{\text{proj}}} \sum_{i=1}^{M_{\text{proj}}} \sum_k P_{\theta_i}(k\tau) h(x\cos\theta_i + y\sin\theta_i - k\tau) \tag{74}$$

and

$$\text{variance}\{\hat{\mathbf{f}}(x, y)\} = \left(\frac{\pi\tau}{M_{\text{proj}}}\right)^2 \sum_{i=1}^{M_{\text{proj}}} \sum_k \frac{1}{\overline{N}_{\theta_i}(k\tau)} h^2(x\cos\theta_i + y\sin\theta_i - k\tau) \tag{75}$$

where we have assumed that the fluctuations in $\mathbf{P}_{\theta_i}^m(k\tau)$ are uncorrelated for different rays. Equation (74) shows that the expected value of the reconstructed image is equal to that made from the ideal projection data. Before we interpret (75) we will rewrite it as follows. In terms of the ideal projections, $P_\theta(k\tau)$, we define new projections as

$$V_\theta(k\tau) = e^{P_\theta(k\tau)} \tag{76}$$

and a new filter function, $h_V(t)$, as

$$h_V(t) = h^2(t) \tag{77}$$

Substituting (70), (76), and (77) in (75), we get

$$\text{variance}\{\hat{f}(x, y)\} = \left(\frac{\pi\tau}{M_{\text{proj}}}\right)^2 \frac{1}{N_{\text{in}}} \sum_{i=1}^{M_{\text{proj}}} \sum_k V_\theta(k\tau) h_V(x\cos\theta_i + y\sin\theta_i - k\tau) \tag{78}$$

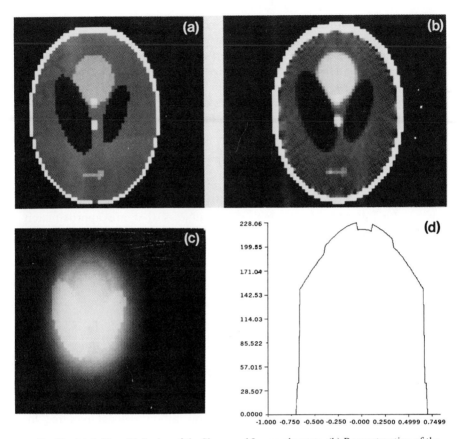

Fig. 23 (a) A 64 × 64 display of the Shepp and Logan phantom. (b) Reconstruction of the phantom from 120 projections and 101 rays in each projection. (c) The relative-uncertainty image for the reconstruction in (b). (d) Graphical depiction of the relative-uncertainty values through the horizontal middle line of (c).

We will now define a *relative-uncertainty image* as follows:[§]

$$\text{relative uncertainty at } (x, y) = N_{\text{in}} \frac{\text{variance}\{\hat{\mathbf{f}}(x, y)\}}{[\exp\{\hat{\mathbf{f}}(x, y)\}]^2} \qquad (79)$$

The relative-uncertainty image becomes independent of the number of incident photons used for measurements, and is completely determined by the choice of the phantom. Figure 23c shows the relative-uncertainty image for the

---

[§] This result only applies when compensators are not used to reduce the dynamic range of the detector output signal. In noise analyses their effect can be approximately modeled by using different N_{in}'s for different rays.

Shepp and Logan phantom (Fig. 23a) for $M_{\text{proj}} = 120$ and $\tau = 2/101$ and for $h(t)$ given by (42). Figure 23c shows graphically the middle horizontal line through Fig. 23c. Relative uncertainty at (x, y) gives us a relative measure of how much confidence an observer might place in the reconstructed value at (x, y) vis a vis those elsewhere.

We will now derive some special cases of (78). Suppose we want to determine the variance of noise at the origin. From (75) we can write

$$\text{variance}\{\hat{\mathbf{f}}(0, 0)\} = \left(\frac{\pi\tau}{M_{\text{proj}}}\right)^2 \sum_{i=1}^{M_{\text{proj}}} \sum_k \frac{1}{\overline{N}_{\theta_i}(k\tau)} h^2(k\tau) \tag{80}$$

where we have used the fact that $h(t)$ is an even function. Chesler et al. [11] have argued that since $h(k\tau)$ drops rapidly with k [see Eq. (42)], it is safe to make the following approximation for objects that are approximately homogeneous:

$$\text{variance}\{\hat{\mathbf{f}}(0, 0)\} = \left(\frac{\pi\tau}{M_{\text{proj}}}\right)^2 \sum_k h^2(k\tau) \sum_{i=1}^{M_{\text{proj}}} \frac{1}{\overline{N}_{\theta_i}(0)} \tag{81}$$

which, when τ is small enough, may also be written as

$$\text{variance}\{\hat{\mathbf{f}}(0, 0)\} = \left(\frac{\pi}{M_{\text{proj}}}\right)^2 \tau \int_{-\infty}^{\infty} h^2(t) \, dt \sum_{i=1}^{M_{\text{proj}}} \frac{1}{\overline{N}_{\theta_i}(0)} \tag{82}$$

Note again that the $\overline{N}_{\theta_i}(0)$ are the mean numbers of exiting photons measured for the center ray in each projection. Using (82) Chesler et al. [11] have arrived at the very interesting result that (for the same uncertainty in measurement) the total number of photons per resolution element required for x-ray CT (using the filtered-backprojection algorithm) is the same as in the measurement of attenuation of an isolated (excised) piece of the object with dimensions equal to those of the resolution element.

Now consider the case of circularly symmetric objects. The $\overline{N}_{\theta_i}(0)$'s for all i's will be equal; call their common value $\overline{N}_0$. That is, let

$$\overline{N}_0 = \overline{N}_{\theta_1}(0) = \overline{N}_{\theta_2}(0) = \cdots \tag{83}$$

The expression (82) for the variance may now be written as

$$\text{variance}\{\hat{\mathbf{f}}(0, 0)\} = \frac{\pi^2\tau}{M_{\text{proj}}\overline{N}_0} \int_{-\infty}^{\infty} h^2(t) \, dt \tag{84}$$

By Parseval's theorem this result may be expressed in the frequency domain as

$$\text{variance}\{\hat{\mathbf{f}}(0, 0)\} = \frac{\pi^2\tau}{M_{\text{proj}}\overline{N}_0} \int_{-1/2\tau}^{1/2\tau} |H(w)|^2 \, dw \tag{85}$$

where τ is the sampling interval for the projection data. This result says that the variance of noise at the origin is proportional to the area under the square of the filter function used for reconstruction. This does not imply that this area can be made arbitrarily small since any major departure from the $|w|$ function will introduce spatial distortion in the image even though it may be less noisy. *None of the equations above should be construed to imply that the variance approaches zero as τ is made arbitrarily small.* Note from Fig. 6 that τ is also the width of the measurement beam. In any practical system as τ is reduced, $\overline{N}_0$ will decrease also.

The preceding discussion has resulted in expressions for the variance of noise in reconstructions made with a filtered-backprojection algorithm for parallel projection data. As mentioned before, filtered-backprojection algorithms have become very popular because of their accuracy. Still the question arises: Given a set of projections, can there be an algorithm that might reconstruct an image with a smaller error? The answer to this question has been supplied by Tretiak [60]. Tretiak has derived an algorithm-independent lower bound for the mean-squared error in a reconstructed image, and has argued that for the case of reconstructions from parallel projection data this lower bound is very close to the error estimates obtained by Brooks and DiChiro [8] for the filtered-backprojection algorithms, which leads to the conclusion that very little improvement can be obtained over the performance of such an algorithm.

8.6 RECONSTRUCTION FROM FAN PROJECTIONS

The theory in the preceding subsections dealt with reconstructing images from their parallel projections such as those shown in Fig. 2. In generating this parallel data a source-detector combination has to linearly scan over the length of a projection, rotate through a certain angular interval, and then scan linearly over the length of the next projection. This usually results in times that are as long as a few minutes for collecting all the data. A much faster way to generate the line integrals is by using fan beams such as those shown in Fig. 3. One now uses a point source of rays emitting a fan-shaped beam. On the other side of the object a bank of detectors is used to make all the measurements in one fan simultaneously. The source and the entire bank of detectors are rotated to generate the desired number of fan projections.

There are two types of fan projections depending upon whether a projection is sampled at equiangular or equispaced intervals. This difference is illustrated in Fig. 24. In Fig. 24a we have shown an equiangular set of rays.

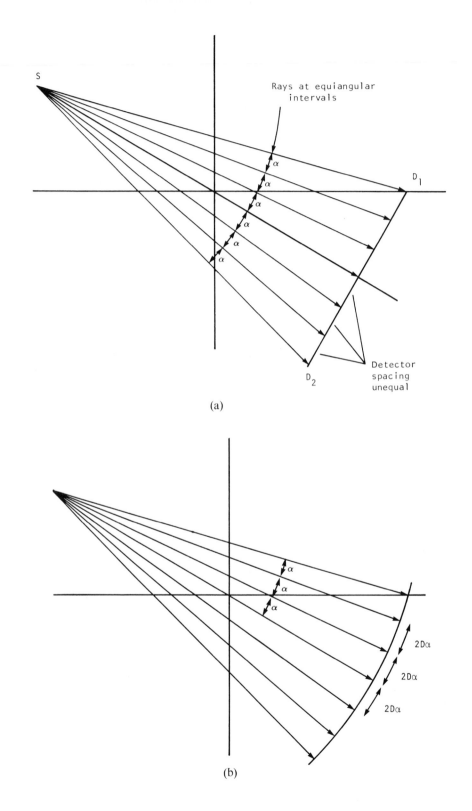

(a)

(b)

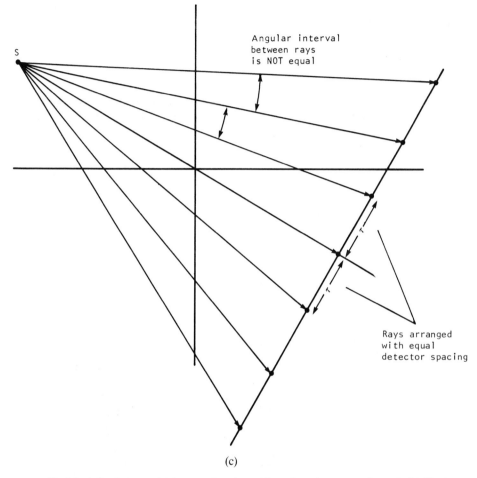

(c)

Fig. 24 A fan-beam projection may be taken with equiangular rays as shown in (a). Equiangular rays imply unequal spacing between the detectors if they are arranged on a straight line. However, if, as shown in (b) the detectors are arranged on a circular arc, the spacing between them will be equal. As shown in (c), a fan-beam projection may also be taken with rays that result in equispaced detectors arranged on a straight line.

If the detectors for the measurement of line integrals are arranged on the straight line D_1D_2, the spacing between them would be unequal. If, however, the detectors are arranged on the arc of a circle whose center is at S, they could be positioned with equal spacing along this arc (Fig. 24b). The second type of a fan projection is generated when the rays are arranged such that the detector spacing on a straight line is equal (Fig. 24c). The algorithms that reconstruct images from these two types of fan projections are different and will be separately derived in the following subsections.

8.6.1 Equiangular Rays

Let $R_\beta(\gamma)$ denote a fan projection as shown in Fig. 25. Here β is the angle that the source S makes with a reference axis, and the angle γ gives the location of a ray within the fan. Consider the ray SA. If the projection data were generated along a set of parallel rays, then the ray SA would belong to a parallel projection $P_\theta(t)$ for θ and t given by

$$\theta = \beta + \lambda \qquad \text{and} \qquad t = D \sin \gamma \tag{86}$$

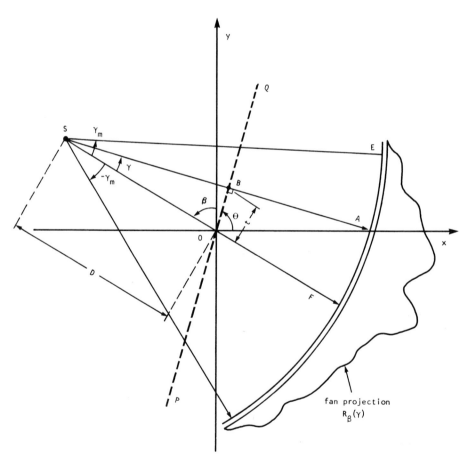

Fig. 25   This figure shows the various parameters used in the derivation of the fan-beam reconstruction algorithm for the case of equiangular rays.

where D is the distance of the source S from the origin O. The relationships in (86) are derived by noting that all the rays in the parallel projection at angle θ are perpendicular to the line PQ and that along such a line the distance OB is equal to the value of t. We know that from parallel projections $P_\theta(t)$ we may reconstruct $f(x, y)$ by

$$f(x, y) = \int_0^\pi \int_{-t_m}^{t_m} P_\theta(t)h(x \cos \theta + y \sin \theta - t) \, dt \, d\theta \tag{87}$$

where t_m is the value of t for which $P_\theta(t) = 0$ with $|t| > t_m$ in all the projections. This equation only requires parallel projections to be collected over $180°$. However, if we wanted to use the projections generated over $360°$, this equation may be rewritten as

$$f(x, y) = \frac{1}{2} \int_0^{2\pi} \int_{-t_m}^{t_m} P_\theta(t)h(x \cos \theta + y \sin \theta - t) \, dt \, d\theta \tag{88}$$

Derivation of the algorithm becomes easier when the point (x, y) (marked C in Fig. 26) is expressed in polar coordinates (r, φ), that is

$$x = r \cos \varphi, \qquad y = r \sin \varphi$$

The expression in (88) can now be written as

$$f(r, \varphi) = \frac{1}{2} \int_0^{2\pi} \int_{-t_m}^{t_m} P_\theta(t)h(r \cos(\theta - \varphi) - t) \, dt \, d\theta \tag{89}$$

Using the relationships in (86) the double integration may be expressed in terms of γ and β:

$$f(r, \varphi) = \frac{1}{2} \int_{-\gamma}^{2\pi - \gamma} \int_{-\sin^{-1} t_m/D}^{\sin^{-1} t_m/D} P_{\beta + \gamma}(D \sin \gamma)h(r \cos(\beta + \gamma - \varphi) - D \sin \gamma)$$
$$\times D \cos \gamma \, d\gamma \, d\beta \tag{90}$$

where we have used $dt \, d\theta = D \cos \gamma \, d\gamma \, d\beta$. A few observations about this expression are in order. The limits $-\gamma$ to $2\pi - \gamma$ for β cover the entire range of $360°$. Since all the functions of β are periodic (with period 2π) these limits may be replaced by 0 and 2π. The value of γ for the extreme ray SE in Fig. 25 is equal to $\sin^{-1}(t_m/D)$. Therefore, the upper and lower limits for γ integration may be written as γ_m and $-\gamma_m$, respectively. The expression $P_{\beta + \gamma}(D \sin \gamma)$ corresponds to the ray integral along SA in the parallel-projection data $P_\theta(t)$. The identity of this ray integral in the fan projection data is simply $R_\beta(\gamma)$. Introducing these changes in (90) we get

$$f(r, \varphi) = \frac{1}{2} \int_0^{2\pi} \int_{-\gamma_m}^{\gamma_m} R_\beta(\gamma)h(r \cos(\beta + \gamma - \varphi) - D \sin \gamma) D \cos \gamma \, d\gamma \, d\beta \tag{91}$$

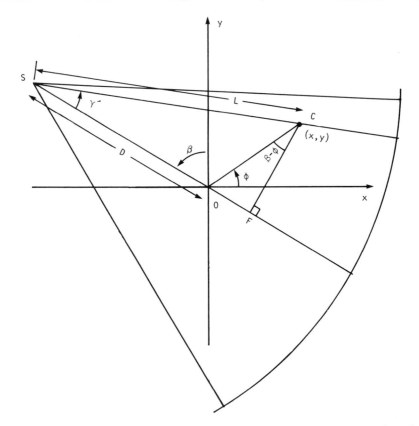

Fig. 26 This figure illustrates that L is the distance of the pixel at location (x, y) from the source S, and γ' is the angle that the source-to-pixel line subtends with the central ray.

In order to express the reconstruction formula given by (91) in a form that can be easily implemented on a computer we will first examine the argument of the function h. The argument may be rewritten as

$$r \cos(\beta + \gamma - \varphi) - D \sin \gamma = r \cos(\beta - \varphi) \cos \gamma - [r \sin(\beta - \varphi) + D] \sin \gamma \tag{92}$$

Let L be the distance from the source S to a point (x, y) [or (r, φ) in polar coordinates] such as C in Fig. 26. Clearly, L is a function of three variables r, φ, and β. Also, let γ' be the angle of the ray that passes through this point. One can easily show that

$$L \cos \gamma' = D + r \sin(\beta - \varphi) \qquad \text{and} \qquad L \sin \gamma' = r \cos(\beta - \varphi) \tag{93}$$

Note that the pixel location (r, φ) and the projection angle β completely determine both L and γ':

$$L(r, \varphi, \beta) = \sqrt{[D + r \sin \beta - \varphi)]^2 + [r \cos(\beta - \varphi)]^2}$$

and

$$\gamma' = \tan^{-1} \frac{r \cos(\beta - \varphi)}{D + r \sin(\beta - \varphi)} \tag{94}$$

Using (93) in (92) we get for the argument of h

$$r \cos(\beta + \gamma - \varphi) - D \sin \gamma = L \sin(\gamma' - \gamma) \tag{95}$$

and substituting this in (91) we obtain

$$f(r, \varphi) = \frac{1}{2} \int_0^{2\pi} \int_{-\gamma_m}^{\gamma_m} R_\beta(\gamma) h(L \sin(\gamma' - \gamma)) D \cos \gamma \, d\gamma \, d\beta \tag{96}$$

We will now express the function $h(L \sin(\gamma' - \gamma))$ in terms of $h(t)$. Note that $h(t)$ is the inverse Fourier transform of $|w|$ in the frequency domain:

$$h(t) = \int_{-\infty}^{\infty} |w| e^{j2\pi wt} \, dw$$

Therefore,

$$h(L \sin \gamma) = \int_{-\infty}^{\infty} |w| e^{j2\pi wL \sin \gamma} \, dw \tag{97}$$

Using the transformation

$$w' = \frac{wL \sin \gamma}{\gamma} \tag{98}$$

we can write

$$h(L \sin \gamma) = \left(\frac{\gamma}{L \sin \gamma}\right)^2 \int_{-\infty}^{\infty} |w'| e^{j2\pi w'\gamma} \, dw' = \left(\frac{\gamma}{L \sin \gamma}\right)^2 h(\gamma) \tag{99}$$

Therefore, Eq. (96) may be written as

$$f(r, \varphi) = \int_0^{2\pi} \frac{1}{L^2} \int_{-\gamma_m}^{\gamma_m} R_\beta(\gamma) g(\gamma' - \gamma) D \cos \gamma \, d\gamma \, d\beta \tag{100}$$

where

$$g(\gamma) = \frac{1}{2} \left(\frac{\gamma}{\sin \gamma}\right)^2 h(\gamma) \tag{101}$$

For the purpose of computer implementation (100) may be interpreted as a weighted filtered-backprojection algorithm. To show this we rewrite (100) as follows:

$$f(r, \varphi) = \int_0^{2\pi} \frac{1}{L^2} Q_\beta(\gamma') \, d\beta \tag{102}$$

where

$$Q_\beta(\gamma) = R'_\beta(\gamma) * g(\gamma) \tag{103}$$

and where

$$R'_\beta(\gamma) = R_\beta(\gamma) \cdot D \cdot \cos \gamma \tag{104}$$

This calls for reconstructing an image using the following three steps.

Step 1. Assume that each projection $R_\beta(\gamma)$ is sampled with sampling interval α. The known data then are $R_{\beta_i}(n\alpha)$ where n takes integer values. The β_i are the angles at which projections are taken. The first step is to generate for each fan projection $R_{\beta_i}(n\alpha)$ the corresponding $R'_{\beta_i}(n\alpha)$ by

$$R'_{\beta_i}(n\alpha) = R_{\beta_i}(n\alpha) \cdot D \cdot \cos n\alpha \tag{105}$$

Note that $n = 0$ corresponds to the ray passing through the center of the projection.

Step 2. Convolve each modified projection $R'_{\beta_i}(n\alpha)$ with $g(n\alpha)$ to generate the corresponding filtered projection:

$$Q_{\beta_i}(n\alpha) = R'_{\beta_i}(n\alpha) * g(n\alpha) \tag{106}$$

To perform this discrete convolution using a FFT program the function $R'_{\beta_i}(n\alpha)$ must be padded with a sufficient number of zeroes to avoid inter-period interference artifacts. The sequence $g(n\alpha)$ is given by the samples of (101):

$$g(n\alpha) = \frac{1}{2} \left(\frac{n\alpha}{\sin n\alpha} \right)^2 h(n\alpha) \tag{107}$$

If we substitute in this the values of $h(n\alpha)$ from (42), we get for the discrete impulse response

$$g(n\alpha) = \begin{cases} \dfrac{1}{8\alpha^2}, & n = 0 \\[2mm] 0, & n \text{ even} \\[2mm] -\dfrac{1}{2} \left(\dfrac{\alpha}{\pi\alpha \sin n\alpha} \right)^2, & n \text{ odd} \end{cases} \tag{108}$$

Although, theoretically, no further filtering of the projection data than that called for by (106) is required, in practice superior reconstructions are obtained if a certain amount of smoothing as shown below is also incorporated:

$$Q_{\beta_i}(n\alpha) = R'_{\beta_i}(n\alpha) * g(n\alpha) * k(n\alpha) \tag{109}$$

where $k(n\alpha)$ is the impulse response of the smoothing filter. In the frequency domain implementation the transfer function of the smoothing filter may be a simple function such as a Hamming window.

Step 3. Perform a *weighted* backprojection of each filtered projection *along the fan.* The backprojection here is very different from that for the parallel case. The difference is illustrated in Figs. 27a and 27b. For the fan-beam case the backprojection is done along the fan (Fig. 27b). This is dictated by the structure of (102):

$$f(x, y) \simeq \Delta\beta \sum_{i=1}^{M} \frac{1}{L^2(x, y, \beta_i)} Q_{\beta_i}(\gamma') \tag{110}$$

where γ' is the angle of the fan-beam ray that passes through the point (x, y). In order to find the contribution of $Q_{\beta_i}(\gamma)$ to the point (x, y) shown in Fig. 27c one must first find the angle, γ', of the ray SA that passes through that point. If the computed value of γ' does not correspond to one of the $n\alpha$ for which $Q_{\beta_i}(n\alpha)$ is known, one must use interpolation. The contribution $Q_{\beta_i}(\gamma')$ at the point (x, y) must then be multiplied by L^2 where L is the distance from the source S to the point (x, y).

This concludes our presentation of the algorithm.

8.6.2 Equally Spaced Collinear Detectors

Let $R_\beta(s)$ denote a fan projection as shown in Fig. 28, where s is the distance along the straight line corresponding to the detector bank. The principal difference between the algorithm presented in the preceding subsection and the one here lies in the way a fan projection is represented, which then introduces differences in subsequent mathematical manipulations. Since the rays in each fan were equiangularly spaced in the preceding case, a projection was represented by $R_\beta(\gamma)$ with γ being the angular location of a ray. Now the intersections of the rays with the detector line are equispaced; we therefore represent a projection by $R_\beta(s)$.

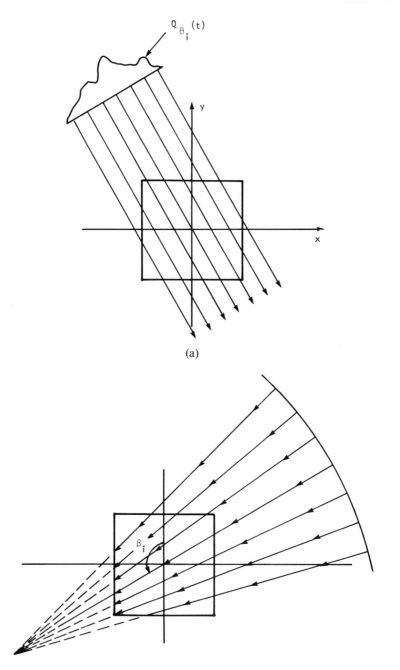

(a)

(b)

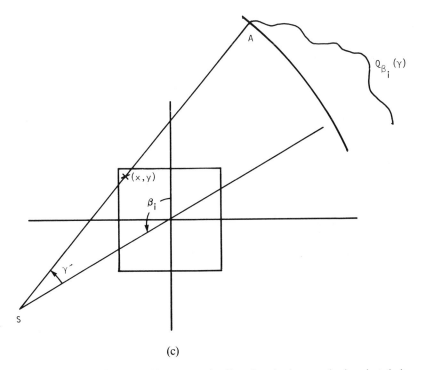

(c)

Fig. 27 While for the parallel-beam case the filtered projections are backprojected along parallel lines (a), for the fan-beam case the backprojection is performed along converging lines (b). (c). This figure illustrates the implementation step that in order to determine the backprojected value at pixel (x, y), one must first compute γ' for that pixel.

Although the projections are measured on a line such as $D_1 D_2$ in Fig. 28, for theoretical purposes it is more efficient to assume the existence of an imaginary detector line $D_1' D_2'$ passing through the origin. We associate the ray integral along SB with point A on $D_1' D_2'$, as opposed to point B on $D_1 D_2$. Thus in Fig. 29 we will associate a fan projection $R_\beta(s)$ with the imaginary detector line $D_1' D_2'$. Considering ray SA in the figure, the value of s for this ray is the length of OA. If parallel projection data were generated for the object under consideration, ray SA would belong to a parallel projection $P_\theta(t)$ with θ and t as shown in the figure. The relationships between (t, θ) and (s, β) are given by

$$ t = s \cos \gamma = \frac{sD}{\sqrt{D^2 + s^2}}, \qquad \theta = \beta + \gamma = \beta + \tan^{-1} \frac{s}{D} \qquad (111) $$

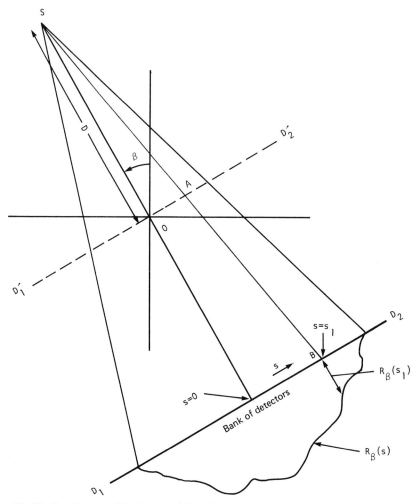

Fig. 28 For the case of fan-beams with equispaced detectors on a straight line, each projection is denoted by the function $R_\beta(s)$.

where use has been made of the fact that angle AOC is equal to angle OSC, and where D is the distance of the source point S from the origin O.

In terms of the parallel projection data the reconstructed image is given by (89) which is repeated here for convenience:

$$f(r, \varphi) = \frac{1}{2} \int_0^{2\pi} \int_{-t_m}^{t_m} P_\theta(t) h(r \cos(\theta - \varphi) - t)\, dt\, d\theta$$

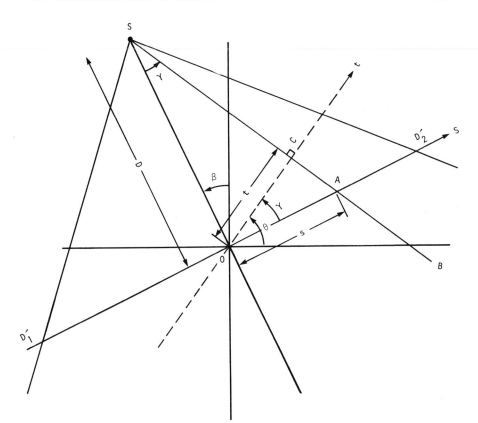

Fig. 29 Shown here are the various parameters used in the derivation of the fan-beam reconstruction algorithm for the case of equispaced collinear detectors.

Using the relationships in (111) the double integration may be expressed as

$$f(r, \varphi) = \frac{1}{2} \int_{-\tan^{-1} s_m/D}^{2\pi - \tan^{-1} s_m/D} \int_{-s_m}^{s_m} P_{\beta+\gamma}\left(\frac{sD}{\sqrt{D^2 + s^2}}\right) \cdot h\left(r\cos\left(\beta + \tan^{-1}\frac{s}{D} - \phi\right)\right.$$

$$\left. - \frac{Ds}{\sqrt{D^2 + s^2}}\right) \frac{D^3}{(D^2 + s^2)^{3/2}} \, ds \, d\beta \qquad (112)$$

where we have used

$$dt \, d\theta = \frac{D^3}{(D^2 + s^2)^{3/2}} \, ds \, d\beta \qquad (113)$$

In (112) s_m is the largest value of s in each projection and corresponds to t_m for parallel projection data. The limits $-\tan^{-1}(s_m/D)$ and $2\pi - \tan^{-1} s_m/D$ cover the angular interval of 360°. Since all functions of β in

(112) are periodic with period 2π, the lower and the upper limits may be replaced by 0 and 2π, respectively. Also the expression

$$P_{\beta+\gamma}\left(\frac{sD}{\sqrt{D^2 + s^2}}\right)$$

corresponds to the ray integral along SB in the parallel projection data $P_\theta(t)$. The identity of this ray integral in the fan projection data is simply $R_\beta(s)$. Introducing these changes in (112) we get

$$f(r, \varphi) = \frac{1}{2} \int_0^{2\pi} \int_{-s_m}^{s_m} R_\beta(s) h\left(r \cos\left(\beta + \tan^{-1}\frac{s}{D} - \varphi\right) - \frac{Ds}{\sqrt{D^2 + s^2}}\right)$$

$$\times \frac{D^3}{(D^2 + s^2)^{3/2}} \, ds \, d\beta \tag{114}$$

In order to express this formula in a filtered-backprojection form we will first examine the argument of h. The argument may be written as

$$r \cos\left(\beta + \tan^{-1}\frac{s}{D} - \varphi\right) - \frac{Ds}{\sqrt{D^2 + s^2}}$$

$$= r \cos(\beta - \varphi) \frac{D}{\sqrt{D^2 + s^2}} - (D + r \sin(\beta - \varphi)) \frac{s}{\sqrt{D^2 + s^2}} \tag{115}$$

We will now introduce two new variables that are easily calculated in a computer implementation. The first of these, denoted by U, is for each pixel (x, y) the ratio of SP (Fig. 30) to the source to origin distance. Note that SP is the projection of the source to pixel distance SE on the central ray. Thus

$$U(r, \varphi, \beta) = \frac{\overline{SO} + \overline{OP}}{D} = \frac{D + r \sin(\beta - \varphi)}{D} \tag{116}$$

The other parameter we want to define is the value of s for the ray that passes through the pixel (r, φ) under consideration. Let s' denote this value of s. Since s is measured along the imaginary detector line $D_1' D_2'$, it is given by the distance OF. Since

$$\frac{s'}{\overline{SO}} = \frac{\overline{EP}}{\overline{SP}}$$

we have

$$s' = D \frac{r \cos(\beta - \varphi)}{D + r \sin(\beta - \varphi)} \tag{117}$$

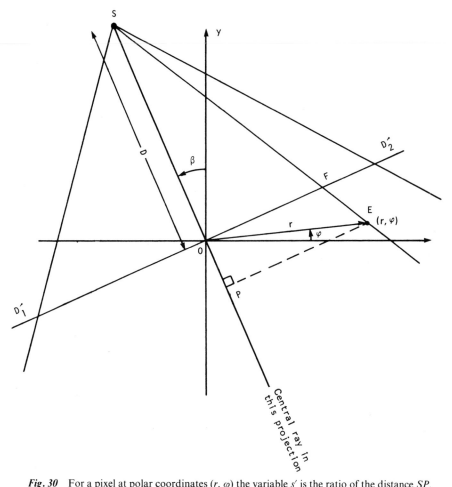

Fig. 30   For a pixel at polar coordinates (r, φ) the variable s' is the ratio of the distance SP, which is the projection of the source to pixel line on the central ray to the source-to-center distance.

Equations (116) and (117) can be utilized to express (115) in terms of U and s':

$$r \cos\left(\beta + \tan^{-1}\frac{s}{D} - \varphi\right) - \frac{Ds}{\sqrt{D^2 + s^2}} = \frac{s'UD}{\sqrt{D^2 + s^2}} - \frac{sUD}{\sqrt{D^2 + s^2}} \quad (118)$$

Substituting (118) in (114), we get

$$f(r, \varphi) = \frac{1}{2} \int_0^{2\pi} \int_{-s_m}^{s_m} R_\beta(s) h\left((s' - s)\frac{UD}{\sqrt{D^2 + s^2}}\right) \frac{D^3}{(D^2 + s^2)^{3/2}} \, ds \, d\beta \quad (119)$$

We will now express the convolving kernel h in this equation in a form closer
to that given by (42). Since $h(t)$ is the inverse Fourier transform of $|w|$ in the
frequency domain:

$$h(t) = \int_{-\infty}^{\infty} |w| e^{j2\pi wt} \, dw$$

we have

$$h\left((s' - s)\frac{UD}{\sqrt{D_2 + s^2}}\right) = \int_{-\infty}^{\infty} |w| \exp\left(j2\,\pi w(s' - s)\frac{UD}{\sqrt{D^2 + s^2}}\right) dw \quad (120)$$

Using the transformation

$$w' = w\frac{UD}{\sqrt{D^2 + s^2}} \quad (121)$$

we can rewrite (120) as follows:

$$h\left((s' - s)\frac{UD}{\sqrt{D^2 + s^2}}\right) = \frac{D^2 + s^2}{U^2 D^2} \int_{-\infty}^{\infty} |w'| e^{j2\pi(s' - s)w'} \, dw'$$

$$= \frac{D^2 + s^2}{U^2 D^2} h(s' - s) \quad (122)$$

Substituting this in (119) we get

$$f(r, \varphi) = \int_{0}^{2\pi} \frac{1}{U^2} \int_{-\infty}^{\infty} R_\beta(s)g(s' - s)\frac{D}{\sqrt{D^2 + s^2}} \, ds \, d\beta \quad (123)$$

where

$$g(s) = \tfrac{1}{2}h(s) \quad (124)$$

For the purpose of computer implementation (123) may be interpreted as a
weighted filtered-backprojection algorithm. To show this we rewrite (123)
as follows:

$$f(r, \varphi) = \int_{0}^{2\pi} \frac{1}{U^2} Q_\beta(s') \, d\beta \quad (125)$$

where

$$Q_\beta(s) = R'_\beta(s) * g(s) \quad (126)$$

and

$$R'_\beta(s) = R_\beta(s) \cdot \frac{D}{\sqrt{D^2 + s^2}} \quad (127)$$

Equations (125)–(127) suggest the following steps for computer implementation.

Step 1. Assume that each projection $R_\beta(s)$ is sampled with a sampling interval of a. The known data then are $R_{\beta_i}(na)$ where n takes integer values with $n = 0$ corresponding to the central ray passing through the origin; and the β_i are the angles for which fan projections are known. The first step is to generate for each fan projection $R_{\beta_i}(na)$ the corresponding modified projection $R'_{\beta_i}(na)$ given by

$$R'_{\beta_i}(na) = R_{\beta_i}(na) \cdot \frac{D}{\sqrt{D^2 + n^2 a^2}} \tag{128}$$

Step 2. Convolve each modified projection $R'_{\beta_i}(na)$ with $g(na)$ to generate the corresponding filtered projection:

$$Q_{\beta_i}(na) = R_{\beta_i}(na) * g(na) \tag{129}$$

where the sequence $g(na)$ is given by the samples of (124):

$$g(na) = \tfrac{1}{2}h(na) \tag{130}$$

Substituting in this the values of $h(na)$ given in (42) we get for the impulse response of the convolving filter

$$g(na) = \begin{cases} \dfrac{1}{8a^2}, & n = 0 \\ 0, & n \text{ even} \\ -\dfrac{1}{2n^2\pi^2 a^2}, & n \text{ odd} \end{cases} \tag{131}$$

When the convolution of (129) is implemented in the frequency domain using an FFT algorithm the projection data must be padded with a sufficient number of zeros to avoid distortion due to interperiod interference.

In practice superior reconstructions are obtained if a certain amount of smoothing is included with the convolution in (129). If $k(na)$ is the impulse response of the smoothing filter, we can write

$$Q_{\beta_i}(na) = R_{\beta_i}(na) * g(na) * k(na) \tag{132}$$

In a frequency domain implementation this smoothing may be achieved by a simple multiplicative function such as a Hamming window.

Step 3. Perform a *weighted* backprojection of each filtered projection along the corresponding fan. The sum of all the backprojections is the reconstructed image

$$f(x, y) = \Delta B \sum_{i=1}^{M} \frac{1}{U^2(x, y, \beta_i)} Q_{\beta_i}(s') \tag{133}$$

where s' identifies the ray that passes through (x, y) in the fan for the source located at angle β_i. Of course, this value of s' may not correspond to one of the values of na at which Q_{β_i} is known. In that case interpolation will be necessary.

8.6.3 A Resorting Algorithm

We will now describe an algorithm that rapidly resorts the fan-beam projection data into equivalent parallel-beam projection data. After resorting one may use the filtered-backprojection algorithm for the parallel projection data to reconstruct the image. This fast resorting algorithm does place constraints on the angles at which the fan-beam projections must be taken, and also on the angles at which projection data must be sampled within each fan-beam projection.

Referring to Fig. 25, the relationship between the independent variables of the fan-beam projections and parallel projections are given by (86):

$$t = D \sin \gamma \quad \text{and} \quad \theta = \beta + \gamma \tag{134}$$

If, as before, $R_\beta(\gamma)$ denotes a fan-beam projection taken at angle β, and $P_\theta(t)$ a parallel projection taken at angle θ, then using (134) we can write

$$R_\beta(\gamma) = P_{\beta+\gamma}(D \sin \gamma) \tag{135}$$

Let $\Delta\beta$ denote the angular increment between successive fan-beam projections, and let $\Delta\gamma$ denote the angular intervals used for sampling each fan-beam projection. We will assume that the following condition is satisfied:

$$\Delta\beta = \Delta\gamma = \alpha \tag{136}$$

Clearly then β and γ in (135) are equal to $m\alpha$ and $n\alpha$, respectively, for some integer values of the indices m and n. We may therefore write (135) as

$$R_{m\alpha}(n\alpha) = P_{(m+n)\alpha}(D \sin n\alpha) \tag{137}$$

This equation serves as the basis of the fast resorting algorithm. This equation expresses the fact that the nth ray in the mth radial projection is the nth ray in the $(m + n)$th parallel projection. Due to the $\sin n\alpha$ factor on the right-hand side in (137) the parallel projections obtained are not uniformly sampled. This can usually be rectified by interpolation.

Exercise 2. Assume that $\alpha = 18°$ in (137). Given 20 fan-beam projections over 360°, show that we can resort them into 10 parallel projections over 180° using only the nonnegatively indexed rays. Also show that if we are given only 10 fan-beam projections over 180°, then we need all the fan-beam rays to generate the 10 parallel projections. (For a solution see [17] and [48].) ∎

8.7 ALGEBRAIC RECONSTRUCTION TECHNIQUES

8.7.1 The Kaczmarz Method

In Fig. 31 we have superimposed a square grid on the image $f(x, y)$, and we assume that in each cell $f(x, y)$ can be considered to be constant. Let f_m denote this constant value in the mth cell, and let N be the total number of

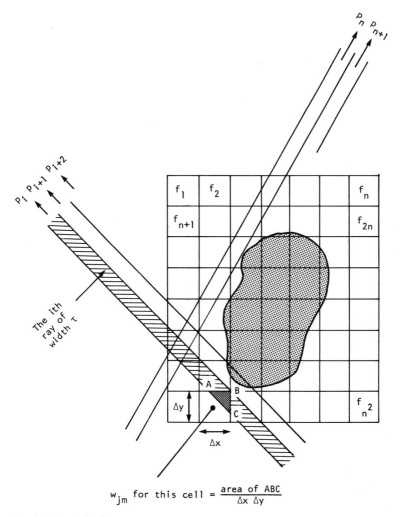

$$w_{jm} \text{ for this cell} = \frac{\text{area of ABC}}{\Delta x\, \Delta y}$$

Fig. 31 In algebraic reconstruction methods, a square grid is superimposed over the unknown image. Image values are assumed to be constant within each cell of the grid.

cells. For the algebraic techniques a ray is defined somewhat differently. A ray is now a "fat" line running through the xy-plane. To illustrate this we have shaded the ith ray in Fig. 31, where each ray is of width τ. In most cases the ray width is approximately equal to the image cell width. A ray-integral will now be called a ray sum.

Like the image, the projections will also be given a one-index representation. Let p_m be the ray sum measured with the mth ray as shown in Fig. 31. The relationship between the f_i's and p_i's may be expressed as

$$\sum_{j=1}^{N} w_{ij} f_j = p_i, \qquad i = 1, 2, \ldots, M \qquad (138)$$

where M is the total number of rays (in all the projections) and w_{ij} is the weighting factor that represents the contribution of the jth cell to the ith ray sum. The factor w_{ij} is equal to the fractional area of the jth image cell intercepted by the ith ray as shown for one of the cells in Fig. 31. Note that most w_{ij}'s are zero since only a small number of cells contribute to any given ray sum.

If M and N are small one could use conventional matrix theory methods to invert the system of equations in (138). However, in practice N may be as large as 65000 (for 256×256 images) and in most cases, M will also have the same magnitude. For these values of M and N the size of the matrix $[w_{ij}]$ in (138) is 65000×65000, which precludes any possibility of direct matrix inversion. When noise is present in the measurement data and when $M < N$, even for small N it is not possible to use direct matrix inversion, and least squares methods may have to be used. When both M and N are large such methods are also computationally impractical.

For large values of M and N there exists a very attractive iterative method for solving (138). It is the "method of projections" first proposed by Kaczmarz [33]. More recently its properties have also been discussed by Tanabe [56]. To explain this method we first write (138) in an expanded form:

$$\begin{aligned}
w_{11} f_1 &+ w_{12} f_2 + \cdots + w_{1N} f_N = p_1 \\
w_{21} f_1 &+ w_{22} f_2 + \cdots + w_{2N} f_N = p_2 \\
&\vdots \\
w_{M1} f_1 &+ w_{M2} f_2 + \cdots + w_{MN} f_N = p_M
\end{aligned} \qquad (139)$$

A grid representation with N cells gives an image N degrees of freedom. Therefore, an image as represented by $(f_1, f_2, \ldots, f_N)$ may be considered to be a single point in an N-dimensional space. In this space each of the above equations represents a hyperplane. When a unique solution to these equations exists, the intersection of all these hyperplanes is a single point giving that solution. This concept is further illustrated in Fig. 32 where, for the purpose of illustration, we have considered the case of only two variables f_1 and f_2 satisfying the following equations:

$$w_{11}f_1 + w_{12}f_2 = p_1, \qquad w_{21}f_1 + w_{22}f_2 = p_2 \qquad (140)$$

In the Kaczmarz method one first makes an initial guess at the solution. Let this guess be $f_1^{(0)}, f_2^{(0)}, \ldots, f_N^{(0)}$. This guess may be represented vectorially

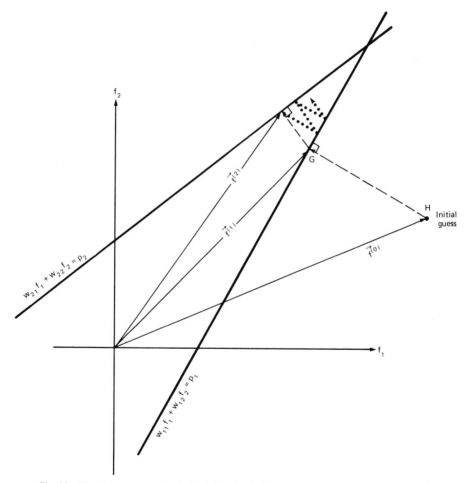

Fig. 32 The Kaczmarz method of solving algebraic equations is illustrated for the case of two unknowns. One starts with some arbitrary initial guess and then projects onto the line corresponding to the first equation. The resulting point is now projected onto the line representing the second equation. If there are only two equations, this process is continued back and forth, as illustrated by the dots in the figure, until convergence is achieved.

by $\vec{f}^{(0)}$ in the N-dimensional space. This initial guess is projected on the hyperplane represented by the first of the equations in (139) giving $\vec{f}^{(1)}$ as illustrated in Fig. 32 for the two-dimensional case. The computer implementation of this step is carried out using the following formula:

$$\vec{f}^{(1)} = \vec{f}^{(0)} - \frac{(\vec{w}_1 \cdot \vec{f}^{(0)} - p_1)}{\vec{w}_1 \cdot \vec{w}_1} \vec{w}_1 \tag{141}$$

where $\vec{w}_1 = (w_{11}, w_{12}, \ldots, w_{1N})$, the coefficients in the first of the equations in (139). To see how (141) comes about we first write the first equation of (139) [or (140)] as follows:

$$\vec{w}_1 \cdot \vec{f} = p_1 \tag{142}$$

The hyperplane represented by this equation is perpendicular to the vector $\vec{w}_1$ as shown in Fig. 33. This equation simply says that the projection of a vector $\overrightarrow{OC}$ (for any point C on the hyperplane) on the vector $\vec{w}_1$ is of constant length. The unit vector, $\overrightarrow{OU}$, along $\vec{w}_1$ is given by

$$\overrightarrow{OU} = \frac{\vec{w}_1}{\sqrt{\vec{w}_1 \cdot \vec{w}_1}} \tag{143}$$

and the perpendicular distance of the hyperplane from the origin, equal to the length of $\overrightarrow{OA}$ in Fig. 33, is given by $\overrightarrow{OC} \cdot \overrightarrow{OU}$:

$$|\overrightarrow{OA}| = \overrightarrow{OU} \cdot \overrightarrow{OC} = \frac{1}{\sqrt{\vec{w}_1 \cdot \vec{w}_1}} (\sqrt{\vec{w}_1 \cdot \vec{w}_1} \, \overrightarrow{OU} \cdot \overrightarrow{OC})$$

$$= \frac{1}{\sqrt{\vec{w}_1 \cdot \vec{w}_1}} (\vec{w}_1 \cdot \vec{f}) = \frac{p_1}{\sqrt{\vec{w}_1 \cdot \vec{w}_1}} \tag{144}$$

To get $\vec{f}^{(1)}$ we have to subtract from $\vec{f}^{(0)}$ the vector $\overrightarrow{GH}$:

$$\vec{f}^{(1)} = \vec{f}^{(0)} - \overrightarrow{GH} \tag{145}$$

where the length of the vector $\overrightarrow{GH}$ is given by

$$|\overrightarrow{GH}| = |\overrightarrow{OF}| - |\overrightarrow{OA}| = \vec{f}^{(0)} \cdot \overrightarrow{OU} - |\overrightarrow{OA}| \tag{146}$$

Substituting (143) and (144) in this equation, we get

$$|\overrightarrow{GH}| = \frac{\vec{f}^{(0)} \cdot \vec{w}_1 - p_1}{\sqrt{\vec{w}_1 \cdot \vec{w}_1}} \tag{147}$$

Since the direction of $\overrightarrow{GH}$ is the same as that of the unit vector $\overrightarrow{OU}$, we can write

$$\overrightarrow{GH} = |\overrightarrow{GH}| \overrightarrow{OU} = \frac{\vec{f}^{(0)} \cdot \vec{w}_1 - p_1}{\vec{w}_1 \cdot \vec{w}_1} \vec{w}_1 \tag{148}$$

Substituting (148) in (145) we get (141).

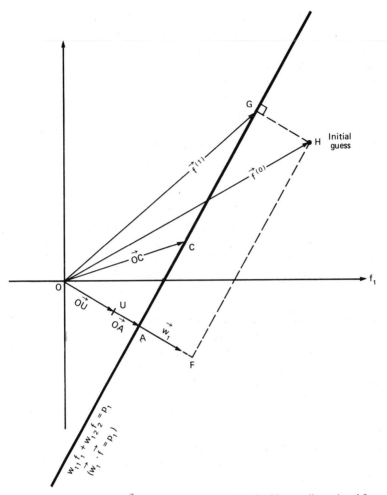

Fig. 33 The hyperplane $\vec{w}_1 \cdot \vec{f} = p_1$ (represented by a line in this two-dimensional figure) is perpendicular to the vector $\vec{w}_1$.

After we get $\vec{f}^{(1)}$, we take its projection on the hyperplane represented by the second equation in (139), which gives us $f^{(2)}$, as is also shown in Fig. 32. This process is repeated with the third hyperplane and so on. The projection on the jth hyperplane may be obtained from that on the $(j-1)$th hyperplane by

$$\vec{f}^{(j)} = \vec{f}^{(j-1)} - \frac{(\vec{f}^{(j-1)} \cdot \vec{w}_j - p_j)}{\vec{w}_j \cdot \vec{w}_j} \, \vec{w}_j \tag{149}$$

where $\vec{w}_j = (w_{j1}, w_{j2}, \ldots, w_{jN})$.

The process of taking projections on different hyperplanes is continued until we get $\vec{f}^{(M)}$, which is obtained by taking the projection on the last equation in (139). *One now iterates by projecting $\vec{f}^{(M)}$ on the first hyperplane again.* For example, for the two-dimensional case shown in Fig. 32 one reprojects $\vec{f}^{(2)}$ on the first hyperplane (in this case a line) to get $\vec{f}^{(3)}$. This process continues until all the M hyperplanes have again been cycled through resulting in $\vec{f}^{(2M)}$. The second iteration is started by projecting $\vec{f}^{(2M)}$ onto the first hyperplane again, and so on. Tanabe [56] has shown that if a unique solution $\vec{f}_s$ to the system of equations in (139) exists then

$$\lim_{k \to \infty} \vec{f}^{(kM)} = \vec{f}_s \tag{150}$$

A few comments about the convergence of the algorithm are in order. If in Fig. 32 the two hyperplanes had been perpendicular to each other, the reader may easily show that given any point in the (f_1, f_2) plane for an initial guess, it is possible to arrive at the correct solution in only two steps like (141). On the other hand, if the two hyperplanes have only a very small angle between them, the value of k in (150) may acquire a large value (depending upon the initial guess) before the correct solution is reached. Clearly the angles between the hyperplanes considerably influence the rate of convergence to the solution. If the M hyperplanes in (139) could be made orthogonal with respect to one another, the correct solution would be arrived at with only one pass through the M equations (assuming a unique solution does exist). Therefore, the value of k in (150) would equal 1 for us to get the correct solution. Although theoretically such orthogonalization is possible using, for example, the Gram–Schmidt procedure, in practice it is computationally not feasible. Full orthogonalization will also tend to enhance the effects of the ever present measurement noise in the final solution. Ramakrishnan *et al.* [51] have suggested a pairwise orthogonalization scheme that is computationally easier to implement and at the same time considerably increases the speed of convergence.

A not uncommon situation in image reconstruction is that of an overdetermined system in the presence of measurement noise. That is we may have $M > N$ in (139) and $p_1, p_2, \ldots, p_M$ corrupted by noise. No unique solution exists in this case. In Fig. 34 we have shown a two-variable system represented by three "noisy" hyperplanes. The dashed line represents the course of the solution as we successively implement (149). Now the "solution" does not converge to a unique point, but will oscillate in the neighborhood of the region of the intersections of the hyperplanes.

When $M < N$ a unique solution of the set of linear equations in (139) does not exist, and, in fact, an infinite number of solutions are possible. For example, suppose only the first of two equations in (140) is given to us for

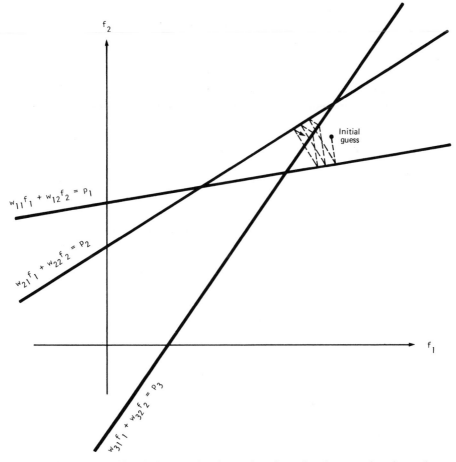

Fig. 34 Illustrated here is the case when the number of equations is greater than the number of unknowns. The lines do not intersect at a single unique point, because the observations p_1, p_2, p_3 have been assumed to be corrupted by noise. No unique solution exists in this case, and the final solution will oscillate in the neighborhood of intersections of the three lines.

the two unknowns f_1 and f_2; then the solution can be anywhere on the line corresponding to this equation. Given an initial guess $\vec{f}^{(0)}$ (see Fig. 32) the best one can probably do is to draw a projection from $\vec{f}^{(0)}$ on the line and call the resulting $\vec{f}^{(1)}$ the solution. Note that the solution obtained in this way corresponds to that point on the given line that is closest to the initial guess. This result has been rigorously proved by Tanabe [56] who has shown that when $M < N$, the iterative approach described above converges to a solution, call it $\vec{f}_s'$, such that $|\vec{f}^{(0)} - \vec{f}_s'|$ is minimized.

Besides its computational efficiency, another attractive feature of the iterative approach presented here is that it is now possible to incorporate into the solution some types of a priori information about the image. For example, if it is known a priori that the image $f(x, y)$ is nonnegative, then in each of the solutions $\vec{f}^{(k)}$, successively obtained by using (149), one may set the negative components equal to zero. One may similarly incorporate the information that $f(x, y)$ is zero outside a certain area, if this is known.

8.7.2 Approximations to the Kaczmarz Method

The difficulty with implementing (149) can be in the calculation, storage, and fast retrieval of the weight coefficients w_{ij} in (139). Consider the case where we wish to reconstruct an image on a 128 × 128 grid from 150 projections with 150 rays in each projection. The total number of weights, w_{ij}, needed in this case is 128 × 128 × 150 × 150 ($\approx 2.7 \times 10^8$), which is an enormous number and can pose problems in fast storage and retrieval in applications where reconstruction speed is important. This problem can be somewhat eased by making approximations such as considering w_{ij} to be only a function of the perpendicular distance between the center of the ith ray and the center of the jth cell. One now only needs to store this function in the computer. In the implementation of (149) using this approach as each equation (ray) in (139) is taken up, the perpendicular distance of the center of a cell from the center of the ray is computed at run time and then the function lookup table is used to approximately determine the corresponding w_{ij}.

To get around the implementation difficulties posed by (149) a myriad of other algebraic approaches have also been suggested, many of which are approximations to (149). To discuss the more implementable approximations we will first recast (149) in a slightly different form:

$$f_m^{(j)} = f_m^{(j-1)} + \left[(p_j - q_j) \Big/ \sum_{k=1}^{N} w_{jk}^2 \right] w_{jm} \qquad (151)$$

where

$$q_j = \vec{f}^{(j-1)} \cdot \vec{w}_j = \sum_{k=1}^{N} f_k^{(j-1)} w_{jk} \qquad (152)$$

These equations say that when we project the $(j - 1)$th solution onto the jth hyperplane, the change $\Delta f_m^{(j)}$ in the value of the mth cell is given by

$$\Delta f_m^{(j)} = f_m^{(j)} - f_m^{(j-1)} = \left[(p_j - q_j) \Big/ \sum_{k=1}^{N} w_{jk}^2 \right] w_{jm} \qquad (153)$$

Note that while p_j is the measured ray sum along the jth ray, q_j may be considered to be the computed ray sum for the same ray based on the $(j - 1)$th solution for the image gray levels. The correction Δf_i to the ith cell is obtained by first calculating the difference between the measured ray sum and the computed ray sum. This difference is then normalized by $\sum_{k=1}^{N} w_{jk}^2$ and assigned to all the image cells in the jth ray, each assignment being weighted by the corresponding w_{ij}. This is illustrated in Fig. 35.

In one of the approximations to (153), which was first proposed by Gordon et al. [22], the w_{ij}'s are simply replaced by 1's and 0's, depending upon whether the center of the jth image cell is within the ith ray. This makes the implementation easier because such a decision can easily be made at computer run time. Clearly, now the denominator in (153) is given by $\sum_{k=1}^{N} w_{jk}^2 = N_j$, which is the number of image cells whose centers are within the jth ray. The correction to the mth image cell from the jth equation in (139) may now be written as

$$\Delta f_m^{(j)} = \frac{p_j - q_j}{N_j} \tag{154}$$

for all the cells whose centers are within the jth ray. We are essentially smearing back the difference $(p_j - q_j)/N_j$ over the these image cells. (This is analogous to the concept of backprojection in the filtered-projection algorithms.) In (154), the q_j's are calculated using the expression in (152), except that one now uses the binary approximation for w_{jk}'s.

Dines and Lytle [19] have recently shown that (154) may also be considered an approximation (perhaps a close one) to the minimax solution of a minimization problem. To illustrate this we subtract (152) from the jth equation in (139) to write

$$p_j - q_j = \sum_{k=1}^{N} \Delta f_m^{(j)} w_{jm} \tag{155}$$

where $\Delta f_m^{(j)}$ is now the difference between the correct, albeit unknown, value of the mth cell and its value after using the $(j - 1)$th equation in (139). Clearly (155) gives us one equation for N unknowns: $\Delta f_1^{(j)}, \ldots, \Delta f_N^{(j)}$. Since this one equation has infinitely many solutions for the unknowns, we must impose additional constraints. For example, one may select a solution that minimizes

$$C = \sum_{m=1}^{N} (\Delta f_m^{(j)})^{2p} \tag{156}$$

If $p = 1$, we minimize the Euclidean distance between the solution $f_m^{(j-1)}$ and the jth hyperplane. Since a perpendicular minimizes the distance between a point and a plane, the resulting solution is identical to (153).

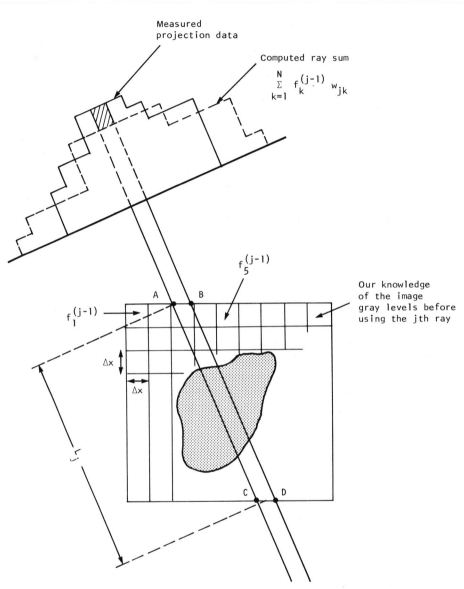

Fig. 35 Another way of looking at the Kacmarz method. After using the $(j-1)$th ray, we first compute the ray sum for all the cells (including fractions thereof) in the jth ray. The computed ray sum is subtracted from the measured projection data for that ray. After normalization, this difference is assigned to all the cells in the jth ray.

If we let $p \to \infty$ in the minimization problem in (156) the resulting criterion is known variously as the L^∞, minimax, or Chebychev norm. The solution of (156) with this norm is given by

$$\Delta f_m^{(j)} = (p_j - q_j) b(w_{jm}) \Big/ \sum_{k=1}^{N} w_{jk} \qquad (157)$$

where

$$\begin{aligned} b(w_{jm}) &= 1 \qquad \text{for} \quad w_{jm} > 0 \\ &= 0 \qquad \text{for} \quad w_{jm} = 0 \end{aligned} \qquad (158)$$

If we again make the approximation that $w_{jm} = 1$ if the center of the mth cell is within the jth ray, and 0 otherwise, we end up with (154).

We will remind the reader that, as was true with (149), the implementation based on (154) is a ray-by-ray approach. We start by making an initial guess for all the image cells (usually they are all set to 0). We then use the first ray (equation) in (139) and modify the corresponding image cells by using (154). This is repeated with each subsequent ray (equation) in (139). When we are through with all the M rays we have finished one iteration. Now we go back to the first equation to begin the second iteration, and so on. Iterations are stopped when the computed change of the image cell values is a negligible fraction of its current value. Criteria for stopping the iterations have been discussed by Herman *et al.* [29].

The approximation in (154), although very easy to implement, was shown by Gilbert [21] to lead to artifacts in the reconstructed images. These are caused by N_j not being a good approximation to the denominators in either (153) or (157). Superior reconstruction may be obtained if (154) is replaced by

$$\Delta f_m^{(j)} = \frac{p_j}{L_j} - \frac{q_j}{N_j} \qquad (159)$$

where L_j is the length (normalized by Δx, see Fig. 35) of the jth ray through the reconstruction region. Gilbert [21] has also proposed another approach for reducing the artifacts. In this approach, which is called the simultaneous algebraic reconstruction technique (SIRT), one computes the changes $\Delta f_m^{(j)}$ caused by the jth ray. However, the values of the image cells are not changed at this point. Before making any changes one goes through all the rays. Only at the end of each iteration are the cell values changed, the change for each cell being the average value of all the computed changes for that cell.

8.8   BIBLIOGRAPHICAL NOTES

The first mathematical solution to the problem of reconstructing a function from its projections was given by Radon [49] in 1917. More recently some of the first investigators to examine this problem theoretically/experimentally (and often independently) include (in roughly chronological order): Bracewell [5], Oldendorf [46], Cormack [12, 13], Kuhl and Edwards [39], DeRosier and Klug [16], Tretiak *et al.* [59], Rowley [52], Berry and Gibbs [4], Ramachandran and Lakshminarayanan [50], Bender *et al.* [3], and Bates and Peters [2].

In Section 8.2 a direct two-dimensional Fourier inversion approach to reconstruction was discussed. This method was first derived by Bracewell [5] for radioastronomy, and later independently by DeRosier and Klug [16] in electron microscopy and Rowley [52] in optical holography. Several workers who applied this method to radiography include Tretiak *et al.* [59], Bates and Peters [2], and Mersereau and Oppenheim [44]. More recently Wernecke and D'Addario [62] have proposed a maximum entropy approach to direct Fourier inversion. Their procedure is especially applicable if for some reason the projection data is insufficient.

The idea of filtered backprojection was first advanced by Bracewell and Riddle [6] and later independently by Ramachandran and Lakshminarayanan [50]. The superiority of the filtered-backprojection algorithms over the algebraic techniques was first demonstrated by Shepp and Logan [54]. Its development for fan-beam data was first made by Lakshimnarayanan [41] for the equispaced collinear detectors case and later extended by Herman and Naparstek [27] to the case of equiangular rays. Many authors [1, 38, 40, 43, 57] have proposed variations on the filter functions discussed in this chapter. The reader is referred particularly to [38, 43] for ways to speed up the filtering of the projection data by using binary approximations and/or inserting zeroes in the unit sample response of the filter function.

Images may also be reconstructed from fan-beam data by first sorting them into parallel projection data. Fast algorithms for ray sorting of fan-beam data have been developed by Wang [61], Dreike and Boyd [20], Peters and Lewitt [48], and Dines and Kak [17].

Aliasing artifacts in image reconstruction have been studied by Brooks *et al.* [9] and Crawford and Kak [14]. The property that when using filtered-backprojection algorithms the variance of the noise in the reconstructed image is directly proportional to the area under the square of the filter function was first shown by Shepp and Logan [54]. This derivation was based on the assumption that the variance of the measurement noise is the same for all the rays in the projection data, which is usually not the case. A more general expression (not using this assumption) for the noise variance was derived by Kak [34] who has also introduced the concept of the relative-uncertainty image.

The algebraic approaches to image reconstruction have been studied in great detail by Gordon *et al.* [22–25], Herman *et al.* [27, 29] and Budinger and Gullberg [10]. To somewhat improve the noise properties of the algebraic techniques, a simultaneous iterative reconstruction technique was proposed by Gilbert [21].

The reconstruction implementations that we presented in this chapter were based on the assumption that uniform sampling is used for the projection data, and that each projection is complete in the sense that it spans the entire cross section. (Of course, in a sense, an incomplete projection could be considered to be a case of nonuniform sampling also.) The reader is referred to [30, 31] for algorithms for nonuniformly sampled projection data; and to [7, 42, 47] for reconstructions from incomplete projections.

The reader's attention is also drawn to [45] for a new scan configuration for generating projection data. Finally, the reader is referred to [35] for some of the most recent advances in computerized medical imaging, an area concerned with and mostly based on the concepts discussed in this chapter.

REFERENCES

1. N. Baba and K. Murata, Filtering for image reconstruction from projections, *J. Opt. Soc. Amer.* **67**, 1977, 662–668.
2. R. H. T. Bates and T. M. Peters, Towards improvements in tomography, *New Zealand J. Sci.* **14**, 1971, 883–896.
3. R. Bender, S. H. Bellman, and R. Gordon, ART and the ribosome: A preliminary report on the three dimensional structure of individual ribosomes determined by an algebraic reconstruction technique, *J. Theoret Biol.* **29**, 1970, 483–487.
4. M. V. Berry and D. F. Gibbs, The interpretation of optical projections, *Proc. Roy. Soc. London Ser. A* **314**, 1970, 143–152.
5. R. N. Bracewell, Strip integration in radio astronomy, *Aust. J. Phys.* **9**, 1956, 198–217.
6. R. N. Bracewell and A. C. Riddle, Inversion of fan-beam scans in radio astronomy, *Astrophys. J.* **150**, 1967, 427–434.
7. R. N. Bracewell and S. J. Wernecke, Image reconstruction over a finite field of view, *J. Opt. Soc. Amer.* **65**, 1975, 1342–1346.
8. R. A. Brooks and G. DiChiro, Statistical limitations in x-ray reconstruction tomography, *Med. Phys.* **3**, 1976, 237–240.
9. R. A. Brooks, G. H. Weiss, and A. J. Talbert, A new approach to interpolation in computed tomography, *J. Comput. Assist. Tomog.* **2**, 1978, 577–585.
10. T. F. Budinger and G. T. Gullberg, Three-dimensional reconstruction in nuclear medicine emission imaging, *IEEE Trans. Nucl. Sci.* **NS-21**, 1974, 2–21.

11. D. A. Chesler, S. J. Riederer, and N. J. Pele, Noise due to photon counting statistics in computer x-ray tomography, *J. Comput. Assist. Tomog.* **1**, 1977, 64–74.

12. A. M. Cormack, Representation of a function by its line integrals with some radiological applications, *J. Appl. Phys.* **34**, 1963, 2722–2727.

13. A. M. Cormack, Representation of a function by its line integrals with some radiological applications, II, *J. Appl. Phys.* **35**, 1964, 2908–2913.

14. C. R. Crawford and A. C. Kak, Aliasing artifacts in computerized tomography, *Appl. Opt.* **18**, 1979, 3704–3711.

15. R. A. Crowther, D. J. DeRosier, and A. Klug, The reconstruction of a three-dimensional structure from projections and its applications to electron microscopy, *Proc. Roy. Soc. London Ser. A* **317**, 1970, 319–340.

16. D. J. DeRosier and A. Klug, Reconstruction of three dimensional structures from electron micrographs, *Nature (London)* **217**, 1968, 130–134.

17. K. A. Dines and A. C. Kak, Measurement and Reconstruction of Ultrasonic Parameters for Diagnostic Imaging, Rep. TR-EE-77-4, School of Electrical Engineering, Purdue Univ., West Lafayette, Indiana, 1976.

18. K. A. Dines and A. C. Kak, Ultrasonic attenuation tomography of soft biological tissues, *Ultrasonic Imaging* **1**, 1979, 16–33.

19. K. A. Dines and R. J. Lytle, Computerized geophysical tomography, *Proc. IEEE* **67**, 1979, 1065–1073.

20. P. Dreike and D. P. Boyd, Convolution reconstruction of fan-beam projections, *Comp. Graph. Image Proc.* **5**, 1977, 459–469.

21. P. Gilbert, Iterative methods for the reconstruction of three dimensional objects from their projections, *J. Theoret. Biol.* **36**, 1972, 105–117.

22. R. Gordon, A tutorial on ART (Algebraic Reconstruction Techniques), *IEEE Trans. Nucl. Sci.* **NS-21**, 1974, 78–93.

23. R. Gordon and G. T. Herman, Three-dimensional reconstruction from projections: A review of algorithms, *Internat. Rev. Cytology* **38**, 1971, 111–151.

24. R. Gordon and G. T. Herman, Reconstruction of pictures from their projections, *Commun. Assoc. Comput. Machinery* **14**, 1971, 759–768.

25. R. Gordon, R. Bender, and G. T. Herman, Algebraic reconstruction techniques (ART) for three dimensional electron microscopy and X-ray photography, *J. Theoret. Biol.* **29**, 1971, 470–481.

26. R. W. Hamming, "Digital Filters." Prentice-Hall, Englewood Cliffs, New Jersey, 1977.

27. G. T. Herman and A. Naparstek, Fast image reconstruction based on a Radon inversion formula appropriate for rapidly collected data, *SIAM J. Appl. Math.* **33**, 1977, 511–533.

28. G. T. Herman and S. Rowland, Resolution in ART: An experimental investigation of the resolving power of an algebraic picture reconstruction, *J. Theoret. Biol.* **33**, 1971, 213–223.

29. G. T. Herman, A. Lent, and S. Rowland, ART: Mathematics and applications: a report on the mathematical foundations and on applicability to real data of the algebraic reconstruction techniques, *J. Theoret. Biol.* **43**, 1973, 1–32.

30. B. K. P. Horn, Density reconstructions using arbitrary ray sampling schemes, *Proc. IEEE* **66**, 1978, 551–562.

31. B. K. P. Horn, Fan-beam reconstruction methods, *Proc. IEEE* **67**, 1979, 1616–1623.

32. C. V. Jakowatz, Jr. and A. C. Kak, Computerized Tomography using X-rays and Ultrasound, Rep. TR-EE-76-26. School of Electrical Engineering, Purdue Univ., West Lafayette, Indiana, 1976.

33. S. Kaczmarz, Angenaherte Auflosung von Systemen linearer Gleichungen, *Bull. Acad. Polon. Sci. Lett. A* 1937, 355–357.

34. A. C. Kak, Computerized tomography with x-ray emission and ultrasound sources, *Proc. IEEE* **67**, 1979, 1245–1272.

35. A. C. Kak (Guest ed.), Computerized medical imaging, a special issue of *IEEE Trans. Biomed. Eng.* **67**, February 1981.

36. A. C. Kak and K. A. Dines, Signal processing of broadland pulse ultrasound: Measurement of attenuation of soft biological tissues, *IEEE Trans. Biomed. Eng.* **BME-25**, 1978, 321–344.

37. P. N. Keating, More accurate interpolation using discrete Fourier transforms, *IEEE Trans. Acoust. Speech Signal Processing* **ASSP-26**, 1978, 368–269.

38. S. K. Kenue and J. F. Greenleaf, Efficient convolution kernels for computerized tomography, *Ultrasonic Imaging* **1**, 1979, 232–244.

39. D. E. Kuhl and R. Q. Edwards, Image separation radio-isotope scanning, *Radiology* **80**, 1963, 653–661.

40. Y. S. Kwoh, I. S. Reed, and T. K. Truong, A generalized $|w|$-filter for 3-D reconstruction, *IEEE Trans. Nucl. Sci.* **NS-24**, 1977, 1990–1998.

41. A. V. Lakshminarayanan, Reconstruction from divergent ray data, Dept. of Computer Science, State Univ. of New York at Buffalo, Tech. Rep. 92 (1975).

42. R. M. Lewitt and R. H. T. Bates, Image reconstruction from projections. *Optik* **50**, 1978, 19–33, 85–109, 189–204, 269–278.

43. R. M. Lewitt, Ultra-fast convolution approximation for computerized tomography, *IEEE Trans. Nucl. Sci.* **NS-26**, 1979, 2678–2681.

44. R. M. Mersereau and A. V. Oppenheim, Digital reconstruction of multidimensional signals from their projections, *Proc. IEEE* **62**, 1974, 1319–1338.

45. D. Nahamoo, C. R. Crawford, and A. C. Kak, Design constraints and reconstruction algorithms for transverse-continuous-rotate CT scanners,, *IEEE Trans. Biomed. Eng.* **BME-28**, 1981, 79–98.

46. W. H. Oldendorf, Isolated flying spot detection of radiodensity discontinuities displaying the internal structural pattern of a complex object, *IRE Trans. Biomed. Eng.* **BME-8**, 1961, 68–72.

47. B. E. Oppenheim, Reconstruction tomography from incomplete projections, *in* "Reconstruction Tomography in Diagnostic Radiology and Nuclear Medicine," (M. M. Ter Pogossian *et al.*, eds.). Univ. Park Press, Baltimore, Maryland, 1975.

48. T. M. Peters and R. M. Lewitt, Computed tomography with fan-beam geometry, *J. Comput. Assist. Tomog.* **1**, 1977, 429–436.

49. J. Radon, Uber die Bestimmung von Funktionen durch ihre Integralwerte langs gewisser Mannigfaltigkeiten (On the determination of functions from their integrals along certain manifolds), *Ber. Saechsische Akad. Wiss.* **29**, 1917, 262–279.

50. G. N. Ramachandran and A. V. Lakshminarayanan, Three dimensional reconstructions from radiographs and electron micrographs: Application of convolution instead of Fourier transforms, *Proc. Nat. Acad. Sci. USA* **68**, 1971, 2236–2240.

51. R. S. Ramakrishnan, S. K. Mullick, R. K. S. Rathore, and R. Subrananian, Orthogonalization, Bernstein polynomials, and image restoration, *Appl. Opt.* **18**, 1979, 464–468.

52. P. D. Rowley, Quantitative interpretation of three dimensional weakly refractive phase objects using holographic interferometry, *J. Opt. Soc. Am.* **59**, 1969, 1496–1498.

53. R. W. Schafer and L. R. Rabiner, A digital signal processing approach to interpolation, *Proc. IEEE* **61**, 1973, 692–702.

54. L. A. Shepp and B. F. Logan, The Fourier reconstruction of a head section, *IEEE Trans. Nucl. Sci.* **NS-21**, 1974, 21–43.

55. D. W. Sweeney and C. M. Vest, Reconstruction of three-dimensional refractive index fields from multi-directional interferometric data, *Appl. Opt.* **12**, 1973, 1649–1664.

56. K. Tanabe, Projection method for solving a singular system, *Numer. Math.* **17**, 1971, 203–214.

57. E. Tanaka and T. A. Iinuma, Correction functions for optimizing the reconstructed image in transverse section scans, *Phys. Med. Biol.* **20**, 1975, 789–798.

58. M. TerPogossian, "The Physical Aspects of Diagnostic Radiology." Harper, New York, 1967.

59. O. Tretiak, M. Eden, and M. Simon, Internal structures for three dimensional images, *Proc. Int. Conf. Med. Biol. Eng., 8th, Chicago, Illinois* 1969.

60. O. J. Tretiak, Noise limitations in x-ray computed tomography, *J. Comput. Assist. Tomog.* **2**, 1978, 477–480.

61. L. Wang, Cross-section reconstruction with a fan-beam scanning geometry, *IEEE Trans. Comput.* **C-26**, 1977, 264–268.

62. S. J. Wernecke and L. R. D'Addario, Maximum entropy image reconstruction, *IEEE Trans. Comput.* **C-26**, 1977, 351–364.

Index

431

Computer Science and Applied Mathematics
A SERIES OF MONOGRAPHS AND TEXTBOOKS

Editor
Werner Rheinboldt
University of Pittsburgh

Hans P. Künzi, H. G. Tzschach, and C. A. Zehnder. Numerical Methods of Mathematical Optimization: With ALGOL and FORTRAN Programs, Corrected and Augmented Edition

Azriel Rosenfeld. Picture Processing by Computer

James Ortega and Werner Rheinboldt. Iterative Solution of Nonlinear Equations in Several Variables

Azaria Paz. Introduction to Probabilistic Automata

David Young. Iterative Solution of Large Linear Systems

Ann Yasuhara. Recursive Function Theory and Logic

James M. Ortega. Numerical Analysis: A Second Course

G. W. Stewart. Introduction to Matrix Computations

Chin-Liang Chang and Richard Char-Tung Lee. Symbolic Logic and Mechanical Theorem Proving

C. C. Gotlieb and A. Borodin. Social Issues in Computing

Erwin Engeler. Introduction to the Theory of Computation

F. W. J. Olver. Asymptotics and Special Functions

Dionysios C. Tsichritzis and Philip A. Bernstein. Operating Systems

Robert R. Korfhage. Discrete Computational Structures

Philip J. Davis and Philip Rabinowitz. Methods of Numerical Integration

A. T. Berztiss. Data Structures: Theory and Practice, Second Edition

N. Christophides. Graph Theory: An Algorithmic Approach

Sakti P. Ghosh. Data Base Organization for Data Management

Dionysios C. Tsichritzis and Frederick H. Lochovsky. Data Base Management Systems

James L. Peterson. Computer Organization and Assembly Language Programming

William F. Ames. Numerical Methods for Partial Differential Equations, Second Edition

ARNOLD O. ALLEN. Probability, Statistics, and Queueing Theory: With Computer Science Applications

ELLIOTT I. ORGANICK, ALEXANDRA I. FORSYTHE, AND ROBERT P. PLUMMER. Programming Language Structures

ALBERT NIJENHUIS AND HERBERT S. WILF. Combinatorial Algorithms, Second Edition

AZRIEL ROSENFELD. Picture Languages, Formal Models for Picture Recognition

ISAAC FRIED. Numerical Solution of Differential Equations

ABRAHAM BERMAN AND ROBERT J. PLEMMONS. Nonnegative Matrices in the Mathematical Sciences

BERNARD KOLMAN AND ROBERT E. BECK. Elementary Linear Programming with Applications

CLIVE L. DYM AND ELIZABETH S. IVEY. Principles of Mathematical Modeling

ERNEST L. HALL. Computer Image Processing and Recognition

ALLEN B. TUCKER, JR. Text Processing: Algorithms, Languages, and Applications

MARTIN CHARLES GOLUMBIC. Algorithmic Graph Theory and Perfect Graphs

GABOR T. HERMAN. Image Reconstruction from Projections: The Fundamentals of Computerized Tomography

WEBB MILLER AND CELIA WRATHALL. Software for Roundoff Analysis of Matrix Algorithms

ULRICH W. KULISCH AND WILLARD L. MIRANKER. Computer Arithmetic in Theory and Practice

LOUIS A. HAGEMAN AND DAVID M. YOUNG. Applied Iterative Methods

I. GOHBERG, P. LANCASTER AND L. RODMAN. Matrix Polynomials.

AZRIEL ROSENFELD AND AVINASH C. KAK. Digital Picture Processing, Second Edition, Vol. 1, Vol. 2

DIMITRI P. BERTSEKAS. Constrained Optimization and Lagrange Multiplier Methods

JAMES S. VANDERGRAFT. Introduction to Numerical Computations, Second Edition

FRANÇOISE CHATELIN. Spectral Approximation of Linear Operators

GÖTZ ALEFELD AND JÜRGEN HERZBERGER. Introduction to Interval Computations. Translated by Jon Rokne

In preparation

LEONARD UHR. Algorithm-Structured Computer Arrays and Networks: Architectures and Processes for Images, Percepts, Models, Information

ROBERT KORFHAGE. Discrete Computational Structures, Second Edition

O. AXELSSON AND V. A. BARKER. Finite Element Solution of Boundary Value Problems: Theory and Computation

MARTIN D. DAVIS AND ELAINE J. WEYUKER. Computability, Complexity, and Languages: Fundamentals of Theoretical Computer Science

PHILIP J. DAVIS AND PHILIP RABINOWITZ. Methods of Numerical Integration, Second Edition